# Living Together

# Living Together

JACQUES DERRIDA'S COMMUNITIES OF VIOLENCE AND PEACE

Edited by ELISABETH WEBER

FORDHAM UNIVERSITY PRESS   NEW YORK   2013

# Contents

CONTENTS

# Acknowledgments

I wish to thank Jacques Derrida, across the distance of time and the proximity of memory, for his illuminating presence, in October 2003, at a gathering that inspired this collection.

I thank Marguerite Derrida for her support.

I thank the contributors to this volume for their everlasting patience on the long road to publication.

I thank Gil Anidjar for his friendship. Without him, this book would not have come into existence.

I thank Thomas A. Carlson for his contributions to the early stages of this project. I thank Helen Tartar at Fordham University Press for embracing it with enthusiasm. I thank the external reviewers for their critique, suggestions, and endorsement, and the editorial staff at the press for their dedication. I thank Charlotte Becker for her astute and meticulous assistance in the preparation of the manuscript. I thank Ariella Azoulay for her inspiration, kindness, and help.

This book wouldn't be without an altogether different gift: I thank Mark Saatjian, David Saatjian, and Ruben Saatjian for the joy of living together.

# Living Together

# Introduction: Pleading Irreconcilable Differences

*Elisabeth Weber*

For Jacques Derrida, the notions and experiences of "community," "living," "together," never ceased to harbor radical, in fact infinite interrogations. The often anguished question of how to "live together" moved Derrida throughout his life and career, animating a host of concepts, most evidently perhaps in the writings on hospitality, "auto-immunity," in all the essays on law, right(s), and justice. Derrida reflected as well, in instances too many to recount, on the folds, difficulties, and aporias of the concept and the experience of responsibility.[1] The "deconstructive unfolding of the tension between justice and law," Christoph Menke succinctly comments, occurs "in the name of an experience that no political stance can capture, but that nevertheless affects any politics as its border, and therefore as its interruption."[2]

During his opening address of the 1989 colloquium "Deconstruction and the Possibility of Justice" at Cardozo Law School, Derrida famously asserted: *"Deconstruction is justice."*[3] This provocative assertion, sharply giving the lie to decades-old criticism of deconstruction as an aestheticizing, apolitical, or ahistorical exercise, recapitulated the stakes of an infinite task and responsibility that, in spite of and because of its infinity, cannot be relegated to tomorrow. "Justice, however unpresentable it remains, does not wait. It is that which must not wait."[4] It is in the spirit of such urgency, of a responsibility that cannot be postponed, that Jacques Derrida was an active and outspoken critic and commentator on issues such as South Africa's apartheid,[5] the Israel/Palestine conflict, the bloody civil war in his native Algeria,[6] human rights abuses, French immigration laws,[7] the death penalty,[8] and on what Richard Falk has termed "the great terror war."[9]

Derrida's oeuvre as philosopher is inseparable from these interventions. In 1997, in response to an invitation to "define, briefly, what an intellectual is for you today," Derrida noted that "never has the task of

1

defining the intellectual rigorously seemed so impossible to me as it does today."[10] He goes on to name several problematic assumptions on which such a definition depends: It assumes first that the "right to speech and writing, in the name of *justice*, should be claimed, assigned, reserved, and specialized" in the name of presumed "rhetorical skills"; it assumes, second, "a division between the private and the political event" and a "particular configuration of the places of public speaking"; and third, "a division of labor between the intellectual and the nonintellectual." Derrida deduces that "now and in the future it would be a betrayal" of a recognized intellectual's "mission" to "write or speak in public, or be an activist in general," without questioning these assumptions that present themselves as "a matter of course," and without "seeking to associate with those who are deprived of this right to speech and writing, or without demanding it for them, whether directly or not. Whence the necessity of writing in different tones—of changing the codes, the rhythms, the theater, and the music." At the same time, Derrida insists "on the responsibilities, rights and powers that I am still recognized as having under the title of 'intellectual,'" to be "at the service both of those 'without a voice' *and* of that which is approaching and offered for 'thinking'—which is always, in a different way, 'without a voice,'" especially considering that "the 'intellectual' (the writer, the artist, the journalist, the philosopher) is the victim, all over the world, of persecutions today that are new and concentrated." The intellectual's task is that of an "inventive engagement," that is, a "transaction that suspends the safe horizons and criteria, the existing norms and rules," in order to "analyze, to criticize, to deconstruct them . . . yet without ever leaving the space empty, in other words open to the straightforward return of *any* power, investment, language, and so on." Such "invention or proposal of new conceptual, normative, or criteriological figures, according to new singularities" can never "lose sight of the macrodimensional—which is not reducible to what is put out about it in dogmatic ideas of globalization." The examples Derrida goes on to name are infinite in their scope:

1. The hundreds of millions of illiterate people; the massive scale of malnutrition, rarely taken into account by the media champions of human rights; the tens of millions of children who die every year because of water; the 40 to 50 percent of women who are subject to violence, and often life-threatening violence, all the time—and so on. The list would be endless;
2. The way that capitalist powers are concentrated into transnational and cross-state monopolies in the appropriation of the media, multimedia, and productions of the tele-technologies and even the languages that they use.[11]

I quote this text at length because it shows how for Derrida the presumed microdimensional (such as the unwavering attention to "new singularities") is always intricately connected to the "macrodimensional"; how community cannot but be at the very heart of the "inventive engagement" of the intellectual, an inventive engagement to which Derrida's entire oeuvre gives powerful testimony. That Derrida almost never uses the word "community" only adds to the challenge of thinking that engagement, that testimony.[12] Commenting on the attacks perpetrated on September 11, 2001, as well as on state-sponsored violence in its variety of forms, Derrida asserts in the dialogue with Giovanna Borradori that "if intellectuals, writers, scholars, professors, artists, and journalists do not, before all else, stand up together against such violence, their abdication will be at once irresponsible and suicidal."[13]

In Richard Beardsworth's succinct formulation, Derrida's "negotiations with the western tradition," rather than "betraying a *reduction* of political possibility—a retreat onto the margins of the political community at the 'closure' of metaphysics—amount to an *active transformation* of the political field." Derrida's "inventive" thought contributes to the necessary "reinvention" of political thought and practice, caught—and paralyzed— "in the increasing tension between internationalization and virtualization, on the one hand, and territorial difference and the corporal realities of human life, on the other."[14] As Pheng Cheah and Suzanne Guerlac note in the introduction to their collection, *Derrida and the Time of the Political*,

> Deconstruction can itself be considered an event and an activity insofar as it brings about a confrontation between philosophemes and categories of knowledge and decisive mutations in the world, causing an interruption of the former by the latter in order to force a mutation in thought so that it can be adequate to the task of thinking these important shifts, instead of being outstripped and rendered irrelevant or *effete* by them.[15]

The present collection might be described as a series of "inventive engagements" with the question of how to live together in a world in which the de-localizing and uprooting forces evoked by the term "globalization" and embodied or transmitted by increasingly complex and ambivalently de-materialized networks (technological, economic, cultural) threaten boundaries of place and time and hence, the integrity and the safety of homes and lands, communities and traditions, languages and cultures, bodies both literal and figurative. Through all of these, globalization renders ever more fragile the possibility (and meaning) of "life" and "together." The violence that dominates international politics makes it clear that any productive reflection on what might appear as irreconcilable differences needs to go beyond the assertions of ecumenism and mutual understanding. The wounds of irreconcilable differences, in other words, need to be addressed as well as the enduring conditions under which such wounds can and do continue to be inflicted. The success of just and peaceful settlements of today's conflicts may well depend on the conviction that irreconcilable differences are not a dead end from which only violence can follow. Otherwise, and without the courage to welcome the unreconciled other, our thinking, instruction, and discussion will do little more than repeat the prejudices that already deepen, on all sides, with every explosion.

In the context of family law, "irreconcilable differences" can be cited as grounds for divorce. But irreconcilable differences do not mark the end of negotiations: On the contrary, issues are resolved *on the basis* of the declaration of irreconcilability. As a result, some states require that spouses live apart before granting a divorce based on irreconcilable differences, yet in many jurisdictions, it is neither logically nor legally impossible to live together, *with* irreconcilable differences. Besides, living apart is still a form of living together. As Jacques Derrida puts it, we have in fact no choice but to live together. Contemporary national and international politics provide countless occasions to witness irreconcilable differences operating on a daily basis, differences that are too often considered dead ends, in which violence is enthusiastically embraced as the only way out or forward. This is a fallacious way, of course, which only turns out to enmesh the parties deeper in their bloody conflict. The challenge then is to learn to live—with differences and irreconcilable differences—to learn to address those differences in new ways, even unheard-of ways, ways that are considered "impossible" in the known and familiar paradigms. Those "impossible" ways are necessarily insecure, even dangerous, but they are also the chance of an arrival of the other whose alterity can be welcome only if time, patience, and respect for complexities are given, a respect that, in Hent de Vries's expression, materializes as "differentialization,"[16] rather than as differentiation, which would leave open the "possibility of an organic, original and homogeneous unity."[17] Derrida "leaves no doubt," de Vries reminds us, that one must be cautious about "translating" motifs such as hospitality and responsibility, "not to mention absolute hospitality, into contemporary 'illustrations.'" Resonating with Derrida's notion of "inventive engagements," de Vries writes that "readers of such philosophical considerations invent the relevant mediations that would allow one to imagine or experience the link—but also the tension—between the idea of hospitality and its pragmatic forms of enactment, engagement, and implementation."[18] Nevertheless, this link "*must*" also "take place," and "it will always be a relation without relation, which can only be thought and lived aporetically, intermittently, and by way of perpetual trial and error, back and forth, for better and for worse."[19] The inventive engagement that materializes as the creation of this "link," as its aporetical thinking and living, occurs as a "singularization and differentialization . . . of the general and the universal—a process that is at the same time a generalization and virtual universalization of the singular, a serialization and infinite substitution of sorts." Of this movement, de Vries asserts that it is "not a mere theoretical procedure, but structures the realm of the ethical and the political, at every step of the way."[20] "At every step of the way": Indeed—this insistence on the obligation to patience often exacerbates Derrida's detractors, and not only them. As Derrida notes in *Politics of Friendship*,

> At a moment when our world is delivered over to new forms of violence, new wars, new figures of cruelty or barbarity (and not always to this "just" and necessary barbarity that Benjamin sometimes called for against the other, the barbarity of the old

culture), at a moment when hostilities are breaking out, no longer resembling the worst that we have ever known, the political and historical urgency of what is befalling us should, one will say, tolerate less patience, fewer detours and less bibliophilic discretion.[21]

To this urging for speed in the name of urgency, Derrida responds in this particular context and in others with a long detour. His faithfulness to patience makes him an heir of Franz Kafka, who surmised that "it is because of their impatience," that "they" (Kafka doesn't specify) were expelled from paradise, and "because of their impatience they don't return."[22] In order to be just, no question, no differentialization, no fold, no detail can be skipped—and no day either. The wisdom of patience should not enable justice to be deferred until tomorrow.

The radicality of such "virtual universalization of the singular" (as opposed to an understanding of the singular as exceptional) is aptly summarized by J. Hillis Miller in his comment on Derrida's meditations on Abraham:

> One might think, or hope, that Abraham's case was exceptional. He was, after all, a great patriarch. His act was the basis of the three great religions of the Book. His progeny, by way of Isaac, ultimately included Jesus Christ, the Messiah. Abraham is not so much to be emulated as admired. Surely God (if you want to call the "nameless" that) will not require of you or me anything like Abraham's sacrifice of his love for his only son to his love for God. The radical strength of Derrida's argument here is to say "no" to this cop-out. No, he says, each one of us, every instant of every day, is in exactly the same situation as Abraham on Mount Moriah with his knife raised over Isaac. Abraham's situation is exemplary, paradigmatic, not exceptional.[23]

Each one of us does the unforgivable. For even if society would prosecute a father murdering his child on the hills of Montmartre, of Hollywood, of Rome, Mecca, or Jerusalem, that same society

> *allows to die* of hunger and disease tens of millions of children (those relatives or fellow humans that ethics or the discourse of the rights of man refer to), without any moral or legal tribunal ever being considered competent to judge such a sacrifice, the sacrifice of the other to avoid being sacrificed oneself. Not only does such a society participate in this incalculable sacrifice, it actually organizes it. The smooth functioning of its economic, political, and legal order, the smooth functioning of its moral discourse and good conscience, presuppose the permanent operation of this sacrifice. And such a sacrifice is not even invisible, for from time to time the television displays—while keeping them at a distance—a series of intolerable images of it, and a few voices are raised to bring it all to our attention. But those images and voices are completely

powerless to induce the slightest effective change in the situation, to assign the least responsibility, to furnish anything other than alibis.[24]

Even though Derrida writes that he won't talk "about wars," he goes on, in this text written in 1992, to bluntly address the first Gulf War, which he places squarely in the tradition of Abraham:

> We are not even talking about wars, the least recent or the most recent ones, in which cases one can wait an eternity for morality or international law (whether violated with impunity or invoked hypocritically) to determine with any degree or rigor who is responsible or guilty for the hundreds of thousands of victims who are sacrificed for what or whom one knows not, countless victims, each of whose singularity becomes each time infinitely singular—every other (one) being every (bit) other [*tout autre étant tout autre*]—whether they be victims of the Iraqi state or victims of the international coalition that accuse that state of not respecting the law. For in the discourses that dominated during such wars, it was rigorously impossible, on one side and the other, to discern the religious from the moral, the juridical from the political. The warring factions were all irreconcilable fellow worshippers of the religions of the Book. Does that not make things converge once again in the fight to the death previously referred to, which continues to rage on Mount Moriah over possession of the secret of the sacrifice by an Abraham who never said anything? Do they not fight in order to appropriate the secret as the sign of their covenant with God, and impose its order on the other, who becomes for his part nothing more than a murderer?[25]

Thus, what the "knights of good conscience" refuse to recognize is that the sacrifice of Isaac, as "monstrous, outrageous" and "barely conceivable" as it might be, is "the most common and everyday experience of responsibility."[26]

In Derrida's reading, "another Abraham" also exemplifies the aporia of forgiveness: "One never asks forgiveness except for the unforgivable. One never has to forgive the forgivable." In Kierkegaard's "fiction," quoted by Derrida, "Abraham himself judges his sin to be unforgivable," the sin, that is, of having "listened" to God "too faithfully," of having "consented to do what God himself had ordered him to do."[27] It is this "other" Abraham, and yet another one, Kafka's, who for Derrida

> conjures up more future to come than many others . . . by calling us to this truth . . . : that anyone responding to the call must continue to doubt, to ask himself whether he has heard right, whether there is no original misunderstanding: whether it was in fact his name that was heard, whether he is the only or the first addressee of the call; whether he is not in the process of substituting himself violently for another; whether the law of substitution, which is also the law of responsibility, does not call for an in-

finite increase of vigilance and concern. It is possible that I have not been called, me, and it is not even excluded that no one, no One, nobody, ever called any One, any unique one, anybody. The possibility of an originary misunderstanding in destination is not an evil, it is the structure, perhaps the very vocation of any call worthy of that name, of all nomination, of all response and responsibility.[28]

I quote Derrida's texts on Abraham at length because they offer intense gatherings of the questions that occasioned this volume. They also offer a sense of the reverberations caused by an ethics that is, to quote Geoffrey Bennington, "ethical only to the extent that it is originally compromised or contaminated by the non-ethical"; otherwise put, the

affirmation of pervertibility as a positive condition of what appeared to be opposed to it. . . . Saying that a positive condition of ethics is an inaugural—structural—perjury does not mean that I am henceforth ethically bound to *approve* actual acts of perjury. This production of a condition of possibility is the aspect of the analysis that prompts its qualification as transcendental. But its specifically *quasi*-transcendental character means that, as always in deconstructive thought, it is impossible rigorously to separate the transcendental from the factical or the empirical, and this entails that, uncomfortably, I cannot use the transcendental aspect of the analysis to provide *a priori* knowledge of which empirical cases, which events arriving, in fact constitute acts of perversion or perversity.[29]

The concept for this collection arose from a conference I organized with Thomas A. Carlson in October 2003. The conference, titled "Irreconcilable Differences? Jacques Derrida and the Question of Religion," would come to pass as Jacques Derrida's last public appearance in the United States.[30] The keynote address, which he gave in spite of the grave illness that claimed his life a year later, was titled "Vivre Ensemble—Living Together." It was the English translation of a slightly shortened version of a lecture (or "lesson") Derrida had given at the 1998 meeting of French-speaking Jewish intellectuals (Colloque des intellectuels juifs de langue française).[31] The full text of this lecture is published in this volume for the first time in English translation: "Avowing—The Impossible: 'Returns,' Repentance, and Reconciliation."

Derrida's starting point, in this lecture, is the possibility that "a *certain* avowal would announce itself as the first *commandment*," an "unheard of and improbable avowal, an avowal that, prior to and beyond any determined fault, declares before the other the unavowable." One figure of this "un-avowable" is forgiveness. But "forgiveness, if there is such, must forgive the unforgivable—and must, therefore, do the impossible. If such were the condition of 'living together,' it would command doing the impossible" ("Avowing," 18–19). The "first commandment" then, of any "living together," is the acknowledgment and avowal of the impossible.

Such "impossibility" finds itself at the heart of several essays in the present collection. Ellen Armour explores Derrida's reflections on the aporias at the heart of the ethical by situating Derrida's essay "Avowing—the Impossible" within the context of his *The Gift of Death* and its analysis of Europe's failure to fully grasp "its roots in a history of and as the emergence of the responsible [Christian] subject." For Derrida, here engaging the work of the Czech philosopher and activist Jan Patočka, the universal obligation inherent in the category of a crime against humanity clashes with an inevitable, but unavowable, preference for "my own" over all others. By responding to the demand of the Other in the form of a particular other, it is impossible not to do violence to another particular other, indeed to *all* particular others. Following Derrida, Armour also offers a reading of Abraham's "gift of death." She explores how Derrida's reconceptualization and recontextualization of the notion of religious identity is particularly productive for a post 9/11 world in which the aporias of forgiveness, pursued by Derrida in his later oeuvre, are intensely acute.

Dana Hollander's essay traces the echoes of Vladimir Jankélévitch's interventions on forgiveness in Derrida's. Hollander reads Derrida's meditations on forgiveness as restating, in a different vocabulary, Jankélévitch's attempts to understand the possibility and impossibility of forgiveness as indissociable realities. For Jankélévitch, as for Derrida, the question of whether there can be forgiveness is entirely distinct from juridical questions about the prosecution and punishment of war crimes. Indeed, for Jankélévitch, there is a necessary and unbridgeable asymmetry between the offended and the offender that results in forgiving being conceived as an act of grace that is not based on reason or reasons. If, as Jankélévitch asserts, one forgives "for nothing," one can never be assured of an identity between the original crime and what is forgiven, between the perpetrator and the one to be forgiven, or between the victim and the one who forgives. Forgiveness thus constitutes an exemplary instance in which the absolutely ethical action is impossible *as* an ethical action; yet, without this impossibility, the very notion of ethical action—as a decision taken as if in response to an absolute command by the Other—cannot but lose its force and meaning.

William Robert also explores the different figures of the "impossible" in Derrida's oeuvre. Robert describes Derrida's calls and responses, and particularly the call for hospitality, as doing "the impossible in the face of the impossible: to open, to affirm, to avow, to give, to save, to bless, to respond, to take responsibility, to welcome. . . . The list is necessarily endless and incalculable." The "impossible" generates an "eventive grammar" that effectuates a "displacement" of ontology by life (such as, for example, of "being" by "mighting") and that consequently disrupts traditional concepts of politics based on the understanding of "together" (in French, the adverb *ensemble*) as a (substantive) "ensemble." Derrida's contribution to this grammar comprises expressions such as "the live-ance of life [*le vivement de la vie*]," a neologism whose English translation is in fortuitous consonance with his famous *différance*, and like the latter, introduces an unheard-of quality into the philosophical discourse, namely a new grammar invented according to "an originary subjunctive"—a grammar of *as if*, of potential and vitality, that names "living to-gether [*vivre ensemble*]" as preceding and exceeding any ontological "being together [*être-ensemble*]" and, thus, Heidegger's "being-with" [*Mitsein*].

"Living together" is thus not a "community" in the common understanding of the term. Kevin Hart observes that this is one of the words that Derrida did not only subject to criticism, or suspend from quotation marks, but rather rejected outright as referring to a "fraternity"-based kinship too intricately associated with fusion to be able to be reclaimed even "*sous rature*." According to Hart, however, Derrida's ethics of "living together" can-not be formally distinguished from "a revival of rational religion" that answers to a natu-ral faith, a faith that is only structurally, and not historically, older than positive religions. In his critique of what he calls "pure" ethics, Hart contrasts Derrida's "impossible apo-rias" with Iris Murdoch's depiction of moral life as a continual engagement rather than an interrupted series of occurrences of moral choices. Derrida's aporias lead to a "hyperbolic ethics of self-sacrifice and sacrifice of the other in each and every direction," requiring an "ethics that cannot be supported, let alone lived." The illusion of a "pure ethics" results from "failing to distinguish the singularity of God from the uniqueness of other people, and the illusion is a dangerous one for ethics and religion alike."

The aporias of forgiveness, gift, and democracy are also at the heart of Michal Ben-Naftali's essay, but with a focus on literature, art, and by extension, politics. Ben-Naftali shows how in Derrida's work, the aporias of democracy are best exemplified in literature, since historically and conceptually the two share conditions of possibility. The fact that both are based upon the right to keep a secret makes "literature inseparable from a de-mocracy to come."[32] In its connection to democracy as "the implementation of the ulti-mate political order," Derrida's "book to come" stands for an "absolute interruption" and "an epistemic mutation" that has made him "a permanent stranger within the philosophi-cal togetherness." Ben-Naftali sees here also a great affinity to modernist painters, such as Wassily Kandinsky, especially in the interpretation given to the latter's work in Michel Henry's notion of "pathetic community." This context allows us to understand Derrida's reflection on himself as a young child in an Algeria subjected to the anti-Semitic legisla-tion of the French colonizer in "Avowing—The Impossible," not so much as an "introspec-tion," than as a crucial starting point for discussing the political, as "the secret that ties togetherness to loneliness and loneliness to togetherness." Living "together," then, de-pends on separation, and mourning needs to be thought of as an "experiential structure at the basis of 'living together.'" "Right from the pledge that binds together two desires," Derrida wrote in 1986,

> each is already in mourning for the other, entrusts death to the other as well: if you die before me, I will keep you, if I die before you, you will carry me in yourself, one will keep the other, will already have kept the other from the first declaration. This double interiorization would be possible neither in monadic interiority nor in the

logic of "objective" time and space. It takes place nevertheless every time I love. Everything then begins with this survival. Each time that I love or each time that I hate, each time that a law *engages* me to the death of the other.[33]

Mourning as fundamental "experiential structure" is also a figure of the impossible.

But what happens if the "law" that "engages me to the death of the other" is rejected, if the other's murder is denied as having ever occurred and mourning is purposefully and perversely rendered impossible? Marc Nichanian's essay probes such impossible mourning by extending Derrida's analyses of forgiveness and "reconciliation" to the extermination committed by the Turkish government before, during, and after World War I against its Armenian population, in parallel with the work of the South African "Truth and Reconciliation" commission which directly occupied Derrida on multiple occasions. Both cases are examples of a "crime without truth," in which "every request for forgiveness would be only a redoubling of the crime, that is to say, a further attack on the victim." As Nichanian shows, political reconciliation is always a "manipulation of mourning," and it is always "monolingual." In the scenes of avowal, and request for forgiveness described by Derrida in "Avowing—the Impossible," we witness a "theater of reconciliation" on a global scale, which is essentially a "theater of testimony." It is precisely through the globalization of testimony that the catastrophe of forbidden mourning unfolds, since the concept and practice of testimony, as Nichanian powerfully shows in his analysis of Gillian Slovo's novel *Red Dust*, implies that the truth is in the hands of the torturer, "once and for all." It is "*always the torturer who testifies, even when it is the victim who speaks*. Testimony always speaks the language of the executioner." Testimony enacts "the monolingual and monochromatic universe of reconciliation," a universe where only one voice is heard, that of the executioner. Consequently, the latter's crime will remain forever a crime without memory, without repentance, without mourning, and without forgiveness. Of this catastrophe, "only literature can speak." The question for "living together" that must remain wide open is whether there can be "another way to request forgiveness, a radical way, *without* the will of reconciliation?"

Mourning is, for Derrida, inseparable from his intense and reiterated preoccupation with the figure of the "specter" or "spirit," which can also manifest itself as a "phantom" or "ghost" that comes to pass as a condition of possibility of any "community." The necessity of welcoming the "memory of the ghost" marks Derrida's commitment to justice in its entirety and is already reflected in concepts, introduced in Derrida's earliest writings, such as the "trace," "différance," and the "supplement." If "deconstruction's affair," in Anselm Haverkamp's words, is not "the proven validity of results, nor the cutting of Gordian knots," if deconstruction rather sets out to find the "most complicated interlacement"[34] of these knots, then one locus of a particularly complicated interlacement visited by Derrida over and over again is the question of memory, as memory of the ghost. The question is not so much how to "address the ghost," and whether one can question or address it, but whether one could "*address oneself in general* if some ghost did not already come back?"[35] Referring to Shakespeare's *Hamlet*, Derrida continues: "If he [or she] loves justice at least, the 'scholar' of the future, the 'intellectual' of tomorrow should learn" to address himself or herself to the other, and learn it "from the ghost." Addressing himself to scholars and intellectuals, Derrida invites them to "learn to live" by learning to live with the ghost: He or she "should learn to live by learning not how to make conversation with the ghost but how to talk with him, with her, how to let them speak or how to give them back speech, even if it is in oneself, in the other, in the other in oneself: they are always *there*, specters, even if they do not exist, even if they are no longer, even if they are not yet."[36] Learning "to live," for the scholar, the intellectual, is thus intimately connected to learning (how to listen, talk, and write) from the phantom, the ghost. In order to address oneself to the other in the search for justice, one has *first of all* "to welcome the law of the phantom," precisely because this "law of the phantom" is the "most effaced and effaceable" and, for that very reason, "the most demanding,"[37] the most urgent.[38]

Derrida's insistence on the specter, phantom, or ghost is also motivated by the necessity, to borrow Samuel Weber's formulation, to analyze how "at least one aspect" of ghostly, spectral life today is the electronic media's contribution "to the institutionalization of death as spectator sport"[39] in the very societies that, in spite of towering military supremacy, use the discourse of legitimate defense and intolerable threats to their security to retaliate against any aggression in massively disproportional ways.[40]

The challenge that Derrida's thought then addresses to us is to realize the need to "learn," from the other, from the nameless, from the phantom or the ghost, how to address ourselves to him, to her; how to learn his, to learn her name with the keen awareness that looking for that name and learning it bears in itself the risk of "losing," forgetting, betraying it in its singularity.

Sherene Seikaly listens to phantoms who cannot be properly mourned in the concrete experience of living as a Palestinian in Haifa, the city where both sides of her family resided before the *Nakba* of 1948. The "interruptions of identity" and the asynchronicity that are described by Derrida as constitutive are experienced acutely and concretely in the everyday life of Palestinian Israelis. For them, the separation, described in Derrida's essay as a condition of possibility for any (adverbial) "together," is painfully and relentlessly lived through war, occupation, the separation wall, and cruel legal regulations (such as the ban on family unification passed by the Israeli Government in 2003). The condition of perpetual and forcible separation inscribes what Edward Said called the "epistemological achievement" of erasure into the very fabric of Israeli culture and society, an erasure that blots out not only the historical Palestinian presence, but also the historical experience of Jewish exile.

To the question raised in Derrida's essay whether "there [is] 'living together' otherwise than among 'first persons,'" Seikaly's essay, just as Michal Govrin's, gives an affirmative answer. Just as "Avowing—the Impossible" evokes a deeply personal, at times confessional tone, these two essays bear witness to and from, respectively, (Arab) Haifa and (Jewish) Jerusalem by relating a unique, personal, irreplaceable history that is interwoven with the life, togetherness, and *"aparthood"* of the community. Govrin's own confession about the "impossibility" of Jerusalem describes Derrida's "charged relationship with Jerusalem" through bearing witness to the friendship she shared with him, and to the "dubious 'role'" Derrida "seemingly 'dedicated'" to her: to be his addressee in Jerusalem. Govrin relates the context in which she introduced Derrida to Jerusalem's ancient cemetery, an experience he comments on at length at the end of "Avowing—The Impossible." The "impossibility" of Jerusalem also comes to stand for the aporias of "prayer" Derrida explores, aporias in which Govrin detects traces of Hassidic piety and Jewish humor. "Jerusalem" is, for Derrida, "perhaps" a prayer, and, at the same time, an "urgent global question." In this regard, Jerusalem exemplifies a gesture amplified elsewhere in Derrida's work, including in "Avowing—the Impossible," namely the refusal to separate "heart, thought, and the political taking of sides."[41]

Formulated positively, and to borrow Peggy Kamuf's words, "a loving movement is the indispensable key to understanding what deconstruction does," because "love's heart" is "that which would be able to hold together in an essential relation the movement toward the animate as well as toward the inanimate, toward life as well as non-life, or death, and, therefore, toward that which can be preserved in life as well as that which has never had or no longer has any life as such to be preserved. At the heart of love, all of these apparent oppositions would be suspended, no longer or not yet in force, or already ruined, in ruins."[42] Political positions or stances, the "political taking of sides," are thus indebted to the suspension or ruin of the "apparent oppositions" of life and non-life, of the "living" and the "phantoms."

Elisabeth Weber's essay proposes a close reading of this particular feature of Derrida's "lesson": its emphasis on the language of the heart and on what is called, in "Avowing—The Impossible," a "fundamental mode . . . of 'living together,'" compassion. It is now well documented that some of the torture methods used by American interrogators in Guantánamo, Iraq, and Afghanistan aim precisely at the destruction of compassion for the torture victim, including in the presumed enemy's own community. As the debate around the systematic use of torture by the most powerful country in the world has amply shown, "The dominant power is the one that manages to impose and, thus, to legitimate, indeed to legalize (for it is always a question of law) on a national or world stage, the terminology and thus the interpretation that best suits it in a given situation."[43] The relentless use of euphemisms such as "enhanced interrogation," the application of "no-touch" or "stealth" torture methods, combined with the persistent use of the singular "the enemy" in the government's statements about detainees in Guantánamo and other American-run prisons overseas hollow out what Frans de Waal calls "the synchronization of bodies," where empathy and sympathy start, not to form a whole, a totality, but to bridge (not overcome) irreducible differences.[44] Compassion as a visceral response (attested in its Hebrew name, *rachamim*, the plural of *rechem*, "the womb") is also systematically undermined in the dichotomies that Derrida scrutinized and deconstructed throughout his career, including the dichotomies between "human" and "animal," and, as the public debate on torture has evidenced all too clearly, the related dichotomy between "friend" and "enemy." However, even if the "enemies" are locked away in faraway offshore detention camps such as Guantánamo, and in overseas prisons such as Abu Ghraib and Bagram in order to deny them a hearing in American courts, one must still live together and, as Derrida underscores, "one must do so well, one might as well do so [*et il le faut bien*]," "one has no choice" ("Avowing").

Priya Kumar's essay gauges the tension between the concepts "ensemble" (ensemble, together) and "stranger" and analyzes the discursive slope between "stranger" and "enemy" in different nationalist discourses in India. She uncovers the "production of the Muslim as a stranger within the ensemble of the Indian nation" not only in a representative Hindu nationalist text, V. D. Savarkar's *Hindutva* (1923), but also, surprisingly, in an emblematic secular nationalist text, Jawaharlal Nehru's magnum opus *The Discovery of India* (1946). The discourse of intolerance and the discourse of tolerance share common ground when it comes to affirming the "autochthony"—and hence the prior claim—of Hindus on the nation-space of India. Any effort then at conceiving possibilities of peaceful coexistence between Hindus and Muslims in India would need to start by fundamentally rethinking the discourses of (Hindu) autochthony and origins that assign Muslims at best a liminal place in those discourses' understanding of Indian nationalism, secularism, and citizenship. Kumar follows Derrida's deconstructions of the "ensemble" and of "hospitality" in analyzing the "demonized narrative of Muslim separatism" as well as the persistent construction of the Indian Muslim as "an undecidable figure, the stranger, whose loyalty is always suspect and must be ritually reaffirmed to quell nationalist anxieties." Kumar's essay thus shows the constitutive and irreparable deficiencies of the concept of "tolerance."

After a careful deconstruction of the intimate connection between "globalization" (that Derrida uncovers as being, in fact, "globalatinization," *mondialatinisation*) and "tolerance," Derrida defines the latter in "Autoimmunity" as being "always on the side of the 'reason of the strongest,' where 'might is right,'" as a "supplementary mark of sovereignty, the good face of sovereignty, which says to the other from its elevated position, I am letting you be, you are not insufferable, I am leaving you in a place in my home, but do not forget that this is my home."[45] It is a "scrutinized hospitality, always under surveillance, parsimonious," in the best cases a "conditional hospitality,"[46] that is, "in spite of itself," a "phenomenon of hostility, with the frightful consequence that war might always be interpreted as the continuation of peace by other means or at least the non-interruption [*l'ininterruption*] of peace or of hospitality."[47]

The particular urgency that the Israeli-Palestinian conflict had for Derrida throughout his life is reflected in its insistence in "Avowing—The Impossible." In his remarks to Giovanna Borradori after the attacks of September 11, 2001, Derrida situated the confrontation "between the state of Israel . . . and a virtual Palestinian state" at the "epicenter, at least metonymically" of the "'wars'" he reflects on in this interview, "wars" that are connected, in different ways, to rivaling political theologies "issuing out of the same stock or common soil" of what Derrida calls "an 'Abrahamic' revelation."[48] Derrida always recognized the necessity of "numerous, complicated" mediations between his discourse and the "current violence," as he put it during a lecture in 1988 in Jerusalem, during the Palestinian uprising that had begun in 1987, mediations that "call for as much patience as caution on our part." But he also underlined that they cannot be used "as a pretext to wait and remain silent before that which demands *immediate* response and responsibility."[49]

In the last interview Derrida gave before his death, he reminds his interlocutor of the difficulty for him to say "we," adding that there *are*, however, "occasions when I do say it," in spite of "all the problems that torment me on this subject, beginning with the disastrous and suicidal politics of Israel and of a certain Zionism."[50] Given the urgency of this conflict in "Avowing—The Impossible," it figures prominently in several of the essays of this collection as well. It is, however, of crucial importance to place a reflection on this "epicenter" in a larger context. This larger context is alluded to by Derrida when he reminds his interlocutor in 2004 that "there has been more than one [Zionism], since the very beginning"[51] and when, as Gil Anidjar notes, Derrida calls "into question the possibility of emancipation as secularization, while calling for a secularization that remains to come." In this vein, Anidjar pursues an analysis of Derrida's decades-long interrogation of the configuration of Judaism and Zionism, from the early texts published in "Writing and Difference," via "Avowing—The Impossible," to the later essays on hospitality. In a close reading of Derrida's *Archive Fever*, Anidjar demonstrates that the rhetoric of secularization isolates and attempts to contain an energy that it calls "religious," an energy that subsequently returns explosively and precisely *as* "religious." According to Anidjar, Derrida's exploration of the "theological and apocalyptic energies and tendencies operative in political Zionism" culminates in a thinking of hospitality that fundamentally questions the "being-at-home" of the host, to the point of dispossessing the host of the security of any belonging and property.

Joseph Massad, proposing a genealogy of the term "Semitism," unfolds the "Palestinian Question *as* the Jewish Question." As both Palestinians and Jews inhabit the taxonomy "Semite," Massad discusses the way their question(s) constitute the Semitic Question—indeed how the Semite became a "question" *for Europe*. Massad's analysis describes anti-Semitism as (in Edward Said's formulation) the "secret sharer" of Orientalism and "Semitism" via the self-invention of the Germans as Aryans in the nineteenth century. Massad also subjects the concept of "the Abrahamic," used by Derrida in his essays on religion, to a critical genealogical reading. Rather than encompassing three monotheistic religions, the "Abrahamic," according to Massad, is "projected" onto "Islam" as one more ruse of an untenable inclusivity that consolidates and maintains the exclusion of the Semite.

Raef Zreik engages Derrida's text as a legal theorist, but also as a human rights and political activist, as a Palestinian citizen of Israel, by exploring the "tension" between the open, de jure infinite, questioning of a deconstructivist reflection on the one hand, and the "demand for closure, finality, and action" that is expected of and fought for by a political activist, on the other. Zreik also analyzes the tension that inhabits the infinite respect for the "other." For, while striving to give a voice to those seen as "other," a deconstructivist practice might come to pass as silencing their power to refute those who are *their others*. Concretely put, while Palestinians, as the subjects of occupation and dispossession, might recognize the solidarity of "deconstruction" with their attempts to make their voices heard, as the *Other* who struggles against hegemonic forces, they may also experience as betrayal its call for endless refinement and universalization,[52] an ever greater complexity of the questions asked, in which sharp distinctions and dichotomies experienced on the ground are blurred. While following Derrida's analysis of the threats and risks latent in the categories of the "whole," "totality," and "telos," Zreik proposes to also consider that the threat does not always emanate from the whole, especially when the latter is a site of resistance.

Richard Falk, since 2008 the United Nations Human Rights Council Special Rapporteur for the Occupied Palestinian Territories, takes Derrida's concept of the "impossible" as the starting point to explore figures of this "impossible that we can neither give up nor believe in" with regard to the Israeli-Palestinian conflict, against the "conventional wisdom" that politics is "the art of the possible." In the Israeli-Palestinian conflict, such a politics can only produce despair for those seeking justice and peace for the Palestinians—and even for the Israelis. Derrida's concept of the impossible, denoting inherently unresolvable dilemmas or aporias of thought and action, is highly relevant in the political context by proposing a "daring conceptual leap from 'impossibility' to 'responsibility,'" which results in detaching the burden of decision from any criteria of guidance as well as from the vague, and sometimes dangerous, admonition to exercise good faith. Given that in this particular conflict, "the probable is stuck in a matrix that seems incapable of yielding a genuine, or even a sustainable, peace for the two peoples," Falk, inspired by Derrida, pursues the hypothesis that "peace with justice" may not be attainable by normal politics but might need "extraordinary politics": "politics as the art of the impossible or the politics of impossibility." While acknowledging the importance of Derrida's analysis of originary violence as accompanying the formation of every sovereign state, Falk asserts that on neither side of the conflict can such "extraordinary politics" continue to rely on violence as the basis of emancipation or security. Falk goes on to describe a series of "impossible" scenarios that might hold the promise of approaching not just "peace," but "peace with justice."

As Derrida noted in different contexts, in the contemporary context of the "war against terror," more than ever,

> radical changes in international law are necessary. . . . I would be tempted to call philosophers those who, in the future, reflect in a responsible fashion on these questions and demand accountability from those in charge of public discourse, those responsible for the language and institutions of international law. A "philosopher" (actually I would prefer to say "philosopher-deconstructor") would be someone who analyzes

and then draws the practical and effective consequences of the relationship between our philosophical heritage and the structure of the still dominant juridico-political system that is so clearly undergoing mutation.[53]

The examples Derrida gives of the tasks awaiting the philosopher-deconstructor manifest the breathtaking extent of the latter's inventive engagements.

> We would have to analyze every mutation in the structure of public space, in the interpretation of democracy, theocracy, and their respective relations with international law (in its current state, in that which compels or calls it to transform itself and, thus, in that which remains largely to come within it), in the concepts of the nation-state and its sovereignty, in the notion of citizenship, in the transformation of public space by the media, which at once serve and threaten democracy, and so on. Our acts of resistance must be, I believe, at once intellectual and political. We must join forces to exert pressure and organize ripostes, and we must do so on an international scale and according to new modalities, though always while analyzing and discussing the very foundations of our responsibility, its discourses, its heritage, and its axioms.[54]

"Deconstruction is justice," then, since it calls for an untiring, in principle infinite, because never "finished," analysis of the philosophical heritage and its juridico-political systems, an analysis that is inseparable from an equally infinite responsibility. As a consequence, it is a call for a "Europe" to come, insofar as, in Rodolphe Gasché's words, for Derrida, "European responsibility is above all the uncompromising willingness to assume the challenge posed by the aporetic nature of inheritance itself, that is, by the constitutive lack of handed-down rules or norms to negotiate contradiction. Consequently, Europe is the name for a responsibility that also goes hand in hand with the necessity of having to invent, each time anew, new ways of meeting mutually exclusive demands."[55] As Jacques Derrida noted in 1990, with respect to the first Gulf War (a war waged for national sovereignty—or for oil), one would need to analyze such conflicts also in terms that would recognize what links the "split genealogy" of the West and its philosophical history "to several great and (despite what people say) irreconcilable monotheisms." And if many today—on all sides—would insist that current military actions by the United States in Iraq, Afghanistan, and elsewhere do not in any way constitute "religious war," we might pause to consider the question Derrida raises in his 1995 essay "Faith and Knowledge": "Wars or military 'interventions,' led by the . . . West in the name of the best causes (of international law, democracy, the sovereignty of peoples, of nations or of states, even of humanitarian imperatives), are they not also, from a certain side, wars of religion? The hypothesis would not necessarily be defamatory, nor even very original, except in the eyes of those who hasten to believe that all these just causes are not only secular but *pure* of all religiosity."[56] It is "not certain," Derrida suggests a few lines earlier in the same essay, "that in

16

addition to or in face of the most spectacular and most barbarous crimes of certain 'fundamentalisms' (of the present or of the past), *other* over-armed forces are not *also* leading 'wars of religion,' albeit unavowed."[57]

To the extent that, as Derrida suggests in his book on "rogue" states, "there is no worse war than that between enemy brothers,"[58] we should reexamine the assumption that peace could be achieved (and should therefore be sought) only through an understanding that somehow overcomes or resolves differences through the realization of identity in difference, or through the subjection of difference to a Hegelian teleology of reconciliation. Such "reconciliation" is all the more unlikely insofar as in the United States and its allied countries, the idea of a "just" or "legitimate" war has, in Avital Ronell's succinct formulation, "been doubled by a just technologization of war, in other words, by the promise of bloodless, sutureless, and surgically precise targeting," which might lead their populations to think that "we can conduct warfare as if it were extraneous, momentary, simulated, and not engaging the very core of our being."[59]

As mentioned above, Marc Nichanian, in his essay for the present collection, explores the constitutive limits of the work of "truth and reconciliation" commissions by showing how the search for and imperative of "reconciliation" cannot but lead to a radical interdiction of mourning, in which there is only one truth, that of the perpetrator. In the case of the Turkish-Armenian conflict of which Nichanian writes, as in so many other wars and struggles, "reconciliation" can mean only "a failure or simulacrum."[60] As Derrida explains in a text on the civil war in Algeria, this would be—it is—a "disaster" that is not only "predictable" but may be "calculated" and that, in any case, "outlines, in the negative, the dream of the impossible that we can neither give up nor believe in."[61] But we can think it, in the form of the "perhaps," which for Derrida "engages the only possible thought of the event—of friendship to come and friendship for the future. . . . There is no more just category for the future than that of the 'perhaps.' Such a thought conjoins friendship, the future, and the *perhaps* to open on to the coming of what comes—that is to say, necessarily in the regime of a possible whose possibilization must prevail over the impossible."[62]

This collection, then, presents attempts to respond to what Derrida called the task of today's intellectuals, the task of "inventive engagements" that do not pursue "reconciliation" but plead for the acknowledgment of those "irreconcilable differences," which might provide the inspiration to go beyond politics as the art of the mere possible and to engage in responses of responsibility.

*September 2010*

# Avowing—The Impossible: "Returns," Repentance, and Reconciliation

## A Lesson

*Jacques Derrida*

*Grâce, oui, grâce.*

Yes, before even starting, I will risk these two words—of *grâce*. First word, *grâce*, second word, *grâce*. In order to attest to my gratitude, indeed, but also in order to avow while asking for *grâce*.

I would like to render thanks [*grâce*], therefore, and also to ask for your forgiveness [*grâce*].

*Rendering* thanks [*grâce*] to those who have granted me the redoubtable honor of speaking, assigning me, as if by the privilege of an election, a task to which I will always feel unequal, I would also *ask* for their forgiveness, and for yours as well. Asking that one forgive what I will soon avow, I will dare to use my avowal as a pretext in order to put forth a general proposition, the formal hypothesis that I submit to your discussion.

Which one?

Well, today—I do say *today*—for those one calls contemporaries, for those who, one thinks, in a supposed synchrony, *live together [pour ceux qui* vivent ensemble] the historical now of a given time, today, therefore, in the same world, facing responsibilities (be they ethical, juridical, religious, and beyond) named by what we call, in so obscure a fashion, in *our* language, "living together [*vivre ensemble*]," well then, a *certain* avowal would announce itself as the first *commandment*.[1]

This is not just any avowal but a singular, unheard of and improbable avowal, an avowal that, prior to and beyond any determined fault, declares before the other the unavowable. For to avow what seems easy to avow, to avow the avowable, let us recognize, would not be to avow. Let us avow that. The avowal, if there is one, must avow the unavowable, and must, therefore, *declare* it. The avowal would have to declare, were it possible, the unavowable, that is to say, the unjust, the unjustifiable, the unforgivable, and even the impossibility of avowing. In the same man-

18

ner, to forgive only that which is forgivable, venial, would not be to forgive. An avowal, if there is such, must avow the unavowable, and forgiveness, if there is such, must forgive the unforgivable—and must, therefore, do the impossible. If such were the condition of "living together," it would command doing the impossible.

I do not yet know whether declaring, manifesting, confessing, or avowing the unavowable already supposes the repentance or the return of some *teshuvah*: an immense enigma, against whose background a globalization[2] of the scene of avowal today presents itself. Everywhere, there is the theatrical process of a *return* to the most proximate or to the most distant past, often with repentance and forgiveness asked for, a process of reparation, indemnification, or reconciliation. However one interprets it, this globalization of avowal and of repentance perhaps affects or already signifies, like an announcement or like a symptom, a certain mutation of the "living together." Thus would resonate the first *commandment*—be it impracticable—dictated by all "living together."

I will not use this word, *commandment*, lightly.

But here is a first avowal before beginning to justify this word of "commandment" with regard to a "living together"—and I will do nothing here but prepare myself, until the very end, to begin again, for there can be no "living together" that is not devoted to this return, this going back upon oneself or back over one's steps, this repetition of inaugurality. I know that there has been here, in the past, a great conference on forgiveness.[3] What would have changed in the world concerning the scene of forgiveness, since that time, thirty years ago, in the time, that is, of one generation? What is new concerning forgiveness and concerning what the scene of forgiveness implies and engages of a "living together"? Since Jean Halpérin has honored me with this invitation by sharing with me the theme chosen for this encounter, namely, "how to live together [*comment vivre ensemble*]?" I avow that I now live differently with these close and familiar words, words which say something about close ones, about the neighbor and the proximate [*qui disent quelque chose des proches, du prochain*], and about *familiarity* itself, even about family. What is a neighbor [*prochain*] when one knows that no known proximity, above all not that of space and time, suffices to define my close ones [*mes proches*] and even less so my neighbor? My neighbor can be a stranger or a foreigner, any other or wholly other [*tout autre*], living very far from me in space and time. This truth has not had to wait for television or the cell telephone. These words, "to live together" and "how" have thus not ceased to accompany me, but they have also and at once failed or escaped my company, becoming for me, in their very familiarity, more and more strange, foreign, enigmatic. "Living together"—yes, but what does that mean? Even before knowing "how"? Is it not both a simple evidence (how could one live otherwise?) and, on the contrary, the promise always of the inaccessible? Suspended in a title and out of context, the tone of this formula remains very unstable. Following the virtual phrases that incline it toward one side or the other, it oscillates between a tone of practical serenity and an accent of tragic pathos, between philosophical wisdom and desperate anguish. Wisdom teaches us: Given that living is always "living together," and that it must be so, let us only learn "how to live together," let us determine rules, norms, maxims, precepts, even an ethical, juridical, and political jurisprudence. But despair protests and replies: "But *how*? How to live together? I will not, you will not, he/she will not, we will not, you will not, they will not, achieve it, ever"—and the variation of these persons speaks also a deeper paradox as to the same concern: Who addresses whom in asking "how to live together?" or still: Does not "living together" take place from the instant that the concern over this question makes us tremble in our solitude and *avow,* yes, declare our despair and share it?

In a kind of discreet and discontinuous meditation, these two words, "living together," this couple of words that go together, that go well together while letting us think of an impossible marriage (one often says of unwed couples: these two "live together"), these two words, therefore, have both harassed and abandoned me, like two words that go together *without* closing themselves up in a togetherness, an ensemble or a gathering— and already there announces itself, between the adverb "together [*ensemble*]" and the noun "ensemble [*ensemble*]," a divorce of which I will make much [*grand cas*]. An intense obsession, if often distracted by the memory I keep of the only time I have attended, without participating, a colloquium such as this one. To attend without participating—is that "living together"? How to "live together" with or for intellectuals said to be French-speaking Jews [*des intellectuals dits juifs de langue française*]? This is not only *my* question, and it is pregnant with so many others. I was attending this colloquium, then, without participating, quite a long time ago, in the 1960s no doubt, probably in 1965. Close to Emmanuel Levinas, near him, perhaps together with him. In truth, I was here thanks [*grâce*] to him, turned toward him. That is still the case today, differently. Another way of recalling, at the moment when I want to salute the name of the admired friend, that one can "live together" with the dead. This will be my conclusion in a moment, when I will return, finally, to Jerusalem and tell you about my first visit to the cemetery of this city the whole of which [*dont l'ensemble*], the being-together of which [*l'être-ensemble*] remain to be thought. "Living together," with the dead, is not an accident, a miracle, or an extraordinary story [*histoire*]. It is rather an essential possibility of existence. It reminds us that in "living together" the idea of life is neither simple nor dominant even if it remains irreducible. "Living together" with the past of those who are no longer and will not be present or living, or with the unpredictable future to come [*avenir*] of those who are not yet living in the present: If this constitutes an indisputable possibility of the being-with-oneself [*être-avec-soi*], of a "living together"—with-oneself, in a self thus shared or divided, enclosed, multiplied, or torn, open too, in any case anachronistic in its very present, at once increased and dislocated by the mourning or the promise of the other in oneself, a larger, older or younger other than oneself, an other outside of oneself in oneself, then "living together" no longer has the simplicity of a "living" in the present pure and simple, no more than the cohesiveness, the self-coincidence of a present whole [*ensemble présent*], living present, present to itself, synchronous with itself, conjoined with itself in a kind of totality. The alterity of irreducible pasts and futures withdraws [*soustrait*] "living to-gether" from the plenitude of a presence to self or from an identity. In order to attempt to think what "living together" might mean [*ce que peut vouloir dire "vivre ensemble"*], one must therefore take into account what occurs [*ce qui arrive*] to that which is called the proximity of the other in the present, and not only by way of technology, from television to Internet and cell phones, wireless communication, or satellites. The alterity of past and future, the irreducible experience of memory and of the promise, of mourning and of hope, all suppose some *rupture*, the interruption of this identity or of this totality, this ac-complishment of a presence to self—a fracturing openness in what one calls *un ensemble* [whole, gathering, ensemble], with the noun *ensemble,* which I will distinguish here from the adverb *ensemble* in the expression "*vivre ensemble.*" This cannot be without conse-quences of all kinds, and not only ethical, juridical, or political, as to what we must medi-tate on *together* [*ensemble*]. The adverb, in the expression "living together," appears to find its sense and dignity only there where it exceeds, dislocates, contests the authority of the noun "ensemble," to wit, the closure of an ensemble, be it the whole of something "living" [*d'un "vivant"*], of a system, a totality, a cohesiveness without fault and identical with it-self, of an indivisible element containing itself in its immanence and simply larger, like the whole [*tout*], than its parts. The authority of the whole [*ensemble*] will always be the first threat for all "living together." And inversely, all "living together" will be the first protes-tation or contestation, the first testimony against the whole [*ensemble*].

Before beginning still, I recall therefore what Emmanuel Levinas told me in an aside on that day and which I had evoked on the day of his death. I narrate in the present tense as is done sometimes in the rhetoric of historians in order to make things more palpable [*sensible*] to representation. On that day, Levinas speaks words that resonate otherwise as to what "living together" might mean *for Jews,* living or not. André Neher is lecturing, and Levinas whispers in my ear: "You see, he is the Protestant—me, I'm the Catholic." This *mot d'esprit* would call for an infinite commentary. I will raise only one question: What must a Jewish thinker be in order to use this language, with the depth of seriousness and the lightness of irony that we hear in it? How can a so-called Catholic Jew (outside of any conversion, any canonization, and outside of any great ecclesial scene of repentance of which we will speak again) "live together" with a supposed Protestant Jew, while remain-ing a Jew together with himself, and while opening himself to another Jew, probable or improbable, in this case me, who has never felt very Catholic, and above all not Protes-tant? A Jew who, coming from another shore of Judaism than Neher and Levinas, a Medi-terranean shore, immediately remarks in the abyss of these doubles or of this Abrahamic, Judeo-Catholico-Protestant, triangle, the absence of the Islamo-Abrahamic? And how does a Jew of whom I know only too well, and from so close, that he will never have been sure of being together with himself in general, a Jew who dares not stop at the hypothesis that this dissociation from self renders him *at once* as less Jewish and as most Jewish—how could such a split or divided Jew [*un Juif aussi partagé ou divisé*] have received this remark? How could he welcome its letter according to the spirit that was undeniably breathing in it, to wit, that nothing of all these differences, dissociations, or indecisions could damage [*entamer*] the complicity of a certain "living together" that had decided for *us* well before *us*—I name thus the supposed friendship, the affinity, the complicity, if not the shareable solidarity of Jews so different within themselves, so different from themselves within themselves and at their core, be they assured or not of a stable and decidable belonging to Judaism? I would not have let my memory speak, at the risk of appearing complacent, if, after lengthy debates, I had not judged it irresponsible to efface, in simple politeness, my signature, that of a Jewish intellectual for whom "living together" with a non-Jewish world was no more serious or more urgent a problem than that of "living together" with all the forms of what one calls the Jewish communities of the world—and first of all, for my generation, the Algerian community, the Algerian communities—the Arab, Berber, French of Algeria, French of France, communities—Israeli community, Israeli communities, and beyond. If I trust what remains for me indisputable or undeniable, to wit, an "I am Jewish," not "I am *first of all* Jewish" but "I am *already and since forever* Jewish and I will it at all cost," this experience of the irrevocable has always tolerated, even demanded, an infinite uncertainty regarding what might be meant by or involved in a "living together" in a Jewish community—and first of all with oneself as Jewish and with oneself in general. It is in this torment that I recall the words of Levinas. In a biography dedicated to him, there is a chapter on the history of the Colloques des intellectuals juifs de langue française which recalls the impressive list of speakers who have participated in its proceedings. One can read there, and I underscore the future tense: "But, among the French philosophers of Jewish origin, one *will* never see Jacques Derrida there." As if I were dead. Or as if the colloquium had already concluded its work and ended the travels of this Booth [*Cabane*] of which Pierre Bouretz spoke so beautifully.[4] This fictitious future, articulating a future anterior, will have belonged, of course, much like the present tense I was invoking earlier, to an unequivocal grammar of the historian of the past; but through its lack of prudence, it announces something else, like my present tense earlier. The thoughtlessness [*légèreté*] of the prediction gives rise to a reflection on time and on what can "occur [*arriver*]" with respect to the "living together," on what can occur to the "living together," and on a certain relation of the arrival, the coming or the event, to the "living together." It is of this relation between the event and the "living together" that I would like to speak. In this respect, the unstable agreement [*accord*] or belonging, the unresolved, divided modality for such a Jew of *his* "living together" in the Jewish and French communities, without speaking for now of the Israeli community, or simply of "living together" with oneself—such is one of the indecisions, even impossibilities whose avowal I would like to unfold in order to draw a few consequences.

I do not, therefore, as I was saying, use the word "commandment" lightly, nor to agree with the spirit of what should be, according to some, a meeting of Jewish intellectuals. No, in its French idiom, "how to live together," in the infinitive and without determined subject, a verb plus an adverb, we hear, in the brevity of its sententious ellipsis, the imperious reminder [*rappel*] of what remains an ineluctable necessity, even a *vital* necessity. One *must* [*il faut*] "live together." Together with the adverb "together," the infinitive "to live" enjoins, it gives at least an implicit assertion: "live together," one must, one might as well "live together" [*il faut bien "vivre ensemble"*]. In any case [*de toute façon*], in any fashion [*de toutes les façons*], "live together" one must, and one must do so well, one might as well do so [*et il le faut bien*].

This "must [*il faut*]," like the *well* of the one must well, can be modulated in any and all keys. Were we to do scales on an instrument in order to test the tuning of its strings, in order to adjust the ear toward the right note, or at least toward a not too discordant note (unless the false note, the right false note [*la juste fausse note*] were not rigorously required when it is a matter of discording [*détonner*] or going out of tune a little in order to think how difficult the accord and agreement are, the harmony of the "living together," a rare and always improbable thing), we would hear the harmonics of this strange expression ("living together"), which has some fairly strict equivalents, it is true, in other languages. Following the French idiom that constitutes, de facto and de jure, and even more than Judaism, even more than the same feeling of supposed belonging to Jewishness, the element of our "being-together," the connotations of the "living together" are distributed from the best to the worst, by way of the last resort, here an inaccessible ideal, there a fatality that itself can be experienced as good, neutral, or infernal. The best of the "living together" is often associated with peace, an enigmatic concept if ever there was one, and I would have liked to have the time for a patient meditation on peace, from Kant to Levinas, a perpetual peace or a messianic peace, whose promise belongs to the very concept of peace and suffices to distinguish it from armistice, from cease-fire, or even from any "peace process." Palestinians and Israelis will live truly together only on the day when peace (not only armistice, cease-fire, or the peace process) comes into bodies and souls, when what is necessary will have been done by those who have the power for it or who, quite simply, have the most power, state power, economic, military, national, or international power, to take the initiative for peace in a manner that is first of all wisely unilateral. At bottom, the question of which I will speak tonight could be summarized as the question of initiative, in avowal: Who takes or must take the initiative? And to whom falls the charge of the unilateral decision before all exchange and all reciprocity to come, in the approach of peace or of reconciliation?

But another connotation of the "*bien vivre ensemble*," that of the last resort, does not wait for peace. It is that of the "one must live together well [*il faut bien vivre ensemble*]," one has no choice. It is, indeed, always a matter of a necessity, and therefore of a law: One cannot not "live together" even if one does not know how or with whom, with God, with gods, men, animals, with one's own, with one's close ones, neighbors, family, or friends, with one's fellow citizens or countrymen, but also with the most distant strangers, with one's enemies, with oneself, with one's contemporaries, with those who are no longer so or will never be so, so many names that I draw from daily language and of which I do not yet presume that we know what they designate. But we sense that the regimes of this law, of the "must [*il faut*]" and therefore of the "well [*bien*]" of "one must *well* live together," can be different. We know (the example will not surprise you, but I could substitute it with so many others) that Israelis and Palestinians, Israelis and Arabs of the Middle East, already must, they must *well* "live together" whether they are or not for "peace now," whether they are or not orthodox, as one says strangely; and the same goes for the Israelis and for all the Jews of the Diaspora (this name which arbitrarily places them in one ensemble, whether they want it or not, be it under the category of dispersion), whether they are believers or not, favoring or not what one calls the "peace process," agreeing or not with those who, here or there, concur in good conscience or cynically to sabotage the said process; well then, all of these, they must well "live together."

In the inflections of what we declare here as our language, these "one must well" of the "one must well live together," can therefore have heterogeneous values to the point of incompatibility. At least two.

*On the one hand,* the "one must well" can announce that one will have to live *badly* [*mal*] together (in hatred or in war—which are also manners of living, even of dying together, in the same space and the same time, in lack of trust, indifference, or resignation to fatality—as when one suggests sometimes that, short of authentic peace, Israel and the countries of the Middle East must well *co*-exist, *co*-habitate, *co*-operate, *col*-laborate. War, cold or not, even apartheid, but also peaceful coexistence, the cohabitation of adversaries, including in the sense of the Fifth Republic, are all forms of the "one must well live together," be it at the price of *not well* agreeing to "live together." And under cohabitation, in the sense of the Fifth Republic, there present themselves at this time, in a nonfortuitous manner, major and conflictual stakes that divide the French community as to "living together": Beyond the thousand problems of Europe and of social justice, in a sharper fashion yet, three fundamental questions of "living together" put this cohabitation to the test today, questions that are no longer only French but to which Jews are particularly sensitive: the question of hospitality to foreigners, immigrants with or without permits, the questions of civil union[5] and of marriage, the question of national memory, in particular (since one could multiply examples) that of World War I, even before the 1930s and 40s, there where another imagery of the trenches of 1914–1918 and thus of so many other structuring phantasms comes to unsettle [*inquiéter*] the most reassuring and the most consensual foundations that are, however, nonnatural, constructed and fragile foundations of the national "living together."

It is true that even in these negative hypotheses of the "one must live together well," the common value of a higher interest is accepted by the partners, even the enemies, that it is better to live than to die (living, surviving, would then be, in this hypothesis, the unconditional imperative, as problematic as it remains). Even if this cohabitation is resigned, armed, organized, at times guaranteed by a contract, a constitution, and some institu-

tional jurisprudence, it answers to a common, and therefore higher, interest. This calculation supposes at least three axioms that are at once powerful and fragile.

1. One cannot not suppose that this reasoned cohabitation represents a temporary situation destined to save the promise of an *avenir,* a to-come, and that the *avenir* of this
   *avenir* should keep the figure of a "living together" free of these negative limits, of this
   statutory surveillance. An authentic peace to come, a peace without end or infinite
   remains the quasi-messianic horizon of this armed peace or of this armistice. What
   goes here for communities, nations, or states can be valid also for families or
   individuals.
2. One cannot not suppose some consensus as to what "living" means, and that it is
   worth more and better than dying—which is far from self-evident, no more than it is
   self-evident that some forms of "dying" do not figure a certain manner of "living together." Dying together, in the *same* place and at the *same* moment, for those whom
   Montaigne calls the "co-dying [*commourans*]," some can see here the supreme ordeal
   of "living together." What does "same" mean in these expressions? Here is an enigma
   that I do not yet touch on.
3. One cannot not suppose that each partner of this coexistence or of this cohabitation
   should be identical to himself, should be one and together with him—which is far
   from self-evident, whether it be a matter of humanity, the nation, or the nation-state
   and therefore the citizen, whether it be a question of no matter what community or
   class of so-called civil society, or whether it be a matter quite simply of a family, of
   each individual and of what one strangely calls one's close ones or one's own, of "me,"
   of whoever says "me" and claims in all conscience—I mean, without taking account
   of some unconscious—to decide and to take responsibility.

But, *on the other hand,* the syntagma "il faut *bien* vivre ensemble" can let itself be
otherwise accented in *our* language, and signal toward a "well [*bien*]," a "living *well* together [bien *vivre ensemble*]," that no longer incidentally qualifies a fundamental or previous "living together." "Living together" then means living together "well [*bien*], according
to the good [*le bien*]: not only some euphoria of living, of the good life, of the *savoir-vivre*
or an art of living, but also according to a good of trust, of accord, or of concord." This
"good [*bien*]" intrinsic to the "living together," no one will *reasonably* think (but it is the
reasonable that we interrogate here) of dissociating from peace, from harmony, from accord, and concord. If "living together" then means "living *well* together," this signifies
understanding one another in trust, in good faith, in faith, comprehending one another,
in a word, being in *accord* with one another. Why then speak of accord? Why this language of the heart [*coeur*], of accord and concord, even of "mercy [*miséricorde*]," and of
the compassion that must bring us closer and a bit more quickly to the question of "forgiveness," with or without *teshuvah*? The language of the heart reminds us that this peace

of "living together," even if it is a peace of justice and equity, is not necessarily under the law of the law, at least in the sense of legality, of law [*droit*] (national or international) or of the political contract; and here, as I often do, I will distinguish, but without opposing them, justice and law [*la justice et le droit*]. Let us turn our ear toward the French idiom: One says, for example, of the partners of a couple (man and woman, man and man, woman and woman) that they "live together" when, outside of the law or the instituted obligations of marriage, even of a civil union, they decide, freely and out of a common accord, to share their life, their time, the places of life (the land on earth), and sometimes, with the time and the land of their history, with their memory and their mourning, the *avenir* of a generation, children engendered or adopted by them (men and women), and so on. (Hence my allusion to the PACS and to the mutineers of World War I, announcement of two earthquakes, the rumbling of which remains still discreet.) Not that "living together" demands a rupture with the normality of law or with marriage (spouses can well "live together," and legality does not exclude "living *well* together"). But even in the cases of the most reassuring juridical normality (with or without civil union), there is a "living *well* together" only to the extent that something that I will elliptically call here the heart, the love or peace of the heart, the *fiance* [of *confiance*, confidence, trust, promise] accord or concord, exceeds the contract guaranteed by law or state legislation. Henceforth, if some ethics of "living together" thus appears to be implied by the idiomatic usage that I content myself for now with analyzing, it supposes accord beyond any statutory condition, not necessarily in contradiction with it, but beyond and across the normality of a legal, political, and state-controlled bond between two or more than one (male or female) who are not only spouses, co-citizens, co-countrymen, congeners, or coreligionist individuals, but remain strangers, (from) others and radically other. The peace of "living together," therefore, exceeds the juridical, even the political, at any rate, the political as determined by the state, by the sovereignty of the state. This "living together," even where it is irreducible to the statutory or institutional (juridical, political, state-controlled) bond, opens another dimension to the same necessity—and that is why I have spoken of the other, of the stranger, of a hospitality to the wholly other who exceeds the statutory convention. The "good" of the "living well together" supposes the interruption of the *natural* as well as *conventional* relation; it supposes even this *interruption tout court* that one calls absolute solitude, separation, inviolable secret. This separation (which was also one of the great themes of Levinas), is precisely that which opens, without contradicting, all the "must" of "one must live together well." Through paradoxes and aporias about which I will even claim shortly that one must avow, one will not say that the parts of one and the same natural, organic, and living ensemble *live together*. The adverb "together" in the expression "living together" does not refer to the totality of a natural, biological, or genetic ensemble, to the cohesiveness of an organism or of some social body (family, ethnic group, nation) that would be measured with this organic metaphor. "Living together" supposes, therefore, an interrupting excess *both* with regard to statutory convention, to law *and* with

26

regard to *symbiosis,* to a symbiotic, gregarious, or fusional living together. I would go so far as to say—this appeared to me serious enough not to be accepted too easily—that all "living together" that would limit itself to the symbiotic or that would be regulated according to a figure of the symbiotic or the organic is a first lapse of the sense [*un manquement au sens*] and of the "must" of "living together." Here is, therefore, a double and paradoxical prescription. It is inscribed in the idiom, that is to say, already in a mode of "living together." "Living together" is reducible neither to organic symbiosis nor to the juridico-political contract. Neither to "life" according to nature or birth, blood or soil, nor to life according to convention, contract, or institution. "Living together," if it were possible, would mean putting to the test the insufficiency of this old couple of concepts that conditions, in the West, more or less any metaphysics, any interpretation of the social bond, any political philosophy or any sociology of being-together, the old couples *physis/nomos, physis/thesis,* nature/convention, biological life/law [*droit*]—law which I distinguish here, more than ever, from justice and from the justice of "living together." One will never think the "living together" and the "living" of the "living together" and the "how together" unless one transports oneself *beyond everything* that is founded on this opposition of nature and culture. That is to say, beyond everything, more or less everything. This excess with regard to the laws of nature, as well as to the laws of culture, is always an excess with regard to the whole [*ensemble*], and I do not take the difficulty lightly. It is almost unthinkable, very close to impossible, precisely. This excess does not signify that law, a nonlegal law or a nonjuridical justice, does not continue to command the sense and the "must" of the "one must live together well." Which law? And can "declaring oneself Jewish," in whatever mode (and there are so many), grant a privileged access to this justice, to this law beyond laws [*cette loi au-dessus des lois*]?

We lack the time to develop this argument in the code of a philosophical analysis that would refer itself to universal and impersonal structures and that would appeal to numerous texts. Under the heading of "declaring oneself Jewish," I would rather confide in you, and perhaps avow that these philosophical necessities have imposed themselves upon me through the modest experience of someone who, prior to becoming what you call a "French-speaking Jewish intellectual [*intellectuel juif de langue française*]," was first a young Jew in French Algeria between three wars (before, during, and after World War II; before, during, and after the so-called war of Algeria). In a country where the number and the diversity of historical communities was as rich as in Jerusalem, West to East, this Jewish child could dream of a peaceful cultural, linguistic, and even national plural belonging only through the experience of nonbelonging: separations, rejections, ruptures, exclusions. If I did not forbid myself any lengthy first-person discourse (but is there "living together" otherwise than among "first persons"?), I would describe the contradictory movement that, at the time of the anti-Semitic zeal of the French authorities in Algeria during the war, pushed a little boy who was expelled from school and understood none of it to rebel, forever, against two ways of "living together": at once against racist gregariousness, and therefore against anti-Semitic segregation, but also, more obscurely, and more unavow-ably, no doubt, against the conservative and self-protective confinement of a Jewish com-munity that, seeking *naturally, legitimately* to defend itself, to constitute or reconstitute its whole [*ensemble*] under the ordeal of these traumas, was folding in upon itself, overbid-ding in the direction that I already then felt as a kind of exclusive, even fusional, commu-nitarianism. Believing that he was beginning to understand what "living together" could mean, the child of which I speak had to break then, in a manner that was as unreflective as reflective, with both sides, with both exclusive—and thus excluding—belongings. The only belonging, the only "living together" that he judged then bearable and worthy of that name already supposed a rupture with identitarian and totalizing belonging, assured of itself in a homogeneous whole [*ensemble*]. In a manner as unreflective as reflective, the child felt at his core two contradictory things as to what this "living together" could sig-nify: on the one hand, that he could betray his own, his close ones, and Judaism, and that he had to avow this within himself, even before others, even before God, but also, on the other hand, that by this separation, this rupture, this passage toward a kind of universal-ity beyond symbiotic communitarianism and gregarious fusion, beyond even citizenship, in this very separation, it could be that he was more faithful to a certain Jewish vocation, at the risk of remaining the only, the last, and the least of the Jews [*le seul et le dernier des Juifs*], in the most ambiguous sense of this expression with which he played without playing—elsewhere and fifty years later, presenting himself or sometimes also hiding himself as a kind of paradoxical Marrano who ran the risk of losing even the culture of his secret or the secret of his culture. For, at the core of this solitude, this child had to begin believing, and he no doubt never finished thinking, that any "living together" supposes and guards, as its very condition, the possibility of this singular, secret, inviolable separa-tion, from which alone a stranger accords himself to a stranger, in hospitality. To recognize that one lives together, well then, only with and as a stranger, a stranger "at home [*chez soi*]," in all the figures of the "at home," that there is "living together" only there where the whole [*ensemble*] is neither formed nor closed [*ne se forme pas et ne se ferme pas*], there where the living *together* [*ensemble*] (the adverb) contests the completion, the closure, and the cohesiveness of an "ensemble" (the noun, the substantive), of a substan-tial, closed ensemble identical to itself; to recognize that there is "living together" only there where, in the name of promise and of memory, of the messianic and of mourning without work and without healing, it welcomes dissymmetry, anachrony, nonreciprocity with an other who is greater, at once older and younger, an other who comes or will come *perhaps,* who has *perhaps already* come—here is the justice of a law above laws, here is a paradox that I believe coherent with what we were saying a moment ago of a "living to-gether" that does not allow itself to be contained, exhausted, or governed, either in a natu-ral or organic (genetic or biologic) whole, or in a juridico-institutional one. And this, whatever the name one gives to these natural or institutional wholes (organism, family, neighborhood, nation, nation-state, with their territorial space or the time of their history). Levinas recalled the bond between Jewish universalism and the respect of the stranger in his lesson, "Toward the Other" with the commentary of a text from Tractate *Yoma* around *teshuvah* (a lesson I will not have time to interrogate in my turn with the attentiveness I would have liked). "The respect for the stranger," he says, "and the sanctification of the name of the Eternal are strangely equivalent. And all the rest is a dead letter. All the rest is literature. . . . The image of God is better honored in the right given to the stranger than in symbols. Universalism . . . bursts the letter apart, for it lay, explosive, within the letter."[6] The faithful child of whom I speak, faithful to this solitude and obligated toward a singular interruption, believed he did not have, in growing up, to salve these first wounds. If the memory of anti-Semitic persecutions, well beyond those he could have suffered himself, remained as unerasable as present in everything he thought, said, wrote, or taught, in return, the same vigilance was warning him, warns him today, against all the risks of the "living together" of the Jews, be they of a symbiotic type (naturality, birth, blood, soil, nation) or conventional (state juridical, in the modern sense): a certain communitarianism, a certain Zionism, a certain nationalism and all that can follow when the motifs of filiation through blood, appropriation of the place, and the motif of election, all run the risk of remaining caught—I am saying "risk" because this is not a fatality, and that is where the moment of responsibility is found—in the grip of nature or of convention. I do not have time here to develop all the philosophical and political analyses that, for the child turned adult, have sharpened this concern, but I must declare, or, if you prefer, avow that this concern was and remains with me without complacency and sometimes without pity. It pushes the said child not only to oppose, sometimes publicly, the politics of the current Israeli government and of a great number of those that preceded it, but also to continue to interrogate himself in the most insomniac fashion regarding the conditions in which the modern state of Israel established itself. If there is a place where I do not have the right to hide this, it is here. I hasten immediately to add at least two things: (1) that one can remain radically critical in this regard without implying thereby any threatening or disrespectful consequences for the present, the future, and the existence of Israel, on the contrary; (2) that I have been able to perceive, and to rejoice at this during my last visit to Israel and to Palestine, that these questions, these "returns" (reflections, repentances, conscious realizations) upon certain founding violences are today more frequent and declared by certain Israelis, citizens and authentic patriots, and by new historians of the state of Israel, the ones and the others having decided to draw political consequences from this return to the past, as some Palestinians do as well. The child of whom I speak and who makes me speak understood in growing up that any juridico-political founding of a "living together" is, by essence, violent, since it inaugurates there where a law [*droit*] did not yet exist. The founding of a state or of a constitution, therefore, of a "living together" according to a state of law [*un état de droit*], is always first of all a nonlegal violence: not illegal but nonlegal, otherwise put, *unjustifiable* with regard to an existing law, since the law is inexistent there where it is a matter of creating it. No state has ever been founded without this violence, whatever form and whatever time it might have taken. But the child of whom I speak asked himself whether the founding of the modern state of Israel—with all the politics and policies that have followed and confirmed it— could be no more than an example among others of this originary violence from which no state can escape, or whether, because this modern state intended not to be a state like others, it had to appear before another law and appeal to another justice. I recall here this classical question because I intend to take into consideration in a moment a certain globalization of law and of scenes of repentance or of forgiveness asked for when the instance in front of which this appearance is instituted is no longer national or belonging to the state.

If I let a Jewish child speak, it is neither to move you cheaply nor to shelter provocations behind an alibi. Rather it is to convince you that my questions, my reticences, my impatiences, my indignation sometimes (for example, when faced with the politics of almost all the Israeli governments and the forces that support them, from within and from without) are not inspired by hostility or by the indifference of distance. On the contrary, shared with so many Israelis who are exposed and concerned otherwise than I am, and together with so many Jews in the world, this innocent concern for compassion (a fundamental mode, in my view, of "living together"), of this compassion of justice and equity (*rahamim*, perhaps), I will claim it, if not as the essence of Judaism, at least as what remains in me inseparable from the suffering and disarmed memory of the Jewish child, there where he has learned to name justice and what in justice at once exceeds and demands law [*le droit*]. Everything comes to me, no doubt, from this source, in what I am about to say, under the title "avowing—the impossible."

"Avowing—the impossible." This can signify at once "one must avow and, therefore, avow the unavowable," and this avowing of the unavowable remains perhaps impossible but an impossibility that must be rendered manifest—even and precisely if it appears impossible. Put otherwise, the truth is that one must do the impossible, and the impossible would perhaps be the only measure of any "must [*il faut*]."

How and why grant *today* such privilege to the avowing of the unavowable? Since I have *chosen* to place this modest address under the sign of the avowal, you have the right to ask me why I am about to do so in such paradoxical and suspicious fashion, to the point of declaring the command to avow to be as necessary as it is impossible.

The choice of this theme was an election, and therefore a selection, therefore an exclusion that I could not justify in a rational fashion, but for which I would account in a solely economic and conditional mode—and this too I must avow. Economical and conditional, because I have committed myself to treating an infinite enigma ("living together") for an hour and a few minutes (on such a topic, this is the time of one of those telegrams that one no longer sends), and to do so in a language shared by all of us who are here together (first response to any injunction of the "living together"), and so a language that resists my temptations, and first of all the temptation that would consist in wagering on the double and abyssal memory that opens upon the immense question of "living together" by multiplying allusions on the side of a philosophical memory, from Aristotle, Rousseau, Kant, Heidegger, or Husserl, to Marx, Nietzsche, or Levinas, to the metaphysics or to the ontology of being-with (*Mitsein*), to the socius, intersubjectivity, the phenomenological constitution of the transcendental *alter ego,* to the social bond and to dissociation, to the relation without relation to the other, to Blanchot's "unavowable community" or Nancy's "inoperative community," and so on. And how to faithfully treat, at this rhythm, a tradition of Jewish thought on the topic of "living together" but also on the return, repentance, pardon, reconciliation, and reparation (on *teshuvah* or *tikkun* in the treasure of canonical texts or their repetition [*reprise*] by Leo Baeck, for example, by Hermann Cohen or Emmanuel Levinas)? If I have chosen the theme of avowal, that is first of all because of what is occurring [*ce qui se passe*] *today* in the world, a kind of general rehearsal [*répétition*], a scene, even a theatrical rendering [*théâtralisation*] of avowal, of return, and of repentance, which seems to me to signify a mutation in process, a fragile one, to be sure, fleeting and difficult to interpret, but, like the moment of an undeniable rupture in the history of the political, of the juridical, of the relations among community, civil society, and the state, among sovereign states, international law, and NGOs, among the ethical, the juridical, and the political, between the public and the private, between national citizenship and an international citizenship, even a metacitizenship, in a word, concerning a social bond that crosses [*passe*] the borders of these ensembles called family, nation, or state. Sometimes accompanied by what one names rightly or wrongly repentance, sometimes preceded or accompanied by what one believes, rightly or wrongly, must condition them, namely confession, repentance, forgiveness asked for, scenes of avowal are multiplied and have been accelerating for a few years, months, weeks, every day in truth, in a public space transformed by tele-technologies and by media capital, by the speed and the reach of communication, but also by the multiple effects of a technology, a techno-politics and a techno-genetics that unsettle [*bouleversent*] *at once* all conditions: conditions of being-together (the supposed proximity, in the same instant, in the same place and the same territory, as if the unicity of a place on earth, of a soil, were becoming more and more—as one says of a telephone and in the measure of the said telephone—*portable*) *and* the conditions of the living in its technological relation to the nonliving, to hetero- or homografting, to prosthesis, artificial insemination, cloning, and so on. Largely exceeding the territory of the state or of the nation, all these scenes of avowal and of reexamination of past crimes appeal to the testimony, even to the judgment of a community, and so of a modality of the living-together, virtually universal but also virtually instituted as an infinite court or a world confessional.

I could recall a great number of different but analogous examples, and intentionally juxtapose the most heterogeneous cases, from the memorable gesture of Willy Brandt in front of the monument of the Warsaw Ghetto, the famous declaration of the bishops of Poland and Germany at the fiftieth anniversary of the liberation of Auschwitz, that of the

French church, of the corporations of physicians and the police, to the speeches of heads of state such as Jacques Chirac, who declared that France had committed the "irreparable." In all these cases, it is a matter of crimes against humanity from which Jews were not the only ones suffering but of which they were massively the designated victims and always named in these declarations of guilt. As problematic as it remains, and whatever the elaborations it still calls for, the concept of crime against humanity (created, as you know, by the international court at Nuremberg in 1945) is the juridical mechanism of this globalization of avowal. This unprecedented event affects at its root a condition of "living together"; but it also marks the aftereffect of a moment in the history of humanity that keeps the wound of the Shoah, even if it is not, of course, reducible to that. This advent of a new juridical concept is the very memory of the Shoah. I would go so far as to say, since I cannot cite so many analogous examples, that the recent promises of the Vatican regarding the examination of conscience as to the Inquisition are inseparable from the same presuppositions, I mean, from the bottomless trauma of the Shoah, of its memory, whether assumed or denied. This globalization of avowal is therefore not thinkable in its inaugural emergence without what happened to the Jews of Europe in the twentieth century, nor is it any more separable from the international recognition of the state of Israel, a legitimation I would also interpret as one of the first moments of this avowal and of this world's bad conscience.

These acts of public repentance address themselves to crimes against the Jews, but one could just as well recall analogous declarations by Vaclav Havel toward the Sudetenland; by Prime Minister Muruyama in his own name a few years ago and, more recently, in the name of the Japanese government as such toward the Koreans, as well as what is happening at this very moment between the Chinese and the Japanese; by President Clinton, not only regarding the sinister and significant matter of the impeachment, but first of all regarding the recognition in 1998 in Africa—without, however, any act of official contrition—of an American responsibility in the history of the African slave trade and the infinite violence of slavery—which, like the violence done to Native Americans, is inseparable from the foundation of the United States. One thinks above all of that extraordinary "Truth and Reconciliation" Commission in South Africa, which was itself preceded by analogous, if not identical, institutions in Chile and Argentina (these, however, did not address violences and traumas affecting communities as different among themselves as in South Africa). These events have, to my knowledge, no antecedents in the history of humanity, in the history of states or of nation-states, which thus find themselves appearing in court, as it were, in front of an instance above the state. Yet all these scenes have in common a feature that is at once double and indivisible. On the one hand, their common presupposition will have been the possibility opened after World War II of recognizing and judging in front of an international instance Nazi violence and, in it, the extermination project called "holocaust," which aimed explicitly and in the first place at the Jews, the Romani, and homosexuals. On the other hand, and with the aim of making this extermination project appear before a universal jurisdiction, the creation of the Nuremberg court and the institution in international law of the new concept of "crime against humanity"—which France in 1964 declared henceforth "imprescriptible." As problematic and insufficient as it remains in my view, as I have said, this concept announces an irreversible progress. It is implied in all the scenes of repentance, of avowal, and of forgiveness asked for. For example, the global and local fight for the abolition of apartheid, followed by the institution of the Truth and Reconciliation Commission, was possible only because of the official recognition of apartheid as a crime against humanity—by the UN among others. This international juridical act provides a reference on whose basis the commission grants itself its authority. It articulates a logic signifying that any state racism (which the "living together" that called itself apartheid was), any racism, and any segregation based on birth, where it is encouraged or permitted in the laws of a state, is a crime against humanity. As imperfect as it remains, this concept is on the horizon of all the progresses to come of international law, of the difficult but irresistible institution of international courts as well as the practical setting to work of any declaration of human rights (something that still remains largely to come if one considers the incommensurable inequalities in the living conditions of human beings); not to speak of what, in the life of what are called animals and in the living together with the living ones that are called, in undifferentiated fashion, animals—for there is also a "living together" with animals—calls up tasks that exceed even the concepts of law and of duty and would have to obligate us to rethink the great question of sacrifice.

I hasten to conclude with the consequences that follow, and I will draw in general lines a series of contradictions that not only do not forbid "living together" but, were they to be declared or avowed, would, on the contrary, provide the condition of "living together" and the chance of a responsibility.

1.  *First aporia. On the one hand,* we know that the globalization of avowal, of repentance and of return upon past crimes, with or without forgiveness asked for, can indeed dissimulate facilities, alibis, perverse strategies, an instrumentalization, a comedy, or a calculation. It calls, then, for an endless vigilance. Yet, it nonetheless resembles those events in which a thinker of the Enlightenment (Kant, in this case) thought he recognized *at least* the sign, *at least* the possibility, of an irreversible progress of humankind. It marks a beyond of national law, even the beyond of a politics measured only by the sovereignty of the nation-state. Nation-states, institutions (corporations, armies, churches) must appear before a court; sometimes former heads of state or military leaders must give account—whether willingly or not—in front of instances that are in principle universal, in front of an international law that does not cease to be refined and to consolidate new nongovernmental powers, to force belligerent parties to recognize their past crimes and to negotiate over the peace of a new "living together," to judge in exemplary fashion governing individuals (dictators or

not) while being careful not to forget the states, sometimes foreign states, that have sustained or manipulated them (the important signal constituted by the removal of Pinochet's immunity would have to go far beyond his own person and even beyond his own country). More generally, with all the questions that these developments leave open, what one calls humanitarian intervention is not the only space of such new interventions.

But on the other hand, if one must salute this progress that sketches a beyond of state-national sovereignty and even of the political inasmuch as it remains, since the beginning, in fact coextensive with the state and with the exercise of citizenship, one can also see emerging possible perversions of this progress: not only a legalism that replaces politics [*politisme*], a reduction of justice to law, a surreptitious appropriation of the universal juridical powers (there is no enforcing law without a force of application, as the same Kant reminded us with good sense), a logic of the alibi or of the scapegoat in the determination of the accused subjects, a hijacking of international law by different forces and camps, by economic or state-national powers that would submit this exercise of law, and even so-called humanitarian action, to unjust strategies and to a disguised politics before which the recourse to the sovereignty of the nation-state would sometimes have to remain an irreducible site of resistance. All the more so since this new legalism, sustained by technological resources of investigation, communication, ubiquity, and unprecedented speed, runs the risk of reconstituting, under the pretext of transparency, a new inquisitorial obsession that transforms anybody into a subject or a defendant summoned to "live together" according to the ensemble, while renouncing not only what one names with the old name of "private life," the invisible practice of faith, and so on; but also, and quite simply, while renouncing this possibility of the secret, of separation, of solitude, of silence, and of singularity, of this interruption that remains, we have seen, the inalienable condition of "living together," of responsibility and of decision. Were the time given to me, I would have offered, in order to sharpen the blade of this aporia, a reading, for today, of what happened [*ce qui se passa*] in the silence and the secret of a certain Abraham on Mount Moriah from this perspective.

If these two exigencies and these two antinomic risks are indisputable and so grave, there are no knowable and prior norms to regulate or finalize our response. The responsibility for the most just decision must be invented each time in a unique fashion, by each one, in a singular time and place. To hold myself to the letter of our theme, well then, for the "living together" that I am proposing we think beyond any "ensemble," there is no "how," there is, in any case, no "how" that could take the form of precepts, of rules, of norms, or previous criteria available to a knowledge. The "how" must be invented by each at each moment. There would be no singular responsibility if a "how" were available in advance to the knowledge of a rule to be applied. What I am saying here is anything but empirical or relativistic; it responds to what I hold as the most demanding in ethical experience [*l'expérience morale*]. One must then at least begin to declare this antinomy, to recognize and acknowledge it, to avow it to oneself, to avow it before the other, every other, before the stranger, and even before the enemy. There where it seems unavowable and because it is unavowable. One must recognize and acknowledge this division, this tearing, this rift, this dissociation from oneself, this difficulty of living together with oneself, to gather in an ensemble, in a totality of cohesiveness and coherence: the first step of a "living together" will always remain rebellious to totalization.

2.  *Another aporia* runs the risk of paralyzing this movement. The ethics of "forgiveness" is, I believe, profoundly divided by two heterogeneous motifs of the Abrahamic tradition, Jewish, Christian, or Islamic, which has bequeathed it to us. Without wanting to reduce these three legacies to the same, far from it, and without being able here to involve myself in the treatment that this immense question would deserve, without stopping either at the profound—actually "Hegelian"—Christianization that marks the language of this globalization of avowal (there is here an effect of what I have called globalization in process [*la mondialisation en cours*], and not only in law), I will mention only one paradox. The heirs that we are feel that the movement of forgiveness is found between two logics, at once heterogeneous to each other and yet undissociable. *On the one hand,* there should be forgiveness only under the form of a gracious, unconditional, free, infinite, and unilateral gift, without an economic circle of reciprocity—that is to say, even there where the other does not expiate, does not repent, and therefore even if the "living together" does not inscribe itself in a horizon of reconciliation, of reparation, of healing, of indemnification, and of redemption. An unconditional forgiveness is an absolute initiative that no calculation, whether sublime or spiritual, should motivate. But, *on the other hand,* the same tradition reminds us, in a prevalent, dominant, and hegemonic fashion, this time, that forgiveness can be granted only in a conditional fashion, there where there is acknowledgment of a fault, avowal, repentance, return upon the past, present or future transformation, forgiveness asked. Although in his book *Forgiveness* [*Le pardon*], Vladimir Jankélévitch had spoken of a *hyperbolic* ethics of forgiveness, he nonetheless firmly declared—especially during the time when, in France, one was debating the imprescriptibility of crimes against humanity—that forgiveness could not be granted to those who never asked for it by pleading guilty. "Forgiveness died in the death camps," he had already said, in a less polemical mode, in his philosophical book on forgiveness. What sense, indeed, would forgiveness have, there where the guilty one does not await it, and first of all does not know or acknowledge the crime? This strong logic, this economy, precisely where it seems to me hardly compatible with this other postulation of unconditional forgiveness—we know that it dominates, even if it does not exhaust them, both the Abrahamic traditions and the actual politics of forgiveness. At the very moment where he recalls that "the principle of Jewish forgiveness" becomes a "pure rule,

unanimously acknowledged by man, and by him uniquely, before the Lord," Hermann Cohen does not dissociate forgiveness from repentance. With this "forgiveness," which is, he says, explicitly designed as the objective of the Torah, he then associates, as if it were one and the same thing, *teshuvah,* which, he recalls, designates repentance and means "return," "change," return to the good, return unto oneself. The instigator of sacrificial worship is also herald of the repentance that figures as a major act in any "ethics and at the core of any divine worship." "Even God cannot redeem me," Cohen dares to say, "without my own moral effort and repentance."[7] As legitimate as it may seem (and I do not want to denounce it), this placing under condition of the unconditional governs the practices of a forgiveness there where the latter remains nonetheless heterogeneous, in its unconditionality, to all these orders (ethical, political, juridical) and to the goals of reconciliation, reparation, amnesty, or prescription. One recognizes the figure of cure, of self-healing, and of "living together" in the South African discourse of the Truth and Reconciliation Commission (above all where it is moderated and interpreted in a Christian sense by Desmond Tutu—something that forces us to ask ourselves whether the globalization of avowal is a planetarization of the Abrahamic concept, or more specifically Christian concept, of forgiveness, or, on the contrary, a new mutation that brings about [*qui fait arriver*] something unexpected, something even threatening to this tradition—I cannot engage here this necessary but immense question). What the South African example brings into evidence, is a process of repentance, of amnesty, or of prescription—which one confuses too quickly with forgiveness—a work of mourning that one interprets as *healing away,*[8] an act of memory as healing that overcomes the trauma and enables wounded communities to "live together." One dreams, of course, that other wounded countries, each in its own way, might be inspired by this motif of "reconciliation" literally inscribed in the foreword to the South African Constitution, in spite of all the ambiguities [*équivoques*] of which I speak. But as equivocal and as conditional as it is, as threatening as it is to the purity of forgiveness, this motif of healing is not only at the heart of all the dominant interpretations of forgiveness. One finds it operating at the heart of the great Jewish reflections on *teshuvah* in this century. One could cite not only Baeck, Cohen, and Buber, but also, as Dominique Bourel recalled in a recent article, Scheler—another Catholic of Jewish origins who spoke of repentance as "*Selbstheilung* of the soul," self-healing of the soul.[9]

Under the sign of *teshuvah,* of what he translates as "return, relation with God," and "absolutely internal event," Levinas appeals to "unconditional justice" in his "Text on Tractate *Yoma,*"[10] but he nonetheless submits forgiveness to condition and asks that it be asked for: "There can be no forgiveness that the guilty party has not sought! The guilty party must recognize his fault. The offended party must want to receive the entreaties of the offending party. Further, no person can forgive if forgiveness has not been asked of him by the offender, if the guilty party has not tried to appease the offended."[11] Here too, I will not follow the subtle trajectory of this meditation, all the paths and the voices [*les voies et les voix*] that cross each other in it, all the way to the double limit where, recalling what he calls the "conditions of forgiveness," Levinas quickly evokes the essential possibility of the offending one's unconscious, which should bring one to conclude, I quote: "In essence, forgiveness is impossible." Levinas also evokes in passing, still a bit furtively perhaps, another border, a decisive one, to my mind, a limit touched upon by an opinion that was preserved in the *Gemara*, that of Rabbi Yehuda ha-Nassi, who speaks of a purifying forgiveness, on the day of Kippur, without *teshuvah, without* repentance.[12] On the edge of that same limit, in an elliptical text that remained unpublished in his lifetime, on "the signification of time in the moral world" and on the Last Judgment, Walter Benjamin too, spoke of a storm of divine forgiveness which blows to its own limit, but without ever merging with a movement or an economy of reconciliation: a forgiveness (*Vergebung*) without reconciliation (*Versöhnung*). Beyond its legal code and its penal limits, the concept of *imprescriptibility* signals toward a Last Judgment: Until the end of times, the criminal (dictator, torturer, nation-state guilty of crimes against humanity) will have to appear before a court and give account. There is no longer an end to responsibility that the guilty one could assume. Ever. It is of this impossible that I would have wanted to speak as the only chance of forgiveness—in all of its ethical and political consequences. It is similar to the avowable and the unavowable: If I avow only what is avowable, I am not avowing. To avow is to avow the unavowable, much like forgiving is forgiving the unforgivable: doing the impossible.

Well, then, since I will never feel justified in renouncing the necessity of a forgiveness conditioned upon repentance, nor in renouncing the demand without demand [*exigence sans exigence*], and without duty, and without debt, of the unconditional forgiveness that gives its sense to any pure thought of forgiveness, the only responsibility I cannot escape is to declare to the other this dilemma; it is to take the initiative, as I do here, of this declaration and to commit myself to drawing its juridical, ethical, political, and historical consequences. By reason of what I have just said, I must do so *alone* and even if I am the only one to take this initiative, without expecting reciprocity, alone and there where I am irreplaceable in this responsibility. It is thus that I understand or accept the concept of election, there where being chosen, well beyond any privilege of birth, nation, people, or community, signifies that no one can replace me at the site of this decision and of this responsibility. And this does not erase, on the contrary, the transgenerational or collective responsibilities that torment the sleep of innocents.

3. One would then have to avow a *third aporia* of "living together." I will never be able to renounce and to say no to a preference for "my own" [*les "miens"*], nor, inversely, to justify it, to have it approved as the law of a universal justice. Those whom I call, in this undeniable but unjustifiable hierarchy, *my own*, are not those who belong to me;

it is the ensemble of those with whom, precisely, it is *given to me*, prior to any choice, to "live together," in all the dimensions of what one calls so easily a community: my family, my congeners, countrymen, coreligionists, my neighbors [*mes voisins*], my close ones, those who speak my language, and I would go so far as to say, my neighbor [*mon prochain*], there where this word, in the biblical tradition, can designate as well the distant stranger, but on the condition that he be my fellow man [*mon semblable*], man and brother in humanity (I have elsewhere interrogated the ambivalences of this notion of fraternity, I cannot revisit this here).[13] How to renounce it, but also how to justify my preference for all the forms of the proximate, of this proximity that, at the limit, in situations of mortal danger, would carry me to the rescue of my children rather than those of another, rather than to the rescue of all those others who are not only my others, to the rescue of a man rather than an animal, and even of my cat rather than a cat unknown to me and dying in Asia? In the eyes of justice or of universal equality, how to justify a preference for one's own children, a preference for one's own, parents and friends, even a preference among one's own, as far as death and ultimate sacrifice, the privilege of Isaac, for example, rather than Ishmael? My own do not belong to me, nor does my "home [*chez moi*]." So go the declensions of the first person, the belonging of belonging [*l'appartenir de l'appartenance*]. "Living together," I belong to that which does not belong to me, to my own, to a language, a site, to a "my home," that do not belong to me and which I will never possess. Belonging excludes any absolute appropriation, even the radical right of property.

How, then, to deny but also how to justify the interior urgency that will make me first nourish my own, the proximate or the neighbor [*le proche ou le prochain*], before rushing to rescue the billions of famished men in the world? For the eloquent and meticulous militants of the rights of men and of social struggles in their countries should never forget that never, in the entire history of humanity, have so many people on earth been lacking bread and drinkable water; and that indifference or passivity on this subject is the beginning of a crime against humanity, a transgression of "You shall not kill"; and whoever says "you shall not kill," if he restricts himself to my neighbor, my brother, my fellow man, man, also avows, what a paradox, the accepted murder of all living others in general, to wit, what one names stupidly [*bêtement*] and confusedly the animal. Well then, this preference, this hierarchy, can give itself distinct manners, brutal or distinguished, odious or refined—no one will ever be able to deny it, in all good faith, nor renounce it. But no one will ever be able to justify it either, what one calls justifying, judging and proving that it is just before a universal justice. In this regard, I will always be indebted and always be failing to fulfill the first duty. To avow this aporia does not suffice, but it is the first condition of a responsible lucidity and a first gesture to open the best possible negotiation, to invent and unilaterally to propose its rule to the stranger, to the unknown one, to the other, even to the enemy, beyond even the neighbor, the fellow man and the brother, all the way to the point where "living together" commits life to all the living, to the gaze of all the living, to the gaze and even beyond the gaze, and even there where no sacrifice can leave my conscience at rest, as soon as one faults or assails the life of a living other, I mean of an animal, human or not. What remains unjustifiable in all good faith remains, therefore, inasmuch as unjustifiable, unforgivable, therefore, unavowable. And it is therefore that which I must begin by avowing.

4. All these aporias obey a common economy, which is none other than economy itself, *oikonomia,* the law of the house, of the proper (*oikos*) and of property. And one would have had to associate the motif of ecology, this large and new dimension of "living together," with the motif of economy. My last example concerns the relation between the living, in the genetic or bio-zoological sense, and technology. More than ever, and every day faster than ever, the techno-scientific and genetico-industrial intervention upon the fetal cell, the genome, the fertility process, homo- or hetero-grafts, and so on, much like the deployment of so many prosthetic structures, obligate us to re-elaborate the very norms of our elementary perception as to what is an ensemble or an organic identity, the "living together" of a proper body. For a proper body is first of all a manner of being together, symbiotically, with oneself and in proximity—a symbiosis that, here too, we can *neither deny nor justify.* Well then, the technological resources that affect the globalization of avowal by transforming the public space (informatization, panoptimization of telephonic and televisual digital communication, etc.), are the same technological resources that engage the living, all the syntheses of the living, all the dimensions of the living being-together (with oneself or with the other) in the space and the time of a *techno-biological prosthesis* that, here again, we can neither love nor reject, neither desire nor refuse, neither justify nor condemn in principle. If it interrupts the naturality of the ensemble, technology is nevertheless since always the very condition of this "living together" that it constantly threatens. It is death in life, as condition of life. That chance should also be a threat, here is what one must acknowledge, avow, here is that for which one must begin to respond, precisely there where, like the avowal of the unavowable, the forgiveness of the unforgivable appears both impossible and the only possibility of forgiveness (forgiving only that which is forgivable is not forgiving). Here too there could be no "how" that would precede, as would a knowledge, the decision or responsibility whose rule each one, singularly, chosen without election, chosen to an irreplaceable place, must invent.

Hastening to my conclusion, in the ellipsis of an image and the furtive passage of a memory, I will gather one question that never waits, the waiting without waiting of these four aporias from which—that is to say, also from Jerusalem—I address myself to you. It is very close to Mount Moriah where Kierkegaard, yet another Protestant, like the Neher of Levinas, said—that is his fiction—that Abraham was tempted to ask God for forgiveness.

But he would have asked him for forgiveness not for having failed at his absolute duty toward God, but rather for having attempted to obey God absolutely and blindly, and so for having preferred this unconditional duty to the life of his own, to his preferred son. Abraham would thus have had this movement, according to Kierkegaard: to ask forgiveness of God for having obeyed him.

I do not have the time to develop, as I would have wished, my interpretation of this interpretive fiction.[14] It associates and dissociates two manners of "living together" with every other (every other is any other; any other is wholly other [*tout autre est tout autre*]). I return for a moment and to conclude, not far from Mount Moriah, but this time closer to the cemetery of Jerusalem. Return, therefore, to end, in Jerusalem. Maimonides, by the way, said that *teshuvah* also meant the end of exile. Return to Jerusalem, therefore, to end, and close to a cemetery. During my first visit, in 1982, an Israeli friend enabled my discovery of this cemetery, showing me the tomb of her grandfather. Then I accompany her, for she must resolve a question in the offices of the Hevra Kadisha, the institution responsible for the difficult administration of the famous cemetery: allocation of plots, decisions as to the "concessions," transport of bodies, often costly operations, from distant countries, and most often the United States, and so on. This is before the cell phone, but I find myself there, in these offices, before a group of "responsible" individuals, busy men, all dressed in black and with traditional headdress. These men appear to run and to be out of breath; they display a feverish activity around walkie-talkies, telephones, and computers that ostensibly link them to all the places in the world from which one begs them, at any cost, for a place in the cemetery. Everything is becoming substitutable in this world, but the irreplaceable resists there, precisely here, now, not only in this place named Jerusalem, but in this very place, the cemetery, in this corner of Jerusalem, in view of orienting the dead.

I asked myself then: What does "living together" mean when the most urgent thing is to choose, while living and in the first place, a last place, an apparently irreplaceable place, desire then dictating not only dying and perhaps surviving or coming back to life in order to rise together upon the arrival of someone, but waiting, here and not there, before this door, unique in the world, this sealed door, the coming or the advent, the to-come of a Messiah? And yet, even before the globalization of the cell phone, of email, and of the Internet, all these little prosthetic machines, telephones, computers, walkie-talkies were beginning to make, yet another time, all these here-nows infinitely proximate and substitutable. New York could appear closer than Gaza (with or without airport), and I could have the feeling of being closer to some other at the other end of the world than to some neighbor, some friend from West Jerusalem or East Jerusalem. To ask oneself then, on a cell phone, whether Jerusalem is in Jerusalem, is perhaps no longer to trust, like others in older times, the distinction between earthly Jerusalem and heavenly Jerusalem. Yet this place of promise appeared to resist substitution and telecommunication. What was signified, then, by the placing of this "taking place" [*l'emplacement de cet "avoir lieu"*]? And of this messianic taking-place?

But I asked myself first, in anguish—and it was the same question: Who can allocate places? Who can authorize himself, while avowing it, to grant here, to refuse there, to grant to one and refuse to the other the chance to make this place his place, to elect it or to believe himself elected to it, be it in order there to bury his dead or there to await some messianic peace, a to-come or a return?

Since that moment and through analogous experiences (a few weeks before this first visit to Jerusalem, I was coming out of a jail cell in Prague), I had to begin thinking that which, in what I have named elsewhere messianic spectrality, or spectral messianicity, exceeds, precedes, and conditions all messianisms. And to think a certain faith older than all religions. This must have occurred to me [m'arriver] a long time ago in Algiers but also during these last years in Jerusalem. I do not know, and I avow it, how to interpret what then occurred to me—or would occur to me still [ce qui alors m'arriva—ou m'arriverait encore]. Nor what was announcing itself above me as a revenant, what was announcing itself by returning upon me [ce qui s'annonçait en revenant sur moi].

1998

*Translated by Gil Anidjar*

# Dying Warring

# *Mal de Sionisme* (Zionist Fever)

*Gil Anidjar*

The increased scrutiny applied of late to the concept of religion, the pulls and pressures it has undergone, has led to a debate, if mostly a muted one, regarding the significance of religion in Jacques Derrida's work. One need only consider the recent puzzling claim that Derrida is best understood as a "radical atheist"[1] or glance at the impressive collection of essays edited by Tom Cohen (titled *Jacques Derrida and the Humanities: A Critical Reader*) in order to wonder about the absence of religion from the rhetoric of interdisciplinarity (or, seemingly, from Derrida's work) on which the volume is predicated.[2] In its unthematized understanding, religion—admittedly so impossible to ignore by now that one rather awaits the exhaustion of its universal popularity—comes to function as the precise opposite of the term's alleged etymology. Rather than link and bind, religion operates a division, splitting Derrida's work between the "secular" humanities and the theologically inclined. Here, the well-remembered, earlier divide between literary scholars and philosophers would be recast between, well, literary scholars and scholars of religion. Religion further produces a split between early and late Derrida, strangely marking a kind of belated victory for past accusations of deconstruction as "negative theology" or as "Jewish mysticism." Thus, whereas some have embraced the radical significance of the "religious turn" and its critical potential (I am thinking here primarily of the work of John Caputo, Hent de Vries, and Samuel Weber), and others, all too enthusiastically perhaps, have located Derrida on a continuum of recognized and less recognized religious traditions (Christopher Wise, who identifies Derrida as "a uniquely *African* theorist of Sephardic, Maghrebian, and Judaic experience," and faults him, among other things, for his "Jewish bias," going as far as to argue that "Jewish peoples will have fewer problems" with Derrida's positions or with his "quasi-atheistic definitions of *spirit*, *revelation*, and the *messianic*—than either Christians or Muslims"), a significant proportion of scholars would

45

rather exercise quiet restraint, a mystical retreat of sorts on the issue of religion.[3] Suspending for the moment the ease with which one could dismiss the gestures, even errors, that maintain such divisions of the Derridean text, it is perhaps equally easy to forget that among Derrida's most important statements regarding what we might now read under the heading of religion, precisely, are those that should have long ago produced a paleonymic concern, a more extended and generalized rethinking of the very term "religion" in its historical and conceptual boundaries and global, or local, significance. We do not need another definition of religion, but we might interrogate its use, the facile and enduring identification—or dismissal—of religions, of "world religions," along with the lavish way it has been extended to proximate and remote corners, by way of documentation and explanation.[4] Invoking Derrida's *Mal d'archive* (translated into English as *Archive Fever*) in my title, and following the turns of its argument, I do not mean to argue that Derrida was or was not religious, nor do I wish to claim him for a particular religious community or aim for more equanimity in his religious inclusiveness, or better yet, strive toward an emancipation (reformation? expansion?) of and after religion. I do want to move along a remedial, if also homeopathic vector and read religion out of a "Jewish question," which articulates itself around another difficult division—if it is one—between the archive and its outside.

## He War

As is well known, *Archive Fever* is a profound interrogation of psychoanalysis as an institution and as a theoretical endeavor, which "should call for a revolution, at least potentially, in the problematic of the archive."[5] *Archive Fever* is also a reflection on the "Jewish question" in psychoanalysis, a reflection on the possibility of a "Jewish science," or the knowability of Judaism. Another easy parallel suggests itself, then, which may require a reading of its own, regarding deconstruction as a Jewish science, or, more pertinently, regarding the possibility of *any* Jewish science. Engaging, if obliquely, Freud's considerations on the constitution and persistence of the Jewish people and their religion, Derrida goes to war *with* (which may also, if not only, mean *against*) science, history and historiography, race and religion.[6] To stay with this last term, one could minimally assert that for Derrida, as for Freud, there is a war of religion, a war on and as religion. This war takes place under the burning evidence of disasters that brand the end of the last millennium.[7] From the opening lines of *Archive Fever*, Derrida refers to these disasters as "archives du mal." These are archives that are themselves "hidden or destroyed, forbidden, hijacked, 'repressed.'" They are treated on the horizon of wars, "during civil or international wars."[8] One need not collapse historical differences in order to recall that it is in the shadow of war that Freud too decides to write and to publish, once again, on religion, and more specifically on "monotheistic religion."

46

Freud famously endeavors thereby "to deprive a people of the man whom they take pride in as the greatest of their sons" and to leave aside "what are supposed to be national interests."[9] Freud also goes on to interrogate the integrity of the Jewish people ("There can be no doubt that very different elements came together in the construction of the Jewish people; but what must have made the greatest difference among these tribes was whether they had experienced or not the sojourn in Egypt and what followed it" [38]), and their psychical, political, and indeed religious unity ("Jewish history is familiar to us for its dualities: *two* groups of people who came together to form the nation, *two* kingdoms into which this nation fell apart, *two* gods' names in the documentary sources of the Bible. To these we add two fresh ones: the foundation of *two* religions—the first repressed by the second but nevertheless later emerging victoriously behind it, and *two* religious founders" [52]).[10] Taking into account the notorious difficulties still lingering regarding the trauma of which Freud then goes on to speak, its contemporary, indeed, prophetic, resonances should not be lost, engaging as they still do the seemingly resolved matter of the unity of the Jewish people: "All of these dualities are the necessary consequences of the first one: the fact that one portion of the people had an experience which must be regarded as traumatic and which the other portion escaped" (52). I recall these well-known moments of the Freudian text in order to underscore that they themselves articulate a response to war—the approaching Second World War calling for yet more "thoughts for the time on war and death," thoughts on a war in which Freud was well aware of being implicated and engaged before it was officially declared. Freud is under attack (still), and scholars have long puzzled over the enigmatic dimensions of his last major work as a potential response to that attack and to the onslaught of National Socialism.

Most puzzling, perhaps, although less commented on, is the fact that Freud clearly formulates that onslaught as a persecution "not only for my line of thought but also for my 'race' [*meiner 'Rasse'*]" (57). Responding to Nazi racial doctrine, Freud pointedly distances himself from the notion of "race" by placing it in quotation marks. This, however, is what is puzzling: Freud (who has elsewhere much to say about race and racial conceptions, not all of which is negative) does not engage in any direct manner the notion of race.[11] Instead, he affirms from the very title of his book (a better translation of which would be, as Samuel Weber has recently reminded us, "The Man Moses and the Monotheistic Religion"), that he will speak of *religion*.[12] At a time when Jews are being inescapably racialized, and to an unprecedented extent, de-theologized, Freud responds, as if on or from another scene, namely, on the terrain of religion.

If only to contrast it with Derrida's, I draw attention to this rhetorical gesture that underscores the difficult and still insufficiently explored rapport between the two terms (race and religion), for I want to argue that Derrida too—who clearly introduces his *Archive Fever* argument as a response—attends to a very different war of religion, a distinct "declaration of war," one to which he emphatically does not respond, this time, with "religion" in an expected sense. Derrida responds instead with science. More precisely, I think, what is at stake in this complex gesture is the very possibility of conducting or offering a scientific or scholarly discourse on Judaism (the latter ostensibly, and in the Freudian context, dominantly a "religion"), be it a science of Judaism or a Jewish science, indeed, and perhaps especially, a Jewish *political* science.[13] What is at stake, therefore, cannot exclude, nay, must include, the ongoing war on Palestine, or to put it another way, the configuration formed by psychoanalysis and Zionism, from declarations of independence to declarations of war. Derrida encourages such interpretations and interrogations when he proposes, in *Archive Fever*, that the path he will follow would have to include, in fact, a meditation on Jewish nationalism, a meditation at any rate on nationalisms and on anti-Semitism. It is on Freud's critique of both that, Derrida writes, "we ought to meditate to-day."[14] And although Derrida himself appears to suspend or delay this meditation, I will try to show that it is pertinently pursued nonetheless throughout *Archive Fever*. On this basis, it becomes doubly relevant to consider that one also finds in Derrida's text the elaboration of something like a *mal de sionisme*, or as Derrida puts it elsewhere, "an evil in Zionism, an inner evil, an evil that is anything but accidental [*un mal dans le sionisme, un mal intérieur, un mal qui n'a rien d'accidentel*]."[15]

### Archives du Mal

Historians have recently begun to explore the thick congruence linking the nineteenth-century emergence of the *Wissenschaft des Judentums*—historically the first among Jewish sciences—with the founding of political Zionism and psychoanalysis.[16] Long before *Archive Fever*, Derrida had already broached an insistent questioning of Judaism on the matter of its "scientific" definition. Derrida critically anticipated thereby the easy assumption that his writings on Judaism could be subsumed under the category of "religion." Instead, Judaism becomes the mark of a reflection about its very status: Is Judaism a religion, Derrida would have been asking from the beginning, something else, or something more than a religion?[17] And earlier yet, is Judaism literature, philosophy, theology? Finally—and this is what will occupy us here—what of a political science of Judaism? What of a Jewish nation, people, or community? What of Judaism and nationalism? Judaism and Zionism?

Since the earliest texts where the figure of Judaism is deployed, Derrida has interrogated the link between Judaism and Zionism, between Judaism, the community, the nation and the state, and territoriality. To mention but one example, already in *Writing and Difference*, Derrida underscores Edmond Jabès's insistence on distance and separation (from the community, from a notion of place and territory as center), an autochthony of the Book and a nomadism of the letter. Further on, in a text written the following year, Derrida reflects on Emmanuel Levinas's opposition to a philosophy of the *lieu*, of the site and of rootedness, questioning the justice of a Levinasian gesture that reads in Martin

Heidegger "a complacent cult of the Sedentary." There is no such cult in Heidegger, Derrida suggests, no "passionate attachment to territory or locality," no "provincialism or particularism." On the contrary, Heidegger's "solicitation of the Site and the Land" is "as little linked to empirical 'nationalism' as is, *or should be*, the Hebraic nostalgia for the Land, a nostalgia provoked not by an empirical passion, but by the irruption of a speech or a promise."[18] If Levinas wanted to interrogate a nationally determined relation to the land, implies Derrida (prefiguring reservations he will reformulate most explicitly in *Adieu to Emmanuel Levinas*), if Levinas wanted to criticize nationalism, he may have directed his attention with equal justification toward Zionist thought and what is, or *should be*, its relation to the Land. Indeed, Derrida himself seems to extend such a criticism in the concluding pages of *Writing and Difference*, where he revisits Jabès's own turn to the Book as a return "that does not retake possession of anything. It does not reappropriate the origin." Instead, "the return to the book is then the abandoning of the book."[19]

What could henceforth be construed as Derrida's textual engagements with a "Jewish question" constitutes a collection of pursuits of this exploration of Judaism in its internal and external differences. Prominent among these are, of course, "Interpretations at War," "Circonfession," *Mal d'archive*, *Adieu*, as well as the more recent texts on Abraham and on "living together," where Derrida engages questions of language, but also matters of election and of "ethnic" difference, signaling toward a history of the national-ethnic refiguration of Judaism as opposed to its "religious" existence. Most important, Derrida interrogates the by now all too accepted notion of a "Jewish people" (one could say, after Freud, Jewish peoples, but this pluralization in itself hardly resolves anything). "Listen," says Derrida in a striking, if oneiric, rendition of an as-yet-unheard interpellation, an as-yet-unheard "Hear! O Israel," another "Hear! O Ishmael!" that is addressed to those who would call themselves his brothers, call themselves his people. "Listen, believe me, do not believe so quickly that you are a people, cease listening without protest to those who say 'listen.'"[20]

Regarding the association of Judaism with Zionism, an association or identification that pivots quite precisely on the notions of people, nation, *ethnos,* and even race, let me state at the outset that it is, of course, a peculiar association, even a paradoxical one insofar as it is the site of a perplexing duality, a contradictory affirmation *and* negation. As the now hegemonic name for a Jewish political science, and more forcefully for a Jewish nationalism and for the national aspirations of the Jewish people—a notion it has done much to constitute and legitimate in its modern understanding—Zionism affirms the connection between Judaism and Zionism either as an essential (if long unrealized) feature of Jewish existence or as its logical evolution, culmination, and superseding conclusion.[21]

But Zionism is also the *end* of Judaism, bringing about a "new Jew," or what Benjamin Beit-Hallahmi has more pointedly called "the anti-Jew," who is both more and less Jewish than the Jew (the "new Jew" as opposed to the exilic "old Jew"), or simply *no longer* Jewish.[22] Following a strict logic of the supplement, Zionism simultaneously adds to and substitutes for Judaism. To the extent that it calls for the end of exile (the Zionist concept of "negation of exile, *shlilat ha-galut*"),[23] to the extent that it embodies what Levinas has described as a way of "escaping or renouncing the fact of the diaspora,"[24] Zionism also has a profoundly negative, even destructive, rapport with Judaism, a rapport that asserts itself most forcefully in the polemical rhetoric that repeatedly equates the Jews with the state of Israel (a state that continues to refer to itself as "the State of the Jewish people" in its entirety), thus claiming to represent them, but also substituting for them, putting itself instead of them and—in a way that is not entirely devoid of menacing echoes—*after* them. However, such complicated equations, routinely made within Zionist discourse (in Israel and elsewhere, often accompanied by highly pejorative and derogatory depictions of "religious" or "orthodox" Jews), become the source of much anxiety when deployed in turn by opponents of Zionism engaging Jewish organizations, communities, or individuals—many of which vocally uphold one form or other of a Zionist ideal. The identification of Zionism and Judaism cuts, in other words, two ways. And the claim that Zionism represents all Jews—that all Jews are or should be Zionists, that they should morph into Zionists—when articulated in a discourse of opposition and resistance to Zionism, is now said to be no more than covert anti-Semitism.[25] There may be more truth to that statement than polemics allow, for if it is anti-Semitic to conflate Jews with Zionism (or vice versa), then it is high time to ask about the anti-Semitism of Zionism (exceeding well beyond the borders of the "Jewish state," into the censoring mechanisms put in place in the name of a permanent concern about "the new anti-Semitism"), which operates precisely on the basis of such conflation. As Joseph Massad has convincingly argued, "The conflation/collapse of the Jewish people into a Jewish state is by Zionist design an attempt to render the Jewish people nonexistent except in the confines of a Zionist time/space called the Jewish state."[26] Indeed, in its fundamental claim to bring about a "solution" to Jewish existence outside of the Jewish state, Zionism has long considered "exilic Judaism" to be abnormal and pathological, or more ominously, fragile and provisional, and finally, endangered. Israeli scholar Stéphane Mosès illustrates this perspective quite well when he recalls that the anti-Zionist Franz Rosenzweig reproached Gershom Scholem, a generally stalwart Zionist and a towering figure of Zionist historiography, for perpetuating such negative views and voicing menacing wishful thoughts *before* World War II, by declaring that "the Judaism of the Diaspora is in a state of clinical death."[27] As unsettling as such statements may seem, they may well prompt us to heed Derrida's pointed question, raised in a proximate context, namely, "What is anti-Semitism not compatible with?"[28]

An interrogation of the link between Judaism and Zionism begins, as I have said, early on in Derrida's writing. By this, I do not mean to suggest that Derrida expresses or even endorses a particular opinion or program, political or otherwise. Nor do I mean to suggest that Derrida was at the forefront of a political struggle or at its subversive edge. Rather, Derrida inquires into the conditions that would enable or disable a treatment of Judaism as a recognizable religious or political community, chosen or not, or even as a bounded unity of any sort.[29] First, and as we began to consider earlier, the link between community and territory undergoes a scrupulous investigation. Commenting again on the work of Edmond Jabès, Derrida reads the wedge that Jabès traces between freedom and its earthly site, between site and Site (*lieu* and *Lieu*), and finally between Judaism and nationalism. This Site, explains Derrida, "whose cult is not necessarily pagan," is neither a mere site nor "an enclosure," not "a place of exclusion, a province, or a ghetto." Signaling toward another topological distinction, that between archive and memory, Derrida continues:

> When a Jew or a poet proclaims the Site, he is not declaring war. For this site, this land, calling to us from beyond memory, is always elsewhere. The site is not the empirical and national Here of a territory. It is immemorial, and thus also a future [*un avenir*]. Better, it is tradition as adventure.[30]

This passage needs to be carefully read as it implies that there are proclamations ("when a Jew or a poet proclaims the Site") that do constitute declarations of war. Whether such can be made by Jews, whether Jews could issue declarations of war (they can, of course, and they have) may very well be contingent on their rapport with site and Site, a rapport with the land that is also a rapport (or perhaps the severing of a rapport) with Judaism. Issuing a call *to* the land (a proclamation of the Site, to the Site) contextualizes and resignifies the prior call *of* the land as declaration of war—or not. The call that constitutes the Jew (and "us" in the quote) as addressee of the land is clearly not a national call and cannot—should not—therefore justify a declaration of war. The call does not address itself to a people or a nation, nor does it quite seek to constitute one, reminding us of the historicity of such national calls. (As I have already mentioned, when addressing members of what might constitute his community in *Monolingualism of the Other*, Derrida will dream of waking them, of impossibly calling upon them to tell them [not] to listen, not to believe those who call upon them as upon a people: "Off you go, on your way, now. Listen, believe me, do not believe so quickly that you are a people, cease listening without protest to those who say 'listen' [*Allez, en route, maintenant. Écoutez . . . ne croyez pas si vite, croyez-moi, que vous êtes un peuple, cessez d'écouter sans protester ceux qui vous disent 'écoutez'*].")[31] Following the logic elaborated by Avital Ronell and by Derrida himself around Kafka's Abraham, the call rather places under interrogation the addressee it constitutes and deconstitutes at that very moment, rather than confirming it as having already existed.[32] Derrida deploys this peculiar logic of the call as making its addressee structurally uncertain when revisiting the rhetoric of authenticity at work in Sartre and in identitarian claims to "Jewishness."[33] Be that as it may, there is no fantasy here, no performativity of a "we, the people" confirming its own preexistence by way of a declaration of independence. The call does not emerge from a national entity validated by divine sources.[34] Nor is it a call that seeks to glorify an exilic or religious mode of existence.

Indeed, existence is hardly what is at stake here, for to speak of a to-come, of an *avenir,* is to refrain from providing, or acknowledging, an ontic or ontological ground upon which to base a programmatic agenda. Rather, much as iterability means the necessary possibility of a mark being torn from context, so the proclamation of a site entails the necessary disjunction, spatial as well as temporal, "beyond memory" and "always elsewhere," an irreducible distance between the Jew (or the poet) and the land, between the memory and the territory, between the land and its (current) occupier. We have never been closer to a thinking of hospitality that would dispossess the current host of his *chez-soi* prior to any belonging, a thinking of hospitality that recognizes the host for the colonizer that he is. This is what Derrida will later elaborate as "the implacable law of hospitality," from which there is yet much to learn and which states that "the *hôte* (or host) who receives, the one who welcomes the invited or received *hôte* (or guest), the welcoming *hôte* who considers himself the owner of the place, is in truth a *hôte* received in his own home. He receives the hospitality that he offers *in* his own home; he receives it *from* his own home—which, in the end, does not belong to him."[35] The one who receives is therefore he who considers and enforces his claim of the home as his own. And it is he who is received. He is, Derrida continues, "receiving hospitality in what he takes to be his own home, or indeed, his own land."[36] We have never been closer, perhaps, to Jerusalem.

One could, in fact, follow the thread of a direct and explicit interrogation—no more, but also no less than an interrogation—of Zionism in Derrida, a recurring gesture that joins a less daring Levinas, who nonetheless "cautions us against a Zionism that would be simply a politics, just 'one more nationalism or particularism.'"[37] Derrida's interrogation in turn seeks to explore and even widen the distinction between Judaism and Zionism, or—as in Levinas again, if at a certain distance from him—the distinctions between different kinds of "Zionisms." Aside from these and from the consistent and barely veiled criticisms of the Jewish state under the general figures of the state and of the nation in "Interpretations at War," and aside, finally, from more explicit political statements made by Derrida on a number of occasions regarding his impatient awaiting for "political invention" in Israel,[38] his suspicions concerning the so-called "peace process" of the 1990s, the plausibility of a "mal de Sionisme" already emerges even from a cursory reading of *Mal d'archive.* Continuing with what we have considered regarding the matter of site and place, Derrida explains that the archive is essentially related to place.

The archive, Derrida writes, is to be distinguished from memory because it occurs; it takes place at the very site where memory fails. The archive "will never be either memory or anamnesis as spontaneous, alive and internal experience. On the contrary: the archive takes place at the place of originary and structural breakdown of the said memory."[39] The production of an archive, always already a repetition, a re-production, entails the construction of what could be called a "lieu de mémoire," precisely there where memory is not, no longer, or ever was. This is why there is no archive without a claim to territory, a declaration or proclamation that seizes a place while at the same time destroying that exteriorized monument, *res publica,* or indeed, state as a certain failure of memory. "There is no archive without a place of consignation, without a technique of repetition, and without a certain exteriority. No archive without outside" (11). This outside is also and constitutively—if one can use that word here—"that which exposes to destruction, introducing *a priori*, forgetfulness and the archiviolithic into the heart of the monument" (12). Monumentalizing memory, the Jew, of which we have already been speaking, offers itself as a "substrate" to the archive that circumcision may be. If so, the question might be asked of the archive that the state constitutes, thereby raising the stake, along with a further interrogation regarding the meaning of the Jew, of the Jewish people, and of the drive to memory and/or archivization, the repetition such as takes place and animates Zionism as a self-proclaimed "return" to the site of Jewish memory. It is precisely at this moment in *Archive Fever*, where such questions are about to emerge, that Derrida recalls, with pointed relevance, Freud's "interesting critique of nationalisms and of anti-Semitism." Derrida also says that "we ought to meditate" on this critique but "cannot possibly enter into [it] here" (13), yet I want to continue suggesting that, this impossibility notwithstanding, Derrida does go into it quite a bit.

### Histoire Juive

Spoken at the site of a private home turned public, a Jewish home if not quite a Jewish national home, Derrida's lecture attends to a site of memory—an archive—which itself sets up and replicates a structure whereby an inscription must be read. It is an inscription to which "one can have access . . . in several languages, beginning with its original in Hebrew" (20). It is written on, if not itself, Holy Writ ("the substrate, in a sense, was the Bible itself, the 'Book of Books,'" says Derrida [21]), and it must be read because, like the archive, it exposes us to layers of memory and destruction, because it evokes an archaeological unconscious.[40] It must also be read because "to read, in this case, requires working at geological or archaeological excavations, on substrates or under surfaces, old or new skins, the hypermnesic and hypomnesic epidermises of books or penises—and the very first sentence recalls, at least by figure, the circumcision of the father" (22). I interrupt the flow of Derrida's own commentary here because even before the explicit recalling of the biblical text on circumcision ("in the seventh in the days of the year of your life"), it is difficult to expect that the circumcised "father" here mentioned would fail to remind the reader of Abraham or Moses, and not only, as Derrida justifiably maintains, of the "father of psychoanalysis." Without entering into Derrida's extended meditations on circumcision and on the way they articulate the impossibility of a covenant—the impossibility, precisely, of a community of fathers, sons, and brothers—let us note that reading here exposes us to an archive that does not amount to a state.[41] Nonetheless, the archives that must be read do multiply, evoking a series of *lieux de mémoire*, memories and monuments, ruins and inscriptions that can only become apparent in their disappearance and even destruction by way of archaeological work. That such work, structured by repetition and return, is itself highly destructive and not simply restorative need not be lingered upon. Here too we would be warranted in thinking that there is enough "to disrupt the tranquil landscape," be it that of "historical knowledge," "historiography," and "scholarship," as well as other not-so-tranquil landscapes that are being shaped and reshaped, constructed and settled, walled, figured, disfigured, and destroyed today, along with so many lives, in or very close to Jerusalem (28).

The series of steps that enable (or disable) the passage from biblical fathers and inscriptions to Jewish (national) homes, be they private or public, from a tribal community to a people and a modern nation and nation-state, from a mythical land to a site of memory and to the construction and monumentalization of a religious tradition, is not to be treated lightly or passed over quickly. I do not seek therefore to render it unproblematic. On the contrary, Derrida's reading of the links and ruptures that relate science to the archive, memory to Judaism, and archaeology to the state, to cite but three examples, are not only subtle and careful, but they also avoid or, more precisely, suspend the explicit translation from the scholarly and scientific to the national and the political; they precisely enable us to follow and interrogate the way in which Freud and, after him, the Jewish historian Yosef Hayim Yerushalmi transpose terms from one sphere to another. Derrida reads the way in which Freud, for example, "speaks the same language" regarding the Jewish people as he does "concerning the land of Israel and the heritage that centuries of inhabitations have perhaps left in 'our blood and nerves'" (35n5), the way in which Freud and Yerushalmi after him move from the psychical to the national, from the structural to the political, from Judaism and psychoanalysis to Zionism. Such translations and transpositions are nothing if not problematic, and yet they signal toward the archive and the archive fever that plague all the domains here explored. Throughout these domains, "the scholar repeats, in a way, the gesture of the father" (38), and so does the politician, one suspects, if only because of Prince Hamlet—or Moses. Throughout these repetitions something "is at work in the concept of the archive and ties it, like religion, like history, like science itself, to a very singular experience of the promise" (36).

If the archive is essentially related to place, and if its question resonates in and for Jerusalem, it is because there too "the question of the archive remains the same: what comes first? Even better: who comes first? And second?" (37). Explicitly or not, we have never been closer to Jerusalem—if not only in Jerusalem. For what indeed "happens to the archive in this situation?" What happens on the day "and from the moment when a science presenting itself as such and under this name binds itself intrinsically not only to the history of a proper name, of a filiation, and of a house, here Freud's house, but to the name and to the law of a nation, of a people, or of a religion"? (45). What happens, in other words, when psychoanalysis becomes, is transposed into, Zionism? Can another science, can a political science "depend on something like a circumcision"? (46). Again, Derrida does not explicitly bring up Zionism in this context, but he does recall the question of anti-Semitism and Freud's treatment of it, Freud's own account for the social and political predicament in which the Jews have found themselves among the nations ("To explain the genesis of anti-Semitism, namely, the jealousy with regard to a people which presented itself, he says, as the favored eldest son of God, Freud evokes in his *Moses* the circumscribed isolation of the Jews, the isolation that cuts them off from the world, the solitude of their exclusion by a circumcision which, according to him, always recalls dreaded castration" [46]). What is at stake, therefore, is, again, nothing else than a discourse that "binds itself intrinsically not only to the history of a proper name, of a filiation, and of a house . . . but to the name and to the law of a nation, of a people, or of a religion" (45). Israel, then, "the memory of Israel" (64), has been implicitly and explicitly mentioned, and although we will do well to remember, as Derrida does in *Adieu*, that "Israel does not primarily name the modern state, the one that bears, that gave itself or took for itself, the name Israel,"[42] it will nonetheless be difficult not to recognize that *Archive Fever* does speak to and about Zionism. It speaks to and about the hegemonic site for and against the very possibility of determining, today, "the essence of Jewishness, if not Judaism" (47).

Paraphrasing Yerushalmi, while reading him against the grain, Derrida makes explicit the terrifying politics of a Judaism, be it scientific or scholarly, that would recognize itself as the unique addressee of a historical (or divine) call, that would locate itself as the privileged *lieu de mémoire* of divine memory, that would affirm itself unique as the recipient of an "extraordinary attribution: the injunction of memory falls to Israel, and to Israel alone" (75). If this sounds all too familiar, it is perhaps because it is. The historian who adjudicates on "the past as something Jewish and *uniquely, exclusively, only Jewish*" may not be a politician but he does affirm (that is, grants himself and the community he proclaims) a political, a theologico-political privilege (75). It is as if

> God had inscribed only one thing into the memory of one *single people* and of an *entire people*: in the future, remember to remember the future. And as if the word "people," in this sentence, could only be conceived of out of the unprecedented uniqueness of this archive injunction. Here is what I call the extraordinary attribution, on the subject of which I will keep a large number of grave questions in reserve. Some of them would have an ethical or political dimension, but they are not the only ones, in spite of their obvious urgency. (76)

But the historian that Derrida engages is not alone, and the urgency grows. I have been arguing that Derrida does not entirely refrain from addressing it by raising the grave questions, both ethical and political, which he here feigns to keep in reserve. There is, or rather, "we are *en mal d'archive*," Derrida writes (91). There is a fever, a burning and a passion which never rests, "interminably, from searching for the archive right where it slips away." There is "a compulsive, repetitive, and nostalgic desire for the archive, an irrepressible desire to return to the origin, a homesickness, a nostalgia for the return to the most archaic place of absolute commencement" (91). Such is "the archaeological outbidding" whereby this fever produces "attempts to return to the live origin of that which the archive loses while keeping it in a multiplicity of places. As we have noted all along, there is an incessant tension here between the archive and archaeology" (92). The archaeological out-bidding also claims "a return to reality, here to the originary effectivity of a base of im-mediate perception. A more profound and safer base" (94). Not so unexpectedly, the claim "takes on a striking, properly hallucinatory, form," one which endangers the ar-chive itself, as having to do with "the nomological *arkhe* of the law, of institution, of do-miciliation, of filiation," as having to do with "the equality and the liberty of brothers" and with "a certain, still vivacious idea of democracy" (95). And so there is an archive fever, which signals in no uncertain terms, even if less explicit ones, toward a Zionist fever, a "mal de Sionisme."

If this Zionist fever has affected and transformed Judaism, if as Franz Rosenzweig thought, Zionism is a "secular form of messianism," a secular form of Judaism, it is per-haps first of all because Zionism constitutes or simply recasts Judaism as its *religious* ante-cedent.[43] The continued and somehow vacuous debates in contemporary Israel concerning the religious/secular divide are noteworthy albeit pale reminders of the "secularization" at work in Zionism, even in so-called religious Zionism. Levinas—in close proximity on that matter with the *Wissenschaft des Judentums*—recognized that theologico-political divide for what it was, namely, an attempt to escape the biblical and talmudic covenant. Para-doxically, Levinas also affirmed the divide when he asserted that "by proclaiming that Judaism was only a religion, [the covenant] asked of Jews more, and not less, than Jewish nationalism."[44] Leaving aside the complex question of what Levinas means here and else-where in his use of the term "religion," one must recognize the distinctive gesture that Derrida in turn extends toward any claim to have crossed over from one allegedly con-tained realm to another—from a religious, traditional domain to, say, politics. Such trans-position, such secularization, was recognized even by a fervent Zionist such as Gershom Scholem to be impossible. Much as the so-called inventors of the modern Hebrew lan-guage could not conceal the abyss sealed within the language, much like "the blind sor-cerers of secularization" failed to recognize "that the abyss does not, any more than language, let itself be dominated, tamed, instrumentalized, secularized," what occurs within and between Zionism and Judaism may be described as a failure of the theologico-political, but also as a failure of secularization.[45] Derrida diagnoses this failure when he explains that Scholem's letter to Rosenzweig "relates, in a paradoxical and fascinating way, to its treatment of the opposition between sacred language and secular language as a *rhe-torical effect*" (201). Why? Because "this secularization one is talking about, that I am talking about, Scholem seems to say, that I accuse and of which I complain, that I warn against, this secularization *does not exist*." Yet, as Derrida reminds us, that such would be the case "does not render the phenomenon—or the symptom—less grave or more incon-sistent, on the contrary" (201). It constitutes an inherent evil, a *mal* and a danger. "This evil of language is also a political evil," Derrida explains, "but it is not an infantile illness of Zionism. This 'necessary consequence' is congenital to every Zionist project for a Nation-State." There is only added irony—is every nation-state essentially Zionist?—in considering, as the historian Amnon Raz-Krakotzkin has suggested,[46] that Scholem went on to deny the recurrence of that apocalyptic danger, the impossibility of secularization, much as he went on to ignore and ultimately dismiss the relevance of that other, less "uncanny" danger that he called "the Arab people" (201). Scholem ultimately denied the theological and apocalyptic energies and tendencies operative in political Zionism, much as he renounced his early political commitment to a binational vision for Palestine. To a large extent, Scholem became a typical example of the kind of practitioner he faulted in his letter. He embraced the rhetoric of secularization and affirmed that Zionism had been secularized, that Zionism, though "Jewish," was not about religion, no longer, in fact, about Judaism.

This is where Derrida's intervention is, I think, key. I will briefly state two reasons for why this is so. First, Derrida demonstrates that it is the rhetoric of secularization that isolates and attempts to contain an energy that it calls "religious," an energy that then explosively proceeds to return precisely *as* religious. To put it somewhat crudely, one could say that there is no theologico-political divide, no religion, before the construction or fiction of a "political" emancipation.[47] Whether such emancipation can be successful as *political* is something about which Marx, for example, had much to say in his own "Jewish question." Derrida renews the spirit of Marx's text by calling into question the possibility of emancipation as secularization, while calling for a secularization that remains to come. But I have left too vague, I am afraid, the second reason to reflect on Derrida's intervention. However, it becomes limpid when, having discussed the epistolary text by Scholem, whose relationship to Jewish nationalism he repeatedly emphasizes, Derrida offers toward his conclusion a somewhat puzzling "remark to the case of national character and the problems it poses."[48] In an earlier discussion of Hermann Cohen's peculiar brand of nationalism and antinationalism, Derrida had turned toward the question of anti-Semitism. This question, this war, is still being fought, of course, but it is less about distinct political options (as if nationalism, or more precisely, Jewish nationalism, was the opposite—the solution—to anti-Semitism, and it is, indeed, in this context that Derrida had raised the question: "What is anti-Semitism not compatible with?").[49] It is less about political options for the Jewish people. Freud had gone to war on the issue of a "Jewish science" by asking what the Jews and science (as intellectual pursuit) had in common, suggesting in his response that science was itself Jewish (that is, Egyptian). Freud was arguing that the initial impulse to worship one invisible God was not only "a triumph of intellectuality," but indeed the opening of a "new realm of intellectuality [*das neue Reich der Geistigkeit*] in which ideas, memories and inferences became decisive."[50] Derrida attends to other wars, but by turning to the archive and to archive fever, he signals toward the claims of Jewish political science. In the same year he published *Politics of Friendship*, Derrida delivered *Archive Fever*. In both texts, Derrida engages war (*polemos*) by asking about the political, the community of fathers and sons (circumcised or not), the community of brothers (for it is, indeed, always a masculine community—and fevers too, like illnesses, are gendered), and the people, love and hate, Judaism, Zionism and (rather than against) anti-Semitism.

In "The Eyes of Language," Derrida points toward another case of anti-Semitism— namely, Kant's—in order to ask again about possible associations and compatibilities. Here, around Scholem's rhetoric, we are again given the task of reflecting on possible and impossible links between Zionism, secularization, and anti-Semitism. For these are all governed by a notion of the political that is predicated on an understanding of the Jewish community and of the Jewish people as "substrate." We are reading Kant, "friend and admirer of Mendelssohn," as Derrida reminds us, Kant, who cannot as of yet distinguish between the Jews' "dispersal throughout the world" (their geopolitical existence) "their union in religion and language" (their spiritual integrity) and their being "a nation of merchants" (their economic identity).[51] Regarding the Jews, in other words, one could not yet speak of secularization, nor could one distinguish between their status as a religious community, an ethnic or national community, and the fact that they may constitute a community of interests. It will take another discourse, another call for solution and resolution, to conclude or make final an emancipation that claims for itself a secularized, cleansed political status. But with that liberation from "religion" (that is, with the simultaneous invention and repression of the religious, in the modern, Christian sense of the term out of the sources of Kant's vagueness), the Jewish people will have to be constituted and de-constituted as a different kind of ground, a distinct kind of archive toward the Zionist monumentalization of the state. Someone, or something, will have to call upon the Jews, to interpellate them and convince them that they are, in fact, a people, an *ethnos*, and perhaps even a race. Such is the Jewish political science of Zionism and such its call—and it calls, still. That is why it is perhaps foremost to those who have felt themselves, who continue to feel themselves, to be the only and exclusive recipients of such a call and of an election that has also become a declaration of war that Derrida calls in turn and says, again: "Listen, believe me, do not believe so quickly that you are a people, cease listening without protest to those who say 'listen.'"[52]

# Forget Semitism!

*Joseph A. Massad*

Memory occupies a significant position in nineteenth- and twentieth-century theories of origins, whether of the species, of the races, of cultures, of civilizations, of religions, of nationalities, or of the psyche. Racial, cultural, and civilizational memories at the level of the group or the individual would indeed become crucial for many of these sciences and systems of knowledge, not least of which was psychoanalysis. Hence Freud's insistence that "ontogeny recapitulates phylogeny" in the development of the human psyche was not merely a continuation of social Darwinist thought but also symptomatic of how the group and the individual came to be seen as related, through memory.

Nationalist movements' attempt to "retrieve" the memory of the "nation" was analogized by Freud to a person's childhood memories. "This is often the way in which childhood memories originate. Quite unlike conscious memories from the time of maturity, they are not fixed at the moment of being experienced and afterwards repeated, but are only elicited at a later age when childhood is already past; in the process they are altered and falsified, and are put in the service of later trends, so that generally speaking they cannot be sharply distinguished from phantasies." Freud proceeds to explain how nations come to write their histories.

> Historical writing, which had begun to keep a continuous record of the present, now also cast a glance back to the past, gathered traditions and legends, interpreted the traces of antiquity that survived in customs and usages, and in this way created a history of the past. It was inevitable that this early history should have been an expression of present beliefs and wishes rather than a true picture of the past; for many things had been dropped from the nation's memory, while others were distorted, and some remains of the past were given the wrong interpretation in order to fit in with contemporary

ideas. Moreover, people's motive in writing history was not objective curiosity but a desire to influence their contemporaries, to encourage and inspire them, *or to hold a mirror up before them.*[1]

In the formation of identities, memory is not only invented, conjured up, or reawakened, but it is also purposely suppressed, erased, and deleted. As identities are elaborated and predicated on the dualism of self and other, identity formation requires of the carriers of identity that they not only remember and forget certain memories about the self but also about the other whose history and present have to undergo a series of operations to guarantee what is to be remembered and what is to be forgotten. Freud's *Moses and Monotheism* is the most illustrative text in this regard.

This is particularly important for European thought as regards Hebrews and Jews and Arabs and Muslims, given their importance as the central other used in consolidating European identity, if not in the consolidation of the very collectivity called Europe, a process that started during the Crusades through the othering discourse of religion and more so since the eighteenth and nineteenth centuries when philology and scientific racism supplemented religion as the primary othering discourse. Whereas modern Europe is produced by the industrial revolution and massive proletarianization in an important relation to colonial adventures, its identitarian ideology retrieves the Crusades as a differentiating moment that sets Jews and Muslims as other. Instrumental for this was not only the new system of knowledge that was grouped under the heading of Orientalism, but also that of philological and racial thinking that was grouped under the heading "Semitism." Both Orientalism and Semitism were dependent on and productive of many of the assumptions of eighteenth- and nineteenth-century knowledge, including racialism, biologism, nationalism, and most of all social Darwinism.

Yet, there is an increasing academic and political trend in the past few years that tells us that we must forget certain formative discourses in order to proceed with politics. Although some have suggested that we must forget feminism in order to have new forms of sexual politics,[2] others insist that we must forget Orientalism and Semitism and only remember *anti-Semitism* in order to abide by the new forms of international politics. In the case of feminism, the proposition famously and recently made by Janet Halley is that the feminist theoretical and political agenda be bracketed but remain accessible when considering other theories of sexuality to which a prescriptive feminism has been an obstacle. In the case of Orientalism, the claim is often made that Said's and the Saidean-derived analysis produce a politically correct straitjacket and/or that Said got it all wrong and that his analysis needs to be thrown out in order for politics, or even cross-racial forms of sexual pleasure, to proceed, as a recent critic of my book *Desiring Arabs* put it.[3] Of course, there is a difference between feminism, which is both a movement and a theory, and "anti-Orientalism," which is a theoretical critique but not a movement. But for the bulk of the critics of Said's and Saidean analysis, this is immaterial. Many among them who emerged with books attacking Said after his death assail the central place he gave to Orientalism in understanding the production of Europe and its relationship to a produced Orient, and misread Said as a demonizer of Orientalists, whom Robert Irwin, for one, wants to show as benevolent seekers of knowledge. Other critics include Zionist apologists who insist that the only thing to be considered when assessing the Palestinian encounter with Zionist colonial settlement is not Orientalism or colonialism but rather, and exclusively, anti-Semitism.[4]

Another memory that has recently been emphasized is that of Abraham through the invocation of the "Abrahamic," ostensibly as a stand-in for the monotheistic. The Abrahamic is said to bring together Jews, Muslims, and Christians, as emerging from a similar tradition and addressing themselves to similar ends. Jacques Derrida deploys the term in his writings on religion in a most productive way. The Derridean Abrahamic, in contrast with the Semitic, purports to eliminate the hierarchy not only among the Semites themselves, and between the Semites and the Aryans, which Orientalism and Semitism consecrated, but also between all three groups in the name of an equalizing gesture. In its elision and forgetting of the Semitic, the memory of the Abrahamic for Derrida, as we will see later, is instrumental for this gesture owing to its emphasis on "religion" rather than race.

I will argue that engaging the politics of memory in the case of Semitism is crucial for our understanding of the lives of those whom Semitism has interpellated and interpellates as Semites to this day. This will bring us to the Jewish Question and to the Palestinian Question, or to the Palestinian Question *as* the Jewish Question. As both Palestinians and Jews inhabit the taxonomy "Semite," I want to discuss the way their question(s) constitutes the Semitic Question—indeed how the Semite became a Question, *for Europe*.

## Semites and Orientals

But what exactly is Semitism, and what does it have to do with the Palestinians? We know much about *anti*-Semitism and how in popular European and American understanding it has much to do with Jews as victims of it. Increasingly the Euro-American depiction has it that Arabs and often Palestinians are perpetrators of it. But what is this Semitism that anti-Semitism is opposed to, that it wants to persecute, to oppress? Why have recent accounts—or memories?—of anti-Semitism forgotten the history of Semitism? Why do they often fail to remember the Semites in their historiography? Are Palestinians in these memories opposed to Semitism, to the Semites, and if so, why would they oppose them? Are they in fact victims or perpetrators of Semitism, or of anti-Semitism? The crucial question that I want to pose is whether anti-Semitism is indeed the enemy of Semitism at all, or if their relationship is of a different order altogether.

When Edward Said embarked on his study of Orientalism, he explained that "by almost an inescapable logic, I have found myself writing the history of a strange, secret sharer of Western anti-Semitism. That anti-Semitism . . . and Orientalism resemble each other very closely is a historical, cultural, and political truth that needs only to be mentioned to an Arab Palestinian for its irony to be perfectly understood."[5] Here I must remind us that the time the Semite became a question was a time when many of the questions Europe had to consider from the late eighteenth century onwards had to do with the Orient; not least among them was the question of the Oriental Ottoman Empire whose presence in Europe and the necessity to evict it from Europe was coded the "Eastern Question." The almost contemporaneous emergence of the "Jewish Question" dealt with the presence of another people, also identified as "Orientals," who had been present for millennia in the heart of Europe. Said's invoking of anti-Semitism as the "secret sharer" of Orientalism, a term he borrows from Joseph Conrad, is instructive. In his famous short story, Conrad identifies his "secret sharer" as a "second self," "my other self," a "double" or, as Said himself put it, as a "mirror."[6] The Oriental and the Semite, the Orientalist and the anti-Semite, Orientalism and anti-Semitism are therefore second selves to one another, doubles, and mirror reflections that must always be read and seen in tandem.

The category of the Semite was invented by European philologists in the eighteenth century and was transformed in the nineteenth century from a linguistic into a racial category. Ernest Renan was perhaps one of the most illustrious Orientalists who helped bring about this transformation. For Renan, the "Semitic spirit" had two forms: "The Hebraic or Mosaic form, and the Arabic or Islamic form"[7] Indeed, according to such representations, as Said summarizes them, "The Semites are rabid monotheists who produced no mythology, no art, no commerce, no civilization; their consciousness is a narrow and rigid one; all in all they represent 'an inferior combination of human nature.'"[8] For Renan (1823–1892), as for Semitic studies, or Semitics, as it was called, "'The Jew is like the Arab' and vice versa."[9] In this regard, the fact that medieval Christians, including the Crusades, referred to Arabs as "Saracens," as in the descendants of Sarah, prefigures this modern identity between the two groups.[10]

The construction of the Semite was, of course, a ruse for the invention of the Indo-European, not only in philological terms but also specifically in racial terms, when the Indo-European becomes the Aryan. Semitism, therefore, is always relational to Europeanism as Aryanism. Hannah Arendt was clear on this in relation to Jews.

Whether the Jews are a religion or a nation, a people or a race, a state or a tribe, depends on the special opinion non-Jews—in whose midst Jews live—have about themselves, but it certainly has no connection whatever with any germinal knowledge about the Jews. As the people of Europe became nations, the Jews became "a nation within a nation"; as the Germans began to see in the state something more than their political representation, that is, as their fundamental "essence," the Jews became a state within a state . . . and since the end of the last century, when the Germans transformed themselves into Aryans, we have been wandering through world history as Semites.[11]

Arendt's astute understanding of the historicity of the category "Semites" is based on her insistent memory that at least, in her case, Jews existed before becoming Semites. Still, however, she does not question the accepted wisdom that anti-Semitism exists *in opposition* to the Semite. This is an important problematic that we must elaborate in order to understand what is required of "our" memory in relation to the Semite. How are we to forget or remember this key Enlightenment and Romantic figure?

Indeed, hegemonic ideas about the Semite would be elaborated further in the nineteenth century through the influence of social Darwinism and evolutionist criteria. The Arab and the Jew were seen in these accounts as manifestations of evolutionary arrest. Said describes how Semiticists represented both groups.

> In no people more than in the Oriental Semites was it possible to see the present and the origin together. The Jews and the Muslims, as subjects of Orientalist study, were readily understandable in view of their primitive origins: this was (and to a certain extent still is) the cornerstone of modern Orientalism. Renan had called the Semites an instance of arrested development and functionally speaking this came to mean that for the Orientalist, no modern Semite, however much he may have believed himself to be modern, could ever outdistance the organizing claims on him of his origins.[12]

This identity between Jews and Muslims was not only made by Europeans hostile to the two groups or even by those hostile to one of them but also by people and thinkers who thought it an objective racial criterion to be traced back to a biblical and Qur'anic genealogy. The Orientalist Louis Massignon, who supported the Palestinian struggle against Zionism, would identify the colonial situation on the ground in 1960 with reference to Semitism: "I think that for the problem of the future of the Arabs, it must be found in Semitism. I think that at the base of the Arab difficulties there is this dramatic conflict, this fratricidal hatred between Israel and Ishmael. . . . The Arabs find themselves in collision with it in the claim of exclusivity among the Semites, the privileged Semites of the right. They, on the contrary, are the outlaws, the excluded."[13] The development of the Semitic idea was such that Jews and Arabs came to identify themselves as "Semites," thereby distancing themselves from their pre-Semitic existence. This would even be put to political use quickly. Indeed, Zionist intelligence, which set up front organizations in Palestine as early as the 1920s between Jews and Arabs under the guise of Arab-Jewish friendship (but which in fact operated as a cover for Palestinian collaborators with Zionism), termed one such organization "The Semitic Union."[14]

## Semites and Anti-Semites

If the designation of people as Semites was precisely a ruse for the designation of their superior other as Aryan, Semitism then begins to look indistinguishable from anti-Semitism. The act of inventing the Semite is the very act of inventing the carrier of that identity as other. It is indeed the act of creating the anti-Semite. In this light, *Semitism has always been anti-Semitism*. The ruse of anti-Semitism is in having us believe that there was a historical gap, a conceptual chronology of sorts, wherein there existed a Semite before Semitism, and that there was Semitism before anti-Semitism. What I am proposing here is that this historicization is itself an effect of the very discourse of Semitism. This is indeed what Arendt had missed in her historiography of anti-Semitism.

Let us consider how Semitism relates to the Jews as an entry point to understanding how Palestinians would figure in this history. In the light of Semitics and based on its taxonomies, anti-Jewish sentiment clustered in the nineteenth century in a full-fledged othering ideological edifice that called itself anti-Semitism. In contrast with Semitism, which was invented by a certain class of intellectuals who were scholars and philologists, anti-Semitism was invented by intellectuals in the political and journalistic professions. The term was coined in 1879 by a minor Viennese journalist by the name of Wilhelm Marr and would first appear as a political program titled *The Victory of Judaism over Germanism*. Marr was careful to decouple anti-Semitism from the history of Christian hatred of Jews on the basis of religion, emphasizing in line with Semitics and racial theories current at the time that the distinction to be made between Jews and Aryans is strictly racial.[15]

In the European world and its American extension where racial theories became the arbiter of rights and privileges by the second half of the nineteenth century, many Jews embraced the Semitic origin story "as a way of establishing the positive impact of their group on world history." In the United States, Jewish philanthropists would endow Semitics departments at universities to "ensure proper recognition."[16] According to the historian Eric Goldstein, "During the nineteenth century the claim of 'Semitic' origin had become something of a badge of honor for American Jews, allowing them to trace their heritage back to the dawn of civilization and take credit for laying the ethical foundations of Western Society."[17] Remembering the Semitic origin, therefore, was part of the process of forgetting the active operation of inventing this origin by philologists.

However, this would change considerably in the twentieth century, especially after scientists began to attribute an African origin to the Semites. This theory was first proposed in 1890 in the United States by the archaeologist and language specialist Daniel Brinton, and within a decade it became so orthodox that when race scientist William Z. Ripley published *The Races of Europe* in 1899, he adopted it and "helped spread it to a large audience."[18] The connection of modern Jews to the ancient Hebrews remained part of an unresolved academic debate at the time, but the question of the origin of the Semites seemed to have been resolved. Indeed, with the increasing identification of Semites with Africa, some Jews seeking full assimilation into whiteness began to retreat from the claim, forgetting it altogether in favor of another memory. Martin A. Meyer, a Reform rabbi in San Francisco and a scholar of Semitic studies, felt it necessary in 1909 to declare that American Jews shared more with non-Jewish white Americans than they did with "the Arab of the desert, the true representative of the Semitic world of yore," or even with the Jews of the Middle East.[19] Meyer claimed that although the ancient Jews who came out of the desert were Semites like the Arabs, their blood was "rapidly diluted." He concluded that "today, but little of that original Semitic blood will be found in the veins of any of us."[20] Another Reform rabbi, Samuel Sale, added that "we can not get away from the bald fact, based on anatomical measurements, that only about five percent of all the Jews bear the characteristic mark of their Semitic origin on their body."[21] Here the act of disavowal is not only a psychic one, but decidedly physiological, when bodies are said to forget their origins except for a few remaining traces.

Another strategy to disavow the African origin hypothesis, however, was to continue to embrace the Semitic identity but to argue that Semites were in fact white, having originated in the Caucasus and not in Africa, as some Jewish anthropologists and some Zionists argued.[22] However, the predominant Zionist explanation for the condition of Jews in Europe would differ from that in the United States, insofar as the European Zionists accepted (anti-)Semitic descriptions of Jews, which they explained by recourse to the Jewish history of persecution, and not necessarily to innate racial characteristics.

Zionism was predicated on the double operation of remembering and forgetting: Zionism stipulated, on the one hand, that modern Jews must remember their peoplehood, that the Hebrews were their ancestors, and that Hebrew culture had always been their heritage, which they could now access through the European Enlightenment, and that Palestine was their ancient homeland to which they must return; on the other hand, it insisted that modern Jews must forget their European Jewish identities and cultures as the historical predecessors of their current identity and that they forget that Palestine had continued to have a living non-Jewish and non-Hebrew population to the present. Although Zionism espoused the goals of the maskilim and other Jewish assimilationists in its understanding that the mark of Jewish otherness had to be removed, it differed from both in affirming that Jews could become Europeans only in Asia. It is in adopting nationalism as the solution—or more precisely, dissolution—of the Jewish Question that Zionism assimilated the most important form of political life unleashed by the French Revolution. If Semitism and anti-Semitism insisted that the Jews were not Aryan or European, that they were a separate race and a separate nation, Zionism could not agree more. Its transformative project would also include the Palestinians whom it sought to transform into Jews in a displaced geography of anti-Semitism.[23] This move would also guarantee that the figure of the Semite, as always already a negative value, would be preserved but would be identified solely with the Arab.

Here, Arendt, who grasped better than most the structural position of Jews in European Christian societies, would still muddle the position of Palestinians and Jews in relation to European Christians more generally. Her insistence on the national principle in defining Jews as a people dominated much of her discussions.[24] She states that "since the days when Polish nobles invited Jews into their country to act as tax collectors, buffering them from the peasants they hoped to suck dry, there has never been such an ideal coordination of interests, such ideal cooperation. In those days, Jews arrived rejoicing in the convergence of so many interests and unaware of their future role. They knew no more about Polish farmers than Zionist officials did about Arabs prior to the Balfour Declaration. In those days the Jews of Central Europe were fleeing from the pogroms of the late Middle Ages to an Eastern paradise of converging interests, and we are still fleeing the consequences of that today."[25] Arendt's placing Palestinians in the same structural position as Polish peasants is both instructive and mishandled: Her description of "Jews" as tax collectors betrays her nationalist historiographical perspective just as her allegation of the ignorance of Zionist officials of the Palestinian Arabs betrays an ignorance of Zionist history. The major conceptual limitation in Arendt's writings on Jews and Zionism, however, is her persistent belief that Zionism and assimilationism are opposed rather than complementary. Despite her incisive criticisms of Zionist practices, her major failure was one of insisting on remembering the Hebrews as the ancestors of the Jews and of reifying European Jews as a people transhistorically. That Zionism sought to normalize Jews was a project that Arendt zealously supported; she would even invoke Kafka's *The Castle* to bolster her argument. Her enthusiasm for Zionism's quintessential racially separatist institution, the kibbutz, was on account of the kibbutz's acting as a transformative institution of Jews from Semites with a negative value into normalized Europeans with a positive one. She celebrates this as Zionism's "greatest achievement," namely its "creation of a new type of man and a new social elite, the birth of a new aristocracy which differed greatly from the Jewish masses in and outside of Palestine in its habits, manners, values, and way of life, and whose claim to leadership in moral and social questions was clearly recognized by the [Jewish] population [in Palestine]."[26] That Zionism transformed the Jew into what the Israeli psychologist Benyamin Beit-Hallahmi called the "anti-Jew," and the Palestinian into the Jew did not deter Arendt from supporting this central Zionist idea.

But how was this transformation of Palestinians effected? It is at the juncture of Semitism that Edward Said locates his intervention. He asserts that "what has not been sufficiently stressed in histories of modern anti-Semitism has been the legitimation of such atavistic designations by Orientalism, and . . . the way this academic and intellectual legitimation has persisted right through the modern age in discussions of Islam, the Arabs, or the Near Orient."[27]

In his book *Semites and Anti-Semites*, the Orientalist Bernard Lewis states that "the argument is sometimes put forward that the Arabs cannot be anti-Semitic because they themselves are Semites. Such a statement is self-evidently absurd, and the argument that supports it doubly flawed. First the term 'Semite' has no meaning as applied to groups as heterogeneous as the Arabs or the Jews, and indeed it could be argued that the use of such terms is in itself a sign of racism and certainly either of ignorance or bad faith."[28] I fully agree with Lewis, and I add that something similar can be said about the Jews. Indeed, to echo Lewis, the argument that is sometimes made that the Jews cannot be anti-Semitic because they themselves are Semites is refuted on the same grounds of the meaninglessness of the term "Semite" when applied to a heterogeneous group like the Jews, as he himself argues.

Lewis, however, adds a qualifier to make untenable the use I have just made of his argument. He maintains that the second reason the argument is flawed is that "anti-Semitism has never anywhere been concerned with anyone but Jews, and is therefore available to Arabs as to other people as an option should they choose it."[29] But, as histories of Zionism have revealed, anti-Semitism has always been made available to those Jews who seek to other themselves and assimilate into European Christian normativity by repudiating the Semite within, namely, their perceived Jewishness—and the Semite without—namely, the Arab Oriental as elaborated by Orientalism. Here, let me recall the function of Freud's mirror. If assimilationist anti-Semitism is the mirror being held up by Zionism before European gentiles, it is merely, as Freud insists, "to encourage and inspire them," to see themselves reflected in the figure of the assimilated nationalist (anti-)Jew. As such, anti-Semitism is also available to the Jews as it is available to the Arabs should they choose to use it.

Freud's own views of the Semites were discordant with his intellectual milieu. As Said notes,

> Freud had his own ideas about European outsiders, most notably Moses and Hannibal. Both were Semites, of course, and both (especially Hannibal) were heroes for Freud because of their audacity, persistence and courage. Reading *Moses and Monotheism*, one is struck by Freud's almost casual assumption (which also applies to Hannibal) that Semites were most certainly not European . . . and, at the same time, were somehow assimilable to its culture as former outsiders. This is quite different from theories about Semites propounded by Orientalists like Renan.[30]

Late in his life, Freud went as far as attempting to rescue modern Jews from Semitism. He insisted that European Jews were not "Asiatics of a foreign race, as their enemies maintain, but composed for the most part of remnants of the Mediterranean peoples and heirs of the Mediterranean civilization."[31] Said wondered about Freud's move: "Could it be, perhaps, that the shadow of anti-Semitism spreading so ominously over his world in the last decade of his life caused him protectively to huddle the Jews inside, so to speak, the sheltering realm of the European?"[32]

In the first half of the twentieth century, anti-Semitism would continue to focus on the figure of the Jew while its double, colonial Orientalism, would focus on the Arab and the Muslim, often conflated as one, as the Semite of choice. In the wake of the Nazi holocaust and the end of colonialism, both would retreat, but only temporarily. Soon anti-Semitism and Orientalism would reemerge with one main racialized Semitic object, the Arab and the Muslim, both seen as one in this racialist economy. This transformative moment in Europe and America, which was consolidated during and after the June 1967 war, would gain momentum quickly, so much so that in the wake of the October 1973 war and the oil embargo, Arabs, as Said observed, came to be represented in the West as having "clearly 'Semitic' features: sharply hooked noses, the evil mustachioed leer on their faces, [which] were obvious reminders (to a largely non-Semitic population) that 'Semites' were at the bottom of all 'our' troubles, which in this case is principally a gasoline shortage. The transference of popular anti-Semitic animus from a Jewish to an Arab target was made smoothly, since the figure was essentially the same."[33] Here, Said deploys the history of anti-Semitism to illustrate his findings about the history of the Arab, and specifically the Palestinian. To clarify what he means, Said states that in depicting the Arab as a "negative value" and as "a disrupter of Israel's and the West's existence . . . as a surmountable obstacle to Israel's creation in 1948," what Orientalist and anti-Semitic representations produce is a certain conception of the Arab that is ontologically linked to the Jew: "The Arab is conceived of now as a shadow that dogs the Jew. In that shadow—because Arabs and Jews are Oriental Semites—can be placed whatever traditional, latent mistrust a Westerner feels towards the Oriental. For the Jew of pre-Nazi Europe has bifurcated: What we have now is a Jewish hero, constructed out of a reconstructed cult of the adventurer-pioneer-Orientalist . . . and his creeping, mysteriously fearsome shadow, the Arab Oriental."[34]

Said's analysis urges us not to remember or forget Orientalism, the Muslim, the Arab, and ultimately the Palestinian without remembering the forgetting of European Jewish history and the history of European anti-Semitism in the context of European colonialism, which made and makes all these historical transformations possible and mobilizes the very discourses that produce them as facts.

**The Abrahamic and the Semitic**

Freud, perhaps, had the most original hypothesis on the relation between the origins of monotheism's God and the Semites. If the chronological story has it that the Arabs, through Islam, recapitulated the Jewish and Christian God as their own, Freud posits that the Jewish God was in fact not only an extrapolation of the Egyptian Aton, but also of the god Jahwe whom the Jewish tribes "took over . . . probably from the neighbouring Arabian tribe of Midianites," in the country "south of Palestine, between the eastern exit from the Sinai Peninsula and the western border of Arabia."[35] This also seems to apply to Moses, whom Freud identifies not only as Egyptian, but, as there was another Moses, also as an Arab Midianite—who together with the Egyptian Moses, constituted what would become the biblical prophet.[36] Either way, it seems the Semites, their prophets, and their gods/God were connected since time immemorial.

But if the Semitic Question brings together Jews, Arabs, and Muslims hierarchically in relation to Aryanism, Semitic monotheism, bringing together Jews, Christians, and Muslims, began to be coded recently as part of the neologism "Abrahamic religions." Although the contemporaneous Judeo-Christian, emphasized after World War II, sought to exclude Muslims from the new alliance, the contemporaneous but less hegemonic "Abrahamic" sought their inclusion. Let us remember that Shem, which means "name" and from which the term Semite is derived, is the biblical son of Noah, and that Abraham is a direct descendant of Shem through his son Arpachshad. Shem and Abraham are biblical figures that have been ambivalently secularized by the Enlightenment tradition. It might have been Gotthold Ephraim Lessing who in 1779 in *Nathan the Wise* started a Christian (or should I call it "Enlightened" or even "liberal"?) trend that he did not name, of insisting on the commonality of monotheisms, but it was left to the Orientalist Massignon to christen it "les trois cultes Abrahamiques" in his 1949 essay "Three Prayers of Abraham."[37] If the Semites and Aryans were grouped as radically other synchronically in racial theories, the Abrahamic was going to link them genealogically as one and the same, or, at least, so hoped Lessing.

In contrast to Semitism, which revolved around language and race as an ontological effect, the Abrahamic would link what was separate under the sign of monotheism as religion, literally as that which links, or what the Orientalist H. A. R. Gibb, in reference to Massignon's efforts, referred to as "the community of Abrahamanic origins."[38] Massignon's interest was to remind Christians to claim an Abrahamic heritage that they had forgotten. He invokes Abraham as the common ancestor for the sake of erasing difference and asserting, if not identity, then at least commonality.

> At that moment when the terror which conceals from us the approach of our final end makes us turn inwards, to return to our origins, when the toxic malice of our disagreements forces us to seek out once again our common ancestors, it is wise to take up once again the links in the spiritual chain of pure witnesses upon which we depend . . . and which leads us back to Abraham, all the more boldly the more desperate our situation.[39]

Massignon affirms that

> Abraham continues to be invoked as their father, by twelve million circumcised Jews, who aspire to take possession for themselves alone of that Holy Land which was long ago promised to him, and by four hundred million Muslims who trust patiently in his God through the practice of their five daily prayers, their betrothals, their funerals,

69

and their pilgrimage. The Jews have no more than a hope, but it is Abrahamic. The Muslims have no more than a faith, but it is Abraham's faith in the justice of God (beyond all human illusions).[40]

The role of the uncircumcised Christians, that is, those who have not kept the covenant with Abraham's God, as Jews, Muslims, and "Eastern" Christians had done, is a historic one, namely, that of love, which they can impart to their brothers in Abraham (let us remember here one of Freud's explanations for anti-Semitism, namely, that it results from the horror felt by Christian boys when they hear of the circumcision of Jewish boys, which they interpret as castration, and which explains the contempt they feel for Jewish men).[41] The context of Massignon's call for a Christian pedagogy of love that could have prevented, but due to its absence failed to prevent, hatred between the Jews and the Muslims, was the "horrible war" of 1948. However, this historic Christian role remains necessary because of geography. Massignon maintains:

> Like history, the geography of today brings us closer to Abraham by focusing our attention on the high place of humanity which began with his own. . . . Here is the physical return of the two inimical brothers to the chosen places of their resurrection (the al-Aqsa Mosque for the Muslims, the Temple for the Jews, only 150 meters apart on the same *Haram*); and only 350 meters from the Anastasis or *Qiyama* (the Holy Sepulcher) of the Christians, who, because they have not developed sufficient consciousness of their "Abrahamic adoption" are not yet concerned about returning to Jerusalem to await the Parousia of the Lord. Nevertheless, there in Jerusalem the Christians have Arab witnesses of their faith and the geographical convergence of the pilgrims of the three Abrahamic faiths in one and the same Holy Land, trying to find there that justice which Abraham through his threefold trial found in his God, led a year ago to a horrible war. Why? Because the Christians have not yet fulfilled their complete responsibility towards their brothers in Abaraham. Because they have not yet explained to them how to love the Holy Land which is one of the two terms of the promise to Abraham.[42]

Note here that Massignon portrays everyone as external to Jerusalem and that everyone wants to return to it. Palestinian Jerusalemites are presented as foreign to their native city, as much outsiders as the colonizing Jews.

More recently, the notion of "Abrahamic religions" has been posited as having a prior Islamicness. Jonathan Z. Smith argued that it was "adopt[ed] . . . from Muslim discourse," a contention that would be adopted in turn by those who have more recently sought to theorize the Abrahamic as that which *links* and *de-links* Jews, Christians, and Muslims.[43] In his introduction to Derrida's work on religion, Gil Anidjar relies on Smith's claim that "the notion of the Abrahamic, like the notion of 'The People of the Book,' is of Islamic origin. It is an ancient notion which, as Derrida notes, was on occasion revived in Europe (Kierkegaard, of course), perhaps most recently by the important Islamicist Louis Massignon."[44] Massignon, to my knowledge, spoke only of "Abrahamic faiths" or "worship," "*cultes*" not religions, even though Derrida, in a discussion of Massignon's work, renders the latter's use of "*cultes*" as "religions."[45] This is a strange rendering given Derrida's knowledge of and engagement with the history of the concept "religion." The French *culte*, like the English cult, is derived from the Latin *cultus*, and *colere,* as in to cultivate, the very same root of the term culture. But the Qur'an (or "Islam" as it is posited metonymically to refer to the "Qur'an") makes no mention at all of "Abrahamic" faiths or religions, or "Abrahamanic religions," as Edward Said used the term in *Orientalism*,[46] and the Qur'an's invoking of "*millat Ibrahim*," where "milla" refers to the "traditions," "ways," and "path" of Abraham (there is no "*din* Ibrahim" in the Qur'an),[47] to encompass all the prophets from Abraham to Moses to Jesus and Muhammad, which is often invoked as evidence of the notion of "Abrahamic *religions,*" was not necessarily or at all a gesture toward the inclusion of Christianity and Judaism qua *religions* (even though the Qur'anic text was always inclusive of the traditions of Judaism and Christianity whose extant scriptures it considered distorted versions of the same word of God). Rather, it asserts an originary Islam which Abraham, Moses, and Jesus preached and to which they belonged and from which Jews and Christians had deviated (the Qur'an announces that "Abraham was neither Jew nor Christian but was a Hanif, a Muslim, and he did not associate anyone with God").[48] In fact, the Qur'an never uses the word "din" in the plural at all, restricting it to the singular throughout. For "*indeed, din*, for God, is Islam,"[49] which is not to mean that for nonbelievers in God, there is not another *din*. Indeed there is, as the Qur'an declares to the unbelievers "For you have your *din* and I have mine."[50] While the Qur'an sublates Judaism's and Christianity's scriptures, it does not call upon Muslims to sublate Jews and Christians, but rather to *include* them as people of the book.

Whether to cultivate or to link, as the etymologies of "cult" and "religion" reveal respectively, "Islam" has no notion of Abrahamic "cultivation" or "linking" in its scriptural or theological history, but more importantly maintains in its very identification with the Qur'an and in its etymology the notion of judgment, accounting, and a continuing debt as *din* and one of "deliverance to God" as *Islam* (often Orientalistically translated as "surrender" or "submission" rather than as "deliverance"). The predominant understanding in Islamic theology, as far as the God of Islam and (the Qur'anic) Abraham are concerned, is that there cannot exist but one *din*, that which delivers humans to God. This is not to say that Abraham is not important in the Qur'an or in Islamic theological traditions and prophetic literature; on the contrary, much importance attaches to him in them. The point is simply that neither the notion of "religion" (let alone "religions") nor "din" is attributed or attributable to him, even while he is recognized as the first prophet to worship the one God.[51]

So what then of the Abrahamic? Why is the Abrahamic, which, it turns out, has an Orientalist, and *not* an Islamic provenance, being projected onto "Islam"?[52] I argue that the Abrahamic is one more ruse of an untenable inclusivity that consolidates and maintains the exclusion of the Semite. It is certainly (and here I differ with Anidjar) not a case of "where religion has emerged, race has all but disappeared."[53] On the contrary, Massignon expectedly links the Abrahamic and the Semitic a priori: "The discoveries of Semitic archeology are bringing us closer and closer to a continuity in the steps which 'external' history had to traverse in order to overtake the Abrahamic milieu and emphasize more and more the exceptional character and monolithic permanence of the two circumcised groups, the Jews and the Arabs, in the face of the Christian apostolate."[54] In analyzing the notion of the Abrahamic, Anidjar tells us that

> this ancient notion . . . has been considered either the original and gathering root of the three major monotheistic faiths or, more pervasively, as the (three) branches of one single faith. It suggests the reclaiming of territorialized roots, the reoccupation and gathering of a site of welcoming togetherness, where old fallen branches can come back to life. . . . This return may promise, minimally, the resurrected togetherness and enabling of "religion," but it also institutes the possibility of comparison under the allegedly unified figure of Abraham, whose name appears in the three scriptural traditions. The modern discourse of comparative religion, which rendered the incommensurable comparable, could hardly have emerged independently of Jewish, Christian, and Muslim medieval disputations that stage the one/three faith(s) in different and complex ways. However, the Abrahamic is not simply a figure that can be subsumed as one theme among many. The Abrahamic is the very condition of "religion."[55]

This conditionality, for Anidjar, is on account of the Abrahamic's separating and linking the theologico-political simultaneously. Indeed, Anidjar adds that the Abrahamic, for Derrida, "dissociates and breaks the dividing movement around which 'Europe'—and religion—constitutes itself."[56]

The term "Abrahamic" would also carry much currency outside theory, and in the heart of international relations. Jimmy Carter, one of those enamored of the brotherhood of the children of Abraham, as he refers to Jews and Muslims, understands Abrahamic descent in racial terms, and, along the lines of Massignon, believes that Christians can access Abraham through faith. He explains this in a 2006 interview in the light of attacks on him as an anti-Semite based on his critical views of Israeli policies.

> I taught this last Sunday as a matter of fact. I reminded people that Abraham's first child from [Hagar] Ishmael was a founder of the Arab nations in general. His second child obviously, by his wife Sarah was a founder of the Jewish people and then after the early Christian church was founded . . . Saint Paul explained that those blessings from God for his children were based not on their race but on their faith. Since Chris-

tians believe, have faith, in God, to have faith in Jesus Christ, then we are also children of Abraham.[57]

The notion of the children of Abraham, however, was not a reactive notion used by Carter to fend off the anti-Semitic label. It was something central to his policies from the 1970s, when he had been considered by the same forces that now accuse him of anti-Semitism as a philo-Semite. When he spoke in 1979 at the signing of the Camp David Accords between Anwar Sadat and Menachem Begin, President Carter declared in the name of the United States: "Let us now lay aside war. Let us now reward all the children of Abraham who hunger for a comprehensive peace in the Middle East. Let us now enjoy the adventure of becoming fully human, fully neighbors, even brothers and sisters."[58] Indeed, since the early 1980s, a large number of books about an inclusive notion of the children of Abraham has been published in English, most likely to bring about this fuller humanity that Carter insisted on. Although I am sympathetic to Carter's, Derrida's, and Massignon's projects of positing the Abrahamic as the filiative and affiliative link between the three monotheistic communities, I am troubled by what it must forget to do so, namely how the Abrahamic is linked to the Semitic, to the Semite.

Perhaps a return to Massignon is in order. Massignon's neologism might have been an outcome of his Catholic faith, which defined much of his life, or an outcome of some other Orientalist passion, or a combination of both. In his discussion of Massignon's notion of the Abrahamic, which he couples with a discussion of Emmanuel Levinas's work, Derrida expresses a need "to answer a concern that you might share with me, I imagine, regarding the ellipsis, if not the exclusion, in any case the active silence with which [Massignon's project of Badalya, which included Arab Christians] suppresses, walls in, chokes all fraternity with those who have, after all some right to figure in an Abrahamic prayer front—to wit, the Jews."[59] Although, on the one hand, Derrida wants to reference Massignon's concern for the Palestinian refugees of the 1948 war (a concern that Derrida himself does not seem to share) by quoting his journal entry from 1949 (while claiming mistakenly that "Three Prayers" was written in 1923), at the same time, he wants to remind his readers of clues to Massignon's position on Jews. Derrida concludes that Massignon's bourgeois French Catholicism "to which one could add other characteristics, leaves us with the feeling of some probability of anti-Semitism."[60] Here Derrida wants to insist that the Abrahamic must be inclusive by demonstrating how for Massignon, it, on occasion, slips into an exclusive realm, one that excludes the Jews.

Although Massignon's motive in conjuring up the Abrahamic was one of self-declared Christian love for the rest of the children of Abraham that was punctuated by racialist criteria, Levinas's views on Palestinians were also troubling. But Derrida does not seem to pay similar attention to Levinas's anti-Palestinian ethics, which exclude Palestinians from the Abrahamic, as he did to Massignon's probable anti-Semitism, though he is careful to remind us that "Levinas declares nothing but the greatest respect for Islam."[61]

Levinas's views of Zionism are important in this regard, as he represents Zionism as a movement geared toward an ethical politics, or what he terms "monotheistic politics."[62] Asked by Shlomo Malka in a radio broadcast following the Sabra and Shatila massacres of 1982, "Isn't history, isn't politics the very site of the encounter with the 'other,' and for the Israeli, isn't the 'other' above all the Palestinian?" Levinas replied,

> My definition of the other is completely different. The other is the neighbor, who is not necessarily kin, but who can be. And in that sense, if you're for the other, you're for the neighbor. But if your neighbor attacks another neighbor or treats him un-justly, what can you do? Then alterity takes on another character, in alterity we find an enemy, or at least then we are faced with the problem of knowing who is right and who is wrong, who is just and who is unjust. There are people who are wrong.[63]

This subtle exclusion of the Palestinians from the Abrahamic through an endorsement of Israeli terror in support of a Maronite Christian neighbor against the Palestinians was justified by Levinas on ethical grounds, even though Said, in a generous move, believed that Levinas's stance, like that of Martin Buber's before him, simply lacked "ethical di-mensions."[64] Derrida also did not seem to want to say much, if at all, about the massacres at Sabra and Shatila, although Anidjar, in an astute reading of Derrida's silence, wants to force him to say what he must but cannot say.[65]

But, I pose the question once again: What kind of labor does the Abrahamic perform in relation to the Semitic? Before I can offer a possible answer, let me recall what Said said about the Semite. Understanding that Zionist ideology emerged as a particular brand of Orientalism and therefore of (anti-)Semitism in the context of Europe's colonial project, Said maintained that "by a concatenation of events and circumstances the Semitic myth bifurcated in the Zionist movement; one Semite went the way of Orientalism, the other, the Arab, was forced to go the way of the Oriental."[66] The journey that the Semite has trav-eled from its eighteenth-century philological origins was one of setting the Arab and the Jew apart from the Aryan until Zionism split the Semite into two kinds in the twentieth century, setting one in alliance with, and the other in opposition to, the Aryan.

For those who have realized the untenability of the Jewish position through Zionism as the Semite who went the way of Orientalism, the notion of the Abrahamic is ambiva-lently useful in leveling the field between the two Semites. Anidjar is more nuanced about this in relation to Derrida than Derrida himself seems to be. Anidjar concludes;

> This trait of the primal father (Abraham) that splits his offsprings, disseminates his sperm, into already politicized entities, factionalized ethnicities, and "religions" grafted and cut off from one another, testifies to the consistently split origin that in Derrida's text fails to gather while inscribing itself in world historical, political explosions. "Reli-gion" as the Abrahamic, while we claim it as "our own" can only disown us.[67]

Derrida's interest in the Abrahamic can be located at this moment of the splitting and might be inspired by an egalitarian impulse to distribute his notion of Jewish messianism seen through a Zionist optic across all three "Abrahamic religions," which he refers to as "Abrahamic messianism."[68] This is most apparent when he strangely calls Zionist occupation and colonization of Jerusalem (which he always calls by its Latinized Hebrew version and never in its Arabic name "Al-Quds," the name by which its inhabitants have called it for a millennium and a half) and the resistance to that conquest as "the war for 'the appropriation of Jerusalem.'"[69] Such a descriptor, echoing Massignon, represents the Palestinians' anticolonial struggle to hold onto their lands and homes in Al-Quds against Zionist colonial-settler theft as much of an "appropriation" of their own city as is the Zionist theft. Indeed, Derrida is even forgiving of the foundational violence of Israel that visited the Catastrophe/Nakba on the Palestinians, for it was not unique, as "no state has ever been founded without this violence, whatever form and whatever time it might have taken" ("Avowing," 29–30). Derrida recalls how as a child he had asked himself "whether the founding of the modern state of Israel—with all the politics and policies that have followed and confirmed it—could be no more than an example among others of this originary violence from which no state can escape, or whether, because this modern state intended not to be a state like others, it had to appear before another law and appeal to another justice" ("Avowing," 30).[70] Derrida seems to have opted for normalizing Israel among the nations, which was, of course, the explicit goal of Zionism. In this democratic and egalitarian spirit, Derrida refuses to pose *the Palestinian question as the Jewish question* and refuses to see it as an anticolonial struggle over land, but rather and instead as the "unleashing of messianic eschatologies" by the three "Abrahamic religions," or what he calls the eschatological "triangle."[71] In this, he does not deviate much from the position of Bernard Lewis, who had identified the Palestinian struggle against Zionist colonialism as "the return of Islam," although Derrida would object to the notion of "return." In rendering Islamic "messianism" or "Islam" the culprit in opposing Zionism, there seems to be an insistence on glossing over the fact that the struggle against Zionism has always been shared by Palestinian and Arab Muslims *and* Christians, and that it is not necessarily supported by all non-Arab Muslims. Said's response to Lewis may also be an apt riposte to Derrida. For Lewis and Orientalists more generally, concludes Said, positing Islam—or any force that speaks in its name—as the motivation of anticolonial Arab struggles, simply means that "history, politics, and economics do not matter."[72]

The most radical position that Derrida had expressed on Zionist colonialism and the Palestinian question did not deviate much from the "international consensus" of the great (Christian) powers, namely: "Palestinians and Israelis will live truly together only on the day when peace (not only armistice, cease-fire, or the peace process) comes into the bodies and souls, when what is necessary will have been done by those who have the power for it or who, quite simply, have the most power, state power, economic, military, national, or international power, to take the initiative for peace in a manner that is first of all wisely unilateral" ("Avowing," 23). When Derrida speaks of opposing certain Israeli policies, it is with the tormented twists and turns of a tortured man fearing excommunication by the community of believers. Having voiced a criticism of Israel, he tells us that he must "hasten immediately to add . . . that one can remain radically critical in this regard without implying thereby any threatening or disrespectful consequences for the present, the future, and the existence of Israel, on the contrary" ("Avowing," 29).[73] This is an ongoing sentiment on the part of Derrida that precedes his manifest interest in the Abrahamic. When he lectured in occupied Al-Quds in 1988, during the first Palestinian uprising against Israeli occupation across the Occupied Territories, he declared his "anxiety" that Palestinians and Arab scholars were not "officially invited" to participate in the conference! It is unclear to what notion of hos(ti)pitality Derrida was appealing when he expressed his wish for an "invitation" to be extended "officially" by the racially privileged citizens of a conquering and racially discriminatory state to their conquered, racially inferior victims.[74] Yet Derrida seemed to grasp the situation on the ground as one of mutual "violence," equalizing once again the violent acts of the conqueror with those of the resisting conquered.

> I wish to state right away my solidarity with all those, in this land, who advocate an end to violence, condemn the crimes of terrorism and of the military and police repression, and advocate the withdrawal of Israeli troops from the occupied territories as well as the recognition of the Palestinians' right to choose their own representatives to negotiations, now more indispensable than ever.[75]

Derrida, however, felt it necessary to assert in his speech that the Israeli State's "existence, it goes without saying, must henceforth be recognized by all and definitively guaranteed," not least, of course, by the Palestinians it conquered and continues to conquer.[76]

Despite Derrida's opposition to white supremacist South Africa in the mid-1980s, he believed that Israel—which defines itself as a Jewish state for all the Jews of the world rather than an Israeli state for all Israeli citizens and guarantees that definition by laws that grant differential rights and privileges to Jews (whether citizens or not) over non-Jewish Israeli citizens—should be recognized by all. His refusal and resistance to see that Israeli colonialism and racism operate with the same force, albeit with different means, inside the Jewish state as they do in the territories Israel occupies seems to be a reflection of an emotional attachment to this Israel, which Derrida expresses openly as the motive for his statement: "As is evident by my presence right here, this declaration is inspired not only by my concern for justice and by my friendship toward both the Palestinians and the Israelis. It is meant as an expression of respect for a certain image of Israel and as an expression of hope for its future."[77] Here, it is not an Aristotelian or a Marxist notion of justice—wherein justice means treating equal people equally and unequal people unequally—that Derrida is invoking, but rather a bourgeois liberal notion of justice—wherein equal and unequal people must be treated equally—to which he seems committed.

The tension between bringing the Semites together for Massignon and Derrida through the filiation and affiliation of the Abrahamic (and here we should remember, as Derrida reminds us twice, that one of his two grandfathers is indeed named Abraham)[78] as a Christian or Zionist position projected onto "Islam," or of separating them through Levinasian Othering and conceptualization of justice characterizes much of the ongoing discourse on the Palestinian Question as the Jewish Question. The problem with the current deployment of the Abrahamic, however, is that it (mis)places religion, eschatological messianism, and, finally, theory over and against, or at the expense of, the political.

Here I want to consider the appeal to the Abrahamic one last time on its own terms. Let us suppose that those thinkers who appeal to it in the context of the Palestinian Question aim to make an ecumenical move, of integrating religions in the "Middle East" under the capacious umbrella of Abrahamic commonality, hoping to provide a theme of unity in the midst of a conflict in which religion has tended to overlay the political aspects. Setting aside for a moment this de-politicizing move, which distracts from the colonial past and present in which the "conflict" lies and in which it is carried out, and avoids the whole question of justice for the Palestinians, the Abrahamic move seems to falter on its own terms and not just because of this de-politicizing effect. For even if integrating, ecumenizing appeals to unity among "religions" were not to distract from the political aspects of the conflict in this way, such appeals can only really be meaningful if this presupposed unity and the presumed integrating elements are syncretic, that is, if the unities and integrations among the religions that are in conflict are part of the lived life of quotidian practice, ritual, festival, custom, community. In such a scenario, then, appealing to these integrating factors may have the effect of demonstrating that the conflict between these "religions" is part of a false and trumped-up political manipulation. But in the appeal to the Abrahamic, the opposite is true. The lived reality of the colonial past and the colonial present is that of the deep, ongoing, and quotidian brutalization of a people by another. In the case of Israeli Jews and Palestinians, there was/is no commonality of living outside the conquest of the land by European Jewish colonists, any more than there was in the lives of white and black South Africans during Apartheid. As for the Arab Jews, whatever memories still survive of a commonality of life between Arab Jewish, Muslim, and Christian neighbors in those Arab countries from which Arab Jews came, they are separated from and contrasted with the conquering relationship that Arab Jews, like their European counterparts (mutatis mutandis), also have to Palestinians. The appeal to the Abrahamic is not therefore an appeal to a lived reality but an appeal to something purely abstract, scriptural, normative.[79]

Here, I want to remind you that the Abrahamic does have a political life of its own in Palestinian history and geography, specifically in the name of one major Palestinian city, al-Khalil, which is the city of Abraham, the friend of God [*Khalilu Allah*]. Al-Khalil's Palestinians, known as Khalilites (in Arabic *khalaylah*), have been enduring some of the worst forms of Jewish settler colonialism in the heart of their city and in their Abrahamic

Sanctuary, where Abraham is said to be buried. Their Abrahamic name is erased in English and other European languages, which insist on using the dead Jewish name of their city, "Hebron," and not the living name that has identified it for almost a millennium and a half: al-Khalil (the same process also applies to other Palestinian cities). In 1994, when Baruch Goldstein, a colonial settler from Brooklyn, massacred twenty-nine Muslim Palestinians while they were praying in the Abrahamic Sanctuary Mosque, Derrida paid attention and referred to them in the context of his discussion of "wars of religion, open war over the appropriation of Jerusalem." Derrida offers the massacre as an example of such wars: "Yesterday (yes, yesterday, truly, just a few days ago), there was the massacre of Hebron at the Tomb of the Patriarchs, a place held in common and symbolic trench of the religions called 'Abrahamic.'"[80] Derrida's insistence on the use of the dead name of al-Khalil, on calling the Abrahamic Sanctuary by its Jewish colonial terminology ("Tomb of the Patriarchs"), on claiming the massacre as part of a religious and not a colonial war, and contextualizing all of this in the Abrahamic, reveals the explanatory potential of the Abrahamic and what it can and cannot include. For a philosopher, like Derrida, so invested in the proper name, to refuse to call Palestinian geography and holy places by their proper Abrahamic names opens him to the *probability* of a similar charge like the one he leveled against Massignon. As Abrahamic Palestinians, Khalilites emblematize the bifurcation of which Said spoke, when they have to live under the terror of armed colonial settlers from Brooklyn in their midst. Palestine's Abrahamic city today is indeed inhabited by four hundred Semites who went the way of Orientalism and one hundred eighty thousand Semites who were forced to go the way of the Oriental. Semitism continues to define their lives precisely because of this bifurcation and the slippage the term experiences with every pronouncement.

But despite the persistence of the Palestinian Question, Derrida did not worry about the survival of the Palestinian people but remained more concerned about the "interminable Jewish Question," as he called it, and worried, as late as 1995, about the disappearance of the Jewish people. The context in which European Jews lived as *Oriental* Semites in Europe and live as *Orientalist* Semites in the Middle East is one that he forgets. He affirms unhesitatingly that Europe and the Middle East are places "in which the Jewish people had such great difficulty surviving and bearing witness to its faith."[81] In March 2000, while visiting Egypt to deliver a series of lectures, Derrida reinvoked his continued opposition to Israeli occupation of the West Bank and Gaza (but not of the whole of Palestine) while echoing his continued concern for *Jews*: "I am also not on the side of anti-Jewish tendencies," he declared, im(ex?)plicitly connecting Palestinian resistance against Israeli Jewish racist violence to "anti-Jewish tendencies," and thus equalizing the anti-Palestinian Israeli occupation with what he (mis)names as "anti-Jewish tendencies" in Palestinian resistance to Israel.[82] The shuttling and oscillation of the Abrahamic in Derrida's work, evidently, can do very little to level the field between Oriental and Orientalist Semites, much as he would have liked it to do.

Here, the Abrahamic demonstrates most clearly its Orientalist origins and functions, no matter how hard it tries to invent an Islamic pedigree for itself. The deployment of the Abrahamic ultimately proves itself to be a liberal move that wants to equate the powerful and the powerless, the Aryan Orientalist, the Semite who went the way of the Orientalist, and the Semite who was forced to go the way of the Oriental. The elimination of hierarchy in the Abrahamic and its commitment to an equalization of the three groups is precisely what is most de-politicizing about the term. Derrida is explicit on this: "Three other messianic eschatologies," he tells us, "mobilize [in the Middle East] all the forces of the world and the whole 'world order' in the ruthless war they are waging against each other, directly or indirectly."[83] The Abrahamic is indeed an antihistorical notion that wants to return us to a nineteenth- and early twentieth-century discourse on Semitism, forgetting the Zionist bifurcation. Like those who insist that when considering Israel, anti-Semitism is all that need be remembered, Derrida declares in the context of a rush by European powers to confess and avow their colonial and genocidal sins that "this globalization of avowal is therefore not thinkable in its inaugural emergence without what happened to the Jews of Europe in the twentieth century, nor is it any more separable from the international recognition of the state of Israel, a legitimation I would also interpret as one of the first moments of this avowal and of this world's bad conscience" ("Avowing," 32). Derrida's account of international support for Israel as motivated by guilt flies in the face of all available histories that have demonstrated beyond any doubt that international support (read: Christian powers) for the establishment of Israel was the result of geopolitical reasons that involved no sense of guilt over the holocaust whatsoever. Indeed, the very same Western (Christian) countries that voted to partition Palestine on November 29, 1947 had voted against or abstained from voting on a UN resolution (introduced by the Arab states) calling on them to take in the Jewish holocaust refugees, shortly before.[84]

Today, as Arabs, as Muslims, Palestinians have become the quintessential Semites. In forgetting Semitism and Orientalism, *and Zionism*, and in urging us to remember only anti-Semitism, Derrida and the Abrahamic readvance the claim that anti-Semitism, rather than Semitism, is what opposes the Semite. That Aryanism and Semitism can only exist as parts of the same discourse of European racial supremacy, which the Abrahamic forgets at its own peril, demonstrates that the Jewish and the Palestinian Questions have never been other than the Aryan and the Semitic Questions. The lesson that Said wanted to commit to Palestinian memory was therefore simple: To forget Semitism, to forget the Semites, we must always remember them.

# Beyond Tolerance and Hospitality: Muslims as Strangers and Minor Subjects in Hindu Nationalist and Indian Nationalist Discourse

*Priya Kumar*

> One will not say that the parts of one and the same natural, organic, and living ensemble *live together*.
>
> —Jacques Derrida, "Avowing—The Impossible"

In "Avowing—The Impossible: 'Returns,' Repentance, and Reconciliation," Jacques Derrida offers a profound meditation on "how to live together."[1] He begins by acknowledging how these familiar, everyday words—*comment vivre ensemble*—have become strange and enigmatic for him; thus much of the essay is devoted to reflecting on the multiple connotations of this phrase before he addresses the question of *how* to live together. "Living together," Derrida points out, encompasses many heterogeneous connotations, ranging from the worst to the best, from notions of the last resort to the idea of living together in peace and in accord. In its French idiom, the phrase "how to live together" enjoins us: "live together," one *must* live together "given that living is always 'living together'" ("Avowing," 19–20). However, Derrida brings out many nuances and fine distinctions in this phrase by pointing out that the "must [*il faut*]" can be accented in at least two ways. On the one hand, the phrase, "*il faut bien vivre ensemble*" (one must *well* live together) reminds us of what remains an unavoidable necessity—one must live together somehow, in any fashion, even if it is badly, in hatred or in conflict, for how can one live otherwise? For example, Israelis and Palestinians, Indians and Pakistanis, simply must coexist and cohabitate in the same space and time; they don't really have a choice. But even, in this negative interpretation of the "must well live together," the two partners accept the notion of a shared higher interest—after all, "it is better to live than to die," so one may as well live together even if it is a resigned, armed, and tenuous coexistence that is contingent on an institutional jurisprudence, a contract, or sheer fear of mutual destruction. On the other hand, this injunction, "must well [*il faut bien*]," can also be otherwise modulated—one must live together *well*—gesturing toward a mode of coexistence that is of trust, concord, and "good faith." For Derrida, "the best of the 'living together' is often associated with peace . . . a perpetual peace or a messianic peace, whose promise belongs to the very concept of peace and suffices to distinguish it from armistice, from cease-fire, or even from any 'peace process.'" Thus Palestinians and Israelis will truly live together only when peace "comes into bodies and souls," when people agree to coexist in accord with one another. This peace or "ethics of 'living together'" does not have to entail a rupture with the law, but it cannot be limited to the contract guaranteed by the law or any sort of state apparatus ("Avowing," 23–24, 26). In fact, it must exceed the uneasy tolerance of the political contract. But *how* does one live well together?[2]

Key to Derrida's vision of living well together are the related concepts of the *ensemble* and the *étranger*. Attending to the gap between the use of "ensemble" as a noun that connotes a whole, a gathering, a totality, and the use of "ensemble" as an adverb—for example in the expression *vivre ensemble* (living together)—Derrida maintains that the authority or closure of the ensemble (as a whole) will always be the first threat to all living together. Hence, the adverb "ensemble" (together) must always exceed, contest, and dislocate the authority of "ensemble" as a noun with its inflections of a whole or a coherent system, whether it is the whole of a biological or genetic organism, or the cohesiveness of a social entity, such as an ethnic group or a nation, that constitutes itself with this organic metaphor. Living together can neither be reducible to "organic symbiosis" (life according to nature, birth, or soil) nor to the juridico-political contract ("life according to convention, contract, or institution") ("Avowing," 27). Hence, one cannot claim that parts of the same ensemble live well together. To live together well, we must be able to interrogate all statutory conventions, all totalizations, and the folding upon itself of any organism or any social body (family, ethnic group, nation) that has been given to us by blood, birth, or belonging. In short, we must be able to think beyond the totality of any ensemble; moreover, we must ask, how do we relate to those who have been excluded from our (various) ensembles—those who have been designated as strangers, foreigners, and enemies?

This essay argues for the critical relevance of Derrida's work for examining the production of Muslims as strangers within the ensemble of the Indian nation, and for thinking about the living together of Hindus and Muslims / Indians and Pakistanis. By reading a representative Hindu nationalist text, V. D. Savarkar's *Hindutva* (1923) in conjunction with an emblematic secular nationalist text, Jawaharlal Nehru's magnum opus *The Discovery of India* (1946), I attend to some of the shared ground between Hindu nationalism and secular nationalism, especially when it comes to affirming the autochthony—and hence the prior claim—of Hindus on the nation-space of India. Both texts were written in colonial prisons (about twenty years apart from each other) and both offer a meditation on the nation as an ensemble and the nation-space as home. In particular, I examine the ways in which Hindus are set up as the organic, original nationals in both Savarkar and Nehru, while Muslims are positioned as enduring strangers (Savarkar) or at best as minor subjects of the nation (Nehru). At the same time, I also emphasize some of the key differences between the two texts: If in Savarkar, the Muslim remains a stranger by virtue of his extraneous religious affiliations, in Nehru, the Muslim outsider is no longer a stranger because he is eventually absorbed into the ensemble of the Indian nation. Moreover, there are vast differences in their visions of India and their approaches to the (problematic) figure of the Muslim: Whereas Savarkar advocates conversion or the return of Muslims to the Hindu fold, Nehru advocates tolerance and diversity as ideals for the nation—however, tolerance is almost always understood as Hindu tolerance of Muslims.

I argue that any effort at thinking about possibilities of peaceful coexistence between Hindus and Muslims calls for a fundamental rethinking of notions of autochthony and origins that establish upper-caste Hindus as the core national subjects, as well as of the liminal place of Muslims, not just in the more blatant fascist rhetoric of the Hindu Right but also in the more "tolerant" discourses of Indian nationalism, secularism, and citizenship. In the final section, I go on to examine the implications of Derrida's treatises on hospitality for thinking the living together of Hindus and Muslims in India. While acknowledging the immense importance of Derrida's injunctions to interrogate our notions of being "at home" and his call for an unconditional hospitality to the stranger (étranger), I also draw attention to some of the risks of absolute hospitality in naturalizing the very categories of host and stranger that it sets out to dismantle. I suggest that if there is to be a living well together, it cannot rely on the ethics of hospitality alone. The stranger must be able to appropriate his or her dwelling-place as a home.

## On the Stranger/Foreigner

The concept of the stranger (étranger) has been at the core of Derrida's ethical philosophy and attests to the influence of Levinasian ethics on Derrida's thinking. In "Avowing—The Impossible," Derrida underscores the importance of the stranger for any living together when he invokes Levinas's lesson on how one should relate to the stranger. Levinas suggests that the respect given to the stranger is equivalent to the sanctity accorded to God; therefore, "the image of God is better honored in the right given to the stranger than in symbols" ("Avowing," 29). In the spirit of this Levinasian dictum, Derrida proposes that one only lives together well with and as a stranger at home, in all the varied senses of home, including the self, the family, the neighborhood, the religious or ethnic community, and the nation-state. To unpack the implications of this statement, we must begin by addressing the category of the stranger in Derrida's thought and its relevance for understanding the anomalous position of Muslims in India.

Derrida writes in French—I read him in English. As he reminds us, the question of hospitality is one of translation; hence, I begin with a meditation on translation. Like the Greek word *xenos*, the French word *étranger* encapsulates both stranger *and* foreigner in English and therefore at once brings out and masks the relationship between these concepts. Although these are indissociable concepts, I suggest they must first be distinguished so as to see the overlaps between them. Because Derrida draws on Emile Benveniste's scholarly treatise, *Indo-European Language and Society* (*Le Vocabulaire des institutions Indo-Européennes*) for his work on hospitality, it is useful to begin with Benveniste's attempt to define *étranger*: "The stranger is 'he who *comes from outside*,' Lat. *advena*, or simply, 'he who is outside the limits of the community,' Lat. *peregrines*" (my emphasis).[3] The English translation of Benveniste's French text deploys "stranger" for *étranger*, but Benveniste's definition (especially the first part of his formulation) seems more closely associated with the English word "foreigner" in its emphasis on an outside space. Whereas a foreigner is clearly someone who comes from abroad—an elsewhere, an outside—the notion of the stranger in modern English allows for more ambivalence and the blurring of categories, such as those between self and other, inside and outside. In modern English (unlike in middle English), the stranger is a newcomer, an unknown and unfamiliar person, but not necessarily one who belongs to another space—another city, locality, or above all, another nation-state—which is typically how we understand "foreigner" today, given the term's inevitable association with citizenship in modernity.[4]

When Derrida uses the French term *étranger*, he draws on both senses of the concept—stranger and foreigner—sometimes moving between the two and at other times privileging one connotation over the other, thus posing a dilemma for those who translate his work into English. This is especially evident in his late work on hospitality where he offers an extended meditation on how one should relate to the stranger/foreigner.[5] A close reading of Derrida's writing on hospitality reveals a slippage in his use of *étranger*—between the notions of foreigner and stranger—precisely because they are so intertwined in French. For instance when, in "The Foreigner Question," he asks: "What does foreigner [*étranger*] mean? Who is foreign? . . . What is meant by 'going abroad,' coming from abroad?" clearly the context justifies the translator's use of "foreigner" (the spatial connotation of *étranger* here veers closer to the English foreigner).[6] For the most part, he proceeds with the assumption that an *étranger* is one who comes from an outside space, a beyond. This is very evident when he writes in "Hostipitality": "*In general it is the birthplace which will always have underpinned the definition of the stranger [étranger] (the stranger as non-autochthonous, non-indigenous . . . ). The stranger is first of all he who is born elsewhere.*"[7]

However, earlier in the same essay, Derrida also draws on the connotation of *étranger* as the strange or unfamiliar person when he suggests that "hospitality is also an intentional experience that proceeds beyond knowledge toward the other as absolute stranger [*étranger*], *as unknown*, where I know that I know nothing of him. . . . Hospitality is owed to the other as stranger" (8). Similarly, in "Avowing—the Impossible," Derrida speaks of the necessity for a hospitality to the "wholly other who exceeds the statutory convention" ("Avowing," 26). Clearly, the term *étranger* in the above contexts is being used to indicate an other "whose foreignness cannot be restricted to foreignness in relation to language, family or citizenship," but one who is the "wholly other, the absolute unforeseeable [*inanticipable*] stranger."[8] Elsewhere in his work, Derrida uses *étranger* to underscore the importance of respecting the alterity of the other in relation to the self, where every other is understood to be wholly other [*tout autre est tout autre*]. Even this very preliminary examination of Derrida's repeated use of the word *étranger* makes it evident that he relies on the dual connotations of *étranger* as both the unknown person (the stranger) and the one who comes from outside (the foreigner). To my mind, the French word *étranger* simultaneously accentuates and obscures the overlap between the categories of stranger and foreigner—that have to do with an affiliation with an outside—which I seek to illuminate and make visible in this essay.

If the question of how one relates to the stranger or foreigner is central to any ethics of living well together, as Derrida proposes, then it is important to differentiate between these two concepts precisely in order to see how they merge and overlap. English is useful here precisely because it has two words—stranger and foreigner—for *étranger*. Zygmunt Bauman's work on the stranger as the "third element"—the hybrid or the monster—is very helpful in allowing us to distinguish the concept of the stranger from the foreigner, as well as to see the intersections between the two. Bauman differentiates between two kinds of unfamiliars: The first are "those who reside in practically remote (that is rarely visited) lands" and denote the limits of familiar territory (i.e., foreigners). Territorial and functional means of separation are used to maintain the unfamiliarity of these (first) kinds of unfamiliars, and exchange with them is outside the everyday web of interactions.[9] The second type of unfamiliars are the strangers:

> Territorial and functional separation cease to suffice once the mere unfamiliar turns to be the stranger, aptly described by Simmel as "the man who comes today and stays tomorrow." The stranger is, indeed, *someone who refuses to stay in the "far away" land or go away* and hence a priori defies the easy expedient of spatial or temporal segregation. The stranger comes into the life-world and settles here. . . . *He made his way into the life-world uninvited*, thereby casting me on the receiving side of his initiative.[10]

A stranger is one who may share your space—who may live in proximity to you—but at the same time is perceived as an *unfamiliar, undecidable* person. The unforgivable sin of "late entry"—and the fact that the moment of entry can be determined or pinpointed—enables the production of the stranger as nonnative, non-autochthonous because he did not belong "originally," from the very beginning, since antiquity. Accordingly, the stranger is an interstitial figure who destabilizes the spatial ordering of the world into friends and enemies. He introduces into "the inner circle of proximity the kind of difference and otherness" that is typically endured and tolerated at a distance.[11] Of course, strangeness and the traits associated with the stranger are not natural; the construction of the stranger as stranger is a continuous process that takes place in everyday life through a nexus of social practices and institutional exclusions that must be reiterated continually. In this way, the stranger is positioned as someone who is other than one's own, who is *outside* one's ensemble, even if he or she does not reside in an outside space or territory (typically the nation-state in modernity). He or she represents an incongruous fusion of nearness and distance, inside and outside.[12]

Thus, both foreigner and stranger have in common the notion of an outside, but, while the association with an outside is very apparent in the instance of foreigner in modern English usage, it is not as evident in the case of the stranger.[13] Only by differentiating between the two can we see how they run together. I argue that the Derridean concept of the *étranger*—when understood as stranger—can be immensely useful for reflecting on the ambivalent place of minority religious and ethnic communities who *are located* within the ensemble of the imagined nation, yet are simultaneously rendered strange and undecidable precisely *because they are haunted by their presumed links to an outside*. In the next section, I reflect on the ways in which Hindu nationalist discourse positions religious minorities as strangers by constructing their particular beliefs and traditions as strange *and extraneous* to the nation. I examine an iconic text of Hindu nationalism, V. D. Savarkar's *Hindutva*, to show how Indian Muslims, in particular, are rendered as non-autochthonous strangers not because they are born elsewhere or because they came from an "outside," but because they follow religious traditions that emerged elsewhere. Savarkar's text illustrates how our notions of being "at home" and in place—especially when they rest on possessiveness and ownership of the home—can often incite hostility and hatred toward those designated as strangers.

## Hindu Nationalism and the Figure of the Muslim

The accelerated ascendance of the Hindu Right, especially since the late 1980s, presents one of the central conundrums of contemporary Indian history and politics. Hindu nationalism's attempts to racialize and militarize Hindus and to Hinduize India has been a matter of much concern for those who believe in the living together of Hindus and Muslims, Indians and Pakistanis.[14] The vision of a homogenous Hindu *rashtra* (nation) that is in accord with upper-caste Hindu beliefs and practices is at the core of the Hindu Right's agenda. Hindu nationalists claim that "Hindus"—a term that elides the many differences of belief, practice, caste, region, and class among the majority community—are the original inhabitants and hence the rightful owners of India, the true guardians of its heritage and its culture. Correspondingly, the construction of insiders and outsiders, natives and aliens, citizens and foreigners, has been central to the Hindu nationalist program. Minority religious communities have been positioned as strangers and outsiders who must either be evicted or assimilated into the fold of the dominant Hindu culture. Although the Hindu Right has targeted all minorities in its goal of making India a Hindu nation, Indian Muslims have merited a special place in its hostile and virulent agenda.

Present-day Muslims are viewed as descendants of cruel and aggressive medieval Muslim rulers who invaded India, destroyed Hindu temples, and forcibly converted many Hindus at the point of the sword. According to this narrative, Hindus have been waging an enduring struggle for liberation against foreign rule for nearly a thousand years, ever since Muslim rulers established their dominance over a large section of Northern India. As Gyanendra Pandey observes, "Hindu 'history' reduces all of India's past to a twofold statement: first the glory of pre-Muslim India; and second the unceasing troubles that have come to reign ever since the Muslims came to the subcontinent. . . . It is a history of perpetual Hindu-Muslim conflict, Muslim aggression and Hindu resistance, Good versus Evil, the Pure versus the Impure."[15] This widely prevalent view reduces the complex history of Muslims—and Islam—in India to a catalogue of barbaric conquests, cruelty, repeated invasions, and the desecration of temples. Muslims are thus viewed as eternal outsiders in much contemporary Hindu nationalist discourse, who must either be expunged from the body of the nation, or at best folded into the internal law of the primordial Hindu hosts.[16]

The notion of *Hindutva* (literally "Hinduness") encapsulates the majoritarian and fascist manifesto of the Sangh Parivar, the "family" of right-wing political, cultural, and religious organizations that make up the Hindu Right, led by the Hindu supremacist organization, the Rashtriya Swayamsevak Sangh or the RSS (the National Volunteers Corps founded in 1925). The word *Hindutva*—a term that connotes a program of Hindu supremacy—is a neologism that was proposed by V. D. Savarkar, an influential icon of the modern Hindu nationalist movement. Savarkar is considered to be the chief inspiration for the Hindu Right's belief that India is the exclusive terrain of Hindus. In his 1923 book *Hindutva: Who Is a Hindu?* Savarkar took on the task of defining the essence of a Hindu by laying out who belongs to the Hindu fold and who must be excluded.[17] Savarkar's work is important for its attempt to racialize and nationalize the category "Hindu" and to establish the intrinsic association of Hindus with the territory of "India." Like many nationalists, Savarkar assumes the fictive continuity of a territorially bound, singular national entity—India or Hindustan—and retrospectively projects it onto the ancient past in an effort to assert majority Hindus as the organic nationals. In fact, the entire exercise of *Hindutva* is devoted to establishing the prior claim of Hindus on colonial India and to excluding Muslims from the ensemble of the nation by designating them as strangers and outsiders.

Savarkar begins his treatise by defining his neologism *Hindutva* and by differentiating it from the "cognate term" Hinduism, which he suggests is only a derivative of *Hindutva*.

> Hindutva is not identical with what is vaguely indicated by the term Hinduism. By an "ism" it is generally meant a theory or a code more or less based on spiritual or religious dogma or system. But when we attempt to investigate into the essential significance of Hindutva we do not primarily—and certainly not mainly—concern ourselves with any particular theocratic or religious dogma or creed. Had not linguistic usage stood in our way, then "Hinduness" would have certainly been a better word than Hinduism as a near parallel to Hindutva. Hindutva replaces all the departments of thought and activity of the whole being of our *Hindu race*. (3–4)

Most of the book is concerned with outlining Hindutva, or the essence of being a Hindu, but in order to appreciate what constitutes Hindutva, Savarkar proposes that one must first understand who or what a "Hindu" is. He goes to great lengths to establish the antiquity of the word *Hindu*, its organic connection with both the land and the people, and its indigenous origin. Like many other nationalists, he locates the origins of the modern "Hindu nation" in Vedic civilization because the Vedas are the "matrix deferred to by the founders and followers of most later strands of Hinduism."[18] Although he proceeds with the (then) widely held assumption that the Vedic Aryans migrated to the northern part of "India" (albeit with the caveat that oriental scholarship doesn't know enough about their original home) and acknowledges the likely presence of already existing "thinly scattered *native* tribes," yet, he also sets up the Aryans as "a people destined to lay the foundation of a great and enduring civilization," who succeeded in developing a "*sense of nationality*" and giving it a "local habitation and a name"—namely Sindhu or Hindu after the river Indus (8, 5, my emphasis).[19] His account of the Aryans is especially interesting because he uses the language of settler colonization and the civilizing mission to describe how they "reclaimed the vast waste and but very thinly populated lands" and "changed the whole face of the wild and unkemp[t] nature." These "intrepid Aryans made it [India] their home and lighted their first sacrificial fire on the banks of the Sindhu, the Indus," and from there "tribe after tribe of the Hindus issued forth from the land of their nursery" in order to conquer the rest of the land. What is noteworthy here is the slippage between the terms Aryan, Hindu, and Indian such that the Vedic Aryans come to constitute the essence and foundation of not just (modern) Hinduism, but also of the imagined Indian nation, which seeks to appropriate state power from the British. Thus Savarkar describes them as "Indians in their forward march" as they moved beyond the land surrounding the Indus. "This strong and vigorous *race*" came to call themselves "Sindhus" and the land as "Sapta Sindhu," while the neighboring Persians came to term them "Hindus"—in a variant of the Sanskrit word Sindhu. Savarkar insists on the autochthony of the term *Hindu* despite its allegedly foreign provenance: "Down to this day the whole world knows us as 'Hindus' and our land as 'Hindusthan' as if in fulfillment of the wishes of our Vedic fathers who were the first to make that choice" (4–15, my emphasis).

As Etienne Balibar tells us, "The name symbolically attached to national existence, *to a territory that remains the same in whole or in part*, or which was that of a neighboring territory (thus 'Germany,' 'Russia,' 'Serbia,'), often contributes to allowing the nation to forge a continuous identity by means of a set of 'national' stories in which it plays a prevalent imaginary role."[20] The notion of "India" as a spatially bound geographical and historical entity only emerged contingently in the last decades of the nineteenth century, in early popular geohistorical nationalist writing from colonial north India, as Manu Goswami has demonstrated.[21] Significantly, the territorial boundaries of colonial India came to constitute the "approximate spatial scale" of the imagined nation in these early nationalist accounts; this imaginative appropriation of colonial territory was in turn attended by the concomitant spatial expansion of the terms—Bharat, Hindustan, or Aryavarta—to effect a nationalization of colonial space.[22] Clearly, "India," "Hindustan," or "Bharat" never was a nation-state in the modern sense of the word during the time of the Vedic Aryans, but like all nationalists, Savarkar insists on the antiquity and the enduring existence of the nation—and its spatially bound territory—by establishing the continuity of the name that is associated with it. It is no coincidence that he chooses "Hindustan" over other variants such as "Bharat," "India," or even "Aryavarta" as the "cradle name" of the nation. While "Aryavarta"—the land of the Aryans—is not expansive enough to encompass the territory of colonial India "from the Indus to the seas," even the ancient name "Bharat" that was affirmed in many popular nineteenth-century nationalist histories is eschewed for "Hindustan"—land of the Hindus—in an effort to claim Vedic Aryans as the founding fathers of the nation, and to validate present-day Hindus as their descendants, the primordial heirs of the nation (14). In Savarkar's account, religious community and territory are fused organically by giving them a version of the same name—Hindu, Hindustan—in order to constitute the nation as an organic ensemble and to assert an isomorphism between people, culture, and territory.

If the migrant Aryans are conjured as fearless and adventurous *settlers* and the founders of the nation, the entry of Muslim rulers from the northwest of the subcontinent many centuries later is described in sharp contrast as a cataclysmic foreign "invasion" that ruptured the peace of the land and its people. Savarkar describes the crossing of Mohammad [Mahmud] of Ghazni across the river Indus as a "dire day" when the "conflict of life and death began" in Sindhusthan. He encapsulates the entire history of medieval north India in a few cursory pages in which his goal is to establish how "India alone had to face Arabs, Persians, Pathans, Baluchis, Tartars, Turks, Moguls—a veritable human Sahara whirling and columning up bodily in a furious world storm." The metaphor of a stormy swirling Sahara is used to describe and lump together different Muslim ethnicities and dynasties as "foreign invaders." What is more, the desert-like qualities of the Sahara are implicitly contrasted with the fertile and life-giving qualities of the river Indus. In many ways, Savarkar reiterates the commonly held colonialist and nationalist view of all Muslim history as invader history: "Day after day, decade after decade, century after century, the ghastly conflict continued and India single-handed kept up the fight morally and militarily." The only qualifier in this sweeping account of different historical figures and moments is when he pauses to acknowledge the Mughal ruler Akbar's ascent to the throne and the birth of his son as a "moral victory" for India (presumably because Akbar married a Rajput princess). At the same time, the "Muslim invasion" of the subcontinent is also seen to have a somewhat beneficial (and unintended) side effect because it worked to unite the entire country into an "indivisible whole" or a "single Being"—recalling Derrida's notion of the ensemble as a totality or a homogenous community—against a monolithic alien oppressor (42–45). In this manner, people belonging to various sects, denominations, castes, and language groups are said to have suffered as "Hindus" and to have emerged victorious against the paradigmatic alien Muslim foe.

Much of the remainder of Savarkar's book is devoted to defining the essential attributes of a "Hindu" (Hindutva), to circumscribing the limits of the posited Hindu "nation," and to designating the figure of the Muslim as a stranger whose loyalties are always suspect *so long as he remains a Muslim*. Accordingly, Savarkar outlines three fundamental aspects of Hindutva: (1) geography or a common territory, (2) a common "race-jati," and (3) a common civilization (*Sanskriti*). At every point of this tripartite formulation, Savarkar pauses to explain why the Muslim cannot be included within the Hindu fold, even if he may be considered a *Bhartiya* or *Hindi* (he uses these terms interchangeably with Indian). He begins by contending that to be a Hindu one must claim this land "as his motherland" and as the land of his patriarchs: "Hindusthan meaning the land of Hindus, the first essential of Hindutva must necessarily be this geographical one." This affiliation with the territory of (colonial) India is first and foremost what makes Hindus a nation. However, geographical ties to the imagined nation-space in themselves are not enough to constitute the essence of a Hindu because "we would be straining the usage of words too much—we fear to the point of breaking—if we call a Mohammedan a Hindu because of his being a resident of India" (82–83). Clearly, dwelling or residence is not enough to claim to be "at home" in a nation.

Savarkar goes on to consider shared descent or what he terms "the bonds of a common blood" between Hindus—"all Hindus claim to have in their veins the blood of the *mighty race* incorporated with and descended from the Vedic fathers, the Sindhus." Hence Hindus are not only a nation, but also a "race-jati," one which has been unified by means of intermarriages between the various castes (84–85).[23] Savarkar relies on biological notions of race to establish Hindus as a homogeneous community. He explains his use of the hyphenated term "race-jati" thus: "The word jati derived from the root Jan[,] to produce, means a brotherhood, *a race determined by a common origin*, possessing a common blood" (84–85, my emphasis). *Jati* is a Sanskrit term derived from the root *jan*, which has the twin meanings of birth and species; significantly, the word *jati* is most often used to describe the phenomenon of caste in India—as it pertains to endogamous descent groups—hence it is noteworthy that Savarkar should use the term *jati* as a translation of the concept of race. Both racism and casteism are deeply harmful forms of social exclusion that justify themselves precisely on principles of biological descent.[24] Thus, it is not inconsequential that Savarkar should amalgamate what are, to his mind, the positively imbued categories of race and caste. The hyphenated term "race-jati" allows him to bring together the categories of race and caste and to constitute Hindus as a bounded organic whole, based on the (fictive) notion of common descent.

Indeed, throughout Savarkar's account of "Hindus" as the organic nationals of the Indian nation, we see a merging of the terms of "race," "jati," and "religion." In his study of the Semites, "an uncannily dangerous group . . . at the internal and external borders of the Christian West," Gil Anidjar has shown how Jews and Arabs similarly functioned at once as race and religion—"virtually the selfsame Semites"—in the work of nineteenth-century Orientalists such that what was said about Jews could equally be said about Arabs.[25] He uses the example of the Semites—who, like the Aryans, were "a concrete figment of the Western imagination"—to show how the categories of race and religion are "discursively co-constitutive, that they operate in concert (regardless of intentionality), particularly where one appears to be irrelevant to the other." Accordingly, Anidjar concurs with William Hart, who suggests that the racial distinctions that are posited between Aryans and Semites are intrinsically connected to religious divisions between Christians and Jews, and Christians and Muslims. The transient, ephemeral figure of the Semite thus emerged from the erasure of a distinction between Jew and Arab, religion and race. Despite (and against) the institutionalized disciplinary divisions that regulate the study of race as distinct from religion, Anidjar calls for a recognition that religion and race are "contemporary, indeed coextensive and, moreover, co-concealing categories, whereby religion often serves as a "mask for race."[26]

These multiple discursive links between race and religion are evident in Savarkar's effort to racialize Hindus. Hindus are at once race, religion, and nationality in Savarkar and the intersection of these categories allows him to constitute Hindus as an indivisible whole—an ensemble in the Derridean sense. Yet, the notion of Hindus as a race—descended from the Vedic fathers—is rendered radically unstable when he acknowledges that many Muslims are in fact local converts: "The story of their conversions, forcible in millions of cases, is too recent to make them forget, even if they like to do so, that they inherit *Hindu blood* in their veins."[27] Once again the figure of the Muslim troubles Savarkar's efforts to establish a closed off and clearly demarcated Hindu whole; still, he must ask, can we afford to "recognize these Mohammedans as Hindus?" Muslims, he claims, must be positioned outside the Hindu fold (even though "their original Hindu blood" may be "almost unaffected by an alien adulteration") because they do not "own" a common culture and civilization—including most importantly a shared religion—with Hindus (91–92).

It is this third principle of Hindutva that allows Savarkar to place the Muslim firmly outside the ensemble of the imagined Hindu—read Indian—nation. Drawing on the nature/culture opposition to claim that civilization is the "secondary creation of man" from "matter," Savarkar argues that Hindu civilization emerges organically as a secondary product of the territory—Hindustan (here understood as nature/matter).[28] What makes Hindus a "cultural unit" or an ensemble is not only the fact that they are a common nation (a people tied to a territory) or a common race (based on shared descent from the Vedic fathers), but "as a consequence of being both," they also have a common *Sanskriti* (culture or civilization) (99). Interestingly, he strives to make the term "Hindu" more capacious in order to include within its conceptual realm all religious traditions that arose *within* the territory of colonial India such as Jainism, Buddhism, Sikhism, and the Arya Samaj. The followers of these "heterodox" or "minority" traditions must be embraced within the fold of Hindutva since they are valuable allies in Savarkar's project of a Hindu nation in the making. Accordingly, he suggests that either the term Hinduism should be restored to its "proper" usage in order to include all religions that emerged in India—"the land of the Saptasindhus or in the other unrecorded communities in other parts of India in the Vedic period"—or failing that, it should be dropped altogether. The "generic term Hindu Dharma" must be used to indicate all these (autochthonous) "Dharmas as a *whole*," while more specific terms may be used to indicate particular religious traditions (107). Noticeably, Islam and Christianity remain extraneous to Savarkar's expanded definition of "Hindu Dharma" because they did not emerge in the territory of the imagined nation.

Accordingly, Christians and Muslims cannot be recognized as "Hindus" even in this expanded sense; they have "ceased to own Hindu civilization" by adopting a different religion, which is viewed as the ultimate betrayal by Savarkar and his descendants in the Hindu Right. The argument is that they feel they belong to a cultural unit that is "altogether different from the Hindu one." Savarkar is willing to concede the possibility of a shared Hindu-Muslim culture such that certain Muslim communities—such as "patriotic" Bohras or Khojas—may share cultural heroes and customs with Hindus, yet even these Muslims cannot be included within the Hindu ensemble *because they follow religions that originated outside of "India."* Thus he proclaims: "For though Hindusthan to them is Fatherland as to any other Hindu yet it is not to them a Holyland too. *Their holyland is far off in Arabia or Palestine.* Their mythology and Godmen, ideas and heroes, *are not the children of this soil.* Consequently their names and their outlook *smacks of a foreign origin.* Their love is divided" (100–101, 113, my emphasis). Herein lies the rub. Savarkar's assertion that Muslims do not quite belong to the Indian nation exemplifies Derrida and Bauman's conception of the stranger as someone who is outside the limits of one's ensemble, an interstitial figure who destabilizes the spatial ordering of the world into friends and enemies. Their affiliation with the nation—Hindustan—is always suspect because they believe in a religious tradition that has been construed as nonnative by relying on the fictive continuity of a territorially bound national entity. Concomitantly, Savarkar's belief that Hindus constitute the organic core of the nation rests not so much on the more typical argument that they are the original inhabitants of the claimed territory—

since he is cognizant of the prevalent Aryan migration theory—but rather upon the autochthony of the diverse religious traditions that he terms "Hindu." India is the land of their revelation: "The system or set of religions which we call Hindu *dharma*—Vaidik and Non-Vaidik—is as truly the offspring of this soil as the men whose thoughts they are or who 'saw' the Truth revealed in them" (110, my emphasis).[29] Territorial origin—itself defined ironically by the nationalization and appropriation of *colonial* space—is used by Savarkar to posit Hindus as the essence of the nation and simultaneously to exclude Muslims and Christians from the ensemble of the nation, or at least to render them strange and undecidable.

Savarkar projects the (modern and colonial) notion of India as a spatially bound, unified entity onto the Vedic past and concomitantly posits a territorial and autochthonous conception of nationhood that affirms a hierarchy of identities—with Hindus firmly established as the core nationals—based on an assumed equivalence between land, culture, and identity. He puts forward a vision of living together that is limited precisely by blood, soil, birth, descent, and belonging in order to set up Hindus as a closed-off ensemble, and eventually to establish India as the land of the Hindus. The limit case in *Hindutva* is always provided by the anomalous figure of the Muslim who must remain extraneous to this vision of a Hindu nation. Although Savarkar also excludes Christians as followers of an alien religion, his examples always return to Muslims as the sites of excess and strangeness, who must be kept out of the Hindu whole. In Savarkar's vision of India as a Hindu nation, Muslims may be considered denizens of India—*Bhartiyas* or *Hindis*—but they cannot claim to be owners or guardians of the nation. Muslims as Muslims cannot be accommodated within Savarkar's fascist project of a Hindu nation in the making. The only way for them to be reabsorbed into the fold is to convert to one of the ostensibly indigenous traditions.[30] Given the prior claim of Hindus on the nation, it is clear that Muslims can only be considered guests or visitors who are there at the largesse of Hindus. Hence they will, at best, be subordinate citizens of a free India.

Although Savarkar's notion of Hindutva emerged in the context of colonial exploitation and anticolonial resistance, there is no escaping the troubling fascism of this book in its effort to draw boundaries and to position the Muslim as a stranger or an internal enemy whose allegiances are suspect. Savarkar's notion that India is the land of Hindus and his vision of a homogenous Hindu nation have been appropriated by the postindependence Hindu nationalist movement in India. Savarkar provides a name—Hindutva—and a manifesto for this movement. (Savarkar himself was part of the Hindu Mahasabha, the Hindu Convention, an organization with close ties to the RSS, and went on to become its leader.) Much subsequent Hindu nationalist discourse positions the Muslim as an outsider and asserts that Hindus are the original and primordial denizens of India. For example, M. S. Golwalkar, the second chief or *sarsanghchalak* of the RSS, asserted, "Undoubtedly . . . we—Hindus—have been in undisputed and undisturbed possession of this land for over eight or even ten thousand years before the land was invaded by any *foreign race*."[31] The language of possession, ownership, and virile mastery is the hallmark of much of this discourse with Hindus established as the autochthons—the representative or core nationals—and Muslims as the perpetual outsiders whose loyalties are always suspect.

More sophisticated voices, following Savarkar's precedent, are willing to concede the possibility of Aryan migration, yet they persist in constituting the Muslim as an unknown, undecidable figure by drawing an explicit contrast between Muslims and the Vedic Aryans. Thus, Shrikant Talageri, a present-day Hindu nationalist writer, argues, "Even if it is assumed that a group of people, called 'Aryans,' invaded, or immigrated into India, . . . *they have left no trace, if ever there was any, of any link, much less the consciousness of any link, much less any loyalties associated with such a link, to any place outside India.*"[32] It is this idea of a trace—a residue—of a link to the "outside" that haunts the figure of the Muslim in Hindu nationalist discourse and allows us to see the shared conceptual ground between the categories of foreigner and stranger. A stranger (unlike a foreigner) may live in proximity to us, but the association with an elsewhere, a beyond, persists in shadowing him. Thus the Muslim may be considered a part of the totality of the Indian nation—he may even share "the same blood"—but his loyalties and allegiances are always open to question, especially since Partition and the creation of Pakistan as a separate homeland for India's Muslims.[33]

If the milder face of the Hindu Right endorses a program of cultural nationalism that upholds assimilation based on Savarkar's notion of Hindutva, more hostile voices support a racist program that makes it acceptable to kill the Muslim. One of the most widespread slogans that was used to mobilize Hindu mobs against Muslims during the Ayodhya agitation of the 1980s and 1990s was *"Babar ki aulad jao Pakistan ya kabristan* [children of Babar (the founder of the Mughal dynasty in India) go to Pakistan or the graveyard]." This horrific attitude was also amply demonstrated in the anti-Muslim pogrom that took place in Gujarat in 2002. The Hindu Right today may not use the term "race" to designate Hindus or Muslims (they speak in terms of Hindu culture/religion and of Hindutva as a "way of life"), but as Anidjar points out, "Religious distinctions, indeed religious identifications, hide the most persistent remnants of a history of racism" and "where religion has emerged, race has all but disappeared (that is to say that though visible, it has been concealed in its power and effects)."[34] In the Hindu nationalist narrative, the Muslim becomes the archetypal outsider, and indeed the enemy of the great Hindu nation.

Balibar is right when he notes that we are witnessing an increasing confusion of the historical and political concepts of the stranger and the enemy throughout the world—a tendency that is in fact inherent in the nation form. Balibar seems to think that this process represents a "new ambiguity" or blurring between these separate categories; however, as Benveniste reminds us, "The notions of enemy, stranger [foreigner], guest, which for us form three distinct entities—semantically and legally—in the [ancient] Indo-European languages show close connections."[35] As I have been arguing, these overlaps persist in modernity, as well, but to appreciate them, we must first be able to distinguish between these interrelated concepts. The structural links between the stranger and the enemy have become very visible in post-Partition India, especially since the rise to political power of the Hindu nationalist movement. Under these prevailing assumptions, India's over one hundred million Muslims are at best guests who live in the country on Hindu sufferance, or at worst the nemesis that must be expunged from the benign and tolerant Hindu nation.

## Nehru's *Discovery of India*

Like Savarkar's *Hindutva*, *Discovery* was written in a colonial prison during the years 1942–46 when Nehru, along with several other Congress leaders, was incarcerated in Ahmadnagar Fort for passing the Quit India resolution against the British government. Part historical narrative, part memoir, and part prison diary, *Discovery* is a paradigmatic expression of the Indian nationalist imagination at the cusp of independence and sovereignty. As Aamir Mufti writes, "Nehru's *Discovery* is, famously, a narrative of the emergence of nationalism out of the great sweep of India's history and an account of the constancy, throughout this process of historical development, *of India's personality*."[36] Published a year before independence, *Discovery* is a colossal work that is at once historical, speculative, and literary in its attempt to imaginatively reconstruct "India's" past.[37] It also anticipates the postindependence Indian state and delineates what sort of shape it should take. In this section, I offer a reading of Nehru's epic narrative in order to trace how Hindus are once again established as the core or original nationals in *Discovery*, whereas Muslims emerge as belated nationals, and eventually as minor subjects of the nation. Yet, *Hindutva* and *Discovery* are also very different works not just in scope and complexity but also in their sensibility: Savarkar's *Hindutva* is fascist and exclusionary in its effort to oust Muslims, whereas Nehru's *Discovery* affirms tolerance and diversity as national ideals.

Much like Savarkar, Nehru assumes a fictive continuity between past and present and takes for granted an already existent bounded national entity—"India"—that he projects on to the classical past. By the time he was writing this book, the findings of the Indus Valley excavations had been widely publicized. The discovery by the archaeological expeditions in the 1920s of this highly sophisticated ancient civilization in colonial India undermined the widely prevalent colonialist and racialized account of blond, white-skinned European Aryans conquering and civilizing the primitive black-skinned natives of India.[38] In view of these findings, Nehru begins his historical account of India with the Indus Valley and suggests that "for all practical purposes" the people of this civilization may be considered "the indigenous inhabitants of India."[39] However, despite this acknowledgment of the (likely) prior existence of the Indus Valley Civilization, he too goes to some lengths to place Vedic culture at the origin of India.[40] This is very evident in the following passage from "The Coming of the Aryans" where he describes the emergence of Indian culture: "We might say that the first great cultural synthesis and fusion took place between the incoming Aryans and the Dravidians, who were probably the representatives of the Indus Valley Civilization. Out of this synthesis and fusion grew the *Indian races and the basic Indian culture*, which had distinctive elements of both" (73).[41] Synthesis and fusion are recurrent tropes in Nehru's biography of the nation: Here, they allow him to set up the Vedic Aryans along with the inhabitants of the Indus Valley as the originary people of India. Imbibing and reproducing Orientalist and colonialist forms of knowledge, Nehru racializes the terms Aryan and Dravidian—which had emerged from linguistics and philology—and sets them up as the first "races" of India. Furthermore, after providing a very brief account of the Rig Veda as possibly "the earliest book that humanity possesses," he asserts that "from these dim beginnings of long ago *flow out the rivers of Indian thought and philosophy*, of Indian life and culture and literature, ever widening and increasing in volume, and sometimes flooding the land with their rich deposits" (79–81, my emphasis). Vedic culture is taken to be not only the foundation of Hindu civilization, but the very basis of Indian civilization. Key to Nehru's effort of constituting Vedic civilization as originary—despite his acceptance of the common theory that the composers of the Vedic hymns migrated to India—is his assertion that the Indo-Aryans elaborated the Vedas "*in the soil of India*" (77). Because the Vedas are considered to be the founding texts by most later strands of Hinduism, it is particularly important for both Nehru and Savarkar to establish their autochthony—"India" as the land of Vedic composition and revelation—all the more so since they accept that the Vedic Aryans came from outside the territorial bounds of the nationalist imagination. This allows them to establish Hindus as the original—and hence representative—national subjects.

In *Discovery*, Nehru goes to great lengths to affirm the continuity of an essential Indian culture that has remained unchanged over the centuries despite the many "foreign" incursions. Consequently, he approvingly cites the archaeologist of the Indus Valley ruins, Sir John Marshall: "In the religion of the Indus people there is much, of course, that might be paralleled in other countries. . . . But, taken as a whole, their religion *is so characteristically Indian as hardly to be distinguished from still living Hinduism*" (71). Although Nehru is very careful to discredit any use of the term "Hindu" (in its present identification with a specific religious tradition) as interchangeable with "Indian," his account fails to avoid the pitfalls of a nativist conception of nationhood that takes territory or land as the natural ground for the constitution of organic cultural identities. Thus, like Savarkar, he posits a stratification of identities by emphasizing the autochthony of certain religiocultural traditions. All religiocultural traditions that originated in "India"—a territory roughly approximating the spatial scale of the colonial state—such as Hinduism, Buddhism, and Jainism (and later Sikhism) are viewed as somehow more authentically or essentially "Indian," whereas Islam and Christianity are external to his narrative of the becoming of the nation. Where Savarkar seeks to provide a more capacious understanding of the terms Hindu, Hinduism, and *Hindu dharma*, Nehru proposes the (related) concept of *Arya dharma* to encapsulate all faiths—Vedic and non-Vedic—that emerged in "India." Thus, he asserts, "Buddhism and Jainism were certainly not Hinduism. . . . Yet they arose in India and were integral parts of Indian life, culture and philosophy. A Buddhist or a Jain in India is *a hundred percent product of Indian thought and culture*, yet neither is Hindu by faith" (75). In contrast, we are told, a Muslim or a Christian "could, and often did . . . *become an Indian* without changing his religion" by adapting himself to the "Indian way of life and culture." The implication is clear—Muslims and Christians are— or were not—a priori Indians. "Indian" in Nehru is akin to Savarkar's expanded sense of "Hindu," where both stand in for a basic or essential national culture. And, although Nehru is willing to admit that this originary "Indian" culture was "greatly influenced by the impact of Islam," he also insists that "it remained basically and distinctively Indian." Thus, "each incursion of foreign elements was a challenge to this culture, but it was met successfully by a new synthesis and a process of absorption. This was also a process of re-juvenation and new blooms of culture arose out of it, *the background and essential basis*, however, remaining much the same" (75–76, my emphasis). What he terms *Arya dharma* is thus located at the core of the nation, whereas Islam and Christianity are rendered ex-traneous to national culture.

Nehru describes the advent of Islam into the space of "India" in a chapter that is no-tably titled "New Problems." In contrast to Savarkar, Nehru emphasizes that Islam came to India as a religion several centuries before it came as a "political force" because of fre-quent trade and cultural contact with the Arab world, especially with Baghdad, which he lauds for being "the biggest intellectual center of the civilized world" in the eighth and ninth centuries. In a typical affirmation of "Indian tolerance," he claims that since "it was the old tradition of India to be tolerant to all faiths and forms of worship," Islam "had taken its place among the many religions of India without trouble or conflict" for over three hundred years. However, things changed with the repeated incursions from Af-ghanistan of Mahmud of Ghazni: "Above all, they brought Islam, for the first time, to the accompaniment of ruthless military conquest," which led to "powerful psychological re-actions among the people" (229, 232, 236). Despite his obvious resistance to Islam as a proselytizing and conquering religion, Nehru goes on to outline how the "invaders" from the northwest were eventually "absorbed into India and [became] part of her life. Their dynasties became Indian dynasties and there was a *great deal of racial fusion by intermar-riage*" (238). This process of naturalization culminates in the figure of the Mughal em-peror Akbar. In a chapter titled "Babar and Akbar: The Process of Indianization," we are told that although Babar, the founder of the Mughal dynasty, remained "a stranger to In-dia," his grandson, Akbar, married a Rajput princess, making Akbar's son and successor Jehangir "half Mughal and half Rajput Hindu . . . thus *racially* this Turko-Mongol dynasty became far more Indian than Turk or Mongol" (259).

The language of race here is reminiscent of Savarkar, but where Savarkar draws on biological conceptions of race (for the most part) to describe Hindus as a "race-jati," Nehru deploys the term "race" in a very loose and capacious sense to designate different cultural, linguistic, and religious entities. For example, once he sets up Aryans and Dravidians as the basic Indian races, he goes on to say: "In the ages that followed there came many *other races*: Iranians, Greeks, Parthian, Bactrians, Scythians, Huns, Turks (before Islam), early Christians, Jews, Zoroastrians; they came, made a difference, and were absorbed." Unlike Savarkar, who lumps together "Arabs, Persians, Pathans, Turks, Moguls" as the monolithic Muslim enemy, in Nehru's considerably more complex and nuanced account of history, it is "wrong and misleading to talk of a Moslem invasion of India. . . . There was a *Turkish* invasion (Mahmud's), and an *Afghan* invasion, and then a *Turco-Mongol* or Mughal invasion" (73, 43, 241). Significantly, each term in this formulation is designated as a "race"—for example, we are told that some of the subsequent rulers who came from Afghanistan (Qutb-ud-Din Aibak, Razia Sultana, and Iltutmish) were in fact "racially Turks" (238). Nehru's culturalist conception of race in these passages resonates with the use of the term in the discourse of race struggle that appeared in Europe in the sixteenth and seventeenth centuries, as traced by Michel Foucault. Foucault notes that "although this discourse speaks of races . . . it is quite obvious that the term 'race' itself is not pinned to a stable biological meaning. And yet the word is not completely free-floating. Ultimately it designates a certain historico-political divide. . . . One might say— and this discourse does say—that two races exist whenever one writes the history of two groups which do not, at least to begin with, have the same language or, in many cases, the same religion."[42] Unlike Savarkar and his contemporaries in the Hindu Right, Nehru is not deploying an anatomicobiological notion of race to describe Hindus or Muslims as a race, but his conception of race does connote a historicopolitical divide between Hindus as the inhabitants of India and the various Muslim rulers who came from the northwest of the subcontinent. Although Nehru also differentiates among the Turks, the Mongols, and the Afghans as diverse "races," he views all of them as invaders and outsiders precisely because they are Muslim.[43] Of course, the key difference from Savarkar's account is that in Nehru's story, eventually, these "foreign" invaders become "Indianized" by means of a process of "racial fusion" and cultural admixture to the extent that they begin to look upon India as their home.

Accordingly, in *Discovery*, the Mughal and Afghan rulers no longer remain foreigners; they become part of the ensemble of the Indian nation such that the "Mughal dynasty became firmly established as *India's own*":

The Mughals were *outsiders and strangers to India* and yet they fitted into the Indian structure with remarkable speed. Through choice or circumstances or both, the Afghan rulers and those who had come with them, merged into India. Their dynasties became completely Indianized with their roots in India, *looking upon India as their homeland, and the rest of the world as foreign.* (261, 241, my emphasis)

While most earlier (and many present-day) nationalist accounts posit a homology between Mughal rule and British colonialism, Nehru emphasizes that unlike the British, who remained "outsiders, aliens and misfits in India," the Afghans and Mughals were absorbed into India and had no outside affiliations. Thus, Akbar and his descendants did not remain strangers in India (238).[44]

Although Nehru's and Savarkar's perspectives on Muslims and the history of Indian Islam are very different, they share the modernist assumption of an already existent, unified national entity—India or Hindustan—that has existed since antiquity and the concomitant fiction of a national people who are organically connected to the land. In both works, we see the production of the nation as a self-constituted organic whole. As Manu Goswami points out in her excellent account of late-nineteenth nationalist narratives:

> Works that regarded the Mughal Empire and by extension Muslims as foreign were formally similar to those that argued that long-run inhabitation had naturalized their status as fellow nationals. Both positions shared in common a historicist understanding of the liaison between territory and identity that rendered Hindus as the original, organic, core nationals. Within this schema, Muslims were regarded as the foreign body, an external element within the corporatist vision of an organic national whole, or at best belated nationals whose relationship to the imagined nation could only be figured as a problem.[45]

This notion of "Hindus" (in an expanded sense) as the core nationals and of Arya/Hindu *dharma* as the originary ethos of India marks the shared ground between Savarkar's account and Nehru's admittedly more sophisticated narrative of the Indian nation. However, while the Muslim remains an enduring stranger in Savarkar—indeed an infiltrator in more recent Hindu nationalist discourse—Muslims are eventually absorbed and become part of the ensemble of the Indian nation in Nehru's *Discovery*. But the fact of their late entry—or rather the late arrival of Islam into the (fictive and enduring) bounded whole of India—enables Nehru to set up a hierarchy of national subjects with Muslims established as minor subjects of the nation.

Accordingly, Nehru can, at best, call for tolerance and protection of minorities when it comes to present-day Muslims. Thus, he is willing to provide "the usual provisions for minority rights," such as those laid out by the League of Nations, including protection of religion, culture, and language for the individual and the group. But he also wonders what more Muslims can ask for as a minority: "It is difficult to conceive what greater protection could be given to any religious minority or group under any democratic system." He reminds his readers that "the whole history of India was witness to the toleration and even encouragement of minorities and of different racial groups. . . . We did not have to go abroad for ideas of religious and cultural toleration; these were inherent in Indian life" (382–83). Nehru repeatedly affirms the essential tolerance of "Indian" traditions, but tolerance is almost always conceptualized as Hindu tolerance toward religious minorities (especially Muslims).[46] As Wendy Brown has shown, tolerance typically expresses the extent to which one group, the "tolerant" (usually conceived as superior), may *withstand* the practices, behavior, or even the existence of another group, the "tolerated" (usually constituted as inferior and marginal).[47] Tolerance, in other words, is mainly granted by those in power who conform to the normative order to those who deviate from it. Thus, the heterosexual tolerates the homosexual; the dominant racial or ethnic group tolerates minority cultures or races; the Hindu tolerates the Muslim, Christian, or the Sikh—though the extent to which tolerance is proffered or withheld differs largely. In each instance, however, the "nonreciprocity" of tolerance discourse is effectively masked since the hegemonic group is typically constructed as universal and "secular," whereas minority groups are viewed as saturated by their religious and cultural identities.

Interestingly, at one point, Nehru does gesture toward a more reciprocal notion of tolerance when he writes, "Religious differences, as such, do not come in the way, for there is a great deal of mutual tolerance for them [in India]" (382). Here, Nehru invokes the idea of tolerance in a more idiomatic sense to connote a notion of mutual or reciprocal tolerance among diverse religious and ethnic groups as a mode of living together. However, the question remains: Can this conception of reciprocal tolerance suffice for the living together that Derrida calls for? Derrida proposes different, more ethical ways of relating to others—especially those who have been excluded from our ensembles—that go not only beyond a liberalist understanding of tolerance but also beyond any relationship of reciprocity, exchange, or mutuality. He suggests that a living together of peace and accord, which exceeds the compulsory tolerance of the juridical contract, can occur only when one opens one's self and one's "home" to the other—the stranger/foreigner who is not considered a natural or organic part of home—without subsuming the other into the self. In the final section, I return to Derrida's meditations on hospitality for thinking the living together of Hindus and Muslims in India, but I also ask: Can we rely on hospitality alone to manifest the living well together? Moreover, what might be some of the risks and pitfalls of Derridean hospitality?

## Hospitality

Derrida calls for a fracturing openness with respect to the ensemble, but it is not merely enough to interrupt the totality of the whole; he also enjoins us to welcome the stranger unconditionally into our home: "This 'living together,' even where it is irreducible to the statutory or institutional (juridical, political, state-controlled) bond, opens another dimension to the same necessity—and that is why I have spoken of the other, of the stranger, of a hospitality to the wholly other who exceeds the statutory convention" ("Avowing," 26). Although Derrida does not elaborate on his thoughts on hospitality in this essay, which is more preoccupied with the question of avowing the impossible and forgiving the impossible, his late work offers many reflections on hospitality. Turning to the concept of hospitality, he deconstructs it from within in order to imbue it with a new significance.[48] He points out that hospitality in the "ordinary sense" is inextricably interwoven with a concept that has traditionally served as its antithesis—hostility—because it requires that the host—he who offers hospitality—must be master in his own home before he can receive the other as a friend or an honored guest.[49] The host authorizes who crosses the threshold by selecting, choosing, and filtering who may/may not pass through the door. He welcomes the other but on condition that the other respects his authority over his home. The other is welcome to the extent that he respects the *chez-soi*—the "being-at-home of my home"—that he adjusts to the order of the house, the language, the nation-state. Hospitality thus rests upon claims of property ownership and a reaffirmation of the host's mastery. Furthermore, this "despotic sovereignty" and the "virile mastery" of the host (who is above all male) is intrinsically related to ipseity—it is "nothing other than ipseity itself, the same of the selfsame," which is why the question of hospitality is also the question of ipseity; it has to do with how we relate to others—as our own or as strangers.[50] The law of identity or the "*being-oneself in one's own home*" thus becomes the very "condition of the gift and of hospitality."[51] Derrida thus locates a violent contradiction inherent in the very concept of hospitality: The host must be assured of his sovereignty over the space that he opens up to the other, which, he suggests, limits hospitality at its origin. It is this seemingly "aporetic paralysis" at the very threshold of hospitality that must be overcome; hence, hospitality can only take place beyond our pre-comprehension of hospitality. Accordingly, Derrida asks us to do the impossible—to put into practice a pure and unconditional hospitality that takes place beyond hospitality.

The absolute hospitality that Derrida calls for "presupposes a break with hospitality in the ordinary sense, with conditional hospitality, with the right to or pact of hospitality."[52] It requires that

> I open up my home and that I give not only to the foreigner (provided with a family name, with the social status of being a foreigner, etc.) but to the absolute, unknown, anonymous other, and that I give place to them, that I let them come, that I let them arrive, and take place in the place I offer them, without asking of them either reciprocity (entering into a pact) or even their names.[53]

Thus, hospitality must not be restricted to the "foreigner"—who is the citizen of a country and endowed with a legal subjectivity—but it must be offered to all others including those we might think of as "barbarians," to whosoever turns up before any determination or any identification, "a human, animal, or divine creature."[54] Derrida diffuses and extends the very meaning of *étranger* beyond its traditional inscription in Greco-Roman and European discourses of hospitality to include the "wholly other," one who is not only beyond the conditional circles of language, family, or citizenship, but also beyond the "its other" of dialectics.[55] What is more, for such an absolute hospitality to take place, the host must become the hostage of the other prior to becoming the host; he must relinquish all claims to mastery and ownership in the instant he receives the other.[56]

The boundless hospitality Derrida calls for transgresses all the laws of hospitality as we know them since hospitality in this revised sense is not about debts, calculations, duties, or contractual obligations. In fact, he goes so far as to suggest that the experience of hospitality is coextensive with ethics itself: "Insofar as it has to do with the *ethos*, that is, the residence, one's home, the familiar place of dwelling, inasmuch as it is a manner of being there, *the manner in which we relate to ourselves and others*, to others as our own or as foreigners, *ethics is hospitality*."[57] Hospitality thus has to do with the claims that the stranger has on us. It is crucial to Derrida's understanding of ethics—our responsibility toward the other—and is inseparable from his thinking of justice and politics.

Throughout, the stranger is understood as one who comes from elsewhere or one who lies beyond the "circumscribed field of *ethos* or ethics," especially in relation to Hegel's three instances: the family, bourgeois or civil society, and the nation-state.[58] Although the relevance and importance of Derrida's arguments about hospitality are fairly evident when thinking about exiles, immigrants, refugees, or asylum seekers, what happens when we consider the question of how to relate to those who have been positioned as strangers *within* the ensemble of the nation by virtue of their ostensibly extraneous religious affiliations? In "Avowing—The Impossible," Derrida maintains that hospitality is also crucial for the living together of peace and accord: "One lives together, well then, *only with and as a stranger, a stranger 'at home [chez soi]' in all the figures of the 'at home,' that there is 'living together' only there where the whole [ensemble] is neither formed nor closed*" ("Avowing," 28, my emphasis). Derrida calls for a reversal of the formula—strangers as enemies—when he emphasizes the importance of living with the stranger, but what is crucial about this formulation is not just the idea of living *with* the stranger, but also living *as* a stranger at home, there where one claims to be at home with oneself, where one stakes ownership.[59] Derrida calls for a radical rethinking of our concepts of identity, residence, and above all, nationality—in its claims over a particular bounded territory. (As Penelope Deutscher reminds us, "A nation state is never properly itself, its territory is never its own," even as it may assert authority over a particular space.[60] This may take the form of literal colonization, as in the case of settler colonies, or it may entail the appropriation and demarcation of a territory in the name of a specific (often the majority) community whose members are designated as the core or representative national subjects.) In his call to live as a stranger at home, Derrida radically interrogates any idea of home that is premised on notions of territoriality, possession, and the prior claim of any one individual or group. To my mind, this is the most important aspect of Derrida's treatise on hospitality and living together and is critical for interrogating notions of autochthony and nativism. Derridean hospitality would enjoin those *who assert authority over a particular nation-space*—such as upper-caste Hindus who claim to be the primordial heirs of the Indian nation—to give up all claims of ownership and sovereignty and to welcome those who have been rendered as strangers without saying "I welcome you" or without seeking to fold the other into the self.[61]

However, the questions remain: Where does hospitality emanate from? Who can extend the gift of hospitality? If there is to be hospitality, as Derrida himself admits, there must be a home, "the own home that makes possible one's own hospitality."[62] And if the question of hospitality is intrinsically related to that of ipseity—whereby the being oneself in one's own home is the very condition of the gift of hospitality (as well as that which limits it at its origin)—then only those who are at home with themselves can welcome the stranger or the foreigner. The imperative to open up their home cannot be placed before those whose very identities are under threat of erasure—in other words, those who have been designated as strangers. At the very least, the host must be "at home" to be able to *give up* his claim on the home and to extend the gift of hospitality. Pointing to some of the risks and paradoxes built into Levinas's and Derrida's discussions of hospitality, Edith Wyschogrod notes that "autochthony persists while engaging in its own deterritorialization."[63] Absolute hospitality thus continues to be bound up with notions of power and agency even as it seeks to radically interrogate and overturn ideas of mastery, ownership, and possession of the home. Like Nehru, Derrida's emphasis seems to be on the (generous) host—he who welcomes (in Nehru's case it would be he who tolerates)—rather than the empowered stranger.

Indeed, one must also ask, does absolute hospitality go far enough in overturning the binaries of host and stranger, or does it risk naturalizing these identities by implicitly placing all power and agency on the host? Does an ethics of hospitality risk fixing the very categories of host and stranger that it sets out to dismantle? More specifically, by using the term "hospitality" to reflect on the relationship of Hindus to Muslims in India, are we in danger of further reifying the identities of Hindus as the primordial hosts and Muslims as the eternal guests/strangers? In my view, reversing the apparently transparent categories of host—the self-designated master of the nation—and stranger might be the more complicated and pressing task. The responsibility for creating a more just and peaceful world must not be limited to the givers of hospitality or those who have assumed the role of the master of the home or the nation.

Writing about immigrants in France, Mireille Rosello cites the story of a migrant worker from Abdelmayek Sayad's *L'immigration, ou, Les paradoxes de l'altérité*, who lived in a *foyer*, a worker's residence that precludes the possibility of dwelling as if one were at home because he can't invite his interviewer to partake of his hospitality. Rosello goes on to ask the important question of what it would take for the "postcolonial guest" to be "at home": "Being at home is being where you can not only eat and drink but also invite some-one to eat, to drink, to chat. Being at home is being where you can be the host, where you can offer hospitality.... The migrant worker shows that the right to offer hospitality would construct his dwelling place as a home that he could, finally, appropriate."[64] Merely dwelling in a place does not amount to being "at home" in a place. Rosello suggests that to be at home, the stranger must be able to offer hospitality—"that is, not reciprocate, but lengthen the chain of possibly incommensurate hospitable gestures."[65] If hospitality has to do with the ethical claims that the stranger has on us, then, there must be room for the stranger *to lay claim* to the very home from which s/he has been excluded or rendered in-determinate.[66] Living well together cannot be contingent on the ethics of hospitality alone.

In the Indian social and political landscape, which has been shaped by the legacies of Partition and the creation of Pakistan as a homeland for the Muslims of the subcontinent, what would it take for Muslims to appropriate the Indian nation-space as a home—and not just as their residence or habitation—and thereby to also claim the position of host?[67] Certainly, Muslims are not "postcolonial guests" in the sense that Rosello uses the term when talking about Maghrebian immigrants in France, but undoubtedly they have been positioned as strangers and unknown entities whose allegiances to the nation are con-stantly suspect, and require ritual performances of patriotism, especially after Partition. I argue that it is only when Muslims will be able to claim the place of the representative nationalist subject—or be one among other representative national subjects—and when they are not constantly obliged to prove their nationalist credentials, will they be able to appropriate their nation as a home. That is, only when the very categories of host and stranger, majority and minority are overturned—which an ethics of hospitality, however generous, does not enable—will we be able to manifest the living well together that Der-rida calls for.

# Rights, Respect, and the Political: Notes from a Conflict Zone

*Raef Zreik*

Reading Derrida is a challenging, even disturbing experience that leaves one feeling anxious, alone, and bruised, and yet, in a certain sense, empowered. In the following essay I engage Derrida's text "Avowing—The Impossible," but I do not limit myself to it; rather, I address the experience of reading Derrida in general. This essay is very much phenomenological. It seeks not to make sweeping judgments, but to domesticate Derrida, to insert him into a certain context to see how he might be deployed, used, or appropriated, and to determine in what ways he might inspire us and in what ways he seems to abandon us, leaving us stranded.

I address those aspects of Derrida's essay that are of greatest interest to me and reflect different aspects of my intellectual and political engagements: as a legal theorist, as a human rights and political activist, as a Palestinian citizen of Israel, and as someone interested in critical theory in general. Activism, be it political or to promote human rights, requires some level of belief in certain values and their attainability, and Derrida questions both assumptions. Legal theory feeds on the analysis of concepts while Derrida undermines their stability and questions their determinacy. Being part of an oppressed and dispossessed Palestinian minority might seduce one to celebrate one's victimhood with a sense of moral immunity, and Derrida would awaken one from one's "dogmatic moralism." Thus I ask how is it possible, after Derrida, to continue to fight for what appear to be "just causes," to do legal theory in the midst of radical instability of concepts, and to save the hope in certain values and their attainability?

My essay is divided into three sections. In the first, I proceed in parallel lines to Derrida's strategies of writing and reading. I extend, deploy, and localize some of Derrida's insights, as well as the way in which he approaches certain questions by uncovering paradoxes, exposing aporias, and unearthing antinomies. In this section I expose and develop some of the internal tensions that inhere in the language of rights and the rhetoric of respect that have surfaced in recent discourses on rights, recognition, and difference. Here I proceed as a deconstructionist legal theorist interested in the language and discourse of rights.

In the second section, I engage Derrida's take on the issue of the nation-state, identity politics in general, and Zionism in particular. This section has a clear political edge and prepares the ground for the third section, addressing the relation between deconstruction and the political. Here I take issue with Derrida's analysis of Israel and Zionism, and in one sense deconstruct his politics, while in another I simply differ from his politics. In this way the section furnishes an example of the tension that exists between deconstruction and politics.

The third section foregrounds the tension between the first section of my essay (on deconstructive strategy) and the second section (where I assert a political view). One objective of this essay is to explore the inherent tensions between Derrida's deconstruction and "the political," or between his deconstruction and his politics, or the possibility of politics in general, something that has been the subject of endless debate and commentary.[1] There is a major tension between the openness and reflection that are required of an intellectual or deconstructivist, and the closure, finality, and action that are required of a political activist. I shall discuss this theme further in the third section of the essay. Derrida's perspectives are particularly disconcerting to political activists who perceive themselves as the victims or subjects of unjustified harm (e.g., abused women or children, or citizens of a dispossessed nation) pursuing what they deem to be their just recompense. Derrida questions not only political authority, but also moral authority. He questions any exclusive privilege one might claim to speak as the ultimate "victim." Thus, in addition to classical foundationalism, Derrida also questions some of its most recent substitutes deployed in the field of "identity politics" or within the discourse of the "politics of difference," including the category of "experience." Experience confers a certain sense of conclusivity, exclusivity, and inaccessibility that may exert silencing power on those who appear not to possess or share it.[2] Experience as such becomes a site of authority that must be interrogated. In other words, while deconstruction gives a voice to those perceived as *Other*, it can also serve to silence them or limit their ability to silence those who are their others. Thus, while Palestinians—as the subjects of occupation, dispossession, or discrimination—might experience deconstruction as supportive of their attempts to make their voices heard, as the other who struggles against hegemonic forces, they may also feel betrayed by its attempts to problematize things or portray a more complex picture in which sharp distinctions and dichotomies are blurred. Whence can one draw the courage and gain the confidence to make clear statements about the justness or unjustness of causes, if after all things are always complex and uncertain?

In this sense the third section could be read as an attempt to investigate the open space between the first section and the second section, though I do not attempt to do so explicitly.

## Paradoxes of Rights, Respect, and Sovereignty

Derrida is suspicious of the "whole," of totalizing theories, of telos,[3] and of overarching schemes that demand obedience or tame manifestations of difference or interruption.[4] Like many before him—Kierkegaard, Max Stirner, Nietzsche, and others—Derrida wants to escape the Hegelian prison of the synthesis, the all-encompassing concept, and the capitalist logic that transforms everything into commodity-like objects and consequently renders them exchangeable. Derrida protests against this whole: "The authority of the whole [*ensemble*] will always be the first threat for all 'living together.' And inversely, all 'living together' will be the first protestation or contestation, the first testimony against the whole [*ensemble*]" ("Avowing," 21). In contrast to the harmony of the whole or the ethics of identity, Derrida suggests the ethics of rupture—the condition of living together that allows space for the other to be, and which is a requisite for any living together.

> The only "living together" that he [Derrida as child in Algeria] judged then bearable and worthy of that name already supposed a *rupture* with identitarian and totalizing belonging, assured of itself in a homogeneous whole. . . . . *There is "living together" only there where the whole [ensemble] is neither formed nor closed [ne se forme pas et ne se ferme pas], there where the living together [ensemble] (the adverb) contests the completion*, the closure, and the cohesiveness of an "ensemble" (the noun, the substantive), of a substantial, closed ensemble identical to itself. ("Avowing," 28, emphasis mine)

Moreover, any living together, instead of being based on a closed whole, should "welcome *dissymmetry*, anachrony, *nonreciprocity with an other who is greater*" ("Avowing," 28, emphasis mine).

In the following section, I develop this theme and interrogate its limits, connecting it to my experience as a civil rights lawyer in Israel. I explore and expand on the threats and risks latent in the categories of the "whole," "totality," and "telos," while arguing that the threat does not always emanate from the whole, for revision is ok sometimes the threat comes from the process of fragmentation itself, and the "whole" is actually a site of resistance and of freedom. In making this case, I refer to two concepts that play an important role in our legal political life: "respect" and "rights." Some of what follows is an elaboration of the different shapes that the "whole" can assume. Sometimes the "whole" can be capitalist logic, and certain aspects of nationalism can be thought of as resistance to the "whole"; at other times, the nation itself is the "whole" and the main source of threat, while capitalist logic may constitute a site of resistance that safeguards a space for the other. At yet other times, science itself may appear to be the "whole," and aesthetics the site of resistance to the hegemony of the concept. I concentrate in the following on respect, rights, and sovereignty.

A great deal of writing has been done in recent years on respect, primarily in the context of debates on minority rights and multicultural societies. After years of discourse on *individual* human rights that argued in favor of treatment of all humans as equals, the discourse has shifted somewhat to emphasize the *group* affiliation of each citizen, thereby granting public recognition to difference.[5] Those who support an emphasis on differences in the public sphere argue against certain processes that produce a "melting pot" and attempts at homogenization, and portray their stance as an act of resistance. Setting their arguments aside, I attempt in the following to outline the argument that the rhetoric of rights has a homogenizing and totalizing logic that reproduces the logic of capitalism itself.

In his essay on the Jewish question, Marx penetrates the nature of the language of rights and the price that is paid for the move to the modern rhetoric of rights, namely the abstraction of the citizen from his particular life and his characteristics.[6] Marx maintains that the state is a modern product that is perceived as having a separate and independent identity only when it can be imagined as abstract and separate from civil society. In feudal times, for example, the state was not separated from civil society. The designations of "lord" and "serf" were, in themselves, both social and political statuses. In the Middle Ages, every sphere of private activity had a political character or theme. Differences that occurred between individuals in private aspects of life had a public aspect. Thus, the right to participate in political life was dependent on ownership of property, which was in turn related to political status. The same was true of religion: Religion was not simply a private affair but entailed public recognition. Belonging to a certain religion meant being subject to a set of legal norms that differed from the norms applicable to members of another religion.

According to Marx, the modern state has actually separated the political (i.e., state) from the social (i.e., civil society). In other words, one might argue that the state does not interfere with civil society, and civil society does not interfere with the state. The state is the "form" or external shell that delineates the outer boundaries of civil society, whereas civil society is the "content" or "matter" of the state. The state is the site of the abstract self; civil society is the sphere of differences and particularities.

The domain of rights in the modern state is the domain of equality between citizens. However, these citizens are equal only because they are abstracted from their particularities and differences (i.e., stripped of their singularity). The equality of individuals with regard to citizenship does not eliminate inequalities, nor does it free individuals from religion or property; on the contrary, equal citizenship presupposes these factors. Legal, formal equality—the domain of rights—is but a guise that masks true relations within civil society. It is a veneer of public sameness beneath which lies a "real" structure of difference in the private sphere.

Marx views the rights revolution as being about the relocation of difference as manifested in property and religion (and every other aspect that makes us particular and concrete). Once ownership of property and religion is privatized, such differences are contained and bear no public or political implication. Only the separation of difference from the public domain, and its consequent confinement to the private domain, allowed the discourse of rights and equal citizenship to enter the political domain. Thus, when we appear in court or "before the law," we appear completely stripped of any singularity; our equality before the law is guaranteed only at the expense of this bracketing and suppressing of difference.

The homology between the form of a commodity and the form of a citizen as the bearer of rights is clear: As long as things have value only as far as they can be used (i.e., their "use value"), they are not commodities.[7] In order for things to become commodities, they must have an "exchange value." In other words, there must be a third abstract medium—money—that allows us to compare their values and render them interchangeable through it. We are able to compare different things or products because we abstract them from their use value—their singularity/difference—and calculate their exchange value, where all products stand faceless, devoid of individual characteristics and differences. The logic of money turns every product into a matter of quantity and all qualitative differences are suppressed. Money is the language that allows commodities to "converse" with each other, that raises things to a universal level, while suppressing their singularity and uniqueness. Thus, the image of the citizen as a faceless rights-bearer is produced in the image of a commodity.[8] This logic has liberating aspects because it allows us to transcend our inherited identities. However, it also has a totalizing logic that is akin to the totalizing logic of capitalism, translated here into political terms.

Thus, within the rhetoric of respect and rights resides a double threat. The first threat is a colonizing, homologizing rhetoric that (a) speaks a universal language, disregarding difference and singularity; (b) understands justice only in terms of the application of universal rules; and (c) associates justice with identity. This threat is the threat of the empire, of the colonial, and of the particular masquerading as universal; it is the beast that wants to devour and assimilate all else, to assimilate, to enforce a vision in the name of some universal truth, and in so doing, it threatens to eradicate alterity.[9] This logic can translate everything into its own language; nothing remains outside it, escapes it, or can resist it. Everything is calculable, interchangeable, translatable, and subject to an overarching logic. Thus the demand of justice is to affirm alterity, incalculability, and singularity.[10]

This mode of "respect" aims to subjugate through assimilation (although it does at least assume that the other *can* be changed, civilized, modified to join *us* or to become like *us*). It does not respect the other for what he or she is, but for what he or she might be—not for his or her actuality, but for his or her potentiality.[11] This is a demeaning kind of respect. It is a respect that one owns without having earned it, that one has without even knowing it, regardless of one's singularity and uniqueness. In other words, it says, "we do not really respect 'you,' but some other entity that we read into 'you,' not the concrete you, but some abstract 'you' that resides within you." This respect is therefore problematic, first, because it exists in spite of and regardless of what one does, and second, because it overlooks one's singularity and does not see one as one really is. In a sense, this kind of respect is actually respect for someone else—an unidentified someone, a faceless entity. It ultimately ends in annihilation; it marks the end of any living together, because it leaves no other with whom to live.

The discussion above might seem, at first glance, highly theoretical and absolutely abstract, bearing no relevance to concrete political/social debates. But this is not the case. One may find it very relevant insofar as it relates to the story of some Jews in Israeli society—primarily Jews from the Arab world[12]—who were forced to assimilate into the melting pot during the first decades after the establishment of Israel. Zionism treated those Mizrachi Jews as potentially but not actually equal, in the following sense: "There is nothing in their genes that hinders them from being like us, if we invest in them; but at this point in time they are not equal and are not civilized as we, Ashkenazi Jews, are." However, the story becomes complicated once Palestinian citizens of Israel enter the scene, because while the Zionist project insisted on identity, insofar as we are speaking of the Jewish people (i.e., one that eliminates differences within the Jewish people), it stressed *difference* from the Palestinians as a complete and absolute other. Palestinian citizens of Israel complicated the picture because they are located inside, but not fully inside, the state. In this sense the case of Israeli Palestinians and the attitude of Zionism toward them sets an example of the second threat that emanates from the rhetoric of respect and rights—the threat of the absolute other, to which I now turn.

The second threat to respect is the way in which the other whose other*ness* seems absolute is dealt with. The absolute other cannot be "tamed" or translated into our language, and there is no bridge to connect us to the absolute other. The absolute other stands beyond universal language and beyond any possibility of communication. She is beyond discourse, and therefore unreachable. Moreover, she resists subjugation through universal language or concepts. The absolute other is the recalcitrant other who resists Hegelian synthesis and is close to the Kantian thing-in-itself. We may respect her utter otherness by trying not to influence it. We do not try to change or modify her, since we know that she is fully shaped and mature, albeit inaccessible. This approach, however, means that there is no dialogue or conversation with the other. Whereas the threat in the first case consisted of everything being translated into a universal language, in this case the threat is the threat of silence, an absolute silence in which words have no opportunity to act. This threat simply positions "us" and "them," with no bridge between us.

This mode of respect incorporates a sense of arrogance toward the absolute other and may therefore be demeaning. One may view as inherent or essential to the structure of absolute others characteristics that hinder their ability to "progress." We view them as unsuitable or unable to join "us"; "we" are an exclusive club. Thus, rather than engaging or negotiating with them, we exhibit total indifference toward them at the first stage, and at the second stage, we engage in war against them: We annihilate them. We treat them as the enemy and struggle with them unto death. We approach them as fully formed, mature subjects, and therefore kill them "out of respect." Notwithstanding this "respect," however, the end result is death and annihilation.

The situation of Palestinians in Israel illustrates these two threats to difference. Israel has no genuine plans to incorporate Palestinians as citizens of Israel within a civic project but rather aims at preserving separation between the two national groups following an ethnic and not a civic logic.[13] In this case, the threat to living together does not stem from the fact that Israel does not take difference seriously, but that it takes it *too* seriously. It is not obliterating difference, but perpetuating difference as a pretext for inequitable treatment and the basis for discriminatory policies that range in motivation from indifference to hostility.[14] The source of the threat is not a project of homogenization aimed at forging a new Israeli nation, but the radical separation of Jews and Palestinians, with a clear privileging of the Jewish majority.

The dynamic becomes yet more distinct when one considers the "two-state" solution and its appropriation by the Israeli and the American right wing. The two-state solution takes the logic of other*ness* to an extreme by supporting each group's right to self-determination and erecting a boundary between them. The boundary itself—perhaps the clearest manifestation of the right to be different—is usually a sign of respect. The two-state/boundary solution highlights the difference between two individuals or two people to such an extent that any unity or overarching whole that could mitigate or overcome their differences is assumed to be radically impossible.

The war on Gaza in the winter of 2009 was a manifestation of the second threat to difference. The logic of two separate entities or two separate sovereign states, held apart by a centrifugal force, erased the image of an occupation in which the occupier has certain responsibilities toward the occupied.[15] At least under occupation, the occupied are part of a whole—actual or constructed—within and under the control of the occupier; hence, both exist within the same entity. Consequently, conflicting interests can and should be governed by universal civil rights norms. However, the two-state solution takes difference to its extreme and creates the possibility of a conflict that cannot be adjudicated (since there is no whole or overarching rule to govern the conflict). It gives rise to a state of "differend,"[16] in which disputes seem irresolvable and war inevitable. No common language is available in such a situation; communication runs out, or more precisely, never begins. Israel's actions in Gaza during the last war would have been inconceivable without its withdrawal from the Strip two years earlier. The withdrawal from Gaza, aimed at creating an image of two states and portraying the conflict between them as war rather than occupation, was a prelude and a priori condition for conceptualizing and waging the recent war. The rhetoric of difference can constitute a prelude to indifference and pave the way to hostility.

There must be space between the threats of erasing difference through homogeneity and through war. Derrida, of course, is very aware that there cannot be difference without identity, without a certain whole.[17] Alone, either poses a certain threat. For example, the more the other is inside the whole, the greater the threat or risk of its being effaced; thus the possibility of living together no longer exists because the other no longer exists. Conversely, pushing the other out beyond any possibility of communication, conversation, or universal rule, and thereby creating situations in which he forms no part of any whole, presents a different array of threats, culminating in war.

Can we have it both ways? It is unsurprising that the category of hospitality occupies such a central position in Derrida's writings, as a zone to which the other can come "in," and yet is not devoured by the colonizing power of the whole because, in some sense, he remains "out." This state of being both "in" and "out," this moment of welcoming, is an invisible and impossible "threshold" that should be capable of avoiding both threats. This relationship between Derrida's art of the impossible and politics—as the art of the possible[18]—will form the topic of the final section of this essay. Before broaching it, though, I first want to take issue with his treatment of Zionism.

## Nationalism, Zionism, and Israel

As in many of his other writings, Derrida is critical and skeptical of the discourse of identity.[19] His whole project, as he stated on numerous occasions, is a welcoming of the other.[20] And yet Derrida seems to acknowledge the fact that we do not have identical duties to all human beings. We owe certain duties to some people that we do not owe to others. This is something we can neither avoid nor justify in universalistic terms.

> How, then, to deny but also how to justify the interior urgency that will make me first nourish my own, the proximate or the neighbor [*le proche ou le prochain*], before rushing to rescue the billions of famished men in the world? . . . No one will ever be able to deny it, in all good faith, nor renounce it. But no one will ever be able to justify it either, what one calls justifying, judging and proving that it is just before a universal justice. ("Avowing," 38)

This perspective treats issues of citizenship almost as fate, neither escapable nor fully justifiable, and bearing the trace of violence as well as a tragic sense of politics. There is a homology between Derrida's views on citizenship and boundedness, and his treatment of friendship and the problem of numbers.[21] One cannot be friends with all humanity, but must choose particular individuals. In doing so, one betrays the rest of humanity. Being a friend becomes the source of duties that are not derived from universal, practical reasons; the friend himself or herself is the reason for the duty. The homology here conveys the aporia that the universal will always need the particular. Having particular friends constitutes a betrayal of the universality of friendship. However, in order to have friendships, we must befriend particular people, otherwise friendship would cease to be a category that can create or generate duties; rather, it would be parasitic on universal ethics.[22]

Derrida's text is most interesting not for its general ideas on nationalism, but for its concrete position toward Zionism. Predictably, Derrida is skeptical of closed politics of identity, of nationalism, and of all other politics that are based on organic, biological affiliation.[23] Reflecting on his early childhood in Algiers and growing up as a Jew, Derrida distances himself from Zionism, stating:

> The same vigilance was warning him, warns him today, against all the risks of the "living together" of the Jews, be they of a symbiotic type (naturality, birth, blood, soil, nation) or conventional (state juridical, in the modern sense): a certain communitarianism, a certain *Zionism*, a certain nationalism and all that can follow when the motifs of filiation through blood, appropriation of the place, and the motif of election, all run the risk of remaining caught . . . in the grip of nature or of convention. ("Avowing," 29, emphasis mine)

Derrida continues, expressing his clear opposition to the politics of current Israeli governments:

> It pushes the said child not only to oppose, sometimes publicly, the politics of the current *Israeli* government and of great number of those that preceded it, but also to continue to interrogate himself in the most insomniac fashion regarding the conditions in which the modern state of *Israel* established itself. If there is a place where I do not have the right to hide this, it is here." ("Avowing," 29, emphasis mine)

Derrida distances himself from Zionism in the same manner that he distances himself from any other form of communitarianism or nationalism. He perceives Zionism simply as a national movement, and his critique of Zionism, in one way or another, derives from his general critique of nationalism at large.[24] Thus, according to Derrida, Zionism requires no special critique: The general critique of nationalism applies. If, however, one were to accept the nationalist approach or rhetoric, it would be difficult to criticize Zionism and Israel. There is no conceptual space that allows us at once to accept nationalism and reject Zionism. In other words, it is not possible to judge Zionism from a nationalist standpoint. Derrida maintains that all nationalisms are effectively homogeneous, thereby normalizing Zionism.

> Any juridico-political founding of a "living together" is, by essence, *violent*, since it inaugurates there where a law [*droit*] did not yet exist. The founding of a state or of a constitution, *therefore, of a "living together" according to a state of law* [*un état de droit*], is always first of all a *nonlegal violence*: not illegal but nonlegal, otherwise put, *unjustifiable* with regard to an existing law, since the law is inexistent there where it is a matter of creating it. *No state has ever been founded without this violence*, whatever form and whatever time it might have taken. ("Avowing," 29–30, emphasis mine)[25]

I agree with Derrida's assertion that the birth of the modern state is basically a violent event.[26] It creates order out of disorder and establishes norms on the basis of sheer violence. Before it lays down rules, there is a moment of exception. For example, the constitution—the normative order itself—is based on will and decision. Beneath the norm stands will, and before the state there was revolution. In many ways, the modern, liberal state, which lauds itself for its rule of law and inclusive nature, suffers from temporal and spatial amnesia. It has forgotten those who were left beyond its borders; it has forgotten the victims of the state-building project who paid the price for its establishment. It does not recall those who suffered ethnic cleansing, dispossession, and transfer, or those on whose ruins a new democratic national regime was founded. In many cases, the other, dark side of nationalism and the celebrated right to self-determination is ethnic cleansing. The project of the modern nation-state—a democratic and liberal state—has a violent and at times colonial aspect. Before Derrida, Carl Schmitt reminded us of the inherent moment of violence that accompanies the birth of the modern state, and the built-in antagonism of friend and enemy, or "us versus them," that liberalism attempts to brush aside.[27]

The admiration that some anti-Zionists have for liberal values, expressed when they compare Israel and Zionism to countries like the United States, France, and Belgium—is, I argue, sometimes misplaced. Israelis may respond by reminding Americans of their history of slaughtering the Native Americans, Jim Crow laws, and the recent Patriot Act. They might similarly remind the French and the Belgians of their colonial practices and the massacres they perpetrated in Algeria and Congo, respectively. Thus, in order to defend itself, Israel taints all modern liberal democracies with traces of violence, racism, and colonialism, which may allow it to feel somehow "justified and at home." In some sense—but only to a certain degree—it is at home. Perhaps Derrida has done only part of the job. Using the extreme case of Zionism, Derrida tells us that the entire modern history of the nation-state, including that of European countries, is one of exclusion and violence, and that we should not let the neat surface of norms and rules deceive us and cause us to forget its dark side. His work leads to the conclusion that Zionism lies within, rather than outside, the paradigm; it is not a special case. Paradoxically, Zionism—in defending itself against its critics—may be carrying out some critical work by forcing the West to confront its own history of violence. Further, in attempting to demonstrate that it is a normal national movement, Zionism may force the modern state to look in the mirror and see what it has striven to conceal.

In maintaining that the establishment of modern nation-states is always a violent event, Derrida locates Zionism within the national paradigm, but he seems to have no criteria with which to evaluate or judge the specific establishment of the State of Israel. While he is critical of the current policies of the Israeli government, he does not critically review its birth.[28] He wonders, for example, if one were to judge Israel at all, whether one would need to appeal to "another law and another justice."

But the child of whom I speak asked himself whether the founding of the modern state of *Israel* . . . could be no more than an example among others of this originary violence from *which no state can escape,* or whether, because this modern state intended not to be a state like others, *it had to appear before another law and appeal to another justice.* ("Avowing," 30, emphasis mine)

In the context of Derrida's work, the following questions arise: Can Zionism be located within a certain paradigm and yet also be evaluated as a project? And can one endorse certain versions of nationalism while being critical of others? Such inquiry is not merely theoretical. Derrida is very aware of the need for nuance. Although, in principle, skeptical of national discourse, he is also conscious of the role that such discourse might play at certain junctures in history.[29]

Derrida stops short of associating Zionism with a particular paradigm (and thereby normalizing it), but he does not attempt to more fully describe its position within the paradigm.

Certain features of Zionism make it appear, if not unique, then at least as an extreme case of nationalism. At its birth, it inherited most of the "genetic diseases" of nationalism. Although Zionism was born as a reaction to certain strains of racism in Europe, and in a certain way does serve to uncover the limits of the Enlightenment ideal, it nonetheless conspires with the colonial against the colonized, and reproduces most of the conceptual frameworks and attitudes deployed against the Jews in Europe. First, although Zionism has national aspects, it is not solely a national movement; in its methods, at least, it is colonial and it collaborates with colonial powers.[30] Second, Zionism is an exilic nationalism designed to provide a solution for Jews worldwide by gathering them together in Palestine. Since Palestine is inhabited by the Palestinian people, ethnic cleansing was almost inevitable: a subtext of the text (as implied in the project). Expulsion of the Palestinians was therefore a foreseeable (though not wholly inescapable) outcome of the practice of self-determination by the Jews in Palestine.[31] Consequently, a certain level of violence and negation of the other—the Palestinian—was built in, inextricable to the project. Third, although it is not the only national movement that deploys religious discourse, Zionism is unthinkable without such a discourse.[32] Fourth, Zionism is an Eastern European, "primordial," organic, closed, ethnic nationalism.[33] Fifth, while it is true that in some sense all nations are "imagined" and impose some level of homogeneity over a deep reality of pluralism and difference, Zionism is outstanding in this regard. Owing to the diverse nature of worldwide Jewry, which speaks a multitude of languages and hails from an array of traditions and backgrounds, Zionism needs a special force of myth, dream, language, rhetoric, and other homogenizing practices if it is to overcome the pluralities and differences among the Jewish people. Sixth, Zionism seeks to be a comprehensive movement that not only achieves statehood and independence but also establishes the "new Jew" as a new character, and revolutionizes all aspects of Jewish life.[34] The mission of ending the exilic life of the Jews through their ingathering in Israel makes the Zionist movement a never-ending project, a constant revolution that has no clear stopping point, and it touches every aspect of life. Thus, it perpetuates the initial violence that typically accompanies the moment of birth of the nation-state—the moment of creation—as Israel is and needs to be reborn anew every day. Israel cannot veil this initial violent moment of creation, of exception that precedes and creates the norm, but rather reproduces it endlessly and violently. Although none of these characteristics is unique to Zionism, Zionism is probably unique in having all of them present all the time.[35]

In "Avowing—The Impossible," Derrida overlooks the details that might allow us to evaluate Zionism critically without being forced to denounce nationalism at large. The fact that nationalism, by definition, has a violent aspect should not stop us from making internal distinctions between the different roles played by different national movements (of course, these distinctions are not carved in stone but could themselves be deconstructed). In order to reject Zionism and oppose its policies in theory and practice, one need not conceptualize it as a unique paradigm, different from any other national movement, or as an aberration in modern history. However, locating Zionism within a certain paradigm need not blind us to the violence it hides and implies. Nationalism can take on various shades and hues; in this case, Derrida fails sufficiently to distinguish them.

Here one can, in fact, deconstruct Derrida himself, and this final note prepares the ground for my final section. By making a general statement on the nature of nationalism or the violence that accompanies the birth of the modern state, Derrida uses an absolute or categorical language that stops the conversation short in its tracks and runs the risk of extinguishing the debate. One can conceive of human existence in general within the context of exile and of existential estrangement after Adam's expulsion from Paradise, and one may consider such forcing of the particular into universal structures or concepts to be a form of violence. But the threat here stems from the fact that by stretching the concepts of violence and exile we may lose our vocabulary for dealing with those who actually live in exile—refugees and the dispossessed—and may lose sight of real physical violence by expanding the term to include other forms of silencing. The same holds true for nationalism as a merely homogenizing violent practice. Something is lost in this expansive use of language, which may amount to something Derrida never tired of warning us against: conceptual imperialism.

## Openness of the Intellectual and Closure of the Political

Debate has been ongoing over whether Derrida's writing has political bite and whether it can take us beyond a negative to a more reconstructive project. Derrida argued from the start that his project was political, and that deconstruction is an intervention or interruption in a setting that always has political dimensions.[36] In fact, at one point—usually associated with his long address at Cardozo Law School, "Force of Law: The Mystical Foundations of Authority"—Derrida turned the tables and responded assertively, though not defensively, to his critics that (a) *deconstruction is justice*" and there is "nothing less outdated than the classical emancipatory ideal,"[37] and (b) deconstruction is a prerequisite for any politically responsible action. Some view these two statements as signaling a return of the ethical and the political in Derrida's writings.[38]

However, for many others, Derrida's approach seems formalist, vague, and uncommitted to any political ideal whatsoever. Moreover, Derrida himself, reflecting on his own practice, has made statements that are difficult to reconcile with the preceding assertions. During a symposium on the topic of deconstruction and pragmatism he made the following claim:

> I would insist that everyone can use this motif (of deconstruction) as they please to serve quite different political perspectives, which would seem to mean that deconstruction is politically neutral. But, the fact that deconstruction is apparently politically neutral allows, on the one hand, a reflection on the nature of the political, and on the other hand, and this is what interests me in deconstruction, a hyper-politicization.[39]

These sorts of statements and many others have caused many to question whether Derrida and deconstruction have any contribution to make to the political.[40]

Covering all aspects of this debate is beyond the scope of this essay. In fact, I am not sure where the debate could lead us, given the different meanings that people intend when they use the word "political." Thus I will engage in a more modest critique and deal with a more limited set of questions, namely, the *concrete ways/senses* in which one might *experience* Derrida as nonpolitical.

Before coming to the sense in which one might experience Derrida as nonpolitical, I want first to convey the basic sense in which Derrida "defends" himself against these charges. Derrida's dealing with the question of justice and law in his "Force of Law" is paradigmatic of the way in which he deals with other concepts, such as the gift, hospitality, forgiveness, and responsibility.[41]

From his early writings on, Derrida insists that undecidability is crucial for justice and responsibility. He theorized that the rules "run out" and we are left in need of decision making. Such decisions, if they are to be real decisions rather than the mechanical application of rules, must contain some new, fresh element. They must be neither repetitions nor replications, but living decisions that constitute interruptions and new interventions. Otherwise, we do not bear responsibility for our decisions; in a sense they must be our own, which is the condition for responsibility itself.[42]

Deconstruction, by focusing on undecidability, forces us to stare at the moment of decision making and recognize the openness of the materials in front of us, so that we cannot "base" our decision on fixed, universal rules. Responsibility is lost when it begins to speak the language of universal rules.[43] This openness brings us to acknowledge that we are not simply applying a rule, but inventing a new one each time we make a decision. The decision can always be otherwise; nothing mandates it entirely; the materials have no immanent rationality, nor can they produce closure by themselves.[44] Rather, they wait for closure to be enforced on them from without, with our "help," our decision. The gap between the universality of rules and the singularity of the concrete decision, as well as the gap between identity and difference that confronts us with responsibility for making decisions, provide the basis for the possibilities of justice, responsibility, and politics.

Derrida applies the same logic in his treatment of other concepts. For example, in order for a gift to be a gift, it must escape the economy of calculation; otherwise it is merely a loan that must one day be returned.[45] Similarly, if forgiveness is conditioned by justice or by the need for each party to pay its due, then it is not a genuine forgiveness, but simply the outcome of a calculation. In order to qualify as true forgiveness, it must escape this calculation.[46]

These perspectives shed some light on why Derrida thinks that deconstruction is the condition of the political. The openness saves us from the jaws of a universal machine that operates itself, and sends us back to ourselves, allowing us to recognize the endless possibilities ahead and the future that awaits us. The undecidability and openness save us from fixed structures and call on us to create a new future, free of any *telos* that seeks to impose itself upon us. It offers hope without guarantees, historical determinism, and "messianicity without any messianism."[47]

I would like to pause here to reflect on some of my experiences as a political activist who reads Derrida. The foregoing reflections highlight the tension that exists between openness and closure. The openness that Derrida describes offers us horizons to the future but is characterized by undecidability, unpredictability, and the impossible. The need for action, however, requires closure and finality. How can one continue to act in the presence of such radical indeterminacy? Would not political acts evoke some level of cynicism in such circumstances?

Derrida's offer of openness and insistence on freedom is valuable indeed. Our acceptance of this offer allows us to tinker with the materials at hand. It frees our imagination and prompts us to think of new combinations that transcend old dichotomies. It acts as a powerful reminder that this world is our own, and in this sense he takes modernity's impulse to denaturalize, which began with Hobbes, to its ultimate conclusion.[48] It can greatly enrich our repertoires and keep us alert to the dark side and dual nature of our every decision. At some point, however, we must decide; one reaches a moment of finality in the moment of action. However, aware of the options, the aporias, and the paradoxes, how are we to reach a decision? Is there not a tension between interpretation, which requires openness, and action, which requires closure, finality, and violence? Are all decisions arbitrary in the same manner? Are they all similarly moments of "madness"?[49] Is there a way to make sense of them? Or do they just come to be? And how are we to manage this tension between openness of the intellect and closure of the political?[50]

Some suggest that openness is the condition of the political, and as such *is* the political. I, however, want to preserve a distinction between a thing that is a *condition* of the political and the political itself. The openness that Derrida suggests exists in the undecidable is perhaps a condition of the political; it is its a priori, without which the political is unthinkable. But is it the political itself? Is making the political possible *equivalent* to being the political? Is creating options the same as choosing between them? What occupies the space between potentiality and actuality, or between openness and closure?

The answer to these questions is both yes and no. It is "yes" in the sense that every intervention that questions hierarchy and interrogates what sounds and looks natural is in some sense a political intervention.[51] In this case, the political is not opposed in any manner to the theoretical or the philosophical.[52] However, it is not political in the specific sense in which I want to employ the concept. What I mean by "political" here is a very limited sense of finality that requires commitment, identification, and accumulation. By commitment and identification, I mean taking sides at a concrete point in time, in a certain conflict. When one does that, one gambles or takes a risk, fully aware that one might do the wrong thing tactically or ethically. Thus, one goes beyond the paradox by taking a gamble; every political action is a gamble. For example, should we advocate autonomy for personal status issues for Muslims and Christians in Israel—as a sign of respecting difference—despite the fact that the religious courts of these groups discriminate against women? Should we commemorate the *Nakba* this year by staging a strike for the Palestinians in Israel? Would that be to overemphasize *difference*? Should the Palestinians within Israel boycott the elections as a result of the massacres in Gaza, or instead use their civic rights to influence wider Israeli society? Should the Palestinians in the occupied territories engage in violent or nonviolent acts of resistance against the occupation?

One might experience deconstruction as nonpolitical in two ways. In one sense, it is not political in that it does not take sides. It might be deployed within a certain political context, but it is the deployment itself that is political. To uncover the patriarchal structures of a certain society through deconstructive practice is, in a way, to intervene in a specific debate and destabilize power relations. However, it is the *decision* to intervene that is political and which is not itself mandated by deconstruction. The tilt—taking sides momentarily—comes not from deconstruction but from elsewhere.[53]

Another sense in which deconstruction is not political is in its formalism and preoccupation with methodological and epistemological issues—and here comes the element of the accumulation of experience. Opponents might argue that they are aware of living in a world riddled with antinomies and paradoxes, but that they have long since relinquished the ambition to solve them. Thus Derrida is fighting a battle that was won long ago. We are not interested in more formulas or ready-made, rule-like answers regarding the way we ought to conduct our affairs, regime, or revolution. The opponents' argument may proceed in the following vein, "Our ambitions are far more modest, and we are merely interested in finding out whether there is anything to be learned from past experiences, as a matter of probability, and nothing more. It is not we who insist on determinacy, decidability, and rule-following, but Derrida himself. Instead of epistemology and methodology, we should take up the study of history. We should move on from 'form' to 'matter,' and from the a priori to the posteriori."

There may be a kernel of truth to this argument. In many ways, deconstruction remains within the horizon of the Kantian paradigm, which asserts negativities and erects borders that we should not cross, as it is the nature of reason to go astray, to wander into foreign lands and stray into metaphysics, and repeat the same old mistakes. The most reason can do in the Kantian paradigm is discipline itself by restraining itself within its own domain. However, as we know, Hegel has already replied to Kant regarding these fears in the preface to the *Phenomenology of Spirit,* where he accuses Kant of being obsessed with the metaphor of the tool (reason itself) and of wanting to ensure beforehand that the tool really works and is capable of making correct judgments before embarking on any inquiry or investigation. For Hegel this mission is impossible, and, moreover, one can only become acquainted with the nature of the tool by using it on the materials themselves, as there are no a priori assurances. In this sense, Kant resembles someone who wants to learn swimming before jumping into the water. Hegel thought that this strategy of retreat and Kant's fear of errors became a fear of truth itself.[54] One could make a similar argument against Derrida, who has not provided us with much guidance during those political moments when we have to make a decision as to what "living together" in Palestine/Israel should look like (e.g., one state or two? A secular state? A bi-national state? Autonomy? A confederation?).

No wonder, then, that in "Avowing—The Impossible" Derrida speaks the language of grace and initiative, for he imagines that forgiveness, justice, and his other concepts would require the transcending of almost everything, in the absence of reciprocity (see "Avowing," especially 18–19, 23, and 26). Such a move requires certain powers and the ability to start ex nihilo, regardless of any economy or causality, and is reminiscent of the image of the sovereign in Carl Schmitt's political theology.[55]

It is both interesting and telling that Derrida goes out of his way in "Avowing—The Impossible" to stress the terminology of love, compassion, and what he terms in general the "language of the heart" ("Avowing," 25–26). Here, again, Derrida manifests a certain level of distrust toward juridical language as a basis for living together. Juridical language that is based on rules and rule-application is obsessed with the universal; it cannot be satisfactorily attuned to the freshness of each new case. Living together requires more than a juridical language that speaks in definite and precise terms of respect: It requires the language of love, which is never calculable, and is always expanding, open-ended, and fragile. Living together demands respect, but is not satisfied with it. If living together is to become possible, respect must be supplemented by love. And as always in the matters of the heart, there are no clear, ready-made formulas; rather, in our relations with others, we must accept our fragile nature and the absence of a reliable safety net.

Is that, then, what Derrida leaves us with as we are trying to cross the abyss, to jump the gap between justice and law, the possible and the impossible, between responsibility as applying rules and as a call for the absolute? Has he left us with a language of the heart, love, hope, initiative, and grace?

# Giving Forgiving

# Responsi/ability, after Derrida

*Ellen T. Armour*

In *The Work of Mourning*, Jacques Derrida speaks of the impossible obligation of putting loss into language to honor the dead.[1] We long to
speak with the deceased, not about him or her. The dissymmetry of the
relationship of mourner to mourned ("Derrida" is now only as we remember him) means that what we say to honor him may miss its mark.
The impossibility of reckoning with loss—the immediate one as well as
those it recalls and anticipates—renders us speechless. "Speaking is impossible," Derrida writes, "but so too would be silence or absence or a
refusal to share one's sadness."[2] Indeed, Derrida himself repeatedly
took on that impossible obligation on behalf of colleagues and friends—
and many of these tributes have found their way into publication. *The
Work of Mourning* is a collection of such addresses. In *Adieu to Emmanuel Levinas,* Derrida honors this particular colleague and friend
with profound yet not uncritical meditations upon concerns that united
and divided them.[3] More recently, Part II of *Rogues* opens with a brief
and poignant acknowledgment of the unexpected death the previous
day of Dominique Janicaud, who was to have attended the conference
Derrida is addressing.[4] Already, then, before even addressing the specific text of Derrida's to which I have been asked to respond, I find myself on well-traveled Derridean terrain—a landscape at once comfortable
and uncanny, familiar and abyssal, marked this time by a redoubled
sense, as this is a work of mourning, of the peculiar interplay of autho-
rial presence and absence (his and my own), speech and writing, responsibility and its limits.

In what follows, I offer my own reading of the essay of Derrida's
that forms the centerpiece of this volume in conjunction with two earlier texts of his that I argue share thematic links with it, *The Gift of
Death* and "Circumfession."[5] I continue to pursue here what has been a
particularly fruitful line of inquiry for me in Derrida's work, one that
attends to what we might call its theologico-ethico-political horizon.

Following what occurs in these texts along that horizon disrupts attempts to keep religion in what many have come to think of as its proper place: as cleanly and clearly delineated from ethics and politics, as confined to the private rather than the public, as an aspect of identity that one can pick up or put down at will, that is clearly and cleanly demarcated from other identities (or aspects/forms of identity)—especially other religious identities. It reframes in more complex ways the problematic of living together that is the volume's topic and title—and our responsibility for responding to the challenges we face, especially in a post-9/11 world.

In his last public lecture, "Avowing—The Impossible: 'Returns,' Repentance, and Reconciliation, A Lesson," delivered at a 2003 conference on Derrida and religion at the University of California, Santa Barbara, Derrida touches on a number of themes familiar to his regular readers: forgiveness, globalization/*mondialisation*, the impossible, messianicity, and so on. These topics arise as Derrida considers the question, "How to live together [*Comment vivre ensemble?*]," the theme of the thirty-seventh gathering of the Colloque des intellectuels juifs de langue française, the occasion for which "Avowing—The Impossible" was originally written.[6] In a manner reminiscent of his 1968 lecture, "The Ends of Man" (written for an international colloquium on philosophical anthropology), Derrida's lecture addresses and problematizes the colloquium's agenda.[7] His address unravels some of the unspoken assumptions that ground such a gathering on such a topic. His reflections simultaneously complicate, deepen, and expand the notion of living together *and* presumptions about identity that underlie such a notion.

**The Personal Is Political**

The problematic of living together invokes a series of concentric circles that ripple outward from one's nearest and dearest to those geographically distant but brought close through globalization. Derrida's reflections on the topic trace its global reach, as he lights briefly on political issues of the day that remain topical. Who can live with whom—and how—is at stake in debates in France over immigration and gay marriage as well as in the Palestinian conflict, all referenced by Derrida. The situations index institutions (legal and political), their limits, and what exceeds them. While living together bears within it a sense of obligation (we *must* [find a way to] live [well] together), it cannot be *simply* legislated. As we know well, hate crime legislation in the United States does not end racism or homophobia. Nor is a legal contract—legal marriage, for example—sufficient to ensure living well together. As any student of family dynamics will tell you, living together does not simply "come naturally"; more than mere biological connection is needed. Indeed, Derrida argues that fulfilling this obligation in all its forms exceeds both nature and culture; in so doing, it exhibits affinities with justice, itself an infinite and inescapable obligation that is, strictly speaking, impossible to fulfill.

It is against this backdrop that Derrida pursues the topic indicated by his title: to avow—the impossible. The title reads doubly, an ambiguity that funds what follows. Read in the imperative, the title articulates the demand that one avow, confess, straightforwardly acknowledge the impossible (itself unspecified, for the moment). Read in the declarative, it suggests that avowing, confessing, straightforward acknowledgment is itself (the) impossible. Of primary interest to Derrida here is the proliferation of avowals (confessions), gestures of repentance, and requests for forgiveness that have taken place on the world stage in recent years. Most memorable, perhaps, are those avowals from political leaders admitting to and seeking forgiveness for acts by their fellow citizens that have left behind deep wounds, which inhibit the ability to live together. These avowals range from public apologies from heads of state (the prime minister of Japan for his military's exploitation of Korean "comfort women," for example) to elaborate and extensive corporate institutions of avowal, the apex of which is the extraordinary Truth and Reconciliation Commission in postapartheid South Africa. The very dynamic itself—unprecedented in the history of humanity, to Derrida's knowledge—is in part a response to a relatively new juridical category, the crime against humanity, created in the wake of the Holocaust. Thus, the "juridical mechanism of this globalization of avowal" is itself both testament and memorial to the "bottomless trauma" ("Avowing," 32) of the Shoah—itself a colossal (many would say singular and unforgivable) violation of living together. No coincidence, then, that this particular trauma in recent years has itself been the subject of a number of avowals by European heads of state and by various organizations (including European church bodies) whose members aided and abetted (actively or passively) the slaughter.

The proliferation of so many highly public instances of avowal seems, at first, to cast doubt on any claim that avowals are impossible. Moreover, many of these avowals work to the public good. And yet, while recognizing and acknowledging the salutary effects of these avowals on living together, Derrida also calls attention to the less sanguine effects of the *demand* for avowal. Both sides of avowal's effects are symptomatic of the aporetic structure of avowal itself and thus its impossibility (strictly speaking). On the one hand, Derrida notes, the advent and active use of the juridical category of a crime against *humanity* is a sign of human progress, of the increasing universalization of human(e) ideals to which Kant looked (cautiously) forward. And yet, in practice, application of this category often falls vulnerable to co-optation and dissimulation (to politics as usual, in other words, among nation-states) and to a tyranny of the "together" that demands a renunciation of singularity, of the secret, of being-together-with-oneself. Insofar as some notion of universal humanity is a necessary condition for living together, then the notion of a crime against humanity carries within it the conditions of its own violation. The obligation to any and all inherent in the category of a crime against humanity sits in tension with a simultaneous preference for "my own" over all others. Recalling what Derrida has said elsewhere, fulfilling one's obligation to the nearest is simultaneously to fail one's obligation to other others.[8] And no rule or regulation can tell us in advance how to wrestle with this aporia in any given instance.

Universality encounters another tension with particularity in these scenes of avowal. A *specific* ethic of forgiveness is being globalized, Derrida argues, an ethic inherited from that triangle of monotheisms (Islam, Judaism, and Christianity) that he calls the Abrahamic. That ethic bears within it an aporetic structure that shows up in its globalized instantiations, as well. On the one hand, strands in the Abrahamic traditions insist that forgiveness has a prerequisite: The violator must avow his or her wrongdoing and request pardon. In exchange, the violator receives forgiveness and finds resolution in reconciliation or healing. On the other hand, the Abrahamic traditions maintain the notion of forgiveness as pure gift, as residing outside the economy of exchange. Derrida reminds his hearers of a claim he has made elsewhere: forgiveness as gift must target the unforgiveable—that for which pardon cannot be earned. Thus, true forgiveness is, at bottom, impossible and, moreover, lies beyond a "horizon of reconciliation" ("Avowing," 35).

All of these aporias are rooted in the foundational notion of the *oikonomia* and the law of proper(ty) that governs it. Here, too, though, boundaries are impossible to fix with great security. Derrida alludes to the advent of developments in technoscience that shake up common-sense notions of self and other and to teletechnologies that simultaneously manifest and enable globalization. Consider, for example, developments in genetic science. Scientists have mapped the genomes for a number of organisms including the human being. Although each person's DNA is unique when considered in its full configuration, it shares most of its substance with others—not just one's immediate relatives, but many others, including animal others. The advent of genetic engineering, via techniques such as cloning and gene therapy, promises to blur the line between self and other even further. Consider as well the economic crises of the fall of 2008, which brought home to all of us the immediate material links that make our economy truly global.

### The Political Is Personal

"Avowing—The Impossible" also makes us aware that the problem of living together, the difficulties of negotiating the aporias that attend avowal and forgiveness, must be worked out not only on global stages but also in much more intimate contexts. And those contexts are not so easily separable from the currents and dynamics of political life. As I noted at the outset, Derrida's lecture was originally crafted as an address to the Colloquium of French Jewish Intellectuals. Cofounded by Emmanuel Levinas in 1957 as a means of reconstituting a community of French Jewish intellectuals after the devastation of the Shoah and the Second World War, the agenda for these gatherings focused on connecting Jewish tradition with contemporary social, philosophical, and political concerns.[9] A gathering of this sort seems to trade on some sense of shared identity among the participants—an identity grounded in shared vocation, language, and religious tradition. Yet Derrida's reflections expose certain fault lines in that assumption, fault lines that align with the particulars of his own personal history.

Just a few pages into his lecture, Derrida recalls attending an earlier meeting of this colloquium some thirty or more years before. There, thanks to his friend Levinas (now deceased, but in a different sense still responsible for his attendance in 1998, says Derrida), he attended but did not participate. That fact in itself calls into question the "together" of living together, he suggests. During a talk by André Neher, Levinas leans over to Derrida and whispers conspiratorially, "'You see, he is the Protestant—me, I'm the Catholic.'" Noting that "this *mot d'esprit* would call for an infinite commentary," Derrida muses for a moment on the rifts, ruptures, and folds in what it might mean for Jews to live together *with each other* that this aside reveals ("Avowing," 21). In particular, how does it position its audience-of-one, a Jew from a different shore of the Mediterranean than either Levinas or Neher, a location where Islam shapes the religious topography, a vector within the Abrahamic omitted from Levinas's off-the-cuff map of religious identity? Derrida remarks on the play of inclusion/exclusion at work in this remark and his reception of it. Even as the remark overlooks a key difference between some Jews and other Jews, it also references and reinforces a "complicity of a certain 'living together' that had been decided for *us* well before *us* . . . the supposed friendship, the affinity, the complicity, if not the shareable solidarity of Jews" regardless of such differences—and regardless of whether any particular Jew is "assured or not of a stable and decidable belonging to Judaism" ("Avowing," 22).

The question of belonging is yet more fraught and complex. Derrida notes that, in a chapter of a biography of Levinas focused on the colloquium, its author writes: "But among the French philosophers of Jewish origin, one *will* never see Jacques Derrida there" ("Avowing," 22, emphasis Derrida's). The use of the future tense is not insignificant, Derrida (rightly) insists. The text plays between the predictive and the declarative: a line is drawn between insider and outsider, the *true* French-speaking Jewish intellectuals and the suspect, those who accede to this identity and those who may not. Derrida's (non)attendance is not so much predicted as proscribed ahead of time. Although we may think of "living together" primarily in spatial terms, this proscription calls attention to its temporal dimension. Living together, Derrida reminds us, rests not simply on the presence of one to another *in* the present, but also bears within it a futural (messianic) dimension; it awaits an arrival (or arrivals) that will bring about the event of living together. Thus, any particular instance of living together also carries within itself an openness to what-may-come that renders its fulfillment always partial and provisional.

Both Levinas's remark and his biographer's proscription call attention to another dimension of identity's relationship to living together: Insofar as living together carries the sense of a commandment or obligation (we *must* live together—well or badly), how one identifies (or is identified) is not entirely within one's control. Derrida notes that one feels the pressures of the "must" in the demand centered on securing peace in the Middle East that Jews live (well) together with Muslims, a demand that, to speak only of Jewish identities, corrals within its purview the orthodox and non, those living in Israel or dispersed throughout the world, irrespective of their differences and disagreements.

Thus, the challenge of how to live together doesn't just afflict those whose identities obviously differ, but even those who seem to share an identity. And it attends even living together with oneself, a site and situation embodied by Derrida as an Algerian Jew. Derrida speaks briefly but movingly of the effects on him of growing up in Algeria during the Nazi era, World War II, and the tumult of the Algerian revolt against French colonial rule. At the time, Algeria was "a country where the number and the diversity of historical communities was as rich as in Jerusalem." One could, as he did, "dream of a peaceful cultural, linguistic, and even national plural belonging only through the experience of nonbelonging: separations, rejections, ruptures, exclusions." As he has elsewhere, he recalls his expulsion from school in Algeria due to Nazi-inflated anti-Semitism, an event that caused him "to rebel, forever, against two ways of 'living together': . . . racist gregariousness" (and thus "anti-Semitic segregation") but also a retreat into an insular community for the sake of identity preservation.[10] Even as a child, he had to acknowledge that the second form of rebellion entailed a betrayal of "his own, his close ones, and Judaism" that he had to avow "within himself, even before others, even before God." Yet this very act of separation, "this passage toward a kind of universality beyond symbiotic communitarianism and gregarious fusion, beyond even citizenship" was simultaneously deeply "faithful to a certain Jewish vocation," that of singularity, of being the stranger ("Avowing," 27–28). Of holding open living together in the name of what is to come and what has been. "There is 'living together' only there where, in the name of promise and of memory, of the messianic and of mourning without work and without healing, it welcomes dissymmetry, anachrony, nonreciprocity with an other who is greater, at once older and younger than it, an other who comes or will come *perhaps*, who has *perhaps already* come" ("Avowing," 28). A difficult politics necessarily follows for this particular French-speaking Jewish intellectual. That he is "*already and since forever* Jewish," and has been irrevocably and irretrievably tied to a deep uncertainty about "what might be meant by or involved in a 'living together' in a Jewish community" ("Avowing," 22). Referring to himself in the third person, Derrida writes that "the memory of anti-Semitic persecutions," including but hardly limited to those he experienced personally, are with him always and reside within "everything he thought, said, wrote, or taught." Yet this "same vigilance was warning him, warns him today, against all the risks of the 'living together' of the Jews" that arise "when the motifs of filiation through blood, appropriation of the place, and the motif of election" risk becoming "caught . . . in the grip of nature or of convention." This two-pronged vigilance has obligated him to criticize—publicly, at times—actions and policies of not only the current Israeli regime, but many of its predecessors, even as he "continue[s] to interrogate himself in the most insomniac fashion" about the conditions that yielded the establishment of modern-day Israel—conditions that are of a piece with the subject of this essay. On the one hand, the establishment of a state is "a juridico-political founding of a 'living to-gether' [that] is by essence, violent, since it inaugurates there where a law [*droit*] did not yet exist," writes Derrida. In that sense, Israel is like any other state, founded upon an originary violence. On the other hand, Derrida asks whether, "because this modern state intended not to be a state like others, it had to appear before another law and appeal to another justice," one that may itself be linked to the globalization of forgiveness. Such questions and criticisms, he insists, do not imply "any threatening or disrespectful conse-quences for the present, the future, and the existence of Israel, on the contrary." Indeed, he was heartened to find, on his last visit to Israel and Palestine, like-minded sentiments ex-pressed seriously by a number of Israelis themselves ("Avowing," 29–30).

Derrida ends the lecture with a recollection of his first visit to Jerusalem, in 1982. He accompanied a friend to the Hevra Kadisha, the institution charged with determining who gets buried in the Jerusalem cemetery (there to await the coming of the Messiah). Families seeking to get their loved ones buried there contact the staff of Hevra Kadisha from all over the world. The office is staffed by a phalanx of orthodox men who determine who gets in and who does not. Derrida's visit predates the advent of the cell phone, but the latest in teletechnologies were very much in evidence as mechanisms for these global ne-gotiations. Walkie-talkies, computers, landline phones, and so on—all effectively altered relationships in time and space, at least for a time. Measuring proximity in terms of access to the cemetery placed New York closer to Jerusalem than Gaza, Derrida writes; one could feel closer to someone on the other side of the world than to a friend in East Jerusalem. But consider the object of these global negotiations—a singular cemetery plot—and such flights of fancy come back to earth. "Everything is becoming substitutable in this world, but the irreplaceable resists there, precisely here, now . . . in this corner of Jerusalem, in view of orienting the dead" ("Avowing," 40). Yet the value of this corner of Jerusalem comes from its orientation toward a yet-to-come, a yet-to-take-place; namely, the coming of a messiah and a heavenly Jerusalem. Indeed, at this site, the two Jerusalems seem to overlap or to blur one into the other. Quite a responsibility to take on, Derrida notes, to determine who gets in and who does not. Who can allocate such responsibility to oneself or to others? Who can shoulder it? With so much at stake?

This experience (among others), Derrida tells us, prompted in him as if it were a returning ghost (*un revenant*) the thought of "a messianic spectrality, or spectral mes-sianicity, [that] exceeds, precedes, and conditions all messianisms" and "a certain faith older than all religions." This notion, too, troubles any linear temporality. How is it possible to think an openness to the future that returns, as a ghost? Indeed, Der-rida closes by acknowledging, "I do not know, and I avow it, how to interpret what then occurred to me—or would occur to me still. Nor what was announcing itself above me as a *revenant*, what was announcing itself by haunting/returning upon me" ("Avowing," 41).

"Avowing—The Impossible" echoes themes found in an earlier essay of Derrida's that also takes up questions of the relationship of religion and politics, *Donner la mort* (titled *The Gift of Death* in English translation).[11] *Donner la mort*, like "Avowing—The Impossible," plays between and among meanings: "to give death (to another)," "to give (oneself) death" (*se donner la mort* is "to commit suicide"). Questions of giving death/the gift of death circulate throughout this text and bear within them implications for the relationships between religion, politics, and ethics. Although Derrida's remarks in "Avowing—The Impossible" foreground Judaism and the landscape of Israel, *Donner la mort* focuses on Christianity and its relation to Europe. In *The Gift of Death*, Derrida takes up a late essay written by the Czech philosopher and activist Jan Patočka, a martyr to the cause of the so-called Velvet Revolution. In this essay titled (in English translation) "Is Technological Civilization a Civilization in Decline, and If So Why?" Patočka considers "what is it that ails 'modern civilization' inasmuch as it is European?"[12] He concludes that the problem lies in Europe's failure to fully grasp its roots in a history of and as the emergence of the responsible subject. That history is itself a quasi-Hegelian history of religion that progresses from the orgiastic and daimonic through the Platonic into the Christian. If Platonism subsumes subjection by desire and mystery into an epistemologically based responsibility to an immortal Good, Christian responsibility subsumes Platonism to yet another order. The Platonic subject was responsible to an external essence (the Good, the One) that is at least indirectly accessible to the human gaze. The Christian subject, however, emerges "in relation to a supreme, absolute and inaccessible being that holds us in check not by exterior but interior force."[13] Thus Christian responsibility eludes epistemological certainty in another asymmetrical and nonreciprocal order based on a terrifying mystery or secret. Drawing on vocabulary reminiscent of that of Rudolf Otto, Patočka calls this secret a *mysterium tremendum*, an experience of transcendence that differs significantly from the Platonic relationship to the Good. "The terror of this secret exceeds and precedes the complacent relationship of a subject to an object,"[14] Derrida writes. Instead of gazing toward its Good, the Christian subject is instead fixed in *its* gaze. Christian responsibility takes its mark from the Other's own gift of death in self-giving love. It is this structure, Patočka suggests, that has yet to be fully thought through. And the very future of Europe rests on its success or failure.

In the four essays that make up *The Gift of Death*, Derrida thinks through Patočka's evocation of Christian responsibility to the point where it is founded and where it founders as (exclusively or simply) Christian and moral, particular or universal, ethical and political. That thinking through goes in two directions: toward the ethical (and its limits) and the political (and its limits) and uncovers aporias familiar to us from "Avowing—The Impossible." The first aporia appears in the early pages of the book where Derrida interrogates the relationships between secrecy, historicity, and responsibility. Patočka seems to be asking for an avowal here, an owning up to/admission of the reality of historicity as foundational for responsibility. Yet, Derrida notes, such an avowal is ultimately impossible insofar as to be responsible is to decide, to act, in spite of (one's) history. That includes the history of religions, especially given that modern ethics claims a secular (and thus universal) ground for responsibility. Despite Patočka's call to resolve it through avowal, historicity and its tie to responsibility must remain an open problem, Derrida asserts. "History can be neither a decidable object nor a totality capable of being mastered, precisely because it is tied to *responsibility*, to *faith*, and to the *gift*," he writes. That is, history is simultaneously ruptured and constituted by the exercise of responsibility in and through "the very ordeal of the undecidable." Insofar as such ordeals are "a form of involvement with the other that is a venture into absolute risk, beyond knowledge and certainty," they require faith. And finally, taking responsibility sets the subject "into relation with the transcendence of the other, with God as selfless goodness," via giving (a new experience of) death. "Responsibility and faith go together, however paradoxical that might seem to some, and both should, in the same movement, exceed mastery and knowledge. The gift of death would be this marriage of responsibility and faith. History depends on such an excessive beginning [*ouverture*]."[15]

This observation opens onto a chain of aporias centered on secrecy. Patočka aims to avow the secret of responsibility, its dependence on historicity. But that secret rests on another: the secrecy and terror inherent in the specifically Christian *mysterium tremendum* engendered by its gift of death. Another aporia appears here: that between the universal and the particular. There is yet more, however. In the final two essays, Derrida continues his pursuit of the terror and secrecy embedded in *mysterium tremendum* taking Christian responsibility down to its Abrahamic roots.

## The Ethical: Singularity and Universality

In "Whom to Give to (Knowing Not to Know)," Derrida turns to Kierkegaard's *Fear and Trembling*, a text focused on the question of the relationship between Christianity and the ethical.[16] As is well known, Kierkegaard's analysis centers on one of the more difficult episodes in biblical tradition, the story of Abraham's near-sacrifice of Isaac. Secrecy and terror attend Kierkegaard's analysis in at least two ways. Abraham tells no one—not even Sarah, the boy's mother—of the reason for his climb up Mount Moriah; he shares with no one the terror that, for the dilemma to truly be a dilemma, Kierkegaard insists he must feel to the fullest. When the boy inquires after the whereabouts of the sacrifice, his father replies—truthfully, but also without really knowing—that God will provide. This gift of death reveals another layer of terror and secrecy as we go deeper into the heart of the *mysterium tremendum*. An infanticide all but committed in the name of the Absolute Other, whose Self (and Will) remains always hidden, gives a different death: The universal is sacrificed in the service of the Absolute. For Kierkegaard, this story properly considered confronts readers with the paradoxical relationship between Christian faith and moral obligation. Although Isaac survives, Abraham is always and forever the giver of death according to a Kantian ethic of universalizable maxims, always and forever a knight of faith in taking the leap of faith. For Derrida, however, Kierkegaard's insight describes an aporia at the heart of ethical obligation per se. All ethical subjects face Abraham's situation. By responding to the demand of the Other in the form of a particular other, we do violence to another particular other, indeed to *all* particular others. Fulfilling the demand of the ethical in any specific instance deals death to the ethical in general. "As soon as I enter into a relation with the other, with the gaze, look, request, love, command, or call of the other, I know that I can respond only by sacrificing ethics, that is, by sacrificing whatever obliges me to also respond in the same way, in the same instant, to all the others."[17] Thus, the ethical itself is founded and founders upon a gift of death.

### The Political Is Personal: Who Is My Neighbor?

In the final essay, "Tout autre est tout autre" (left in French in the English translation), Derrida continues his interrogation of Patočka and Kierkegaard with an eye now toward the question of Christian *political* responsibility. Derrida moves from the story of Isaac's near-sacrifice to the Gospel of Matthew. To a theologian such as myself, this site calls to mind the long tradition of Christian anti-Judaism inherited from Luther, among others, which pits Christianity as the religion of grace against Judaism, the religion of law. One can, of course, cite innumerable aspects of Jewish tradition that belie this pernicious stereotype; the Gospel of Matthew is arguably one such citation from the side of Christian tradition. If anything, Matthew's Jesus depicts the demands of the law as more strenuous than competing versions of first-century Judaism. (It is in Matthew that one finds the passage that got President Jimmy Carter in trouble years ago when he acknowledged lusting after a woman in his heart, a form of adultery, Matthew's Jesus says in Matthew 5:28). Derrida notes that Matthew's Jesus advocates giving alms in secret (Matt. 6:3), anticipating themes of self-forgetfulness and self-giving essential to the economy of gift. Here, however, gift seems to resolve into exchange when Matthew's Jesus promises reward from "your Father who sees in secret" (Matt. 6:3).[18] (Gift resolves into exchange in Abraham's life, too, one could argue. YHWH rewards Abraham for his faith by making him the father of nations through Isaac and Ishmael.)

In Matthew, Jesus is asked which commandment is the greatest, and he replies (quoting Deuteronomy 6:5 and Leviticus 19:18), "You shall love the Lord your God with all your heart, and with all your soul, and with all your mind" (Matt. 22:37) and "You shall love your neighbor as yourself" (Matt. 22:39). But the critical question becomes who is one's neighbor? How are we to distinguish between friends and enemies? Carl Schmitt, author of *Political Theology*, argues that the reference here is solely interpersonal and direct: Love those who, via daily intercourse, abuse you.[19] No obligation exists here to the stranger, the foreigner, the political other. Against Schmitt, Derrida argues that, if the obligation is excessive, then it cannot be contained within such narrow boundaries.

Although this marks the threshold of an excessive obligation to the political other (an obligation that history suggests Christianity has as often honored in the breach as in the fulfillment), symptoms of the same paradoxical relation between the singular and the universal that we found in Christian ethical responsibility emerge in this account of Christian political responsibility. In Derrida's reading, the logic in the Matthean text asserts Christian superiority to both Jew and Gentile. Matthew's Jesus contrasts the standard of obligation that he is advocating not only with Leviticus, but with that of "the Gentiles [ethnikoi, peoples, nations]" (Matthew 5:47). Yet Derrida suggests that consideration of Leviticus (and I would add larger strands of the Hebrew canon) belies Christianity's claim to free and clear title to the standard of excessive obligation. Leviticus, after all, lays out obligations not only to one's next of kin or neighbor, but also to the stranger and the foreigner, and stops well short of advocating revenge against such others.[20] The effects of this insight gain in significance when we place Matthew into its historical context. Like much of the New Testament, Matthew predates Christianity's emergence as a religion in its own right; the line between Judaism and proto-Christianity in Matthew is not altogether clear and is, arguably, a matter of contestation. Thus, what seems a properly Christian obligation rests on an Abrahamic foundation.

This foundation is no stable platform upon which the three traditions stand side by side as peers. Rather, it is the site of the emergence of competing claims to the patronymic legacy (who are the *real* heirs to the promise given by God to Abraham?), a competition that has often issued in violence and violation. Though it begins in Europe, *The Gift of Death*, like "Avowing—The Impossible," concludes by returning to the singular landscape of Jerusalem. If Derrida's focus in "Avowing" was on Jerusalem as the site of a messianic future, his focus here is on Jerusalem as the site of a violent past. Here the history of violent conflict among the Abrahamic traditions over the patronymic legacy takes geographical form—and at the site of the originary violence of Isaac's near-sacrifice. Central to Jerusalem's significance is the location where the two Jewish temples stood, now home to the Dome of the Rock, a Muslim holy site. Traditionally, this spot is believed to be the location of Abraham's near-sacrifice of Isaac, which all three structures claimed to commemorate. (Nearby, of course, is the Way of the Cross, the route Jesus of Nazareth is said to have taken on his way to his own sacrificial death, traditionally viewed as prefigured in Isaac's near-death.)

In my closing comments, I want to honor Derrida by remaining for a while at this particular site in the presence of the *revenants*—past and future—that haunt it. Few places are as freighted as Jerusalem with the promise of living together (well) and the past and present reality of the failure of that promise. The significance of this place—literally and symbolically—has become even more acute in the wake of 9/11. All of us who are heirs of Abraham regardless of where we reside are brought near to this site and its significance by this weight. How might we find a foothold?

## Religious Identity Redux

In "Avowing—The Impossible," Derrida reconceptualizes and recontextualizes our notion of religious identity in ways that are particularly apt for a post-9/11 world. This is not the first time that Derrida has written incidents from his life into his texts. But in tone and function—at least, at first glance—the autobiographical references here seem rather different from, say, Derrida's 1993 quasi-autobiographical essay, "Circumfession," Derrida's contribution to *Jacques Derrida*, a volume coauthored with the literary theorist Geoffrey Bennington.[21] *Jacques Derrida* entices readers by seeming to promise to produce "the real" Jacques Derrida—one way or another. Bennington's primary contribution, "Derridabase," an essay that attempts to "describe . . . at least the general system of [Jacques Derrida's] thought,"[22] runs across the top two-thirds of the pages of *Jacques Derrida*. Derrida's contribution, "Circumfession," occupies the bottom third and includes considerable autobiographical detail. The final pages of the book, "Acts of Genre," feature a brief biography of Derrida complete with timeline and a few photos. Yet all is not quite as straightforward as it seems. If Bennington aims to systematize and offer a clear account of "Jacques Derrida" the philosopher, his subject's stream-of-consciousness quasi-autobiographical meanderings do quite the opposite. Which is not say they are in any simple or straightforward way self-revelatory. Despite its immediacy (the very real impending death of Derrida's mother, Georgette, features prominently), "Circumfession" obscures as much as it reveals, thus to a degree thwarting *Jacques Derrida*'s ostensible aim. True to one reading of its title, "Circumfession" circumvents (autobiographical) confession as much as it engages in it (an appropriate ploy, given that Derrida names Augustine's *Confessions* as his template).[23] Derrida's use of the autobiographical in "Avowing—The Impossible" is more straightforward—confessional, even (*avouer* means "to confess," after all). One might even call it conventional, insofar as Derrida explicitly links—even roots—certain long-term intellectual concerns to incidents from his past. Thus, "Avowing—The Impossible" seems to finally give us what *Jacques Derrida* tantalizingly promised but perhaps (and, if so, intentionally) failed to deliver: a glimpse of "the real" Derrida. Like all true gifts, it comes without announcing itself in advance and without demanding acknowledgment. Giving an account *of himself* is not, after all, the ostensible topic of "Avowing—The Impossible." This possibility is particularly seductive coming as it does in such immediate proximity to Derrida's death. Yet "Circumfession" and "Avowing—The Impossible" may have more in common in their use of the autobiographical than it may seem, at first. Though the tone and, to some degree, the substance of the autobiographical in each case differs, circumvention *and* avowal respectively deploy the autobiographical in the service of rendering legible *as* impossible the project of fixing identity once and for all.

Recall again the original context for which "Avowing—The Impossible" was produced: the colloquium of French-speaking Jewish intellectuals. Up to this point, Derrida's published comments on his religion (or religion without religion, to borrow John Caputo's well-known phrase) have come largely in response to attempts by others to fix him in place according to the boxes we in the West tend to use to define (and confine) religious identity. One is either a believer or not, a theist or not; we assign you an identity based on the content of that belief, the specific shape of that theism (or lack thereof, in the case of some forms of Buddhism, for example). Derrida's use of and reflections on the auto-bio-graphical defies such boxes and modes of assignation. In doing so, he offers what seems to me a productive route toward an alternative conception of religious identity—one perhaps better suited to our time and place.

The schematic of religious identities as a set of clearly delineated boxes (Jew, Christian, Muslim, Hindu) reflects the larger taxonomy of the "world religions" and the ostensibly shared domain, religion, it purports to map. Both the specific taxonomy and the concept of "religion" are troubled and contested today in religious studies scholarship as well as in what can be observed in "lived religion" (where, for example, Christians celebrate Eucharist in the sanctuary and practice yoga in the fellowship hall).[24] To check off one box or another is to concede to the taxonomy's implicit demand for avowal, for auto-bio-graphical confession: "I *am* a Muslim; I confess it and own up to it."

Yet Derrida's reflections on (his) Jewishness in "Avowing—The Impossible" belie such a one-dimensional understanding of religious identity and its relation to avowal. Constituted in relation to social and historical forces over which one has little if any control, religious identity, Derrida's reflections suggest, exhibits affinities with gender and race or ethnicity as understood in much contemporary theory.[25] Like them, religious identity is as much a matter of public performance (sometimes on command) and/or perception as private conviction, of acquiescence *and* resistance to taking up one's (assigned) place in the world. Like other identities, religious identities are embedded in social realities that extend well beyond one's immediate circle (of coreligionists, in this case) whether self-selected or not. Religious identities bear not only the imprints of the past (religious and world history broadly conceived) but are also imbricated in the present (globalization) and the future (insofar as they anticipate a yet-to-come).

Derrida's ruminations also belie understanding religious identities as independent one from the other. This becomes clear in a particularly potent and significant way in Derrida's notion of the Abrahamic. Contemporary adherents of Islam, Judaism, and Christianity may consider themselves members of very distinct religious traditions, but relations between them and their adherents still bear the marks of the history of the divisions that gave birth to them, as Derrida's autobiographical references here make clear. Thus, these identities are constituted by one another and by their roots in the Abrahamic—for good or for ill. Not only Derrida, but any of us who claim or are claimed by the Abrahamic, must acknowledge this history that haunts us. The personal is indeed the political—and vice versa. But how to take responsibility for and respond to these *revenants*?

## Responsi/ability, after Derrida

In response to 9/11, the American administration launched the so-called "global war on terror," which some have depicted as a clash of Christian and Muslim civilizations. Islam is demonized as an inherently violent religion and Christianity lionized and equated with American-style democracy. Following Derrida in thinking Christian responsibility through to its Abrahamic foundations reminds us that Christianity's roots, too, lie in violence and violation. As Gil Anidjar puts it, "All the parties involved with Mount Moriah, beginning with God, are implicated in a war that is, daily and horridly, not just a war of occupation but a fight to the death."[26] We are haunted, then, by the ghosts of the violent past as well as the bodies of the violent present; all are casualties of this originary violence that haunts the Abrahamic. We are haunted as well by the yet-to-come, by the messianic, an open future, a literal u-topia (not-place) characterized simultaneously (and undecidably) by hopes for justice and fears of terror. To take responsibility for this history and this future is not to claim mastery over either. Indeed, Derrida's analysis makes it clear that we cannot. To take responsibility, to act, is to take a leap into the unknown and unknowable—to simultaneously make and break with history, to simultaneously fulfill and fail our obligations to others and our dreams/fears for the future. Learning to live together, it seems, will require taking up responsibility for these gifts of death that remain our legacy, a taking up that, in whatever small way we take it on, follows after and thus honors Derrida and his *revenants*.

# Contested Forgiveness: Jankélévitch, Levinas, and Derrida at the Colloque des intellectuels juifs

*Dana Hollander*

## "Why the Duty to Forgive Has Today Become Our Problem"

> It is not difficult to understand why the duty to forgive has today become our problem. Forgiveness is . . . an event that has never occurred in history.
> —Vladimir Jankélévitch, *Le Pardon*

These two sentences are from the opening paragraph to Vladimir Jankélévitch's classic study on the topic of forgiveness, *Le Pardon* (published in 1967).[1] They can be taken to frame a paradoxical, dual approach to what the question of reconciling differences, of irreconcilable differences, can mean when it comes to responding to historic wrongs or evils within contemporary political realities. If we consider the duty to forgive to be our problem "today," then we thereby acknowledge that we inhabit a movement, within or in relation to the history of evils that have been perpetrated, in which whether to forgive is a new sort of problem. At the same time, Jankélévitch's pronouncement that "forgiveness is an event that has never occurred in history" indicates that there is something about the concept of forgiveness, about forgiveness as we understand it, that exceeds the empirical-historical realm—something, in other words, that goes beyond, or escapes, the idea of an empirical forgiveness that could actually take place or take effect in history.

Looking at Derrida's considerations of forgiveness, which date from the 1990s, we can see that they are similarly informed by the tension between a duty or demand to forgive and the elusiveness of a true forgiveness.[2] An important occasion, or frame of reference, for those considerations is what Derrida described as a proliferation of public-political-official acknowledgments of wrongdoing that were presented to those who had been wronged as a plea for forgiveness, and a step toward reconciliation. Derrida cites acts of this kind by the Japanese

137

prime minister, by the Catholic Church in France and Poland vis-à-vis the victims of the Holocaust, as well as the Truth and Reconciliation Committees in South Africa. (Indeed, this latter example was of special importance, since Derrida delivered his major lecture on forgiveness to audiences in South Africa, and he pays special attention to this example in his discussions of forgiveness.) Derrida emphasizes particularly forgiveness as a postwar leitmotif of French policy: he cites the fact that insofar as responsibility was claimed for the crimes of the Occupation and the Algerian War, it was in order to effect a national reconciliation, by means of an amnesty for such crimes.[3] Pointing out that such "public manifestations of repentance" constitute something new in the history of politics,[4] Derrida would like to guard against taking for granted the seemingly automatic success of such gestures: that is, against the idea that forgiveness can be asked for and granted in these public rituals, and that reconciliation between erstwhile perpetrators and victims can thereby be achieved. In questioning whether forgiveness is a possibility, Derrida is thus in sympathy with Jankélévitch's efforts to show where this possibility might have its limits.

At the same time, Derrida refuses what appears to be Jankélévitch's final verdict, that for some crimes, and in particular for the crimes of the Holocaust, forgiveness is impossible— and indeed unethical.[5]

In the opening to *Le Pardon*, Jankélévitch sums up our paradoxical relationship to forgiveness by juxtaposing the impossibility of forgiveness with the obligation to forgive— that is, a theoretical observation with a moral demand. We can think of this as a Kantian imperative along the following lines: We must not give up on the possibility of forgiveness, on the duty to forgive, even if we have not experienced forgiveness as an empirical reality. On the other hand, Jankélévitch points out an inverse paradox: If forgiveness is a matter of the will, then the very fact that we desire to forgive, if this is a sincere desire, means that it is in our power: "Vouloir c'est pouvoir." For how could we imagine—much less take on—an ethical precept that is in principle inachievable? Here, Jankélévitch draws on a verse from St. Paul's First Epistle to the Corinthians.

> No temptation has overtaken you that is not common to man. God is faithful, and he will not let you be tempted beyond your strength, but with the temptation will also provide the way of escape, that you may be able to endure it. (1 Cor. 10:13)

According to this logic, sin is always humanly resistible and always inexcusable, and divine commandments, if they are to be more than what Jankélévitch calls "Platonic recommendations," or, even worse, disingenuous sophisms, always command the possible.[6] Jankélévitch begins, then, from two inverse paradoxes: a Kantian one, according to which to do one's duty is practically possible and commanded for the very reason that it is theoretically unthinkable; and a Pauline one, according to which the command is binding only in that I am up to fulfilling it.

In a move that makes clear that what he is aiming at is a concept of forgiveness that is authentic, pure, and radical, and thus free of the temptation toward compromise or conciliation for their own sake, Jankélévitch structures the larger part of his study of forgiveness as a successive discussion of a number of scenarios that he calls *produits de remplacement*: "substitute products" for real forgiveness that we might commonly encounter or be tempted by in everyday life. These scenarios are similar to forgiveness—he calls them instances of *simili-pardon* / simili-forgiveness or pseudo-forgiveness—in that they seem to achieve "more or less the same external effects" as we expect forgiveness to achieve.[7] However, they fail to capture what he calls the "hyperbolic problem that we are called upon to face, the problem of forgiveness which imposes itself before evil, malice, perversity—forgiveness before the unforgivable."[8] For Jankélévitch this failure can be boiled down to the absence of any "intention to forgive"; instead, simili-forgiveness is exclusively directed toward an external aim, that of

> putting an end to a situation that is critical, tense, abnormal, and that ought to be resolved one of these days. For chronic hostility that is passionally rooted in a rancorous memory, such hostility, like any anomaly, demands to be resolved. Rancor feeds a cold war, which is a state of exception; and forgiveness, whether true or false, does the opposite: it suspends the state of exception, liquidates what resentment maintained, resolves the vindictive obsession. The knot of rancor is loosed.[9]

Admitting that in seeking a definition of forgiveness by successively describing its false alternatives he is producing an "apophatic or negative philosophy of forgiveness," Jankélévitch identifies two broad types or classes of such pseudo-forgiveness.

1. The first of these are, broadly speaking, appeals to time as a process that diminishes or erodes the unforgivability of the fault. Under this heading, "the wearing effect of time [*l'usure par le temps*]," Jankélévitch includes both appeals to historical progress—e.g., the idea that we have to move on, that being prepared for the future, for innovation, for life, requires letting go of the past—and appeals to the idea that the passage of time itself wears out the severity of the fault, perhaps because the intensity of its memory has lessened. Against these tendencies, which Jankélévitch, writing in the 1960s, finds in abundance in postwar Europe, he proposes a simple formula: Time cannot be, or figure in, an argument for forgiveness, or about any moral issue for that matter.[10] "Time—which brings with it forgetting, effacement, erosion—time is of the order of facts; but it does not in itself have any influence on the just and the unjust, on good and evil . . . which are [instead] . . . moral, ethical, atemporal, super-natural conflicts, outside of time."[11]

2. The second major type of pseudo-forgiveness discussed by Jankélévitch is what he names "excuses," by which he means efforts to come to a mitigating understanding of the fault, or, we might say, efforts to mitigate the fault, or its unforgivability through understanding, or explanation, or reasoning. Excuses are philosophical arguments, unlike the

appeals to the healing effects of time, which are pragmatically oriented. They work by denying the severity of the fault, by downgrading unforgivable evil acts to excusable transgressions. Indeed, at the limit, the excuse would amount to a denial of any such thing as a radical evil or an unforgivable crime. Forgiveness, Jankélévitch says, would then be left without an object.[12]

Reviewing the phenomena that fall within these two classes of pseudo-forgiveness allows Jankélévitch to also highlight three important minimal criteria for true forgiveness: that it ought to have an event-like character; that it involve a personal relationship between the one who forgives and the one to be forgiven; and that it be total and without reserve.[13] For instance, we can understand the inadequacy of excuses to lie in their being formulated in objective, impersonal terms, rather than taking the form of a dialogue between the offended and the offender (i.e., an asking and a granting of forgiveness).[14] Similarly, the idea that forgiveness is a punctual event serves to clarify the inadequacy of appeals to the progressive passage of time. It also helps Jankélévitch bring into view a third kind of pseudo-forgiveness: a punctual "liquidation" of the fault by means of a sort of arbitrary act. Jankélévitch speaks here of a gesture of drawing a line under all that has happened, deciding that enough is enough, a brusque "I've had enough" or "good riddance [bon-débarras]." This "liquidation" of the fault may fulfill Jankélévitch's third requirement: it might be a total, unreserved doing-away with the fault. But because it is not founded on any reasons, nor on any relationship to the offender, it too does not satisfy the criteria for true forgiveness.

After Jankélévitch's apophatic procedure, then, what is left of pure forgiveness? The third "pseudo-" category of "liquidation" serves as a bridge of sorts to what Jankélévitch calls pure or hyperbolic forgiveness: If the non-forgiving liquidation of a fault required no reason and no excuse, this, it turns out, is something it shares with true forgiveness, which is an act of grace, bestowed on the offender. Such an act, which is the only kind of forgiveness that could be asked, has no reason. (This is why Jankélévitch can say in his book that while we can speak of the inexcusable, there is no such thing as the unforgivable—a statement that we will come back to.[15]) Jankélévitch goes so far as to term it a *pardon fou*, a mad pardon.[16] It can be effected only

> graciously, gratuitously, for nothing [*pour rien*], not out of magnanimity, nor out of greatness of soul, for in greatness of soul there is something a bit contemptuous, a bit disdainful, and the sentiment that we are so large that the offense can no longer touch us ... but for NOTHING ...[17] or, even better, *because the crime is a crime*.[18]

For Jankélévitch, this hyperbolic, true forgiveness appears "almost ungraspable" and "is not, properly speaking, something that one could truly live."[19] It would thus be an attitude "so hyperbolical, so super-natural, that we can hardly conceive of it and that in most cases, even for this kind of forgiveness, there enter elements that naturalize it. Super-natural pardon is naturalized after all."[20] It is difficult, if not impossible, not to rationalize, to resort to excuses or project positive outcomes toward which forgiveness would be merely a means, in place of forgiving purely, hyperbolically, madly, "for nothing."

Derrida too reflects on the paradox of forgiveness—as he does elsewhere in considering ethical phenomena such as the gift and hospitality—in terms of conditions of possibility and impossibility. Responding to Jankélévitch's meditation on the impossibility of forgiveness, he writes, "We will have to ask ourselves, again and again, what this 'impossible' might mean, and if the possibility of forgiveness, if there is such a thing, is not to be measured against the ordeal [*épreuve*] of the impossible."[21] The kind of thinking-together of possibility and impossibility alluded to here will be familiar to anyone who has followed the trajectory of what have become known as Derrida's "ethical-political" writings, in which the question of whether ethical events are possible is examined from the point of view of their radical difference from models of economic exchange, and in which the affirmation of the possibility of such events—the basis for our striving for them as possibilities—is at the same time grounded in what Derrida calls conditions of impossibility.

If we recall, for instance, Derrida's analysis in *The Gift of Death* of Kierkegaard's meditation on the binding of Isaac in *Fear and Trembling*, what stands out is Derrida's emphasis on the distinction between what Kierkegaard calls the ethical—an action that may be communicated as just, that is, may be justified in public, to a community, or even to oneself, and therefore accords with a responsibility only in a *relative* sense—and what Kierkegaard terms an act of faith, but which he equates with an absurdity, an act of madness, and a scandal: Abraham's heeding of God's command to kill his son is not communicable or justifiable in public, but represents what Derrida calls an *absolute* responsibility or an absolute decision. For Kierkegaard, this kind of act goes beyond ethics understood as something reducible to general, universalizable principles or imperatives. Derrida takes up Kierkegaard's ethics-faith distinction because he believes that it reveals something crucial about the ethical: If heeding God's absolute command means doing something uncommunicable and absolutely secret, then absolute responsibility is, as Derrida puts it, "not a responsibility; at least it is not general responsibility or responsibility in general."[22] For how could we conceive of a duty that would not be defensible or justifiable or even capable of being conveyed to other people? On the other hand, something about the very idea of ethical action would be lost if it did not encompass the idea that it issues from something like an absolute command. This is what Kierkegaard captures with his famous distinction, and what Derrida then calls the "aporia of responsibility," the possibility of the ethical founded in its impossibility. The absolutely ethical action is impossible *as* an ethical action; yet, without this impossibility, it appears that the very notion of ethical action—as a decision taken as if in response to an absolute command—loses its force. It is in this sense that Derrida can evoke, in the lecture "To Forgive," "the possibility of forgiveness" as something that "if there is such a thing" would have to be "be measured against the ordeal of the impossible."[23] Derrida adds the following:

We constantly struggle in the snares of an aporia whose abstract and dry form, whose logical formality is as implacable as it is indisputable: There is only forgiveness, if there is such a thing, of the un-forgivable. Thus forgiveness, if it is possible, if there is such a thing, is not possible, it does not exist as possible, it only exists by exempting itself from the law of the possible, by impossibilizing itself, so to speak, and in the infinite endurance of the im-possible as impossible.[24]

For Derrida, this aporia "enjoins us to try to think the possible and the impossible otherwise, the very history of what one calls the possible and 'power' [i.e., *potentia*—D.H.] in our culture and in culture as philosophy or as knowledge."[25]

When Derrida remarks in "To Forgive" that "this lecture could also have been a lecture on the possible and on the 'im-' that comes in front of it, of an im-possible which is neither negative, nor non-negative, nor dialectical,"[26] we can take this as a restatement, in a different vocabulary, of what Jankélévitch tries to accomplish in his study of forgiveness, in that it attempts to understand the possibility and impossibility of forgiveness as indissociable realities.[27]

## "It Is a Matter Here of Our Problem"

It is not difficult to understand . . . why we have chosen such a subject, which is an old subject of moral theology, discussed since always by Christian and Jewish theologians. But our reasons are not only theological; we have our very own reasons. It is a matter here of our problem [*il s'agit là de notre problème*].
—Vladimir Jankélévitch, "Introduction au thème du pardon"

In his writings on forgiveness Derrida is particularly struck and disturbed by a contrast between the philosophical discourse on forgiveness that makes up the book *Le Pardon* and Jankélévitch's more polemical tone in the essay "Pardonner?" that was his contribution to the French debate about the so-called "imprescriptibility" of the Nazi-era crimes against humanity. "Imprescriptible" is the French legal term for a crime that is not subject to any statute of limitations. If the 1960s were an era of intensified public debate and awareness of the legacy of the Holocaust crimes, an intensification that was partly due to the fact that the Nazi extermination campaigns now lay twenty to twenty-five years in the past, this intensification was also tied to the landmark Eichmann trial (1961–62) and the Frankfurt Auschwitz trial, which began in 1963. A further reason lay in the fact that, as that twenty-year mark approached, the question arose of whether an exception to the statutes of limitations that were in force in countries throughout Europe ought to be sought. In France, as in Germany and throughout Eastern Europe,[28] various legal means were found circa 1964–65 to suspend the existing statutes of limitations for these crimes.

The French law concerning the imprescriptibility of crimes against humanity was enacted in 1964; in Germany, relevant laws were enacted in two stages, in 1965 and in 1969; and there was also a United Nations resolution in 1967 "On the Non-Applicability of Statutory Limitation to War Crimes against Humanity."

As Derrida points out, Jankélévitch's writings on forgiveness come out of these intense preoccupations in the early to mid-1960s with the legal and ethical ramifications of the Nazi-era crimes. They began with a course on forgiveness that Jankélévitch gave in 1962–63 at the Sorbonne,[29] and culminated in the 1967 book *Le Pardon*. Along the way, in 1965, Jankélévitch published, first in *Le Monde* and then in a journal of administrative law, his essay on imprescriptibility, which he titled, simply, "L'Imprescriptible."[30] In 1971 he published an expanded version of this essay under the title "Pardonner?" which has been translated into English as "Should We Pardon Them?"[31] and is discussed, along with the book, by Derrida in "To Forgive." But another station along the way deserves to be highlighted: Jankélévitch's preoccupations with the problem of forgiveness prompted him to take a leading role in organizing the October 1963 meeting of French-speaking Jewish intellectuals, the Colloque des intellectuels juifs de langue française. This annual French-Jewish institution, which was launched in 1957 and continues to thrive to this day, is best known among American readers of French thought as the forum in which Emmanuel Levinas regularly delivered his "Talmudic readings"; these readings became a regular fixture of the Colloques and also form an important corpus in Levinas's published oeuvre.[32] In October 1963, then, Jankélévitch took a leading role in the Colloque (the fifth of its kind), which was devoted to the same theme that had been the focus of his own teaching the previous academic year: forgiveness. His was the very first address at the colloque; its task was to provide a philosophical "Introduction to the Theme of Forgiveness." This address is an extremely important and helpful text, in part because it already contains an account of forgiveness that is very close to the one he would put forward in the 1967 book.

In my preceding account of Jankélévitch's views, I have been drawing interchangeably on the book *Le Pardon* and on the text of this address, since indeed the accounts of forgiveness they offer are very close, but I now want to begin to differentiate them. There is a striking contrast between the 1967 book, which includes the axiom that there are things that are "inexcusable" (in the sense elaborated by Jankélévitch, that is: incapable of being mitigated by means of explanations or arguments), but that no crime is unforgivable, and the polemical essay "Pardonner?" (1965/1971), which states, "Forgiveness died in the death camps." This contrast allows us to hypothesize with Derrida that the polemical message of the latter text, which addressed head-on the problem of forgiveness as what Jankélévitch calls "our" problem (i.e., as an existential historical problem) contradicts that of the book, which at least laid out the conditions for forgiveness, however hyperbolic and "mad." Indeed, as Derrida points out, Jankélévitch himself seems to encourage such a reading in his preface to the expanded 1971 version of the essay, in which he points out that, in its "answer to the question, Must we pardon?" the essay "seems to contradict" his earlier book, which he describes as "a purely philosophical study on *Forgiveness* [*Le Pardon*]."[33] But if we add to these two apparently contradictory texts the address to the 1963 Colloque, which seeks to provide a philosophical introduction to the topic of forgiveness, but is nevertheless, like the polemical essay, written from a "we"-perspective—this time, from the perspective of an explicitly Jewish "we" that is called upon in a particular way to answer the challenge of whether to forgive—then this might help us shed a more differentiated light on the "seeming contradiction" between the philosophical study and the polemical essay. Let me recall again the quote that I placed at the opening of the second part of this essay. It is drawn from Jankélévitch's Colloque address:

> It is not difficult to understand . . . why we have chosen such a subject, which is an old subject of moral theology, discussed since always by Christian and Jewish theologians. But our reasons are not only theological; we have our very own reasons. It is a matter here of *our* problem [*il s'agit là de notre problème*].[34]

Recalling Jankélévitch's criteria for pure forgiveness, and his taxonomy of pseudo-forgiveness, it becomes clear that the idea that forgiving is an act of grace not based on reasons means that the question of whether there can be forgiveness is going to be quite distinct from juridical questions about the prosecution and punishment of war crimes or crimes against humanity. Jankélévitch underscores this point at the Colloque when he states that this third condition of forgiveness, that it be granted totally and without reserve, means that forgiveness is strictly "extra-juridical."[35] Nevertheless, he also follows the opposite intuition, equally familiar to us, that jurisprudence is surely meant to capture and reflect ethical views, in that he closely aligns the problematic of forgiveness with the question of legal prescriptibility. Forgivability and prescriptibility are treated as one and the same problem in the 1965 essay "L'Imprescriptible," and even more so in the 1971 expanded version, "Pardonner?" And in the context of the Colloque, Jankélévitch makes the link between the two issues when he introduces his audience to the first type of pseudo-forgiveness, the appeal to the wearing effects of time:

> The wearing effect of time is not properly speaking an argument in favor of forgiveness, but it is the one most commonly invoked today when we are invited to forgive. You know that the law records the legality, the validity of this kind of forgiveness in the notion of prescription. Thus, it appears that after twenty-five years, after a certain number of years, the unforgivable evil could be forgiven, and the malicious person would cease to be malicious. From this point of view it would be comprehensible, after fifteen years, to bear a grudge against those who burned six million Jews, while twenty years after, this inexpiable crime would become expiable as if by magic.[36]

The phrase in this passage, "when we are invited to forgive," reflects an important aspect of the context in which Jankélévitch is speaking. The Colloque's organizers—among them Jankélévitch, Levinas, and André Neher, another eminent French-Jewish thinker, chose "forgiveness" as the annual theme in response to a pressure they perceived the Jewish community to be under. Levinas (who presided over this particular Colloque as its host, since it was held on the premises of the École Normale Israélite Orientale, of which he was the director) comments on this in his welcoming address. He introduces the annual theme of the Colloque in the name of André Neher, who has unexpectedly been prevented from attending the opening session:

> This theme emerged from an experience on which I don't want to elaborate, which he [Neher] himself lived, in which, precisely believing that everyone would understand him, he observed that we are being reproached for not knowing how to forgive—a reproach about which I shall leave aside the anecdotal aspect, but which arose under rather impressive conditions. It is this that we have chosen as our theme.[37]

As one might well imagine, such a stage-setting, in 1963, for a French-Jewish conference on forgiveness, made for dramatic and powerful conversations among participants well-versed in philosophy and other disciplines, and existentially affected by all the questions that concerned the legacy of the Holocaust—not only the prosecution and jurisprudence of genocidal crimes and war crimes, but also German-French reconciliation and the place of Germany in the postwar order, as well as the matter of German reparations to the victims of Nazism. It is not possible to convey, within the bounds of this essay, all that can be gleaned from the published proceedings about the intensity of these discussions. But reading Jankélévitch's pronouncements on forgiveness in this context gives one, I would argue, a richer sense of the dilemma he finds himself in, and finds himself compelled to perform, when he writes the disclaimer of sorts that he attaches to "Pardonner." Let me quote it now in full:

> In a purely philosophical study on *Forgiveness* that I have published elsewhere, the answer to the question "Must we pardon?" seems to contradict the one given here. Between the absolute of the law of love and the absolute of vicious liberty there is a tear that cannot be entirely sundered. I have not attempted to reconcile the irrationality of evil with the omnipotence of love. Forgiveness is as strong as evil, but evil is as strong as forgiveness.[38]

The tone of this statement reflects, I believe, the very real dilemma in which Jankélévitch and others find themselves. As Jankélévitch writes of hyperbolic forgiveness, it would have to be a *pardon fou*, and an un-livable attitude. Whereas in the book *Le Pardon*, he can nevertheless lay out philosophically the conditions of such a forgiveness, in these shorter works—which are more closely tied to the discursive context I have been highlighting, he expresses the same paradox in more existential terms—in terms that reflect why, in dealing with forgiveness, "It is a matter here of *our* problem."

### "But Have They Ever Asked Us for Forgiveness?"

The contrast or contradiction that Derrida points to between what he calls (picking up on Jankélévitch's own description of his works on forgiveness) the "polemical [*pamphlétaire*]" logic of "L'Imprescriptible"/"Pardonner?" and the logic of hyperbolic ethics reflected in the philosophical book on forgiveness is most strikingly exemplified in Jankélévitch's abrupt exclamation, toward the middle of the essay: "Forgiveness! But have they ever asked us for forgiveness?"[39] This exclamation, which may easily be read as a response to Neher's observation that Levinas said had served as the occasion for the 1963 Colloque, comes after Jankélévitch has stated his opposition to the prescriptibility of crimes against humanity and to a reconciliation that would serve to efface the Nazi atrocities by equating them with the casualties of warfare.[40] Where Jankélévitch's hyperbolical account of pure forgiveness clearly resonates with Derrida's understanding of the possibility and impossibility of ethical decision, this line is a plea and a protest that clearly belongs to a different register. Its tone is one Jankélévitch adopts at several points in his address to the colloque, and if many, including Derrida, have been disturbed by it, this is surely in line with Jankélévitch's intentions in speaking this way. Given Jankélévitch's early insistence that true forgiveness must involve a relationship between the offended and the offender, it is quite startling to find him claiming here, in effect, that *this* Jewish survivor experiences no such relationship as possible with the Germans. His reason for this is simple. It is that *they have no idea*. Commenting in "L'Imprescriptible" on the necessary disproportion between the Nazi crimes and any punishment, Jankélévitch writes

> Strictly speaking, what happened is *inexpiable*. One does not even know any more whom to attack, whom to accuse. Will we accuse those honest bourgeois from the provinces who formerly were officers of the SS? . . . Will we accuse those placid and easygoing German tourists who look so well and must surely have good consciences? They would certainly be astonished to be thus taken to task and would wonder what we could want them for and what it was all about. No one here below has a bad conscience, that is well known. No one is guilty because no one was ever a Nazi; thus the monstrous genocide, a catastrophe in itself like earthquakes, tidal waves, and the eruptions of Vesuvius, is not the fault of anyone. One may as well accuse the devil![41]

And in a similar passage in the Colloque address, Jankélévitch adds an example that hits much closer to home.

> Whom to accuse? One cannot accuse anyone. First of all, because no one was a Nazi, as you know, no one was responsible! And then they show us these young men and women who don't know what is at issue, who would be very surprised if one were to expel them from the Sorbonne, as I often feel like doing.... Indeed, they are so placid ... and all we can do is to perform symbolic, powerless, negative gestures ... or [to adopt] attitudes that are themselves philosophical and symbolic, such as remembering, communing with ourselves, or feeling [*ressentir*].[42]

Where there is no recognition of guilt or evil on the part of the offender, Jankélévitch seems to be saying, how can there be forgiveness? But the problem, as Derrida shows us in "To Forgive," is that Jankélévitch thereby introduces a condition of symmetry and exchange into a relation that was supposed to be gratuitous and asymmetrical. And this is in an obvious tension with Jankélévitch's acknowledgment that such an asymmetry is necessary for forgiveness to take place, that forgiveness must be "for nothing" and merely "because the crime was a crime"—or as Derrida puts it, that "one can only forgive the unforgivable." What I want to suggest, however, is that Jankélévitch's protest that there isn't anyone to accuse or dialogue with can also be read as a further reflection of that necessary asymmetry between the offended and the offender. That is, his protest is itself an extension of his view that one forgives "for nothing" and that one can thus never be assured of an identity between the original crime and what is forgiven, between the perpetrator and the one to be forgiven, or between the victim and the one who forgives. That he does not view this as a reason to fully give oneself over to rancor is reflected in the following lines from the Colloque address. Note that they echo the prefatory disclaimer that he attached to "Pardonner?"

> We see that there is ... an equivalence between the unforgivable and forgiveness, between the evil and the act by which we forget or absolve it, and which has the effect that in the end the one is not stronger than the other, just as the Song of Songs says that love is as strong as death.... The Song of Songs doesn't say that love is stronger than death, it says that it is as strong as death.... [Thus,] There is between love and death an infinite debate ... such that our spirit is perpetually sent from one to the other.[43]

## "Even Though No One in This Hall Has Asked That the Descendants of Our Torturers Be Nailed to the Rocks"

Derrida's insistence, in the work on forgiveness and elsewhere, that responsibility must be absolute, without condition, and that this entails an asymmetry between the doer and the recipient of the deed, is of course closely tied, as he again makes evident in his contribution to this volume, to the approach to ethics developed by Emmanuel Levinas. When we look back at the proceedings of the 1963 Colloque in search of ways to extend or intensify the conversation between Derrida and Jankélévitch on forgiveness, it is therefore also worth looking for signs of a conversation between Jankélévitch and Levinas in that very charged historical context. How does the Levinasian insistence on asymmetry play out when confronted with Jankélévitch's insistence that a dialogue with the perpetrator, initiated by the perpetrator, is needed?

Besides presiding over the Colloque as its host, Levinas also delivered there one of his best-known Talmudic readings, "Envers autrui" ("Toward the Other"), which is also discussed by Derrida in "Avowing—The Impossible." This is a rich and complex text, and I cannot do more here than point to one strand of what Levinas does there that appears to me particularly pertinent to the Jankélévitch-Derrida conversation that is my focus. In doing so, my aim is not only to contribute to the contemporary discussions of Levinas's Talmudic readings—which grow out of an ongoing recognition that to study his philosophy requires exploring the passages between the body of work he designated as his "philosophical" texts and those writings of a more occasional nature that were originally presented in public Jewish contexts, and which he called "confessional"—but also to do so in a way that recognizes that interpretations of such texts, particularly the Talmudic readings delivered at the annual Colloques, benefit greatly from reading them in conjunction with what we can glean of their specific discursive contexts.[44]

I thus want to begin by returning to Levinas's words of welcome to the Colloque. Immediately after the remark I quoted earlier about André Neher and the thinking that inspired the choice of forgiveness as a theme, Levinas adds:

> But intellectuals are people who are sincere, the only ones who ought to tell the truth, and we thought . . . Monsieur Neher thought . . . I am always reduced to doing commentary on other people's thought . . . Monsieur Neher thought that the theme of forgiveness that one ought to bestow or not to bestow cannot be posed unless, at the same time, one asks oneself whether it can be bestowed on us, whether we are not also, to a certain degree, responsible.[45]

And Levinas goes on to announce that the second part of the Colloque is going to be devoted to this self-critique, and in particular to the relationship between Jews and non-Jews. In line with this theme, in the main part of "Toward the Other," Levinas examines a passage from Tractate Yoma that sheds light on what is required, in the case of offenses against others and against God, for repentance [teshuvah] to take place and for the offenses to be forgiven. Having completed his reading,[46] he adds a coda of sorts. Its starting point is a biblical story, and Levinas expresses his hope that by recalling this story he might be able to link up to that aspect of the Colloque which he here calls its "principal theme": "the problems confronting us regarding our relations with the Germans and Germany."[47] The story, from 2 Samuel 21, is of a famine that hit the kingdom of David, which, David is told by God, is due to the "bloodguilt on Saul and because he put the Gibeonites to death." This goes back to the story of the Gibeonites told in Chapter 9 of Joshua, in which the Gibeonites enter into an alliance with the Israelites, but under false pretenses: They claim to be a tribe that has journeyed from far away to meet and make peace with the Israelites, rather than being a neighboring tribe, residing in Canaan. They are thus spared, and when the ruse is discovered, their oath of allegiance continues to be honored, but they are reduced to the status of woodcutters and water carriers for the people of Israel. In 2 Samuel 21, David declares that "the Gibeonites are not of the people of Israel," and we learn that "although the people of Israel had sworn to spare [the Gibeonites], Saul had tried to wipe them out in his zeal for the people of Israel and Judah." When David asks the Gibeonites how this ancestral wrong can be expiated or atoned for, they renounce any claim to material compensation ("It is not a matter of silver or gold between us and Saul or his house") or any demand for a blood vengeance that would extend to all of Israel ("neither is it for us to put anyone to death in Israel"). Instead, they make a specific demand for vengeance, which David grants:

> The man who consumed us and planned to destroy us, so that we should have no place in all the territory of Israel—let seven of his sons be handed over to us, and we will impale them before the Lord at Gibeon on the mountain of the Lord. (2 Sam. 21:5–6)

Now, in his discussion of this story, Levinas moves to a Talmudic interpretation it receives, in Tractate Yevamot. The interpretation is given in the context of a discussion of intermarriage laws. According to interpretative tradition, the Gibeonites are accorded the legal status of *netinim*, allied with Israel, members of the congregation, but prohibited from intermarriage with the congregation. Within this discussion, the rabbis are led to examine the origins of this special status between total outsider or enemy and full member of the people of Israel, partly by reading the story of vengeance in Samuel. To the objection, drawn from Deuteronomy 24, that children ought not to be punished for the faults of their parents, one of the rabbis replies: "It is better that a letter be rooted out of the Torah than that the divine name shall be publicly profaned."[48] Levinas draws out the lesson to be learned from this line as follows:

> To punish children for the faults of their parents is less dreadful than to tolerate impunity when the stranger/foreigner is injured. Let passersby know this: in Israel, princes die a horrible death because strangers were injured by the sovereign. The respect for the stranger and the sanctification of the name of the Eternal are strangely equivalent. And all the rest is a dead letter. All the rest is literature. The search for the spirit beyond the letter, that is Judaism itself. We did not wait until the Gospels for that.[49]

The passage in Yevamot also gives a supplementary explanation for David's declaration that the Gibeonites are foreigners, that they do not belong to the people of Israel. It has David saying to the Gibeonites: "This nation [Israel] is distinguished by three characteristics: They are merciful, bashful, and benevolent. . . . Only he who cultivates these three characteristics is fit to join this nation." That is, rather than having the right to vengeance accorded to them because of their status as foreign (and, more particularly, as allied foreigners), the Gibeonites now, as Levinas puts it, "excluded *themselves* from Israel" *because* they sought revenge.

Here is how Levinas pinpoints the significance of this story for the theme of the Colloque:

> I have the impression that I have come back to the theme evoked by Monsieur Janké-lévitch when he opened this *colloque*, even though no one in this hall has asked that the descendants of our torturers be nailed to the rocks. The Talmud teaches that one cannot oblige men who demand retaliatory justice [or "law of talion"; *justice du talion*] to grant forgiveness. It teaches us that Israel does not deny this imprescriptible right to others. But it teaches us above all that if Israel recognizes this right, it does not ask it for itself and that to be of Israel [*être d'Israël*] is to not claim it.[50]

Can we read this conclusion as an answer to the question Levinas posed in his welcoming remarks: whether the Jews are responsible for forgiveness? The hierarchy of virtues given by the story, as told by Levinas, drawing on a combination of the biblical and the Talmudic sources, is at the same time an assertion or reassertion of what exactly separates Israel from the Gibeonites. In order to repair the relationship with the Gibeonites, the distinction between Israel and them must be reasserted and clarified, along with the hierarchical relationship between the right to revenge and the renunciation of that right in favor of forgiveness.[51] We are in the midst of the difficult problematic of election, as it is also evoked by Derrida in "Avowing—The Impossible." If the Jews now are in the same position vis-à-vis the Germans as were the Gibeonites to the people of Israel, then Levinas wants to see today's Jews as called upon to renounce the right to vengeance, *in their being Jews*. The dilemma, then, between unconditional, hyperbolic forgiveness, and a forgiveness that is contingent upon gestures of appeasement, expiation, or repentance on the part of the one to be forgiven, turns into a dilemma between the particularism and universalism of "being of Israel."

Though Derrida does not discuss Levinas's "Toward the Other" or Jankélévitch's discussions of forgiveness within the context of the Colloque of 1963, he does, in "Avowing—The Impossible," make the following note connecting "living together" (the Colloque's theme in 1998) and "forgiveness":

> I know that there has been here, in the past, a great conference on forgiveness. What would have changed in the world concerning the scene of forgiveness, since that time,

thirty years ago, in the time, that is, of one generation? What is new concerning forgiveness and concerning what the scene of forgiveness implies and engages of a "living together"? ("Avowing," 19; "Avouer," 182–83)

The Colloque of 1963 is long past; today's ethical-political challenges are other ones,
though they are, as Derrida also made clear, framed and confronted in ways that would be
unthinkable without the varied trajectories of coming to terms with the Holocaust. In
"Avowing—The Impossible," Derrida cites part of Levinas's concluding observations to
his interpretation of the story of the Gibeonites in "Toward the Other," some of which I
already cited above.

> The respect for the stranger and the sanctification of the name of the Eternal are
> strangely equivalent. And all the rest is a dead letter. All the rest is literature.... The
> image of God is better honored in the right given to the stranger than in symbols.
> Universalism ... bursts the letter apart, for it lay, explosive, within the letter.[52]

Derrida cites these lines because they bespeak "the bond between Jewish universalism
and the respect of the stranger." At the same time, as he has done elsewhere in discussing
the experience of Jewishness, Derrida calls for a "vigilance ... against all the risks of the
'living together' of the Jews," which he links to "the motifs of filiation through blood, appropriation of the place and the motif of election"—a "concern [that] was and remains with
me without complacency and sometimes without pity" ("Avowing," 29; "Avouer," 197–98).[53]
And yet, the motif of election is also an enabling one for Derrida, one that provides a
glimpse of a forgiveness that must indeed be avowed as necessary:

> Since I will never feel justified in renouncing the necessity of a forgiveness condi-
> tioned upon repentance, nor in renouncing the demand without demand [*exigence
> sans exigence*], and without duty, and without debt, of unconditional forgiveness that
> gives its sense to any pure thought of forgiveness, the only responsibility I cannot es-
> cape is to declare to the other this dilemma; it is to take the initiative, as I do here, of
> this declaration and to commit myself to drawing its juridical, ethical, political, and
> historical consequences. By reason of what I have just said, I must do so *alone* and
> even if I am the only one to take this initiative, without expecting reciprocity, alone
> and there where I am irreplaceable in this responsibility. It is thus that I understand
> or accept the concept of election, there where being chosen, well beyond any privi-
> lege of birth, nation, people or community, signifies that no one can replace me at the
> site of this decision and of this responsibility. ("Avowing," 37; "Avouer," 210)

If we take seriously this appropriation and mobilization by Derrida of the concept of election, then it would not be anachronistic, across the span of forty years, to express the hope

that Levinas's conclusion that the Talmud teaches that "to be of Israel" is to not claim the right to revenge can be heard not as a particularist assertion of the Jew over the non-Jew, but in terms of the ethical dilemmas of election: The oscillation—one that Jankélévitch also performs and defends—between unconditional forgiveness and forgiveness contingent on repentance leaves one only with the inescapability of responsibility, with the obligation to affirm it and take it on as both universally commanded and, in Derrida's words, "even if I am alone . . . without expecting reciprocity."

# To Live, by Grace

*William Robert*

*Living together begins with grace.*

Jacques Derrida affirms that living together begins with grace by beginning his essay "Avowing—The Impossible" with "*grâce*." As he writes, "first word, *grâce*, second word, *grâce* . . . in order to avow while asking for *grâce*"—asking for, desiring, calling or even begging for "*grâce*," and doing so "before even starting [*avant même de commencer*]" ("Avowing," 18).[1] His text opens with an avowal of these two words of "*grâce*" and the risk that this invocation or provocation entails.

Before the beginning, then, there is risk, which includes the possibility that this pre-preliminary petition for "*grâce*" might go without response or might not receive the "*grâce*" requested. Any act of address involves this risk, since address always involves self-exposure and self-sending, even self-dissemination, with no promise of return. Address remains a particularly risky endeavor in this case of "*grâce*," which performs in multiple registers at once. One might even, or therefore, say that "*grâce*" overperforms, that its performance overflows and surpasses any regular or regulatory conception of performativity, for this invocatory "*grâce*" opens and affirms, avows and requests, gives and saves, blesses and welcomes—all at once, even before the beginning.

By commencing with "*grâce, oui, grâce,*" followed by "*oui,*" Derrida's text opens with "*grâce, oui*" twice, so that "*oui*" is the second word, twice following and affirming "*grâce*" in a quasi repetition. "*Oui*" appears twice, before the beginning, as what Derrida calls "the opening *and* the cut [*l'ouverture* et *la coupure*]" that "institutes and opens . . . exceeds and incises" his text as well as the possibility of performativity.[2] "*Oui*" does so, according to Derrida, as a preontological and "transcendental [or quasi-transcendental] condition of all performative dimensions," which means that "any event brought about by a performative mark, any writing in the widest sense of the word, involves a *yes*, whether this is phenomenalized or not, that is, verbalized or adverbalized as

153

such."³ Hence "*oui*" is implicated in any performative scene, such as address, as what engenders the possibility of performativity.

Though "*oui*" is never present "as such," this arche-originary, quasi-transcendental nevertheless, Derrida writes, "opens the eventness of every event [*ouvre l'événementialité de tout événement*]," though "it is not itself an event."⁴ An event names that which comes very quickly and always unexpectedly, which is why Derrida suggests that "an event implies surprise, exposure, the unanticipatable" and is "by definition an absolute exception, even grace maybe [*peut-être la grâce*]."⁵ An event arrives unforeseeably, as an eruption of the impossible in the possible. An event is, in short, when the impossible happens. "*Oui*" opens the way for this impossible eruption, as the condition of the unconditional, but as second: "*oui*" is not the first but the second word, twice, in Derrida's doubled invocation "*grâce, oui.*" Though "*oui*" conditions performativity from before the beginning, before language and even before being, "*oui*" only ever appears second—and twice, since according to Derrida "*oui*" "begins by responding," by addressing an other and asking this other to say "*oui*" in response—asking, that is, "only for another *yes*, the *yes* of an other," thanks to which "*oui*" becomes "*oui . . . oui.*"⁶

Derrida deploys this "*oui . . . oui*" at the beginning of his text, punctuating it with "*grâce . . . grâce,*" so that "*grâce*" and "*oui*" call and respond to each other, twice. "*Grâce*" and "*oui*" responsively avow and affirm each other, twice, at and as the incisive opening of Derrida's text. This points already to "*grâce*" as avowal and request: "*grâce*" avows "*oui*" as well as itself in its affirming, responsive, double re-call, and in doing so, avows the possibility of testimony. "*Grâce*" becomes itself testimony, for Derrida risks two words of "*grâce*" (and two affirmations of "*oui*") "in order to attest to my gratitude, indeed, but also in order to avow while asking for [*demandant*] grâce" ("Avowing," 18; "Avouer," 181). His calls and re-calls for "*grâce*" at once avow and request "*grâce,*" addressing an other and asking this other to avow, to say "*oui*" to "*grâce.*" In responsively avowing "*grâce,*" this other would render "*grâce*" performatively as Derrida does when he writes, "I would like to render *grâce*, therefore, and also to ask for your *grâce* [*grâce, donc, je voudrais rendre, et grâce demander*]" ("Avowing," 18, translation slightly modified; "Avouer," 181). He renders "*grâce*" as thanks and requests "*grâce*" as pardon: pardon from any other whom his text addresses.

His rendering-request solicits pardon on behalf of or in the place of his text—and does so in advance, for (in his words) "what I will soon avow" ("Avowing," 18; "Avouer," 181). He begs for pardon ahead of time, asking an other whom his text addresses for an anachronistic decision and gift of forgiveness. In doing so, he asks this other to do the impossible. To decide (especially beforehand) can never be an active matter of self-mastery but is instead a passive experience of alterity that one undergoes and through which a decision of an other arrives. This is why, for Derrida, "my decision can never be mine; it is always the other's decision in me," and this decision "should tear . . . should disrupt the fabric of the possible."⁷ Any decision thus remains impossible, but a decision to performatively grant pardon, as in "I forgive" addressed to an other, is doubly impossible since, as

Derrida succinctly states, "forgiving is impossible [*le pardon est impossible*]."[8] Pardon would become possible only as impossible: only in forgiving the unforgivable. Pardon, if it takes place, takes place extraordinarily, as an absolute and unforeseeable exception that arrives, according to Derrida, "*as* the coming of the impossible, where a 'perhaps [*peut-être*]' deprives us of all assurance and leaves the future to the future [*laisse l'avenir à l'avenir*]."[9] This "perhaps [*peut-être*]," allied to "*oui*," reiterates that the impossible remains unpredictable and that the coming of the impossible, as an event, *might* or *might not* happen, remaining "perhaps" to come (*à-venir*) in the unforeseeable future (*l'avenir*). Pardon would thus be one name (or nickname) of the impossible, because for forgiveness to happen, the impossible would have to become possible, as an event. The same would hold for avowal; Derrida affirms in writing that "an avowal, if there is such, must avow the unavowable . . . and therefore do the impossible [*l'aveu, s'il y en a, doit avouer l'inavouable . . . et donc faire l'impossible*]" ("Avowing," 19; "Avouer," 182).[10]

Giving (already implied in forgiving) would be another instance of doing the impossible, since a gift must come by surprise, from an other, not as part of an economic exchange and not with any expectation or even hope of return. A gift must never present itself as such, making it what Derrida calls "the very figure of the impossible," yet he insists that "the impossible must be done. The event, if there is one, consists in doing the impossible [*il faut faire l'impossible. L'événement, s'il y en a, consiste à faire l'impossible*]."[11] Though the gift figures the impossible, one must nevertheless give—and give in the face of its very impossibility, beyond calculation or condition.

Derrida gives "*grâce*" in a polyperformative rendering-request that renders "*grâce*" as a gift of thanks and requests "*grâce*" as a gift of pardon, indulgence, even mercy. He requests "*grâce*" as a gift that saves, for an offering of mercy offers clemency that protects and keeps safe. Such saving "*grâce*" arrives idiomatically, by way of "*grâce à*," or "thanks to": saving thanks to "*grâce*," which gives safety "*grâce à*" or via *sauf* (save, safe, unscathed). An eventful donation of "*grâce*" might, in a Christian idiom, include the gift of salvation, which in this context represents the gift that exceeds all other gifts since it grants ultimate safety as well as eternal life. Thus, "*grâce*" can give a life-saving gift, as it does in an Abrahamic idiom, particularly one definitively marked by the *Akedah*. In this scene of near-sacrifice, "*grâce*" names a double gift that saves twice, saving Isaac's life and saving Abraham from killing his son. The angelic double call to Abraham on Mount Moriah gives (however impossibly) "*grâce*" as a gift of *sauf*, which keeps Isaac unscathed and his life safe.[12]

In view of this Abrahamic event of "*grâce*," it is not surprising that *sauf* refers more broadly to religion. Indeed, Derrida links *sauf* to the two sources of religion, which he identifies as sacrality and faith. By giving safety, *sauf* keeps someone or something safe and sound by marking it as set apart, distinct, special, extraordinary—in other words, sacred. In addition, Derrida asserts, "the word '*sauf*' leads back to the origin of faith and religion itself."[13] Hence religion bears two genealogies, two sources, and two names: *sauf* and *foi*.

These two source names come together in the gift of testimony, which, according to Derrida, reveals "*a* convergence of *these* two sources: the *unscathed* (the safe, the sacred or the saintly) and the *fiduciary* (trustworthiness, fidelity, credit, belief or faith)."[14] This confluence takes place in any experience of testimony as well as any scene of performativity, any address, any attestation or avowal, such as Derrida's invocatory avowal-affirmation, "*grâce, oui, grâce*," which, as a performative (in this case, a polyperformative), pledges faith and asks an other for a pledge of faith. This pledge calls for incredible faith, of the sort required by a miracle, for in this performative scene, Derrida asks an other "to believe the other that I am" and "'to believe what I say as one believes in a miracle.'"[15] A miracle is, after all, an event par excellence; a miracle is one name for the impossible becoming possible and a call to believe in the unbelievable. Only belief in a miracle, then, would be belief; as Derrida writes, "To believe should then lie and reside only in this impossible faith in the impossible. Then one could believe only in miracles [*Alors on ne pourrait croire qu'au miracle*]. And to believe *would be* the miracle, the magical power of the miracle. The miracle would be the ordinary of belief."[16] As a name, faith would remain *sauf*, in reserve, saving itself only to refer to miracles. The name "faith" would, in this way, become sacred.

Faith, like "*grâce*," would become a benediction, a *benedictum*, a *bien dire*, that grants "*grâce*" as blessing, since to bless extends a gift marked by *sauf* and "*grâce*." Derrida's "*grâce, oui, grâce*" thus opens his text with a blessing, an offering of benediction in the form of a prayer, which (like any address) depends upon a pledge of faith. His text begins with a benediction that blesses and welcomes its addressee, no matter whom. The double "*grâce, oui*" affirms Derrida's avowal: "Let us say *yes to who or what arrives*, before any determination, before any anticipation, before any *identification*, whether it be or not be a question of a foreigner, an immigrant, an invited guest or an unexpected visitor, whether the arrival be or not be the citizen of another country, a human, animal, or divine being, living or dead, male or female [*disons, oui, à l'arrivant, avant toute détermination, avant toute anticipation, avant toute* identification, *qu'il s'agisse ou non d'un étranger, d'un immigré, d'un invité ou d'un visiteur inopiné, que l'arrivant soit ou non le citoyen d'un autre pays, un être humain, animal, ou divin, un vivant ou un mort, masculin ou féminin*]."[17] This Derrida does in offering, "before even starting," an affirming gift and welcoming avowal of "*grâce, oui, grâce*," to whomever his text addresses. Derrida thus does the impossible by granting hospitality to one or ones who, like an event, arrive unforeseeably and without warning—and, like an event, whose arrival calls for a response, in this case a giving and forgiving under the sign of "welcome."

"*Grâce, oui, grâce*" announces and enacts this welcome as an offering of hospitality, which is a performance that avows, or an avowal that performs, the impossible. Hospitality enmeshes and intermingles all of these calls and responses, by way of "*grâce*," to do the impossible in the face of the impossible: to open, to affirm, to avow, to give, to save, to bless, to respond, to take responsibility, to welcome . . . the list is necessarily endless and incalculable. In giving the gift of hospitality, then, one impossibly recalls and responds to all of these performative invocations and provocations in *"grâce, oui, grâce."*

*Living together takes place by grace.*

"Living together [*vivre ensemble*]" depends on the hospitality extended in the name of *"grâce"*—a hospitality exceeding any conditions that might be inscribed in a pact, a law, or a right. Hospitality, as an event of *"grâce,"* must remain unconditional; it must entail a willingness to exceed bounds, to cross thresholds, and to welcome an *arrivant*, no matter whom or what. Such absolute hospitality requires, Derrida writes, "that I give . . . to the absolute, unknown, anonymous other, and that I *give place* to him, that I let him come, that I let him arrive, and take place in the place I offer him, without asking of him either reciprocity (entry into a pact) or even his name [*que je donne . . . à l'autre absolu, inconnu, anonyme, et que je lui donne lieu, que je le laisse venir, que je le laisse arriver, et avoir lieu dans le lieu que je lui offre, sans lui demander ni réciprocité (l'entrée dans un pacte) ni même son nom*]."[18] Absolute hospitality calls for this response that transgresses limits to make room for an *arrivant* who, like the impossible, happens to arrive. Hospitality would performatively begin with an instantaneous affirmation, *"oui,"* and a welcoming word of *"grâce,"* however (and especially when) impossible, for hospitality means, according to Derrida, "to let oneself be overtaken [*surprendre*]" by anyone who shows up, thereby partaking of what Derrida calls "the madness *of* hospitality" (madness naming a different kind of transgressing limits).[19]

Any *arrivant* calls for this same excessive hospitality, this welcoming avowal and affirmation (*"grâce, oui, grâce"*) granted to any other who arrives. One must, then, follow the example of Abraham and offer the same unrestrained and unreasonable welcome to any other who unexpectedly comes, whether human or divine (or something else), known or unknown. Abraham welcomes any *arrivant*, no matter whom or what, avowing in his acts Derrida's contention that "every other (one) is every (bit) other [*tout autre est tout autre*]," which implies that any other is as other as God (the name of the wholly other) would be and therefore that "God, as wholly other, is to be found everywhere there is something of the wholly other," so that "what can be said about the relation of Abraham to God can be said of my relation without relation to *every other (one) as every (bit) other* [tout autre comme tout autre]."[20] Hence, any gift of hospitality is marked by the Abrahamic and the mode of radical hospitality that it entails.

Nevertheless, any gift of hospitality remains just that: a gift—which is to say, impossible, yet taking place singularly. Hospitality of this kind can never be acculturated, routinized to the point of expectation, for this would deny its eventful character. Hospitality must remain impossible, called for by an unexpected and unexpectable *arrivant* who catches one off guard, unprepared or unavailable. With each call of hospitality and affirmative response to this call, both each time unique, the impossible takes place without condition or reservation—or regularization. Granting hospitality (particularly to the unwelcomable) must, like avowing the unavowable or pardoning the unpardonable, remain (perhaps thanks to *sauf*) an instance of doing the impossible as an avowing and affirming response to a disruptive, unanticipatable event—and, Derrida avers, "one must do the impossible [*il faut faire l'impossible*]."[21]

This would be the impossible possibility, the chance and the risk, of "living together [*vivre ensemble*]." In other words, "living together [*vivre ensemble*]" requires doing the impossible—more than once.

But to do the impossible remains and must remain impossible. It can take place only as impossible, arriving as an event that one avows and affirms, particularly since one can avow only the unavowable. "Living together [*vivre ensemble*]" would thus stand as another name for the event—if there is such [*s'il y en a*]. This relational nexus of "living together [*vivre ensemble*]" and the event figures the hinge of Derrida's text, which he affirms in writing: "It is of this relation between the event and the 'living together [*vivre ensemble*]' that I would like to speak," namely, "on what can 'occur [*arriver*]' with respect to the 'living together [*vivre ensemble*],' on what can occur to the 'living together [*vivre ensemble*]' and on a certain relation of the arrival, the coming or the event, to the 'living together [*vivre ensemble*]'" ("Avowing," 22; "Avouer," 187).[22] (To speak about this relation would involve addressing "living together [*vivre ensemble*]" *as if* it were possible, *as if* all of its preconditions were possible, *as if* one could do the impossible. Speaking about this relation would proceed by way of this *as if*, which might be one reason that Derrida enframes "living together [*vivre ensemble*]" with quotation marks throughout his text.)

Whatever can "occur [*arriver*]" via "living together [*vivre ensemble*]" occurs through life. "Living together [*vivre ensemble*]" is an event of life; even better, "living together [*vivre ensemble*]" is a matter (and manner) of living. This makes it a matter of "*grâce*," for on Derrida's account, "grace grants life for life [*la grâce accorde la vie pour la vie*]."[23] "*Grâce*"—"*grâce, oui, grâce*"—performatively opens and affirms, avows and requests, gives and saves, blesses and welcomes life, and life traces its genealogy to "*grâce*." Life begins with "*grâce*" and begins again with "*oui*," which affirms life in affirming "*grâce*" before the beginning. "*Grâce, oui, grâce*" avows and affirms life in advance, ahead of time.

Hence life takes place already ("before even starting") in "*grâce*"—"yes, life [*oui, la vie*]," Derrida writes, "from the first syllable. The first syllable is literally *alive* [*en vie*]," and "life is kept alive [*en vie*], beginning again from one word, one syllable to the next."[24] Derrida goes on, citing Hélène Cixous's "*je vis des lettres*" (whose translations might include "I live letters" or "I live on letters") to reiterate that every word, every syllable and letter, performs a "*oui*" that reaffirms life, that repeats the gift of life and, in doing so, keeps life alive.[25] Language revives life with every syllable, every letter, so that life lives on (though it remains untranslatable). This reviving gift, moreover, is already given and given again, twice, in the double "*grâce, oui*" that commences Derrida's text even before commencing. "*Grâce*" gives life so that life might live and live on, so (in Derrida's words) "that life should live, oh, that the living of life . . . in all times and tenses *might* live, that life may live for life [*que vive la vie, vivement que* puisse *vivre le vivre de la vie . . . sous tous les temps, que vive la vie pour la vie].*"[26] Given that "grace grants life for life" so "that life may live for life," one might risk avowing and affirming that "*grâce*" is for life: *grâce, c'est pour la vie.*

What *for*? What is the force or might of this *for* (*pour*)? It conditions the meaning of life, so that life would remain unthinkable before and without *for*. Life, in the phrase "it is *for* life [*c'est pour la vie*]," must be approached and thought by way of *for*, rather than the reverse. As Derrida writes, "The world 'life [*vie*]' would not be thinkable in its meaning . . . before what, grammatically, gives itself as a preposition, namely, 'for [*pour*].'"[27] In giving itself, *for* also grants the way through which "*grâce*" grants life, which means that life must pass by way of *for*—and not only life, but anything, since *for* makes way for everything that might pass into existence.

This *for* owes to its genealogy, tracing its lineage to *pro*, a Latin preposition that can mean "for," "before," "in front" or "in place of," "by virtue of." These potential meanings give *for* transitive as well as matrixial, even originary, features (thereby granting *for* a kinship with ℵ and *khōra*, which engender place). According to Derrida, "this 'for,' this *pro-* would become the prolegomenon of everything, it would be said [or would say itself] before any *logos*, it goes in all directions, that of finality or of destination, of gift, of donation and of dativity, but also of substitution and of replacement. . . . Absolutely preliminary, the *pro* of *for* thus pronames and prenames everything [*ce 'pour,' ce* pro- *deviendrait le prolégomène de tout, il se dirait avant tout* logos, *il va dans toutes les directions, celle de la finalité ou de la destination, du don, de la donation et de la dativité, mais aussi de la substitution et du remplacement. . . . Préalable absolu, le* pro *de* pour *pronomme ainsi et prénomme tout*]."[28] *For*, then, also relates to "*oui*" as what comes before and makes possible any performativity, any language, any naming, any being. Like "*oui*," *for* arrives before the beginning, preceding and proceeding from everything by pronaming and prenaming everything. *For* performs the act of giving names in advance, ahead of time. As Derrida asserts, "Everything happens on the side of 'for' [*tout se passe du côté de 'pour'*]."[29]

Like "*oui*," *for* also operates in every performative scene, as the threshold through which every possibility of performativity passes in its teleological transitivity, crossing from one to an other: from addresser to addressee, from giver to receiver, and so on. *For* designates a passage through which performativity moves, conditioning any possibility of taking place and of taking the place of any emplacement or replacement. Derrida's avowed hypothesis thus becomes what this passage, in all of its excessive surplus, passes in the "life" of "for life" by way of *for*, thus reiterating that "'for' conditions the meaning [*sens*] of 'life.'"[30] If "*grâce* grants life for life" before the beginning, and *for* stands as "the prolegomenon of everything," then *for* comes even before "before the beginning"; it precedes, makes way for, and gives birth to life, so that *for* is always (already) *for* life.

To be *for* life means, among other things, to side with life, to take and to stand on the side of life. Taking sides in this way would seem to require plurality in the possibility of taking one of two or more sides, but such is not the case with life. Life is a singular side without an other. Life, Derrida repeatedly insists, "has no other, it has no other side" which means that "there is no other side than this side, the side of life [*il n'y a pas d'autre côté que ce côté-ci, le côté de la vie*]" and, therefore, that "there is no side for nonlife."[31] Life is the only side. It remains, Derrida continues, "a unique side without another side, and this would be life itself . . . this unique side, this unilaterality is *of life for life*, life itself, life promised to life [*de la vie pour la vie, la vie même, la vie promise à la vie*]."[32] There is only the side of life *for* life.

Death, therefore, is no side and has no side. Death is a nonside. But this does not amount to a denial of death—far from it. It amounts instead to a confounding of traditional oppositions that set life and death as binary poles, on opposite sides, symmetrically siding against each other. Often in such a configuration, death becomes life's negative, defined by a lack of life: Life is something, and death is nothing, nothing but a lack. Phrased in ontological terms, life is being, and death is nonbeing. Derrida's suggestion displaces this kind of binary, oppositional structure based on plenitude and lack, with each taking a side. If life remains a side without an other, if life is the only side, then death (as a nonside) must be on the side of life. Life and death, then, are on the same side, so that even death must in this way be *for* life. Furthermore, if life and death stand on the same side, they become no longer opposed or even opposable but undecidable—and, Derrida avers, "Because it is undecidable, one can decide and settle only *for* life."[33]

If life and death remain undecidable, so do finitude and infinitude. They, too, must both reside on the side of life as the only side. Thus, Derrida writes, "Life, which is undecidable, is also, in its very finitude, infinite. What has only one side—a single edge without an opposite edge—is in-finite [*in-fini*]. Finite because it has an edge on one side, but infinite because it has no opposable edge."[34] *For* life, then, is bounded and boundless, limited and unlimitable, as in-finite, with the infinite impossibly within the finite. The finite and the infinite are on the same side, just as the possible and the impossible are, with the latter conditioning and making way *for* the former. Like the possible and the impossible, the finite and the infinite are not opposed but dwell on one side (*côté*), next to (*à côté de*) each other. But their cohabitation on the side *for* life does not efface death and mortality in a wish for immortality or eternal life. Instead, it shifts the possibilities of immortality or eternity so that, in Derrida's words, "there is neither immortality nor eternity in the old sense of these words—unless [*sauf si*] the unharmed [*sauf*] being, the spared [*sauve*] and thus pardoned [*graciée*] life, in its finite moment of life, deserves to be called immortality or eternity, in the grace of the finite instant."[35] Derrida thus redefines immortality and eternity, via the infinite, in terms of *sauf* and "*grâce*," so that eventfully granting these gifts within life gives gifts of life, gifts *for* life.

Every reiteration of "*oui*" that affirms "*grâce*," which gives life *for* life, avows and affirms this commitment *for* life, one that is (in Derrida's words) "a commitment of life to life and unto death, whether it will be life or death [*un engagement de la vie à la vie à la mort, si ce sera la vie ou la mort*]."[36] Because they are both *for* life on the side of life, life and death here remain undecidable, in a space of "life death." Like the possible and the impossible, like the finite and the infinite, life and death fall on the same side and co-implicate each other, so that any experience of one is engendered thanks to the other. Because no *for* life can decide or disentangle life and death, living and dying, living and the living cannot shield themselves from dying and the dead. All of the possibilities of the event and the *arrivant* entail avowing and affirming whoever or whatever arrives or returns, alive or dead, with unconditional hospitality, since "*tout autre est tout autre.*" Consequently, any experience of or possibility of living—and, therefore, of "living together [*vivre ensemble*]"—must include living with others, alive or dead. One can and one must "live together" with the dead, *for* life and on the side of life, as a condition of the possibility of living. Indeed, Derrida attests, "'Living together' [*vivre ensemble*] with the dead, is not an accident, a miracle, or an extraordinary story [*histoire*]. It is rather an essential possibility of existence," particularly since an experience of the impossible engenders any possible experience ("Avowing," 20; "Avouer," 184).

Living and thus "living together [*vivre ensemble*]" with the dead take place on the side of life thanks to *tekhnē*. *Tekhnē* names a practice, a "doing," that brings together performativity and repetition, the unique and the recurring, what arrives and what returns, commencement and recommencement. *Tekhnē* thus reaffirms Derrida's axiomatic avowal, "no to-come without heritage and the possibility of *repeating*. No to-come without some sort of *iterability* . . . and *confirmation* of the originary *yes*. No to-come without some sort of messianic memory and promise, of a messianicity older than all religion, more originary than all messianism. No discourse or address of the other without the possibility of an elementary promise. . . . No promise, therefore, without the promise of a confirmation of the *yes*."[37] *Tekhnē* binds the possibility of the unforeseeble spontaneity of life and the event to the possibility of repetition and automation—the possibility to come (*à-venir*) of an *arrivant* and the possibility of return in a *revenant*. In doing so, *tekhnē* binds the unscathed and the fiduciary, *sauf* and *foi*, as the two sources of religion.

*Tekhnē* also binds life and death, the living and the dead, which "live together" on the side of life thanks to a bond between life and *tekhnē*. This bond includes iterability, address, faith, and performativity (along with *oikos* and *oikonomia*) according to a risk and a chance: the risk and chance of life *for* life, which open the risk and chance of "living together [*vivre ensemble*]." *Tekhnē* offers both the possibility and impossibility of "living together [*vivre ensemble*]" via the "*grâce*" of faith, which itself conditions every performative scene of address, every possibility of reiteration, and thus every chance for community as "living together [*vivre ensemble*]," with no matter whom or what. This faith is implied in "*oui*" as affirmation, serving as what Derrida names "the testimonial pledge of every performative" that calls for faith *as if* in a miracle to allow for the possibility of "*oui*" as reaffirmation, reavowal, reiteration.[38] Both faith and the future, as the copossibilities of an *arrivant* and a response, depend on *tekhnē* as itself, according to Derrida, "the possibility, one can also say the chance, of faith. And this chance must include in it the greatest risk

161

*[la possibilité, on peut aussi dire la chance, de la foi. Et cette chance doit inclure en elle le plus grand risque].*"[39]

That risk is, for life, death as mortal finitude and, for "living together [*vivre ensemble*]," what Derrida identifies as a "death-drive that is silently at work in every community . . . constituting it as such in its iterability, its heritage, its spectral tradition."[40] *Tekhnē* bears an affinity with death as the impossible condition of possibility for life and for "living together [*vivre ensemble*]." Though *tekhnē* is exemplarily *for* life, it owes this to its relation with death, for *tekhnē* is, according to Derrida, "death in life, as condition of life" ("Avowing," 39; "Avouer," 213). *Tekhnē* haunts life and "living together [*vivre ensemble*]" with the specter of death, which it manifests particularly in technologies of life, technologies *for* life, that, Derrida writes, "engage the living, all the syntheses of the living, all the dimensions of the living being-together [*l'être-ensemble vivant*] (with oneself or with the other) in the space and the time of a *techno-biological prosthesis*" ("Avowing," 39; "Avouer," 213).[41] This prosthesis inserts a *tekhnē*, a technology, into life that performs a denaturing move by interrupting the apparent naturality of life. Thus *tekhnē*, like death, is on the side of life, as the side without an other that interrupts traditional structures of binary opposition. This interruption takes place thanks to an excess that moves, in Derrida's words, "*beyond everything* that is founded on this opposition of nature/culture. That is to say, beyond everything, more or less everything" ("Avowing," 27; "Avouer," 194).[42] *Tekhnē* enables and performs this excessive interruption by surpassing the nature/culture distinction thanks to its intervention in the very nature of life.

This excessive disruption or disruptive excess extends *for* life, *for* the whole of life, since "grace grants life for life."[43] Indeed, Derrida writes, "grace gives in every sense, it gives birth but it also pardons sovereignly, it grants life by interrupting dying [*mourance*], it lifts the sentence and literally *regives* life, forgives, gives itself without reserve body and soul . . . and, at the last minute, it gives and forgives life as for the first time, life *for* life [*elle donne et pardonne comme pour la première fois la vie, la vie pour la vie*]."[44] Every reiteration of "*grâce*" regives and every reiteration of "*oui*" reaffirms life *for* the duration of life, each time entwining uniqueness (in the name of *sauf*) and repetition (in the name of *foi*) in a *tekhnē* of donation that continues *for* the whole of life.

But this whole does not signify a closed totality or a process of totalization, akin to a sealing of "together [*ensemble*]." Whole and "together [*ensemble*]" instead name events, instances in which these donations and redonations happen, each time bringing to pass what Derrida terms a "substitution of the irreplaceable [*remplacement de l'irremplaçable*]" thanks to a successive reavowal of faith (in the performative act Derrida calls "fiding [*fiance*]") each time uniquely.[45] Such a reaffirming reavowal performs a *revenir*, even before the beginning, that recalls what Derrida idiomatically refers to as an "advent [*avènement*]," namely, a "globalization of avowal [*mondialisation de l'aveu*]" ("Avowing," 32; "Avouer," 202).[46] Thinkable only in the traumatic wake of the Shoah (and the subsequent invention of "crimes against humanity"), this advent allies with *tekhnē* in ways that might unsettle at once all conditions of living and of "living together [*vivre ensemble*]," with the living and with the dead, with animals, and with techno-biological prostheses that install death at the heart of life, *for* life.

Nevertheless, this "globalization of avowal" does not efface the uniqueness of every avowal and every affirmation, every "*grâce*" and every "*oui*," as well as every opening, giving, saving, blessing, welcoming that these words perform. Nor does it minimize questions of life and of "living together [*vivre ensemble*]," for these remain open and vital questions whose responses must be invented each time, *as if* for the first time. Furthermore, that this globalization reveals an element of *tekhnē* in every scene of avowal and affirmation does not provide prefabricated, globalized, or globalizable answers to questions such as "how 'to live together'? [*comment 'vivre ensemble'?*]" As Derrida attests, "There is no 'how' [*il n'y a pas de 'comment'*] . . . that could take the form of precepts, of rules, of norms, or previous criteria available to knowledge. The 'how' must be invented by each at each moment" ("Avowing," 34; "Avouer," 206). These questions thus persist *for* the whole of life, coming and coming again, bringing each time a risk and a chance, and demanding inventive response and responsibility each time.

Every avowal and affirmation, every response *for* life, arrives via *for* as an event that critiques and cancels ontology. Ontology here stands as a nickname for what Derrida elsewhere calls metaphysics: a science of presence that attempts to naturalize particular valuations, elisions, and erasures (the most notable for Derrida being the debasement of writing by speech), often in the name of being (*être*). This makes "it is [*c'est*]" ontology's most concise and powerful self-assertive self-expression—a simple, indicative statement of predication based on presence, on that which *is*. But *for* is older, more primordial and more originary, than anything that *is*; as the prolegomenon that "pronames and prenames everything," *for* "is" already on the scene long before ontology. *For* comes before the beginning (and even before "before the beginning"), since the beginning marks the beginning of being and all that it entails: ontology, metaphysics, presence, essence—and grammar, especially a grammar that operates by predication in the indicative verbal mood. *For* precedes and exceeds any grammar, for which it remains inexpressible. Therefore, Derrida writes, "It is *as if* one had to invent a new grammar," *as if* a new grammar were necessary, called for by *for*.[47] This grammar would have to take place in the subjunctive, the verbal mood of *as if*, of possibility rather than actuality, used to refer to an event not certain to happen or to a nonconcrete reality. The subjunctive remains more abstract than the indicative, expressing conditions of volition, doubt, and necessity as well as matters of judgment and emotion. The subjunctive would thus take place under the sign of "might [*puisse*]," expressing possibility and impossibility, chance and risk.

This newly invented grammar in the subjunctive would be a grammar of life rather than of being, given Derrida's assertion that "life *is* mighty might [*la vie est puissance puissante*]," that life and might "are basically the same [*sont au fond le même*]," especially since life might or might not continue—life might or might not encounter death at any moment, on the side of life.⁴⁸ The impossible might arrive at any time, unexpectedly and unforeseeably. An eventive grammar of life would thus have to locate life beyond ontology, beyond any discourse of "it is [*c'est*]," in a different grammar of "it might" (or "it might not"). Life would become no longer a matter of being (*être*) but of "mighting" (*puissant*), and what "might" or "might not" would have to be able to arrive in life, as an event, by overcoming the traditional opposition that would no longer hold between *dynamis* and *energeia*.

Under the aegis of *for*, in this vital grammar of the subjunctive, life would arrive before being and, therefore, before the beginning. Like might, life (in Derrida's words) "in advance eludes the 'it is [*c'est*].' Just as a certain performative eludes the constative and a certain subjunctive the indicative."⁴⁹ In short, life precedes being, eluding being by coming before: before the beginning, like "*grâce, oui, grâce.*" Life precedes and exceeds being, since "up to the end," Derrida writes, "'for life' has no end, it knows no end."⁵⁰ Derrida continues: "This 'for life' is not a *being* for life symmetrically opposed to the famous *Sein zum Tode*, being-toward-death, as its other side. It is on the same side."⁵¹ Here Derrida reaffirms his insistence that life and death both come on the side of life, which is qualitatively different from any ontological structure of Martin Heidegger's.

Just as life *for* life does not stand opposed to *Sein zum Tode*, "living together [*vivre ensemble*]" does not stand opposed to *Mitsein*, "being-with" (another Heideggerian variation of *Sein*). On the side of life, *for* life, "living together [*vivre ensemble*]" precedes and exceeds any ontological "being together [*être-ensemble*]" and, with it, Heidegger's *Mitsein*. "Together [*ensemble*]" would therefore be a matter of living rather than of being. This displacement of ontology by life (of being by "mighting") significantly disrupts traditional concepts of politics based on "together [*ensemble*]," as Derrida observes: "'Living together [*vivre ensemble*],' if it were possible, would mean putting to the test the insufficiency of this old couple of concepts that conditions, in the West, more or less any metaphysics, any interpretation of the social bond, any political philosophy or any sociology of the being-together [*l'être-ensemble*], the old couples *physis/nomos*, *physis/thesis*, nature/convention, biological life/law [*droit*]" ("Avowing," 27; "Avouer," 194). Here Derrida maintains life's priority over being by writing "living together [*vivre ensemble*]" in terms of *as if*, which keeps "living together [*vivre ensemble*]" outside of the domain of being, outside of any regime of metaphysics (particularly figured in terms of nature-culture).

Instead, Derrida names "living together [*vivre ensemble*]" as an "interruptive excess" with respect to this ontometaphysical opposition and with respect to any formed whole: "Living together [*vivre ensemble*]" remains "always an excess with regard to the whole [*ensemble*]" ("Avowing," 27; "Avouer," 194–95). This "interruptive excess" shatters any possibility of "together [*ensemble*]" as a noun—as a definite and definable object in an ontological grammar. In this newly invented grammar, "together [*ensemble*]" would function only as an adverb, as in "living together [*vivre ensemble*]," thereby locating what Derrida identifies as its "fracturing openness" only "there where it exceeds, dislocates, contests the authority of the noun 'ensemble,' to wit, the closure of an ensemble," for "the authority of the whole [*ensemble*] will always be the first threat for all 'living together [*vivre ensemble*]'" ("Avowing," 21; "Avouer," 185).

"Living together [*vivre ensemble*]" thus remains and must remain open, unclosed, incomplete, and incompletable, *for* the whole of life. "Living together [*vivre ensemble*]" remains always to come, *à-venir*, welcoming with a reavowing, reaffirming "*oui*" any *arrivant* who might come unforeseeably. "*Oui*" would, again and again, revitalize life by reiterating what Derrida terms "the live-ance of life, before and beyond being [*le vivement de la vie, avant et au-delà de l'être*]," in a new grammar invented according to "an originary subjunctive"—a grammar of *as if*, of potential and vitality.[52] This would be a grammar of experience and of experimentation, since Derrida conceives of experience in terms of living rather than of being: experience, according to him, is "living for living [*vivre pour vivre*]."[53] Here experience effects a translational displacement, from life *for* life to living *for* living, which revives the noun "life" with the gerund "living," an open, in-finite, vital process that happens and that provides the medium in which the impossible takes place, as in a miracle. But this gerund already effects another displacement in translation, since "living" stands in for *vivre*, the infinitive form of the verb "to live." The infinitive highlights the sense of futurity, as expressed in the infinitive construction *à-venir*, "to come" (which plays homophonically on *l'avenir*, the future). The infinitive stands as an ideal way to name an unanticipatable event, particularly since this verb lacks a subject, so that the infinitive makes way or leaves room for an event to occur. This newly invented grammar in the subjunctive—a grammar of *as if*—would, then, have to make room for the infinitive (or, perhaps, the in-finitive), reiterating the verbal rather than nominal quality of this open-ended, eventive grammar.

This bears on any question or instance of living, particularly the question of "living together [*vivre ensemble*]," since "living together [*vivre ensemble*]" renders an infinitive gerundive in translation. But "living together [*vivre ensemble*]" is, according to Derrida, "in its French idiom . . . in the infinitive and without a determined subject, a verb plus an adverb" ("Avowing," 22–23; "Avouer," 188). "Living together [*vivre ensemble*]" might be better translated as "to live together [*vivre ensemble*]," further accenting its unforeseeable, in-finite character that remains open-ended, *as if* it were a question. "To live together [*vivre ensemble*]" cannot but retain an interrogatory trace, haunted by a spectral "how? [*comment?*]" that calls for a unique answer each time, thus keeping the infinitive open to whoever or whatever might arrive—remaining open, then, *for* the whole of life. Furthermore, because "to live [*vivre*]" remains constitutively open to a possible arrival—no matter how impossible—of an *arrivant*, an event, a future, it is haunted by the specter of "together [*ensemble*]."

Such a specter carries with it a messianic trace, for the messianic names par excellence the event that remains to come (*à-venir*). The messianic might or might not come, perhaps as an *arrivant* or a *revenant* (or, impossibly, as both); regardless, it names what

Derrida calls "messianic spectrality, or spectral messianicity" and avows "a certain faith older than all religions" ("Avowing," 41; "Avouer," 215).[54] This would be the faith *as if* in a miracle, the faith that recalls and reavows *"grâce, oui, grâce"* as it affirms every performative possibility, every possibility of performativity. To live (*vivre*) would partake of this faith insofar as to live (*vivre*) would always already mean "to live together [*vivre ensemble*]"— together with the messianic as the quintessential eventful possibility that might arrive unforeseeably any time. In this way, the messianic would name the impossible possibility of any event, of any *arrivant*, of alterity and thus of "living together [*vivre ensemble*]"; it would name, in Derrida's words, "the opening to the future or to the coming of the other . . . but without horizon of expectation and without prophetic prefiguration. The coming of the other can emerge as a singular event only when no anticipation *sees it coming*, when the other and death—and radical evil—can come as a surprise at any moment. . . . Interrupting or tearing history itself apart, doing it by deciding, in a decision that can consist in letting the other come. . . . The messianic exposes itself to absolute surprise."[55] In this way, the messianic bears on what Derrida calls "a 'general structure of experience'"—which is to say, of living (*vivre*).[56] The messianic, as the impossible possibility that might nevertheless happen, would condition and would keep open any possibility of living (*vivre*)—in other words, of "living together [*vivre ensemble*]."

Just as Derrida affirms, "'To live' is always 'to live together' ['*vivre*,' *c'est toujours vivre ensemble*]," so that "one cannot not 'live together' [*on ne peut pas ne pas 'vivre ensemble*']," to live is always to *live on* ("Avowing," 19–20, 23, translation slightly modified; "Avouer," 183, 189). One cannot not live on. The infinitive *vivre* contains this eventive potentiality by remaining itself to come, *à-venir*, open to the future and to any *arrivant* or any event that comes, no matter what. From before the beginning, then, the infinitive responds affirmingly to the call to do the impossible. To live (*vivre*) avows before the beginning, thanks to *"grâce, oui, grâce,"* to do the impossible insofar as to live (*vivre*) is always already to live on (*survivre*). Because to live (*vivre*) predates and outlives any ontology, any nominal grammar, any condition, this *sur* of *survivre* is inscribed from before the beginning and *for* the whole of life. This *sur*, Derrida insists, "is *not to be added on* to living and dying. It is originary: life *is* living on, life *is* survival [*la vie* est *survie*]," meaning that "this surviving is life beyond life, life more than life [*la survivance, c'est la vie au-delà de la vie, la vie plus que la vie*]."[57] *Sur* therefore designates an excessive, elemental surplus intrinsic to living (*vivre*), aporetically making the value of life worth more than life—in other words, incalculable. This excess value allows living (*vivre*) to grant "living together [*vivre ensemble*]" and living on (*survivre*) *for* life, for the risk and chance of these two vitalities depend on life's absolute value. As Derrida formulates this aporia, "Life has absolute value only if it is worth *more than* life," and life's absolute value conditions any chance and opens any risk of "living together [*vivre ensemble*]."[58]

Living on (*survivre*) therefore acts as the impossible condition that makes living (*vivre*) possible, to which living (*vivre*) must respond by avowing the unavowable in what

Derrida calls "the performance of its own event of affirmation" that opens "to the impossible possibility of what comes about [*arrive*]" in living (*vivre*) as living on (*survivre*).[59] This also extends to "living together [*vivre ensemble*]," since living (*vivre*) is, from before the beginning, "living together [*vivre ensemble*]." Furthermore, "living together [*vivre ensemble*]," as "living on together [*survivre ensemble*]," exemplarily names in the infinitive, *as if* in a new grammar, that which remains to come (*à-venir*) and thus revitalizes living by keeping it faithfully open to whoever or whatever might arrive: an event, an other, death, the future, love, messianism, peace, even "*grâce, oui, grâce.*" Because any of these might come at any instant, "living on together [*survivre ensemble*]"—from before the beginning, thanks to "*grâce,*" and into the unforeseeable—remains, in Derrida's words "a *vital* necessity" ("Avowing," 23, "Avouer," 188). "*Oui,*" "living on together [*survivre ensemble*]" would be a necessity *for* life.

# Four or Five Words in Derrida

*Kevin Hart*

I would like to start by considering three words in Derrida, three words that he rejects in his writings, words that, at one time or another, he subjects to criticism, reformulates, holds at arm's length, or suspends from quotation marks. These words are "life [*la vie*]," "experience [*l'expérience*]," and "community [*la communauté*]." When Derrida asks us to think "how to live together," he does so at a point in his life when he has long since called these three words into question. And he presents "how to live together" in two registers. First, it is given as a matter of moral urgency in today's world: How *are* we to live together in peace, given our conflicting ideologies, our clashing religious beliefs, and our diminishing resources? And, second, it is given as a phenomenological problem: We must pass from the "what" of the case, living together, to its "how." It is a call for us to convert the gaze from the natural to the phenomenological attitude, although of course Derrida will make further moves that will distance him from phenomenology, removing him from all talk of absolute phenomenological life, lived experience, the sphere of transcendental being called "monadological intersubjectivity" in the fifth of Husserl's *Cartesian Meditations* (1950), and the community of phenomenological investigation of which Husserl dreamed. His path will take him away from life, experience, and community, as we usually understand those words, although distance is not the main issue here. The path does not take him so very far away, just to the side of these words, or even, perhaps, inside them, in order to reveal them to be not entirely closed upon themselves. Other words that he will affirm in particular contexts will show this: "friend" and "neighbor," and, of course, "Other," but also more abstract words familiar to those who read the works of the last phase of Derrida's writing life. I am thinking of "democracy," "forgiveness," "heritage," and "hospitality."

Also, I would like to draw attention to the theological framing of "living together" that Derrida undertakes. "Avowing—The Impossible" leads us, after some twists and turns, and through some aporias that take the ground from under our feet, to a scene of Derrida's theological awakening in Jerusalem. In 1982 he visits with a friend the Old Cemetery on the Mount of Olives, and must enter the offices of the Chevra Kadisha, the organization that administers the cemetery, allocating burial plots, arranging for the transportation of dead Jews from Europe, the United States, and elsewhere, back to the Holy Land. What he sees is a frenzy of activity: "These men appear to run and to be out of breath; they display a feverish activity around walkie-talkies, telephones, and computers that ostensibly link them to all the places in the world from which one begs them, at any cost, for a place in the cemetery" ("Avowing," 39).[1] For the devout who are close to death, or for those they have left behind, to have a plot in this cemetery facing the Golden Gate on the Temple Mount's eastern wall is of absolute importance, for it is through there, they believe, that the Messiah will enter, and the dead who are raised to new life in that cemetery will be the first to look upon the longed-for face. The messianism apparent here frightens Derrida, not least of all because of the air of fanaticism he breathes in the cemetery, of people trading in a peace that is held to lodge securely in a future present. And he begins to think, or recall, "a certain faith older [*une certaine foi plus vieille*] than all religions" ("Avowing," 41). We in turn will think of an earlier remark of Derrida's, that *la différance* is "'Older' than Being itself" [*Plus "vieille" que l'être lui-même*].[2] And we are likely, and rightly, to assimilate the later remark to the earlier. This faith that is older than the faith of the positive religions is a "spectral messianicity" that "exceeds, precedes, and conditions all messianisms [*messianicité spectrale, excède, précède et conditionne tous les messianismes*]" ("Avowing," 41). We are asked, then, to correlate *la différance* and faith.

So the fourth word I wish to consider is "faith [*foi*]," or maybe not this word but another one almost like it, "belief [*croyance*]," which Derrida sometimes prefers.[3] It is this belief, *croyance*, that will inform how we are to live together. If we children of Abraham are to live well, in justice and peace with one another, we must reject a concept of full presence that has been usually associated with life, experience, and community; we must also modify or reject traditional styles of religious belief and embrace another. Judaism will point Derrida to that new notion, because he is a Jew and because his theological awakening occurred in a Jewish cemetery, although the faith he has in mind is "older" than any positive religion, not by dint of historical precedence but by quasi-transcendental status. This faith passes beneath Judaism, as well as beneath Christianity and Islam, as a doubled condition of possibility and impossibility.

Three questions immediately reveal themselves: What exactly is the theology of "living together"? What does this theology tell us of life, experience, and community? And is this theology adequate to the complexities it seeks to address? To answer even one of these questions would take a long essay, and I shall not answer any one of them in detail. But I shall try to remain answerable to all of them.

. . .

Derrida begins his writing life by contesting the concept "life" in the name of "writing," and he does so by reading Husserl very closely. In the opening pages of *Speech and Phenomena* (1967) he quickly identifies the main thing to be addressed. "The ultimate form of ideality, the ideality of ideality, that in which in the last instance one may anticipate or recall all repetition, is the *living present*, the self-presence of transcendental life."[4] And he adds, "We will come back to the enigma of the concept of life in such expressions as 'living present' and 'transcendental life'" (6). Indeed he does. Four pages later we are told that phenomenology, "the metaphysics of presence in the form of ideality," is also "a philosophy of life," and this for two reasons: "not only because at its center death is recognized as but [*qu'une*] an empirical and extrinsic signification, a worldly accident, but because the source of sense in general is always determined as the act of *living*, as the act of a living being, as *Lebendigkeit*." Husserl may bracket empirical life but only to bring transcendental life, "the transcendentality of a *living* present," more surely into the light (10).

Death cannot be excluded from this philosophy of life, however. Husserl may wish to do so by securing a pure realm of "solitary mental life," an inner world of expression that is merely represented by sensible signs. The living act, the *Lebendigkeit* that motivates expression, "does not risk death in the body of a signifier that is given over to the world and the visibility of space" because it can "*show* the ideal object or ideal *Bedeutung* ["sense" or "meaning"] connected with it without venturing outside ideality" (77–78). Yet, as Derrida adduces in a meticulous reading of Husserl, expression itself relies on sensible signs. Death is marked in the signifier because, being a sensible sign, it stands outside pure phenomenological life; and because expression necessarily relies on the sensible sign, the living presence that guarantees expression "had already from the start fallen short of itself": It is "deferred *ad infinitum*" (87, 99). Phenomenology cannot remain a philosophy of life, pure and simple; it must be extended in a new direction, taking death into account, becoming what Derrida calls "deconstruction" or, in an expression he uses on one or two occasions, "life death" (*la vie la mort*).[5] Toward the end of his life, when responding to Hélène Cixous's writings, he will come to recognize that (in a sense) he has always taken the side of death, while disputing the value and pertinence of "side." "Death would be on my side," he says, "and life on hers."[6] True as this wry remark is in certain respects, it does not diminish the more general truth that *la différance* is fundamentally an "unconditional affirmation of life": not life as *bios* or *zōē* or even *psuchē* (see John 10:17) but as structural survival.[7]

"Life death" was the title of Derrida's seminar at l'Ecole Normale Supérieure in 1975, part of which is excerpted in *The Post Card* (1980). In *Speech and Phenomena* he had called the movement of infinite deferral of full presence that is set in motion by the sensible sign by the nickname "*la différance*."[8] Then, in 1975, he developed his thoughts in the area of psychoanalysis while discussing Freud's *Beyond the Pleasure Principle* (1920). "Death is inscribed, although non-inscribable, 'in' *différance* as much as it is in the reality principle which is but another name for it, the name of another 'moment,' since pleasure and reality are also exchanged within it" (*Post Card*, 286). *Différance*, he goes on to argue, subtends life and death but not as opposed concepts: "Life-death" is "the law of the proper" (*Post Card*, 359), there is an economy in which all departures from life are returned to it, albeit spectrally, and in which life is always and already conditioned by the possibility of death.[9] His reading of Freud's "beyond [*Jenseits*]" is informed by Maurice Blanchot's *L'Arrêt de mort* (1948) and *Le pas au-delà* (1973). Neither title is translatable: The first means both "death sentence" and "stay of execution," while the second means "the step beyond" and "the not beyond." This doubling allows Derrida to determine a complex logic—strictly, a logic and a "graphic"—that will guide his reading of Freud in particular and his understanding of "life death" in general.

> In a word, from the first session on, it had been stated that a "logic" of the *beyond*, or rather of the *step beyond* [*pas au-delà*], would come to overflow the logic of the position: without substituting itself for this logic, and above all without being opposed to it, opening another relation, a relation without relation, or without a basis of comparison, a relation with what it crosses over via its step or with what it frees itself from at a stroke. But neither the stroke nor the step has any indivisible characteristic here. (*Post Card*, 260, translation slightly modified)

The task will be to uncover two texts in Freud's *Beyond the Pleasure Principle*, one that presents a position about the relation between pleasure and death, a clear and potent logic, and another based on writing (a "graphic") that exceeds this position and cannot be reduced to it. Death is not conceived as the negation or dialectical opposite of life; rather, the two subsist in a "relation without relation," that is, a relation marked by an interruption that renders it impossible to compare the two terms or to bring them together in a higher synthesis. What we have then is, "Neither life nor death, but the haunting of the one by the other."[10]

"Relation without relation" has come to be known as one of Maurice Blanchot's signature expressions, although Emmanuel Levinas uses it as well, albeit in a slightly different way.[11] Where Levinas conceives the other person as transcending me, Blanchot sees that the other and I transcend each other. Derrida had been devoting himself to a study of Blanchot's narratives at the same time that he was lecturing on "life death."[12] Life and death abide, for Derrida, in what Blanchot calls a *"neutral relation,"* in which *"the relation of the one to the other is doubly dissymmetrical."*[13] This means that my death is not an event or nonevent that waits to confront me in a future present; it is always and already here, not lodged in the present moment but marked in my reliance on the sensible sign and its condition of possibility. To return to the argument of *Speech and Phenomena*: "The relationship with *my death* (my disappearance in general) thus lurks in this determination of being as presence, ideality, the absolute possibility of repetition. The possibility of the sign is this relationship with death."[14] Each and every time I write or say a word, my death is announced; moreover, the very possibility that I can write or say a word bespeaks my death. Similarly, whenever I say the name of a living person his or her death is declared: I do not have to wait for an empirical death to take place before mourning begins. There is no *one* "end of life," then, for death is dispersed in the proper name, my name or yours, and is always loose in the world.[15] As Derrida says, "We *already* are . . . dead for one another."[16] If we are "hollow men" it is not in T. S. Eliot's sense, for Derrida is making a structural and not an existential remark. It is not a matter of a shadow falling "Between the idea / And the reality" but of a trace passing through both "idea" and "reality" and resituating both in terms of its economy.[17]

Whether before or after an actual death, more than mourning is involved, Derrida will say, because I do not only introject an image of the beloved but also incorporate it. The distinction is Sandor Ferenczi's, and was taken up by Freud and then elaborated by Nicolas Abraham and Maria Torok.[18] If I successfully introject an image of the dead beloved, I take that image fully into myself, digest it, and can complete my mourning; but the image of the beloved can resist being interiorized, and his or her otherness can remain in me, giving rise to melancholy. Resistance to introjection is known as incorporation. If incorporation happens, I form what Abraham and Torok call a "crypt" in my ego, a place for the living dead. For Derrida, incorporation is not an aberrant or pathological state but the very law of "life death"; no mourning is complete, it always leads to melancholy. This means that the living are always haunted by the dead, and the dead are always living a half-life in one or more crypts. A terse, memorable image says it all: "The Self: a cemetery guard."[19] And doubtless specters frighten this guard by day and by night.[20]

It will readily be seen that Derrida is quite unlike Michel Henry and Gilles Deleuze who, in their different ways, think of life entirely by way of immanence.[21] There can be no life without transcendence, and no melancholy either, Derrida says: Any text can survive its author, even before the author's death takes place. Something I write, even my proper name, can return to haunt me, or those I leave behind. This is nothing to do with a present being that becomes a nonbeing or an absent being (in some other world, say) and that then comes back in a manner that is only quasi-present, held between life and death. Not at all: There is a spectral return because the being in question was never fully present in the first place.[22] Despite what philosophers of different stripes have presumed, there never has been a completely filled intuition.[23] The structure of all texts, regardless of genre or value, is that of survival or "living on," which is not just to do with living longer but of living "*more and better*, beyond its author's means."[24] Note how different this idea of survival is from Kafka's. The novelist tells his diary on October 19, 1921: "Anyone who cannot come to terms with his life while he is alive needs one hand to ward off a little his despair over his fate—he has little success in this—but with his other hand he can note down what he sees among the ruins, for he sees different (and more) things than do the others; after all, dead as he is in his lifetime, he is the real survivor."[25] Despair lets us experience ourselves as already dead, Kafka says; for Derrida, though, we are already dead in a structural manner, regardless of whether or not we experience despair. Kafka sees transcendence, of a sort, in what the one who despairs can see in life, while Derrida construes transcendence as survival by dint of quasi-transcendental structure.

Transcendence as structural survival is Derrida's alternative to immortality as conceived by Socrates, or resurrection as witnessed by Paul. Socrates and Paul tell us that immortality and resurrection are true. By contrast, Derrida's concern with survival has to do with meaning, not truth. There can be meaning in language only if death is possible, the death of the author and the intended reader or readers. His concern is not quite Blanchot's, which focuses on the objection that "before the work, the writer does not yet exist; after the work, he is no longer there."[26] Instead, the claim turns on the text, not the existence or nonexistence of the author: What has been written signifies, has meaning, regardless of whether the author or the original audience is present. The economy of "life death" is prior to the living presence of author or intended reader, and the question whether human beings survive death or do not survive death is not one that Derrida poses, let alone answers. Instead, he considers another mode of transcendence that is interwoven with structural survival: When a text passes from the interest of the signifier to that of the signified. Even a work such as Stéphane Mallarmé's "Plusieurs sonnets" or Geoffrey Hill's "Lachrimae"—each of which suspends a straightforward relation with the signified by dint of words that point legitimately in two or more directions—nonetheless cannot maintain the suspension indefinitely. Each set of poems maintains its singular idiom by folding its relation to the signified in diverse ways, and thereby remaining close to the signifier.[27] After a while, we can make decent sense of "Le vierge, le vivace et le bel aujourd'hui" and "Martyrium," even though we can never account for all the meaning that each poem generates. Derrida seems to assume that the idiom that survives will be more cryptic than clear, but the assumption is unwarranted. A good reader will find more and more meaning in George Herbert's "Love" (III), for example, which seems pellucid in its semantics and syntax, every time it is reread. A true poem of whatever style is always ahead of us because of its singularity, not because of obscurity or difficulty, fragmentation or anything else.[28]

I shall return to transcendence in a moment. Now, though, I pass to the second word that Derrida criticizes. In *Of Grammatology* (1967), in a discussion of Louis Hjelmslev's linguistics, Derrida allows himself a general philosophical comment: "'Experience' has always designated the relationship with a presence, whether that relationship had the form of consciousness or not."[29] This is not a sufficient reason, though, to reject the word and the concept; indeed, we might well wonder whether it would be possible to do so.[30] Derrida's next sentence is the more telling of the two: "At any rate, we must, according to this sort of contortion and contention which the discourse is obligated to undergo, exhaust the resources of the concept of experience before attaining and in order to attain, by de-construction, its ultimate foundation."[31] Nothing more is said of the topic in *Of Gramma-tology*, nothing overt, at least. Yet the tenor of the discussion of Rousseau and Lévi-Strauss is perfectly at one with a later statement, in 1971, to do with "all 'experience' in general."[32] When considering the three predicates of writing—the mark, its force of breaking with its original context, and the spacing that constitutes the mark—Derrida observes that they are found in all language, spoken or written, "and ultimately in the totality of 'experi-ence.'" And he concludes, "There is no experience of *pure* presence, but only chains of differential marks."[33] These signifying chains are presumably the "ultimate foundation" of what we call "experience," and therefore offer no solid ground at all.

Can we talk coherently of experience if we have no fulfilled intuition but only differ-ential marks that have no binding relation to an original context of production? Yes, Der-rida thinks. A more detailed answer is given in an interview granted in 1991. Asked whether he draws his sense of responsibility from his philosophy, Derrida demurs over the interviewer's choice of the one word "philosophy" as a description of his teaching and writing and offers an alternative. "I prefer to speak of *experience*, this word that means at the same time traversal, voyage, ordeal, both *mediatized* (culture, reading, interpretation, work, generalities, rules, and concepts) and *singular*—I do not say immediate (untranslat-able 'affect,' language, proper name, and so forth)."[34] In his teaching and writing, Derrida goes on to say, he looks always for the point where "work and singularity cross, where universality crosses with that *preference* of singularity which it cannot be a question of renouncing, which it would even be immoral to renounce." This is not an affair of a sub-jective predilection but of an inclination for the singular each and every time that it crosses the universal. Derrida finds himself "inscribed" in this preference, for it "embod-ies the singular decision or the responsibility without which there would be neither mo-rality, nor right, nor politics."[35] Experience, then, is redefined so that it does not answer directly to the sense experience of empiricism but is always a negotiation of an aporia. As he asks rhetorically elsewhere, "Is an experience possible that would not be an experience of the aporia?"[36]

We feel here the full etymological weight of "experience," the state of having been exposed to danger, specifically the danger of arriving at a limit and having no guide to the territory ahead.[37] It is usual to consider the singular case as falling under a general rule, so that the rule is applied to the singular case. Not so for Derrida: The singular case and the general rule are incommensurable, and yet they cross one another whenever one acts and takes responsibility for that act. Elucidating this notion gives Derrida the opportunity to bring together several of his most important late ideas in an arresting formulation. "The condition of possibility of this thing called responsibility is a certain *experience and ex-periment of the possibility of the impossible: the testing of the aporia* from which one may invent the only *possible invention, the impossible invention*."[38] What is impossible is, precisely, a satisfactorily resolution of the aporia formed by the singular and the universal;

and yet one is required to do that in each and every moral act. Responsibility is to be invented freshly each time one acts because each moral act involves someone whose singularity is qualitatively different from the singularity of everyone else. If this is not so, then responsibility is no more than the application of a rule; it is thoughtless and hence irresponsible.

Derrida's demurral over "philosophy" as a description of what he does suggests that it is worth pausing to make a couple of general remarks about his style of philosophizing. In the first place, his affirmation of experience rather than philosophy does not result in anti-intellectualism, although it breaks with the Greek heritage of ethics as contemplation. His moral thinking goes by way of Levinas and Kant, and it makes considerable adjustments to each. Like Levinas, he rejects the critical philosophy of the subject and the universality of the moral law, while retaining Kant's notion of respect and relaunching the project of a moral religion in terms of another law, the reality principle or *la différance*. Unlike Levinas, he affirms justice over the good. In a bold move, Levinas plucks Plato's "good beyond being"[39] from metaphysics or theology and reinscribes it in ethics: "The Other, in his signification prior to my initiative, resembles God [*ressemble à Dieu*]."[40] Derrida takes Levinas's remark and pushes it a little further, maintaining that the other person, like God, is absolutely singular. Hence ethics is formally unable to be distinguished from religion, and both are set in the register of justice, not the good. Like Levinas more than Kant, Derrida is primarily concerned with *Ur*-ethics rather than with a multitude of first-order moral problems, and attempts to rethink this *Ur*-ethics by way of a criticism of the autonomy of the subject in Kant and by a deepening of Levinas's affirmation of the otherness of the other person.

Accordingly, we will look in vain for Derrida's views on a wide range of topics in moral philosophy and metaethics, including a firm distinction between them, for it is sometimes difficult to tell if Derrida is doing ethics or elaborating the conditions for doing so. Certainly, there is no sense in which his moral thinking could be said to be normatively complete, offering a full ethical account of a wide range of actions. He is an unusual philosopher in that he addresses many major thinkers—Plato and Kant, Hegel and Kierkegaard, Husserl and Heidegger, among others—and illuminates them from new angles, but without coming up, as they do, with first-order positions on the usual repertoire of philosophical problems. It does not follow, though, that we cannot put well-known distinctions in moral philosophy to Derrida in an attempt to elucidate his position or metaposition. We may wonder, for instance, whether the structural preference he speaks of with respect to the singular case is a justifying or a motivating ground for action, and whether he takes himself to be telling us something new about morality or whether he is merely outlining a new way of understanding what we already know. It is notable that Derrida does not defend his position on ethics (or metaethics) against rival claims by philosophers outside his heritage. He takes it for granted, for example, that the moral life is discontinuous, worked out by negotiating one aporia after another, and offers no arguments against those philosophers who construe the moral life as turning on a vision of the good (as in Platonism) or as holding that the good is simple and indefinable (as in G. E. Moore's ethics). Everything for Derrida turns on choice, even if it is a question of structures rather than freedom (as it was for Sartre), and we may well wonder if that can be the basis of an adequate view of the moral life. For there seems to be no sense in his account of ethics as a growing awareness of values over the course of life, or the development of the virtues, so that some moral decisions are not, and need not be, freshly made with respect to moral rules.

One assumption at the base of Derrida's notion of moral experience is the absolute singularity of each person, which is to be distinguished from another assumption that he rejects, autonomous agency, which is part and parcel of the metaphysics of the subject. As Derrida phrases things, in an apparently tautological statement, "Every other is completely other [*Tout autre est tout autre*]."[41] This is not a skeptical or solipsistic assertion that one can have no experience of the other person. On the contrary, it is an intensification of what we mean by "experience." As Derrida says, "experience itself . . . is always experience of the other [*l'autre*]."[42] I will examine the assumption of absolute singularity a little later, although now it can be seen to explain why Derrida is not at ease with the notion of community. Just as "life" and "experience" are criticized and reworked, so too is "community," though this last word is not rehabilitated: It becomes recast as "living together," "culture," "heritage," "hospitality," or "democracy." Derrida is clear about the profile of "community" that disturbs him: "If by community one implies, as is often done, a harmonious group, consensus, and fundamental agreement beneath the phenomena of discord or war, then I don't believe in it very much and I sense in it as much threat as promise."[43] Community as *communio* (a group that isolates itself from all others) is rejected here, but so too is community as *commercium* (a group formed by mutual exchanges).[44] Kant distances himself from *communio* and *Gemeinschaft*; Derrida does so as well while also going further, registering concern with both *commercium* and *Gemeinwesen*.

Almost immediately after saying all this, however, Derrida begins to think "community" in a more affirmative manner, and does so in terms that are already becoming familiar to us.

> There is doubtless this irrepressible desire for a "community" to form but also for it to know its limit—and for its limit to be its *opening*. Once it thinks it has understood, taken in, interpreted, *kept* the text, then something of this latter, something in it that is altogether *other* escapes or resists the community, it appeals for another community, it does not let itself be totally interiorized in the memory of a present community. The experience of mourning and promise that institutes the community but also forbids it from collecting itself, this experience stores in itself the reserve of another community that will sign, otherwise, completely other contacts.[45]

A community that closes upon itself, having its social and political principles fully present to itself in the form of a complete program of laws, would form a static unity and would be an image of death without any structural survival. If one is attentive to the structure of community, Derrida thinks, one can see that this self-enclosure does not happen: A community mourns its founding fathers and mothers, its exemplary leaders, and great citizens, incorporating them, while also opening itself to those who are to come and to transform the community by reinterpreting the desires of the founders and those who have followed them. (The emphasis needs to fall on *reinterpreting* those first desires; simple appeals to the founding fathers and mothers can reinforce homogeneity.) The same is true of a heritage, which, properly understood, involves a transcendental community partly of one's own choosing. And as Derrida makes clear in a dialogue with Elisabeth Roudinesco, "heritage" crosses "life" in a decisive manner: "Life—being alive—is perhaps defined at bottom by [the] tension internal to a heritage, by [the] reinterpretation of what is given in the gift, and even what is given in filiation."[46] Once again, *la différance* is life, understood as structural survival.

Without a degree of distance or dissociation from its putative origins and ends, there can be no community that lives and breathes, and were one's heritage to be grasped solely in terms of complete fidelity to one or more figures in the past, one's intellectual life would be no more than arid repetition. In order to remain alive, Derrida says to Roudinesco, a heritage "demands reinterpretation, critique, displacement, that is, an active intervention, so that a transformation worthy of the name might take place."[47] As stated at this level of generality, as is often the way, the idea of community or heritage as *différance* is not all that surprising. Let us stay with community. One may insist that there are, after all, communities that are neither fascist nor Stalinist. Yet Derrida's point is subtler than this objection allows. A community that is based on fraternity, regardless of how democratic and free it proclaims itself to be, is nonetheless less open to women, or male-female relationships, than it seems to be. Hence Derrida's reservations about Blanchot's "unavowable community" and Nancy's "inoperative community," each of which relies implicitly on a notion of fraternity that needs to be exposed and criticized.[48] Were such criticism to take place, "community" could perhaps be used again, ventured *sous rature*, yet Derrida seems to think that its associations with fusion are too many and too close for the word to be rehabilitated in our day.

"Culture" is a preferable word to "community," Derrida thinks, although even here one must be wary of overtones of fusion and conformity.[49] "Democracy" and "friendship" offer more interesting possibilities: The one is reimagined as a "democracy to come," a society always open to more democracy, while the other conceives friends as "alone because they are incomparable and without common measure, reciprocity or equality. Therefore, without a horizon of recognition."[50] Again, we find the assumption that the other person is "every bit other [*tout autre*]," wholly transcendent, and one can find it unnamed in the third word that Derrida colonizes, "hospitality." As he interprets the word, "Hospitality is the deconstruction of the at-home; deconstruction is hospitality to the other, to the other than oneself, the other than 'its other,' to an other who is beyond any 'its other.'"[51] Here the other person is freed from the conceptual dyad of "self" and "other" and is outside any fusion or dialectical recuperation. I and the other person abide in a relation without relation, each transcending the other.

. . .

The theology of "living together" turns on a revival of rational religion: the spectral return of Kant's *Religion within the Limits of Reason Alone* (1793) to a world that is "out of joint" in part because of religious conflicts today.[52] Of course, "rational religion" does not return to exactly the same place it occupied in late eighteenth-century Europe; it is now "at" the limits of reason alone, not within them. It has arrived at a border and must negotiate one or more aporias, which is to say that it must undergo an experience, as must anyone who proposes to rethink "religion" in the wake of Kant. One's experience of "religion" cannot be confined to conditions of possibility but must involve a relation to the impossible. There is a peril involved: One may lose religion as we know it, and one may lose deconstruction as we know it.

To be sure, Derrida does not use the word "possibility" in the same way as Aristotle (in either sense considered in the *Prior Analytics* 1.32b5–20) or in the same way as Kant (as analyzed in the *Critique of Pure Reason* A220–25). For Derrida, "possibility" characterizes law, method, rule, and program, which makes anything that outplays those things "impossible"; and in this sense "deconstruction loses nothing from admitting that it is impossible."[53] So the two concepts, possible and impossible, do not arrange themselves in the form of a contradiction but of an aporia. The impossible is not that which cannot happen; it is the way in which we talk of how something genuinely inventive comes to be and thus extends the realm of the possible. It comes as the answer, for example, to a rigorously posed question, one whose answer is far from apparent.[54] And it is far from apparent for as long as one does not convert the gaze from the "what" to the "how." Accordingly, deconstruction "itself" must risk being rethought freshly each time it is practiced. If it is not, it lapses into one more method of reading and writing. And if it is, it may well be translated into something other than what it has been; it may find "itself" in the midst of a context dominated by theology, for example, rather than literature or philosophy, or indeed revealed theology rather than rational theology.

The barb just felt should be pulled out and inspected for traces of poison. Derrida insists that his rethinking of rational religion does not lead to the God of the Abrahamic religions and, moreover, that the theology in which his thought is implicated presumes the death of that God.[55] Now, it is true that Derrida's theology allows no space for God, as he understands the concept; it is also true that he offers no arguments against the compatibility of God with his position or indeed against the existence of God. There is, I think, no coercive reason why we need to think of God as self-presence, but let us do so for the sake of the argument. If God is eminent self-presence, Derrida will seek to show that this self-presence can never be represented in speech or writing without falling short of itself. This does not constitute an argument for the nonexistence of God, however, only an indication that God's self-communication will be unable to maintain its absolute idiom in human language. No parallel exists between Derrida's case against Husserl's "solitary mental life" and a similarly phrased argument against the reality of the divine life. The reasoning directed against Husserl establishes that there is no "private language," as Wittgenstein called it, that human beings can use; it makes no ontological claim about the being of human beings, and it cannot be extended to include the being of God. There is nothing in deconstruction that can deny the existence of *ipsum subsistens esse*, although there is a good deal that can tell us about what happens if God, thus conceived, tries to represent himself in a natural language.

It is worth setting Derrida's remarks about phenomenological manifestation beside those about divine revelation. To be sure, Derrida has reasons to think that there can be no full intuition of phenomena, while of course allowing that there is manifestation of phenomena. Doubtless he would have grounds to say that there can be no full intuition of revelation (many theologians, including Karl Barth, would agree with him, pointing out that every revelation involves a re-veiling); but instead he bypasses revelation as such. He does so by choosing *Offenbarkeit* over *Offenbarung*: the condition of possibility for revelation precedes revelation itself and is independent of it, even though one needs revelation (or what one takes to be a revelation) in order to discern it. And yet one could argue that it is revelation that reveals, among other things, its own conditions of possibility. The God who reveals himself to those who believe in him seldom imposes himself in the register of presence: theophanies, levitations, stigmata, and visions may be experienced, although even here full intuition of God is rarely given: A holy man or woman may receive the stigmata, say, but it may remain quite unclear whether it has been received by the imposition of Christ or by a combination of a hysterical condition and extreme religious devotion.[56] In any case, for most Christians, including the saints, God reveals himself while also re-veiling himself. We are to love God *modus sine modo*, at the limit of our capacities, yet God mostly comes to us *modus sine modo*, understood slightly differently, as a way without a way, from beyond creation and its categories. Most of the time, God comes to us between thoughts, unable to be netted by our concepts, not as a blinding revelation in the present moment.[57] And if we translate this into Derrida's vocabulary what we end up with is that God's coming is more like a trace than a presence. It is not, though, mere structural survival.

That said, let us listen to Derrida characterize the theology at the base of "living together." It requires us to distinguish messianism and messianicity: The former posits a historical messiah who presents or embodies divine revelation, while the latter is a structure that has been revealed by acts resulting in bids for messianic entitlements. Derrida's theology arises from this structure, *"the most anarchic and unarchivable place possible,"* otherwise known as *la différance*.[58] (For all his foxiness, Derrida is at heart a hedgehog.) We can distinguish two propositions: (1) A structure of messianicity precedes and conditions all messianisms (or, as he also says, *Offenbarkeit* is prior to *Offenbarung*), and (2) the positive revelation of all messianic religions is precluded by the structure of messianicity (which would mean that we have *Offenbarkeit* but not *Offenbarung*). As already noted, Derrida states that his thesis is (1) messianicity "precedes and *conditions* all messianisms" (my emphasis). It would follow from this proposition that messianic claims are always divided and equivocal, calling for subtle interpretation by the faithful, needing to be held in tension with the hold that ethics has upon us. In fact, though, since he disregards or even dismisses revelation, he actually urges us to accept (2), which would mean that positive religions should be replaced with his reformulated religion of reason. Revelation would give way to ethics, as he understands it, which is to say that it would yield to the undecidable relation between ethics and religion, what we might call *"l'éthique la religion."* What is clearly decided is that the historical yields to the structural, the old is captured by the "older."

Consider the following passage, where Derrida outlines the expectation of the coming of the other person.

> *An invincible desire for justice is linked to this expectation. By definition, the latter is not and ought not to be certain of anything, either through knowledge, consciousness, conscience, foreseeability or any kind of programme as such. This abstract messianicity belongs from the very beginning to the experience of faith, of believing* [la foi, du croire], *of a credit that is irreducible to knowledge and of a trust that "founds" all relation to the other in testimony. This justice, which I distinguish from right, alone allows the hope, beyond all "messianisms," of a universalizable culture of singularities, a culture in which the abstract possibility of the impossible translation could nevertheless be announced. This justice inscribes itself in advance in the promise, in the act of faith* [l'acte de foi] *or in the appeal to faith* [l'appel à la foi] *that inhabits every act of language and every address to the other. The universalizable culture of this faith* [cette foi], *and not of another or before all others, alone permits a "rational" and universal discourse on the subject of "religion." This messianicity stripped of everything, as it should, this faith* [cette foi] *without dogma which makes its way through the risks of absolute night, cannot be contained in any traditional opposition, for example that between reason and mysticism.*[59]

The essential movement here is from faith (or belief) to justice, and it takes place by way of distinguishing itself from Kant's account of human rights being founded on the autonomy of the will. At the same time, it considers faith or belief in Kant's sense of "reflective faith," although Derrida relies more surely on an older notion of "natural faith" that goes back to Aquinas and Cicero.[60] Not that Derrida will accept the adjective "natural": For him his *Ur*-faith is given in a quasi-transcendental manner, and what seems natural has been naturalized. At any rate, there is no consideration of belief in moral intuitions, say, and no place assigned to faith regarded as a theological virtue. The naturalized faith I have in you is sufficient, Derrida thinks, to ground justice. Supernatural faith is superfluous, mere *Aberglaube*. Yet will naturalized faith in an utterly undetermined "you" suffice to ground acts of extreme endurance of suffering and extraordinary goodness, such as those we associate with the martyrs and saints, whether canonized or not? Perhaps, but I suspect that those people need an absolute commitment to something more concrete than an undetermined "you" who is invited to come.

Ethics turns on the categorical imperative, Kant holds, a purely formal law that requires no appeal to a heteronomous end such as God, the good, or a list of specific goods. The categorical imperative, in any of its versions, is the very basis for establishing conditions of autonomy and equality, and of giving warrant for a universal community of rational individuals. The same would be true of Kantian intuitionism.[61] Derrida will resist this movement toward a universal community, just as he will resist the communities of Blanchot and Nancy, preferring what he calls *"a universalizable culture of singularities."*[62] It should also be noted, though, that Derrida allows this rejection of rights to exclude, without argument, the standard case for natural law, namely, that the good precedes rights. The good or goods do not appear in Derrida's ethics; it has no teleology except for a formally empty and aimless one of calling "come" to whatever may enter the field of the possible, without determining it in any way in advance, or prescribing its manner of behavior on arrival. Only because there is no determination of who or what may come in actuality can there be justice, Derrida thinks. It is a transcendental condition for ethics, and particular acts of justice will always weigh the deeds and material circumstances of each and every new arrival, giving the new arrival a structural preference over general rules and laws.

At this point one might usefully evoke Iris Murdoch, a very different sort of moral philosopher from Derrida, to indicate an alternative way of thinking, one that she set against an earlier and highly influential existential moral philosophy found explicitly in Sartre and implicitly in Stuart Hampshire. She draws on Simone Weil's notion of attention as developed in her *Cahiers* (1970). "Attention, taken to its highest degree," Weil says, "is the same thing as prayer. It presupposes faith and love."[63] Murdoch will distance herself from the view that attention *is* prayer, but will work with the notion. "If we consider what the work of attention is like," she says, "how continuously it goes on, and how imperceptibly it builds up structures of value round about us, we shall not be surprised that at crucial moments of choice most of the business of choosing is already over."[64] Without having the opportunity to examine a range of particular cases, it can at least be said that Murdoch's picture of the moral life fits more closely with one's experience of moral life than either Sartre's picture (difficult choices) or Derrida's picture (impossible aporias). "The moral life," Murdoch says, "is something that goes on continually, not something that is switched off in between the occurrence of explicit moral choices."[65] To which one might add, "whether they are existential or structural."

Religion, Derrida says at the conscious risk of pleonasm, is always "the religion of the living" ("Faith and Knowledge," 49). Even so, religion answers to both an affirmation of life as an absolute value and the sacrifice of life. A second long quotation is needed to see how Derrida frames this "double postulation" of life by the faithful.

> *On the one hand*, the absolute respect of *life*, the "Thou shalt not kill" (at least thy neighbour, if not the living in general), the "fundamentalist" prohibition of abortion, of artificial insemination, of performative intervention in the genetic potential, even to the ends of gene therapy etc.; *and on the other* (without even speaking of wars of religion, of their terrorism and their killings) the no less universal sacrificial vocation. It was not so long ago that this still involved, here and there, human *sacrifice*, even in the "great monotheisms." It always involves sacrifice of the living, more than ever in large-scale breeding and slaughtering, in the fishing or hunting industries, in animal experimentation. Be it said in passing that certain ecologists and certain vegetarians—at least to the extent that they believe themselves to have remained pure of (unscathed by) all carnivorousness, even symbolic—would be the only "religious" persons of the time to respect one of these two pure sources of religion and indeed to bear responsibility for what could well be the future of a religion. ("Faith and Knowledge," 50; Derrida's emphases)

Some qualifications are called for here, since religious sacrifice does not always involve "sacrifice of the living." In the central ritual of the Catholic Church, the Mass, the sacrifice takes place by way of a sacrament, without affecting the natural body of Jesus, who died only the once, while in the Episcopal Church a "sacrifice of praise" is an expenditure of time and energy by the faithful. Also, Derrida's critical remarks on religion's reliance on sacrifice sit oddly with his great emphasis that sacrifice and self-sacrifice are essential to the moral life as he conceives it. For every time I perform a moral act, he says, I am also sacrificing others I have overlooked or ignored in order to do that one just act. Here the concern is not a preference for singularity over a general state of affairs but the impossibility to elect one singularity over another when more than one presses on me, which is each and every moment.

After considering Kierkegaard's treatment of Abraham's willingness to sacrifice his son, Isaac, on Mount Moriah, Derrida generalizes the conclusion he has reached.

> By preferring my activity as a citizen or as a professorial and professional philosopher, writing and speaking here in a public language, I am perhaps fulfilling my duty. But *I am sacrificing and betraying at every moment* all my other obligations: my obligations to the other others whom I know or don't know, the billions of my fellows

(without mentioning the animals that are even more other others than my fellows), my fellows who are dying of starvation or sickness. I betray my fidelity or my obligations to other citizens . . . to those I love in private, my own, my family, my son, *each of whom is the only son I sacrifice to the other, every one being sacrificed to every one else in this land of Moriah that is our habitat every second of every day.*[66]

Not only is sacrifice inevitable (though not desirable) but also the moral life, as Derrida conceives it, is endless self-sacrifice and, indeed, hyperbolic self-sacrifice. My choices of where to sacrifice myself in the service of others involve me sacrificing further others whom I may or may not know, as well as sacrificing the opportunity to sacrifice myself elsewhere.

Again, Murdoch offers a useful counterweight: "A moral philosophy should be inhabited."[67] Yet no one can inhabit this mental torture chamber called ethics, as Derrida describes it, let alone use it to promote human flourishing. Perhaps Derrida concludes that ethics is tragic; one could also conclude that he has given the reductio ad absurdum of "pure ethics." If I decide when young to set myself on a course to be a professor of theology in the United States and not a physician helping the poor and sick in Africa, I can still optimize the good in my chosen way of life, and can do so by addressing unjust states of affairs, keeping promises, repairing wrongs I have committed, developing my virtues, acting with beneficence, and so on: In other words, by recognizing a plurality of basic moral obligations to a wide range of people who come within my compass.[68] Of course, those obligations can conflict with one another, but this problem can be resolved by appealing to what presses on me as a final obligation in a given circumstance. And, of course, I could have chosen differently what to do in life, and even if I embrace my choice, I may still feel the pressure of a life I have not lived, except, perhaps, in fantasy. Yet the moral demands on me of people I cannot help simply because I have chosen to help others is, if I may borrow an expression from Robert Audi, "ineradicable but overridable."[69] Those demands retain moral weight even though I may override them in the interest of properly performing my duties where I happen to be. And of course my commitments to pursuing my moral life here are not indefeasible: I may adjust them and spend time and money where I am in order to help people in Africa whom I will never meet. Also, it is far from clear that in choosing as I have done I have *sacrificed* helping other people. I can sacrifice myself without any external sign of doing so (as Jesus did on Calvary), but I cannot sacrifice others without an intention to do so and without a ritual that would make it a sacrifice. If I am indifferent to other people, I may be morally culpable, but I am not thereby sacrificing anyone.

Derrida reaches an extreme conclusion partly because of an assumption in his moral epistemology and partly because of another in his ethics. In the first place, one does not need a completely fulfilled intuition in order to sense the weight of a moral obligation; yet if one frees ethics from all intuitions and all laws (except *la différance*) one has no basis for responding to one call over another. And in the second place, Derrida bases his ethics on the presumption that ethics as such must be pure, by which he means that it does not originate in any presumed similarity of myself and the other person. "I tried to argue in my seminar this year," he writes in 2003, "that pure ethics, if there is any, begins with the respectable dignity of the other as the absolute *unlike* [*l'absolu* dissemblable], recognized as nonrecognizable, indeed as unrecognizable, beyond all knowledge, all cognition and all recognition."[70] The displaced theology at the root of this claim is immediately apparent. If we go back to the twelfth century, for example, we can see that *homo interior* is characterized by sheer otherness, by the God who leaves the *imago dei* in one's self. One approaches that otherness by introspection.[71] Derrida removes the otherness from the self and places it in the other person, while asserting it to be the mark of the absolutely singular, of which God is one example among others.[72] This would be his justification for speaking of sacrifice, for one can sacrifice only to a god or God. Yet even if the other person is like God in being absolutely singular, it does not follow that he or she is sufficiently like God to justify the language of sacrifice. The other person is unlike God in that he or she needs my help, and in choosing which people to help (with reference to my skills) I must look to features in those people other than absolute singularity: their lack of education, their poverty, their sickness, natural and political dangers facing them, and so on.

Now one might observe that the "purity" of ethics need not turn on the other person as wholly unrecognizable but on what one recognizes as objective moral truths. I may take the other person to be wholly unlike me, or I may take him or her to be very much like me; either way, I may hold in addition that certain moral truths are properly basic: that I should keep my promises, that I should address manifestly unjust states of affairs, and so forth. If we are pointed outside the self in quest of a ground for a pure ethics we need not end with the otherness of the other person but in the objectivity of moral truths. That is, we need not end in a radical noncognitivism based on the absolute unknowability of the other person (as distinct from approval or disapproval of his or her actions). We may end by affirming that the good is simple and indefinable, that it variously abides in states of affairs, and that we pursue it in following moral truths. Does this commitment also bind us to a notion of full presence?

An endorsement of moral intuitionism, even a Kantian intuitionism, need not require one to prescribe that there be full intuition of moral concepts.[73] It is sufficiently clear to me, as an attentive and mature person, that I should not tell lies; I do not need theoretical confirmation of the judgment. My aim need not be truth but only right action, and practical reason will suffice for that. Even so, the appeal to objective moral truths is one that Derrida would resist on the ground that it would deny the fundamental asymmetry of myself and the other person. Were there objective moral truths, both the other person and I would be rendered equal before them, whether they are natural or nonnatural, and this situation would foreclose the transcendence of the other person and, in the end, construe ethics in terms of exchange. What seems to be an alternate pure ethics, Derrida would conclude, is in fact compromised by what seems to make it pure: its objective status. Two clarifications are required, each of which points to a need to modify Derrida's general thesis about the relation between ethics and religion.

1.  Derrida figures the other person in terms of transcendence: His or her otherness is absolute, completely unconditioned, and to be affirmed without reference to any category or natural quality that we may share. Coordinate with this positing of the otherness of the other person is the claim of his or her singularity. On the one hand, the other person is held to be absolutely singular, unlike me in every way, and yet like God (or at least the God of Kierkegaard and the young Barth: the deity who is "wholly other"). In addressing another person I cannot have recourse to any rigorous distinction between him or her and God, and consequently I cannot properly draw a sharp, continuous line between ethics and religion. On the other hand, the absolute character of the other person's singularity must withdraw as soon as one considers him or her as a human being, someone with whom one lives in the world, and who is only relatively singular. Derrida tells us time and again that the absolute character of any singularity becomes a trace.[74] So neither by fact nor by right can one actually affirm the absolute otherness of the other person. The transascendance that is one with the other person's extreme elevation is entangled with the transdescendance that is coordinate with the trace.[75] In effect, the absolute singularity in question is not an *ousia* or "beyond *ousia*" of the other person but a relationship that I take myself to have a priori with him or her, formed on the basis of needing to exceed any program or general moral law. A pure ethics would require me to assume the other person's complete otherness even though I have no intuition of it or reason to think that he or she actually is wholly other than me. Yet there is no need to make such an assumption: All I need to treat the other person as irreducible to me are notions of uniqueness and relative singularity. A "pure ethics" is a name for an ethics in which the absolute singularity of God has been inserted in ethics to the benefit of neither ethics nor theology.

2.  At the base of Derrida's moral philosophy is a strict distinction between exchange and gift. I am called to give to the other person, without any thought of reciprocity and without any limit to what I give. Yet if I take the other person to be knowable, even analogically, then what may appear to be a gift is in fact no more than an exchange. I give to the other person in the awareness that he or she will also regard me as knowable and thus deserving of the same treatment. Even if I am not so treated by the other person, my sense of entitlement fulfills the requirement of exchange. Attention has generally been given to Derrida's notion of gift, either saying that there is no need for a pure gift or noting that purity should be repositioned at the level of intention.[76] Yet the problem abides more surely in his understanding of exchange. For it relies on a model of synchronic structure and evacuates all temporality and narrative from consideration. A return gift is not necessarily a calculated exchange, an equal

sum game, for it has imaginative and narrative dimensions that introduce differences and enrich living together. I receive a gift from you and, at the same time or later, I give you something back. My gift involves gratitude, to be sure, but may also be of itself a good deed, involve a degree of self-denial, be kind and thoughtful, have been chosen by imagining your pleasure at receiving it and, indeed, your flourishing in the use or enjoyment of it. An act of generosity or justice has a history, one that involves my past and yours, your imagined future as well as mine, both separate and together. Exchange is flattened out when it is a matter of theoretical confirmation, as in working out a zero-sum game, or an asymmetry that you or I can turn to advantage. Exchange is affirmative when it calls for narrative confirmation, meaning rather than truth, when I can fruitfully ask questions such as these: Does the story I tell myself about my gift ring true? Does the gift point to a reduction of you, or my relationship with you, or does it encourage the flourishing of both? My counter-gift cannot properly be reduced in any significant way to your original gift to me or, without crass reduction, brought before a neutral state of affairs, such as a dollar amount. The narrative and imaginative dimensions of gift giving are what make living together possible, various, and enriching.

. . .

Derrida's theology of living together involves replaying a liberal Protestant theology of the late eighteenth century so that this rational religion answers to a natural faith that is structurally, not historically, older than positive religions. It seeks to refigure "life," "experience," and "community" by way of a quasi-transcendental structure called *la différance*, which has the benefit of keeping the heritages of those notions open and alive, but which forbids, Derrida thinks, anything more than structural survival. Rather than lauding the transascendant deity, Derrida affirms a transdescendant quasi structure. Derrida says nothing about the kingdom, the community of Jesus' disciples, for example, but he indicates what is needed for the concept "kingdom" to be repeatedly reformulated in philosophy and theology. He says nothing about life in the Spirit, or how that life is possible by way of Jesus' death, but he gives us an idea of how and why "life" gets reworked in Christian theology. And he tells us nothing of the experience of God, although once we learn to distinguish the otherness of *différance* from the otherness of God we can perhaps be more precise in our theological formulations. Were Derrida to offer his views as an account of religion, it is unlikely that anyone would confess a religion so thin, and in fact he is not actually offering us a renewed rational religion as such. His theology turns on a claim that, if there is an ethics, a pure ethics, one would not be able to decide formally between it and religion. Yet that claim cannot be sustained: The God of Abraham is absolutely singular, as we Jews, Christians, and Muslims have come to see, and the other person, though unique, is relatively singular. God is "other" in a different sense than is available in the "self-other" distinction, and "other" too than the transdescendant otherness of *différance*. On realizing this, and holding still to Derrida's later thought in its word rather than in its intent, we are left with a rational religion without historical roots and a hyperbolic ethics of self-sacrifice and sacrifice of the other in each and every direction. Living together, in Derrida's understanding, is something that requires belief in the other person, a naturalized faith, yet it also requires an ethics that cannot be supported, let alone lived.

There never has been any "pure ethics"; the illusion that there is, or might be, comes from failing to distinguish the singularity of God from the uniqueness of other people, and the illusion is a dangerous one for ethics and religion alike. What we can gain from Derrida's theology is not his stronger thesis in which historical faiths are to be replaced by a structural one but rather his weaker thesis, that *la différance* "precedes and conditions" not any revelation but the statement of any revelation. The faithful are enjoined to take all due care when interpreting those statements in sacred texts and in commentaries on them, and not to rely on a priestly hierarchy for interpretation.[77] It is not so much a new thought in the history of religion as a heavy underlining of what we have long known, but no less valuable for that in a world that wants certainty in preference to interpretation. What is new and valuable is what Derrida taught us years before his theological awakening: how to read texts, sacred or otherwise, with infinitely more care, precision, and openness to unexpected meanings, than we ever thought possible.

# Surviving Mourning

# Mourning and Reconciliation

*Marc Nichanian*

To Catherine Coquio

On December 17, 2008, a group of Turkish intellectuals posted a petition online. Its phrasing, every single word of it, was as follows:

> *1915'te Osmanlı Ermenileri'nin maruz kaldığı Büyük Felâket'e duyarsız kalınmasını, bunun inkâr edilmesini vicdanım kabul etmiyor. Bu adaletsizliği reddediyor, kendi payıma Ermeni kardeşlerimin duygu ve acılarını paylaşıyor, onlardan özür diliyorum.[1]*

As I write these lines, the petition has been signed by approximately 29,000 people, and threats of judicial proceedings or of investigation have already been issued against them by the authorities. I do not know Turkish, so I am incapable of glossing the text of the petition. Its translation into some of the languages I do know, moreover, fails to help me in glossing them any better. Here, for instance, is the English version:

> My conscience does not accept the insensitivity showed to and the denial of the Great Catastrophe that the Ottoman Armenians were subjected to in 1915. I reject this injustice and for my share, I empathize with the feelings and pain of my Armenian brothers and sisters. I apologize to them.

Are they apologizing or are they asking for forgiveness? "I apologize." "*Ich entschuldige mich.*" "*Chiedo scusa.*" In the face of such a disparity, I will not risk an interpretation. I simply refer the reader to the authorized commentaries. I wish merely to register my discomfort with the public reaction of some artists of Armenian origin to this apology or this begging for forgiveness. Why discomfort? Because they replied "Thank you."[2] And since, despite everything, I am unable to avoid it, I will cite Vladimir Jankélévitch: "Get ahead of one's victim, that was the thing;

ask for a pardon! We have waited for a word for a long time, a single word of understanding and sympathy. . . . We have wished for it, this fraternal word! Certainly, we did not expect that they would beg our forgiveness. But the understanding word, we would have received it with gratitude, with tears in our eyes."[3] But also and inversely: "I do not see why it should be up to us, the survivors, to pardon. Let us rather beware that complacency about our beautiful soul and our noble conscience, that the opportunity to assume a pathetic attitude and the temptation of playing a role do not one day make us forget the martyrs. It is not a question of being sublime, it is enough to be loyal and serious. In fact, why should we retain for ourselves this magnanimous role of pardoner?"[4] I have no sympathy to spare for Jankélévitch and his palinodes on forgiveness. His sovereign contempt for the "other cases" of collective destruction disgusted me some time ago ("If the Jews were exterminated, it was ultimately the fault of Abdülhamīd").[5] I have cited him for this phrase only: "How we have hoped, for this fraternal word. . . . But the word of understanding, we would have welcomed it with *gratitude*, with tears in our eyes." Is this not troubling?

## 1.

Political reconciliation is always a manipulation of mourning; moreover, it is always monolingual. That is what I would like to show in the present essay.

It is so, it has been so from the beginning, since the most distant past, since this past which it seems is ours, that of the Western world, since its first utterance, since the first moment in which it narrated itself to itself, constructing its origin in such a powerful and cunning way, since the moment it narrated to itself its mournful conciliation with itself. It has remained so through its transmission, from Homer to Virgil, from Priam to Aeneas, from one political empire to another, and all the way down to us, we who play the game of reconciliation, we who delight in watching our political origins played and replayed on the stage of our being-together, our *Gemeinwesen* (of which, Hegel said, Antigone—this theatrical figure par excellence—is the "eternal irony"),[6] the stage of democracy as conqueror. And what a conqueror democracy is! It conquers with its bombs as much as with its commissions of truth and reconciliation. Bombs are monolingual. But commissions are just as monolingual, even if, officially, they speak so many languages (eleven official languages for South Africa). They all speak the one and only language of the Western world, that of universal right.[7]

Without transition, I will transport myself first to that most distant past, to what takes place in Chapter 12 of the *Iliad*, the moment when Hector and Achilles are finally facing each other. Hector has desisted from fleeing the fight; he has finally returned to himself. He is finally going to face his destiny, which is to die there, now, in just a moment. In order to preserve the symmetry of the fight, and despite everything, the poet makes them into equals. It is a semblance of equality, a semblance of symmetry, everyone knows it well, because the gods have made their decision. The scales have been tipped. The fatal day has descended upon Hector; he will go to Hades. Phoebus Apollo has abandoned him. The Greeks were particularly fond of this symmetry between the warriors. A symmetry conceals a dissymmetry that was there already, at the moment they narrated this story to each other with delight; a dissymmetry that, in reality, had nothing to do with the gods (it is not that the gods are not embroiled there, that they do not play their roles; it is rather that the dissymmetry precedes them and encircles them). The gods easily bear this blame. Now, by the ruse of Athena, the warriors are facing each other and Hector turns to Achilles. He speaks to Achilles; Achilles responds. They understand each other. Is it because they had the time, during so many years of uninterrupted combat, to get to know each other? We must suppose in any case that they speak the same language, as in the American Sword and Sandal movies, where the Romans speak English (or Galileo French, in the period films of Parisian cinemas). For the *Iliad* is just that, no doubt: a peplum for centuries to come and a popularization, reenacting the early Greek debates on some rather worn-out topics, about which the decision was made long ago and unanimously. Here, we must assume that Hector and Achilles both speak Greek, the language of the grand peplum of history. Ah, yes, by the way! What language did the Trojans actually speak? Did they speak Greek, like the Greeks? Does this matter in any way? The fact is that the Greeks never asked themselves that question. At the end of the story, at any rate, there is no one but the Greeks to narrate the story of the destruction of Troy for us. At least they narrated it; they did not cease narrating it to themselves. They reenacted, at least, in their narrative, their own genocidal will. Or is it the case that the symmetry they are so fond of is there in order to erase for good all traces of genocidal will? Is it not the very mark of denegation situated forever at the heart of this will, the mark of genocidal denegation at the origin of history? Let us be even more direct, even more anachronistic: Is it not the mark of *negationism* at the origin of history? But if it is, and from the beginning, then there is no longer any history. There is no longer any origin.

At least, then, Hector and Achilles speak. Or rather, first, Hector speaks. He calls on the gods to witness. And the first thing he says, in an altogether intelligible manner, is this: He will not maim the body of Achilles. Yet, this is only a rhetorical overture. In fact, what he really asks from his adversary is an oath. Hector asks Achilles to swear that he will respect his body, Hector's body, that he will not maim or mutilate it, that he will not leave it to the dogs, that he will give it back to his family, to his kin, who will then conduct the ritual of mourning over his body. Certain that he will be killed, Hector thus begs Achilles to give due respect to mourning. He asks him not to *forbid mourning*. He proposes an agreement in advance, an accord and the only way of making a future coexistence possible. He offers a pact of reconciliation that is immediately connected to mourning—again in a perfectly intelligible manner. Reconciliation will be possible if and only if mourning is respected on both sides, even before the adversaries kill each other.

Reconciliation will be possible only on the condition of forbidding in advance, by a mutual accord, the interdiction of mourning. But Achilles' heart is hardened. He refuses categorically. He does not want to hear of an accord or of a pact. This is verse 261 of chapter 12, a verse that has resounded in our ears for so very many years: "*Do not come,* álaste, *to speak to me of accords.*"

It is this word, *álastos*, which troubles me. It is extremely difficult to translate. In French, it can perhaps be translated as "*maudit* [cursed]" (Mazon), or perhaps "*inoubliable* [unforgettable]." In English, I find "unforgivable" (Robert Fagles) and also "You, cursed" (A. T. Murray).[8] Several studies have treated the question anew since 1988 when Nicole Loraux established her cartography of "nonforgetting" in the Greek world. For *álaston* is nonforgetting, which retains throughout the undecidability between the "unforgetful" and the "unforgettable" the very thing which "in the Greek poetic tradition . . . does not forget and inhabits the mourner to the point of saying 'I' in the mourner's voice."[9] There is, of course, an interdiction of mourning, decreed by Achilles, the modalities of which we are going to follow. But even before this interdiction, there is that terrible power of nonforgetting, something that inhabits and remains, that does not erase itself, something that we are in fact obliged to call "mourning" again, but which rather resembles a complete disordering of mourning, a hard thing, rigid, choleric, criminal.[10] It is this unhinged mourning that we must know how to conjure, prior to any politics, prior to any foundation or restoration of democracy, prior to every accord, every contract, every pact and every reconciliation. This is what the Greeks, in their obsession, called *álaston penthos*, mourning that does not pass, which nothing could make one forget.

## 2.

Nicole Loraux's analyses of amnesty in ancient Greece (where amnesty is not amnesia, she says, even if it resembles it in many ways; it is not forgiveness either, of course) fascinated her readers well before the question arose in South Africa of granting amnesty to the crimes of apartheid. Between these analyses and the modern situation there were similarities that Loraux did not even need to mention in *The Divided City* in 1997, as they were obvious to everyone. At the same time, it seems to me that this self-evidence has not been sufficiently interrogated. Loraux's readers, who were also fascinated by the postapartheid democratic restoration and the foundation of democracy, contented themselves in this regard with a few footnotes. Instead, we read political analyses of the process of "reconciliation by truth," that is, analyses that rely most often on the publication of the final report of the Truth and Reconciliation Commission, officially delivered to Nelson Mandela in 1998 and later completed. One is thus forced to read such analyses of the eminently political process of reconciliation, foremost in them the idea (said to be novel) that reconciliation can be accomplished only by way of an enunciation of the truth, that is to say, purely and simply by way of avowal and testimony. In these analyses, one must know how to read the fascination with the Greek model, with the *repetition* of the Greek model in 1991 or in 1996–97, under our very eyes. It seems that this repetition would allow our re-thinking of politics and of democracy in their historical origin and in their operation. Is this true? Does repetition truly allow a rethinking of politics and of democracy? Well, this is what we are going to examine.

Consider the essay written by Barbara Cassin in the special 2004 volume of *Le Genre Humain,* titled *Vérité, réconciliation, réparation.* The essay is titled "Amnistie et pardon: Pour une ligne de partage entre éthique et politique."[11] It begins with the enunciation of a necessity. One must "decouple" forgiveness and amnesty, Cassin says (37). One must not envision them together. One can draw a parallel between them, or envision the relation of exteriority between one and the other. But one must not confuse them. Such necessary separation would correspond to a distinction that philosophy has always, it seems, insti-tuted and respected: the distinction between ethics and politics. The reading here offered by Cassin of the Truth and Reconciliation Commission's texts is therefore not necessarily entirely "sympathetic." To the contrary, she forcefully insists on the fact that the commis-sion is a juridico-politico-ethico-religious "imbroglio" (38–39). She recognizes that the commission's report, in chapter 9 of volume 5 ("Reconciliation"), has a section titled "Rec-onciliation without Forgiveness," and thus that even the commission has envisioned, in fine, the possibility of "untying" ethics and politics. But this is a chapter without substance, one that does not carry out the consequences of the presentation that the commission gives of its own work. The imbroglio, then, dominates. Why is there such interference between two orders of reality that should be distinguished at all costs? Because of the nature of the crime: apartheid as a "crime against humanity." Nevertheless, says Barbara Cassin, one must know how to distinguish. Killing, whether it be for a just cause or not, is always illegal. Therefore even those who were on the side of "democracy" had to confess their crimes. (This at once brings us to a situation that is perceptibly different from what Nicole Loraux describes: In Athens, the amnesty decree and the will to reconciliation it ex-presses, emerged, it seems, from a need to obliterate the victory and not from a necessity to confess the crime. This, at least, is Loraux's interpretation.)

Such an altogether welcome introduction to the difficulty of distinguishing between ethics and politics does not, however, prompt Cassin to question the very idea of a "poli-tics," of a "living-together," of a *Gemeinwesen,* in which forgiveness (an "ethical" category) would have no place. Quite the contrary: From here on out, the project is to read the pan-els of the commission with Greek eyes (40), in fact with the eyes of sophistry, which is to say, to read in them after all the operation and the success of a political project, abstract-ing entirely from the supposedly ethical dimension (and thus also, without doubt, from the nature of the crime and from the inevitable interference caused by the crime against humanity).

Cassin's purely political reading begins with a commonsense observation. Had the security forces (those who, in the final count, were the agents of the crime) been incriminated, judged, and condemned, then elections would not have been possible in South Africa immediately after the apartheid (41). That is what is called pragmatism. All living-together would thus require a deep-seated pragmatism. I do not see any other way of understanding the matter. Whence at any rate comes the necessity of a *deal* (a *contract* between those who were yesterday still sworn enemies, no less so than Hector and Achilles; a contract and a matching oath, in view of a reconciliation) and consequently the fact of a "double blackmail": I give you amnesty, and you give me the maintenance of order and the means of putting in place the institutions of democracy. If need be, we will rewrite history together, as the Greeks did, by inserting symmetry within the epic struggle we conducted and in which we prevailed—happily after all (even if our analysts, doubling the *political* gesture of reconciliation, assure us that it is not *we* who have prevailed, it is rather democracy and living-together). Such are the terms of the contract that are to be examined in the essay by Barbara Cassin, by way of a detailed presentation of the conditions of amnesty, which we already know. If justice must absolutely be the issue, it will be a justice that is administered piecemeal. It will be neither a general amnesty, nor an amnesty of the individual as such. Only actions will be granted amnesty, and only if it is possible to do so. For politics, the author comments, the "concrete particular" is always at issue. Nevertheless, as we know well, only acts of a strictly political nature can be granted amnesty, with the demand for truth (in English: *full disclosure*) as a consequence. The first condition of amnesty is that only those who operate within a structure of command, who execute orders, are eligible for amnesty. A suitable translation: There can be no "idiocy" in politics. A politician acts always as an agent of a group, within a community. He cannot authorize himself. This remark therefore confirms (even if in a somewhat circular manner) Cassin's original choice with regard to the mode of reading the events: We are indeed within the realm of politics. Then comes the next requirement, namely, that liberty be exchanged for truth, for a communication of truth, a truth made therefore "common" [*la vérité communiquée, "communisée"*] (43). There would have been a procedure of transformation, therefore, which would correspond to what the Greeks called *metanoia* or *metabôle*. Is it one or the other? Even before posing the question, one must understand that it is indeed this transformation of *human wrongs* into *human rights*, and brought about by the campaign of confessions, that would merit a Greek reading.[12] We have thus arrived at the heart of the political operation.

Let us now see what is meant by *metanoia* and *metabôle*. Should we translate these Greek terms to "repentance"? Perhaps. But in the word "repentance" there is nothing political. Political reconciliation has no need for such repentance. Here again, the question was purely rhetorical. In fact, reconciliation needs no *metanoia*, because it constitutively ignores the subjective conversion of minds. Instead, it wants *metabôle*, an "objective inversion of states [*inversion objective des états*]" (44)—this is Cassin's terminology. Political reconciliation (and, with it, democracy restored) does not want to convert, it just wants to transform. We are within the relativism of Protagoras. Sophistic relativism is the "rational choice of something better," a choice that is "rendered objective [*objectivable*]." It is therefore an "authentic political choice" (44). The sophist is a physician of society. Whence transitional justice, which does what it can with a view to healing.[13] This much-vaunted justice would thus be, again and always, a Greek justice. The demonstration is concluded.

One can proceed to envision further points of contact between Greek politics as thought by sophistry and modern politics as rediscovered through the report of the Truth and Reconciliation Commission. Let us mention three points, only to confirm what the preceding demonstration has already established.

1. The first point of contact concerns the political nature of truth. Moderns are here rediscovering what the Sophists already knew in their relativism. One must know how to interpret this politically, in terms of social and democratic reconciliation, and not in Platonic terms. It is the truth-result that matters in this neighborhood. In the time of negotiation, it has to do with a manufactured reversal, where what is realized is a *kairos*, a sort of breach in time. One labors with an opportune and constructed truth. The resumption of four definitions of truth proposed by the commission (which therefore busied itself also with philosophy, let it be said frankly) intervenes here: Factual or *forensic* truth; narrative truth, which proceeds from the hearings; social truth, that of dialogue; healing truth, that of restorative justice (45).[14] Political truth would therefore be made of these four things, the factual, the narrative, the social, the curative. It would produce a consensus regarding the past. It would insist on this concrete particular, in order to say that it is neither a matter of the "inner heart [*for intérieur*]" nor of the universal (46).

2. The second point of contact concerns language as an element. The commission is here supposed to incarnate the connection between rhetoric and law, which had already been surreptitiously proclaimed by sophistry, twenty-five centuries ago. The rhetorical use of language establishes a common world. It provides an effective force through its performativity. Finally, it institutes a therapy against the evils that would otherwise risk tearing apart society and sociality. In sum, language humanizes anew, it constructs and it heals.

3. The third point of contact is what Cassin calls the "autolock of the amnesty apparatus [*l'autoverrouillage du dispositif d'amnistie*]" (50). There again, Cassin describes an exemplary success, one that drove the leaders of the apartheid regime to appear before the commission for the murder of Siphiwe Mthimkulu. Interpreted in sophistic and therefore Greek terms, this means that the power of the weak resides in using the power of the strong to their profit. Such would be one of the constitutive paradoxes of democracy at the moment of its foundation. Or else, in fact (it is the moment of avowal), wildly proclaim your own injustice, and this very proclamation will make

you just. Become thereby a member of this community that creates itself in the name of reconciliation. Or again, and to the contrary, refuse to seek amnesty, pretend to have always acted justly and in the name of justice. But this is to say that you have never ceased belonging to this community. In both cases, you recognize justice. It is enough to speak, and it is done. It matters little whether in speaking you incriminate yourself or whether you thereby defend yourself of ever having acted against justice. In both cases, you speak in the name of justice and you subsequently respect the community that establishes itself by grounding itself performatively on justice.

I have tried to reproduce Barbara Cassin's argument as faithfully as possible, because it seems exemplary to me. She does not omit the confusion of genres, which reigns in spite of everything in the reasons adduced in the commission's work and in its final report. She insists on the specifically political character of reconciliation. She reads the modern event as a way of revisiting the Greek event, underscoring thereby a sort of perennial dimension of the political. Such would be the way in which the political constitutes itself: suspending between parentheses the conflict that nonetheless inhabits its origins; choosing a pragmatic definition (dialogic, narrative, curative) of the truth; ignoring the effects of the inevitable manipulation of mourning within the reconstitution of the city reconciled with itself. Here then is a politics that speaks Greek, that is, therefore, perfectly monolingual. To such politics, one could oppose another, equally Greek idea, that of the *gigantomachy* of origins. It seems to me that this is what Nicole Loraux has explored and brought to light with a rare steadfastness. It would be obsessed by three things: (1) the constitutive conflict of the city; (2) another definition of truth, which the commission obviously could not take into account in its philosophical deliberations, a truth dictated this time by the will to power, that is to say, very simply, by domination (how indeed could the victim of *yesterday* escape *today* the truth of the domination to which she had been so intensely subjected?);[15] and (3) the inaugural interdiction of mourning. When the political city presents itself as an ideality, must we have faith in its constitutive operations? Should we not rather ask how an ideality constitutes itself historically?

It also turns out that one can read an essay by Jacques Derrida in the same issue of *Le Genre Humain*, perhaps the very last essay he published in his lifetime. The essay is titled "*Versöhnung, ubuntu, pardon: Quel genre?*" (it is the transcription of a session of Derrida's seminar on "Pardon and Perjury," of 1998–99). To ask about the "genre" of reconciliation is to suggest that the rupture was avoided (and not repaired), which is to say that it was denied in the double mode of denial and denegation (I shall explain this further on). It is also to suggest that the truth remains subjected to the will to power, and finally that mourning was manipulated once more. These are the three points I wish to develop here on the bases of other premises. Derrida himself describes a *theater* of reconciliation, which is another way of asking how the ideality of the political city, which is presumably reconciled with itself, is constituted historically. This concerns the (resolutely monolingual) theater of the spirit. That is why Derrida's essay starts with a sharply ironic development ("Spirit, are you there? [*Esprit, es-tu là?*]") on Hegel's word concerning the word (of) reconciliation. *Das Wort der Versöhnung ist der* daseinde *Geist.*[16] The spirit is finally there, when the word is pronounced and the globalized scene of reconciliation is created, which grants to each their role as victim or as executioner. The spirit is among us. That is where we are henceforth. "We hear the offstage voice of Hegel's specter, no doubt wondering, as it witnesses today, on this very day, the scenes of repentance that are increasingly spreading, whether this globalization of avowal is not, finally, the self-presentation of the spirit."[17] I would add that today, the being-there of the spirit is translated by the omnipotence of testimony, of the word of testimony. The theory and practice of the Truth and Reconciliation Commission are built entirely on the act of testimony; thus, it matters little whether the latter be accompanied by "repentance" or not. What does matter is this theater of reconciliation, which is also essentially a theater of testimony. At bottom, testimony (as practice, as concept) managed successfully to impose itself only through its theatricalization on a global scale. Obviously, once one sets out to read the politics of reconciliation in terms of denial, of will to power, and of the manipulation of mourning, or else through a historical deciphering of the operation that makes us imagine the Greek city as the grandiose or stammering announcement of the advent of the spirit in its being-there, the political interpretations of the foundation of democracy (and of the reinvention of the political) become somewhat problematic. That is no doubt why, in Barbara Cassin's introduction to the issue of *Le Genre Humain* which has concerned us so far, she describes the responses given as "not always convergent."[18]

## 3.

It is not the report of the commission that will teach us how an ideality is constituted historically, under the name of the political city, through the theater of reconciliation and therefore (in fact) through the universalized scene of testimony today. It will tell us nothing about the "genre" of reconciliation, about the inaugural tear negated and denied, about the truth detained forever by the executioner of yesterday, today repentant—nothing about the encrypted mourning, or about the interdiction of mourning. The report of the commission will not tell us what happens behind the scenes of the political theater of reconciliation, where what counts is only what takes place before our very eyes. We must therefore turn elsewhere. Derrida addresses testimony, by way of the work of Antje Krog.[19] For our part, we shall turn to a novel, *Red Dust*, by Gillian Slovo.[20] This requires a brief explanation.

I do not believe that the novel is better suited than any other literary genre to speak the reality of an epoch, to scrutinize consciences, or to interrogate the truth (even if Gillian Slovo selected a fragment of Shakespeare as an epigraph to her novel, "Is not the truth the truth?" [*Henry IV, Part I*, 2.4]). In some extreme moments, it might be capable of speaking its own truth, the truth of its "genre," while struggling with the event. It is, therefore, the site where an experience can sometimes be inscribed, by chance or by miracle, an experience which is never independent, however, from the writing of novels as such, an experience that is each time quite specific. Today, the novel is necessarily faced with the global theater of testimony, with the representation of the city reconciled with itself, with the being-there of the spirit in the word of reconciliation, as Hegel understood it two hundred years ago. The commissions of reconciliation speak the truth of the process, the whole truth (and not only the political truth, of course). They cannot, however, speak its limit, *that which remains*[21] once the whole truth has been spoken. The role that has been allotted to the novel is to explore this limit. In other words, its role is to stage itself, to put itself into play as genre, faced with its double or its other, that is, testimony. That, I am convinced (even if nothing confirms it explicitly), is also why the session of Derrida's seminar devoted to South Africa and to the works of the commission, as it was published in 2004, is called "*Versöhnung . . . :* Quel genre?" Yes, what genre remains after reconciliation, if testimony henceforth occupies the entire stage? That is the question. The novel is what takes on the burden of this *remainder*. That is what allows it to ask, along with Shakespeare: Could the truth be, by chance, the truth? What is at stake, of course, is the truth of testimony.[22]

And so I come to the novel by Gillian Slovo, with no other protocol, in order to ask myself first: at bottom, of what use are the avowals of executioners and their supposed repentance? Of course, it is a naive question, which has been posed so many times and to which so many varied responses have been given. Let us grant that the avowals represent the truth. But for all that, do they assuage the survivors and the parents of the victims? Is the truth sufficient to heal their wounds? Let us even grant that the executioner, present in flesh and blood, asks for forgiveness. Is the sole request for forgiveness sufficient in order to begin a sort of mourning on a societal scale? Surely these questions are too general. But the novel does pose them in this way.

Justice and truth? "Only the closest relatives, parents like Steve's, managed to hold on to a normal, human grief. You could spot them at every Truth Commission hearing, sitting in the front row, staring numbly at their children's killers as if that way they could understand what had happened and that way could accept *that the result would not be justice but the truth*" (171).[23] Toward the end of the novel, the investigation is stopped because the victim does not want to continue to be confronted with his torturer. Sarah, the lawyer, regrets the interruption, because they were finally getting "towards a type of justice," she says. To this her mentor responds: "But the Truth Commission is not about justice, it has never meant to be" (318). Let us assume still that this may be true, and that for the purpose of doing justice, there are courts. But she responds to him: "Is it about truth? . . . Hardly. If the new rulers of South Africa think justice is complicated, well, they should know that the truth is even more elusive. So what else is there? Reconciliation? That's what the churchmen preach. . . . But I defy you to find reconciliation between the individuals either in this case or in a score of others" (318).

Forgiveness and mourning, mourning without forgiveness? In part, the novel expresses itself on this too. The body of Steve, the youth who died under torture, is recovered by his parents thanks to the self-interested avowals of one of the torturers. They bury him with dignity. Would mourning be possible then, in individual cases, despite the absence of forgiveness? Perhaps. We know that in reality the remains of the militants who died under torture were not always given back to their families. I shall return to this. In the novel, Steve's murderer does not confess, nor does he present himself before the commission to seek amnesty, except in the very last instance, in reality in order to evade justice, to be able to commit suicide in peace, to implicate Steve's father along with him in the crime, and thus to humiliate the victims one last time (but forever). Even if Steve has been buried, there is no peace for the survivors and their families. James, Steve's father-turned-murderer, is dispossessed of himself three times: first in being forced to hear and to swallow the insanities that the torturer (Pieter) reels off about his son; then, in killing the torturer not of his own will but according to the torturer's; finally, in being robbed of his own vengeance, because the wife of the torturer accuses herself of the murder. James ultimately acquiesces, since he does not react against the woman's lie. He is nothing anymore but a wreck in human guise: "First [Pieter], by involving James in his final act, had taken the choice out of James's hand, and then his wife had gone further. She'd stood by and watched, without interruption, as James had twisted in the agony of what Pieter had told him and then she had taken up the gun, *and stopped James from being James, from telling the truth*. She had kept James as her sort had always tried to keep him: securely, in his place" (303). Pieter and his wife have refused the terms of the accord that establishes concord between the two parties. Doing so, even in death, they maintain their high-handedness over the situation.

And yet, these are only subsidiary questions within the novel. The guiding thread still remains the unbearable face-to-face encounter between the other torturer, who begs absolution from his crimes (Dirk Hendricks) and his victim (Alex Mpondo). Of course, the torturer does not distill the truth except drop by drop, when he is forced to do so. He makes public the fact that Alex Mpondo cracked under torture. He enjoys anew this atrocious instant in which the prisoner is forced to reveal everything and even to betray. But he still keeps a part of the truth to himself—the truth that tortured Mpondo for fourteen years, the thought that he may have been responsible, in some measure, for Steve's death. Only the torturer could tell Mpondo whether Steve had already died when he gave in to the torture and gave away his name. What reassured him somewhat during all those years was the idea that perhaps (or surely) Steve had betrayed him first. And yet he realizes within the course of the novel that this was not the case. Mpondo is therefore entirely abandoned to the thought that he was the cause of the death of his brother-in-arms: "Alex was no longer sure of anything. The nightmare from which he had been running ever since his release had caught up with him. The terror of the answer to a single question: had he, by his cowardice, been responsible for Steve's death?" (204). Meanwhile, the novel narrates the fear, the hold that the perpetrator maintains on the victim: "Dirk Hendricks hadn't changed at all . . . what he wanted now was the same thing he had always wanted—to obliterate Alex" (237). As a result, Alex is one with the will of the torturer. And here again is the central question of the novel: "That's what the future holds, he thought: people wanting to know without asking whether my betrayal ended in Steve's death. A question, the only question. One he could not answer because he genuinely did not know. Only Dirk Hendricks knew. The irony of it. *Dirk Hendricks as repository of his past*" (244, my emphasis).

The pivotal scene comes a little later. Sarah, the lawyer, requests one last interview with Dirk Hendricks, in order to know the truth about the moment that Alex spoke. Had Steve already died? Dirk Hendricks answers in the negative, of course. "Alex Mpondo broke first. He pointed the finger at Sizela. He exposed his friend. . . . What Mpondo said made all the difference. It sealed Sizela's fate. . . . Sizela had never mentioned Mpondo, you see—he protected his friend to the last. But now it was obvious that they knew each other well. That infuriated Pieter. He was determined to crack Sizela. . . . Your friend Mpondo . . . was responsible for Steve's death . . . *and that's the truth of it*" (326, my emphasis). As a result, Hendricks remains master of the truth to the very end. He remains the repository of the truth. And yet in her capacity as a third party, the lawyer decides to absolve Mpondo, whom she now believes culpable. She decides to conceal from him what she believes to be the truth. For whatever the executioner says, *what he says will become the truth of the third party, the truth for the rest of the world*. The truth speaks one sole language. And it is always that of the executioner. From then on, nothing remains except absolving the victim. Therefore, during her last walk with Mpondo, Sarah lies to him. She tells him the opposite of what Dirk Hendricks told her. She tells him that Steve had already died when he spoke. Her rationale is that "this reassuring of Alex was much *more important than the truth could ever be*" (331). Such is Sarah's point of view on the truth. But it is not quite that of the novel, not yet. There is also, there is at least, the point of view of the executioner: "The only consolation for this whole calamity was the look that had passed over Sarah Barcant's face when Dirk Hendricks planted the seeds of his lie in her. What a fool she was. To have asked him, of all people, when exactly Sizela had died! What had she expected—*that he would tell the truth*? The truth that Mpondo only broke after Sizela's death? That Pieter was just clumsy? That it was an accident?" (335). Ah, it was therefore a lie? If we believe this page, Dirk Hendricks lied (which we did not know before); he enjoyed one last time (but, here again, once and for all) his power over the victim. But (and I am going to repeat this question several times) how does the novelist know that it was a lie? From where does she grasp, for her part, the truth that the torturer alone possesses? There is, finally, Alex's point of view. He knows that she lied (she? I mean Sarah, of course, within the novel, not the novelist).

She'd been trying to let him off the hook. . . . The fact that she'd assumed Alex would believe what she'd told him showed how long she'd been away. . . . He knew the man's twisted mind and how it worked. He knew what gave him pleasure. And in knowing Dirk Hendricks he also knew that even if the sequence of events had been exactly as Sarah had described them, if Steve had died before Alex named him, Hendricks would never admit to it. No matter the truth of what happened, Hendricks would have lied, most certainly said anything to keep Alex on the hook. (336)

When it adopts the point of view of the torturer, the novel seems to say that Mpondo is innocent of the death of his friend. Sarah therefore wants, in reality, to make him innocent of a crime of which he is (according to the author) innocent, objectively so. She grants him an *absolution* which, all things considered, he should not need. But all this means nothing. How, indeed, does the novelist know that Mpondo is innocent of the crime of betrayal, if (constitutively) only the torturer can know, if the torturer alone possesses the truth of the crime? Of course, Mpondo does not believe what the lawyer tells him in her gesture of absolution. Indeed, if Steve had died before Mpondo had betrayed him, the torturer would not have admitted it in any way. He would have kept the truth for himself. What is important here, therefore, is certainly not Mpondo's innocence. It is the fact that he could know nothing of the truth, absolutely nothing. The truth is in the hands of the torturer, once and for all. Here lies the truth of testimony. *It is always the torturer who testifies, even when it is the victim who speaks.* Testimony always speaks the language of the executioner.

I do not know if this really needed a proper demonstration. But the commission confirmed it in a magisterial and spectacular way. And since it is a grave affirmation, I return to it again, I insist on it, in remaining within the very terms of the novel: Only the torturer possesses the truth of the crime. In other words, there is no truth of the crime. Is this really understood? This is what the novel, *as genre*, had to oppose to the commission's report. One must, therefore, choose one's genre, as one chooses one's camp. It could then be said that Barbara Cassin—with all the respect due to her for her erudition and despite her welcome denunciation of the politico-juridical-religious "imbroglio" of the commission—chose her camp. This camp is not (or not only) that of politics against morality. It is the camp of the theatrical stage of reconciliation, this stage on a global scale, which, despite her reservations, remains a Christian stage, the stage of the Son. She chose the theatrical genre of testimony which today dominates the world, this philosophical genre where the spirit is joined with itself and finally dwells among us. For the novel, there no longer remains anything but remains. That is why the novel alone can suggest this sentence: *There is no truth of the crime* (even if this novel also says the opposite through the voice of the author who, in her all-too-human weakness, believes she knows what the truth of the crime is). The victim will remain always, and forever, in a state of indecision with regard to the truth. This sentence, yes, only the novel could suggest it. No report of any commission could inscribe it in black on white in its pages, even if the report of the Truth and Reconciliation Commission approximates it by pretending to limit its usage of the truth to the narrative and curative effect. To say that there is no truth of the crime, is that a relativism? If you will. But if it is a relativism, it is certainly not Protagoras's nor the commission's, which works politically for the good of the society to be reconciled, and for democracy to be founded through the efficacy of language.

About this crime (the crime about which the "truth" *as fact* is entirely possessed by the torturer), there can be no truth. This is why it will also remain forever a crime without memory, without repentance, without mourning and without forgiveness. I cannot even imagine that someone could ask forgiveness for such a crime without truth. Because this crime without truth is a crime only because it is "without truth," precisely. For what could one henceforth ask forgiveness? Every request for forgiveness would be still more insulting than the crime, because it would obviously mean that the executioner had not understood what it is about, or alternatively that, having perfectly understood, *he doubles the crime with the request for forgiveness.* What's more, whose forgiveness would he ask? A crime without truth, by definition, is also a crime without a witness, and, subsequently, without victim. It makes both victim and witness disappear, without return, without any possible reconstitution, without any "retrospective construction," granting that such a thing could even be envisioned. In the final analysis, who can receive the request for forgiveness? In order to receive it, one would have *to constitute oneself* as victim. One would have to change the nature of the crime, which would immediately cease to be what it is, this crime without truth. To constitute oneself as a victim by receiving the request for forgiveness would be to reconstitute the crime as a fact, to affirm its truth, that is to say, once again radically to ignore its nature.[24] It is a renewed insult, this time self-inflicted, an indelible shame. And regarding this shame, I can only repeat what I have already said in another context: Every retrospective construction of the position of the witness, every reconstitution of the victim, every act of receiving forgiveness "appeals to the power of the archive," because it asks that "the event be recognized as a fact in the world of mortals." It renews the shame, therefore, incessantly.[25] Ignoring the irreversible, unavowable, and therefore unforgivable nature of the crime without truth, pretending to repair the witness who died by the will of the torturer—this doubles denegation with denial. Denegation is the act of the executioner, what constitutes him as an executioner. Denial is the act of the victim, what constitutes one as victim. Of course, Alex Mpondo did not thereby become white. But it's just as if he did. He speaks and from his own mouth we hear the voice of the torturer. Thus, by the grace of forgetfulness (all at once negation, denial, and denegation), I mean, by the grace of the forgetfulness of the crime without truth insofar as it is without truth, we henceforth find ourselves within the monolingual and monochromatic universe of reconciliation, a universe where only one voice is heard, forever, a universe that is one with the being-there of the spirit. A universe without remainder? Perhaps. Only the novel can speak of the remainder, I have said. I now add: Only literature can speak of the Catastrophe. But it can do this only in a dead language, dead forever, inaudible therefore, a language that will never be, never again; a theatrical language that will never be a reconciling and reconciled language. In sum, a language without mourning. And yet, a language that will be obliged to refer to the theater, to the theater of the Greeks, to rival it.

**4.**

It remains for me to speak of the manipulation of mourning.

In reality, that is where we began, by following the very first exchange between Achilles and Hector. But then some tortuous paths returned us to the present, the present of political reconciliation, of living together, the present that is always inspired by the Greek example. It seems that we are condemned to this back and forth between Greek reconciliation and modern reconciliation, jumping over the "Hegelian" moment. And it is a safe wager that it is this Hegelian moment that forces upon us this exhausting return, either to show that the truth that is expressed in the modern practice of reconciliation had already been set to work by Greek sophistry, or, inversely (and this is what I began to do here), to show that Greek reconciliation knew much about its own compromises, its own manipulations, its own denials and denegations, much more than we suspect. This is also why, when Derrida signals (without wanting to linger there, he says) the "profound . . . Christianization that marks the language of this globalization of avowal," he immediately corrects himself by indicating that it has to do, in fact, with a "Hegelian" Christianization ("Avowing," 35).[26] And the reason, of course, is not that the practitioners of modern avowal, from Turkey to South Africa, would have suddenly started reading Hegel, or that the powerful Hegelian reconciliation would have begun to impregnate the world with its historic influence. No, the reason for this is much more complex, and that is why it requires scare quotes around "Hegelian." I am going to explain this in a few sentences.

The "Hegelian" Christianization goes, among other things, through the emergence of philology as an institution of mourning. Philology invented the native, and required therefore an immense enterprise of reconciliation between the philologist and his native, in order for the "knowledge of the philologist" about the native to be justified as the "knowledge of the native" about himself.[27] It was a Christian philology, a colonizing philology, if you will, and of course an orientalist philology. But it is precisely the philology that is in question here, that is to say, a knowledge. A knowledge of the native. And what governs henceforth, and in secret, the enterprise of reconciliation is a strange "structure of testimony," put in place by philology overnight. The native bears witness for his culture, but he cannot do so except as a vestige, in the beyond of a supposed disaster, a disaster of which he knows nothing himself, of course. A witness of his culture, he is also the witness of his own disaster. The native is thus, from the start, a mourning creature. He cannot bear witness for his culture except in mourning, by mourning his culture, in a mourning instituted entirely by philology. It is through this absolutely constraining situation that we are obligated to rethink mourning and the manipulation of mourning. It is this situation which confirms itself and destroys itself (or reveals itself) at once through the rhetoric of reconciliation that followed in the wake of the catastrophes of the twentieth century but also in the practice of avowal and in the management of mourning set in place by the commissions that, the world over, work at reconciliation by the utterance of the truth. Hegel, in his madness for reconciliation, is only the first aftershock of the structure of testimony proper to philology and its institution of mourning. It is the power of this aftershock that obligates us today to revisit the interdiction of mourning decreed by Achilles and the monolingualism of Greek reconciliation, within which, already, the victors (in reality, the perpetrators) take charge of the writing of history, and do so once and for all, in proving the evidence *that there is no other history.* And that one must therefore work against history, if one wishes to understand anything about what occurs there, at the supposed origin of our mourning, of our disaster and of our frenzied reconciliation. I am going to explain all this in a few points.

1.  I did not have any idea of the constraining structure of testimony when I wrote, a few years ago, the essay on Zabel Essayan. A reminder, therefore: Essayan, a writer who was already well known, had returned to the town of her birth, Constantinople, in 1908, just after the Young Turk Revolution. She became part of the delegation that was sent to Cilicia (in the Adana region) by the Armenian Patriarchate in order to gather together the orphans of the pogroms of April 1909, three months after the events. She came back a few months later, powerless and absolutely shattered. The local authorities had not authorized the opening of an Armenian orphanage. Her departure resembled an escape. She identified too deeply with the victims and the survivors. She could have lost her mind. Two years later, in 1911, she published *Among the Ruins,* which is one of the great books of the twentieth century in the Armenian language. She described what she had seen; she expressed her confusion; she raised a plaint that is still heard today, a century later. This was, of course, a testimony, even if this word was not used at the time. It is only now that this designation can be coupled with it. But it was also a monument of mourning. And yet the same Zabel Essayan was incapable of raising again a similar monument of mourning after 1915–16 (at that time she was in the Caucasus). She could not do anything other than gather together the testimonies of the survivors, transcribe them, translate them into French, in the hope that they would be heard by the civilized world. Mourning, from then on, was impossible. The interdiction of mourning pronounced by the perpetrator could still be opposed by the fierce resistance of a woman in 1909. The same interdiction, which is found at the heart of the genocidal will, was final after 1915. Of course, the interdiction of mourning had not been advertised by the perpetrator or shouted out from the rooftops from city to city. It is the experience of this woman, it is the disparity be-

tween the two situations, that of 1909 and that of 1915, which makes me say that she reacted to an interdiction of mourning in writing *Among the Ruins*. That is why I have called her a "modern Antigone."[28] True, she had dared to defy the interdiction. But I myself obeyed; I was obeying already (or still) another necessity: that which obligated me to take recourse in a Greek figure, the very figure, moreover, that occupies finally a central place in the Hegelian understanding of reconciliation.

2.  After the interdiction, there is the manipulation. The interdiction characterizes the time of the crime. The manipulation operates on the contrary in time of "peace," in the time of reconciliation, precisely. I take up again, briefly, the rich argumentation of Mark Sanders, as outlined in his article "Ambiguities of Mourning."[29] The article centers around the testimony and the claim of a Zulu woman, Lephina Zondo, whose son had been executed for his activism as a member of the African National Congress. This woman wants to recover the ashes of her son in order to practice the funerary rites. Immediately, and once again, it is Antigone who comes to the mind of the author, but at the price of a detour. This detour is "custom." The woman addresses herself to the president of the session (who was, in this hearing, Alex Boraine) in order to claim the possibility of mourning, to be sure, against that which she perceives as an interdiction of mourning; yet she does this in the name of custom. "Because it's our custom," the translation makes her say.[30] Not to show the body to the family—is this a violation of human rights? Logic demands, Sanders seems to suggest, that this claim should not have been submitted before the commission. What calls for analysis is the fact that the mother's reaction to the implicit interdiction of mourning is an appeal to law, to civil and civilized law. She appeals to civilized law so that the latter might recognize custom, not as its "other," but from within itself. Indeed, according to Mark Sanders (and if I understand his argument correctly), this claim alone enables the questioning of the identity of civilized law; it "makes the law speak," it makes it speak of itself, it invites it, forces it to return to its foundation, and therefore to understand something that is found in itself beyond itself. It should henceforth have the potential to provoke a crisis within the law that founded the Truth and Reconciliation Commission.

What we thereby see is the organization of a confrontation between custom and law, custom and the rights of man. The question, says the author, "is the 'legal' denial of customary funeral rights, of the usual process of laying the dead to rest."[31] It seems that this confrontation quite naturally invites an exploration of what happens in Sophocles' *Antigone*, or of its interpretation by Hegel. But this can be done on one condition only: that one understand what is meant by this "custom" defended by the South African Antigone against the law. In a word: Customary law is not so customary. In the colonial system, customary law could not be independent of the hierarchy of power. The British had discovered this system in India toward the end of the eighteenth century. The civil and civilized law did not directly govern the natives. They had to be governed by themselves, and so they had to *discover their own proper law*. The principal task of the philologists was therefore to translate into English the law books of the natives, or rather to transform them into law, which was not yet called customary, a law issued from native customs, such as the colonizers read them in their books. Modern colonization begins here. It begins with philology. From then on, the colonized is no longer a raw body treated as a simple resource, as was still the case with the Spanish a century earlier. The idea of a "proper law," of a government of one's own, by one's own law, had to mature over the course of the entire eighteenth century in order to succeed, and finally become this prodigious modern invention, the modern invention par excellence: the invention of the native. The native is the one who lacks the knowledge of custom within himself. Fortunately, the colonizer is there to reactivate custom within the space of his knowledge and to give it back to the native in the form of law, of customary law. And yet who can reactivate custom within the space of knowledge—by translations into English or French if need be, in order finally to make the native profit from it—if not again the philologist? Thus, philology works hand in hand with the colonizer. This powerful lesson in government, which is also a lesson in the fabrication of the native, of the notion and of the reality of the native (of the figure of the native), by philology and by colonial power—this powerful lesson discovered by the English in India after a slow maturation in the course of the eighteenth century was subsequently extended to the whole world and to all colonial practices, in Africa in particular, where it enjoyed remarkable favor during the entire nineteenth century. The civil law of the citizen thus played the role of philology in relation to customary law, which was the law of the native.[32] The law proper to the native could function as law and as system of representation (as much as of government) only within the relation of translation and of knowledge established by philology. It is indeed through the philology of the native that colonial government made (that is, imposed) itself.

What I have just explained in a few lines[33] forces us to read Mark Sanders's analyses with a high degree of uncertainty. In fact, custom is never in a position of exteriority in relation to civilized law, even though the protagonists are never aware of this intimate dependence of custom in relation to civilized law. That is precisely why the intervention of Lephina Zondo before the commission and the request that she formulates can be read as subversive. They are not subversive with respect to the law that decreed an interdiction of mourning. They are subversive with respect to the very idea of reconciliation. The latter, in fact, knows nothing of the interdiction of mourning, or does not want to know anything about it. So much is quite obvious. But above all it knows nothing of the structure of domination in which this interdiction exercised itself. This subversion of the idea of reconciliation seems to be a good thing, in Mark Sanders's eyes, because it provides access to a dimension that the instigators of the commission had not foreseen. The entire enterprise of reconciliation was therefore necessary, along with the avowals, the testimonies, and the confrontations, in order for these two things to appear in filigree, which reconciliation could not foresee: the interdiction of mourning and domination, this very peculiar form of domination that forces the native to think his mourning, his own mourning, through the categories of the colonizer. Even his mourning has not been recognized as his. This would, in any case, be a great success of reconciliation, even if presented in this paradoxical form (reconciliation works against itself), and this would in no way contradict the data of the theater of reconciliation prepared by Hegel. Or would it not be the opposite instead? If it is true that the mourning of the native was not recognized as his *yesterday* because it was forbidden by the law of the state, if it is true that the right of mourning had been refused to him, what of *today*? Is a Truth and Reconciliation Commission in a position to denounce the domination that made "custom" (in its knowledge and in its practice) depend entirely on the hierarchy of colonial power? Is it in a position to change anything about this at all? Has not the mourning of the native been taken away once and for all? Is it not the case that the native must still and always justify his mourning before a commission, by virtue of civilized law? Hence the degree of uncertainty. In any case, the manipulation of mourning is blatant. There cannot be any reconciliation without the manipulation of mourning.

The sons will reconcile themselves beyond death, under the gates of Thebes. This will be called *Versöhnung*. They will be reconciled as sons. They will speak the language of sons, the historical language of struggle and of hard symmetry. Antigone will remain locked up forever within her living tomb. From there she will make her claim heard. In no living language. Forever the survivor. It is indeed *as* survivor that Antigone will forever remain the irony of being-together,[34] of this being-together reconciled in the one and only language of the repentant perpetrator, in the monolingualism of Western law and of history. She will make her claim and her interrogation heard through her dead yet surviving language, in her "nearly lost" language. At the dawn of the modern epoch, Hölderlin is the only one to remember it.

And yet, someone will say, is it not the case that one must distinguish between a nondemocratic state and a democratic state? That one must help (if not love) those who, within the nondemocratic state, are working to liberalize their own society? That one must be at their sides, if it is so needed? Must one not, nolens volens, work at reconciliation, therefore? Must we not do all this, and above all, when the nondemocratic state rests in its foundation and in its renewed existence on the "crime without truth" and on the "interdiction of mourning," in a perfectly reflected way, overt, bluntly, with no hidden agenda and without a shadow of repentance? Let us imagine for a moment what such a nondemocratic state could be. A pure hypothesis, of course. It sends ambassadors throughout the world in order to assure and confirm that the "crime without truth" is indeed "without truth." It humiliates the victim and the survivor (well, those who pretend to be such). It erects monuments to the memory of Hitler and Goebbels in the center of Berlin. It opens offices of denegation, where very serious historians work to drive out the absurd affirmations of the pseudovictims. It employs an army of scholars to this effect. It uses universities to spread the good word. It establishes prizes awarded to the best students who will have been able to write a dissertation at the end of their studies proving once and for all, if there were need for it, that the allegations of crimes against humanity are ridiculous and that they should be returned against those who expound and foment them. It sets in motion the machine of the state in order to resist throughout the world the slightest attempts to lend an ear to these allegations and to translate them into articles of right, and it also uses a few historians in Western universities, who gladly make themselves the apostles of this good word, all in good faith. A situation eminently different from that which prevails in South Africa, you will agree.

None of this was addressed in the present essay, because this was in no way its object. All the apostles of reconciliation would do well to reflect on this again. Yes, one should distinguish. Yes, one should help and even love those who work at the liberalization of their own society. But, on the one hand, one should know with whom one is "reconciling." One should not confuse friendship and reconciliation. One should be capable of carrying out a "politics of friendship" instead and in lieu of a "politics of reconciliation." And, on the other hand, one must in any case know what will never be reconciled within reconciliation (and with this I have occupied myself here). Tomorrow, we shall be reconciled. The crime without truth will remain all the more without truth, there is no need of a nondemocratic state for that. And the interdiction of mourning will not cease to resound in our ears. Antigone will not leave her crypt. Achilles will continue to drag the body of Hector in order to tear it to shreds. The gods will intervene always too late to give him the order to put an end to mourning, in order to convey to him that "too much mourning harms." And history, historicist or not, will always be the accomplice of the perpetrators, whether they were victorious or not. "Even the dead will not be safe," said Benjamin.[35] But it is too late. They *are* in danger; they always were. Only the Greeks will remain forever to speak of the destruction of Troy, of this crime without truth, in the one and only language of mourning usurped. Unless irony is mixed in. The irony of being-together, the sole surviving language.

*Translated from the French by Alison Bjerke*

# The Painter of Postmodern Life

*Michal Ben-Naftali*

Derrida's readers are apparently divided between two opposite types. On the one hand, there are those who seek after affective intimacy, and on the other, those who join a political gravity on the basis of Derrida's effort to rethink the very notion of the political, an effort whose consistent presence as a question Derrida emphasized throughout his work. But one can recognize that the limit between intimacy and polis is not clear-cut. Not only because formal issues that characterized deconstruction from its early days were shown to imply a political dimension through and through (the thought concerning *différance* has always been the thought of the political, Derrida wrote in *Rogues*),[1] and not only because friendship led as if spontaneously to "politics of friendship," but also because what seemed to be an introspection—a confession or an avowal—has always already involved an outside, an outside that is not what could be named a political outside: an absolute outside, a Blanchotian outside, where the voice of the first person heard is both personal and neutral, a voice that maps therefrom the existential questions that life, or rather "living together," poses. And thence—the distinction between the political and the intimate becomes secondary and perhaps less critical.

There is no doubt that within the massive Derridean work of incorporation and contamination, this lesson "Avowing—The Impossible" constitutes a particularly hybrid effort. One can say that, in general, Derrida's writing has unfolded a wide thematic repertoire in which, time after time, a motif that has been moving implicitly in a specific essay or book, seems to have been waiting for the right moment where it could be formulated in a more explicit way, in order to become a principle of thought or a prism through which ideas could be reexamined. This continuity within dissemination, this insistence upon the same motifs using an old vocabulary or neologisms, is what has made the cumulative touch of such a delicate, weak thought into a powerful one.

In *Rogues*, Derrida describes that cyclic movement of rotation around an axis that remains immutable. This is the potter's gesture, he writes, which resembles that of the musician, the sculptor, the rhetorician and perhaps the philosopher, perhaps Derrida himself, who has been drawing his self-portraits through different materials and in different rhythmic variations.[2] In "Avowing—The Impossible," however, Derrida not only joins together different ideas and different semantic fields (such as avowal, confession, his adolescence in Algeria during World War II, globalization or "globalatinization," the Israeli-Palestinian conflict), he actually presents them in different rhetorical registers: from first-person *mémoires* to contemporary political philosophy, from conceptual meditation to historical discussion. It is as if this lesson constitutes a gathering point for issues that were discussed in the past, issues that we are invited to rethink now, although not a single canonical work mentioned (from Aristotle to Nancy) is being interpreted—we are invited to read "pure and simple" Derrida, apparently liberated from a textual crypt in which he is involved, more naked and vulnerable on the one hand, although seemingly closer to the conventional philosophical discourse on the other. Nevertheless, the simultaneity of dispersion and of "living together" in what is conceived as a textual totality evokes restlessness instead of calm, for it is not clear where exactly this lesson was written from, why and for what purpose, from what distance or proximity to the one who writes, or toward which "life" and which "together." It is not clear what the precise register of the discussion—or of thought's slow and dense elaboration—is, and whether all this indeed accumulates into a political statement concerning the contemporary world order, or rather into an aesthetic, ethical, or confessional one. Even if we can find in this lesson an echo to each one of these existential orders, the embarrassment it provokes is not only a function of the anticipated deconstruction of dominant concepts in each and every domain. It has to do rather with the place without place from which Derrida's phenomenological or postphenomenological *epoché* is being made while considering the idea of "living together," there where his earliest landscapes constituted a basic mood and tonality, emphatically prepolitical ones. In this sense, while not explicitly connecting his avowal to specific parental figures, it seems that Derrida approaches here that thrilling phrase of Hélène Cixous's, which he tackled at length in another book: "The author is the daughter of the dead-fathers. *I am on the side of my living mother* [*L'auteur est la fille des pères morts. Moi je suis du côté de ma mère vivante*]."[3]

But he is no longer among the living. And things he said and suggested about others apply to us, Derrida's readers, as well. Indeed, most of us have been fortunate enough to listen to him as well during conferences, in the "living together" that is called forth by a temporary sojourn in a lecture hall, within a temporality that always exceeded the common lecture timetable, from him who was given a place but also took a place, serving both as a guest and a host, and enabling for us all a "living together" in a more comprehensive and profound sense, even when we do not read the same texts written by him, even when we read altogether different texts of which he is not the author, texts written in different

212

languages that belong to different cultures. That is why we cannot write about him without crossing the question, if only within ourselves: What does he say to us today, to each one of us, about his or her concerns. We cannot write about him without giving an account of what we attach ourselves to in his work, whether we are drawn to his deep skepticism or to his profound faith, how we hear the tone of him who divided his writing at least into two voices, into an ensemble of voices, in fact, that were heard alternately as a demand or a request or an imploration or a prayer: How should we "live together"? It was he who spoke in *Adieu to Emmanuel Levinas* about the "intimate exchange that always links one, deep inside, to a dead friend or master,"[4] he who transformed an essay into a homage, who absorbed many others within the very texture of his writing, but in a complicated manner that avoided narcissistic projection and posed perhaps the most radical challenge writing could pose: that movement of de-subjectification, a point zero or a minus point zero, in terms of the *Monolingualism of the Other*, a promise of an unknown language, an unheard language, which does not let itself be reappropriated by normative schemes of grammar or semantics. From this absolute outside, from that speech he did not yet know, and that he will never know, radical considerations concerning "living together" were made. And we should, each one of us, search after his or her place in what constitutes at the same time a Babel of languages and an absolute tongue, avoiding repeating his gesture, keeping ourselves from becoming a mimetic community, a symbiotic Derridean school, grateful to him as we are. Again, it was Derrida, always in brackets, who unfolded Echo's cunning, who in the guise of compulsive repetitions found her way to express her own speech: "(as if Echo had not invented the necessary ruse for speaking in her own name, for reclaiming the floor, for calling the other while feigning to repeat the ends of sentences)."[5]

What then is the register of this lesson? In order to try to touch on this question we should first look at Derrida from a formal perspective, even when he deals, here and elsewhere, with concrete and burning historical and political issues. But this is not the familiar formal perspective. It involves what I shall call an avant-garde or a lyrical abstract in its philosophical expression. Apparently no distance is bigger than the one that lies between philosophy and lyrical abstract, whose origin does not occur within philosophical discourse but within the history of plastic art, and therefore does not seem to be contained in philosophy but, on the contrary, pushes it aside in order to found a singular event. But here it seems that Derrida's continuous attachment to Blanchot becomes prominent: The philosophical text does not constitute only a language and a style that already exist, but first and foremost a "writing" in Roland Barthes's sense, a writing without a priori, a writing from a vacuum, a writing without "writing," a "neutrality that every writer seeks, deliberately or without realizing it, and which leads some of them to silence."[6] The philosopher does not only rewrite the philosophy of the past—and no one has enacted as consciously and as intensively as Derrida this spectral inheritance—but at the same time and perhaps even more insistently the "book to come," a book that involves the antinomy of gathering and dispersion, says Derrida,[7] following Blanchot, who discusses in his turn Mallarmé's project: a book that contains what cannot be contained, a "movement of diaspora" that constitutes a new literary space.[8]

The "book to come" is being suggested every time that literature and "democracy to come" are being discussed. Derrida speaks repeatedly about the common conditions of possibility, historical as well as conceptual, of both literature and democracy: Both lack an essence and a proper meaning and involve a dizzying semantic abyss; both will never be present in a rigorous sense but in changing historical manifestations; both are based on the right to say everything and not to say anything, namely to keep a secret, a secret concerning the real and the fictive and therefore concerning the speaker's responsibility which is at once an irresponsibility and a hyperresponsibility;[9] both are exposed to the destruction of their defenses and to the possibility that the freedom they presuppose will be held against their very notion. But "the book to come," on the one hand, echoing Blanchot and his literary vision, and, on the other, its connection to democracy as the implementation of the ultimate political order, is much closer to painting's radical modernism, being an absolute interruption, an epistemic mutation, one that has indeed made Derrida a permanent stranger within the philosophical togetherness.

It is as if there were two procedures or two dominant sensibilities in Derrida's writing, living together in one corpus: the somewhat more familiar procedure of incorporating others' writings in a hyperbolic and impossible mourning, which was present in every textual meditation that became in a certain sense a eulogy, a mise-en-abyme which was expressed thematically throughout Derrida's writing as a complex act of both an uncontainable paternal inheritance and an invention of the father. At the same time, and perhaps against our permanent search after the Derrida of the Book, of the Book of Books, as much as he studied the books of the past, he studied the book to come, and beside or against his implication within continuity and inheritance, though uncanny, he was looking after the absolute interruption of revolution. Kafka, in Derrida's description, wrote a letter to his father not under his father's name (as did Kierkegaard), but to a father that became a spectral father, as the fathers Cixous points at. The dead father or the killed father becomes a multiplicity through writing, in an Oedipal movement that turns into an anti-Oedipal one, one that undermines the nucleus in which it is apparently implicated. Kafka the son does not try to resemble his father. He describes himself in "a Letter to the Father" as a born delinquent, as a transgressor of law—while the law is the law of normative life, of marriage, of "taking a wife." Paradoxically, contrary to what is described in Freud's *Totem and Taboo*, the law of the father is the law of desire while the son's transgression constitutes a flight from the father and a sublimation of the desire for a woman. Parricide involves fighting for one's de-socialization, for one's freedom of imagination, fighting to liberate oneself from the father and from the bonds of the community in order to live in solitude. Fiction is therefore a usurpation, "a parasitism" that transforms the law of the father and the father tongue, the polis and the social space; it is the capacity to deceive the father, to interrupt the genealogical chain and to dissociate oneself from obligation to continuity. Such is "the law of the father that speaks through the mouth of the son speaking through the mouth of the father,"[10] and that is why the son asks for forgiveness. We shall come back to the son's forgiveness.

The formal disposition of Derrida's "writing," or rather the fictive turning of philosophical writing, is enacted through the aporetic double bind, namely the undecidable tension between the economy of the possible and the aneconomy of the impossible absolute. This repetitive gesture (concerning notions such as forgiveness, hospitality, the gift, or the avowal—as in our case) draws Derrida's map of questioning, and thereby reflects what he avoids putting into question or saying, what he cannot say or would not say. Writing thus maps the conditions of saying and of doing, lingering upon the form, for example, the form of political decision, the form of asking forgiveness in the face of its theatrical "globalatinization" in the contemporary world, in order to formulate an aporia. Never sensational, writing often renounces the sheer narration of a plot ("I have never known how to tell a story," says Derrida at the beginning of his *Mémoires for Paul de Man*)[11] through an antimimetic position that displaces concrete questions, articulating a network or else a grid of ideas and of concepts whose rules are formed by Derrida himself. The further he devotes himself to the world, the more he resists it, through a sort of a rejection of that which is undigestible, of what he cannot digest, in a discursive economy that lets him say things about the worst in a restrained excessiveness. There is nothing like the beginning of the discussion of the sacrifice of Isaac and the lengthy lingering on the sensation of trembling which stays at the body's level in "Mysterium Tremendum," and which pays no attention to bodily tortures, to express this restraint.[12] But Derrida speaks explicitly of this choice at the end of his *Gift of Death*, in an independent section called "Literature in Secret." This chapter deals with the ambiguous speech, as it were, of the one who keeps silent. The secret of the one who wouldn't speak is linked here to the secret of literature and to Abraham's secret, or in other words, to the biblical genealogy of literature that is thus torn from its epic origin, "as though the essence of literature, in its strict sense, in the sense that this Western word retains in the West, were essentially descended from Abrahamic rather than Greek culture."[13] In his elaboration of Kierkegaard's analysis Derrida points out Abraham's renouncement of ethical discourse—of what belongs to the order of communicating, explaining and justifying his deed. All this—in order to fulfill a singular religious responsibility whose ultimate expression is silence and not speech. The discussion articulates the relations between silence, secret, and forgiveness: "Pardon for not meaning (to say . . . )." Here it is not the spectacular theater of forgiveness that Derrida introduces in his lesson. It suggests another forgiveness, an intimate, silent forgiveness, like a weak echo of confession. As in those "affairs" in which it seemed that Derrida kept silent or perhaps did not say enough in the burdened juncture of speech and silence, the question that is posed here implicitly would be whether a philosopher, a thinker, or an intellectual could let himself or herself not speak, refuse the liberty of speech, the democratic freedom

215

of expression and thus the constitutive role he or she plays in this freedom. Would his or her obligation consist in saying, always saying, in every circumstance, always speaking in front of others? Isn't philosophy defined as that genre of discourse that precisely over-comes secrets, aiming to found a space of transparency and intelligibility? "Never has the task of defining the intellectual rigorously seemed so impossible to me as it does today," says Derrida in an interview.[14] In "Literature in Secret" he describes the complex relation between saying and not-saying; not-saying involves, as mentioned above, asking for for-giveness: "Pardon for not meaning." But forgiveness, through its very aporetic condi-tions of possibility, implies the unforgivable. In other words, the choice not to speak, asking thereby for forgiveness, is unforgivable, and he who chooses it, or is forced to choose it, is not exempt from responsibility. On the contrary, he is absolutely responsi-ble for his silence.

The formal antimimetic gesture is not, however, philosophical in any common sense, neither is it narrative. Abstraction does not resemble discursive abstraction, so that some-times philosophy, when encountering it, does not recognize itself. It is closer to the picto-rial abstract, to drawing or to brush paintings whose power or weakness does not lie in what they represent, but in what is created by the composition or the tonality of the colors in a way that in a certain sense transforms Derrida the philosopher into a painter of post-modern life. In *Memoirs of the Blind* he makes another avowal using the child's voice. It is an episode in a family novel. His elder brother had a gift for painting, and his paintings—copies of family photos—were hung on walls throughout the house, arousing his little brother's envy. He recognized that he was punished, but that he was nevertheless secretly chosen, as if called by another line, another graphé: writing. But this recognition, at the beginning of a discussion on the abyssal night (again, Blanchotian night) at the basis of drawing, a drawing which is altogether foreign to the day's phenomenality, a drawing whose origin is memory and not perception even when the model is present in front of the artist, a drawing that is therefore at the basis of an absolute heterogeneity between the drawing line and the thing drawn—this recognition of the latent and ambivalent de-mands of brotherhood pervades in unexpected ways. This does not apply only to those works in which he dealt directly with painting or drawing (*The Truth in Painting, Memoirs of the Blind*).[15] It applies to the very philosophical act, to the philosopher as an abstract painter who responds to the imperative of silence that is essential to painting, and who thus makes a weak gesture, much like drawing is a weak painterly gesture, which has nothing to do with the drawer's affective sensibility or the intensity of his hold on the brush. Drawing itself, the decision to draw and not to paint in color, to make a fragile line, a sign or a trace of a sign, constitutes a decision to inhabit a weak register, though Derrida with the same determination imposes a powerful affective tonality in some of his brush paintings.

As far as I know, Derrida never wrote about Michel Henry, and Henry's phenomenol-ogy of the flesh, which is implicated within a self-conscious metaphysical language, might

seem misplaced in relation to a thinker who devoted a life work to deconstructing immanent presence and the living present. But Henry's vocabulary as well as the rigorous distinctions he makes between "life" or "absolute life" and "world," between "interiority" and
"exteriority" or "object," should not keep us from looking at those moments where one
can sense in Derrida the same self-affection that Henry describes and names "life." Those
moments of trembling, of the self-absorbed trembling body, and in a much more complex
sense, those insane moments of transcending the aporia of decision, of taking a singular
responsibility, moments that last forever, being divided only by representation that comes
after the fact.

Henry's starting point was indeed a categorical distinction between "world," namely
what appears to us as an exterior object, and "interiority," which constitutes a different
order of revelation, an unseen one, which cannot be related to as an "inner world." This
interiority is what we mean when we speak about "life." Life is experienced before any
look and independently of it. It lies at the basis of our pathetical subjectivity. When we
experience pain or happiness, we do not open ourselves to exteriority or toward a transcendent instance. We open ourselves to life itself, to that self-affection that recognizes no
distance. However, we rarely experience life in full. In this context, Henry addresses art in
general and Kandinsky's both painterly and theoretical work in particular—work that
formulates, in spite of its revolutionary character, the axioms that stand at the origin of
any art. In a certain sense, every art is abstract. It is wrong to see art as a means to copy
either a model or the world of nature. There exists an art worthy of its name only inasmuch as life does not appear in it as an object. Art should make us see what is not seen and
what cannot be seen by constructing a new ontological dimension. In this sense it appears
as an expression of life by intensifying life and thereby our experience of it. Art's theme is
life—its tonality, its force, those unseen emotions through which one does not cease to
experience oneself in a relation of absolute immanence. In ordinary life this pathetic force
is not in use, or else it might become a source of anxiety. Art enables us to experience this
force not through intellectual reflection, but through the growth of sensation by pathetic
identification which is woven between an artist and a spectator who build together, in
their imaginary, a "pathetic community." Those who experience art experience, then, the
same pathos as those who made it.[16]

Introducing Michel Henry inside the frame of Derrida's family scene is important, in
my view, for several reasons: It enables us to think seriously of Derrida's pathos, and even
of a "pathetic community" involved with him. It enables us to formulate those moments of
implication or contamination or even "contemporaneity" enacted between reader and
writer, or moreover, those moments of reflexive identification between the one who forgives and the one who is forgiven. Furthermore, Henry enables us to return via a nonvital-
istic philosophy to the essential notion of "life" and to give it the full weight that seems to
be given to it in Derrida's lesson on "living together." Henry, by describing Kandinsky and
his privileged place in the world of figurative art, also helps us think of Derrida as someone

who articulated an aesthetics of philosophy. Just as Kandinsky's lines or points unfolded the axioms at the origin of art, Derrida, in both his abstract though material way and his lyrical or "pathetic" way, unfolded the principles and the ambitions of canonical discursive philosophy. And, much like Kandinsky, Derrida did so from a marginal, if not revolutionary, place.

Abstraction (and the pathos that accompanies it) has various manifestations in Derrida's writing. First, it is enacted as a generalization. But it is not a modest one, namely a generalization that is being induced from several elements that seem to have a common denominator. Derrida's generalization is much more far-reaching. He takes a notion (such as "Shibboleth," "sacrifice," "mourning"—there are plenty of examples) that becomes flexible and virtuosic enough to encompass a large and heterogeneous repertoire of phenomena that belong to different zones of being and cognition—concrete as well as virtual, as if it were a metaphor performing a poetic act of joining. But what is called a "metaphor" in fact becomes a quasi-transcendental condition of thinking a constitutive structure in human experience. In our lesson, Derrida not only connects what applies to communities, nations, or states and what applies to families and individuals (thus crossing Arendt's distinctions between different spaces of the human condition and between a domestic subjectivation and a political individuation), but the very concept of "living together" gets crystallized on the basis of the individual body in order to reach, finally, via the intimate life of the couple and of home, the polis and the global "living together" and thus become a condition of possibility of thinking this ensemble ("Avowing," 24). The harmony or the disharmony in which the body is orchestrated, the way my body relates to my psychic existence, whether I live in peace with myself, with certain parts of myself, whether I put them aside or kill them altogether, the expression I give them, all these aspects—which are of course articulated differently—come up in Derrida's spectral conversation with himself, which is thus never an introspection in the regular sense. It is a crucial starting point for discussing the political. But what seems to be a common measure between the intimate and the political via the metaphor or the quasi-transcendental principle of "living together" must not lead us astray. The body and the house, since those days when the child-that-he-was did not yet talk in terms of territory, possession, or place, have always supplied an affective color to Derrida's writing, and perhaps they also stand at the basis of the "pathetic community" of his readers. However, we all sense the deception that a too-quickly-felt intimacy might create. People may share a flat but not live together; sometimes they must avoid dwelling together in order to live together; families can share a common space with no exchange but that which has to do with common functioning: All the aporias henceforth in Derrida's lesson will result from the secret that ties togetherness to loneliness and loneliness to togetherness, and will have to do with earlier and later texts he wrote, texts that reexamine the manner in which our thinking of "living together" is indeed a broadening of the Oedipal nucleus, one that is vulnerable to mystifications and populist rhetorical perversions, but that at the same time opens up to spectralization that takes its distance from spontaneous belonging, thus founding a moral alliance.

What specifies this lesson is that the formal principle of abstraction, which is present in many of Derrida's works, receives another pathetic dimension—to use Henry's terms—in fact a biographical intensification. This is of course not the first time that we hear those details about childhood or adolescence in Algeria before and during World War II, about the complex ethnic context, about the powerful experience of separations and expulsions that was not yet articulated or else understood in terms of citizenship and its negation, but that became little by little the basis of his continuous rebellion against two ways of "living together": racist gregariousness, on the one hand, and defensive segregation, on the other. But it is clear that a person who lives with his memories recounts them each time differently, and that here, even if he once said he couldn't tell a story, concrete narrative is nevertheless necessary, for it lies at the heart of the question that constitutes the title of this whole lesson: "Avowing—The Impossible." Moreover, as does every text written by Derrida, it implies another impossibility—that textual excessiveness which cannot be reduced to hermeneutic understanding, and which necessarily makes the experience of reading an experience of the unreadable.

What characterizes this avowal, this confession? Who is its addressee? What is the language of avowal? And why is this low-key avowal in the first person juxtaposed to the collective act of avowal and forgiveness, which characterizes "living together" in the epoch of technology and "globalatinization"? What is the relation between the global scene, which results from recognizing the crimes of the past, namely crimes against humanity, and Derrida's avowal? Why is biography introduced within a semantic field of repentance and forgiveness? Does he ask for forgiveness? And if so, from whom? Indeed it seems that, if the theatricalization of global forgiveness is at issue here, this is not the same theater, this is not the same drama, these are not the same actors, even though in both cases, the private and the public, avowal is taken to the point of the impossible.

Derrida says that he is going to speak in the first person, but in this avowal, which lasts about three pages, he speaks alternately in the first and in the third person: the portrait of the philosopher as a child. In other places as well, when asked to describe his childhood, he emphasized the incapacity to reproduce what was passing in the mind of a little boy facing such events, what he was thinking about, what he was feeling, whether he was hurt by the very shock of changes and the intuitive knowledge that followed, namely that "living together" might not hold, might not be what it used to be, that times will never be what they were, that there will sometimes be more togetherness and sometimes less togetherness.[17] There are biographical details that arise in other contexts and do not appear in this lesson. They are linked to his brother and sister who were expelled from school and to the fact that no one in the family talked about what was happening or supplied explanations. Here Derrida does not describe his home; he describes the outside without saying how the family reacted, what the adults were saying, what the persecution did to the feeling of coherence or to the unraveling within. In what way did the boy become his family's chosen, representing in his sensitivity the unknown that became a burden or a task? In other words, at the time the events were taking place, Derrida the child experienced them through the same double movement of affective tension, namely involvement and distance, the very "within without" that would become the deconstructive double bind. The fact that the speaker is an adult naturally creates a split in the whole procedure. No one bears witness for the witness; he cites Celan elsewhere.[18] The adult who testifies here for the child, in the place of the child, making the child speak, giving words and concepts to what was then prereflexive, deprived of words, and never articulated as a consolidated position or an active rebellion—leaves the child's avowal silent. The first person who writes "I" is juxtaposed to the child's third person, whose childhood wounds are still open, so that there exists an almost fatherly continuity between past and present, a thread that ties early times to later times also in conditions of splitting and multiplicity. "Is there a 'living together' otherwise than among 'first persons'?" Derrida asks ("Avowing," 27). But the interesting thing here is indeed the division of personal pronouns, since he could have spoken about his past in the first person. Derrida chooses to bring closer and to distance his testimony at once, because avowal is impossible. And the pathos of his words results not only from what they say—from what relates to the burdened biographical and historical figure of the "Jewish child"—but also from what they keep in secret. Why did the child react that way, while his environment reacted differently? Why did the environment mark its belonging while the child marked his alienation? What caused his repulsion? From what did he isolate himself? One cannot confess, he says; this is an impossible act that relates to the impossible ("Avowing," 37). Nevertheless, and for this very reason, it is necessary. In *Monolingualism of the Other*, Derrida writes that one cannot testify but to the unbelievable.[19] What can be proven belongs to the order of knowledge. The order of testimony, on the contrary, presupposes the miraculous.

Choosing the language of avowal, then, places Derrida's discussion of "living together" within the order of the faith and faithfulness that the listeners are invited to show in the child's experience, which the adult tries to reconstruct. This is the untold alliance, a temporary alliance of "living together," between the witness and his audience. Derrida's axiomatic declarations on the conditions of the possibility and the impossibility of "living together"—on what it presupposes and what keeps it alive—derive, therefore, from the main gesture of lyrical abstraction, namely, an act of generalization that carries structural characteristics that constitute experience, and which is painted by the child's affective experience: "Everything comes to me, no doubt, from this source," he says ("Avowing," 30). In this way he enables us, his audience, to accept his assertions or reject them, but thereby he also transforms us, in Henry's terms, into a pathetic community.

An intriguing moment in this avowal is connected with the conclusions Derrida drew from what had happened to him, somatic conclusions, as it were, that became a

*Weltanschauung* at the foundation of deconstruction, if it has one. At an early phase Derrida felt, in his words, his capacity to betray his relatives and to recognize his betrayal if only within himself ("Avowing," 28). In other words, even when young he felt the untying of togetherness at the heart of togetherness. He felt that his instinctive reaction to anti-Semitic persecutions was opposite to that of the community, in a way that perhaps made him doubly haunted, by xenophobic exclusiveness from without and by Jewish exclusiveness from within. (It is important to note that in other descriptions of childhood scenes, Derrida speaks about a Jewish community with a much more complex cultural tissue, a community that was in fact alienated from the Jewish culture and copied Christian rituals: synagogues were called churches, Bar Mitzvah was turned into a communion, circumcision became baptism.)[20] As a boy he felt the terror imposed by a togetherness that can suffocate thinking. Furthermore, he felt his own suspicion toward this togetherness that, in times of unbearable distress, made of these difficult circumstances a constant characteristic and even a privilege or else an election. He felt then the option given to him to retreat, to defend himself in his turn from the self-defense of the community, to refuse belonging or possessing, or simply to betray: to speak to the community in another language, which is not the language of "living together," if it has one single language. The word "betrayal" is surely prominent here, all the more so in the face of Derrida's intensified preoccupation with faith, belief, faithfulness, and credibility, which form the conditions of possibility of any speech.

We cannot ignore Abraham in this context and the thought Derrida dedicated to him in *The Gift of Death* and in "Abraham, the Other": Abraham the father of faith, who betrays his relatives, there where faith and betrayal live together, if only as a part of a certain Judaism or Jewishness.[21] Abraham, according to Kierkegaard's reading, preferred the togetherness with God to living together with the others. Abraham thus renounced the ethical or social norms of "living together." For this reason there was no language among world languages that could let him explain his deed or justify it in the face of the community he seemingly represented. It is a supreme moment of faith in which faithfulness to the One, to the absolute Other, implies betraying the other other. Each betrayal, each sacrifice, according to Derrida, implies betraying the one for the other. But Derrida's betrayal involves here an unknown addressee, a totally other, identity-less addressee, a neutral voice that commands him from within or from without, making a delinquent out of him. This unknown addressee becomes to a major extent a haunting or spectral figure for Derrida. Throughout his work, this figure would sometimes take the form of a friend, and in this sense, unique as it is, would become at once singular and replaceable. But here this figure tells him or says through him much more than what Abraham said, what he could say or let himself say. It tells him that saying "no" to togetherness is crucial in order to make togetherness possible. In other words, the religious "no" (or the aesthetic "no," for these orders are not so different from one each other after all) addressed to the ethical order not only transgresses "living together" but conditions it as well. Abraham's sacrifice, as Derrida tries to show in *The Gift of Death*, is an integral part of daily life, an inevitable act that is implicated in the very normal economy of "living together."[22] Isaac too was to sacrifice one of his sons for the sake of the other.[23]

What is left then is the complementary layer of this scene—this scene of Derrida's avowal: asking for forgiveness. Asking for forgiveness for what is by definition unforgivable. Abraham asked God for forgiveness, Derrida writes in *The Gift of Death* (following Kierkegaard's fiction), although he could not have acted otherwise, although he would have done the same in any similar situation. Abraham did not ask Isaac or his relatives, those whom he betrayed, for forgiveness. Derrida, in his turn, does not address his relatives. On the contrary, he defines the conditions of the possibility of "living together" as containing crypts of retreat and solitude. The adult is therefore not the young delinquent who has changed and became transformed. Moreover, the adult is the one to have made the child's insights into constitutive axioms of "the ethics of deconstruction." The adult who in other theatrical scenes performed alternately as Derrida-Abraham or as Derrida-Shylock[24] became the one who is looking for a place without a place, after the night from which forgiveness is being delivered: "Pardon for not meaning," that reflexive though evasive forgiveness, which leans on a narcissistic chain of identifications, and which is crucial for any forgiveness—a forgiveness in which the one who asks and the one who gives finally ask forgiveness from themselves. Like the forgiveness we ask from the dead, a forgiveness that is as necessary as "living together," a forgiveness that Judaism celebrates in the grand Day of Forgiveness, when God inscribes the Book of Life, as Derrida recalls in another book.[25] A supreme moment of "living together" in which "we let ourselves pray with the delinquents."[26]

The child that became a man defines, then, the principles of "living together" beginning from that spectral darkness that accompanies all his life, a darkness that is connected with conscious and unconscious memories, and which makes him recognize the ambiguous moments of the community's embrace as necessary precisely for honoring the solitude of each of its members. Since he fears his solitude, but at the same time, and perhaps even more, he fears losing it. "Living together" therefore involves an essential solitude for those who take part in it, a de-socialization that is necessary for their very socialization, a possibility of accompanying from afar, of separation, of interruption: "Does not 'living together' take place from the instant that the concern over this question makes us tremble in our solitude and *avow*, yes, declare our despair and share it?" ("Avowing," 20). "Living together" is not based on recognizing commonality, but on making solitude common. That would be the widest common denominator, and in this sense, the most solid one of a "non-operative" community of those who lack community. In *Adieu to Emmanuel Levinas*, Derrida adds, following Levinas's articulation between hospitality and interruption: "The social bond is a certain experience of unbinding without which no respiration, no spiritual inspiration, would be possible. Recollection, indeed being-together itself, presupposes infinite separation."[27]

Throughout *Politics of Friendship*, Derrida discusses the tension that prevails between essential solitude and the relational asymmetry that is thereby implied: "We are first of all, as friends, friends of solitude, and we are calling on you to share what cannot be shared: solitude. We are friends of an entirely different kind, inaccessible friends, friends who are alone because they are incomparable and without common measure, reciprocity or equality. Therefore, without a horizon of recognition. Without a familial bond, without proximity."[28] Still, the affective zones that preoccupy Derrida, those "Abrahamic" limit zones are much more threatening. And what apparently looks like a condition of the possibility of pacified "living together" might ruin it altogether in the most desperate manner. This was indeed what was asked of Abraham: to murder the child of the promise, the child of the future to come, for the sake of the wholly Other; Abraham was about to commit a crime against humanity. The potential for perversion that Derrida seems to be fighting for, insisting on keeping secrets and keeping distance as crucial for responsibility as such, the interval of solitude necessary for decision making—all these are pregnant with evil as much as they anticipate the good. Derrida repeats it time and again.

> To love in love or friendship would always mean: I can kill you, you can kill me, we can kill ourselves. Together or one another, masculine or feminine. Therefore, in all cases, we *already* are . . . dead for one another.[29]

The implication of love within hatred, of pleasure within pain, of friendship within animosity, constitutes a structural possibility that is morally indifferent,[30] whether we stand with Kant, who presupposes animosity as the state of nature beginning from which we should establish our life together, or whether we are inclined to think, following Levinas, that a pacified hospitality is at the basis of human events.[31]

Living is living together. It is a vital necessity and an inevitable imperative that is imposed at random on everybody. Even if we do not know how to do it or how to do it well—even in fighting or in hatred or in war, even in innocence, in indifference or in obscure familiarity, even in what seems to be a total ejection from the "living together" (of the *sans-patrie*, the refugees, the exiles)—life is happening together, already constructed by an originary symbolic formation of togetherness, even before it is subordinated to a logos that supplies it with an inner justification and makes it meaningful. Although Derrida relates to the distinction between the togetherness on which we are projected and that which is founded by a political or juridical act, recognizing thereby the process of socialization and politicization as crucial for "living together" in harmony and peace; although he raises the question of whether the globalization of forgiveness constitutes a symptom of contemporary "living together" that has changed its temporality and space as well as its very notion; although he unfolds the aporias that lie in the apparent definite answers to massive fascist and totalitarian attacks on "living together," but which perpetuate in their turn logocentric homogenization using market economy and the media—the focus of his lesson is not the political order and is not an attempt to search for a scheme that mediates between the prepolitical and the political. Derrida stops at the prepolitical, affective, or pathetic level of "living together." He stops before the law, in that place without place where a bare "living together" takes place, life of maturation, of expectation and aging, that place without place that lacks a world, where the world is put within brackets and the "most necessary, the most logical, but also the most insane" experience of *epoché*, the phenomenological gesture, becomes possible.[32] Only therefrom, without that mediation of world or polis, independent of world's existence or destruction, can he define a "living together" worthy of its name. The hypothesis about the ruin of the world—he has already written in his early introduction to Husserl's *Introduction to Geometry*[33]—does not threaten the pure sphere of phenomenological existence. "Living together" involves the existence of an absolute other and is inscribed, therefore, in every relational gesture that displaces the self from its essential solitude toward the other, in avowal as in forgiveness, in responsibility as in promise.

But the radicalism of this phenomenological (and then, with Levinas, postphenomenological) description lies in the fact that its conditions of possibility are formulated in terms of crisis, of accident, or, moreover, through the experience of absence as an originary relational experience. "Living together" presupposes a separation and is dependent on it, and therefore the two options he rejected as a youth, gregarious symbiosis on the one hand and defensive segregation on the other, are not worthy of the name "living together." Consensual community is neither the condition of "living together" nor its telos. "Living together" is manifested at its most as surviving, as *sur-vie*, when we lose the togetherness necessary for us and feel we are unable to continue living. Mourning is thus the experiential structure at the basis of "living together."[34] "Living together" is at once a deprived life, and we should consider togetherness beginning from deprivation, from the anticipated departure of the other, from the melancholic wound that keeps the memory of "living together" and foretells its future; beginning with the interruption that abandons us to our solitude, in the light of which togetherness does not continue to prevail except within him or her who should carry henceforth the other and its disappearing world. To come back to Michel Henry's language, "living together" could also exist in the absence of a world, after the end of the world, in an acosmic situation, acutely described by Hannah Arendt.[35] Derrida does not say so when he comes to deal with the Israeli-Palestinian conflict, but perhaps for him as well, acosmic melancholy, which conditions the crystallization of subjectivity, might become apolitical and reflect a pathology in political life, which is manifested through the incapacity to ask for forgiveness.

But the claim implied in his words is much more far-reaching. In fact, when he leads us through his avowal to the aporias of "living together" and to the question of the relations between Israelis and Palestinians, Derrida renounces the common vocabulary of the "peace process," suggesting another semantic field. And he asks without asking why, in a state where forgiveness constitutes a formative element in the very process of calendar temporality with its annual renovation, forgiveness is not possible. And he asks without asking if we can imagine a third party involved in forgiveness, if forgiveness can be mediated. And he asks without asking if political forgiveness is enough in order to create real reconciliation.[36] And he asks without asking whether the global theater of forgiveness would work in this case as well, in face of these wounded communities. And he asks without asking whether sons would be able to do what fathers were unable to do.[37]

These are the words of Derrida the son or Derrida the child, "the child of whom I speak and who makes me speak," the child who interrogates himself "in the most insomniac fashion" ("Avowing," 29). The child is the one to object sometimes publicly to the politics of the state of Israel; the child is the one to question the violence implicated in the very foundation of this state, the one to ask if it illustrates a violence that no state can be exempt from, or whether it is another state, appearing before "another law" and "another justice." The child is he who wishes to reflect on the articulation between avowal and forgiveness beginning from de-socialization, via individual prayer, away from the crowd. The only possible questions, Derrida wrote in the book dedicated to Hélène Cixous, are the impossible ones.[38] Possible questions are those we can answer and are therefore not true questions—although elsewhere, he said that the proof for the existence of an answer is that one cannot face the question. Knowledge is too terrible.

The scene of forgiveness Derrida imagines in *Literature in Secret* belongs to literary fiction. Literature is the event in which impossible forgiveness takes place. It presupposes that the law of the father brings forth murder. In order for the son to forgive the father, he should identify with the father, that is, become in his turn a potential murderer. "One of the causes of this aporia of forgiveness is the fact that one cannot forgive, ask, or grant forgiveness without this specular identification, without speaking in the other's stead and with the other's voice. Forgiving by means of this specular identification is not forgiving, because it doesn't mean forgiving the other *as such* for an evil *as such*."[39] At the same time, in order for the father to ask for forgiveness, he should identify himself with the victim, that is, show that he realizes the harm he has done to the other: "Can one ask someone other than oneself for forgiveness? Can one ask one's self for forgiveness?"[40] Specular identification or reflexive narcissism would thus lead to the following conclusion: "Undeniably, the letter from father to son is also a letter from son to father and from son to son, a letter of one's own [*une lettre à soi*, also 'to itself, to himself'] whose stakes remain those of forgiving the other by forgiving oneself. Fictive, literary, secret, but not necessarily private, the letter remains, without remaining, between the son and himself."[41] Forgiving the other is at the same time an inner movement. "Forgiveness is thus always asked—by means of retraction—of oneself or of another, of another self."[42]

We do not know whether "Avowing—The Impossible" is indeed Derrida's (fictive) letter to his father, the son who speaks of his guilt toward the Jewish community, performing thereby the ultimate scene of literature. It is clear, however, that the peace that "comes into bodies and souls" ("Avowing," 23), peace that expresses the pathetic texture of "living together," must hold to this intimate specularity; it must be, after all, forgiveness that a "Jewish child" asks of himself as of another.

If we join Derrida's profound belief, ignoring the profound skepticism that lived together with it, perhaps we will discover that the drama of forgiveness is the history of God: a drama between father and son that ultimately takes place between God and himself, suggesting God's implication in every forgiveness. "Forgiveness comes to pass as a covenant between God and God through the human."[43]

# Return to the Present

*Sherene Seikaly*

> Your father is your father. Whenever you sat with him the two of you
> spoke quickly. He didn't show his wound in front of his son. You don't
> know how you hid from him the severity of your compassion for him,
> and so you inherited his wound.
>
> —Mahmoud Darwish, *Before Absence*

In "Avowing—The Impossible: 'Returns,' Repentance, and Reconciliation," Jacques Derrida reflects on the aporia of "living together" as both
a simple evidence and the promise of the inaccessible. To explore "living
together," Derrida breaks open the possibility of the unified self, the unified whole or ensemble, and the notion of synchronous time. His reflections on avowal and living together take him to Israel and Palestine, an
example, he remarks, that "will not surprise you" ("Avowing," 24).

Drawing on Derrida's lessons of the alterity of past and future,
mourning and hope, and the fractured self, I offer a set of reflections
on the experience of asynchronous time in the eastern Mediterranean
city of Haifa. Since the late Ottoman period, Haifa has sustained a repu-
tation of historical and cultural "coexistence," what Derrida might have
called resigned cohabitation ("Avowing," 24). I read Derrida's lesson
on avowal from another shore, that of a Palestinian diasporic experience of "returning" to my city of origin—where both sides of my family
resided before 1948—through both my research and my marriage to a
Palestinian-Israeli (yet another shore of experience that I tentatively,
partly share). Reflections on the web of wounds, memory, and forgetfulness contribute a layer to the writing on Palestinians operating in and
against the constraints of Israeli Jewish "enforced hospitality," and pon-
der avowal, betrayal, and the togetherness and *aparthood* of living in
Haifa.[1] How can we imagine a living together that contains a whole,

neither "formed nor closed"? And indeed, "Who can allocate places? Who can authorize himself . . . [to make] this place his place?" ("Avowing," 18, 41).

## Time, Self, and Other

"Living together," for Derrida, oscillates between the tone of practical serenity and tragic pathos, between philosophical wisdom and desperate anguish. He explains that the wise tell us we must live together and prescribe rules for doing so—norms, precepts, and jurisprudence. Others declare that living together is unachievable.

Yet, Derrida insists, "In any case, in any fashion, 'live together' one must" ("Avowing," 23). This "one must" can be heterogeneous to the point of incompatibility; it ranges from an inaccessible idea to a fatality that can be experienced as good, neutral, or infernal. There is the living badly together (in hatred, war, apartheid, lack of trust, indifference, resignation). Yet at its best, "living together" can be an "interrupting excess" that transports self and *ensemble* beyond all that is based on the opposition between nature and culture, threatening the totality of the whole ("Avowing," 26–27).

"Living together" as a source of serenity and pathos, wisdom and anguish, is also linked to the proximity of the other in the present. This other in the present is the alterity of past and future, the experiences of memory (of a younger self) and promise (of an older self), of mourning and hope. All of these conditions are interruptions of identity, inextricably linked to the experience of asynchronous time. One lives with the other (the dead, the not yet born) and the other in the self (the younger, older, larger self).

The experience of asynchronous time in turn interrupts the idea of a unified subjectivity and self-presence.[2] The self in the very moment of self-awareness is "anachronistic," as a result of experiencing, living, the past in the present. Thus living together with the dead is not accidental, miraculous, or extraordinary. It is an "essential possibility of existence." This possibility of existence is a reminder that "the idea of life is neither simple nor dominant even if it remains irreducible." Thus, "living together" cannot have the simplicity of "a 'living' in the present pure and simple" ("Avowing," 20). For Derrida, living in the present is as philosophically impossible as the cohesiveness of a self, living synchronously with itself, conjoined in a totality.

The resonance between the dislocated self and the always open, never-formed collective unfolds at various moments in "Avowing—The Impossible." One such moment is Derrida's recollection of his departed friend Emmanuel Levinas. At a meeting of the Colloques des intellectuels juifs de langue française, as André Neher is speaking, Levinas turns to Derrida and quips: "You see, he is the Protestant—me, I'm the Catholic." Derrida asks: "How can a so-called Catholic Jew . . . 'live together' with a supposed Protestant Jew, while remaining a Jew together with himself, and while opening himself to another Jew, probable or improbable, in this case me, who has never felt very Catholic, and above all not Protestant?" ("Avowing," 21).

Derrida conjures the Algeria that inhabited him long after his departure from its Mediterranean coast as "another shore of Judaism."[3] In doing so, he names the absence of "the Islamo-Abrahamic" in the triangle of Jew, Protestant, and Catholic, thereby opening the idea of a Jewish whole to interrogation. Levinas's witticism is an opening for Derrida's reflections on living together. This aporia begins with the split self—"And how does a Jew of whom I know only too well . . . that he will never have been sure of being together with himself in general . . . how could such a split or divided Jew have received this remark?" It moves to the division and cohesion of the *ensemble*, or the whole—"the supposed friendship, the affinity, the complicity, if not the shareable solidarity of Jews so different within themselves"—and beyond, since for Derrida the "'living together' with a non-Jewish world was no more serious or more urgent a problem than that of 'living together' with all the forms of what one calls the Jewish communities of the world" ("Avowing," 21–22).

Yet in all this Derrida leaves the possibility of a Muslim Jew unnamed. When he conducts a "return" of sorts to Jerusalem, he reflects—"Maimonides, by the way, said that *teshuva* also meant the end of exile" ("Avowing," 40). Maimonides, who "defies categorization"[4] for his prominence both as a Jewish thinker and leader and as an Islamic philosopher, provides an opportunity to reflect on the possibility and impossibility of a Muslim Jew,[5] a "living together" of another sort.

Derrida's entry into reflections on living together in Israel and Palestine is also, and not surprisingly, through that other shore of Judaism, Algeria. He reflects on his life as a young Jew in Algeria, where he "could dream of a peaceful cultural, linguistic, and even national plural belonging only through the experience of nonbelonging: separations, rejections, ruptures, exclusions" ("Avowing," 27). That child in Algeria rejected the virulent anti-Semitism of the French authorities as well as the constitution and reconstitution of a Jewish whole (*ensemble*).

For the child in Algeria, the only "living together" that was bearable was one that "supposed a rupture with identitarian and totalizing belonging." The turning away from communitarian symbiosis carried both the risk of betrayal and the potential of being more, perhaps the most, faithful to "a certain Jewish vocation" ("Avowing," 28).

Risking betrayal is one aporia of avowing the impossible and living together: "I will never be able to renounce and to say no to a preference for 'my own' [*les 'miens'*], nor, inversely, to justify it, to have it approved as the law of universal justice." It is this position, perhaps, as "the only, the last, and the least of the Jews" that made both the wounds of anti-Semitic persecutions and a vigilance against being "contained, exhausted, or governed" by a natural, organic, or a juridico-institutional whole "unerasable" in everything Derrida said, wrote, or taught ("Avowing," 37, 27–29). It is through this child's vigilance in Algeria that Derrida reflects on Israel, Zionism, and the living together of Jews: "The same vigilance was warning him, warns him today, against all the risks of the 'living together' of the Jews, be they of a symbiotic type (naturality, birth, blood, soil, nation) or conventional (state juridi-cal, in the modern sense): a certain communitarianism, a certain Zionism, a certain na-tionalism and all that can follow [from] the motifs of filiation through blood, appropriation of the place, and the motif of election." This vigilance against containment in the "motifs of filiation through blood" further "pushes the said child not only to oppose, sometimes pub-licly, the politics of the current Israeli government and of a great number of those that pre-ceded it, but also to continue to interrogate himself in the most insomniac fashion regarding the conditions in which the modern state of Israel established itself" ("Avowing," 29).

Having laid the groundwork for the critique of Israel, Derrida "hasten[s] immediately to add at least two things":

(1) that one can remain radically critical in this regard without implying thereby any threatening or disrespectful consequences for the present, the future, and the existence of Israel, on the contrary; (2) that I have been able to perceive, and to rejoice at this during my last visit to Israel and to Palestine, that these questions, these "returns" (reflections, repentances, conscious realizations) upon certain founding violences are today more frequent and declared by certain Israelis, citizens and authentic patriots, and by new historians of the state of Israel, the ones and the others having decided to draw political consequences from this return to the past, as some Palestinians do as well. ("Avowing," 29)

## Past

Living in Haifa in the present entails a delicate balance of asynchronous time. Holding U.S. citizenship, and standing as outsider-insider, I do not return to the past in Haifa, for it rarely leaves me, offering instead a web of experiences of debt and death.

Judith Butler has powerfully delineated the link for Derrida between "debt" and "death." Noting an urgency in Derrida to acknowledge the people who translated him, read him, defended him, and made good use of his thinking and words, Butler recounts:

I leaned over and asked whether he felt that he had many debts to pay. I was hoping to suggest to him that he need not feel so indebted. . . . He seemed not to be able to hear me in English. And so when I said "your debts," he said: "My death?"
"No," I reiterated, "your debts!" and he said: "My death!?"[6]

Butler further reflects on the debt-death link for Derrida through the act of mourning, citing him: "There come moments when as mourning demands [*deuil oblige*], one feels obligated to declare one's debts. We feel it our duty to say what we owe to friends."[7] Der-rida has shown us, Butler explains, how the very act of mourning is a "continued way of 'speaking to' the other who is gone, even though the other is gone, in spite of the fact that the other is gone, precisely because the other is gone."[8]

Derrida ponders acts of mourning as a living together with the dead in "Avowing—The Impossible" as well. Remembering Levinas, and repeatedly referring to him, is for Derrida "another way of recalling, at the moment when I want to salute the name of the admired friend, that one can 'live together' with the dead" ("Avowing," 20).

For Derrida, this living with the dead and the not yet born renders temporal immediacy impossible.[9] For the descendant of two families expelled from the city, now scattered over three continents, living in Haifa entails living with the dead, mourning both their death and their past presence in this city. Recalling the memories of my elders' favorite haunts and corners in pre-1948 Arab Haifa is an act of debt, an act of mourning, and at times an act of betrayal. A measure of trepidation lingers around mundane acts of the everyday. A sense of betraying "my own" overtakes me as I drive by what is now the Haifa Museum of Art and what was once my grandmother's school; its name still engraved in the wall teases my memory of her memory. My grandmother was not one to ask about the city's present. Uprooted from her home with her husband and children in 1948, her commitment to forging life anew despite instability and displacement required active forgetting. Simon, my uncle, was a different case. Born in 1935 in Haifa, and expelled in 1948, he carried the city with him everywhere—its shores, its staircases, its cinema houses. Simon held in the spaces of his memory the twists and turns of the city's hilly streets. I thought the city never left him, but I came to understand that he had never left it.

He often asked about a particular cinema house: "Is it still there? We loved that place. Its roof opened and shut. Does it still?" We were confused about the exact location of the theater, thinking it was the old building with the battered billboard near the vegetable market. Later we realized it was another location: the mini mall, where we go to the pharmacy and the bank. With the car double-parked in rush hour and a list of items to buy, I recently stole a few minutes in the crevices of the mundane to walk around and imagine. Looking up, I found the roof was indeed exposed.

As the older generations that remember living together in Haifa before 1948 pass under the weight of time, the city crystallizes even more as a site of mourning, a place to recall the other who is gone and the time that has passed.

## Present

> Another connotation of the "*bien vivre ensemble,*" that of the last resort, does not wait for peace. It is that of the "one must well live together [*il faut bien vivre ensemble*]," one has no choice.
> —Jacques Derrida, "Avowing—The Impossible: 'Returns,' Repentance, and Reconciliation"

Ben Gurion Boulevard, Zionism Avenue, Independence Street, and Balfour Way: These are the names of the main streets of Haifa. Street names and monuments commemorating Zionist triumph are among the daily reminders that a Palestinian is "a stranger 'at home'" here. The naming and renaming can take on an inconsequential character as you learn the roads, walk, drive, take and give directions. On one level, the naming and renaming function as one of the various structures of Palestinian "nonbelonging: separations, rejections, ruptures, exclusions" ("Avowing," 28, 27). But their deeper force is their role in the public conquest of, and the inner contest over, memory.

One hot July morning in 2006, we sat at our favorite hummus place in Haifa. Abu Maron's was usually busy: Israeli soldiers and Palestinian and Israeli workers, hipsters, families, and activists all gather in search of the best plate of hummus in the city.

Abu Maron's shares a wall with the Istiqlal mosque, where in the 1930s 'Izz ad-Din al-Qassam organized Palestinian sharecroppers, recently dispossessed of lands that absentee Lebanese and Palestinian owners sold to the Jewish National Fund. A student at the al-Azhar University and a fighter in the Syrian revolt of 1925–27, al-Qassam was an Islamic modernist who used the mosque as a site of social service for and politicization of the newly landless and proletarianized farmers in the budding industrial center of Haifa. The Istiqlal mosque still stands fully functional, with Friday sermons. During Ramadan, the Haifa municipality permits mosque leaders to raise the volume on the call to prayer. For one month of the year, a welcome sound bellows over Haifa's hilly terrain.

Abu Maron's plastic outdoor seating is in the center of Wadi al-Salib, a valley that holds some of the most extensive among the ruins of Arab Haifa. The intricate architecture of three-windowed porches and the arched two-story houses of the nineteenth and early twentieth centuries hint at a past prosperity that is now a weak presence, precariously confronting erasure.

The Haifa municipality launched attempts to re-create Wadi al-Salib as a center for artists and bohemians, a place where Israeli Jews could revel in rehabilitating living ruins, valuing what had been left behind while actively forgetting previous inhabitants. Although comparable projects have been successful (in the old city of Jaffa and the artist colony of Ein Hod),[10] this endeavor failed miserably in Wadi al-Salib. The valley continues to be a dilapidated area, its main street lined with Mizrahi-owned antiques stores; on Saturday evenings the flea market is an all-night affair where one can peruse abandoned archives of photographs and furniture. The municipality opted instead for the expansion of the courthouse and of ministerial buildings in the area; the severe angles of twenty-first-century architecture infiltrate the valley's streets. It was a hollow relief that the attempts to "invest" in the valley would come to naught; the Arab ruins remain a standing, if rapidly eroding, remnant. More than a reference to the state's "founding violences" ("Avowing," 29), more than a trace of Palestine— these remnants constitute Israel. "The trace is not only the disappearance of origin . . . it means that the origin did not even disappear, that it was never constituted except reciprocally by a non-origin."[11] The origin has not disappeared, indeed Palestine is the always-already absent-present of Israel.

That particular July morning, amid the heat and humidity reminiscent of Beirut, and after a considerable period, the experience of asynchronous time moved me again. Sometimes it is easier to eat hummus at Abu Maron than to remember, easier to forget, temporarily, to remember. That morning, surrounded by the remnants of pre-1948 Haifa and intoxicated by the proximity of the other in the present, I impetuously asked a question for which there was no immediate answer: "Do you think my parents were ever here? Did they know this street or see that building?"

Haifa, from the lens of an impossible "return"—since as Elias Khoury put it: "One does not *return* to Palestine, one should simply *go*"[12]—is a palimpsest. Subject to the state's active denial and erasure, its underlying layers come in and out of visibility in the everyday. Thus living in Haifa is a struggle of finding a mode of conviviality "in the present with the spectral presence of . . . figure[s] who contributed decisively to shaping this present but did so without ever fully entering it."[13] These spectral presences may be invisible to the other—either to "my close ones" or the stranger ("Avowing," 38). In this way, remembering *and* forgetting are acts of betrayal.

### Living Together . . . in War

> *You know, of course, that one does not count the dead in the same way from one corner of the globe to another. . . . For Europe, for the United States, for their media and public opinion, quantitatively comparable killings, or even those greater in number whether immediate or indirect, never produce such an intense upheaval when they occur outside European or American space (Cambodia, Rwanda, Palestine, Iraq, and so on).*
> —Jacques Derrida, in Jürgen Habermas, *Philosophy in a Time of Terror*,
>    interviewed by Giovanna Borradori

That summer of 2006 in the house with many windows on Masada Street (Masada is the famous site of that collective suicide now central to Israeli mythologies of martyr-victim-hero), which is parallel to Hillel, and Arlozoroff, I learned a morbid lesson in the differentiated acts of counting the dead.

Most of that July I read my Mandate Palestine documents and newspapers, looking up at the news, but only briefly as the Israeli army brutally struck down Palestinian lives during summer strolls and barbecues on the beach in Gaza. The early-twentieth-century daily *Filastin* reported on the dead of the Arab Revolt (1936–39) as the current toll in Gaza continued to mount. "Martyrs of the nation," that ever-shrinking nation, they were all labeled.

Counting the Palestinian dead, in the past and the present, had become part of an inane routine. It was the news of Hizbollah capturing two Israeli soldiers that halted daily life. Soon we were treated to (yet another) show of Israeli military machismo. Dan Halutz, chief of staff at the time, with no uncertain measure of distance and rationality, echoed Donald Rumsfeld that day when he spoke to U.S. troops on their way to Iraq: "Six days, six weeks . . . [but not] six months."[14] This war, Ehud Olmert announced, enjoyed "unprecedented" international backing.[15] Israeli intellectuals drew celebratory comparisons with the war of 1948 and the pure struggle for Israel's threatened will, right, destiny to exist.[16] Lebanon, Halutz proclaimed, would be put back twenty years.[17]

We waited with bated breath. What would the Israelis do with their unprecedented U.S. license to "uproot terror"? Would they destroy Lebanon? How many would they kill? Would they assassinate Nasrallah as they had assassinated so many of the Palestinian leadership—left, right, and center?

We slept and woke to the sounds of the Israeli arsenal annihilating the Lebanese south. I heard the F16s tear up the sky on their way to Beirut—where my family took refuge in 1948, my city of birth, and another site of being a different sort of "a stranger 'at home'" ("Avowing," 28).

The first katyusha rocket hit Haifa when I was standing on the porch in the kitchen. It was distant, meek, and failed to bring down an iron fence. We occupied the complicated position of Palestinians living in that part of Palestine that was now Israel. We were in Haifa—our city and our home. Yet we wanted to see the swaggering defeated—that hubris that allowed Israeli military commanders to express pride that West Bank children sketched warplanes in the skies of their drawings.[18]

Subject and object of Israel's colonial settler project, we watched as consensus was born. Many Israeli Jews bought the faulty merchandise their government sold: This was a war of existence; Hizbollah was the long arm of Iran waiting for the right moment to wipe Israel off the map. The few but steadfast voices of opposition in Israeli society were shamefully dismissed as treacherous.

Israeli media, for their part, struck an uneasy balance between celebrating militarism and performing normality. In the first days of the war, the national TV station broadcast directly from an air force base. The anchors delivered the news, fully adorned in fetching outfits, against the background of an F16. And as if this aesthetization of violence was not enough, one could always watch *Milu'im* (Reservists), a reality show that documents the trials and tribulations of Israeli reservists as they effortlessly move from civilian to military life. The rituals of consumerism, in stark emulation of the U.S. model, proceeded unchecked. At any given time, the television spectacle of "the war in the north," as it was billed, competed with Israeli renditions of "Who Wants to Be a Millionaire" and "The Biggest Loser." Life went on. The incoherence of the sole nuclear power in the Middle East being threatened by twelve thousand katyusha rockets was lost on most.

As over one thousand Lebanese lay dead under the rubble, and a million Lebanese were displaced, that Israeli hubris was momentarily shaken. There was a distinct sense of malaise. A friend explained: Everyone is depressed. Halutz was hospitalized with stomach ailments. Shim'on Peres rushed to explain in his testimony to the Winograd Commission, "War is a competition of making mistakes, and the biggest mistake was the war itself."[19]

When the sirens sounded, my spouse and I took to standing in the small corridor that we hoped would protect us from the possibility of shattered glass. I began recalling memories of war in Beirut in the 1970s, when long nights in corridors and stairwells were the norm. One day that July a rocket hit our neighborhood post office, a seven-minute walk away. Our eyes met and in a rushed and unspoken decision, we ran to the stairwell. Thus, we began sharing moments of the sixth war with our neighbors in the building. All were new Russian immigrants, some donning crosses, mostly poor, and predominantly marginalized; they hesitated to look at us. They seemed more apprehensive of us than of the rockets. They deemed us suspect because of our Arab-ness, discernible from our names and language. Even in the face of the new immigrant who was teetering around the edges of the Jewish nation's language and acceptance, we were the unwanted guest, the barely tolerated alien.

The Palestinians in Israel soon became a subject of curiosity in U.S., British, and Israeli reports that presented vulgar renditions of that colonial category—"Israeli Arabs." On August 7 an unguided katyusha hit Wadi al-Nisnas, one of the oldest and most densely populated neighborhoods of Arab Haifa, dating back to the nineteenth century. Another katyusha managed to strike the historic building of the communist paper *al-Itihad*, which was established in the mid-1940s and housed the minds and pens of Emile Habibi, Emile Touma, Samih al-Qassim, and Mahmoud Darwish. The victims, three killed and tens injured, were Arab.

Reporters swarmed to discern how these Arabs "caught in the middle" felt and where their loyalties lay. The most sympathetic accounts drew on the lack of shelters in Arab cities and villages and their proximity to military sites. But beyond the disenfranchisement of an ethnic minority, the deeper story was erased.

The Palestinian citizens in Israel must ask for hospitality on the land of their ancestors, in a language that is not their own. As the novelist and scholar Anton Shammas has explained, the "original deterritorialization and scattering of the Palestinians in 1948 was done in the language of grace."[20] The Palestinians who were "spared the fate of the wanderers" and remained on the land were then subject to the military governor's Hebrew permits that allowed them to "move around in the scenes of [their] homeland which had turned overnight into 'the homeland of the Jewish people.'"[21] The Palestinian, forced to learn Hebrew for beginners, became "a new immigrant to his own country."[22] It is in this way that the territorialization of Hebrew in the Jewish state, and the deterritorialization of Arabic from the land of Palestine, continue to render Palestinians in Israel as external to its territory. This is not for Palestinians the first act of violence against them; it is one measure of many in which they, the host, have been forcibly made into strangers. The definition of the state and its territory means, ultimately, that the Palestinian can never be "at home politically"[23] or otherwise.

Impregnable borders make the short distances between Beirut and Haifa immeasurable. I traveled between the cities in my archival search, coming across documents that reminded me of their painful proximity: "A strategic road was constructed along the Northern Frontier from Ras en Naqura on the coastal road between Haifa and Beyrouth eastward to km.217 on the Rosh Pinna-Metulla road, North of Lake Hula. . . . The length of the road is about 66 kilometers."[24]

These borders were temporarily bridged as correspondents from Beirut and Haifa shared the same screen. Friends from all over the world wrote, commenting on the irony and absurdity of our location in Haifa. We were stuck on the wrong side, they noted. But as the days and years pass, it can only become clearer that the position of Palestinians in Israel is not the wrong side, but a core of this long, arduous struggle.

This struggle contains two battles taking place at once: one for what Edward Said called a "remembered presence"[25] and another to remain in the present.

As a student of British-ruled Palestine, I am often inspired by the city's squares, buildings, and markets to ruminate about life in twentieth-century Palestine—its visions and projects and the possibilities of its "alternative futures"[26] beyond, before, sometimes without the *nakba*. The *nakba* is that formative event in Palestinian history when the majority of the people living in historic Palestine were expelled or fled from their ancestral lands. It is the event that often stands in Palestinian historiography as the beginning and the end of the story, yet it appears in "Avowing—The Impossible" only as "the conditions in which the modern state of Israel established itself" and "certain founding violences" (29).

The remnants of Palestine in Israel—a house, the Istiqlal mosque, Wadi al-Salib—are both traces and lived spaces. They hold the past and they constitute the present. They mean what they are today—an old store, an abandoned building, an elegant cinema house transformed into a bank—and contain what they once were. There is a Palestine, one that continues to exist after and through the *nakba*; it is suspended in imagination and is a presence to be daily contended with.


**Returns to the Present**


In January 2009, as Israeli drones rained indiscriminate and brutal death on the Palestinians of the embattled Gaza Strip, Simon passed away. When I heard my father cry for the first time, I felt the sting of the still-open wound. The burial of my uncle shone a harsh light on the depths of dispersal. The widely scattered family of seven that began in Haifa would bury their dead far from each other and from their city. As they bid their eldest brother adieu across three continents, they also buried a memory of togetherness. Simon's last resting place in the United States, many miles from Haifa, brought the issue of land, and its lack, starkly and once again to the surface. Dispersal would continue in death; who would remember togetherness?

Living together, or more accurately, living *apart*, in Haifa is best understood as an extended experience of asynchronous time, the past in the present, despite the *nakba* and because of it. For this reason it is as important to draw political consequences from a return to the present as it is from Derrida's counsel to "return to the past" ("Avowing," 29).

What "living together" means for Palestinians inside Israel, in the West Bank, in Gaza, and in the diaspora, is living *separate* from other Palestinians. This relentless separation of Palestinians continues today through war, occupation, the separation wall, and less noted legal machinations such as the racialized ban on family unification passed in 2003.[27] It is this condition of perpetual separation that makes any "living together" premised on the erasure of a remembered presence.

The layered and heterogeneous character of what Edward Said called the "epistemological achievement"[28] of erasure fuels the historical myths that underlie Israeli culture. The historian and critic Gabi Piterberg analyzes this erasure in his discussion of the "negation of exile" as a myth that cemented "continuity between an ancient past, in which there existed Jewish sovereignty over the land of Israel, and a present that renews it in the resettlement of the land of Palestine."[29] The "return to the land of Israel" thus recovered the land, which itself was condemned to exile as long as it lacked Jewish sovereignty, and functioned as a normalization of Jewish existence, no longer docile, passive, and deterritorialized in exile, now normal, complete, and authentic on the land. This normalization continues to be intricately dependent on the heterogeneity of erasure "of the historical experience both of the Jews in exile, and of Palestine without Jewish sovereignty."[30]

Israel's function as normalizing—indeed, its status as a normal state as opposed to the promise of exceptionalism—is a recurring question. Joseph Massad reminds us of the antagonism between the Zionists' slogan: "We are not a people like any other" and the Palestinian cry: "We are a people like all others."[31]

The question of the exceptional versus the normal finds unique resonance in "Avowing—The Impossible" as part of the broader reflections on the impossibility of living together with the self, the other, and the ensemble that drive the piece. For Derrida, the adverb "together" in living together does not refer to the totality of a natural, biological, or genetic ensemble. Therefore, living together "supposes . . . an interrupting excess *both* with regard to statutory convention, to law *and* with regard to *symbiosis*." Living together is not reducible to organic symbiosis or the juridico-political contract. Indeed, "if it were possible," living together would test the "the old couple *physis/nomos, physis/thesis,* nature/convention, biological life/law [*droit*]." Derrida distinguishes this law, "more than ever, from justice" ("Avowing," 26–27). To live together requires transporting oneself beyond "almost everything" that founds itself on this opposition between nature and culture. And here Derrida reflects on "declaring oneself Jewish," law, justice, and exceptionalism.

> One will never think the "living together" . . . unless one transports oneself *beyond everything* that is founded on this opposition of nature and culture. That is to say, beyond everything, more or less everything. This excess with regard to the laws of nature, as well as to the laws of culture, is always an excess with regard to the whole [*ensemble*], and I do not take the difficulty lightly. . . . This excess does not signify that law, a nonlegal law or a nonjuridical justice, does not continue to command sense and the "must" of "one must *well* live together." Which law? And can "declaring oneself Jewish," in whatever mode (and there are so many) grant a privileged access to this justice, to this law beyond laws [*cette loi au-dessus des lois*]?" ("Avowing," 27)

Derrida moves from these remarks to revisit the child he was in Algeria; he recounts the "conditions in which the modern state of Israel established itself" that drove him to insomnia.

> But the child of whom I speak asked himself whether the founding of the modern state of Israel—with all the politics and policies that have followed and confirmed it—could be no more than an example among others of this originary violence from which no state can escape, or whether, because this modern state intended not to be a state like others, it had to appear before another law and appeal to another justice. ("Avowing," 30)

These very remarks, Massad points out, assimilate Israel's founding violence as "normative and normal."[32] They also take a particular approach to temporality, an approach that resonates with the figure of the child who continued "to interrogate himself . . . regarding the conditions which the modern state of Israel established itself."

These founding conditions and certain violences that took place in the space of the "nonlegal," that is, "not illegal but nonlegal, otherwise put, *unjustifiable* with regard to an existing law" ("Avowing," 29), emerge as temporally distinct from the policies of the current Israeli government and those that preceded it. That the violence of the *nakba* remains unnamed in the text, as noted above, is itself significant of an erasure. This unnaming and erasure is what allows for the problematic distinction between the "founding" and the policies of governments as temporally distant and independent from one another.

Indeed, separating "certain founding violences" from "the politics of the current Israeli government and a great number of those that preceded it" will not suffice.

Israel's founding violences were a result of the formation of an exclusively Jewish state. That imperative did not begin in 1948, nor did it end there. The process of partitioning land and labor into Jewish and non-Jewish categories began with the onset of European

Jewish settlement. The anxieties about the Jewish state's "demographic integrity" continue today, as do the relentless policies and machinations of separation. Thus separation, indeed *aparthood*, appears in Israel and Palestine as in other contexts, "less as a discrete event than as interminable condition."[33]

The tremendous rupture of the *nakba* and its significance in making Palestinian "living together" impossible is not, then, a founding or originary event but a heterogeneous and continuous experience. On the one hand, the memory and the remnants of the *nakba* and Palestine, in Israel, constitute Israel as its always-already absent-present. On the other hand, the *nakba* also stands for the ongoing, uninterrupted process of separating Palestinians from one another. Thus, to "remain radically critical . . . without implying from it any threatening or disrespectful consequences for the present, the future, and the existence of Israel" ("Avowing," 29) is impossible. Remaining radically critical of Israel requires stepping away from that decidedly identitarian, totalized, "self-identical"[34] figure that Derrida so vigilantly guarded against and so rigorously deconstructed but that nevertheless makes a startling appearance in "Avowing—The Impossible," in the formulation of the Israeli "authentic patriots" (29). A radical stance necessarily and explicitly means consequences for Israel's present and its future. As long as the right to a remembered presence is denied, the living together will continue to be based on an *aparthood* that can allow for only a shallow performance of conviviality with Palestinians in Israel and requires an armed cohabitation in the West Bank and Gaza.

To better explore living together in Israel and Palestine, we must regard the "conditions in which the modern state of Israel established itself," through the very prism of asynchronous temporality. A temporality that avows the *nakba*, a temporality that names the conditions that constituted Israel, and denounces the conditions this state continues to require as long as its present and future remain by juridical definition an exclusively Jewish territory.

# Remembering Living

# Living—with—Torture—Together

*Elisabeth Weber*

In the introduction to his monumental *Torture and Democracy*, Darius Rejali relates the story of Mordehy Petcho, a member of the Jewish guerrilla group Irgun, who, in 1939, lay in a cell after being tortured by the British CID.

> [Petcho] describes how an old Arab brought food. As he could not eat, the Arab fed him, and when Petcho felt sharp pains, the old man asked to lift the blanket. Then he saw the bruises and "cursed the English as the worst of savages." One can scarcely imagine a stranger scene in which a Palestinian Arab and an Irgun supporter bind themselves in common recognition of each other's humanity. Sixty years later, Palestinians had a hard time appreciating the suffering Israeli positional torture effected on their own relatives, and the Israelis denied torture had happened at all, since it left no marks. It took hard work for people to learn how to read the bodies that were subjected to *shabeh* technique, to question state power and accord respect to its victims.[1]

This account of the interaction of a member of a militant Zionist group[2] and an Arab man in what was then the British Mandate of Palestine exemplifies in a striking way what Derrida calls "a fundamental mode . . . of 'living together'": compassion.[3] More precisely, it offers a glimpse into the moving power of compassion (in the sense of "moving to action")[4] that is not limited to members of a defined "community," of a constituted "*ensemble*."

As Derrida emphasizes in his "lesson," "Avowing—The Impossible: 'Returns,' Repentance, and Reconciliation,"

> The adverb, in the expression "living together" [*vivre ensemble*], appears to find its sense and dignity only there where it exceeds,

dislocates, contests the authority of the noun "ensemble," to wit, the closure of an ensemble, be it the whole of something "living" [*d'un "vivant"*], of a system, a totality, a cohesiveness without fault and identical with itself, of an indivisible element containing itself in its immanence and simply larger, like the whole [*tout*], than its parts. The authority of the whole [*ensemble*] will always be the first threat for all "living together." And inversely, all "living together" will be the first protestation or contestation, the first testimony against the whole [*ensemble*]. ("Avowing," 21)[5]

Rejali's description of the scene between a Jewish guerrilla fighter and an Arab man offers a glimpse into a mode of "*vivre ensemble*," "living together," that, indeed, offers a "protestation or contestation . . . against the whole," a mode of "living together" in which the "together" is one not between allies, but between enemies sworn to the other's death. Moreover, this "together" makes "living," in the most concrete and basic sense, possible for one of them.

Rejali introduces his account by stating that "communities treat victims that have marks of violence upon their bodies entirely differently from those who have no marks to show." The visibility of wounds thus kindles this "fundamental mode . . . of 'living together'" that is compassion. The absence of such visibility, caused by the use of what Rejali has termed "stealth torture,"[6] is the result of a deliberate calculation to avoid the radar and publicity of human rights monitors, as well as compassion's power to cause public outcry and activism, by stifling this "fundamental mode" of "living 'together'" with the torture victim, *both* in the community of the perpetrator *and* in the torture victim's own community. Some stealth methods have been scientifically developed or refined at prestigious North American universities.[7] They are often belittled as "torture lite" but are as brutal as they are, in the words of the CIA Inspector General's Torture Report, "precise, quiet and almost clinical."[8]

This essay proposes to read Derrida's reflections about "living 'together'" in the context of the use of torture by the most powerful country in the world. Its title does not refer to what it might mean to live "with" torture after having suffered it. It would not dare to. Rather, it refers to the fact that after the Bush administration's official espousal of torture (under the euphemism of "enhanced interrogation") in the summer of 2002,[9] every person living in the United States lives knowingly or unwittingly with the legacy of this fateful policy decision.

To my knowledge, Derrida has not written about torture other than mentioning it in the context of other forms of violence.[10] "In any case [*de toute façon*]," Derrida writes in his "lesson," "in any fashion [*de toutes les façons*], 'live together' one must, and one must do so well, one might as well do so [*et il le faut bien*]. . . . One has no choice" ("Avowing," 23). Is torture, however, not the limit of the "we must live together"? If "forgiveness, if there is such, must forgive the unforgivable," must then "living together," if there is such, live the unlivable? ("Avowing," 19). Would Derrida's thinking lead us to this conclusion?

## I.

Right from the start of Derrida's text, the question of how to live together "makes us tremble":

> Wisdom teaches us: Given that living is always "living together," and that it must be so, let us only learn "how to live together," let us determine rules, norms, maxims, precepts, even an ethical, juridical, and political jurisprudence. But despair protests and replies: "But *how*? How to live together? I will not, you will not, he/she will not, we will not, you will not, they will not, achieve it, ever"—and the variation of these persons speaks also a deeper paradox as to the same concern: Who addresses whom in asking "how to live together?" or still: Does not "living together" take place from the instant that the concern over this question makes us tremble in our solitude and *avow,* yes, declare our despair and share it? ("Avowing," 19–20)

In the context of this essay, the "despair" that must first be declared and shared, avowed, is over what appears to be a bolstered public acceptability of torture, and, especially in the aftermath of the attacks of September 11, 2001, the despair over a massive campaign to relegitimize torture undertaken by American officials up to the highest levels. In the foreword to a collection titled *Torture,* published in 2004, Ariel Dorfman observes that

> we live in a world where torture is practiced on a regular basis in more countries than ever—132 at the latest count, but who knows if there are not more—and where torture is being contemplated as inevitable and even beneficial in nations that call themselves democratic and respectful of the rights of their citizens. . . . I live in a country—the United States—where a leading civil rights lawyer has suggested that the courts might issue 'torture warrants' as a way of fighting terrorism. . . . We live in times where people, in this land and in so many other supposedly "civilized" nations, are so filled with primal fear that they look on with apparent indifference at the possibility of extreme maltreatment of their presumable enemies—indifference, indeed, at the evidence and televised images of this sort of maltreatment.[11]

The increased presence of the issue of torture in the public debate in the United States should not blind us, however, to the fact that U.S. endorsement of torture did not start with the infamous "torture memos"[12] or the signing into law of the Military Commissions Act in October 2006. As Alfred McCoy has shown, when in December 1984, "after years of global grass-roots agitation," the UN General Assembly adopted the Convention Against Torture, it took the United States ten years to ratify it. McCoy sees the reason for this long delay in the "CIA's clandestine maneuvering," through the State and Justice

245

Departments, to protect the "torture paradigm" it had developed over at least three decades from international sanction. To this effect, the U.S. administration proposed "a record nineteen reservations that stalled the convention's ratification in the Senate." Among those, the Reagan administration "focused, above all, on the issue of psychological torture." The result was a redefinition of "mental harm" and the exclusion, from the U.S. ratification, of "sensory deprivation (hooding), self-inflicted pain (stress positions), and disorientation (isolation and sleep denial)—the very techniques the CIA had refined at such great cost over several decades. . . . Through this process, the United States, in effect, accepted just half the UN Convention Against Torture—affirming only the ban on physical methods. This decision, unnoticed when Congress finally ratified the convention in 1994, would effectively exempt the CIA's interrogation methods from international law."[13]

The publication, in February 2006, of the infamous Abu Ghraib photos, and the passing into law of the Military Commissions Act in October 2006, which was tantamount to the official adoption of torture (without mention, of course, of the word "torture") by the U.S. government, can be understood as two answers to the question of "living 'together,'" two answers that deny the possibility of any "together." To the question how one can live with the presumed "enemy," when this enemy is suspected of plotting the deaths of thousands of people and massive destruction, these answers reply that one cannot, ever, live together. These two answers also betray a fundamental refusal to be answerable to the question how those targeted as enemies might answer the question of "living together," considering that they have had to "live together" with *their* enemy ever since he colonized, bombed, exploited them. Those two answers' radical refusal and denial notwithstanding, even if "the enemy"[14] is locked away in faraway offshore detention camps such as Guantánamo, and in overseas prisons such as Abu Ghraib and Bagram, in order to deny him, or rather the many men and women lumped together in this demagogic singular, to be heard in American courts, "'live together,' one must," as Derrida emphasizes, and, moreover,

> one must well "live together" [*il faut bien "vivre ensemble"*]. In any case [*de toute façon*], in any fashion [*de toutes les façons*], "live together" one must, and one must do so well, one might as well do so [*et il le faut bien*]. . . . One has no choice. It is, indeed, always a matter of a necessity, and therefore of a law: One cannot not "live together" even if one does not know how or with whom, with God, with gods, men, animals, with one's own, with one's close ones, neighbors, family, or friends, with one's fellow citizens or countrymen, but also with the most distant strangers, with one's enemies, with oneself, with one's contemporaries, with those who are no longer so or will never be so, so many names that I draw from daily language and of which I do not yet presume that we know what they designate. ("Avowing," 23–24)

Living together "one must," and, as Derrida underlines, one must even "live together" with the dead. The "nightmare" of Eric Fair, a former interrogator in Iraq, who is haunted frequently during his sleep by the memory of the man he tortured,[15] starkly illustrates this, and his plea to the American public demonstrates that he is not the only one living with the dead: "The scars of guilt are no longer mine alone. They are carried now by this entire nation, its people, its institutions, and its leaders. The failure of men like me to prevent these egregious acts is now eclipsed by the failure of the nation to bring 'enhanced interrogations' to an immediate end," and those responsible to trial.[16] Fair's testimony confirms, to quote Derrida's text again, that "'living together', with the dead, is not an accident, a miracle, or an extraordinary story [*histoire*]. It is rather an essential possibility of existence. It reminds us that in 'living together' the idea of life is neither simple nor dominant even if it remains irreducible" ("Avowing," 20). Although films such as Rory Kennedy's *Ghosts of Abu Ghraib* and Alex Gibney's *Taxi to the Dark Side* suggest that shame and guilt haunt some of the torturers, the impunity of those who devised and ordered the torture at the highest level of government evince that we seem to have learned all too easily to live with torture and torturers.

While politicians, pundits, and scholars discuss in editorials, in academia, and at the highest levels of the U.S. administration whether torture under the Bush administration should be prosecuted, and whether the use of torture may be justified in some cases,[17] the prohibition of torture has a distinctive status in the pantheon of international rights: It is absolute. It cannot be derogated under any circumstances, as the 1984 "UN Convention on Torture and Other Cruel, Inhuman or Degrading Treatment or Punishment" states in unequivocal terms: "*No exceptional circumstances whatsoever, whether a state of war or a threat of war, internal political instability or any other public emergency, may be invoked as a justification of torture.*"[18] The use of torture thus flagrantly violates international law. For Derrida, international law (whose importance he underlines repeatedly and consistently) or any other "law" is not sufficient to "live together well," not only because they often are not respected or because "radical changes in international law are necessary."[19] Rather, the incommensurability of any "law" with "justice" pits the generality of the rule against the irreplaceable singularity of the event. When Derrida calls compassion a "fundamental mode of living together," he clearly does not consider it a derivative. While compassion may be kindled most easily by the witnessing of the other's suffering (as in the scene of recognition between the old Arab man and Mordehy Petcho), it is not exhaustible in a reaction. Rather, for Derrida, who follows Levinas here, it suspends the economy of "being," in Levinas's terms, the economy of the "third," to plunge the witness into the exorbitant call of the other, the "face to face" in which it is impossible not to respond. Again, in Levinas's concepts, compassion could be described as an-archic living-with, where I have been called before being able to say "I."

Torture destroys this most fundamental "with" or "together" between the perpetrator and the victim.[20] "Clean," "democratic torture" is designed to undermine the future of any "together" as well: In the words of Veena Das, whom Rejali quotes, "denial of the other's pain is not about the failings of intellect, but the failings of spirit. In the register of the imaginary, the pain of the other not only asks for a home in language, but also seeks a home in the body."[21] Stealth torture "denies precisely this home in the body, tangling the victims and their communities in doubts, uncertainties, and illusions."[22] Rejali distinguishes between "different kinds of inexpressibility that follow from torture" and focuses on the "inexpressibility that matters politically," which is "not the gap between the brain and the tongue, but between victims and their communities, a gap that is cynically calculated, a gap that shelters a state's legitimacy."

What does it take then, for a community to respond, for "citizens [to] learn to hear torture victims and read their bodies"? According to Rejali,

> What enables us to reconstitute our ability to speak with each other about pain is an activity different from capturing pain in works of art, stories, statues, and other objects of worldly making. What it takes is something fundamentally more powerful and fragile, the ability to create a common political space. When the old Arab reached across that prison cell, lifted the blanket, and read Petcho's body, for a brief moment he and Petcho occupied such a space. Such reading has become much harder in modern times, and, consequently, the spaces in which we can appear before each other in our pain have become more scarce.[23]

The "fragile" together of a "common political space" is created in Rejali's account through the surge of compassion. Using Derrida's language one could say that the occurrence of compassion bridges the aporia between the singular and the general, between the radical singularity of pain and the potential generality of a common political space. Stealth torture is designed to quell the surge of compassion in the victim's and the perpetrator's communities where it is most easily stirred: In the possibility of witnessing the other's pain, not just intellectually, but in the flesh. Compassion, far from being reducible to an emotional response, is critical in serving as powerful motivation for the creation of a "common political space," however fragile it may be, of protest, opposition, and activism. The purpose of democratic torture is to thwart this critical activism by undermining this incalculable source.

## II.

The "fundamental mode" of compassion is a nodal point in Derrida's "lesson," because just as in Rejali's example, it has the capacity of bridging aporetic incompatibilities. Compassion is the tangible affect or emotion, at least in a young boy's experience, that taught him to "name justice and what in justice at once exceeds and demands law." In other words, it is in compassion where the child first encounters what the philosopher will later gauge as aporetic impossibilities of "living 'together.'" After depicting the hardship he suffered as a "little black and very Arab Jew"[24] in his native Algeria for his audience consisting mostly of "intellectuals said to be French-speaking Jews,"[25] Derrida concludes:

> If I let a Jewish child speak, it is neither to move you cheaply, nor to shelter provocations behind an alibi. Rather it is to convince you that my questions, my reticences, my impatiences, my indignation sometimes (for example, when faced with the politics of almost all the Israeli governments and the forces that support them, from within and from without) are not inspired by hostility or by the indifference of distance. On the contrary, shared with so many Israelis who are exposed and concerned otherwise than I am, and together with so many Jews in the world, this innocent concern for compassion (a fundamental mode, in my view, of "living together"), of this compassion of justice and equity (*rahamim,* perhaps), I will claim it, if not as the essence of Judaism, at least as what remains in me inseparable from the suffering and disarmed memory of the Jewish child, there where he has learned to name justice and what in justice at once exceeds and demands law [*le droit*]. Everything comes to me, no doubt, from this source, in what I am about to say, under the title "avowing—the impossible." ("Avowing," 30)

"Compassion . . . (*rahamim,* perhaps)" is the "source," then, for thinking the adverbial "*ensemble*/together" that fractures the substantive "*ensemble*/whole" and thereby makes "living together" possible. As always in Derrida's texts, the parenthesis is not to be taken lightly. Derrida has written extensively on the modality of the "perhaps," which does not, as he specifies, belong "to a regime of opinion," nor does it signify "haziness and mobility, the confusion preceding knowledge or renouncing all truth." If the "perhaps" is "undecidable and without truth in its own moment (but it is, as a matter of fact, difficult to assign a proper moment to it), this is in order that it might be a condition of decision, interruption, revolution, responsibility and truth."[26] In Derrida's *Politics of Friendship*, "perhaps" indicates the interruption of a politics and a justice reduced to rationality, calculability, predictability. "Perhaps" introduces the chance of an event that for once deserves its name: a radical arrival, which Derrida, in the creation of the neologism "arrivance," invites to enter into resonance with another term of invention of the future: *aimance* ("lovence").[27] The difficulty to think such an event becomes apparent in the words themselves. The French word for "perhaps," "*peut-être*," is, as Derrida points out, "perhaps, too rich in its two *verbs* (the *pouvoir* [literally: to have the power to do . . . ] and the *être* [to be])"[28], whereas the English *perhaps* and the German *vielleicht* still resonate with the chance of an unforeseeable happening.

The first word of the parenthesis, *rachamim*, is no less decisive. It is the Hebrew word for "compassion," deriving from רחם, "rechem," the womb. In the Bible, God is recognized as the "Compassionate" (רחמן); one of the Jewish memorial prayers invokes the Father of Compassion (אב הרחמים).[29] The plural of *rechem*, the womb, *rachamim* means both "entrails" and "compassion," the entrails as the seat of compassion. *Rachamim* inspired Emmanuel Levinas's description of the "subject" as immemorially "persecuted," as "maternity, gestation of the other in the same" and as "the groaning of the wounded entrails."[30] The metaphor of the "wounded entrails" that stands for maternity in Levinas's later work, however, does not necessarily give preference to one's "own," one's own children in particular. According to Levinas, the subject's infinite responsibility is *first* an entirely involuntary being-held-hostage by the compassion toward the orphan and the stranger. In Levinas's thinking, this is a "fundamental mode" of the very constitution of the subject, even if, in the concrete "living together," counting and calculability, that is, the imposition of an "economy" on such infinite compassion becomes unavoidable. However, as Levinas's own metaphor of "maternity" and the origin of *rachamim* in *rechem* suggest, *rachamim* points to a difficulty that Levinas does not directly address, and that Derrida's essay confronts by describing it as the site of one of the "aporias" of "living 'together.'"

"I will never be able to renounce and to say no to a preference for 'my own' [*les "miens"*], nor, inversely, to justify it, to have it approved as the law of a universal justice." My "preference for all the forms of the proximate, of this proximity that, at the limit, in situations of mortal danger, would carry me to the rescue of my children rather than of those of another, rather than to the rescue of all those others who are not only my others, to the rescue of a man rather than an animal, and even of my cat rather than a cat unknown to me and dying in Asia," is as undeniable as it is unjustifiable. Derrida continues: "In the eyes of justice or of universal equality, how to justify a preference for one's own children, a preference for one's own, parents and friends, even a preference among one's own, as far as death and ultimate sacrifice, the privilege of Isaac, for example, rather than Ishmael? My own do not belong to me, nor does my 'home [*chez moi*]'" ("Avowing," 37–38).

In Derrida's text, "*rachamim,* perhaps" is the "source" of his meditation on "living together," because, as mentioned above, it is here that the aporias of "justice," and thus the aporias of "living 'together,'" are acutely lived, viscerally and in the flesh. By the same token it is here that the binaries defining a thinking that is de facto still all too metaphysical ("nature"/"culture," "human"/"animal," "friend"/"enemy," etc.) are vividly questioned. Derrida forcefully states that there will not be any "living together" if those binaries are left standing.

> One will never think the "living together" and the "living" of the "living together" and the "how together" unless one transports oneself *beyond everything* that is founded on this opposition of nature and culture. That is to say, beyond everything, more or less everything. This excess with regard to the laws of nature, as well as to the laws of culture, is always an excess with regard to the whole [*ensemble*], and I do not take the difficulty lightly. It is almost unthinkable, very close to impossible, precisely. ("Avowing," 27)

One of the "impossibles" that through *rachamim* might take place, for example, is a profound rethinking of "what one names stupidly and confusedly the animal" ("Avowing," 38). The aporia of the preference for the "proximate" would logically need to lead to a rethinking of the "cardinal criteria of the anthropological difference," from Aristotle to Heidegger (and certainly beyond) that consolidate the "abyss" (in Heidegger's formulation) between the human being and the animal.[31] Derrida does not deny this "abyss," but asserts that it needs to be fundamentally, that is, radically rethought. Its destructive potential is conjured when human beings are identified with animals in order to justify their exploitation, persecution, torture, and murder. Well-known historical examples would include the justification of slavery in the United States before the Civil War and the ideology of National Socialism, but the practices of American military personnel and CIA operatives who dehumanized their victims in prisons such as Abu Ghraib, Bagram, and Guantánamo must also be listed. In spite of the many and deep differences between the two huge issues of human torture and animal mistreatment (that according to Derrida has known an unprecedented acceleration over, roughly, the last two hundred years),[32] they overlap on at least three points that are constitutive of both: the "indubitable" knowledge that the victims suffer, an undeniability that "*precedes* any other question";[33] the doubtless possibility "within us," of a "surge of compassion, even if it is then misunderstood, repressed, or denied"; and an ongoing "war" that is "waged over the matter of pity."[34] In his great lesson on animals, which focused on "the immense question of pathos and the pathological, . . . of suffering, pity, and compassion; and the place that has to be accorded to the interpretation of this compassion, to the sharing of this suffering among the living, to the law, ethics, and politics that must be brought to bear upon this experience of compassion,"[35] Derrida writes that this "war" is "passing through a critical phase. We are passing through that phase, and it passes through us. To think this war we find ourselves waging is not only a duty, a responsibility, an obligation, it is also a necessity, a constraint that, like it nor not, directly or indirectly, no one can escape."[36]

Without conflating the two enormous issues, then, "*rachamim*, perhaps" is the nodal point from which Derrida's appeal regarding the necessity and urgency to rethink the suffering of animals can be transposed verbatim on the issue of torture.

## III.

The rupture of an established "whole" or "totality" in *rachamim*, in the compassion for the other, does not concern only a collective. It concerns oneself, one's "self" or "one"'s self as well: "The alterity of past and future, the irreducible experience of memory and of the promise, of mourning and of hope, all suppose some *rupture*, the interruption of this identity or of this totality, this accomplishment of a presence to self—a fracturing openness in what one calls *un ensemble* [whole, gathering, ensemble], with the noun *ensemble*, which I will distinguish here from the adverb *ensemble* in the expression '*vivre ensemble*'" ("Avowing," 21). For Derrida, there will be no "living together" without the recognition and acknowledgment of "this division, this tearing, this rift, this dissociation from oneself, this difficulty of living together with oneself." He continues, "The first step of a 'living together' will always remain rebellious to totalization," including the "totalization" of one's "own" "self" ("Avowing," 35). This "fracturing openness," this "dissociation from oneself" implies that one is a "stranger" to oneself, in a "strangeness" inseparable from an "inviolable separation" between "oneself" and others. For Derrida, "any 'living together' supposes and guards, as its very condition, the possibility of this singular, secret, inviolable separation, from which alone a stranger accords himself to a stranger, in hospitality. To recognize that one lives together, well then, only with and as a stranger, a stranger 'at home [*chez soi*],' in all the figures of the 'at home'" is the "very condition" of a living together in "the justice of a law above laws" ("Avowing," 28).

Torture is the *achieved* destruction of compassion, of the moving and groaning of the "entrails" that, to quote Levinas, have always already, immemorially contested the sovereign assurance of "self-identity." In a perverse twist, torture also assaults this immemorial "fracturing openness" or "strangeness" to oneself (that *is* the "self") by forcing the victim to betray what could be called *rachamim*, compassion, for oneself. This is where Derrida's argument resonates with one of the most powerful voices against torture of the early Enlightenment, Christian Thomasius, who identifies such self-betrayal as *constitutive* of torture.[37]

In 1705, almost sixty years before Cesare Beccaria's famous *Crimes and Punishments*, Thomasius published a short treatise in Latin, *On the torture that needs to be banned from Christian courts*.[38] Of course, Thomasius's treatise is separated from today's torture practice by what Michel Foucault has described as the redistribution of "the entire economy of punishment" in the eighteenth and nineteenth centuries, and the resulting disappearance, as Foucault puts it, of "the body as the major target of penal repression," otherwise described as the "humanization" of penal justice, an expression Foucault lists as an example of the proliferation of "inflated rhetoric."[39] What Foucault describes as the "disappearance of torture as a public spectacle" has, on the one hand, been completed with the invention of the so-called "no touch" or stealth torture by democratic societies, but, on the other hand, has also been thoroughly refuted with the publication of the infamous photos of Abu Ghraib, and the increasing popularity of torture as manifested by TV series such as *24*.[40] Foucault writes that "physical pain, the pain of the body itself, is no longer the constituent element of the penalty. From being an art of unbearable sensations punishment has become an economy of suspended rights." This may accurately describe most of modernity's penal practices, but it is doubtful that it can be said of the practice of torture. On the contrary, torture could be described as the "art of unbearable sensations" that is *inseparable* from an "economy of suspended rights."[41]

At the outset of his text, Thomasius reiterates Cicero's condemnation: The "goal" of the *quaestio*, the "question," or, as the German expression specifies, the "painful question [*peinliche Frage*],"[42] does not seem to be to investigate the truth, but to force the tortured person to give "false statements."[43]

Thomasius observes that "because of torture, the poorest of the poor of all accused, whose guilt has not been proven yet, receive punishments that surpass hugely the punishments they would receive if proven guilty." That proves the "godless perversity in punishing" and there is nothing "more unjust."[44] But Thomasius's decisive argument against torture, not mentioned by the opponents of torture before him, is the following: "The miserable defendants are pushed towards their demise under the torments of torture, in order to supplement what, due to the absence of witnesses or proofs, is missing in the judge's certitude to condemn them. They are forced to fight against themselves through their own confession, and thus, become traitors of themselves [*sui ipsius proditores torti constituuntur*]" (170–71).[45]

This argument of "self-betrayal" needs to be considered in the context of Thomasius's "demand for a fundamental equality in rights,"[46] which sharply contradicted the prevalent notion of "rights" of his time. As a consequence, Thomasius emphasizes one of the principles of his understanding of natural law: Nobody should be prevented from defending himself (168–71). This principle is "entirely exterminated" with state-sponsored torture that forces human beings—Thomasius calls them sometimes "mortals"[47]—"to prepare their own demise [*exitium/Untergang*]" (168–71), by incriminating themselves (170–71), and thus hasten their condemnation to capital punishment. With the abolition of the above-mentioned principle of natural law, torture victims are instead pushed (*adiguntur*) to their own ruin/destruction (*sui perniciem/Verderben*) by supplementing what the judge is lacking for their condemnation. Through their confession, they are "forced to conduct battle against themselves,"[48] to, "as it were, cut their own throat with a sword [*quasi gladium ad illud iugulandum, exigere/so dass er sich gleichsam selber das Messer an die Kehle setzen muss*]" (170–71). And: "Can it be reconciled with natural reason to force human beings [*homines*] to their own slaying/slaughter/carnage [*caedem*]?" (174–75).[49]

Torture victims are forced into becoming traitors of themselves (*sui ipsius proditores*): They are coerced into the betrayal not only of their existence, but of their very "nature."

As Werner Riess recalls, in the early modern period in certain Northern German cities, someone who had undergone torture had lost his or her honor forever, even if he/she was able to prove his/her innocence.[50] The mere suspicion of being guilty of an infamy so great that it warranted torture in the eyes of the juridical system was thus sufficient for the expulsion from civil society.[51]

Thomasius presents the flip side, and perhaps even the unspoken motivation of this expulsion: One cannot be tortured without being forced to betray oneself. I would claim here that this is the case even if no confession is made. Thomasius asserts that torture was a pagan practice, initially applied by the Romans[52] only to slaves who were "treated as equal with four-legged creatures (animals) [*quadrupedibus/Vierfüsslern (Tiere)*]" (176–77). The betrayal of oneself is, one the one hand, the hastening of one's own slaughter through false statements, but on the other, even if this is only intimated in Thomasius's text, such forced crossing over into bestiality.[53]

It is, one could say, the betrayal of the human community.

Let me recall that in Abu Ghraib, humiliation, including the leashing of victims as if they were four-legged creatures, was part and parcel of the use of torture: the intent to shame the victims to such a degree as to virtually exclude them from their own communities.[54] In our days, then, three hundred years after Thomasius's treatise, one of the arguments that branded torture for him as an unconscionable, godless perversity, has returned as one of the principal goals of "enhanced interrogation" methods.

Even if the confession obtained under torture is no longer automatically followed by capital punishment as was still the case in Thomasius's time, the latter's argument also holds for victims of torture of later centuries, and for victims of the least admitted form of torture, that inflicted by Western democracies. The "stealth" techniques do not only undermine the power of activism that compassion is susceptible to kindle, but also threaten to lock up victims in unavowable shame. "Physical scars can be shown without shame; they win sympathy and recognition from families and communities. But the photographs at Abu Ghraib put the survivors in a vicious bind."[55] In revealing their ordeal, they would repeat the utter humiliation that not only shamed them to the cores of their beings, but was also purposefully designed never to be revealable. The victim who would publicly expose what was done to him would be treated as if he had betrayed his extended self, his community, but also his very humanity. In other words, he cannot hope for the compassion of others, nor for compassion for himself. "'Shoot me here,' said an Abu Ghraib prisoner pointing to the space between his eyes, 'but don't do this to us.'"[56]

Marc Nichanian's analysis of the aporias of "testimony" to genocide is perspicacious for the present context as well: "There is no testimony of shame. It might even be the only thing for which there cannot be testimony. Shame itself is its own testimony." There is no testimony, because giving testimony means to become a "living proof of one's own death. . . . That is the moment of shame. Testimony is shame."[57] The shame of the torturer, if it occurs as in Eric Fair's statement, is thus of a different nature.

Given that the victims of American-sponsored torture are almost exclusively Muslim men, it is necessary to follow Rejali even further.[58] In a piece entitled "The Real Shame of Abu Ghraib," Rejali notes that "in the beginning, Muslim states did not carry forward many of the worst tortures (including crucifixion) of the Persian and Roman empires they replaced. They did introduce tortures of their own, from the amputation of limbs to the common beating of the soles of the feet, the *falaka*, that are cruel by our standards. But Muslim societies were guided by ideals and values that Westerners can recognize and which still animate penal reform today."[59] Rejali moves on to focus on the most abhorred of ancient torture practices, crucifixion. Ancient societies regarded it as "the worst of executions" for the following reasons.

"Crucifixions displayed victims naked in public without honor. They subjected victims to the vengeful feelings of a crowd," transforming the onlookers into a jeering mob and allowing them "to take pleasure in pain and breach the bonds of civility. They extended suffering for days. They left victims as food for wild beasts and birds, denying them a proper burial." In short, Muslim societies rejected crucifixion, because it was "the practice of savages and tyrants who did not respect the law."[60] In the Roman empire, this punishment, which subjected "the victim to the utmost indignity,"[61] was usually reserved for criminals considered nonhuman (slaves and pirates) or for citizens convicted of high treason who, by their acts, were considered to have excluded themselves from the political and by extension the human community.[62] Rejali's analysis shows that the "real shame of Abu Ghraib" and of other American detention facilities lies in what those methods, discussed and approved by the highest ranking government officials and their advisors, stir up in the collective cultural memory of Muslim countries. All of the characteristics of crucifixion were explicitly or implicitly present in the infamous techniques used in Abu Ghraib prison. The hooded man standing on a box with wires attached to his fingers whose photograph became the icon for American brutality in Abu Ghraib, was, according to Rejali, subjected to an "old" technique

> dubbed the "crucifixion" by British solders during World War I. The CIA had hired experts to study it who had reported that the technique caused enormous swelling in the feet, intense pain in the hips, shortness of breath, and after three days, kidney failure. Forced standing on an elevated object is known only in three countries in the late twentieth century, Venezuela, South Africa and Brazil. And only Brazilian torturers used electricity as means of forcing the prisoner to maintain an erect position voluntarily, a technique dubbed "the Vietnam."[63]

Torture techniques like those used in Abu Ghraib that perpetrate an assault on "cultural identity"[64] with their use of intense shame revive, according to Rejali, the cultural memory of that "'barbaric' form of execution of the utmost cruelty," that already for the people of the ancient world was "an utterly offensive affair, 'obscene' in the original sense of the word."[65]

It can be assumed that what happened at Abu Ghraib would be considered intensely shameful for any victim from any cultural background, and for many so shameful that it would threaten to destroy not only their community's compassion, but also their compassion for themselves. At the same time, it is essential not to belittle the fact that the approved techniques were designed to target specific cultural sensibilities, or, bluntly speaking, to humiliate Muslim men. According to Alfred McCoy, "The war on terror would develop a conscious strategy of sexual humiliation as an adjunct to the CIA's [torture] paradigm."[66]

Moreover, the fact that the technique known in intelligence circles as "crucifixion," a technique intensely studied by the CIA, has become the "icon" of American torture all over the world, and particularly in Muslim countries, may indicate the necessity to research what Avital Ronell has termed the "phantasmatic history" of the United States, especially when considering that the Brazilian version of this technique, adopted in Abu Ghraib, is known as "the Vietnam." What Ronell wrote about the first war in Iraq, Operation Desert Storm, might be said of Operation "Infinite Justice," rebaptized on September 25, 2001, as "Operation Enduring Freedom": "The war was less a matter of truth than of rhetorical maneuvers that were dominated by unconscious transmission systems and symbolic displacements but which nonetheless have produced material effects."[67] The torture techniques used in Abu Ghraib might be understood as "material effects" of such "unconscious transmission systems and symbolic displacements." They fit Thomasius's formulation: Even without confessions, and without the certainty of a death penalty following the confession, they push victims to strive for their own annihilation. "'Shoot me here,' said an Abu Ghraib prisoner pointing to the space between his eyes, 'but don't do this to us.'" The sworn statement of another Abu Ghraib prisoner, Ameen Saeed Al-Sheik, read: "They said we will make you wish to die and it will not happen."[68]

## IV.

"Living together" supposes, as Derrida insists, an "interrupting excess . . . with regard to *symbiosis,* to a symbiotic, gregarious, or fusional living together." It also supposes an "interrupting excess . . . with regard to statutory convention, to law" ("Avowing," 26–27). One of Thomasius's arguments speaks to this "interrupting excess," as I hope to show in concluding.

As I have mentioned, Thomasius recalls that torture was a pagan practice, initially applied by the Romans only to slaves who were "treated as equal with four-legged creatures (animals) [*quadrupedibus/Vierfüsslern (Tiere)*]" (176–77). He insists that torture is "dangerous and irreligious" (134–35, 146–47), that the Holy Scriptures "curse" and "abhor" it (162–63), and that it "should have been banned from the courts of the Christians a long time ago" (176–77, 186–87). But, he observes, even though torture cannot be reconciled with the scriptures, "the Christian people nonetheless persist in holding on to so many pagan things [*tam multa gentilia*] with all their strength [*mordicus*: literally, with their teeth; doggedly], as if they [those pagan things] were the most religious" (or "the holiest" [*religiossima*]) (176–77), and this in spite of the Christian teaching that obliges the believers to "always" hold "a meekness" or "gentleness corresponding to the Gospels" in or "near their heart [*cordi esse debet mansuetudo/ Sanftmut am Herzen liegen muss*]." Thomasius calls on gentleness as a matter of the heart in the same paragraph in which he brandishes the Roman doctrine that slaves cannot be subjected to injustice (*iniuria/Unrecht*) because they are the equals of animals, and they can be "killed without punishment" (176–77).

Torture, then, was an accepted practice by Christian states in Thomasius's time, even though the Holy Scriptures "curse" and "abhor" it, and even though forgiveness and compassion are portrayed in the Gospels as specifically Christian. In our time, torture has been and for many still is a practice accepted by citizens of democratic states, even though their constitutions "curse" and "abhor" it.[69] And this may, in Derridean terms, not be so surprising. Derrida has argued that Western democracies are haunted by their unquestioned, repressed foundation in the blood ties that link brothers of noble birth and exclude everybody else.[70] In the context of the adoption of torture as official U.S. policy under the Bush administration, and of the growing acceptability of torture (as evidenced in the dramatic increase of torture scenes in TV shows),[71] one may wonder whether an aspect of the foundation of secular states in Christianity remains as of yet unthought: the mostly forgotten second meaning of the symbol that stands erect at its center as "the most religious" or "the holiest." As unthought, this second meaning of the cross may be "haunting" what, in Derrida's words, "*in fact* governs not the principles but the predominant reality of American political culture," that is, "despite the separation in principle between church and state, a fundamental biblical (primarily Christian) reference in its official political discourse and the discourse of its political leaders."[72] The second meaning of the cross is synonymous with the most despised and abhorred ancient form of torture and capital punishment. The torture technique dubbed "crucifixion" might be the most visible "material effect" of the "symbolic displacements" in which the "phantasmatic history" of the United States is acted out.[73]

In his study on suicide bombings, Talal Asad pursues a related argument. In the "indirect suicide" of Jesus' crucifixion, "the violent breaking of the body is not an occasion for horror" (such as suicide bombings are in our days), but "becomes the source of a transcendent truth." Most significantly, "it also constitutes, in and through violence, the universal category of 'the human' to whom the gift is offered." In other words, "in Christian civilization, the gift of life for humanity is possible only through a suicidal death."[74] Asad shows how the "Crucifixion represents the truth of violence" even in the "popular visual narratives" of our "secular" age, where the lonely male hero suffers "severe physical punishment or torture," and his excruciating pain comes to pass as "the very vindication of truth."[75]

Following Derrida's logic, the forgotten or repressed "foundation" of a state is not within reach of the "law" nor of "statutory convention" (such as the Holy Scriptures for Thomasius, and the Constitution for us), because it is its "origin." The fact that the Hebrew Bible, or in Christian parlance the Old Testament, "abhors" torture doesn't solve the problem that the New Testament finds its foundational origin in a practice abhorred as the quintessence of torture. Crucifixion figures itself among those "pagan things" defended doggedly as the holiest.

257

In a believer's perspective, the central symbol of Christianity declares Jesus's radical and revolutionary solidarity with the least of the least (one might say *rachamim*), and declares those expulsed from the human community as being not only human, but belonging to God's kingdom (at the condition, though, of their repentance). Allowing for the forgotten or repressed memory of this symbol to be addressed might come to signify a "mutation" in a sense similar to that evoked by Derrida with regard to the "globalization of avowal." In his lesson, Derrida argues that the scenes of public avowals and repentance he analyzes might

> signify a mutation in process, a fragile one, to be sure, fleeting and difficult to interpret, but, like the moment of an undeniable rupture in the history of the political, of the juridical, of the relations among community, civil society, and the state, among sovereign states, international law, and NGOs, among the ethical, the juridical, and the political, between the public and the private, between national citizenship and an international citizenship, even a metacitizenship, in a word, concerning a social bond that crosses [*passe*] the borders of these ensembles called family, nation, or state. ("Avowing," 31)

The scenes of public avowal bear thus the promise of an opening of these "borders" and thus the promise, perhaps, of rethinking what "ensemble" might signify. A few pages later, Derrida evokes the concept of "mutation" again, this time with even greater insistence. He notes that the discourse of institutions like the Truth and Reconciliation Commission in South Africa "forces us to ask ourselves whether the globalization of avowal is a planetarization of the Abrahamic concept, or more specifically Christian concept, of forgiveness, or, on the contrary, a new mutation that brings about [*qui fait arriver*] something unexpected, something even threatening to this tradition—I cannot engage here this necessary but immense question" ("Avowing," 36).

This question may become pressing with regard to the present and future legacy of the use of torture by the United States against Muslim detainees in Iraq, Afghanistan, Guantánamo, most of whom were or are innocent of any crime. Facing the "real shame" of Abu Ghraib and other torture chambers might bring about a mutation, "something unexpected, something even threatening" to the dominant understanding of the central symbol of Christianity and the concept of forgiveness that is inseparable from it.

# From Jerusalem to Jerusalem—A Dedication

*Michal Govrin*

**At the Close of Time**
On the Sabbath before Rosh Hashanah
At the close of time
Before it opens forth again
Unsure
We are immured in straits
Dire as judgment, blind
And absolute.

On the Sabbath before Rosh Hashanah
Not the Sabbath of Return, not "By your might"
For of what use in your sight is all our striving
If not to disclose these crimps of
The soul, to recall them
Like a dove that finds
A moment's respite in the cleft.

On the Sabbath before Rosh Hashanah
In this city clamped
Like an ant-infested
Orange rind
Cast into the dust heap where the
Cats of devastation prowl
On the night of the mantled moon.

On the Sabbath before Rosh Hashanah
The city unfolds like the draper's shop
In creases of the shaded alleyways
And the stairs we climbed to the rooftop

When a tingling whiteness flowed
From belfry towers
So close to the sky

—Still our feet shall stand before you
Unsounded polyglot of many faces,
You who watch as we tread the flagstones,
You to whom all words flow—
Even the orange-vendor drawing near
Breaks into smile
Before the pen that
Draws us both together
If only for a moment
In your alphabet.
(Shabbat before Rosh Hashana, 2003)

—Michal Govrin, *And So Said Jerusalem, Poems and Hymns*, translated from the
Hebrew by Betsy Rosenberg

At the margins of what is said, life gapes. Nameless. Beyond the boundaries of life and
death. At the point of connection and separation.

Like the positioning of my lecture, at the first sitting of the conference, near its margins.[1] I'll allow myself therefore to speak in my marginal voice. At the margins of a philosophy that is not foreign to the question of "margins." And I'll proceed from outside, as
a witness, a storyteller. From within being. And by reading among other things the words
that were written in the margins of books. Outside. Dedications.

I'll approach from Jerusalem—which is the "navel of the world" and simultaneously a
place beyond all boundaries.

And I'll start right away with an apology, from that same marginal standpoint, for my
choosing a speech that is vulnerable, poetic. Dangerous. "Exposes itself to the accident," like
the poematic porcupine [*hérisson*] in "What Is Poetry?"[2] A choice of a poematic speech in
order to reawaken the place of danger and tremor. To indicate it.

And in a confessional tone.

An embarrassing genre. For how can one confess? And not just according to the
words of Derrida, about how confession is always of what cannot be confessed. But rather,
how to confess without it immediately being a concealment, precisely because of being
public? And how to confess, to give a name, without it being a contradiction—by the very
giving of a name—to what remains implicitly nameless. Up to the end.

It will be a confession about Jerusalem. About the "impossibility" of Jerusalem. And
through Jacques Derrida's journey from Jerusalem to Jerusalem.

Not what is Jerusalem, but how to say it with the performative power of language. As Paul Celan requests in his poem "The Poles": "Say that Jerusalem *is*."[3] How to say Jerusalem, out of and against the political, the social reality. In the here and now but also in a messianic expectation, in an apocalyptic time. Jerusalem as the place of holiness and Eros. Jerusalem as the poematic place, which exists by the power of saying.

"To Michal, from Jerusalem to Jerusalem, with all my heart, Jacques," was Jacques Derrida's dedication of his book *Adieu à Emmanuel Levinas* when he gave it to me on his arrival to Jerusalem, in January 1998.[4]

This dedication did not just happen. Derrida's route to Jerusalem went via his extended dialogue with Emmanuel Levinas, and my route to the meeting with Jacques Derrida went via my meetings with Levinas.[5] The words of the dedication allude metonymically also to the very motion of approach to Jerusalem with which the book ends:

Let us return for a moment to Jerusalem.
We are approaching the gates of Jerusalem.
What is an approach? Will such an approach ever end?[6]

[Nous approchons les portes de Jérusalem.
Qu'est-ce que l'approche? Et cette approche cessera-t-elle jamais?][7]

The question of Judaism, of the Hebrew language, Israel, and Jerusalem were central to our close friendship of twenty-five years. Our first meeting, in Paris in the autumn of 1979,[8] revolved around the Hebrew word *temunah*, which appears in the second commandment: "Thou shalt not make unto thee any graven image [*temunah*],"[9] and whether the term "representation" is its accurate translation. At his request, I lectured on the subject at his seminar on Hegel at École Normale Supérieure.[10] And at the meeting afterward Derrida spoke emotionally about his starts at writing about circumcision. At that same meeting he expressed the still hesitant request to visit Israel, Jerusalem, if he were invited. And indeed in the spring of 1983 Derrida arrived at the invitation of the Hebrew University of Jerusalem for his first visit.[11] We went out then to the landscape, and so we continued on his four subsequent visits to the city, in the course of which I became a kind of guide. *A deux ou à trois*, along with Marguerite Derrida.

Following the visits there were books, letters, and phone calls arriving, from Paris to Jerusalem. In our telephone conversations during the short time of peace and many periods of tension and war, always, at a certain point in the conversation, a change in his voice would occur and with it the question: "How is Jerusalem?"

It will require a detailed examination to get to the bottom of Derrida's charged relationship with Jerusalem. I will attempt here to bear witness, as far as is possible, to what was lived and transmitted. And in the name of that same dubious "role" that Jacques Derrida seemingly "dedicated" to me: to be the addressee in Jerusalem. And maybe even the addressee of Jerusalem, in the name of Jerusalem.

The first dedication was sent from Paris to Jerusalem and was attached to a consignment of books and articles, dated June 1, 1983.

> Dear Michal,
>
> These little texts, like open postcards, I dare send only because we discussed them. All of them, from now on will have for me one meaning, "Jerusalem," how much I blessed all that I lived there, and how happy I was, a little while ago, to feel that all of them would converge toward the seal which I have still not deciphered, down below, to the left of the last page of the little book . . .
>
> Jacques Élie, June 1st '83.

Among the books there was a little book: *Of an Apocalyptic Tone Newly Adopted in Philosophy,*[12] and on its final page a reproduction with the caption: "Magic. Apocalyptic key. The seven seals of Saint John." In that same seal "which I have not yet deciphered, down below, to the left of the last page," was written in Hebrew letters: "Holy the / Jerusalem [*Hakdosh/Ha/Yerushalaim*]."

I will not pause here over the choice of name "Jacques Elie" for the signature, which hints at what will be expressed by Derrida further on. I will emphasize the expression "how much I blessed all that I lived there, and how happy I was" and the echo found in it of the epiphany at the beginning of the cycle of "Jerusalem" poems by Paul Celan, written after his only visit to Jerusalem, in 1968. Years later, at the "Passage des Frontières" conference at Cerisy in 1992, I read Paul Celan's walking in Jerusalem through those poems. As I was preparing the lecture, Ilana Shmueli's first publication appeared, and it transpired that it was a walk *à deux*.[13] Actually, through Celan's poems I also tried to obliquely read the stages of a *tour à deux*, and to open the question, is it possible "to reach Jerusalem"?

It was a late spring day, fairly hot. In the flush of the renewed meeting after Paris in Jerusalem it was agreed that I would take Derrida for a tour. I borrowed a car for that purpose. I had to decide on a route. How to write on the landscape. And what? I had to listen to his expectation. Unfold it in the place. And to follow a parallel trajectory of my own state of mind, which, perhaps, despite all the differences, was not so different from his.

For any walk *à deux* is simultaneously the walk of each one on his own trajectory through the place as well as the walk toward the place of the other, and from within it. And what opens up at that moment and revives the place, is precisely by the power of the other place, the place of the other.

I was then in the midst of a "pilgrimage" to and from within Jerusalem and to the "danger of the sacred" while writing a novel, *The Name*, and following the footsteps of its heroine.[14] Simultaneously, I had been typing the manuscript of my father, Pinchas Govrin's memoirs, in which he describes the arrival of four generations of my family from the

Ukraine to Palestine throughout the twenties, each by his own route: my Hassidic great-grandfather, my modern Orthodox grandfather and my father, his brothers and nephew, the socialist pioneers.[15] The family elders all died before I was born, but in his book my father passed on to me their longings for Zion. My great-grandfather passed away in 1936 and was buried on the Mount of Olives. In 1948 this part of Jerusalem was conquered by Jordan and access to it was blocked. Since the transfer of Eastern Jerusalem from Jordanian to Israeli rule during the Six-Day War in 1967, my father yearned to find his grandfather's grave, if it remained intact and had not been vandalized, as had many of the graves in the ancient graveyard. He got as far as verifying the initial details of the burial and of the grave's location, but in the meantime his health deteriorated, and he could no longer continue his search. In the course of typing up his notes I understood that the role had been transferred to me. And so I set off for the offices of the Chevra Kadisha (Burial Society) of the Wohlyn Community in Mea She'arim, who had dealt with my great-grandfather's burial in decades past, and from there in a gravedigger's jeep, I ascended to the Mount of Olives. It was one of those dizzying conjunctions of eras and places on the slopes of Jerusalem, when to the sound of the gravediggers' walkie-talkies we reached the headstones of my great-grandfather and great-grandmother Isaac and Glikel Hayot (Globman) on the southern slope of the Mount of Olives, where they had stood, alone, all those years.

And so on that morning when we set out to "visit in Jerusalem" I decided to "include" Jacques Derrida in my personal quest and turned the steering wheel toward the Mount of Olives. I did so out of my own compulsion—but believed it was also in attentiveness to what was said in silence. I drove up the slope toward A-Tur, through the grounds of the Intercontinental Hotel and to the Mount of Olives, the place where according to tradition the Messiah's feet will stand when he reaches Jerusalem on the day of redemption and the resurrection of the dead. All around stretched the antique Jewish graveyard, some of whose headstones are over two thousand years old. And around them the dust of multitudes of bones from generations upon generations. New headstones, old ones, smashed, restored. And across the valley on Mount Moriah, the ruins of the Temple Mount, and above them, Haram al Sharif with the El-Aqsa Mosque and the golden dome of the Omar Mosque. At the eastern wing, opposite the Mount of Olives, is the blocked Mercy Gate, through which believers say the Messiah will enter. According to family lore, my great-grandfather, Reb Itzik, asked for his grave to be turned directly toward the gate, so that on the day the Messiah comes, in the midst of the hullabaloo of the resurrection of the dead and their arrival as rolling bones from every part of the diaspora, he would not need to ask the way, simply rise and walk straight into the open gate of redemption.

I parked at the summit. Morning clouds chilled the air a little. We stood before the expansive, breathtaking view that spreads across the horizon above Jerusalem. Silence reigned, and out of it Derrida started talking about his father, about his grave on the mountainside over the sea in Nice, drawing a line thereby from there to here. And as the morning

263

went on, already in the alleyways of Mea She'arim, he drew the line on to his childhood in Algiers, and told of his grandmother who worked with his father in the charitable trust for the burial of the dead. "The Truest Act of Kindness" was its name, coined after this commandment. Another link between there and here.

Then, in 1983, Derrida had still hardly spoken publicly of his Judaism, his family, or of his childhood in Algiers. Therefore I had not expected such an echo. Not so much of one. Not such a personal, biographical one. The previous evening he'd lectured at the Van Leer Institute in Jerusalem about the parable "Before the Law" by Kafka. He spoke in particular about the threshold. His remarks rocked me. They stirred in me the most secret desire to cross over the threshold into the beyond. A beyond of darkness and denial, maybe. God's absence, or the hiding of the divine face during and after the Holocaust, which preoccupied me in my writing. The next day, in the side streets of Mea She'arim I brought before him the parable of Rabbi Israel Baal Shem Tov, the founder of Hassidism, about the king who surrounds his palace with walls and gates, and strews treasures in the way, so that all who seek him recoil from the barrier or are content with the gold, and return the way they came—apart from the one who truly longs to see the king and sees that all the barriers are merely an illusion, and goes straight past them to the king.[16] A parable which seeks to illustrate the Hassidic belief that "no place is empty of the divine presence": There is no distance and no partition, because the divinity exists in every single place. Did Kafka know the Baal Shem Tov's parable and enter into dialogue with it in "Before the Law"? Is the threshold within us? Was it the blindness of the one waiting before the law, that he did not cross what was merely an illusion, did not see that he was *already* inside, at any place?

On that day of shared touring, at a certain moment, it seemed to me that it was necessary to cross a threshold. To leave the one reality and mark the existence of another. And so, in an adventurous decision with no knowledge of the consequences, I knocked on the doors of the Chevra Kadisha of the Wohlyn Community in Mea She'arim. I made up some administrative excuse to get us inside, to the dim interior, and asked something about repainting the names on the headstones of my ancestors. We were invited to sit down. To wait. Left so before the pious Jews wreathed in their long beards, who tended their own business. For a long while.

The room whirled. Something gaped there.

Did I imagine it?

The tears. The tremor of emotion.

In silence.

A certain kind of dedication. That was bestowed there. That was received.

Something was engraved, like a seal, or perhaps a seal that was awakened.

And I cannot—now—after all that has happened—not tremble when I think of another mark that was sealed and erased and is unceasingly awakening, claiming its name—

the number which was impressed into my mother at the gates of Auschwitz, the one she had surgically removed when she reached Israel, and whose absence, years after her death, still leads me after her.

As only years after, with Derrida's public and impossible confession, "Avowing—The Impossible," the mark, the wound, will indeed return and be named, and it will be what we run from and to. What marks being Jewish, can perhaps only be confessed without words, in silence, or tears, or in Jerusalem.

Our friendship was lived between Jerusalem, Paris, and New York. And again Paris and Jerusalem. On work trips, when I stayed with my husband, the French mathematician, Haim Brezis, and our two daughters born not long after the passing away of my two parents and the passing of Jacques Derrida's mother. At family meetings. Meetings *à deux*. In phone calls. But all through the years that scene, at the offices of the Chevra Kadisha in Mea She'arim in Jerusalem has remained unspoken. I was sure I imagined it. And yet, it continued to reverberate.

In 1992 at Cerisy I left encrypted the echo of the tour *à deux* of nine years before. It is hidden in the address of the dedication and it elliptically seals my words.

> And meanwhile, it is possible to pass the place one morning like any other. Me, for example, on the Mount of Olives, searching for the grave of my great-grandfather. Fifty years after it was dug, beyond all the wars that have been waged here since then. . . . A morning like any other, searching after this grave, with a grumpy resistance to this mission from beyond the grave. My odd companions, the men of the Chevra Kadisha . . . with their wispy beards blown by the wind, cradle their walkie-talkies trying to pinpoint some last detail. One moment of rest. A stolen moment of calm, high on the slope, facing the sealed Gate. In the silence of mid-morning. As if, for all time, there had never been anything but these mountains all around, Mount Moriah opposite, this silence. To the end of time.[17]

In Derrida's long response to my lecture at Cerisy, in an echo of his first public references to Jerusalem in "How to Avoid Speaking?", the question already arose of whether it is possible to approach Jerusalem, to enter its gates, and if so how? Is it possible only to "go around," like Celan in his poem "Die Glut"? Or to call it by name, like in the poem "The Poles": "*say* that Jerusalem *is*"?[18] And is it possible to approach through the poetic to the political? "Celan, enigmatically, goes around . . . a way he gives us in a kind of reserve. But nevertheless it is clear that the holy places, those three holy places which are also sites of possession and of war, as such oppose, or reject, the poetic speech, the aspiration to bring Jerusalem, 'to being' through speech, by the mere 'naming it.'"[19]

The dialogue in Cerisy took place after Derrida had visited Jerusalem three times already, and in his remarks he insisted that nowadays Jerusalem is a global question, and not just a local one, as he repeatedly expressed it later on. He isolated the question of Israel from the question of Jerusalem, and posed the latter as the world's nucleus question. And later in his response, referring to the "circumnavigating way" of Celan, he said:

> And if so, if there is a kind of alliance between these two motions, it is possible, to a certain extent, to ask what will be the politics of poetics. That is to say, what shall we do with that calling of Jerusalem by name? And anyhow, in what language shall it be called by name? Who will call her name? And in what tongue? And what will be the way to make an utterance, that poetic obligation within the name of Jerusalem? What relationship will it have to the stone, with what is here called stone? That is to say, the irreplaceableness of a place such as this which leads to a war of religions, to religious war?[20]

It was in 1986, on his second visit to Jerusalem, at the conference on "Absence and Negation" at the Hebrew University, that Derrida delivered his famous lecture "How To Avoid Speaking," in which he addresses—for the first time—the question: *Suis-je à Jérusalem?*

> Am I in Jerusalem? This is a question to which one will never respond in the present tense, only in the future or in the past. . . . In other words, am I in Jerusalem or elsewhere, very far from the Holy City? Under what conditions does one find oneself in Jerusalem? Is it enough to be there physically, as one says, and to live in a place that carries this name, as I am now doing? What is it to live in Jerusalem?[21]

In the course of this visit Stéphane Mosès gave him his translation of Scholem's unpublished letter to Rosenzweig in 1926, "A Declaration of Faith in Our Language," found in Scholem's estate.[22] A year later Derrida lectured on this letter, and through it formulated the gaping dichotomy at the heart of the apocalyptic and political place, the messianic place and the place of stone, all at once. A contradiction in which we live. In his remarks on Scholem's letter, Derrida stresses the catastrophic expectation of the apocalypse embedded in language, and especially Hebrew, according to Scholem. But he includes himself in the first person plural of those who have found "an apocalyptic way, which in any event, *we* follow."[23]

Then too, during that visit, we ascended to the Mount of Olives, to that same spot, visited near Scholem's house and stood, together with Marguerite, by the window of a *yeshiva*, to hear the voices of the children reading the Torah together. A question regarding the Hebrew translation for the term "performance," which he put to me at the end of my lecture in that same conference, became the urge to write about Hebrew in a book of lyrical prose, *The Making of the Sea, A Chronic Exegesis.*[24] The book raises the erotic aspect of the speech act, and the longing for a place that is embedded in Hebrew, and is set as a page of Talmud, with an allusion to *Glas*. And later, during the several months of the winter of 1987–88 when our family stayed in Paris, Derrida also asked that we hold Hebrew lessons.

Those lessons were conducted between the fundamentals of the alphabet and grammar and a reading of the first chapter of the book of Genesis.

Jacques Derrida's third visit to Jerusalem was in the spring of 1988. It was a few months after the outbreak of the first, popular Intifada, which broke the barrier of denial in Israeli consciousness and led over the years to a recognition of the rights of the Palestinian people. In the light of these events it was necessary to say Jerusalem again, and perhaps to uncover the contradictions in Zionism, and in being Jewish.

We planned therefore a bi-vocal book, *On Zionism*, and began to work together on intercrossing texts. But my literary urge overpowered it, and instead of a theoretical text was created the novel *Snapshots*,[25] and from the conversation informing it what remained was the motto from Derrida's "What Is Poetry?" and the metaphor of the porcupine thrown on the highway, waiting for an accident, which reverberates with the fate of *Snapshots*'s heroine, the architect, Ilana Zuriel. She draws the inspiration for her architectural plan for a monument—or, more precisely an antimonument—for peace in Jerusalem from the temporary structure of the Sukka, and the commandment of the Sabbatical Year. It was my way of opening the possibility of "nonholding," which is part of the Jewish concept of ownership. It was my way of continuing the conversation.

After that, Derrida's exposure of his Jewish identity grew apace in his writings, and in parallel he elaborated his Jewish-Arab identity. His public criticism toward Israel and its policies grew, joining his voice to others. Yet at the same time, another seemingly opposite and intimate voice has continued—in bursts of worry, anxiety even. In phone calls to Jerusalem at the time of the first Intifada, at the time of the Gulf War, in the years of the terrorist attacks of the Second Intifada. Always, at a certain point in our conversation the sigh "Ahh, Jerusalem" was uttered, and in it distance and closeness, criticism and worry, "the escape from . . ." and "drawing close to" were all interwoven.

A posteriori I found an effective acknowledgment of this complexity in "Avowing— The Impossible," in the self-analysis of the "boy" wounded forever by antisemitism, and by the conflict between identification and denial—particularly in moments of peril. The contradiction between the desire to be "chosen" and the compulsion to "flee"—two terms identical in their Hebrew root letters (B.Ch.R / B.R.Ch. ‫ב.ח.ר‬ / ‫ב.ר.ח‬).[26]

I would describe the contradictory movement that, at the time of the anti-Semitic zeal of the French authorities in Algeria during the war, pushed a little boy who was expelled from school and understood none of it to rebel, forever, against two ways of "living together": at once against racist gregariousness, and therefore against anti-Semitic segregation, but also, more obscurely, and more unavowably, no doubt, against the conservative and self-protective confinement of a Jewish community that, seeking *naturally, legitimately* to defend itself, to constitute or reconstitute its whole [*ensemble*] under the ordeal of these traumas, was folding in upon itself, overbidding in the direction that I already then felt as a kind of exclusive, even fusional, communitarism.

Believing that he was beginning to understand what "living together" could mean, the child of which I speak had to break then, in a manner that was as unreflective as reflective, with both sides, with both exclusive—and thus excluding—belongings. The only belonging, the only "living together" that he judged then bearable and worthy of that name already supposed a rupture with identitarian and totalizing belonging, assured of itself in a homogeneous whole [*ensemble*]. In a manner as unreflective as reflective, the child felt at his core two contradictory things as to what this "living together" could signify: on the one hand, that he could betray his own, his close ones, and Judaism, and that he had to avow this within himself, even before others, even before God, but also, on the other hand, that by this separation, this rupture, this passage toward a kind of universality beyond symbiotic communitarism and gregarious fusion, beyond even citizenship, in this very separation, it could be that he was more faithful to a certain Jewish vocation, at the risk of remaining the only, the last. and the least of the Jews [*le seul et le dernier des Juifs*], in the most ambiguous sense of this expression with which he played without playing—elsewhere and fifty years later, presenting himself or sometimes also hiding himself as a kind of paradoxical Marrano who ran the risk of losing even the culture of his secret or the secret of his culture. ("Avowing," 27–28)

And maybe more than anywhere else, Jerusalem became [*avoir lieu*] for Derrida the *topos,* the place for this contradiction, a sort of a concrete *Chora.*

In January 1998 Jacques Derrida visited Israel once more. Ten years after his previous visit. It was already after the murder of Yitzhak Rabin, the high point of the peace process (which he calls a kind of war), the New Historians and post-Zionism were in full swing, and, underneath the surface, tension was rising in preparation for the second Intifada of El-Aqsa which would break out in the millennium year at the Temple Mount. From the stage of the Opera in Tel Aviv Derrida was asked about politics. And refrained. Together with Moshe Ron we conducted a tripartite public conversation. But before an opera hall full of a crowd who had streamed to a mass public event, it was not possible to speak in a voice of silence and in contradictions.

Echoes of that visit to Jerusalem appear in the book *La Contre-allée* by Catharine Malabou and Jacques Derrida, and they lurch between opposite poles.[27] In the remarks dedicated to his visit to Israel a moment of hospitality is described which did not occur in Jerusalem but rather in Ramallah and for some moments in Tel Aviv. The hospitality of the colleagues and audience in Jerusalem stir repulsion and refusal in Derrida. Had an emotional process, already traced in Celan, here turned the memory and the (messianic) emotion to disappointment and anguish? Had the sacred become the abject?[28] Had the political paralyzed the obligation (moral, philosophical, theological, historical, and personal) to ask, *suis-je à Jérusalem?* And to ask it from the heart, the irreplaceable place, and the place of contradiction. In a telephone conversation between Paris and Jerusalem in response to this section of the book, we agreed to disagree.

Yet, during the visit, Jacques Derrida asked that we drive to "take a picture" in the place where our journey began, in the ancient Jewish cemetery on the Mount of Olives. In *La Contre-allée* that photograph appears opposite a description of the remnants of the Jewish community of Istanbul. And there, Derrida lingers in a self-analysis of that same ongoing movement of denial and of eschatological, fatal search. At that same place Derrida compares with some irony this expectation for a revelation to the messianic expectation of "those buried in the ancient Jewish graveyard of Jerusalem, opposite the gate," and again borrows the identity of the "marrano."

> Like certain Marranos I would have begun by forgetting, by believing that I have simply forgotten my own filiation. I have the feeling that the people I meet while travelling, or who flock to hear me speak, can sense that. They expect one day to see the Thing or the Cause revealed. Like those who get buried in the old cemetery in Jerusalem, facing the Gate. They want to be being-there, one day, standing (as one says for a "standing ovation"). They wait so as to reserve their place in the cemetery or lecture hall, like in Jerusalem.[29]

And immediately the loaded retreat from closeness is renewed, "I'm over-doing, as usual, the messianic scenes . . . yet at the same time they fill me with terror [*J'exagère, comme toujours, avec ces scènes messianiques . . . elles me terrifient en même temps*]."[30]

When Derrida visited in January 1998, he offered me many books with dedications. This one on a copy of the essay "Un ver a soie": ". . . back to Jerusalem"; or this one on a copy of *Le monoliguisme de l'autre* which he gave me at the end of the visit: "To Michal, beyond all the crazy languages of Jerusalem / from year to year / to thank her [*pour lui rendre grâce*] / if possible—/ Jacques / Jerusalem, Tel-Aviv, Jerusalem, 4–11 January 1998." And the dedication on the book *Adieu à Emmanuel Levinas* with which I began.

This book includes—in a kind of tripartite debate with Levinas's conception of the feminine—the question of the desire for Jerusalem. Derrida addresses the erotic feminine aspect of Jerusalem as a place of lust, referring to my reading in Cerisy. The phonetic proximity in French between to live and to desire [*désirer-résider*] leads Derrida to pursue the question: not only is it possible to reach Jerusalem, but what is the meaning of residing in it, of dwelling in it, and is it possible to separate desire from dwelling?

"To desire, to reside. In singing the election of Zion by the desire of Yahweh—yes, the desire of Yahweh—a psalm (132:13) names Jerusalem as the chosen lover or spouse for a dwelling. God says that he desires to reside in Zion. 'There I will reside, for I desire it,' says one translation. Desiring to reside, as if it were a single word, a single and same movement, for there is no desire without this elective claim, without this exclusive request for a singular residence.

"'Yes, Yahweh has chosen Zion, He has desired it for his habitation. This is my resting place forever; here I will reside, for I have desired it.'"[31]

Is it therefore necessary to regard Eros, to regard the desire in belief, as a mode which cuts through the political, which gives it foundation? And how to render this desire a responsible one?

The following autumn in New York we held the symposium "Body of Prayer"[32] with the poet David Shapiro, at the Cooper Union School of Architecture. The symposium took place at the time when Derrida was preparing his lecture, "Avowing—The Impossible," which he would give on his return to Paris. It was held to coincide with the publication of the English translation of my novel *The Name*. In *Body of Prayer* Derrida presents a series of contradictions at the very heart of prayer itself. Contradictions which paradoxically inform what embodies true prayer in his eyes, prayer that retains a tremor of hesitation, the recollection of how much it is "impossible." To pray one must first pray for the possibility of praying— *prier pour la prière*. Derrida says in a kind of echo of the opening of the silent Amidah prayer: "Lord, open my lips and let my mouth say your praises." And to whom should one pray? Here as well one has no confidence that there is indeed someone who listens.

> Michal said that in the Jewish prayer we "produce" the God, so to speak; we make the God present, so that the presence of God depends on the prayer. Yes, yes, and possibly no. Possibly no. If we were sure that at the other end of the prayer God would show up, and that we produce the addressee, that wouldn't be a prayer. The possibility that God remains eternally absent, that there might be no addressee at the other end of the prayer is the condition for the prayer. If I was sure that my prayer would be received by some addressee, there would be no prayer. So that's why I would go so far as to say there should be a moment of atheism in the prayer. The possibility that God doesn't answer, doesn't exist. And I pray God that He, but that's up to Him, that He be there. But the possibility for Him not to listen to, not to respond to His name, is included in the essence of the prayer. If you want to pray, if you have to know how to pray, to learn how to pray, you have to accept the hypothesis that you may pray for no one, for nothing. . . . That's why there is something trembling, some tremor within the prayer. There is no quiet prayer. Because there is an anxiety about the authenticity of the prayer. And I'm not the one who can decide about the authenticity of the prayer. Only the other can decide. And the other one is just a question mark. It's not just a question mark, but a possibility which remains a possibility.[33]

At the conclusion Derrida touches on the contradiction between despair and hope, which informs prayer. One of the meanings of the root of the Hebrew words "prayer," "to pray" [*Lehitpalel*] P.L.L [*Peh, Lamed, Lamed*] is "to hope" [*Lephalel*]. Through it Derrida speaks of

> another possibility that I can't exclude. The possibility of a hopeless prayer. You may pray without any reference to the future, just to address the other, hopelessly, hope-

lessly: in reference only to the past. There is only repetition, no future. And, nevertheless, you pray. Is that possible? To pray hopelessly? And is it possible to pray hopelessly, not only without request, but even by giving up hope? If one agrees that there is such a possibility of prayer, a pure prayer, that is hopeless, then shouldn't we think that finally the essence of the prayer has something to do with this despair, with this hopelessness? The pure prayer doesn't ask for anything, not even for the future. Now, I can imagine the response to this terrible doubt: that, even in that case, if I pray hopelessly, there is a hope in the prayer. I would hope, at least, for someone sharing my prayer or someone listening to my prayer, or someone understanding my hopelessness and my despair and so in that case there is, nevertheless, a hope and a future. But, perhaps not. Perhaps not. At least perhaps, this is for me also, a terrible condition of the prayer.[34]

To pray without hope. The powerful despair of belief.

Is there an echo here, conscious or unconscious, of the secret teachings of Hassidism? And perhaps no less of the Jewish humor so desperate and full of hope? The "nevertheless" facing an impossible history?

And the continuing longing to be a guest, to enjoy hospitality. In his commentary on Frédéric Brenner's photographs in *Diaspora* (which was written in 2000), Derrida finds hospitality in the recollection of a moment that occurred in the Hasidic courts in Jerusalem, to which I took him and Marguerite on the eve of Sabbath during their 1986 visit.

> Jerusalem. I have had the experience of dancing, in Mea She'arim, with some Hasidim. I had entered as a visitor, like a somewhat nervous tourist, and was immediately noticed, because of my clothes, by the dancers who for a long time pretended they didn't even see me. Then one of them came up to me, we spoke in the English of New York, which he knew well. Hospitality: The visitor becomes a guest. I was invited to join them, and after a few minutes, everything was shared with me: food, song, good cheer. For a long time I danced with these Hasidim, observed by Marguerite, my wife, and Michal Govrin, who was our guide. The women had to remain outside, of course, excluded from the dance reserved for men. I saw them looking at us, and from the corner of my eye I saw them laughing through a kind of fence.[35]

Was it there, in Mea She'arim and via New York, that a peculiar sense of community was momentarily shared?

In December 2000 the conference "Judéités: Questions pour Jacques Derrida" was held in Paris, against a backdrop of the first wave of deadly terror attacks in Jerusalem after the outbreak of the second Intifada.[36] In my lecture I quoted my soon-to-be published novel *Snapshots*, in which I interpret the law of the Sabbatical year as a unique form of having property in remembrance of the impossibility of really possessing a land that belongs to God. Beyond the violent terms of the conflict, I offered the laws of the Sabbatical year as a "third" possibility of "dwelling" in Jerusalem, by relinquishing the exclusivity of desire, freeing Jerusalem from her mythic position as the desired and fought-for woman. In a long debate between Derrida and me following the lecture, we discussed the tension between relinquishing desire and sacrifice.[37] In the coming years, again, as they always did in periods of political violence and terror, anxious phone calls reached Jerusalem from Paris with nearness and distance intertwined.

And then Jacques Derrida's last visit in Jerusalem. In 2003, to receive an honorary doctorate from the Hebrew University. At the height of the Intifada. It was not certain that he would accept the invitation. In the enlightened West voices were on the rise at the time rebuking and calling for a boycott of Israel and its academy. Derrida accepted the honor and the hospitality. The ceremony was scheduled for the end of June.

It was a few days after he'd learned of his fatal illness. He stayed for less than two days. Immediately upon his arrival and disclosing the diagnosis, he asked me to take him later to the Western wall. Fragility accompanied all his movements. It was a long day with a lecture on Celan, a ceremony in the amphitheater facing the desert, and a supper during which he removed from his pocket with special attention his note and read the words of criticism and closeness this time voiced together. And the next day, at the meeting with Israeli colleagues, he addressed the audience, saying, for the only time I ever heard, "we."

Late at night, at the end of the formal celebrations, he reminded me of his wish that we drive to the Western wall. He didn't say to pray, just "to the Wall." With urgency, as if it were the only reason for his having come. We drove through the empty roads around the Old City.[38] We entered the gate, and went down the road leading to the Temple Mount. At midnight, alone, in a body bent ahead of time in the knowledge of the torments awaiting him, Jacques Derrida strode toward the lit rampart, empty of worshippers. Not with a prayer book, which he did not know how to read, but with a Bible. In French. Standing alone wrapped in silence. In a prayer of "perhaps," of the despairing hope for existence. Of a Jew who saw himself, at the peak of pride and peak of despair as "the last of the Jews." As if only thus would he pray from within the contradiction. As if only thus he would be a Jew.

It was only after his death that Claude Sitbon brought me the proceedings of the thirty-seventh "Colloque des intellectuels Juifs de langue française," with Derrida's lecture "Avowing—The Impossible," which I had not known.[39] And there, surprisingly and so late, in a kind of public dedication addressed across death, I found the echo of the ancient cemetery and of that moment beyond the threshold.

> I return for a moment and to conclude, not far from Mount Moriah, but this time closer to the cemetery of Jerusalem. Return, therefore, to end, in Jerusalem. Maimonides, by the way, said that *teshuva* also meant the end of exile. Return to Jerusalem, therefore, to end, and close to a cemetery. During my first visit, in 1982, an Israeli friend enabled my discovery of this cemetery, showing me the tomb of her grandfather. Then I accompany her, for she must resolve a question in the offices of the Hevra

Kadisha, the institution responsible for the difficult administration of the famous cemetery: allocation of plots, decisions as to the "concessions," transport of bodies, often costly operations, from distant countries, and most often the United States, and so on. This is before the cell phone, but I find myself there, in these offices, before a group of "responsible" individuals, busy men, all dressed in black and with traditional headdress. These men appear to run and to be out of breath; they display a feverish activity around walkie-talkies, telephones, and computers that ostensibly link them to all the places in the world from which one begs them, at any cost, for a place in the cemetery. Everything is becoming substitutable in this world, but the irreplaceable resists there, precisely here, now, not only in this place named Jerusalem, but in this very place, the cemetery, in this corner of Jerusalem, in view of orienting the dead.

I asked myself then: What does "living together" mean when the most urgent thing is to choose, while living and in the first place, a last place, an apparently irreplaceable place, desire then dictating not only dying and perhaps surviving or coming back to life in order to rise together upon the arrival of someone, but waiting, here and not there, before this door, unique in the world, this sealed door, the coming or the advent, the to-come of a Messiah? And yet, even before the globalization of the cell phone, of email, and of the Internet, all these little prosthetic machines, telephones, computers, walkie-talkies were beginning to make, yet another time, all these here-nows infinitely proximate and substitutable. New York could appear closer than Gaza (with or without airport), and I could have the feeling of being closer to some other at the other end of the world than to some neighbor, some friend from West Jerusalem or East Jerusalem. To ask oneself then, on a cell phone, whether Jerusalem is in Jerusalem, is perhaps no longer to trust, like others in older times, the distinction between earthly Jerusalem and heavenly Jerusalem. Yet this place of promise appeared to resist substitution and telecommunication. What was signified, then, by the placing of this "taking place" [*l'emplacement de cet "avoir lieu"*]? And of this messianic taking-place?

But I asked myself first, in anguish—and it was the same question: Who can allocate places? Who can authorize himself, while avowing it, to grant here, to refuse there, to grant to one and refuse to the other the chance to make this place his place, to elect it or to believe himself elected to it, be it in order there to bury his dead or there to await some messianic peace, a to-come or a return?

Since that moment and through analogous experiences (a few weeks before this first visit to Jerusalem, I was coming out of a jail cell in Prague), I had to begin thinking that which, in what I have named elsewhere messianic spectrality, or spectral messianicity, exceeds, precedes, and conditions all messianisms. And to think a certain faith older than all religions. This must have occurred to me [*m'arriver*] a long time ago in Algiers but also during these last years in Jerusalem. I do not know, and I avow it, how to interpret what then occurred to me—or would occur to me still [*ce qui alors m'arriva—ou m'arriverait encore*]. Nor what was announcing itself above me as a *revenant,* what was announcing itself by returning upon me [*ce qui s'annonçait en revenant sur moi*]. ("Avowing," 40–41)

At Jacques Derrida's funeral no Kaddish was said, but he was buried wrapped in a prayer shawl. Waiting?

On his book *Adieu à Emmanuel Levinas,* the opening of which was said as a eulogy at the open grave of his revered mentor, he left a dedication, and in it a journey, beyond the border of life and death, "From Jerusalem to Jerusalem."

And to us, the living, who stand at the gates of Jerusalem even as we are within it, Derrida left the open contradiction, which cannot be soothed or confessed. An urgent global question. Or perhaps, after all, a prayer. Drawing a meridian from Jerusalem to Jerusalem. Adding, thus, his own, irreplaceable voice to those who say: "Jerusalem *is.*"

*Translated from the Hebrew by Atar Hadari*

# How to Live Together Well: Interrogating the Israel/Palestine Conflict

*Richard Falk*

## Comprehending the Israel/Palestine Ordeal as of 2010

Derrida, in his illuminating essay "Avowing—The Impossible: 'Returns,' Repentance, and Reconciliation," directly and indirectly sheds light on the Israel/Palestine conflict in ways that circumvent and transcend a widely endorsed conventional wisdom that has led nowhere but to recurrent cycles of violence and deepening distrust for more than six decades. Yet to take advantage of Derrida's distinctive and suggestive modes of understanding requires distancing and differentiating, as well as appreciating. This distancing and differentiating is both a crucial theoretical feature of Derrida's approach, but it is also pertains to the unreflexive polarization that has long been characteristic of most presentations of the Israel/Palestine conflict. If this impasse is ever to be broken in a manner that produces genuine peace rather than a truce or a new framework of oppression, then an exchange of ethical commitments to the well-being of the other must become a core ingredient of communications, and especially negotiations.[1] Although Derrida's fundamental discourse is metapolitical, albeit with a variety of political implications that he explicates in valuable ways, the assessment offered here is basically political in the sense of seeking to identify and understand conflict-resolving and conflict-sustaining aspects of the Israel/Palestine struggle.

The argument of this essay is thus anchored in Derrida's thought in a dialogic and critical spirit that highlights his approaches, but also takes account of some alternative ways of improving the life circumstances of Israelis and Palestinians.[2] These alternatives are less philosophically probing of the underlying conflict, but seem somewhat more promising as historically realizable political projects for living together well in the context of future relations within Israel/Palestine. This essay will then engage in a comparison between Derrida's radical thinking about impossibility (as permanently embedded in human experience and yet

morally essential as horizon and to encourage the striving needed to fulfill human potential) and a more unidimensional and mundane view of impossibility (as currently not
plausibly realizable, accepting the conventional realist limitation of imagination that can
only be overcome by unanticipated historical developments). It is important to realize
that for Derrida the impossible needs to become operative to fulfill the potential of the
possible. Without the affirmation of a seemingly unrealizable potential, the wisdom of
"going beyond" is denied, and unconditional deference is accorded to the feasible and
realistic.

Derrida is aware on several levels of the seemingly endless dance of death that has for
so long entrapped the Israeli and the Palestinian peoples. He is also sensitive to the connections of the Israel/Palestine conflict with the intensification of current lethal combat
zones, both regional and global. Such concerns are explicit in Derrida's final phase of
philosophizing undertaken in the shadow of the 9/11 attacks on the World Trade Center
and the Pentagon. In *Philosophy in a Time of Terror* Derrida interprets this global setting
as dominated by "two political theologies, both, strangely enough, issuing out of the same
stock or common soil of what I would call an 'Abrahamic' revelation."[3] Derrida makes
explicit this linkage between the macrolevel geopolitics of counterterrorism in the in-
flamed Middle East and the Israel/Palestine microlevel struggle. He asserts, "It is highly
significant that the epicenter . . . of all these 'wars' is the confrontation between the state
of Israel (another 'democracy' . . . ) and a virtual Palestinian state (one that . . . has not yet
given up on declaring Islam the official state religion . . . )."[4] Derrida also observes here
that Israel has "not cut the umbilical cord with religious, indeed with ethnoreligious authority."[5] Such a deepening of reflective awareness strengthens the case for casting the net
of inquiry far beyond the horizons of conventional wisdom, and simultaneously warns us
that the Abrahamic legacy is disposed toward an exterminist outlook toward the other,
whether that other be the 9/11 attackers or Palestinians demanding an authentic peace
based on equality and mutuality.[6]

## Conventional Wisdom and Unconventional Justice

Conventional wisdom with respect to Israel/Palestine continues to control public discourse on the conflict despite its unbroken record of futility. It basically reaffirms the
concept of partition as applied to historic Palestine, although not as an initiative of the
UN between two equal claims on the territory as was controversially attempted in 1947.
The idea in recent decades has been to bring about a meeting of minds on the part of representatives of the antagonists seated at an international negotiating table, with the United
States sitting at its head both purporting to be neutral in *this* role while acting openly and
essentially in an unbreakable partnership (labeled "special relationship") with whatever
Israeli government is in power at the time. The hoped-for end result of achieving "peace"

is generally asserted to be two nominally sovereign states, geographic neighbors coexisting peacefully side by side. (The gross disparities between the two "neighbors" in their present condition and with regard to any likely negotiated outcome has been treated by mainstream commentators in the West as unmentionable, inevitable, realistic, and intrinsic.) One state, Israel, would remain a regional superpower with a formidable arsenal of nuclear weapons; the other, Palestine, would struggle for oxygen if it is, in fact, allowed to come into existence as a nominal sovereign state accepted as a member of international society. This Palestine would have to be willing to accept total vulnerability as an assured feature of its own demilitarization, disempowered as a state by being denied in advance any discretion or capabilities to uphold its own security in the face of perceived future threats to its existence and interests, however real, and consigned to living under humiliating conditions of constant economic, political, and social subordination to its Israeli neighbor.

Such a "peace" is so emptied of justice and elemental collective dignity as to be almost certainly challenged from within the wider Palestinian community, which will be likely interpreted in the West not as a consequence of a response to injustice and indignity, but as a vindication of those Israeli voices who proclaimed over and over again the "impossibility" of any peace with the Palestinians, or more generally, the Arabs. Even aside from the asymmetry of such a peace between two peoples, now equal only in their shared humanity, there are two intractable problems with this conception. First of all, with an evolving set of circumstances that has continued for more than sixty years, the smaller Palestinian reality contracts further and further, while the Israeli reality expands in such a way that what may have seemed somewhat mutual and equitable decades ago now appears as one-sided and deformed. Israel has established such weighty facts on the ground (e.g., settlements, Judaization of Jerusalem) and heavy nonnegotiable demands (e.g., no right of return for Palestinian refugees, no shared or divided control of Jerusalem) so as to repeatedly reshape the bargaining process of realist diplomacy to the disadvantage of the Palestinians. Indeed, in many respects, what is treated as de jure occupation is more aptly described as de facto annexation.

In effect, the Palestinians are force-fed an increasingly one-sided arrangement that is given a totally misleading imprimatur of reasonableness by whoever happens to be "the honest broker" in the White House at the time. For the Palestinians what is called "peace" is ever more a slap in the face designed not only to legitimize unlawfully achieved disparities but also to depict the Palestinians as rejectionist and determined to eliminate Israel when, in reality, they are only resisting a permanent condition of subordination of future Palestinian security and development to Israeli will and whim. As Derrida affirms, the fears of the Jewish mainstream in Israel for their own future are genuine, associated with the long dark shadow still cast by memories of the Holocaust, and for Derrida himself, in his own personal inerasable memories of life as a Jewish child in the antisemitic atmosphere of colonial Algeria. These are genuine elements of an Israeli Jewish collective consciousness that *partly* explains Israeli nonnegotiable security requirements, which are interwoven in complex ways with territorial ambitions and biblical claims. What such a reality induces at mainly Palestinian expense, however, is a lethal spiral between escalating Israeli demands for security (which to the extent accepted, give rise to intensifying Palestinian insecurity) and various deprivations associated with being expected to swallow unacceptable demands.[7]

Second, the current Israeli leadership that seems completely resistant to striking a fair compromise is probably not prepared to accept even an arrangement that is slanted so strongly in its favor. Ironically, such stubborn Israeli rejectionism may disclose the hollowness of the conventional wisdom on the conflict as habitually seen from the perspective of the favored Israeli side. Such a disclosure suggests that the peace process could have been all along for Israel nothing more than a diversionary theater piece whose primary role was to facilitate the accumulation of ever more irreversible facts on the ground until the goal of a genuine Palestinian state no longer seems plausible to its most ardent advocates. The separation wall, draconian occupation, ethnic purification policies in East Jerusalem, relentless expansion of settlements and a Jews-only road network on the West Bank, appropriation of water in occupied Palestine, undisguised refusal to repatriate refugees—all are creating a growing impression that the peace process, if not always, at least lately, has become a charade masking the annexationist reality.

Negotiations probably never have been intended by the Israeli leadership to culminate in an actual peace agreement, but at best were designed to give an acceptable public relations exhibition of an unacknowledged, yet real, Palestinian surrender of self-determination rights coinciding with an Israeli dynamic of creeping annexation ("facts on the ground") relentlessly taking place on the West Bank and in East Jerusalem. If this is so, the peace process from beginning to end was nothing more than a cruel mind game played over and over for the sake of the liberal West and undoubtedly for portions of the Israeli populace and diasporic Jews. Neither the West nor Israeli public opinion exerted genuine pressure on Israel to make peace, and the United States, with multiple forms of leverage, was particularly culpable. It was sufficient for Israel to make periodic *rhetorical* avowals, however disingenuous, of its commitment to a consensual process that would bring about a new condition of coexistence. If this happened, it was hoped that it would undercut anti-Western popular sentiments in the region with a variety of geopolitical benefits. Such a perception fused in the political imagination some kind of "solution" to the conflict with the promotion of Western, especially American, strategic interests in the Middle East, especially related to the oil reserves. This geopolitical dimension of diplomacy has become particularly pronounced in the twenty-first century given the priority accorded to energy reserves and counterterrorism in Western grand strategy. The unresolved encounters in Iraq, Afghanistan, and Iran are by-products of this global problematique. All of these geopolitical potholes would be easier to repair, so prevailing political reasoning supposes, if the Israeli/Palestinian conflict could be finally resolved, and the irritant of the conflict removed from the regional and global setting, with little concern devoted to whether the substance of such a removal would be consistent with international law, and even less, with the requirements of justice.

There is also an influential and related argument that, since "peace" now seems unachievable by the parties to the conflict, and yet is such a high geopolitical priority, it must instead be imposed from outside. In effect, it is contended that the United States as the main producer and consumer of the conventional wisdom on the conflict must redeem its own fable by rescuing the peace process from total disillusionment. Exponents of this reasoning hold that this can be done only by dictating the terms of coexistence in a manner that ratifies most of Israel's essential demands while purporting to be guided by a sense of justice beneficial for both sides.[8] Such an approach turns the historic clock of diplomacy back to the colonial era where it was common practice for European diplomats to draw the boundaries of political communities in the Global South without consulting the populations affected. The results were generally disastrous—natural communities divided in often arbitrary fashion by European ignorance, arrogance, and ambition, postponing for generations efforts to reconstitute more natural political communities based on ethnic, religious, spatial, and cultural affinities. Indeed, much of the bloody turmoil afflicting the peoples of the Middle East can be traced to the dirty work of British and French diplomats who divided the spoils of the collapsed Ottoman Empire after the end of World War I.

The United States, as unconditional ally of Israel and arbiter of the conflicting claims of the two sides, combines this imperial role of past colonial powers with a contemporary normative pretension that supposedly provides parties with the guidelines as to what is fair and just. Of course, past colonial empires also claimed higher justifications, summarized crudely as the "white man's burden" or some equally self-serving variant. Yet here too such a scenario for solution is wishful thinking as the postcolonial historical circumstances matter, and a conflict as fundamental as that between Israel and the Palestinians cannot be solved by a diktat from Washington even if, as is not the case, the United States had the capacity and will to impose a just solution. The process of envisioning a solution has become more and more difficult without breaking the bonds of conventional wisdom altogether by abandoning the presumed basis of peace as some arrangement of permanent partition (the two-state consensus) rather than in a restored unity for Palestine, which until recently has been advocated only by isolated and idealistic voices in the wilderness. Somewhat surprisingly there has recently surfaced in Israel a right-wing version of a one-state solution in the following form: relinquishing Gaza forever, thereby getting rid of 1.5 million Palestinians; expanding the settlements indefinitely; denying the Palestinian diaspora any right of return; promising an eventual Israeli citizenship to the captive Palestinian population; and extending the hegemony of a Jewish state to the West Bank and East Jerusalem.

Different understandings of "impossibility" inescapably confront any effort at this stage to point the parties toward the only peace that might be genuine and sustainable.[9] It will be explained in a later section that this represents a deliberate repudiation of the conventional wisdom that politics is "the art of the possible." The claim here is that such a politics of "the possible" can produce only despair for those seeking justice and peace for the Palestinians, and even for the Israelis. Derrida's thinking, although using impossibility in a less immediately political sense, but rather in a profound series of "deconstructions" denoting inherently unresolvable dilemmas or aporias of thought and action bearing on living together, is highly relevant in this context by proposing a daring conceptual leap from "impossibility" to "responsibility," that is, detaching the burden of decision both from any criteria of guidance and from the vague, and sometimes dangerous, admonition to exercise good faith. Many individual and collective disasters have emanated from the good faith and sincerity of fanatics, perhaps most definitively, the Holocaust. By referencing the Nuremberg trials against surviving Nazi leaders, Derrida convincingly treats the Holocaust as a historically definitive turning away from deference to the unconditional sovereignty of states and unaccountability of their leaders.[10] In effect, sincerity is never enough. Respect for fundamental human rights must be retained as the Archimedean threshold of political acceptability without surrendering to an unjust fait accompli.

What is distinctive about Derrida's coupling of impossibility with responsibility is the realization, in common with such existentialist forebears as Kierkegaard and Sartre, that there are no Kantian universal norms available to ensure a responsible decision and no calculus of risk that narrows down the uncertainties. In this sense to be responsible is meaningless, and impossible. Responsibility means risking on behalf of a desired end without the slightest assurance of attainability. Responsibility can thus be associated with both freedom and desire.

## Derrida's Relevance

Against such a discouraging background of assessment, and taking note of the daily torment experienced by the Palestinians, Derrida's guidance to living together well is refreshing and possibly liberating, but only if understood as a series of signposts for thought and not solutions for the policy puzzles. Derrida both encourages detachment from the conventional dead-end wisdom that has long shaped the mainstream discourse of the Palestine/Israel conflict, and avoids the correlative temptation to advocate some type of colonialist intervention disguised as conflict resolution achieved through the exercise of global leadership.

Derrida is suggestive both at the level of generality and of particularity. He points to "peace" as "an enigmatic concept if ever there was one" ("Avowing," 23), and makes clear that it is not to be confused with "armistice," "cease-fire," or "peace process" ("Avowing," 23), nor with the sort of ultimate or utopian peace associated with such words as "perpetual" or "messianic" that provide an imaginative horizon for that which is desired and desirable.[11] These visionary signposts point to outcomes that are not within the realm of attainable futures, and hence, appear *politically* irrelevant in the narrow sense of projects that are undertaken with the means envisioned to attain the end. So what could be a relevant horizon of ( just) peace for these two peoples locked so rigidly in conflict?

Of course, Derrida gives no easy answers or clear paths, only hints and calls for responsible decisions in the presence of radical and irreducible uncertainty, decisions that are hence inseparable from accepting high risks and dangerous uncertainties. Among the hints is the clear differentiation between the absence of war under conditions of cease-fire and armistice, and even worse, occupation (gradations of *living together badly*), and an avowal of peace that involves a search for *how* within a given set of conditions the process of living together can be transformed into *living together well*, or at least, much better. Derrida insists that this quest for peace requires sensitivity to the demands of law but is far from synonymous with the implementation of legality. In Derrida's words: "I do not wish to grant too great a privilege to the juridical sphere, to international law and to international institutions, even if I believe more than ever in their importance."[12] To succeed with law and beyond law, a peace process must engender such movements of the heart as trust, good faith, and compassion, taking the fears and perceptions of "the other" into account ("Avowing," 25–26). More specifically, "Palestinians and Israelis will truly live together only on the day when . . . peace comes into bodies and souls" ("Avowing," 23). By putting the threshold of peace so high for these peoples so long mired in distrust, bad faith, and hostility, Derrida is perhaps here unwittingly encouraging a politics of despair, with which I disagree for reasons made clear below.

It needs to be appreciated that diplomacy as practiced by governments is much more modest about its idea of peace, and even more humble in its accomplishments. In general, the diplomat proclaims success, and may even receive a Nobel Peace Prize, if antagonistic parties can only be made to agree, even if the agreement reflects the unfair outcome of coercion or bribery rather than genuine consent and fulfillment of respective rights. President Jimmy Carter's Camp David Accords in 1978 were properly celebrated as bringing an end to a condition of war between Israel and Egypt, including Israeli withdrawal from the Sinai peninsula, but this was achieved only by offering the parties large continuing annual subsidies and by leaving the Palestinians adrift. From such diplomacy the best that Palestinians and Israelis can expect is a less violent form of unjust living together, that of a durable cease-fire and armistice, a long-term truce, and above all, an end to occupation, achieved at the high costs of inscribing illegality, injustice, and hierarchy on the lives of both peoples, but with grossly unequal effects as between oppressor and oppressed.

At the same time, despite these difficulties, it would be irresponsible in the special sense imparted by Derrida to abandon the search. There are other valuable hints in Derrida's text. I find especially crucial the stress on the additional ethical burdens placed on the strong, thereby taking a more humanistic account of disparities of power than is customary for realists. It is the worldly "realist" stance that reduces collective human interaction to working out the implications of disparities of power, what "experts" refer to as facts on the ground in the Palestine/Israel setting. The ultimate expression of this realist feature of international relations is to consider as legal the "peace treaties" that ratify the fruits of aggressive war. Derrida reserves this kind of calculus, insightfully and realistically, for his more compelling sense of the real as always incorporating a sense of the impossible as enhancing potential. He suggests that an initiative for peace must proceed "in a manner that is first of all wisely unilateral" ("Avowing," 23), a willingness by the stronger side to act without seeking an exchange or a reciprocal action, a genuine search for reconciliation. One suspects that such an Israeli posture, if genuine, would have a contagious effect, leading quickly to Palestinian countermoves that could create a benign circle of respect and engagement, and might constitute the start of a true peace process.

It should be carefully observed that Derrida puts the enigmatic qualifier "wisely" before the word "unilateral," suggesting limits perhaps intended to be associated with avoiding a provocative vulnerability in the form of a repudiation from within (as enraging one's own constituency by giving away too much without receiving anything in return) or without (creating a temptation for adversary extremists by the seeming exhibition of weakness). Suggestive of the issue in the Israeli/Palestinian context was the assassination in 1995 of the Israeli prime minister, Yitzhak Rabin, by a right-wing Israeli extremist, Yigal Amir, who seems to have acted in good faith, seemingly at the behest of others in a right-wing sect, intending to save the country from the peace that Israeli extremists believed would follow the recently signed Oslo Accord, and either doom the Jewish state over time or at least forfeit its maximalist vision of reconstituting biblical Israel. As subsequent events have shown, Amir need not have thrown his life away, nor taken the life of Rabin, as it is highly unlikely that had Rabin lived, a viable Palestinian state would have emerged from the ensuing negotiations in any event.

Similarly, the assassination of Anwar Sadat, president of Egypt, in 1981 was attributed to Egyptian extremists who were deeply opposed to Sadat's normalization of relations with Israel, especially his signing of the Sinai Peace Treaty in 1979, widely viewed as an unforgivable betrayal of Arab unity and the Palestinian struggle. Sadat's gestures were interpreted differently depending on national and ideological perspective. For the Israeli mainstream and liberal Americans, Sadat was perceived at the time to be an angel of peace, but for Palestinians, and the Arab "street," Sadat was a cowardly and opportunistic figure ready and willing to turn his back on Palestinian claims and rights, while subscribing to the word "peace" without concern for its substance.[13]

There is a parallel path of respect for rights leading toward genuine peace that Derrida does not consider, although he is acutely sensitive to the role and limits of law, and more generally, to the importance and yet insufficiency of a juridical framing of living together, either well or badly. Such a framing is particularly problematic in the Israel/Palestine context because it is insufficiently sensitive to the circumstance of *these* two peoples living together better in the early twenty-first century. As Derrida perceptively notes, both positive and negative potentialities can be realized along a spectrum of endlessly varied permutations. A positive law-based initiative would entail a belated Israeli acknowledgment that reconciliation depends on a mutual acknowledgment of respective *rights*, but coupled with an attitude of reconciliation and compassion. Such an acknowledgment would come as an utter surprise, amounting to a rupture with the consistent and effective Israeli insistence on shifting the diplomatic conversation away from respective rights toward the need to work out adjustments to existing facts, that is, in effect, ratifying prolonged unlawfulness.

If we contemplate this rupture, however unlikely it seems, there is a further benefit: The Palestinians would then have something to give in exchange as well as to receive. Despite their anguish over the *nakba*, they themselves could also, if so inclined, help construct an atmosphere of trust by recognizing the anguish of the Holocaust, thus framing the interaction of the two peoples as based on a shared compassionate appreciation of the historical suffering of "the other." With the help of such a manifested and mutual awareness, a turn away from facts on the ground and toward law/rights could *begin* to overcome the deepening imbalances and open wounds arising from long sustained and acute disparities in power and decades of failure to protect Palestinian rights. It is not that the discourse of law is inherently generative of justice, but it can be, as here, a partial corrective for embedded injustice, that is, where rights have been systematically occluded by force and facts. This has long been the disillusioning experience and ordeal of the Palestinians, who point to the consistent failure over many years to implement dozens of UN resolutions affirming their rights. As a result many Palestinians held the view until recently that only violence would yield any results, pointing to Hizbollah's success in prompting Israeli withdrawal from Lebanon in 2000 and Israeli "disengagement" from Gaza in 2005. Yet there has been in the last several years an encouraging development—this Palestinian sense of dependence on violent resistance is giving way to a soft power strategy, epitomized by the worldwide boycott, divestment, and sanctions (BDS) campaign, or more broadly, to engagement in a global legitimacy war of the sort that toppled the apartheid regime in South Africa in the early 1990s.

Against this background, the willingness of Israel to acknowledge the relevance of Palestinian rights under international law, as conditioning the politics of reconciliation, would exhibit Israeli sincerity and seriousness to an extent never previously displayed. Yet from another vantage point, as significant as such a turn would seem, it would still only amount to a belated recognition of entitlements on the Palestinian side that were long suppressed by Israeli diplomatic muscle and force of arms. Derrida constructively points out that a reconciling process is unlikely to move very far ahead without some real and perceived *sacrifice* being made on all sides, but to qualify as a "sacrifice" an action must come from within each of the antagonists rather than be imposed from without by a powerful geopolitical actor. Derrida's presentation also makes it clear that an act of sacrifice should never be confused with a *concession* made as a result of negotiations or even as a calculated step to achieve an eventual advantage (for instance, dismantling some or all of the West Bank settlements in the expectation of permanent unified control of Jerusalem or of Palestinian abandonment of demands associated with the right of return of refugees).

Such a rights-based approach to peace, from the perspective of the sort of rational calculations that dominate realist diplomacy, would seem to suggest dramatic benefits for the Palestinians and major drawbacks for the Israelis. It would from this worldly viewpoint seem impractical in the extreme, and even irrational. On every major contested issue in the conflict (refugees, Jerusalem, settlements, borders, water) international law is clearly (at least as clear as law can ever be) on the side of Palestinian claims to a degree that would make legal counterarguments seem puerile and unpersuasive. That is, there are several Israeli legal counterarguments that could certainly be advanced, but they are so much against the grain of prevailing and neutral legal (and ethical) understanding as to carry little weight if objectively assessed. If a rights-based approach to peace negotiation were to be adopted, it would almost certainly resolve issues in contention in favor of Palestinian claims. Put differently, Palestinians' post-1967 grievances seem overwhelmingly legitimated by international law.[14]

And significantly, since the PLO National Council declaration in 1988, the most substantial pre-1967 Palestinian grievances (with the exception of the refugee issue) have been effectively renounced, including the earlier insistence that the establishment of a Jewish state within the British-mandated territory of Palestine was unlawful from its moment of origin, as well as the subsequent, more limited contention that Israel, as a territorial entity, should be confined to the borders of the 1948 armistice that had already greatly enlarged Israeli territory beyond the UN partition boundaries established by the international community as a fair apportionment as between the two entities.[15] In effect, without demanding or receiving reciprocity, the Palestinians have already made major, largely unacknowledged concessions to the Zionist project of establishing a Jewish state on Arab lands, moves that Derrida might have termed a wise unilateral initiative. This Palestinian self-limiting posture definitively *sacrificed* significant law/justice claims arising from the establishment of a Jewish state within the Palestinian Mandate as a colonialist scenario.[16] What makes this gesture toward reconciliation particularly impressive is that Palestine was (and remains) the obviously weaker party, and despite its vulnerability made such a pronounced effort more than twenty years ago to transform a frozen conflict so as to establish a new reality of living together, hopefully well.

The Palestinian side was almost certainly inhibited from describing its behavior in the language of sacrifice owing to an entirely understandable anxiety about generating fury among the Palestinian people for giving away that which was inalienable, and hence could and should not have been given. In retrospect, it can be seriously asked in Derrida's suggestive language whether this was a *wise* instance of Palestinian unilateralism, which has now been inscribed in the political consciousness of all parties as the baseline from which any serious negotiations should start. Even Hamas demands only withdrawal to the

1967 boundaries as the precondition for long-term peaceful co-existence. In effect, since the Palestinian initiative of 1988 gained little or nothing from the Israelis, it may not seem to have been a wise sacrificial initiative, at least as viewed retrospectively. Perhaps at the time it seemed like a bold gamble given the limited options at the disposal of the Palestinians.

Later, after the societal mobilization of the Intifada (1987), followed by the Gulf War (1991), there seemed to be a serious American-led effort to find a solution for the conflict through providing an international framework. Edward Said strongly argued that the main result of this effort, the Oslo Declaration (1993) was to give effect to an unwise and subservient unilateralism on the Palestinian side. Subsequent developments have largely upheld his otherwise cynical assessments of the so-called peace process.[17] Can Israel ever be expected to shift the fulcrum of their negotiations from "facts" (that is, power and status quo) to "rights" (that is, sacrifice and withdrawal) for the sake of reconciliation and in the spirit of compassion? And if not, can the Palestinians ever be expected to give their consent to a set of circumstances that is disastrously disadvantageous from the perspective of their rights, hopes, aspirations? If these questions are answered negatively, as would seem to be the case from a political perspective, but not from *certain* religious perspectives, then deep or real peace is necessarily part of that messianic horizon that Derrida identifies, and not a worldly possibility. This is a depressing realization, and hopefully not the whole story. What we should by now know is that the political processes, as so far known to us, can only be expected to achieve either a victors' peace or a nominal peace (essentially dictated by Tel Aviv, ratified by Washington, and swallowed in Ramallah). Such a peace, at best another armistice or truce given a different description, would need to be harshly enforced at every stage to be at all stable, unless ethnic cleansing or a consummated genocide would eliminate the Palestinian presence altogether. Short of a Palestinian surrender, continuing resistance by the Palestinians would almost certainly be the inevitable by-product of such a peace. Any such outcome would certainly be trumpeted as a genuine peace by the mainstream media and negotiating governments, and might mislead public opinion in the West. At the same time it is almost certain to be greeted with great suspicion by those who have in the past and present acted in solidarity with the Palestinian struggle.

In some respects an illuminating analogy is the deceptive acquiescence of many surviving indigenous communities to their dismal fate. Of course, this acquiescence takes a variety of forms, ranging from hidden opposition at the margins of various modern societal arrangements to different degrees of co-optation and opportunism, but it should never be confused with acceptance or a satisfactory rendering of justice.[18] One expression of the tension wrought by such forms of peace is the behavior of Puerto Ricans who vote for statehood in the afternoon and then go to a local bar to sing independence songs. In effect, the calculative advantages of tax breaks and food stamps for an impoverished island people induces a pragmatic vote for a subordinated affiliation associated with statehood within the federal structure of the United States, while the impractical dream of most Puerto Ricans is to be a fully independent and sovereign state standing on its own.

In the face of the discouraging prospect of genuine peace being achieved by intergovernmental diplomacy, a shift to religious orientations by both Palestinians and Israelis has been observed. When religion is put forward as an alternative to politics, this shift must be clarified. For one face of religion is the accentuation of the worst tendency of politics to extinguish compassion and to interpret conflict in a completely narcissistic, absolutist, friend/enemy dualistic, and belligerent manner. The extremist wings on both Israeli and Palestinian sides have grown in influence while the conflict has persisted through the decades, exhibiting this abandonment of politics in favor of religion. Reliance on fundamentalist religious identities gives rise to nonnegotiable demands that are completely indifferent to the consequences for the feared and hated "other."

But there is more to religion than such extremist versions. Religion should not be treated as the essential foundation for peace, but neither should it be demonized. Demonization of the Islamic other became an acceptable component of public discourse, especially in the United States, after the 9/11 attacks and in response to the rise of the so-called "religious right" and evangelical Christianity.[19] It should be remembered that the inclusive potentialities of religion provide the strongest and most widely adhered-to basis for a compassionate and ecumenical approach to conflict and reconciliation, as well as offering a serious engagement with the imperatives of universal principles of justice.[20] Both Judaism and Islam have strong inclusive traditions that have recently been hidden or marginalized by the politically motivated prominence given to the minority views of exclusivist extremists. This misleading and exaggerated presentation of religion exerts a baneful historical influence, accentuated if allied with lifeworld expansionist and xenophobic undertakings.[21] If there is to be societal support for actualizing the mainly hidden compassionate and inclusive potentiality of religion as an indispensable basis of reconciliation for Israel and Palestine, it will depend on a reconfiguring of religion along these more universalistic lines.

In an elemental sense, a peace process that is truly about peace is necessarily and inevitably, albeit partly, a religious undertaking that cannot be adequately grasped by reliance on the language of the bazaar or even of world politics. And maybe for that reason the existential outcome for the parties locked in conflict will likely not be genuine peace because their respective imaginations are set too securely within a *politically* grounded mind-set, or worse, rendered unconditional, that is, *apolitical*, by exclusivist religious affirmations.[22] Tragically, this suggests that what we have been calling a "peace process" is almost certain to give rise to one of several nonpeaceful outcomes: new cycles of violence, eventual annihilation or surrender by the weaker side, or, at best, a permanent cease-fire and an end to occupation, whether negotiated or imposed, and whether or not denominated as "peace."

By moving outside of politics in the direction of religion, the main civilizational custodian of both compassionate and narcissistic ethics, we observe more clearly the unfolding tragedy afflicting in different ways and in distinct registers of suffering the adversaries called Israel and Palestine. In effect, peace is not attainable by political means at least as administered by governments, a depressing conclusion to be sure. It should be depressing for both sides, because it means that even the dominant party can never relax, can never trust, and must constantly act to instill fear and loathing on the part of the dominated other. Such a pattern of neither peace nor war has been increasingly evident in Israeli security policy: building an unlawful separation wall of further encroachment on occupied Palestinian territory, attacking a defenseless Gaza with ultramodern and cruel weaponry, and even threatening aggression against Iran, rationalized in advance as a necessary "preventive war."

There are at least three other ways of conceiving the political in relation to the Palestine/Israel conflict that pave the way to more hopeful scenarios, which will be discussed in descending order of plausibility. Each is improbable, and for that reason, promising as a vector for constructive thought. As argued above, the probable is stuck in a matrix that seems definitely incapable of yielding a genuine, or even a sustainable, peace for the two peoples. None of these ways being proposed here is directly considered in Derrida's essay, but each could be incorporated in his presentation without disturbing his overall framing of the inquiry.

A first alternative would involve exploring analogous conflict patterns to discover the conditions under which progress toward peace was made. For instance, the Irish experience of recent years qualifies as one where an apparently irreconcilable conflict was resolved to a significant, although as yet still uncertain degree. The context suggests that many factors led to this generally favorable set of developments, but the most crucial seemed a change of heart on the part of the main external actors, the United Kingdom and the United States, in their approach taken toward the Irish Republican Army (IRA). What changed was the willingness to see the IRA as a political other, with grievances and legitimate claims, rather than as a terrorist spoiler of the status quo that must be eliminated and could not be treated as a negotiating partner. Such a shift, never publicly acknowledged, appeared to make a crucial difference, inducing a spirit of reconciliation, compromise, and mutuality culminating in the Good Friday Agreement. Despite some bloody setbacks, a momentum for reconciliation produced a set of conditions that comes close to achieving a sustainable peace (although doubts and grievances remain and regressive incidents occur), which while falling far short of realizing the full meaning of peace in Derrida's sense, of course an impossibility, did achieve an outcome that had seemed "impossible" in the lesser sense used here, and was desirable as compared to what had previously existed.[23]

Could not some similar process emerge in Israel, or on the part of the United States or the European Union as external actors, treating the Palestinian other, including Hamas, as a human subject and political actor with rights, status, and feelings, as well as seeking enough common ground to be able to redeploy the language of peace and peace process in a credible manner *for the first time*?[24] Derrida has some interesting and pertinent comments on his hopes that Europe might become a different kind of political actor, more swayed by law and justice, but admits that he discerns no present evidence supportive of such a hope.[25]

What makes this approach unlikely to be embraced is the width and depth of disparity in material conditions, intensified by a prolonged occupation that deliberately sought to give this constructed reality an appearance of permanence. The extent of common ground seems too minuscule to enable any dramatic movement from the *here* of occupation (really annexation) to the *there* of Palestinian self-determination in the form of a distinct sovereign state. That is why humane skeptics on the Palestinian side, from Edward Said to Saree Makdisi, have increasingly opted for a single democratic secular state (one polity for two peoples) that entails the abandonment of a Jewish state, and thus of the main Zionist rationale.[26] In other words, both sides would have to renounce their separate nationalistic goals in exchange for the benefits of a sustainable peace by adopting a merger (or partial submergence) of their respective nationalisms, signaled by a new name for this sovereign entity that would be more or less coterminous with the British Mandate of Palestine. In effect, then, the one-state solution would be an Israel/Palestine version of the Irish breakthrough toward accommodation, but taking into account the drastically different circumstances, and hoping for the best under the most difficult of circumstances. And some qualified observers of the conflict express concern that this hope for the best could end up as an embodiment of the worst, which would be a single state dominated by Zionist ideology and Israeli secular control. Increasingly, a Zionist version of a one-state solution is being espoused by the Israeli right wing, in which Palestinians would eventually be given a diluted form of citizenship and the state would remain avowedly "a Jewish state."

When describing the formation of states, and specifically Israel, Derrida observes that their birth is always accompanied by what he calls "originary violence," a violent imposition on what previously existed and a set of exclusions bearing on the future that arises as soon as defensible borders are drawn, from which "no state can escape" ("Avowing," 22).[27] On the Israeli side especially, and particularly on the part of dedicated Zionists, we might expect a renewal of originary violence if a wider Israeli swing toward a one-state outcome were ever to occur, but that should not necessarily doom the project. As Derrida also points out, the imposing of law requires reliance on force to achieve compliance even if its goal is the elimination, or at least the mitigation, of violence. The political preconditions for the formation of a single state to embrace the two peoples are difficult to set forth in advance. These would likely reflect a political form that expressed the popular will of both communities as discerned by legitimate representation at the leadership level and consent and consensus at the popular level, which does not currently exist, nor is it easily imagined. An additional difficulty of implementation, even if some degree of political resistance could be somehow brushed aside or rendered minimal, is that the disparities that presently exist would undoubtedly be preserved and reproduced in new forms in a unified state. Eliminating or at least mitigating these disparities would depend on a religious revisioning of the conflict through an outpouring of empathy on both sides that could hardly be imagined, stretching imaginative projections to a breaking point. The South African compromise miraculously achieved by Nelson Mandela nevertheless allowed the white elite to retain their privileged material and social positions. Such an outcome, itself an illustration of the impossible happening to an extent, suggests the problems contained in what remains an inspiring instance of a largely nonviolent transformation under the extremely violent circumstances of acute abuse and exploitation during the last stages of apartheid. Even if we embrace the ambiguous utopianism of a one-state "solution" to the Palestine/Israel conflict as a practical political project, there are these further concerns about the persistence of originary violence and the degree to which law is invoked to protect regimes of unequal rights and opportunities so as to maintain preexisting economic, social, and cultural hierarchies.

A second alternative approach takes seriously the eventual possibilities of bottom-up politics associated here with the mobilization of global civil society in the shape of a Palestinian global solidarity movement.[28] Social change has throughout history been dependent on such struggles, and some argue that most successful challenges to oppression have resulted from them.[29] The American civil rights movement was one impressive example, but undoubtedly the most relevant example for this essay is the anti-apartheid movement that exerted such pressure on the South African racist regime as to bring about an entirely unexpected change of heart and mind, featuring Nelson Mandela's release from jail and the subsequent, equally unexpected, consensual establishment of a multiracial constitutional democracy. This came about not because of a sudden moral awakening on the part of the Afrikaner leadership in South Africa, but because of the multiple pressures exerted through a worldwide movement, fully supported by the UN, leading to the isolation and delegitimation of the apartheid government as resting its authority on its territorial sovereignty and on what had been officially declared a crime against humanity. Derrida persuasively stresses this development of criminalizing the behavior of sovereign states and their leaders as a decisive moment in the moral evolution of humanity. He traces the emergence of this sovereignty-transcending criterion of "crime against humanity" directly to the Holocaust, which allowed international law to move morally and legally forward via the Nuremberg Judgment.

In important respects, the Palestinian Solidarity Movement is correctly perceived as the successor to the anti-apartheid movement. Particularly since the Gaza attacks of 2008–9, a mobilization of support for Palestinian justice and self-determination has taken hold in all parts of the world, but to a far lesser extent at a governmental or intergovernmental level. There is under way a robust BDS movement (that is, boycott, divestment, and sanctions) modeled on the anti-apartheid movement, and achieving some symbolically important results, including an escalating spiral of economic, sports, and cultural boycotts in recent months.[30] It is difficult to evaluate the effectiveness of this mobilization because it will be denied any impact by the established centers of power and opinion until the target government decides on making a radical and entirely unexpected, and likely abrupt, move in the direction of accommodation. This was the case with regard to South

Africa, and it is likely to be so for Israel, assuming that a moment of transformation does eventually arise. At this time, such an eventuality seems totally implausible, but so it did in the case of South Africa just months before it began happening. Visiting there in the apartheid era, I was struck over and over again by how the white consensus was articulated in survival terms—it's either us or them—while the African consensus was equally captive to the hard power mythology of conflict and violence—we will prevail, but it will take a long time and be bloody. The idea of reconciliation and transformation was not acknowledged on either side even in private conversation until it began to happen!

Of course, Israel/Palestine is not South Africa. The Palestinians are not blessed with a Mandela. The Israelis are burdened by a history of persecution that makes its leadership risk-averse and overly reliant on force to achieve security. Beyond this, Mandela made it easier for the white establishment by his refusal to challenge economic and societal apartheid, limiting his demands to the dismantling of political apartheid. For this reason, it may be that a fierce struggle lies ahead in the likely event that the remnants of apartheid come under increasing pressure from an impoverished and still exploited African majority. What is relevant, however, is to take note of how often political struggles are not settled by force of arms, but rather on the symbolic battlefields of legitimacy wars. Whether we consider the American defeat in Vietnam, the collapse of Communism in Eastern Europe and the Soviet Union, or the removal from power of despotic leaders in Iran (1979) or the Philippines (1985), the importance of victory in legitimacy wars is repeatedly demonstrated. But winning a legitimacy war is a far cry from ensuring a corresponding political result. The plight of the Tibetans or Chechens or any number of entrapped ethnicities in hostile political frameworks demonstrates the sad historical truth that legitimacy matters *decisively* only under certain conditions. The Palestinians waging their struggle at the present time have yet to show that they have the capacity to make the outcome of this legitimacy war matter enough to the Israeli leadership to make the option of reconciliation an attractive alternative to conflict.

A third mode of hopeful conceiving is to take serious account of the unanticipatable as an element of the wider reality of the Palestine/Israel conflict. At present, given the circumstances described above, and the outlook of the relevant political actors, the rational and realistic political mind cannot conceive of genuine peace as an outcome, that is, a peace based on living together *well*. The most that can be rationally imagined is a somewhat better cease-fire, agreed upon and reinforced by a partial Israeli withdrawal and sweetened by international economic assistance, but built on unacceptable and unlawfully constructed disparities and by a persisting lack of respect for Palestinian rights, especially in relation to refugees, exiles, and Jerusalem. In contrast, what Derrida seeks and demands by way of peace is an entirely different modality of living together than as occupier and occupied or as Jew and Arab, differentiations of identity inevitably tinged with bitterness and the reinstitutionalizing of ethnic hierarchy. Perhaps the optimal form of a mutual agreement was developed a few years ago by the concerted and courageous efforts of civil society peace representatives of both Palestinian and Israeli peace camps, with the Israeli participants being fringe political players, while the Palestinian participants were closely allied with the core leadership at the time of Yasser Arafat. Reflecting this disparity in representation, what could be agreed was inscribed in arrangements proclaimed to the world as "peace" but retaining the core inequities to the Palestinians that had been accumulating over the years. These Geneva proposals certainly diminished the one-sidedness of intergovernmental horizons but still came nowhere close to prescribing a just peace, sensitive to the fundamental rights of both peoples, and may even have fallen short of achieving a sustainable peace, the form of *necessary* impossibility insisted on here. There is no doubt that good faith and a search for reconciliation animated this effort, as well as a disavowal of the sterile Oslo peace process. Nonetheless, the participants in this alternative search were pragmatists influenced by considerations of realism, making the outcome of their efforts to find a more balanced conception of peace still far too deferential to the demands of Israel as the more powerful party. This kind of realism may enhance the prospect of agreement between unequal parties, but it is almost certain to fail in its principal aim to produce a sustainable peace, much less a genuine and just peace.[31] Such an outcome reinforces the impression that a sustainable peace is presently unattainable despite maximizing rational efforts, and thus fails the litmus test of lifeworld politics as the art of the possible. It also confirms Derrida's admonition that peace for Israel/Palestine will not and cannot be achieved through bargaining or calculating relative advantages via governments. An altered will in society and among elites is also indispensable.

But suppose instead, in a situation where peace with justice is not attainable by normal politics, that there is recourse to what might be called "extraordinary politics," politics as the art of the impossible or the politics of impossibility. The viability of such considerations rests on our confirmed inability to anticipate the future, and our experience of being consistently surprised by the unanticipated.[32] Many historical struggles for social and political justice succeeded despite the seeming impossibility of such an outcome. This was true of the antislavery movement, of many anticolonial struggles, more recently of the anti-apartheid movement, and throughout history of the many movements of resistance that defied the logic of superior military and material power. In relation to the Palestinian struggle it appears concretely to mean at present investing hopes for the future in the conduct of the legitimacy war without calculating or depicting in advance how to achieve a just outcome or what its contours would be. As suggested earlier, the structures and practices of a prolonged coercive occupation amount to a continuing crime against humanity in the Nuremberg sense, and this adds clarity and consensus to solidarity with the Palestinian quest for rights and justice as the foundation of peace. Because of such moral/legal pressure, an alternative to an oppressive stalemate or an unsustainable long-term cease-fire is gradually implanting itself on global collective consciousness, as well as among Palestinians and Israelis, and might over time encourage outside actors to play a constructive peacemaking role.

In such a "hopeful" understanding of the Palestinian plight, it has been necessary to break the bondage of reasonable expectations or feasible proposals. Only the unreasonable and infeasible appear presently useful. And what was discussed above needs to be considered in combination, not as a matter of alternatives. Of course, there are no assurances of success, far from it, and that is part of the point. The search for any assurance in advance as the prudential basis for concerted action contradicts the foundational engagement of a politics of impossibility in a mysterious, counterintuitive kind of hope that arises out of the depths of hopelessness, and cannot be validated by an appeal to evidence. Implicit in this exploration of impossibility has been a skepticism about any further reliance by either side on violence as the basis of emancipation or security, while acknowledging the importance of Derrida's analysis of originary violence as accompanying the formation of every sovereign state. If the Palestinians are to enjoy the benefits of a sustainable peace, it must be accompanied by some realization of justice, remembering that there are gradations of "sustainability" that also cannot be calculated, and that even a sustainable peace falls short of the goal of a genuine peace in which the interests of the other are merged and equated with the interests of the self. Moving from here closer to there will almost certainly be largely, although neither exclusively nor necessarily, the result of a globalized nonviolent movement that undermines the stability of existing structures at the level of mind and heart. This is the major teaching of late twentieth- and twenty-first-century conflict, and the most enduring lesson of the South African transformation. Yet even here, truthfulness requires the acknowledgment that the remarkable achievement of South African multiethnic constitutionalism embedded some of the injustices associated with economic and social apartheid, and in this sense was itself susceptible to Derridean criticism as an *irresponsible* compromise.

Irresponsible, but still moving forward toward justice by acting within the domain of the impossible.

# Notes

## Elisabeth Weber, *Introduction: Pleading Irreconcilable Differences*

1. For a detailed account of the philosophical background for Derrida's thinking of the aporetical, see Richard Beardsworth, *Derrida and the Political* (London: Routledge, 1996).

2. Christoph Menke, *Für eine Politik der Dekonstruktion*, in *Gewalt und Gerechtigkeit. Derrida—Benjamin*, ed. Anselm Haverkamp (Frankfurt: Suhrkamp, 1994), 286.

3. Jacques Derrida, "Force of Law," trans. Mary Quaintance, in *Acts of Religion*, ed. Gil Anidjar (New York: Routledge, 2002), 243.

4. Ibid., 255.

5. Jacques Derrida, "Racism's Last Word," in *Psyche: Inventions of the Other,* vol. 1, ed. Peggy Kamuf and Elizabeth Rottenberg (Stanford, Calif.: Stanford University Press, 2007), 377–86; "The Laws of Reflection: Nelson Mandela, in Admiration," in *Psyche: Inventions of the Other,* vol. 2, ed. Peggy Kamuf and Elizabeth Rottenberg (Stanford, Calif.: Stanford University Press, 2008), 63–86.

6. Jacques Derrida, "Taking Sides for Algeria," in *Negotiations: Interventions and Interviews 1971–2001*, ed. and trans. Elizabeth Rottenberg (Stanford, Calif.: Stanford University Press, 2002), 117–24.

7. For example, in "Derelictions of the Right to Justice," in *Negotiations*, 133–44.

8. See, for example, "For Mumia Abu-Jamal," in *Negotiations*, 124–29; "Open Letter to Bill Clinton," in *Negotiations,* 130–32.

9. Richard Falk, *The Great Terror War* (New York: Olive Branch Press, 2002).

10. Jacques Derrida, "'But . . . No, but . . . Never . . . , and Yet . . . , as to the Media': Intellectuals. Attempt at Definition by Themselves. Survey," in *Paper Machine*, trans. Rachel Bowlby (Stanford, Calif.: Stanford University Press, 2005), 33.

11. Derrida, *Paper Machine*, 36–39, translation modified.

12. See Kevin Hart's essay in this collection.

13. Jacques Derrida, "Autoimmunity: Real and Symbolic Suicides," in *Philosophy in a Time of Terror: Dialogues with Jürgen Habermas and Jacques Derrida*, ed. Giovanna Borradori (Chicago: University of Chicago Press, 2003), 125.

14. Beardsworth, *Derrida and the Political*, xiv. "The names of Somalia, Rwanda and Bosnia—together with the many that are already there, joining these names in the public of the electronic and digital gaze, or will join them in the future of this gaze—testify to the present paralysis of political thought and practice." Beardsworth's book was published in 1996; its analyses are of course still valid today.

15. Pheng Cheah and Suzanne Guerlac, "Introduction: Derrida and the Time of the Political," in *Derrida and the Time of the Political*, ed. Pheng Cheah and Suzanne Guerlac (Durham, N.C.: Duke University Press, 2009), 7.

16. Hent de Vries, *Religion and Violence: Philosophical Perspectives from Kant to Derrida* (Baltimore: Johns Hopkins University Press, 2002), 368.

17. Jacques Derrida, *Margins of Philosophy*, trans. Alan Bass (Chicago: University of Chicago Press, 1982), 13.

18. Vries, *Religion and Violence*, 368.

19. Ibid.

20. Ibid., 368–69. By contrast, the hegemonic adoption or abduction of the concept of "friendship" in the Western tradition shows, as de Vries demonstrates in his comment on Derrida's *The Politics of Friendship*, that the assertion of its "general or even universal validity" results in "the expression of a particular—and all too often particularist—politics that mistakes itself for the natural order of things" and therefore mobilizes a "discourse on birth and on nature" that "informs all nationalisms, all ethnocentrisms, all racisms" (369).

21. Jacques Derrida, *The Politics of Friendship*, trans. George Collins (London: Verso, 1997), 78–79.

22. Franz Kafka, *Nachgelassene Schriften und Fragmente*, vol. 2, ed. Jost Schillermeit (Frankfurt: S. Fischer 1992), 113.

23. J. Hillis Miller, *For Derrida* (New York: Fordham University Press, 2009), 219.

24. Jacques Derrida, *The Gift of Death and Literature in Secret*, 2nd ed., trans. David Wills (Chicago: University of Chicago Press, 2008), 86.

25. Ibid., 86–87.

26. Ibid., 68.

27. Jacques Derrida, "Literature in Secret," in *The Gift of Death*, 125–27.

28. Jacques Derrida, "Abraham, the Other," in *Judeities: Questions for Jacques Derrida*, ed. Bettina Bergo, Joseph Cohen, and Raphael Zagury-Orly, trans. B. Bergo and Michael Smith (New York: Fordham University Press 2007), 34.

29. Geoffrey Bennington, "Deconstruction and Ethics," in *Deconstructions: A User's Guide,* ed. Nicholas Royle (New York: Palgrave, 2000), 72.

30. The paragraphs, above, on "irreconcilable differences" are derived from the conference description that Thomas Carlson and I coauthored.

31. Jacques Derrida, "Avouer—l'impossible: 'retours', repentir et reconciliation," Comment vivre ensemble? Actes du XXXVIIe Colloque des intellectuels juifs de langue française (1998), ed. Jean Halpérin and Nelly Hansson (Paris: Albin Michel, 2001), 179–216. For more details on this "annual French-Jewish institution" see Dana Hollander's essay in this collection.

32. Derrida, "Literature in Secret," 156.

33. Jacques Derrida, "Aphorism Countertime," trans. Nicholas Royle, in *Psyche: Inventions of the Other*, ed. Kamuf and Rottenberg, 132.

34. Anselm Haverkamp, *Kritik der Gewalt und die Möglichkeit von Gerechtigkeit: Benjamin in Deconstruction,* in *Gewalt und Gerechtigkeit*, 7.

35. Jacques Derrida, *Specters of Marx*, trans. Peggy Kamuf (New York: Routledge, 1994), 176.

36. Ibid.

37. Derrida, "Force of Law," 259.

38. See Nicholas Royle, *In Memory of Jacques Derrida* (Edinburgh: Edinburgh University Press, 2009), 149.

39. Samuel Weber, *Targets of Opportunity: On the Militarization of Thinking* (New York: Fordham University Press, 2005), 58.

40. The names of U.S. military interventions are telling in this regard: The military response to the attacks of September 11, 2001, was named at first "Operation Infinite Justice" before being changed to "Operation Enduring Freedom" after the protest of Muslim groups. The 2003 invasion of Iraq was called "Operation Iraqi Freedom." The same can be said of the names of Israeli military interventions, such as "Operation Summer Rain" on June 27, 2006, and "Operation Cast Lead" in December 2008. For an analysis of the names of Israeli military interventions see Colin Dayan, "Reasonable Torture, or the Sanctities," in *Speaking about Torture*, ed. Julie Carlson and Elisabeth Weber (New York: Fordham University Press, 2012).

41. See Derrida, "Taking Sides for Algeria," 119.

42. Peggy Kamuf, *Book of Addresses* (Stanford, Calif.: Stanford University Press 2005), 26–28.

43. Derrida, "Autoimmunity," 105.

44. Frans de Waal, *The Age of Empathy* (New York: Three Rivers Press, 2009), 48. On the centrality of euphemism in current conflicts, see Fred Halliday, *Shocked and Awed: A Dictionary of the War on Terror* (Berkeley: University of California Press, 2011). See also Julie A. Carlson and Elisabeth Weber, "For the Humanities," in *Speaking about Torture*, 14–15.

45. Derrida, "Autoimmunity," 127.

46. Ibid., 128.

47. Jacques Derrida, *Adieu to Emmanuel Levinas*, trans. Pascale-Anne Brault and Michael Naas (Stanford, Calif.: Stanford University Press 1999), 95.

48. Derrida, "Autoimmunity," 117–18.

49. Derrida, "Interpretations at War: Kant, the Jew, the German," in *Acts of Religion*, ed. Anidjar, 137. See Gil Anidjar, "A Note on 'Interpretations at War'," in *Acts of Religion*, 135.

50. Jacques Derrida, *Learning to Live Finally: An Interview with Jean Birnbaum*, trans. Pascale-Anne Brault and Michael Naas (Hoboken, N.J.: Melville, 2007), 39.

51. Ibid., 39.

52. See Derrida, "Autoimmunity," 114.

53. Ibid., 105–6.

54. Ibid., 126, translation slightly modified.

55. Rodolphe Gasché, "European Memories: Jan Patočka and Jacques Derrida on Responsibility," in *Derrida and the Time of the Political*, ed. Cheah and Guerlac, 154.

56. Jacques Derrida, "Faith and Knowledge," in *Acts of Religion*, ed. Gil Anidjar (New York: Routledge, 2002), 63.

57. Ibid.

58. Jacques Derrida, *Rogues: Two Essays on Reason*, trans. Pascale-Anne Brault and Michael Naas (Stanford, Calif.: Stanford University Press, 2005), 50.

59. Avital Ronell, *Finitude's Score: Essays for the End of the Millennium* (Lincoln: University of Nebraska Press 1994), 297.

60. Derrida, "Taking Sides for Algeria," 118.

61. Ibid.: "We are in effect in the aftermath of the so-called conference of reconciliation, that is, of a failure or simulacrum, of a disaster in any case so sadly predictable, if not calculated, one that outlines, in the negative, the dream of the impossible that we can neither give up nor believe in." (In *Papier machine* (Paris: Galilée 2011), 221, the quotation reads in French: *"Nous sommes en effet au lendemain de la conférence dite de réconciliation, c'est-à-dire d'un échec ou d'un simulacre, d'un désastre en tout cas si tristement prévisible, sinon calculé, qui dessine, comme en négative, le rêve de l'impossible auquel nous ne pouvons ni renoncer ni croire."*) The conference referred to by Derrida was called "National conference of consensus."

62. Derrida, *Politics of Friendship*, 29.


## Jacques Derrida, *Avowing—The Impossible: "Returns," Repentance, and Reconciliation*

Translation revised by Thomas A. Carlson for the keynote address of the conference "Irreconcilable Differences? Jacques Derrida and the Question of Religion," University of California, Santa Barbara, October 2003.

1. Translator's note: The expression "vivre ensemble" refers to the title of the conference where Derrida gave this lecture: *"Comment vivre ensemble?* [How to live together?]" As will become clear, Derrida attends to and produces subtle displacements with and within this expression.

2. Translator's note: On the problems associated with a translation of *mondialisation* as globalization, and what Derrida calls *mondialatinisation*, see Samuel Weber's translator note in Jacques Derrida, "Faith and Knowledge," in *Religion,* ed. Jacques Derrida and Gianni Vattimo (Stanford, Calif.: Stanford University Press, 1998), 67.

3. See *La conscience juive face à l'histoire: Le pardon,* ed. Eliane Amado Levy-Valensi and Jean Halpérin (Paris: Presses Universitaires de France, 1965).

4. Translator's note: An allusion to *Sukkot,* the Feast of Booths, and to a remark by Levinas, recalled by Pierre Bouretz, which referred to the Colloque itself as a traveling booth.

5. Translator's note: The pacte civil de solidarité or PACS was instituted in October 1999 by the French legislature. According to the French foreign ministry, PACS "has enabled couples unwilling or unable to marry to live in stable and more comfortable conditions. PACS constitutes a contract binding partners by rights, and obligations as well [*PACS a ouvert la possibilité aux couples, qui ne veulent ni ne peuvent se marier de vivre dans des conditions stables et plus confortables. Le PACS constitue un contrat liant les partenaires par des droits, mais aussi des devoirs*]" (http://www.diplo matie.gouv.fr/france/fr/societe/societe02_2.html). PACS is also defined as "a contract between two persons of legal age, of different or same sex, toward the arrangement of a common life. It creates rights and obligations for the partners, notably with regard to mutual and material assistance [*un contrat conclu entre deux personnes majeures, de sexe différent ou de même sexe, pour organiser leur vie commune. Il crée des droits et obligations pour les partenaires, notamment une aide mutuelle et matérielle*]" (http://www.france.diplomatie.fr/etrangers/vivre/pacs).

6. Emmanuel Levinas, *Nine Talmudic Readings,* trans. A. Aronowicz (Bloomington: Indiana University Press, 1990), 27–28; *Quatre lectures talmudiques* (Paris: Minuit, 1968), 60–61. Aronowicz's translation slightly altered.

7. See Hermann Cohen, "Die Versöhnungsidee" and "Der Tag der Versöhnung" in *Jüdische Schriften,* vol. 1 (Berlin: C.A. Schwetschke, 1924), 132, 143; *Reason and Hope,* trans. E. Jospe (Cincinnati: Hebrew Union College Press, 1993), 206, 212. Jospe's translation slightly altered.

8. Translator's note: The phrase "healing away" is in English in the original text.

9. Dominique Bourel, "Note bibliographique: La *teshuva* dans la pensée juive du XXe siècle," in *Retour, repentir et constitution de soi*, ed. Annick Charles-Saget (Paris: Vrin, 1998), 210.

10. Levinas, *Nine Talmudic Readings*, 18.

11. Ibid., 19.

12. Ibid., 17.

13. Most notably in *Politics of Friendship,* trans. G. Collins (London: Verso, 1997).

14. I attempt to do so elsewhere in *Donner la mort* (Paris: Galilée, 1999).

## Gil Anidjar, Mal de Sionisme (*Zionist Fever*)

This essay, first presented at "Irreconcilable Differences? Jacques Derrida and the Question of Religion," a conference convened by Elisabeth Weber and Thomas A. Carlson (University of California, Santa Barbara, October 23–25, 2003), is a revised version of my "Zionist Fever" published in *Umbr(a): A Journal of the Unconscious* (2004): 93–114. I gratefully acknowledge permission to republish from Joan Copjec and the editors of *Umbr(a)*.

1. Martin Hägglund, *Radical Atheism: Derrida and the Time of Life* (Stanford, Calif.: Stanford University Press, 2008).

2. *Jacques Derrida and the Humanities: A Critical Reader*, ed. Tom Cohen (Cambridge: Cambridge University Press, 2002).

3. Christopher Wise, *Derrida, Africa, and the Middle East* (New York: Palgrave, 2009), 1, 48.

4. Tomoko Masuzawa has compellingly enjoined us to rethink this benevolent universalism, its roots, and its history in *The Invention of World Religions, or, How European Universalism Was Preserved in the Language of Pluralism* (Chicago: University of Chicago Press, 2005).

5. Jacques Derrida, *Mal d'archive* (Paris: Galilée, 1995), 2 ("Prière d'insérer"). I could not find this passage in the English edition.

6. These two words by and for James Joyce are read by Derrida in "Two Words for Joyce," where Derrida offers a "first translation: HE WARS—he wages war, he declares or makes war, he is war, which can also be pronounced. . . . He war: he was—he who was ("I am he who is or who am," says YAHWE). Where it was, he was, declaring war, and it is *true*" (Derrida, "Two Words for Joyce," trans. Geoffrey Bennington in *Post-Structuralist Joyce: Essays from the French*, ed. Derek Attridge and Daniel Ferrer [Cambridge: Cambridge University Press, 1984], 145). A few lines later, Derrida adds that "this madness of writing" is one "by which whoever writes effaces himself, leaving, only to abandon it, the archive of his own effacement." The writer, here Joyce, is leaving—he is "leaving us caught in his archive" (146). War, religion, the archive, and sexual difference. We are already reading Freud, obviously, and more specifically, *Archive Fever*.

7. Freud's argument linking religion to war, to the hostility of the individual toward civilization, but also to the state of war that is the state of nature (a Hobbesian war of all against all), and to the struggle against helplessness is famously made in *The Future of an Illusion*, in *The Standard Edition of the Complete Psychological Works of Sigmund Freud* (London: Hogarth Press and the Institute of Psycho-Analysis, 1961).

8. I paraphrase and quote again from the untranslated "*prière d'insérer*" in *Mal d'archive*, 1.

9. Sigmund Freud, *Moses and Monotheism,* in *The Standard Edition of the Complete Psychological Works of Sigmund Freud* (London: Hogarth Press and the Institute of Psycho-Analysis, 1964), xxiii, 7. Subsequent citations are given parenthetically in the text. For a wider discussion and recapitulation of the relations between psychoanalysis and war see Jacqueline Rose, *Why War?— Psychoanalysis, Politics, and the Return to Melanie Klein* (Oxford: Blackwell, 1993), and Derrida, "Psychoanalysis Searches the State of Its Soul," in *Without Alibi,* ed. and trans. Peggy Kamuf (Stanford, Calif.: Stanford University Press, 2002).

10. I am indebted to Samuel Weber's discussion of these passages in his "Doing Away with Freud's *Man Moses,*" in *Targets of Opportunity: On the Militarization of Thinking* (New York: Fordham University Press, 2005), 63–89.

11. Sander Gilman somehow confirms the enigma inherent in this particular moment when he argues that for Freud, in fact, "the definition of the Jew had a further dimension" than a religious one: "Being Jewish meant being a member of a race" (*Freud, Race, and Gender* [Princeton: Princeton University Press, 1993], 6). In *Freud and the Non-European,* Edward Said would thus signal toward a shift (an uncertain one, in the light of Freud's invocation of his "race," however suspended), a turn or return of sorts to religion, by pointing out that Freud argues that Jews are not a race, "they are not Asiatics of a foreign race [*sie sind nicht fremdrassige Asiaten*]" (Freud, *Moses and Monotheism,* 91). Later on, Freud goes on to recast National Socialism as a hatred of religion, of the two monotheistic religions (Edward Said, *Freud and the Non-European* [London: Verso, 2003], 39).

12. Weber, "Doing Away," 69. Elsewhere, I have tried to raise some questions on the difficult matter of "race and religion," most specifically around the nineteenth-century invention of the Semites, the effects of which linger in Freud's writings.

13. It is difficult to ignore the insistence with which many of Derrida's striking assertions about psychoanalysis resonate as and with political assertions about (if not exclusively) Palestine and Israel (by which I do not mean simply to recognize, much less resolve the weight of the unsaid here, precisely regarding Israel and Palestine, but only to indicate, as I will do throughout this essay, a fruitful area of reflection). "Psychoanalysis," Derrida writes, "has not yet undertaken and thus still less succeeded in thinking, penetrating, and changing the axioms of the ethical, the juridical, and the political, notably in these seismic places where the theological phantasm of sovereignty quakes and where the most traumatic, let us say in a still confused manner the most cruel events of our day are being produced" (Derrida, "Psychoanalysis Searches," 244).

14. Jacques Derrida, *Archive Fever,* trans. Eric Prenowitz (Chicago: University of Chicago Press, 1995), 13.

15. Jacques Derrida, "The Eyes of Language," in *Acts of Religion,* ed. and trans. Gil Anidjar (New York: Routledge, 2002), 194. I quote from the French version now published in *Cahier de l'Herne: Jacques Derrida,* ed. Marie-Louise Mallet and Ginette Michaud (Paris: L'Herne, 2004).

16. Daniel Boyarin, *Unheroic Conduct: The Rise of Heterosexuality and the Invention of the Jewish Man* (Berkeley: University of California Press, 1997); Susannah Heschel, *Abraham Geiger and the Jewish Jesus* (Chicago: University of Chicago Press, 1998); Susannah Heschel, "Revolt of the Colonized: Abraham Geiger's *Wissenschaft des Judentums* as a Challenge to Christian Hegemony in the Academy," *New German Critique* 77 (1999): 61–86; Mitchell B. Hart, *Social Science and the Politics of Modern Jewish Identity* (Stanford, Calif.: Stanford University Press, 2000); and see also Edward Said's extensive discussion of psychoanalysis and Zionism, underscoring their potential differences in *Freud and the Non-European.*

17. Inspired in part by Derrida's work, Daniel Boyarin has developed the argument that, while construed by Christianity as a religion, Judaism does not abide by the definitions of the term (*Border Lines: The Partition of Judaeo-Christianity* [Philadelphia: University of Pennsylvania Press, 2004]).

18. Jacques Derrida, *Writing and Difference*, trans. Alan Bass (Chicago: University of Chicago Press, 1976) 145; emphasis added.

19. Ibid., 295; and recall that in "Two Words for Joyce," the archive "itself" is abandoned.

20. Jacques Derrida, *Monolingualism of the Other, or The Prosthesis of Origin*, trans. Patrick Mensah (Stanford, Calif.: Stanford University Press, 1998), 34. In *Politics of Friendship*, Derrida has interrogated the gendered dimension of a call to "fraternity" inherent in the history of Western political thought (*Politics of Friendship*, trans. George Collins [London: Verso, 1997]). On the question of Zionism and gender, see, among others, Joseph Massad, "The 'Post-Colonial' Colony: Time, Space, and Bodies in Palestine/Israel," in *The Pre-Occupation of Postcolonial Studies*, ed. Fawzia Afzal-Khan and Kalpana Seshadri-Crooks (Durham, N.C.: Duke University Press, 2000), 311–46; also Boyarin, *Unheroic Conduct*.

21. For a discussion of the congruence between the development of a Jewish (social) science and Zionism on the existence of a Jewish people, even a Jewish race (in the accepted and widely affirmed terminology of the nineteenth century), see Mitchell Hart, *Social Science*. Hart underscores "the ability to unite a myriad of Jewish groups under the banner of Jewish statistics," an ability that demonstrated in turn "the ability of Zionism to unify the Jewish *Volk* under the banner of national regeneration. This 'unification' occurred first of all (perhaps could only occur) at the conceptual or imaginary level. Jewish social scientific narratives united Jewry at a representational level by positing a *Volk* and nation bound by genetic as well as historical ties, transcending the geographic and cultural disjunctions characteristic of the Diaspora" (55).

22. B. Beit Hallahmi quoted in Joseph Massad, "The Post-Colonial Colony," 337; and see also Susannah Heschel, who describes how the Zionist revolt, in Europe, "turned out to be a revolt against Judaism, not a revolt against the West" (Heschel, "Revolt of the Colonized," 69). Nadia Abu El-Haj also describes the way in which "Zionism sought to distinguish the new Hebrews from their Jewish counterparts in the Diaspora. The new Hebrew/Israeli person was imagined as secular/modern as opposed to religious/traditional, active as opposed to passive, and connected to the land, as a *laborer*, as opposed to disconnected from it, most fundamentally, as a diasporic person" (*Facts on the Ground: Archaeological Practice and Territorial Self-Fashioning in Israeli Society* [Chicago: University of Chicago Press, 2001], 16).

23. Amnon Raz-Krakotzkin, "Exile within Sovereignty: Toward a Critique of the 'Negation of Exile' in Israeli Culture" [in Hebrew], *Theory and Criticism* 4–5 (1993).

24. Levinas quoted in Derrida, *Adieu to Emmanuel Levinas*, trans. Pascale Anne-Brault and Michael Naas (Stanford, Calif.: Stanford University Press, 1999), 151n129.

25. For a discussion of the way in which the label "anti-Semite" is now being deployed see *The Politics of Anti-Semitism*, ed. Alexander Cockburn and Jeffrey St. Clair (Oakland: Counterpunch and AK Press, 2003).

26. Massad, "The Post-Colonial Colony," 335.

27. Stéphane Moses, quoted in Derrida, "Eyes of Language," 193. For some years now, one of the most prominent writers and public intellectuals in Israel, A. B. Yehoshua, has elaborated on this view of diasporic existence as "neurotic." Derrida recently pointed out that "the one who says 'it's not going well' already announces a repairing, therapeutic, restorative, or redemptive concern. It is

necessary to save, it is necessary to assure the salvation. . . . This salutary, sanitary, or immunitary concern triggers simultaneously a gesture of war: the militant would like to cure or save by routing, precisely, a resistance" (Derrida, "Psychoanalysis Searches," 243). In its attempt to renew a diagnostic of a "mal de Sionisme," such is obviously the predicament of my own writing here.

28. Jacques Derrida, "Interpretations at War: Kant, the Jew, the German," trans. Moshe Ron, in *Acts of Religion*, ed. Gil Anidjar (New York: Routledge, 2002) 166.

29. Catherine Malabou has persuasively argued that election is one of the most recurring motifs against which Derrida struggles (see "La compulsion de révélation," in *Judéités: Questions pour Jacques Derrida* [Paris: Galilée, 2003]).

30. Derrida, *Writing and Difference*, 66.

31. Derrida, *Monolingualism of the Other*, 34.

32. Avital Ronell, *Stupidity* (Urbana: University of Illinois Press, 2002), and Jacques Derrida, "Abraham, l'autre," in *Judéités: Questions pour Jacques Derrida* (Paris: Galilée, 2003). I have tried to further read the logic of the call, of naming and interpellation, in Derrida in my "*Traité de Tous les Noms* [What Is Called Naming]," *Epoché: A Journal for the History of Philosophy* 10, no. 2 (2006): 287–301.

33. See Derrida, "Abraham, l'autre."

34. On declarations of independence as declarations of war see Jacques Derrida, "Declarations of Independence," trans. Thomas Keenan and Thomas Pepper, in *Negotiations: Interventions and Interviews*, ed. Elizabeth Rottenberg (Stanford, Calif.: Stanford University Press, 2002), 46–54.

35. Derrida, *Adieu*, 41. Although the criticism of any nativism as territorial claim is here obvious, it clearly does not level the field of power as it stands today. As Derrida explains in his lecture "Avowing—The Impossible," the responsibility for the claim to territory concerns first of all the state, which has the power to make that claim. Derrida, in other words, clearly lays the *responsibility* on the Israeli state.

36. Derrida, *Adieu*, 42. Derrida will later pointedly ask, "Who are the *hôtes* and the hostages of Jerusalem?" ( 105); and cf. also Derrida and Anne Dufourmantelle, *Of Hospitality*, trans. Rachel Bowlby (Stanford, Calif.: Stanford University Press, 1999), and Derrida's "Hostipitality," in *Acts of Religion*, ed. and trans. Gil Anidjar (New York: Routledge, 2002).

37. Derrida, *Adieu*, 113.

38. Ibid., 81.

39. Derrida, *Archive Fever*, 11, subsequently cited parenthetically in the text.

40. For a rigorous reading of Zionism's investment in archaeology and of the state of Israel's deployment of its "scientific" discourse, see Nadia Abu El-Haj, *Facts on the Ground*; also see Said, *Freud and the Non-European*, beginning at page 45.

41. From *The Post Card* and *Glas*, through *Shibboleth: For Paul Celan* and, of course, "Circumfession" and *Archive Fever*, Derrida's meditations on circumcision engage much more than the question of community and would obviously require a more patient commentary than I can provide here.

42. Derrida, *Adieu*, 66.

43. Rosenzweig, quoted in Derrida, "Eyes of Language," 193. On the invention of Judaism as "religion" see Heschel, *Abraham Geiger,* and see also Amnon Raz-Krakotzkin, *The Censor, the Editor, and the Text: The Catholic Church and the Shaping of the Jewish Canon in the Sixteenth Century*, trans. Jackie Feldman (Philadelphia: University of Pennsylvania Press, 2007).

44. Levinas, quoted in Derrida, *Adieu*, 151n129.

45. Derrida, "Eyes of Language," 198; Subsequent citations are given parenthetically in the text.

46. Amnon-Raz-Krakotzkin, *Exil et souveraineté: Judaïsme, Sionisme et pensée binationale* (Paris: La Fabrique, 2007), especially following page 131.

47. This is. of course, Talal Asad's argument in *Formations of the Secular: Christianity, Islam, Modernity* (Stanford, Calif.: Stanford University Press, 2003).

48. Derrida, "Eyes of Language," 220.

49. Derrida, "Interpretations at War," 166.

50. Freud, *Moses and Monotheism*, 113. The structure of this argument recalls Freud's universalization of castration out of the particular predicament of circumcision.

51. Derrida, "Eyes of Language," 221. Kant echoes enduring perceptions, enduring equations, often stereotypical, of Jews and merchants. Thus, for example, "Old Christians," who, in Portugal at least, referred to descendants of Jewish converts (*conversos* and "New Christians") as "*homens de negócios* [men of commerce]," a phrase that was synonymous with "*gente de nação hebrea* [men of the Hebrew nation]" (see Miriam Bodian, *Hebrews of the Portuguese Nation: Conversos and Community in Early Modern Amsterdam* [Bloomington: Indiana University Press, 1997], 64, 147). Earlier yet, Jewish converts in medieval Italy were labeled *mercanti* (cf. Yosef Hayim Yerushalmi, *Sefardica* [Paris: Chandeigne, 1998], 262).

52. Derrida, *Monolingualism of the Other,* 34.

## Joseph A. Massad, *Forget Semitism!*

This chapter was presented at two conferences on the works of Edward Said. I thank Gil Anidjar, Nadia Abuelhaj, and Stathis Gourgouris for inviting me to give the keynote address at the "Orientalism from the Standpoint of Its Victims" conference held at Columbia University on November 7, 2008, and Nahla Abdo for inviting me to give the keynote address at the "Counterpoints: Edward Said's Legacy" conference, held at the University of Ottawa and the University of Carleton, on November 1, 2008. I am grateful to Ahmad Atif Ahmad, Talal Asad, Wael Hallaq, Neville Hoad, Rosalind Morris, and Lecia Rosenthal for reading and commenting on earlier versions of this chapter and Gil Anidjar for his engagement with me on the section dealing with Derrida. An earlier version of this chapter was published in French in Joseph Massad, *La persistance de la question palestinienne*, trans. Joelle Marelli, (Paris: La fabrique, 2009).

1. Sigmund Freud, *Leonardo da Vinci and a Memory of His Childhood*, in *The Standard Edition of the Complete Psychological Works of Sigmund Freud* (London: Hogarth Press, 1953–74), 11:83–84, published originally in 1927; emphasis added.

2. See, for example, Janet Halley, *Split Decisions: How and Why to Take a Break from Feminism* (Princeton: Princeton University Press, 2008). On the critique of *Desiring Arabs*, see Amr Shalakany, "On a Certain Queer Discomfort with Orientalism," unpublished paper delivered at the Queering International Law conference, and available on its website at http://www.thefreelibrary.com/Queering+international+law.-a0177100773.

3. Joseph Massad, *Desiring Arabs*, (Chicago: University of Chicago Press, 2007).

4. See Robert Irwin, *For Lust of Knowing: The Orientalists and Their Enemy* (London: Penguin, 2007). As for Zionists, see the post by Martin Kramer about the conference "Orientalism

from the Standpoint of Its Victims," held at Columbia University, on November 7–8, 2008. Kramer insists that anti-Semitism is the main reason for Palestinian suffering, something shared according to him from the "Mufti [al-Husayni] to [Joseph] Massad." Martin Kramer, "Muftis of Morningside Heights," October 13, 2008, posted on http://www.martinkramer.org/sandbox/blog/page/14/.

5. Edward W. Said, *Orientalism* (New York: Vantage, 1978), 27–28.

6. I thank Andrew Ruben for alerting me to this connection to Conrad. See Joseph Conrad, *The Secret Sharer,* in Conrad's *The Nigger of the "Narcissus" and Other Stories* (New York: Penguin Books, 2007), 171–214. See also Edward W. Said, *Conrad and the Fiction of Autobiography* (New York: Columbia University Press, 2008), 127. The book was first published in 1966.

7. Quoted in Gil Anidjar, *Semites: Race, Religion, Literature* (Stanford, Calif.: Stanford University Press, 2008), 32.

8. Said, *Orientalism,* 142.

9. Quoted in Anidjar, *Semites,* 32.

10. Here I am not interested in whether this is a necessarily correct etymology of Saracens, but rather that many see it as such (see note 52 below). Other proposed etymologies have it that "Saracens" is derived from the Arabic word "Sharqiyyin" meaning "Easterners" or "Orientals."

11. Hannah Arendt, "Antisemitism," in *The Jewish Writings,* ed. Jerome Kohn and Ron H. Feldman (New York: Schocken Books, 2007), 69.

12. Said, *Orientalism,* 234.

13. Louis Massignon, 1960, cited in Anouar Abdel-Malek, "Orientalism in Crisis," in *Orientalism, a Reader,* ed. A. L. Macfir (New York: New York University Press, 2001), 51. See Said on Massignon and Berque in *Orientalism,* 270.

14. See Hilel Cohen, *Army of Shadows, Palestinian Collaboration with Zionism, 1917–1948* (Berkeley: University of California Press, 2008), 25.

15. See Bernard Lewis, *Semites and Anti-Semites: An Inquiry into Conflict and Prejudice* (New York: W. W. Norton, 1986), 94.

16. Eric Goldstein, *The Price of Whiteness, Jews, Race, and American Identity* (Princeton: Princeton University Press, 2006), 20.

17. Ibid., 108.

18. Ibid.

19. Cited in ibid., 109.

20. Ibid.

21. Cited in ibid.

22. See ibid., 111, 179.

23. I elaborate on this process in Joseph Massad, "The Persistence of the Palestinian Question," *Cultural Critique,* no. 59 (Winter 2005): 1–23.

24. On Arendt's complex relationship with Zionism, see Richard J. Bernstein, "Hannah Arendt's Zionism?" in *Hannah Arendt in Jerusalem,* ed. Steven E. Aschheim (Berkeley: University of California Press, 2001), 194–202.

25. Arendt, "Antisemitism," 58–59.

26. Hannah Arendt, "Peace of Armistice in the Near East?" in *The Jewish Writings,* 443.

27. Said, *Orientalism*, 262.

28. Lewis, *Semites and Anti-Semites*, 117.

29. Ibid.

30. Edward W. Said, *Freud and the Non-European* (London: Verso, 2003), 16–17.

31. Sigmund Freud, *Moses and Monotheism*, in *The Standard Edition of the Complete Psychological Works of Sigmund Freud* (London: Hogarth Press, 1953–74), 23:90.

32. Said, *Freud and the Non-European*, 40.

33. Ibid., 286.

34. Ibid.

35. Freud, *Moses and Monotheism*, 33.

36. Ibid., 35. On Freud's intellectual precursors on the question of Moses and monothesim, see Jan Assmann, *Moses the Egyptian: The Memory of Egypt in Western Monotheism* (Cambridge, Mass.: Harvard University Press, 1997).

37. Louis Massignon, "Trois prières d'Abraham, père de tous les croyants," in *Parole Donnée* (Paris: Julliard, 1962), 261. See Jacques Derrida, "Hostipitality," in *Jacques Derrida, Acts of Religion*, ed. Gil Anidjar (New York: Routledge, 2002), 369.

38. Said, *Orientalism*, 265.

39. Massignon, "Three Prayers of Abraham," in *Testimonies and Reflections: Essays of Louis Massignon,* ed. Herbert Mason (Notre Dame: University of Notre Dame Press, 1989), 6.

40. Ibid., 7.

41. Sigmund Freud, "Analysis of a Phobia in a Five-Year-Old Boy," in *The Standard Edition of the Complete Psychological Works of Sigmund Freud* (London: Hogarth Press, 1953–74), vol. 10, n. 36. Freud repeats this hypothesis in *Moses and Monotheism*, 90.

42. Massignon, "Three Prayers," 8.

43. See Jonathan Z. Smith, "Religion, Religions, Religious," in *Critical Terms for Religious Studies*, ed. Mark C. Taylor (Chicago: University of Chicago Press, 1998), 276.

44. Gil Anidjar, "Introduction, 'Once More, once more': Derrida, the Arab, the Jew," in *Acts of Religion* (New York: Routledge, 2002), 3.

45. Derrida, "Hostipitality," 369.

46. Said, *Orientalism*, 268.

47. Indeed the Qur'an is explicit on this in *The Holy Qur'an*, Sura 6:161 "Say, my Lord has guided me to the straight path, to an upright *din*, in the ways of (millat) Abraham, the Hanif, and he associated no one with God." According to the Qur'an, the word "Hanif" refers to the earliest form of monotheistic worship, which the Qur'an recognizes by the name "Islam."

48. *The Holy Qur'an*, Sura 3:67.

49. *The Holy Qur'an*, Sura 3:19. To bolster his claim that "Abrahamic *religions*" (in the plural, no less) have an "Islamic," rather than an Orientalist, provenance, and that the word "milla" and "din" have the very same meaning and significance in Arabic, which he (mis)translates into English as "religion," Anidjar cites the authority of a short inconclusive study by Gerald Hawting, a Bernard Lewis–trained British Orientalist scholar (and Guy Stroumsa, an Israeli scholar of Judaism from Hebrew University). See Gil Anidjar, "Yet Another Abraham," paper presented at Columbia University, Middle Eastern, South Asian, and African Studies Departmental colloquium, fall, 2011, December 8, 2011, 3n.

50. *The Holy Qur'an*, Sura 109:6.

51. For an informative study of the place of Abraham in Islamic theological literature, see Tuhami al-'Abduli, *Al-Nabiyy Ibrahim fi al-Thaqafah al-'Arabiyyah al-Islamiyyah* [The Prophet Abraham in Islamic Arab Culture] (Damascus: Dar al-Mada lil-Thaqafah wa al-Nashr, 2001).

52. This is not unlike how the European Christian appellation "Saracens" to refer to Arabs was projected onto the Arabs themselves who are said to have made the claim of descent from Sarah. Indeed, according to the Oxford English Dictionary's entry for "Saracen," "St. Jerome (Ezek. VIII. xxv) identifies the Saracens with the Agareni (Hagarens, descendants of Hagar) 'who are now called Saracens, taking to themselves the name of Sara.'"

53. Anidjar, *Semites*, 21.

54. Massignon, "Three Prayers," 7.

55. Anidjar, "Introduction," 3.

56. Ibid., 7.

57. "Those Who Call Me an Anti-Semite Are a Small Fringe of Radical People in My Country, An Inteview with Jimmy Carter," December 12, 2006, interview with al-Jazeera, reproduced on Counterpunch, December 14, 2006: http://www.counterpunch.org/khan12142006.html.

58. Remarks by President Jimmy Carter at the Signing of the Peace Treaty between Egypt and Israel, March 26, 1979; see http://www.historyplace.com/specials/calendar/docs-pix/mar-carter-cdavid.htm.

59. Derrida, "Hostipitality," 418.

60. Ibid.

61. Ibid., 367.

62. Emmanuel Levinas, "The State of Caesar and the State of David," *Beyond the Verse, Talmudic Readings and Lectures*, trans. Gary D. Mole (London: Athlone Press, 1982).

63. Leora Batnitzky, *Leo Strauss and Emmanuel Levinas: Philosophy and the Politics of Revelation* (West Nyack, N.Y.: Cambridge University Press, 2002), 153.

64. Edward W. Said, *The End of the Peace Process, Oslo and After*, (New York: Pantheon, 2000), 208. I should note here that three years later, while recalling a conversation with Levinas that had taken place at a conference in 1965, Derrida expressed a passing concern that Levinas had identified himself as a Catholic and André Neher as a Protestant, absenting the "Islamo-Abrahamic" ("Avowing," 21).

65. Anidjar, "Introduction," 25–26.

66. Said, *Orientalism*, 307.

67. Anidjar, "Introduction," 20.

68. Jacques Derrida, *Specters of Marx* (London: Routledge, 1994), 210.

69. Ibid., 73.

70. In *Specters of Marx*, Derrida maintains that "one would have to analyze . . . in particular since the founding of the State of Israel, the violence that preceded, constituted, accompanied and followed it on every side, *at the same time* in conformity with *and* in disregard of an international law that therefore appears today to be at the same time more contradictory, imperfect, and thus more perfectible and necessary than ever" (72–73).

71. Ibid., 73. See also Christopher Wise, "Deconstruction and Zionism: Jacques Derrida's *Specters of Marx*," *Diacritics* 31, no. 1 (2001): 61–62.

72. Said, *Orientalism*, 207.

73. On the question of Derrida's ambivalence regarding the necessary courage required for him to speak in defense of the Palestinians, see Caroline Rooney, "Derrida and Said: Ships That Pass in the Night," in *Edward Said and the Literary, Social, and Political World*, ed. Ranjan Ghosh (London: Routledge, 2009), 45–46.

74. Jacques Derrida, "Interpretations at War: Kant, the Jew, the German," in *Acts of Religion*, ed. Gil Anidjar (New York: Routledge, 2002), 137.

75. Ibid., 138.

76. Ibid.

77. Ibid.

78. Jacques Derrida, *Archive Fever: A Freudian Impression* (Chicago: University of Chicago Press, 1996), 78, 89.

79. I thank Akeel Bilgrami for his engagement with me on this point.

80. Jacques Derrida, "Faith and Knowledge: The Two Sources of Religion and the Limits of Reason Alone," in *Acts of Religion*, ed. Gil Anidjar (New York: Routledge, 2002), 45.

81. Ibid., 91.

82. Muna Tulbah, "Jak Drida: Thaqafat 'al-Tafkik' takhtalif min balad ila akhar wa laysa kul naqid adabi muhayya' l'imtilakiha [Jacques Derrida: The Culture of "Deconstruction" Differs from One Country to Another and Not Every Literary Critic Is Ready to Acquire It]," *Al-Hayat*, March 3, 2000, 16.

83. Derrida, *Specters of Marx*, 72.

84. See Evyatar Friesel, "The Holocaust and the Birth of Israel," *Wiener Library Bulletin* 32, no. 49/50 (1979); Joseph Massad, "Palestinians and Jewish History: Recognition or Submission?" *Journal of Palestine Studies* 30, no. 1 (2000): 52–67.

## Priya Kumar, *Beyond Tolerance and Hospitality: Muslims as Strangers and Minor Subjects in Hindu Nationalist and Indian Nationalist Discourse*

This essay provides an elaboration of some of the arguments in my book, *Limiting Secularism: The Ethics of Coexistence in Indian Literature and Film* (Minneapolis: University of Minnesota Press, 2008). Many thanks to my father Tapishwar Kumar—the Nehruvian man par excellence—for his careful reading of this essay and for always being willing to think with me. I am grateful to Elisabeth Weber for generously sharing Derrida's essay with me and for her editorial suggestions. I am also indebted to Gil Anidjar for his instructive comments and questions. Claire Fox, Kathy Lavezzo, and Ajay Skaria provided many thoughtful questions and suggestions on earlier drafts of this paper. Many thanks, as well, to Amit Baishya and Murli Natrajan for some stimulating conversations on the intersections of race and religion in Hindu nationalist discourse.

1. Jacques Derrida, "Avowing—The Impossible: 'Returns,' Repentance, and Reconciliation," in this volume. Hereafter cited in text with page numbers.

2. Derrida claims there is no "how" in the sense of precepts and rules, but it must be invented by each one in every singular situation. He underscores the importance of avowing the unavowable and forgiving the unforgivable—often through returns to the proximate or distant past—as the

very conditions of a new living together. He differentiates between two kinds of forgiveness: one that is dependent on and demands repentance, and the other, a pure forgiveness without expectation of confession or reconciliation. For more on the importance of avowing the impossible past of Partition, see Priya Kumar, *Limiting Secularism*, especially chapter 3, "Acts of Return: Literature and Post-Partition Memory."

3. Emile Benveniste, *Indo-European Language and Society*, trans. Elizabeth Palmer (Coral Gables, Fla.: University of Miami Press, 1973), 293.

4. The *Oxford English Dictionary* provides us with the following meanings for stranger: (1) one who belongs to another country, a foreigner; chiefly (now exclusively), one who resides in or comes to a country to which he is a foreigner; an alien. (2) One who is not a native of, *or who has not long resided in*, a country, town, or place. Chiefly, a newcomer, one who has not yet become well acquainted with the place, or (cf. 4) *one who is not yet well known*. (3) A guest or visitor, in contradistinction to the members of the household. (Now chiefly with mixture of sense 4) (4) *An unknown person; a person whom one has not seen before; also in wider sense, a person with whom one is not yet well acquainted* (my emphasis). The *OED* indicates that definition 1—the notion of the stranger as a foreigner—is now somewhat rare, and that recent examples show a mixture of senses 2 and 4—the stranger as a newcomer or as the unknown one.

5. Often his translators provide qualifying footnotes explaining their choice of term. For example, in *Of Hospitality*, Rachel Bowlby explains her choice of "foreigner: because "it was more appropriate in most of the contexts" and notes that she would occasionally substitute "stranger" "where necessary or conventional," whereas Barry Stocker and Forbes Morlock in their translation of "Hostipitality" state that *étranger* has been translated variously as "stranger," "foreigner," or "foreign," "depending on the context." Gil Anidjar, in contrast, refers to use the term "stranger "in his translation of "Avowing—the Impossible" in this collection. See Rachel Bowlby, "Translator's Note," in Jacques Derrida, *Of Hospitality: Anne Dufourmantelle Invites Jacques Derrida to Respond*, trans. Rachel Bowlby (Stanford, Calif.: Stanford University Press, 2000), ix; Jacques Derrida, "Hostipitality," trans. Barry Stocker and Forbes Morlock, *Angelaki* 5, no. 3 (2000): 3–18, 16.

6. See Derrida, *Of Hospitality*, 43.

7. Derrida, "Hostipitality," 14.

8. See Derrida, "Hostipitality," in *Angelaki*, 8, and "Hostipitality," trans. Gil Anidjar, in *Acts of Religion*, ed. Gil Anidjar (New York: Routledge, 2002), 361. In *Of Hospitality*, in a somewhat contradictory manner, Derrida differentiates between *étranger* as foreigner and the "absolute other" where the *étranger* is one with whom one has reciprocal rights of hospitality in the form of a pact, whereas the absolute other does not have a name or a family name ("the social status of being a foreigner"), but hospitality is owed to this absolute, unknown other (25).

9. Zygmunt Bauman, "Modernity and Ambivalence," in *Global Culture: Nationalism, Globalization and Modernity*, ed. Mike Featherstone (London: Sage, 1990), 148.

10. Ibid., 149, my emphasis.

11. Ibid., 150.

12. Derrida himself veers closer to Bauman's understanding of stranger when he explains the term *étranger* thus: If we had to give the term *étranger* a "determinate scope," a "normal usage"—especially where the context remains unspecified—"*étranger* is understood on the basis of the circumscribed field of *ethos* or ethics," especially in relation to Hegel's three instances: the family, bourgeois or civil society, and the state (or the nation-state) (*Of Hospitality*, 45). A similar understanding is also at work in the second part of Benveniste's formulation of *l'étranger*: "he

who is outside the limits of the community, Lat. *peregrines*" (*Indo-European Language and Society,* 293).

13. The connection with an "outside" becomes apparent when we look at the etymology of both "stranger" and "foreigner." "Stranger/strange" derives from the Old French *estrangier/ estrange*, and from the Latin *extrne-us* where the *extr* connotes something external or outside. (The *OED* gives the meaning of "extraneous" as "of external origin; introduced or added from without.") "Foreigner" derives from the Old French *forain*, and from the Latin *for nus*, and the *OED* notes that the prefix "for-" occurs only in words adopted from French, and (like *extr*) represents an outside, an out. I am grateful to Jonathan Wilcox and Denise Filios for some useful discussions on these concepts and their etymology.

14. See Balmurli Natrajan's "Searching for a Progressive Hindu/ism: Battling Mussolini's Hindus, Hindutva, and Hubris," *Tikkun* magazine, September/October 2009, for an illuminating account of Hindu nationalists' fascination with fascism and their attempts to racialize Hindus: http://www.tikkun.org/article.php/sept_oct_09_natrajan.

15. Gyanendra Pandey, "The Civilized and the Barbarian," in *Hindus and Others: The Question of Identity in India Today*, ed. Gyanendra Pandey (New Delhi: Viking, 1993), 12.

16. For an insightful analysis of the politics of the Hindu Right, see Tapan Basu et al., eds., *Khaki Shorts and Saffron Flags: A Critique of the Hindu Right* (New Delhi: Orient Longman, 1993).

17. V. D. Savarkar, *Hindutva: Who Is a Hindu?* (1923; Bombay: Veer Savarkar Prakashan, 1989). Hereafter cited by page numbers parenthetically in the text.

18. Edwin Bryant, *The Quest for the Origins of Vedic Culture: The Indo-Aryan Migration Debate* (Delhi: Oxford University Press, 2001), 272.

19. On the two-century-old Aryan migration debate and the origins of Indo-Aryan-speaking peoples, see Bryant's *Quest for the Origins of Vedic Culture.*

20. Etienne Balibar, *We, the People of Europe?: Reflections on Transnational Citizenship* (Princeton: Princeton University Press, 2004), 22.

21. Manu Goswami, *Producing India: From Colonial Economy to National Space* (Chicago: University of Chicago Press, 2004).

22. Ibid., 181.

23. Here, Savarkar seeks to correct Orientalist notions of caste as a fixed and unchanging system. He speaks in a pedagogical vein: "For the very castes, which you owing to your colossal failure to understand and view them in the right perspective, assert to have barred the common flow of blood into our race, have done so more truly and more effectively as regards the foreign blood than our own" (*Hindutva: Who Is a Hindu?* 85). He goes on to outline how "intermarriages between the chief four castes" [the varnas] resulted in the creation of many new castes and eventually a unified Hindu race (86).

24. See *Against Stigma: Studies in Caste, Race and Justice Since Durban,* ed. Balmurli Natrajan and Paul Greenough (Hyderabad: Orient Blackswan Press, 2009) on racism and casteism as descent-based forms of discrimination.

25. This used to be the case until the Nazis differentiated between Jews and Arabs precisely along the lines of race and religion: "What had been for Ernest Renan virtually the self-same Semites (Jews and Arabs), at once race and religion, became for the Nazis highly differentiated groupings, differentiated in the very terms and deployments of race and religion." Thus, where the Nazis racialized and de-theologized the Jew—for example, in *Mein Kampf*, Hitler claimed that the Jews'

"whole existence is based on one single great lie, to wit, that they are a religious community while actually they are a race"—they also deracialized Islam, which they seemed to have considered strictly a religion rather than a racial signifier. See Gil Anidjar, *Semites: Race, Religion, Literature* (Stanford, Calif.: Stanford University Press, 2008), 6, 19, 109n20.

26. Anidjar, *Semites: Race, Religion, Literature*, 6, 117–19.

27. Race also becomes a radically unstable category in Savarkar when he draws attention to the invention of race as a concept: "After all there is throughout this world so far as man is concerned but a single race—the human race kept alive by one common blood, the human blood. *All other talk is at best provisional, a makeshift and only relatively true. Nature is constantly trying to overthrow the artificial barriers you raise between race and race.* To try to prevent the commingling of blood is to build on sand. Sexual attraction has proved more powerful than all the commands of all the prophets put together. . . . Truly speaking all that any one of us can claim, all that history entitles one to claim, is that one has the blood of all mankind in one's veins. The fundamental unity of man from pole to pole is true, all else only relatively so" (*Hindutva*, 90).

28. In sharp contrast, Derrida states that living together would entail interrogating the insufficiency of the old couple of concepts: "*physis/nomos, physis/thesis,* nature/convention, biological life/law." One will never be able to think the living together, he claims, unless one "transports oneself *beyond everything* that is founded on this opposition of nature/culture." See "Avowing," 27.

29. This is a paradoxical claim since he begins with the assumption that the Vedic Aryans migrated to India and came as "newcomers."

30. Accordingly, Savarkar extends an invitation to the other: "Ye, who by race, by blood, by culture, by nationality, possess almost all the essentials of Hindutva and had been forcibly snatched out of our ancestral home by the hand of violence—ye, have only to render wholehearted love to our common Mother and recognize her not only as Fatherland (Pitribhu) but even as Holyland (punyabhu); and ye would be most welcome to the Hindu fold" (*Hindutva: Who Is a Hindu?* 115). Conversion becomes the means to reenter the Hindu fold for Muslims and Christians.

31. Cited in Gyanendra Pandey, "Which of Us Are Hindus?" in *Hindus and Others*, 239. Indeed, Golwalkar took Savarkar's efforts to constitute India as a Hindu nation even further; in 1939, he explicitly compared the RSS vision with fascism: "To keep up the purity of the Race and its culture, Germany shocked the world *by purging the country of the Semitic races—the Jews.* Race pride at its highest has been manifested here. Germany has also shown how well nigh impossible it is for Races and cultures, having differences, going to the root, to be assimilated into one united whole, a good lesson for us in Hindusthan to learn and profit by." Cited in Natrajan, "Searching for a Progressive Hindu/ism," 1.

32. Cited in Bryant, *Quest for the Origins of Vedic Culture*, 274.

33. As I have argued in *Limiting Secularism*, the dominant narratives of secular nationhood tend to construct Partition as the logical culmination of the Muslim separatist impulse. However, recent revisionist historical scholarship on the Partition suggests that Jinnah did not really want Pakistan—the separate nation—but held up the specter of Pakistan as a cleverly disguised tactical maneuver, a bargaining chip with which to extract specific concessions for Muslims from Nehru and Gandhi's Congress party. Indeed, as Aamir Mufti argues, Partition must be read as a development necessary to the discourse of Indian nationhood, "a turning of two thirds of the Muslims of India [the largest Muslim polity in the world at the time] into non-Indians" (Pakistanis) so that the remaining one-third could successfully be contained in the role of national minority. The Muslim separatist impulse in India, enunciated most explicitly by the Muslim League and Jinnah, must be

understood primarily as a refusal to accept this ambivalently coded anomalous citizenship, a refusal to be cast in the excluded and cast-out position of minority. Such a fundamental rethinking of the very origins of the Indian nation-state is crucial for thinking coexistence in the present. It enables us to reconsider the demonized narrative of Muslim separatism as well as the persistent construction of the Indian Muslim as an undecidable figure, the stranger, whose loyalty is always suspect and must be ritually reaffirmed to quell nationalist anxieties. See Ayesha Jalal, *The Sole Spokesman: Jinnah, the Muslim League and the Demand for Pakistan* (Cambridge, U.K.: Cambridge University Press, 1985); Aamir Mufti, "Secularism and Minority," *Social Text* 14, no. 4 (1995): 75–96, see especially 86–87.

34. Anidjar, *Semites: Race, Religion, Literature*, 20–21.

35. See Etienne Balibar, "Strangers as Enemies: Further Reflections on the Aporias of Transnational Citizenship": http://www.globalautonomy.ca/global1/article.jsp?index=RA_Balibar_Strangers.xml, and Benveniste, *Indo-European Language and Society,* 294.

36. Aamir Mufti, *Enlightenment in the Colony: The Jewish Question and the Crisis of Postcolonial Culture* (Princeton: Princeton University Press, 2007), 133.

37. Amit Baishya has usefully drawn attention to the literary dimension of the text by attending to its tropology—its use of the recurrent "concept-metaphor" of "life" for constructing the Indian nation—and the ways in which it functions as a mode of "literary self-making," which seeks to understand the past by bringing it in relation to Nehru's present (31–32). Although *Discovery of India* is not a fictional work, it also asks the reader to "suspend the referential illusion" that is crucial to the "historiographical effect." Thus, he proposes that we read it as a "literary non-fiction of the nation-form" (35). See "Conjuring the Nation-State: The Vicissitudes of 'Life' in *The Discovery of India*," *Postcolonial Studies* 12, no. 1 (2009): 29–46.

38. In his official account of the excavations carried out at Mohenjo-Daro between 1922 and 1927, Sir John Marshall writes: "Hitherto it has commonly been supposed that the pre-Aryan peoples of India were . . . black skinned, flat nosed barbarians. . . . Never for a moment was it imagined that five thousand years ago, before the Aryans were heard of, Panjab and Sindh . . . were enjoying an advanced and singularly uniform civilization of their own . . . even superior to that of contemporary Mesopotamia and Egypt" (cited in Bryant, *Quest for the Origins of Vedic Culture*, 159). It is noteworthy that Nehru also cites Marshall in his chapter on the Indus Valley Civilization.

39. Jawaharlal Nehru, *The Discovery of India* (1946; Delhi: Oxford University Press, 1989), 72. Hereafter cited by page numbers parenthetically in the text.

40. The question of whether the Indus Valley Civilization preceded, coexisted, or was coterminous with Vedic civilization continues to be a matter of immense debate. For a lucid account of proponents on both sides, see Bryant's *Quest for the Origins of Vedic Culture*.

41. Nehru moves from hypothesis to assertion when he claims that Dravidians were the inhabitants of the Indus Valley Civilization. Since the script of the Indus Valley is yet to be decoded, it is very difficult to establish whether the inhabitants of the Indus Valley Civilization were Indo-Aryan, Dravidian, or Munda speakers.

42. Michel Foucault, *Society Must Be Defended: Lectures at the Collège de France 1975–76* (New York: Picador, 1997), 77. Foucault sees this discourse of race struggle as a powerful form of counter-history—"a direct challenge to the history of sovereignty and kings—to Roman history" (71). He goes on to trace how this discourse of race-struggle is recoded in the nineteenth century in terms of a biological and medical understanding of races and "postevolutionist" notions such as natural selection and the survival of the fittest. He suggests that this is the point at which actual racism appears. Now the theme of a binary society divided into two warring groups or "races" is replaced by

a society that is "biologically monist." It is threatened by a number of heterogeneous elements that are not essential to it—hence the idea that foreigners (*étrangers*) have infiltrated this society—and that the state must be the protector and the guarantor of integrity and the purity of the race (80–81). We see this discourse of racism at play in the discourse of the Hindu Right, which makes it permissible for Hindus to kill the Muslim as the paradigmatic figure of the infiltrator.

43. However, the figure of the Afghan is especially curious in *Discovery of India* because it troubles and interrupts Nehru's assumption of discrete races/cultures and a bounded and stable geopolitical entity called "India." Thus, while Mahmud of Ghazni's invasion of certain parts of north India is described as a "*foreign* Turkish invasion" and the Mughals are a "Turco-Mongol" dynasty who were (initially) "*outsiders and strangers*" to India, the Afghans are designated as a "border Indian group, hardly strangers to India" such that the period of their rule may well be termed the "Indo-Afghan period" (238, 241). Rather, they are an "Indo-Aryan race closely allied to the people of India" because their language, Pashto, "basically derived from Sanskrit" (238). Since "Aryans" and "Dravidians" are taken to be the proto-Indian "races," Afghans can be viewed as an "Indo-Aryan race," even if they are Muslim and other.

44. Of course, the paradox remains that Akbar was born in a place (Umerkot Fort, Sindh) that was very much part of the nationalist imagination of "India," yet he must "become" Indian through a process of racial fusion and synthesis. Nehru's account of Akbar undermines from within his previous emphasis on nativity as a significant marker of nationality—for example, his affirmation of those religious traditions that were born on the "soil of India" as more authentically Indian than Islam and Christianity.

45. Goswami, *Producing India*, 188.

46. This, of course, has been the dominant understanding of Indian secularism.

47. See Wendy Brown, "Reflections on Tolerance in the Age of Identity," in *Democracy and Vision: Sheldon Wolin and the Vicissitudes of the Political*, ed. Aryeh Botwinick and William E. Connolly (Princeton: Princeton University Press, 2001), and Wendy Brown, *Regulating Aversion: Tolerance in the Age of Identity and Empire* (Princeton: Princeton University Press, 2008).

48. See, for example, "Hostipitality," *Angelaki; Of Hospitality: Anne Dufourmantelle Invites Jacques Derrida to Respond*; "Hostipitality," in *Acts of Religion*; and *Adieu to Emmanuel Levinas*, trans. Pascale-Ann Brault and Michael Naas (Stanford, Calif.: Stanford University Press, 1999).

49. In fact, as Derrida points out, there is also a semantic and etymological link between hostis (as host) and hostis (as enemy) and hence between hospitality and hostility. See "Hostipitality," in *Angelaki*, 15.

50. Ibid., 14–15.

51. Ibid., 4.

52. Derrida, *Of Hospitality*, 25.

53. Ibid.

54. Ibid., 77.

55. "Hostipitality," in *Angelaki*, 8, and "Hostipitality," in *Acts of Religion*, 363–64.

56. See "Hostipitality" in *Acts of Religion* for an elaboration of the themes of holding oneself hostage and as the substitute of the other in the work of Levinas and Massignon.

57. Jacques Derrida, "On Cosmopolitanism," in *On Cosmopolitanism and Forgiveness*, trans. Mark Dooley and Michael Hughes (London: Routledge, 2001), 16–17.

58. Derrida, *Of Hospitality*, 45.

59. On reversing the notion of the stranger as the enemy, see also Balibar's "Strangers as Enemies," 13.

60. Penelope Deutscher, "Hospitality, Perfectibility, Responsibility," in *Jacques Derrida: Deconstruction Engaged: The Sydney Seminars*, ed. Paul Patton and Terry Smith (Champaign: University of Illinois Press), 96.

61. In fact, the very act of saying "I welcome you" or "I invite you" becomes a way of insinuating that one is at home here, and hence of appropriating a place of ownership and mastery for oneself.

62. Derrida, *Of Hospitality*, 53.

63. Edith Wyschogrod, "Autochthony and Welcome: Discourses of Exile in Levinas and Derrida," *Journal of Philosophy and Scripture* 1, no. 1 (2003): 36–42, 40.

64. Mireille Rosello, *Postcolonial Hospitality: The Immigrant as Guest* (Stanford, Calif.: Stanford University Press, 2001), 17–18.

65. Ibid., 18.

66. In "It's My Home, Too: Minoritarian Claims on the Nation," I discuss the importance of Hindi films such as Mahesh Bhatt's *Zakhm*, Khalid Mohamed's *Fiza*, and Shyam Benegal's *Mammo*, which make a powerful case for Muslim claims on the Indian nation. See *Limiting Secularism*.

67. This is not to undervalue the everyday affects of home or ties to a place, but to mark the difference between the power to assert authority over a particular (nation-) space and the inability to do so. For more on the significance of what the geographer Yi-Fu Tuan terms "homely pleasures accumulated over time" and how they make up the homelike qualities of a particular place, see my essay "Karachi as Home and the Uncanny Homecoming of Muhajirs in Kamila Shamsie's *Kartography*," *South Asian Review* 32, no. 3 (2011).

## Raef Zreik, *Rights, Respect, and the Political: Notes from a Conflict Zone*

1. See, e.g., Catherine Zuckert, "The Politics of Derridean Deconstruction," *Polity* 23, no. 3 (1991): 335; Nancy Fraser, "The French Derrideans: Politicizing Deconstruction or Deconstructing the Political," in *Working through Derrida*, ed. Gary Madison (Evanston, Ill.: Northwestern University Press, 1993), 51; Richard Kearney, "Derrida's Ethical Re-Turn," in *Working through Derrida*, 28; Richard Beardsworth, *Derrida and the Political* (London: Routledge, 1996); Richard Bernstein, "Serious Play: The Ethical-Political Horizons of Derrida," *Journal of Speculative Philosophy* 1, no. 2 (1987): 93; Martin McQuillan, ed., *The Politics of Deconstruction* (London: Pluto Press, 2007); Nicholas Dungey, "(Re)Turning Derrida to Heidegger: Being with Others as Primordial Politics," *Polity* 33, no. 3 (2001): 455; A. J. P. Thompson, *Deconstruction and Democracy: Derrida's Politics of Friendship* (London: Continuum, 2005).

2. See Joan Scott, "The Evidence of Experience," *Critical Inquiry* 17, no. 4 (1991): 773. See also 780–90, where Scott discusses the authority of experience.

3. See, e.g., Derrida's take on the nature of the new international in Jacques Derrida, *Specters of Marx: The State of the Debt, the Work of Mourning, and the New International*, trans. Peggy Kamuf (New York: Routledge, 1994), 90. Any overarching system will ultimately become totalitarian, and Derrida understands the aim of his project of deconstructive reading as to "*free oneself of totalitarianism as far as possible*," argue Derrida and Peggy Kamuf, "Like the Sound of the Sea Deep within a Shell: Paul de Man's War," *Critical Inquiry* 14, no. 3 (1988): 648 (emphasis added).

4. Some read this relation to the other, expressed by Derrida in his early writings, as lying at the heart of his ethics. As Kearney puts it, "For to safeguard the *other* from all logocentric strategies to objectify and reify is to guard the other as an irreducible locus of address and response—arguably the sine qua non of all ethical discourse" ("Derrida's Ethical Re-Turn," 47).

5. To mention just two major works, see Charles Taylor, "Politics of Recognition," in *Multiculturalism: Examining the Politics of Recognition*, ed. Amy Gutmann (Princeton, N.J.: Princeton University Press, 1994), and Bhikhu Parekh, *Rethinking Multiculturalism* (Cambridge, Mass.: Harvard University Press, 2000).

6. For Marx's analysis of feudalism, see Marx, "On the Jewish Question," in *Early Writings* (London: Penguin Books, 1992), 211, 232–33.

7. See Isaac Balbus, "Commodity Form and Legal Form," *Law and Society Review* 11, no. 3 (1997): 571.

8. For such a Marxist reading, see Terry Eagleton, *On Ideology* (London: Verso, 1991). See mainly chapter 3, where Eagleton analyzes Marx and the relation between ideology and commodity, and chapter 5, where he analyzes Adorno's understanding of ideology.

9. To review, in general, Derrida's insistence on the other the reader may consult "Deconstruction and the Other," in Richard Kearney, *States of Mind: Dialogues with Contemporary Thinkers* (Manchester: Manchester University Press, 1984).

10. Jacques Derrida, "Force of Law: The Mystical Foundation of Authority," *Cardozo Law Review* 11, no. 5–6 (1990): 919, 929.

11. See Charles Taylor's discussion of this point in "Politics of Recognition," 42–44.

12. For a critical reading of the way in which Mizrachi (Eastern) Jews have been treated in Israel, see Yehuda Shenhav, *The Arab Jews: A Postcolonial Reading of Nationalism, Religion, and Ethnicity* (Stanford, Calif.: Stanford University Press, 2006); Ella Shohat, "Sephardim in Israel: Zionism from the Standpoint of Its Jewish Victims," *Social Text* 19/20 (1988): 1.

13. For Israel's policy of separatism and the ethnic dominance of Jews over Palestinians, see Oren Yiftachael, *Ethnocracy: Land and Identity Politics in Israel/Palestine* (Philadelphia: University of Pennsylvania Press, 2006); Nadim Rouhana, *Palestinian Citizens in an Ethnic Jewish State: Identities in Conflict* (New Haven, Conn.: Yale University Press, 1997).

14. For a general review of the legal status of the Palestinians in Israel, see David Kretzmer, *The Legal Status of the Arabs in Israel* (Boulder, Colo.: West Review Press, 1990). See also a report by Adalah—The Legal Center for Arab Minority Rights in Israel, *Legal Violations of Arab Minority Rights in Israel: Report on Israel's Implementation of the International Convention on the Elimination of All Forms of Racial Discrimination* (Shafa Amr, Israel, 1998). For a comparative framework, see Ilan Saban, "Minority Rights in Deeply Divided Societies: A Framework for Analysis and the Case of the Arab-Palestinian Minority in Israel," *New York University Journal of International Law and Politics* 36, no. 4 (2004): 885. Here I emphasize that my position toward difference is not shared by many Palestinians, and in fact many Palestinians prefer to emphasize their right to be different before the Israeli state. See, e.g., the National Committee for the Heads of the Arab Local Authorities in Israel, *The Future Vision of the Palestinian Arabs in Israel*, 2006, available at http://www.adalah.org/newsletter/eng/dec06/tasawor-mostaqbali.pdf; Mada al-Carmel—Arab Center for Applied Social Research, *The Haifa Declaration*, 2007, available at http://www.mada-research.org/UserFiles/file/haifaenglish.pdf.

15. I have developed this point further in Raef Zreik, "The Palestinian Question: Themes of Power and Justice—Part I: The Palestinians of the Occupied Territories," *Journal of Palestine Stud-*

*ies* 4, no. 32 (2003): 39. See also Neve Gordon, *Israel's Occupation* (Berkeley: University of California Press, 2008), especially the final chapter, where the author analyzes the separation principle.

16. To use Jean-François Lyotard's term from *The Differend: Phrases in Dispute*, trans. George van den Abbeele (Minneapolis: University of Minnesota Press, 1983), xi.

17. See, e.g., his clear formulation in *Deconstruction in a Nutshell* (ed. John Caputo [New York: Fordham University Press, 1997], 13): "Now, this does not mean that we have to destroy all forms of unity wherever they occur. I have never said something like that. Of course, we need unity, some gathering. Some configuration. You see. Pure unity or pure multiplicity—when there is only totality or unity and when there is only multiplicity or dissociation—is a synonym of death. What interests me is the limit of every attempt to totalize. To gather . . ." (The question is whether Derrida would find anyone other than some fundamentalists to disagree with this rather mild formulation.)

18. To borrow the title of the article by Derek Attridge, "The Art of the Impossible," in *The Politics of Deconstruction: Jacques Derrida and the* other *Philosophy*, ed. Martin McQuillan (London: Pluto Press, 2009).

19. Derrida's critique of identity is at the core of his approach, and his early readings in language and critiques of "logocentrism" and "presence" are critiques of identity. This critique was later spelled out in his political writings, such as *Specters of Marx*, where he adopts a suspicious attitude toward almost all forms of nationalism. See Jacques Derrida, *Specters of Marx*, trans. Peggy Kamuf (London: Routledge, 1994), 169. For a more nuanced reading of nationalism in Derrida, see Jacques Derrida, *The Monolingualism of the* other, trans. Patrick Mensah (Stanford, Calif.: Stanford University Press, 1998). For the way in which Derrida has been deployed by others in order to deconstruct the nationalist discourse among the many, see Homi Bhabha, "DissemiNation: Time Narrative and the Margin of the Modern Nation," in *Nation and Narration*, ed. Homi Bhabha (New York: Rutledge, 1990).

20. Derrida writes that his entire project of deconstruction is geared toward the other. "The critique of logocentrism is above all a search for the other," and deconstruction is in fact an antitotalizing project and form of "openness to the other." See Derrida, "Deconstruction and the Other," 105, 125.

21. See Jacques Derrida, *The Politics of Friendship*, trans. George Collins (London: Verso, 1997), 19. For an elaboration on this homology, see A. J. P Thomson, *Deconstruction and Democracy: Derrida's Politics of Friendship* (Continuum: London, 2005), 15–16. Of course, the problem of numbers was originally raised by Aristotle in *The Nicomachean Ethics* (Baltimore: Penguin Books, 1953–69), 282.

22. See a similar argument in *the Gift of Death* (trans. David Wills [Chicago: University of Chicago Press, 1999], 69), where Derrida states, "I am perhaps fulfilling my duty. But I am sacrificing and betraying at every moment all my other obligations: my obligations to the other others whom I know or don't know, the billions of my fellows who are dying of starvation or sickness. I betray my fidelity or my obligations to other citizens, to those who don't speak my language and to whom I neither speak nor respond."

23. See, e.g., his reservation toward the way in which Rousseau approaches the differences between nations as expressing some deep, essentialist character. In *Of Grammatology* (trans. Gayatri Spivak [Baltimore: John Hopkins University Press, 1976], 267–68), he is already questioning Rousseau's essentialist reading in his *Essay on the Origins of Language*.

24. See Christopher Wise's criticism of Derrida for his relative silence regarding Zionism and his normalization of Zionism: "He does not criticize Israel in *Specters*, and so deflects attention. He

makes it appear that all nationalisms are the same. All nationalisms are religious or mythological. Every ideological phenomenon is marked by a degree of religiosity." Christopher Wise, "Deconstruction and Zionism," *Diacritics* 31, no. 1 (2001): 56, 68. Wise mentions that, while Fukuyama is conservative in many ways, he is at least strongly critical of Israel's policies and is very clear in his denunciation of the Israeli occupation, in contrast to Derrida.

25. With the exception of "unjustifiable," which Derrida emphasizes.

26. See Raef Zreik, "Notes on the Value of Theory: Readings in the Law of Return—A Polemic," *Journal of Law and Ethics of Human Rights* 2, no. 1, article 13. Available at http://www.bepress.com /lehr/vol2/iss1/art13.

27. Carl Schmitt, *The Concept of the Political*, trans. George Schwab (Chicago: University of Chicago Press, 2007). See also Carl Schmitt, *The Crisis of Parliamentary Democracy*, trans. Ellen Kennedy (Cambridge, Mass.: MIT Press, 1985), where Schmitt traces one of the weakest points in liberal thinking, namely its inability to make sense of the concept of borders and citizenship, which is by definition based on excluding certain groups of people from the polity, without any ethical justification.

28. In principle, Derrida would not argue that because all founding moments are violent, all are indistinguishable and equally bad, although he does not state clearly how he would draw such a distinction. See Drucilla Cornell, "The Violence of the Masquerade: Law Dressed Up as Justice," in *Reading through Derrida*, 77. My critique of Derrida is local and related to the State of Israel.

29. While his attitude is very skeptical of any national discourse, see his discussion in *The Monolingualism of the* other where he seems to be more nuanced. Toward the end of his life, Derrida urged resistance to globalization and called on Europe to devise a policy to resist U.S. hegemony, which leaves the impression that Derrida is willing, at times, to deploy a certain identity for the sake of emancipatory ideals. See Benjamin Ross and Heesok Chang, "JacquesDerrida, the Last European," *SubStance* 35, no. 2 (2006): 140. See also note 26 above.

30. For the colonial paradigm in approaching and analyzing Israel, see, e.g., Maxime Rodinson, *Israel: A Colonial-Settler State?* (New York: Monad Press, 1973). See also a more recent study of Israel as a settler-state: Gershon Shafir, *Land, Labor and the Origins of the Israeli-Palestinian Conflict, 1882–1914* (New York: Cambridge University Press, 1989). For the colonial paradigm in relation to Israel and its internal Palestinian minority, see Elia Zuriek, *Palestinians in Israel: A Study in Internal Colonialism* (Boston: Routledge and K. Paul, 1979).

31. National self-determination need not materialize within a separate state but may be achieved in another form that is less than a state, such as autonomy and federalism. See in this regard Chaim Gans, *A Just Zionism: On the Morality of the Jewish State* (New York: Oxford University Press, 2008). See mainly chapter 3, where Gans discusses self-determination and hegemony.

32. See Lilly Weissbrod, "Religion as National Identity in a Secular Society," *Review of Religions Research* 24, no. 3 (1983): 188. See also Menachem Freidman, "The State of Israel as a Theological Dilemma," in *The Israeli State and Society: Boundaries and Frontiers*, ed. Baruch Kimmerling (Albany: State University of New York Press, 1989), 165.

33. See Zeev Sternhell, *The Founding Myths of Israel: Nationalism, Socialism, and the Making of the Jewish State* (Princeton, N.J.: Princeton University Press, 1992). For the distinction between the two kinds of nationalisms, ethnic and civic, see Roger Brubaker, *Citizenship and Nationhood in France and Germany* (Cambridge, Mass.: Harvard University Press, 1992).

34. See David Ben-Gurion, "The Imperatives of the Jewish Revolution," in *The Zionist Idea: A Historical Analysis and Reader*, ed. Arthur Hertzberg (New York: Doubleday, 1959), 606.

35. See Raef Zreik, "Persistence of the Exception: Some Remarks on the Story of Israeli Constitutionalism," in *Thinking Palestine*, ed. Ronit Lentin (London: Zed Books, 2008), 141.

36. See, e.g., his essay "The Ends of Man," which opens with the bold statement that, "Every philosophical colloquium necessarily has a political significance." Jacques Derrida, "The Ends of Man," in *The Margins of Philosophy*, trans. Alan Bass (Chicago: University of Chicago Press, 1982), 111. See also his assessment of the nature of deconstructive reading in his essay "Critical Response" (*Critical Inquiry* 13, no. 1 [1986]: 168), where he argues that deconstruction is political by nature, stating that "deconstructive readings are . . . interventions, in particular political and institutional interventions, that transform contexts without limiting themselves to theoretical or constative utterances." In his interview with Kearney, he replied to the charge that deconstruction is mere method and that there is nothing beyond language as follows: "Deconstruction is not an enclosure in nothingness but an openness toward the other" ("Deconstruction and the Other," 124.)

37. Derrida, "Force of Law," 919, 945, 971.

38. For the ethical significance of Derrida's work in general, see Kearney, "Derrida's Ethical Re-Turn," 28.

39. Chantal Mouffe, ed., *Deconstruction and Pragmatism* (New York: Routledge, 1996), 85.

40. The list is long; to mention but a few, see Simon Critchley, *Ethics of Deconstruction: Derrida and Levinas* (West Lafayette, Ind.: Purdue University Press, 1999); Thomas McCarthy, "The Politics of the Ineffable: Derrida's Deconstructionism," *Philosophic Forum* 21, no. 1–2 (1989–90): 146. See also note 1, above.

41. On the gift, see Derrida's discussion of the gift in "Force of Law," 965. See also Jacques Derrida, *Given Time: I. Counterfeit Money*, trans. Peggy Kamuf (Chicago: University of Chicago Press, 1991). If the gift is subject to a certain economy of circulation and calculation, it is no longer a gift. See also Derrida, *The Gift of Death*, p. 35.

On hospitality, see Jacques Derrida, *Adieu to Emmanuel Levinas*, trans. Pascal-Anne Brault, Michael Naas (Stanford, Calif.: Stanford University Press, 1999). See also François Raffoul, "On Hospitality, Between Ethics and Politics: Review of 'Adieu a Emmanuel Levinas' by Jacques Derrida," *Research in Phenomenology* 28, no. 11 (1998): 274, a book review in which the author argues that the main theme of the book is hospitality. See also John Caputo's discussion in *Deconstruction in a Nutshell*, 106. The same applies to hospitality, where the conditions of its possibility presuppose its impossibility. In order for there to be real hospitality, the host must cease being a host and allow the guest to feel "at home"; however, by doing so, hospitality threatens to negate itself, which is, again, the "art of the impossible."

On forgiveness, see Jacques Derrida, *On Cosmopolitanism and Forgiveness*, trans. Mark Dooley and Michel Hughes (London: Routledge, 2001), where he once more stresses the incalculable nature of an act that transcends universal rules and argues against the economic logic of forgiveness as a type of exchange (34), which is why he insists that forgiveness should be given without being asked for (see 35), and that forgiveness means forgiving the unforgivable (32), as it is not subject to questions of calculable justice (43). Otherwise, it would be merely an act of exchange and subject to the rules thereof, and consequently lose its independent and unique nature.

On responsibilty, see Derrida, *The Gift of Death*, mainly 54–82.

42. In his *Adieu to Emmanuel Levinas* (117), Derrida writes that "without silence, without the hiatus, which is not the absence of rules but the necessity of a leap at the moment of ethical, political, or juridical decision, we could simply unfold knowledge into a program or course of action. Nothing could make us more irresponsible; nothing could be more totalitarian." See also Peter

Krapp, "Between Forgiveness and Forgetting," in *Derrida and Legal Philosophy*, ed. Peter Goodrich et al. (New York: Palgrave Macmillan, 2008), 165.

43. In *The Gift of Death* (61) Derrida writes, "The first effect or first destination of language therefore deprives me of, or delivers me from, my singularity. By suspending my absolute singularity in speaking, I renounce at the same time my liberty and my responsibility."

44. See David Bates, "Crisis between the Wars: Derrida and the Origin of Undecidability," *Representations* 90, no. 1 (2005): 1.

45. For his treatment of the gift, see Derrida, *Adieu to Emmanuel Levinas*.

46. See Derrida, *On Cosmopolitanism and Forgiveness*.

47. Derrida writes in *Adieu to Emmanuel Levinas* (119) that "the same duty to analyze would lead me to dissociate with all the consequences that might follow, a structural messianicity, an irrecusable and threatening promise, an eschatology without teleology, from every determinate messianism: a messianicity before or without any messianism incorporated by some revelation in a determined place that goes by the name of Sinai or Mount Horeb."

48. Hobbes in many ways began this process of denaturalization by questioning the state as a natural phenomenon. However, since then much of political philosophy has reflected this oscillation between moments of denaturalization/awakening/critique and other moments of positing/naturalizing/sleeping. Each philosopher questions the naturalness of the premises of his predecessor and shows that they are either constructed or presumed.

49. See Derrida quoting Kierkegaard approvingly in *The Gift of Death*, 66.

50. Derrida is fully aware of this tension and, unlike some of his supporters, does not aim to conceal it, but instead lives with it as an open wound. In one of his interviews he stated the following, "The difficulty is to gesture in opposite directions at the same time: on the one hand to preserve a distance and suspicion with regard to the official political codes governing reality; on the other, to intervene here and now in a practical and *engaged* manner whenever the necessity arises. This position of dual allegiance, in which I personally find myself, is one of perpetual uneasiness. I try where I can to act politically while recognizing that such action remains incommensurate with my intellectual project of deconstruction." Quoted in Thompson, *Deconstruction and Democracy*, 27.

51. One can cite Derrida's conversation with Giovanna Borradori on terrorism following September 11, 2011, as an example. Derrida questions the whole conceptual scheme that guides the United States and its allies in the so-called War on Terror, as well as the concept of terrorism itself, which he tries to problematize by comparing it to neighboring concepts, such as war, policing, liberation movements, etc. In so doing, he is clearly protesting against the use and deployment of the rhetoric of war against terror. This in and of itself has clear political implications for the nature of the political conversations we engage in. See Giovanna Borradori, *Philosophy in a Time of Terror: Dialogues with Jürgen Habermas and Jacques Derrida* (Chicago: University of Chicago Press, 2003), 100–109.

52. When Marx wrote that he thought the role of philosophers was not to explain the world but to change it, he was thinking of accomplishing change theoretically, through study. One clearly needs to go beyond the simple dichotomy of theory versus practice or materiality versus ideality; the distinction I am suggesting has nothing to do with words and action, nor theory and politics; writing can be political, while certain practices have theoretical value.

53. Again, Derrida can serve as an example for the stand he took against apartheid. See Jacques Derrida, "Racism's Last Word," *Critical Inquiry* 12, no. 1 (1985): 290. In his conversation in *Philosophy in a Time of Terror*, he clearly takes sides and stands opposed to the terrorist attackers

and Bin Laden's strain of Islamic fundamentalism. See Borradori, *Philosophy in a Time of Terror*, 114. However, these examples raise the question of the basis upon which Derrida decides to take sides in these concrete cases and not others. What is significant here is not whether Derrida himself but his approach will enable, or even direct us to, a way of making such interventions and taking sides, as he did. One must admit that, at least politically, these cases were relatively easy ones on which to take sides, although far less so philosophically.

54. G. W. F. Hegel, *Phenomenology of Spirit*, trans. A. V. Miller (Oxford: Oxford University Press, 1977), 47. Clearly, the fact that Hegel made this argument does not in itself validate it. What I want to stress here is the need to overcome the a priori mode of thinking, which, by virtue of its nature, ends up being formalistic. Of course, this does not commit me to any Hegelian "concept" or "synthesis."

55. See Carl Schmitt, *Political Theology: Four Chapters on the Concept of Sovereignty*, trans. George Schwab (Chicago: University of Chicago Press, 2005). I am indebted to Christoph Schmidt, who brought this comparison to my attention.

## Ellen T. Armour, *Responsi/ability, after Derrida*

1. Jacques Derrida, *The Work of Mourning*, ed. and trans. Pascale-Anne Brault and Michael Naas (Chicago: University of Chicago Press, 2003).

2. Ibid., 73.

3. Jacques Derrida, *Adieu to Emmanuel Levinas*, trans. Pascale-Anne Brault and Michael Naas (Stanford, Calif.: Stanford University Press, 1999).

4. Jacques Derrida, "The World of the Enlightenment to Come (Exception, Calculation, Sovereignty," in *Rogues: Two Essays on Reason* (Stanford, Calif.: Stanford University Press, 2005), 117.

5. Jacques Derrida, *The Gift of Death*, trans. David Wills (Chicago: University of Chicago Press, 1995); Jacques Derrida, "Circumfession," trans. Geoffrey Bennington, in Bennington and Derrida, *Jacques Derrida* (Chicago: University of Chicago Press, 1993).

6. Jacques Derrida, *"Avouer—l'impossible: 'retours,' repentir et réconcilation,"* in *Comment vivre ensemble? Actes du XXXVIIe Colloque des intellectuels juifs de langue française*, ed. Jean Halperin and Nelly Hansson (Paris: Albin Michel, 2001). See Jacques Derrida, "Avowing—The Impossible: 'Returns,' Repentance, and Reconciliation: A Lesson," trans. Gil Anidjar (this volume).

7. Jacques Derrida, "The Ends of Man," in *Margins of Philosophy*, trans. Alan Bass (Chicago: University of Chicago Press, 1985), 109–36.

8. See, e.g., Derrida, *Gift of Death*, which I discuss below.

9. Simon Critchley, "Emmanuel Levinas: A Disparate Inventory," in *The Cambridge Companion to Levinas*, ed. Robert Bernasconi and Simon Critchley (New York: Cambridge University Press, 2002), xxiv.

10. We might describe these kinds of living together with a term Derrida has used elsewhere; as an autoimmune response. For a particularly relevant discussion, see "Autoimmunity: Real and Symbolic Suicides—a Dialogue with Jacques Derrida," in *Philosophy in a Time of Terror: Dialogues with Jürgen Habermas and Jacques Derrida*, interviewed by Giovanni Boradorri (Chicago: University of Chicago Press, 2003), 85–136.

NOTES TO PAGES 130-36

11. Jacques Derrida, *Donner la mort*, in *L'Ethique du don: Jacques Derrida et la pensée de don*, ed. Jean-Michel Rabaté and Michael Wetzel (Paris: Métailié-Transition, 1992). For a complete reference to the English translation, see note 5 above.

12. Derrida, *Gift of Death*, 3. Jan Patočka, "La civilisation technique est-elle une civilization de déclin, et pourquoi?" in *Essais hérétiques sur la philosophie de l'histoire*, trans. Erika Abrams (Lagrasse: Verdier, 1981).

13. Patočka, "La civilisation," 116, quoted in *Gift of Death*, 31, 93. Christianity does not simply replace the orgiastic or the Platonic. Just as the orgiastic is taken up into the Platonic, so Christianity incorporates both—and both are always ready to return. Patočka identifies symptoms of its post-Christian return in the orgiastic fervor that accompanies every revolution. Derrida sees the return of Platonism in the vulnerability of the Christian economy of gift to recapitulation by an economy of exchange.

14. Derrida, *Gift of Death*, 38.

15. All quotes in this paragraph are from Derrida, *The Gift of Death*, 5, emphases in the original.

16. Søren Kierkegaard, *Fear and Trembling/Repetition*, *Kierkegaard's Writings*, vol. 6, trans. and ed. Edward V. Hong and Edna H. Hong (Princeton: Princeton University Press, 1983).

17. Derrida, *Gift of Death*, 68.

18. The biblical quotations contained herein are from the New Revised Standard Version Bible, Division of Christian Education of the National Council of the Churches of Christ in the United States of America, 1989.

19. Carl Schmitt, *Political Theology: Four Chapters on the Concept of Sovereignty* (Chicago: University of Chicago Press, 2006).

20. In addition to Lev. 19:18 previously cited, see also Lev. 19:34: "You shall love the alien as yourself" (NRSV).

21. Derrida, "Circumfession."

22. Geoffrey Bennington, "Derridabase," in Bennington and Derrida, *Jacques Derrida*, 1.

23. For more on this, see Ellen T. Armour, "Beyond Belief? Sexual Difference and Religion after Ontotheology," in *The Religious*, ed. John Caputo (New York: Blackwell Press, 2002), 212–26.

24. See Tomoko Masuzawa, *The Invention of World Religions* (Chicago: University of Chicago Press, 2005) and *In Search of Dreamtime: The Quest for the Origin of Religion* (Chicago: University of Chicago Press, 1993); J. Z. Smith, *Relating Religion: Essays in the Study of Religion* (Chicago: University of Chicago Press, 2004); Richard King, *Orientalism and Religion: Post-Colonial Theory and the Mystic East* (New York: Routledge, 1999); Talal Asad, *Genealogies of Religion: Discipline and Reasons of Power in Christianity and Islam* (Baltimore: Johns Hopkins University Press, 1993).

25. See, e.g., Judith Butler, *Gender Trouble: Feminism and the Subversion of Identity* (New York: Routledge, 1990) and *Bodies That Matter: On the Discursive Limits of "Sex"* (New York: Routledge, 1993); Frantz Fanon, *Black Skin, White Masks*, trans. Richard Philcox (New York: Grove Press, 2008; originally published in France as *Peau noire, masques blancs* [Paris: Éditions du Seuil, 1952]); Kwame Anthony Appiah and Henry Louis Gates Jr., eds., *Identities* (Chicago: University of Chicago Press, 1996).

26. Gil Anidjar, "Hosting," in *Derrida and Religion: Other Testaments*, ed. Kevin Hart and Yvonne Sherwood (New York: Routledge, 2004), 65. See also Anidjar's important study of the his-

318

tory of the Abrahamic identities and "Europe," *The Jew, The Arab: A History of the Enemy* (Stanford, Calif.: Stanford University Press, 2003).

## Dana Hollander, *Contested Forgiveness: Jankélévitch, Levinas, and Derrida at the Colloque des intellectuels juifs*

I thank Thomas Carlson and Elisabeth Weber for inviting me to the "Irreconcilable Differences?" conference held in October 2003 at University of California, Santa Barbara, for which I originally wrote this essay, and Craig Perfect for his research assistance in support of this project.

1. Vladimir Jankélévitch, *Le Pardon* (1967), in *Philosophie morale* (Paris: Flammarion, 1998), 997. Available in English as *Forgiveness*, trans. Andrew Kelley (Chicago: University of Chicago Press, 2005). Page citations are to the French original.

2. Derrida's treatments of forgiveness date roughly from 1996 to 1999, when "le parjure et le pardon" was the topic of his courses at the Ecole des Hautes Etudes en Sciences Sociales and at the University of California, Irvine. They can be most readily referred to in the published lecture "To Forgive," delivered in South Africa and at Villanova University in 1999 (trans. Elizabeth Rottenberg, in *Questioning God*, ed. John Caputo, Mark Dooley, and John Scanlon [Bloomington: Indiana University Press, 2001]; original French text: "Pardonner: L'impardonnable et l'imprescriptible," in *Jacques Derrida*, ed. Marie-Louise Mallet and Ginette Michaud [Paris: L'Herne, 2004]) and in an interview with Michel Wieviorka, "Le Siècle et le pardon," in *Le Monde des Débats* 9 (1999), reprinted in *Foi et savoir, suivi de Le Siècle et le pardon* (Paris: Seuil, 2000), which is the edition referred to here. The text of Derrida's answers in that interview was translated into English as "On Forgiveness," trans. Michael Hughes, in *On Cosmopolitanism and Forgiveness* (London: Routledge, 2001). For these and other works, I have modified the published translations wherever necessary.

The theme of forgiveness was especially pertinent in the context of the "Irreconcilable Differences?" conference at which I first presented this essay: The lecture Derrida presented on that occasion, included in this volume under the title "Avowing—The Impossible: 'Returns,' Repentance, and Reconciliation," is also in part a discussion of forgiveness. For more on the background of that lecture, see note 32 below.

3. Derrida, "Le Siècle et le pardon," 115; "On Forgiveness," 40.

4. Derrida, "Pardonner," 543; "To Forgive," 25.

5. Derrida, "Pardonner," 544; "To Forgive," 27.

6. Jankélévitch, *Le Pardon,* 997–99.

7. Ibid., 1000.

8. Vladimir Jankélévitch, "Introduction au thème du pardon," in "Cinquième colloque des intellectuels juifs de langue française: Le Pardon" (1963), in *La Conscience juive face à l'histoire: le pardon*, ed. Eliane Amado Lévy-Valensi and Jean Halpérin (Paris: PUF, 1965), 248.

9. Jankélévitch, *Le Pardon,* 1001.

10. Jankélévitch, "Introduction au thème du pardon," 250–52; and Jankélévitch, *Le Pardon,* 1031.

11. Jankélévitch, "Introduction au thème du pardon," 250.

12. Ibid., 253.

13. Ibid., 249.

14. Jankélévitch, *Le Pardon,* 1059.

15. Ibid., 1095, 1141.

16. Ibid., 1095ff.

17. Suspension points in the original.

18. Jankélévitch, "Introduction au thème du pardon," 256.

19. Ibid., 255.

20. Ibid., 256.

21. Derrida, "Pardonner," 544; "To Forgive," 27.

22. Jacques Derrida, *Donner la mort* (1990), in *L'Ethique du don: Jacques Derrida et la pensée du don,* ed. Jean-Michel Rabaté and Michael Wetzel (Paris: Métailié-Transition, 1992), 62, and in *Donner la mort* (Paris: Galilée, 1999), 88–89. *The Gift of Death,* trans. David Wills (Chicago: University of Chicago Press, 1995), 61.

23. Derrida, "Pardonner," 544; "To Forgive," 27.

24. Derrida, "Pardonner," 558; "To Forgive," 48.

25. Ibid.

26. Ibid.

27. In his interview with Michel Wieviorka, noting the tension in the Western tradition between viewing forgiveness as a "gracious gift" "without condition" and as something that requires "the repentance and transformation of the sinner," Derrida insists that "these two poles, the unconditional and the conditional, are absolutely heterogeneous, and must remain irreducible to one another. They are nonetheless indissociable. . . . It is between these two poles, irreconcilable but indissociable, that decisions and responsibilities are to be taken" ("Le Siècle et le pardon," 119; "On Forgiveness," 44–45). Asked by Wieviorka whether he thus remains "permanently divided [*partagé*] between a 'hyperbolic' ethical vision of forgiveness, pure forgiveness, and the reality of a society at work in pragmatic processes of reconciliation," Derrida replies:

> Yes, I remain "divided," as you put it so well. But without being able, nor wanting, nor having to choose [*départager*]. The two poles are irreducible to one another, certainly, but they remain indissociable. In order to inflect politics, or what you just called the "pragmatic processes," in order to change the law . . . , it is necessary to refer to a "'hyperbolic' ethical vision of forgiveness." Even if I am not sure of the words "vision" or "ethics" in this case, let us say that only this inflexible exigency can . . . inspire here, now, in urgency, without waiting, response and responsibilities. ("Le Siècle et le pardon," 125; "On Forgiveness," 51)

For an exploration of the dual tendency to see forgiveness as a gift and as based on repentance, especially with a view to Judaism, see Solomon Schimmel, *Wounds Not Healed by Time: The Power of Repentance and Forgiveness* (Oxford: Oxford University Press, 2002), chap. 6. That the question of whether repentance conditions forgiveness is not an either/or matter is suggested, for example, by Mariano Crespo's discussion of the role of remorse in forgiveness, which highlights the complicated structure of remorse as it is understood by the Christian tradition (though he oddly includes Philo in the category of "Christian philosophers") in terms of a *metanoia*, or conversion, in which the acknowledgment that one has sinned *coincides* with the discovery of God's mercy. Mariano Crespo, *Das Verzeihen: Eine philosophische Untersuchung* (Heidelberg: C. H. Winter, 2002), 78–84, esp. 79n143. A version of this idea is pursued by Rémi Brague, for whom sin, in Christian thought, is defined from the outset as an offense viewed from the point of view of forgiveness; it is thus visible only "after the fact," and the two terms are linked from the outset. Rémi Brague, "Du pardon et, accessoirement, du péché," *Magazine littéraire* 367 (1998): 32–34.

28. See G. Levasseur/A. Decocq, "Infractions Internationales," in *Encyclopédie juridique Dalloz: Répertoire de droit international*, ed. Phocion Francescakis (1968–69), 2:188.

29. Cf. Jankélévitch, "Introduction au thème du pardon," 247.

30. Vladimir Jankélévitch, "L'Imprescriptible," in *La Revue administrative* (January/February 1965): 37–42. Cf. "L'Imprescriptible," *Le Monde,* January 3–4, 1965.

31. Vladimir Jankélévitch, "Pardonner?" (1971), in *L'Imprescriptible. Pardonner? Dans l'honneur et la dignité* (Paris: Seuil, 1986). "Should We Pardon Them?" trans. Ann Hobart, *Critical Inquiry* 22 (Spring 1996): 552–44.

32. Note that Derrida's contribution to the present volume, "Avowing—The Impossible," is a version of his address to the 1998 Colloque, whose theme was "How to Live Together?" "Avouer—l'impossible: 'retours,' repentir et reconciliation" / "Leçon de Jacques Derrida" in Colloque des intellectuels juifs, *Comment vivre ensemble? Actes du XXXVIIe Colloque des intellectuels juifs de langue française* (1998), ed. Jean Halpérin and Nelly Hansson (Paris: Albin Michel, 2001). In this address, Derrida emphasizes that his personal experience of the colloque is also bound up with Levinas's role in it: "I was attending this colloquium, then, without participating, quite a long time ago, in the 1960s no doubt, probably in 1965. Close to Emmanuel Levinas, near him, perhaps together with him. In truth, I was here thanks [*grâce*] to him, turned toward [*tourné vers*] him. That is still the case today, differently" ("Avowing," 20; see also 21, 22; "Avouer," 184; see also 185–86, 187. The version of the address included in this volume also contains references that connect with the original context of its presentation, notably the reflections on what it might be to be a "French-speaking Jewish intellectual" ("Avowing," 27).

33. Jankélévitch, "Pardonner?" 14; "Should We Pardon Them?" 553.

34. Jankélévitch, "Introduction au thème du pardon," 247, emphasis added.

35. Ibid., 249.

36. Ibid., 248.

37. Emmanuel Levinas, "Allocution de bienvenue," in "Cinquième colloque des intellectuels juifs de langue française: Le Pardon," 245.

38. Jankélévitch, "Pardonner?" 14–15; "Should We Pardon Them?" 553.

39. Jankélévitch, "Pardonner?" 50; "Should We Pardon Them?" 567.

40. Jankélévitch, "Pardonner?" 47–48; "Should We Pardon Them?" 565–66.

41. Jankélévitch, "Pardonner?" 29–30; "Should We Pardon Them?" 558–59.

42. Jankélévitch, "Introduction au thème du pardon," 260.

43. Ibid.

44. Levinas himself gave these discursive contexts particular weight when it came to his Talmudic readings, and to the nature of reading Talmud in general. In the introduction to *Quatre lectures talmudiques*, his first published collection of such readings, all of which were originally delivered at the Colloque, he writes that "the pages of Talmud," because they "register an oral tradition and a teaching which came to be written down accidentally," must be "[brought] back to their life of dialogue and polemic [*leur vie dialoguée et polémique*] in which multiple, though not arbitrary, meanings arise and buzz in each saying" (Introduction to *Quatre lectures talmudiques* [Paris: Minuit, 1968], 13. English translation in *Nine Talmudic Readings*, trans. Annette Aronowicz [Bloomington: Indiana University Press, 1990], 5). To this he adds in a footnote:

Dialogue is not easily brought to life again in its written remains. We have, at any rate, kept our commentary in the form of oral discourse that it had at the Colloques, not even eliminating from it the addresses to this or that friend or interlocutor present in the hall. (Ibid., 13n/10n4)

45. Levinas, "Allocution de bienvenue," 245. Suspension points in original.

46. For discussions of this first part of "Toward the Other," see Robert Gibbs, "Returning/Forgiving: Ethics and Theology," in *Questioning God*, as well as *Why Ethics? Signs of Responsibilities* (Princeton: Princeton University Press, 2000), 321–24; also see Edith Wyschogrod, *Emmanuel Levinas: The Problem of Ethical Metaphysics*, 2nd ed. (New York: Fordham University Press, 2000), 188–94.

47. Emmanuel Levinas, "Envers autrui" (1963; originally in "Cinquième colloque des intellectuels juifs de langue française: Le Pardon"), in *Quatre lectures talmudiques*, 57; "Toward the Other," in *Nine Talmudic Readings*, 25.

48. Tractate Yevamot 79a, cited according to the *Soncino Press Babylonian Talmud*, ed. Isidore Epstein.

49. Levinas, "Envers autrui," 60–61; "Toward the Other," 27–28.

50. Levinas, "Envers autrui," 63; "Toward the Other," 28–29.

51. Drawing on Levinas's reading, Solomon Schimmel interprets the treatment of the story in Yevamot 79a as reflecting an ambivalence between recognizing individual responsibility and condoning collective/transgenerational retribution. While "the Bible does not condemn David or the Gibeonites," the rabbinic interpretation recasts the biblical story so that the tension is resolved in favor of individual responsibility. This is done by introducing "another moral-religious value, protecting the vulnerable—the alien, foreigner, stranger, convert—from oppression and persecution," which is applied "on a one-time, emergency basis" in order to justify "the application of a strict law of talion that relied on more primitive conceptions of retribution." Although Schimmel's account is helpful in calling attention to the different layers of interpretation, biblical and rabbinic, that Levinas is mobilizing, his point is different from Levinas's in that he encourages us to imagine a historical development of Judaism from holding "more primitive" conceptions, such as that of the law of talion, to "introducing" "moral-religious values," such as that of protecting the stranger, in order to overcome problems arising from the more primitive conceptions. As one might expect given his ethics of alterity, and its indebtedness to Jewish sources, Levinas instead treats love of the stranger as an overarching (if problematic) theme in Judaism and is not interested in setting up any kind of genealogy between the Bible and Talmud. More particularly, Levinas takes the "one-time emergency" relapse into retributive justice, which is justified by the rabbis with respect to the value of love of the stranger, as an occasion to highlight the fact that assertions that the stranger is to be loved or protected always entail definitional and hierarchizing operations such as characterizing Israel as "merciful, bashful, and benevolent" and on that basis permanently excluding the Gibeonites from Israel (Schimmel, *Wounds Not Healed by Time*, 26–28).

52. Levinas, "Envers autrui," 60–61; "Toward the Other," 27–28, quoted in "Avowing," 29; "Avouer," 197.

53. I discuss Derrida's treatments of election and Jewishness at greater length in *Exemplarity and Chosenness: Rosenzweig and Derrida on the Nation of Philosophy* (Stanford, Calif.: Stanford University Press, 2008), and in "Is Deconstruction a Jewish Science?" *Philosophy Today* 50, no. 1 (2006), special issue on "Jewish Philosophy Today," ed. Claire Katz.

## William Robert, *To Live, by Grace*

1. Jacques Derrida, *"Avouer—l'impossible: 'retours,' repentir et réconcilation,"* in *Comment vivre ensemble? Actes du XXXVIIe Colloque des intellectuels juifs de langue française*, ed. Jean Halperin and Nelly Hansson (Paris: Albin Michel, 2001), 181; "Avowing—The Impossible: 'Returns,' Repentance, and Reconciliation," trans. Gil Anidjar, this volume. It is important to note that Derrida's opening words, "*grâce*" and "*oui*," remain untranslated.

2. Jacques Derrida, *"Nombre de oui,"* in *Psyché: Inventions de l'autre* (Paris: Galilée, 1987), 639, 644; "A Number of Yes," trans. Brian Holmes, *Qui Parle* 2, no. 2 (1988): 120, 126.

3. Jacques Derrida, *Ulysse gramophone: Deux mots pour Joyce* (Paris: Galilée, 1987), 126; "Ulysses Gramophone: Hear Say Yes in Joyce," trans. Tina Kendall and Shari Benstock, in *Acts of Literature*, ed. Derek Attridge (New York: Routledge, 1992), 298.

4. Derrida, "A Number of Yes," 129; *"Nombre de oui,"* 648.

5. Jacques Derrida, *"Une certaine possibilité impossible de dire l'événement,"* in *Dire l'événement, est-ce possible?* (Montreal: L'Harmattan, 2001), 81; "A Certain Impossible Possibility of Saying the Event," trans. Gila Walker, *Critical Inquiry* 33, no. 2 (2007): 441. Jacques Derrida, *H.C. pour la vie, c'est à dire . . .* (Paris: Galilée, 2002), 19; *H.C. for Life, That Is to Say . . .* , trans. Laurent Milesi and Stefan Herbrechter (Stanford, Calif.: Stanford University Press, 2006), 14.

6. Derrida, "Ulysses Gramophone," 301, 299; *Ulysse gramophone*, 130, 128. That *"oui"* is not first but second, though it remains preontological and takes place before the beginning, resonates with the opening of Genesis, in which creation begins not with the first but with the second letter of the Hebrew alphabet: not א but ב. This ב begins בראשית [*bereishit*], the word that begins creation. At least one recent translation of the Hebrew Bible (by the Jewish Publication Society) translates its opening words not as "in the beginning God created" but "when God began to create," which suggests a time before "time," in which an arche-originary *"oui"* would position itself, as before the beginning, thereby according it a preontological kinship with א.. In a different register, *"oui"* also bears a kinship with the Platonic figure of *khōra* (χώρα), which becomes an important element in Derrida's thought, particularly in his reflections on religion. On this latter point, see Derrida, *Khōra* (Paris: Galilée, 1993); "Khōra," trans. Ian MacLeon, in *On the Name*, ed. Thomas Dutoit (Stanford, Calif.: Stanford University Press, 1995), 87–127.

7. Derrida, "Certain Impossible Possibility of Saying the Event," 455; *"Une certaine possibilité impossible de dire l'événement,"* 102.

8. Derrida, "Certain Impossible Possibility of Saying the Event," 456; *"Une certaine possibilité impossible de dire l'événement,"* 103. See also Derrida's extended meditation on forgiveness in *On Cosmopolitanism and Forgiveness*, trans. Michael Hughes (New York: Routledge, 2001), 25–60, esp. 32–33.

9. Jacques Derrida, *"Comme si c'était possible, 'within such limits' . . . ,"* in *Papier Machine* (Paris: Galilée, 2001), 285; "As If It Were Possible, 'Within Such Limits' . . . ," trans. Benjamin Elwood and Elizabeth Rottenberg, in *Negotiations: Interventions and Interviews, 1971–2001*, ed. Elizabeth Rottenberg (Stanford, Calif.: Stanford University Press, 2002), 344. Derrida goes on to elaborate: "One forgives only the unforgivable [*on ne pardonne que l'impardonnable*]. By forgiving what is already forgivable, one forgives nothing. Consequently, forgiveness is only *possible, as such*, where, faced with the unforgivable, it seems thus *impossible*," so that "the 'condition of possibility' is a 'condition of impossibility.'" See Derrida, "As If It Were Possible," 349; *"Comme si c'était possible,"* 291–92.

10. In "Avowing" see also 30 and 37; "Avouer," 199 and 210. Here, *s'il y en a* points toward a metonymic kinship that bonds itself, *peut-être*, and the subjunctive as figures of *as if*, which plays

important roles throughout Derrida's corpus. I thank Francis Sanzaro, Nell Champoux, and Wilson Dickinson for reading and discussing with me in French a number of Derrida's texts—discussions out of which this point emerges.

11. Jacques Derrida, *Donner le temps: 1. La fausse monnaie* (Paris: Galilée, 1991),19; *Given Time: 1. Counterfeit Money,* trans. Peggy Kamuf (Chicago: University of Chicago Press, 1992), 7. Derrida, "Certain Impossible Possibility of Saying the Impossible," 449; *"Une certaine possibilité impossible de dire l'événement,"* 94. Derrida extends this exorbitantly excessive character of the event, arriving under the sign of *as if,* in writing that "the event as such, if there is any [*s'il y en a*], couldn't care less [*se moque*] about the performative or the constative." See Jacques Derrida, *Le toucher, Jean-Luc Nancy* (Paris: Galilée, 2000), 94; *On Touching—Jean-Luc Nancy*, trans. Christine Irizarry (Stanford, Calif.: Stanford University Press, 2005), 79. See also Derrida's remarks on the symptom vis-à-vis the event (and the infinitive) in "Certain Impossible Possibility of Saying the Event," 456–58; *"Une certaine possibilité impossible de dire l'événement,"* 104–7.

12. Derrida offers a compelling reading of the *Akedah*, written in response to Søren Kierkegaard's own compelling reading in *Fear and Trembling*, in *The Gift of Death*, trans. David Wills (Chicago: University of Chicago Press, 1995), esp. 53–81. For a very different but provocative take on Abraham in the *Akedah*, see Franz Kafka's "Abraham," in *The Basic Kafka* (New York: Washington Square Press, 1971), 172–74. For an excellent commentary on the Abrahamic more broadly, see Gil Anidjar's "'Once More, Once More': Derrida, the Arab, the Jew," in *Acts of Religion*, ed. Gil Anidjar (New York: Routledge, 2002), 1–39.

13. Derrida, *H.C. pour la vie,* 90; *H.C. for Life,* 80. Derrida offers a provocative meditation on religion, and negative theology in particular, under the name *sauf.* See Jacques Derrida, *Sauf le nom* (Paris: Galilée, 1993); *"Sauf le nom,"* trans. John P. Leavey Jr., in *On the Name*, ed. Thomas Dutoit (Stanford, Calif.: Stanford University Press, 1995), 35–85.

14. Jacques Derrida, *"Foi et savoir: Les deux sources de la 'religion' aux limites de la simple raison,"* in *La religion*, ed. Jacques Derrida and Gianni Vattimo (Paris: Seuil, 1996), 83; "Faith and Knowledge: The Two Sources of 'Religion' at the Limits of Reason Alone," trans. Samuel Weber, in *Religion*, ed. Jacques Derrida and Gianni Vattimo (Stanford, Calif.: Stanford University Press, 1998), 63. Derrida considers religious themes of name, promise, and testimony in a different vein in "How to Avoid Speaking: Denials," trans. Ken Frieden, in *Derrida and Negative Theology*, ed. Harold Coward and Toby Foshay (Albany: State University of New York Press, 1992), 73–142.

15. Derrida, "Faith and Knowledge," 63–64; *"Foi et savoir,"* 83–84.

16. Derrida, *H.C. for Life,* 4; *H.C. pour la vie,*11.

17. Jacques Derrida, *De l'hospitalité* (Paris: Calmann-Lévy, 1997), 73; *Of Hospitality: Anne Dufourmantelle Invites Jacques Derrida to Respond*, trans. Rachel Bowlby (Stanford, Calif.: Stanford University Press, 2000), 77, translation modified.

18. Derrida, *Of Hospitality*, 25, translation modified; *De l'hospitalité, 29.*

19. Jacques Derrida, "Hostipitality," trans. Gil Anidjar, in *Acts of Religion*, ed. Gil Anidjar (New York: Routledge, 2002), 361, 362. For a commentary on these points, particularly vis-à-vis Abraham, see Gil Anidjar, "Hosting," in *Derrida and Religion*, ed. Yvonne Sherwood and Kevin Hart (New York: Routledge, 2005), 63–71. For other helpful treatments of hospitality, see Hent de Vries, "Hospitable Thought," in *Jacques Derrida and the Humanities: A Critical Reader*, ed. Tom Cohen (Cambridge: Cambridge University Press, 2001), 172–92, and Michael Naas, *Taking on the Tradition: Jacques Derrida and the Legacies of Deconstruction* (Stanford, Calif.: Stanford University Press, 2003), 154–69.

20. Jacques Derrida, *Donner la mort* (Paris: Galilée, 1999), 110; *The Gift of Death*, trans. David Wills, 2nd ed. (Chicago: University of Chicago Press, 2008), 78.

21. Derrida, "Certain Impossible Possibility of Saying the Event," 449; *"Une certaine possibilité impossible de dire l'événement,"* 94.

22. See also "Avowing—The Impossible," 18; "Avouer," 182.

23. Derrida, *H.C. for Life,* 53; *H.C. pour la vie,* 50.

24. Derrida, *H.C. for Life,* 61; *H.C. pour la vie,* 57.

25. Derrida, *H.C. for Life,* 60; *H.C. pour la vie,* 56.

26. Derrida, *H.C. for Life,* 61; *H.C. pour la vie,* 57.

27. Derrida, *H.C. for Life,* 87; *H.C. pour la vie,* 78.

28. Derrida, *H.C. for Life,* 87, translation modified; *H.C. pour la vie,* 78. *Pro,* too, has a genealogy, which connects it to the Greek πρό.

29. Derrida, *H.C. for Life,* 88; *H.C. pour la vie,* 78.

30. Derrida, *H.C. for Life,* 87, and see 12; *H.C. pour la vie,* 78, and see 17–18. See also "Avowing," 26–27; "Avouer," 193–95.

31. Derrida, *H.C. for Life,* 39, 113; *H.C. pour la vie,* 39, 98. See also pages 29, 47 and 31, 46, respectively, where Derrida discusses "side (*côté*)."

32. Derrida, *H.C. for Life,* 52; *H.C. pour la vie,* 50.

33. Derrida, *H.C. for Life,* 48; *H.C. pour la vie,* 46.

34. Derrida, *H.C. for Life,* 48; *H.C. pour la vie,* 46.

35. Derrida, *H.C. for Life,* 81; *H.C. pour la vie,* 73.

36. Derrida, *H.C. for Life,* 134; *H.C. pour la vie,* 116. (This might also be translated as "a promise from life to life to death, whether it will be life or death.") Derrida discusses this point in *Aporias,* trans. Thomas Dutoit (Stanford, Calif.: Stanford University Press, 1993), 46. Derrida also repeats his formulation *"tout autre est tout autre"* in this text.

37. Derrida, "Faith and Knowledge," 47; *"Foi et savoir,"* 63.

38. Derrida, "Faith and Knowledge," 28; *"Foi et savoir,"* 41.

39. Derrida, "Faith and Knowledge," 47, translation modified, and see 41–42; *"Foi et savoir,"* 63, and see 56–57. See also *H.C. for Life,* 120; *H.C. pour la vie,* 104.

40. Derrida, "Faith and Knowledge," 51, *"Foi et savoir,"* 69.

41. For a different but resonant consideration of *tekhnē* and life, see Jean-Luc Nancy, *The Creation of the World or Globalization,* trans. François Raffoul and David Pettigrew (Albany: State University of New York Press, 2007), pp. 93–95. With this in mind, this "living together [*vivre ensemble*]" can suggest a new mode of biopolitics.

42. The nature-culture distinction occupies a place at the heart of Derrida's work since its very beginning, with Derrida having devoted two of his earliest texts, "Structure, Sign, and Play in the Discourse of the Human Sciences" and *Of Grammatology,* to careful and inventive critiques of it. These critiques relate to his discussions of structuralism and poststructuralism, modernity, mourning, psychoanalysis, genealogy, sexual difference, technology, and politics—all vital issues that recur throughout Derrida's corpus. I explore some of these issues, in different contexts, in "Witnessing the Archive: In Mourning," in *Religion, Violence, Memory, and Place,* ed. Oren Baruch Stier and J. Shawn Landres (Bloomington: Indiana University Press, 2006), 37–50; "Antigone's Nature," *Hypatia* 25, no. 2 (2010): 412–36; and *Trials: Of Antigone and Jesus* (New York: Fordham University

Press, 2010), esp. 20–35. For some of the many excellent considerations of these topics, see Gil Anidjar, *The Jew, the Arab: A History of the Enemy* (Stanford, Calif.: Stanford University Press, 2003), esp. 40–60; Geoffrey Bennington, "Derridabase," in *Jacques Derrida*, ed. Jacques Derrida and Geoffrey Bennington (Chicago: University of Chicago Press, 1993); Judith Butler, *Bodies That Matter: On the Discursive Limits of "Sex"* (New York: Routledge, 1993), esp. 1–23; Peggy Kamuf, *Book of Addresses* (Stanford, Calif.: Stanford University Press, 2005); Bernard Stiegler, *Technics and Time, 1: The Fault of Epimetheus*, trans. Richard Beardsworth and George Collins (Stanford, Calif.: Stanford University Press, 1998); Hent de Vries, *Religion and Violence: Philosophical Perspectives from Kant to Derrida* (Baltimore: Johns Hopkins University Press, 2002); Elisabeth Weber, "Elijah's Futures," in *Futures: Of Jacques Derrida*, ed. Richard Rand (Stanford, Calif.: Stanford University Press, 2001), 201–18; David Wills, *Prosthesis* (Stanford, Calif.: Stanford University Press, 1995), esp. 130–75; and the essays in *Jacques Derrida and the Humanities: A Critical Reader*, ed. Tom Cohen (Cambridge: Cambridge University Press, 2001).

43. Derrida, *H.C. for Life,* 53; *H.C. pour la vie,* 50.

44. Derrida, *H.C. for Life,* 127, translation modified; *H.C. pour la vie,* 110.

45. Derrida, *H.C. for Life,* 95; *H.C. pour la vie,* 84. See also "Avowing," 40; "Avouer," 215, where Derrida mentions "a certain faith older than all religions."

46. See also "Faith and Knowledge," which offers lengthy considerations of globalization, globalatinization, and the religious (especially Abrahamic) imports of such *tekhnē* for possibilities of living and "living together [*vivre ensemble*]."

47. Derrida, *H.C. for Life,* 70; *H.C. pour la vie,* 64.

48. Derrida, *H.C. for Life,* 69; *H.C. pour la vie,* 63.

49. Derrida, *H.C. for Life,* 10, and see 19, 23; *H.C. pour la vie,* 16, and see 23, 34. For an approach to these questions of life from a different angle, see Leonard Lawlor, *The Implications of Immanence: Toward a New Concept of Life* (New York: Fordham University Press, 2006).

50. Derrida, *H.C. for Life,* 88; *H.C. pour la vie,* 78.

51. Derrida, *H.C. for Life,* 88; *H.C. pour la vie,* 78.

52. Derrida, *H.C. for Life,* 84, and see 61; *H.C. pour la vie,* 76, and see 57. Derrida goes on to insist that "one should henceforth . . . use the word *vivement* as a verbal noun rather than as an adverb: one would say le *vivement* [the live-ance], *le vivier du vivement* [the life-pool of the live-ance]." See Derrida, *H.C. for Life,* 150; *H.C. pour la vie,* 128.

53. Derrida, *H.C. for Life,* 89, translation modified; *H.C. pour la vie,* 79. Though I cannot explore this in detail here, the themes of experimentation, test, and trial run through *H.C. for Life, That Is to Say . . .* and bear specifically on questions of experience and undecidability, especially vis-à-vis life and death. For a provocative consideration of these themes, see Avital Ronell, *The Test Drive* (Urbana: University of Illinois Press, 2005). For a complementary discussion of experience, see Derrida's interview with Jean-Luc Nancy, "'Eating Well,' or the Calculation of the Subject," trans. Peter Connor and Avital Ronell, in *Points . . . : Interviews 1974–1994*, ed. Elisabeth Weber (Stanford, Calif.: Stanford University Press, 1995), 255–87.

54. See also Derrida, "Certain Impossible Possibility of Saying the Event," 461; *"Une certaine possibilité impossible de dire l'événement,"* 111–12, where Derrida suggests that "maybe religion starts here," namely, with the messianic as an event that might (or might not) take place and the attendant "act of faith having already commenced."

55. Derrida, "Faith and Knowledge," 17, and see 47; *"Foi et savoir,"* 27–28, and see 63.

56. Derrida, "Faith and Knowledge," 18; "*Foi et savoir,*" 28.

57. Jacques Derrida, *Apprendre à vivre enfin: Entretien avec Jean Birnbaum* (Paris: Galilée, 2005), 26, 54–55; *Learning to Live Finally: The Last Interview*, trans. Pascale-Anne Brault and Michael Naas (Hoboken, N.J.: Melville, 2007), 26, 52. Elsewhere, *sur-vie* is translated as "more-than-life."

58. Derrida, "Faith and Knowledge," 50; "*Foi et savoir,*" 68.

59. Jacques Derrida, "*Survivre,*" in *Parages* (Paris: Galilée, 1986), 149; "Living On: Border Lines," trans. James Hulbert, in *Deconstruction and Criticism*, ed. Harold Bloom, Paul De Man, Jacques Derrida, Geoffrey H. Hartman, and J. Hillis Miller (New York: Seabury/Continuum, 1979), 103–4.

## Kevin Hart, *Four or Five Words in Derrida*

1. Also see Catherine Malabou and Jacques Derrida, *Counterpath: Traveling with Jacques Derrida*, trans. David Wills (Stanford, Calif.: Stanford University Press, 2004), 15.

2. Jacques Derrida, "Différance," in *Margins of Philosophy*, trans. Alan Bass (Chicago: University of Chicago Press, 1982), 26. Here Derrida places quotation marks around "older," which he forgets to do in the later, similar remark.

3. See Jacques Derrida, "Faith and Knowledge: The Two Sources of 'Religion' at the Limits of Reason Alone," in *Religion*, ed. Jacques Derrida and Gianni Vattimo (Cambridge: Polity Press, 1998), 64. Also see Derrida's comments on "belief" in *H.C. for Life, That Is to Say . . .* , trans. Laurent Milesi and Stefan Herbrechter (Stanford, Calif.: Stanford University Press, 2006), 3.

4. Jacques Derrida, *Speech and Phenomena: And Other Essays on Husserl's Theory of Signs*, trans. and intro. David B. Allison, preface by Newton Garver (Evanston, Ill.: Northwestern University Press, 1973), 6. Citations in the immediately subsequent paragraphs are given within parentheses in the text.

5. See Jacques Derrida, *The Post Card: From Socrates to Freud and Beyond*, trans. Alan Bass (Chicago: University of Chicago Press, 1987), 259.

6. Derrida, *H.C. for Life,* 158.

7. Jacques Derrida, *Apprendre à vivre enfin*: *Entretien avec Jean Birnbaum* (Paris: Galilée, 2005), 54.

8. I call *la différance, le supplément*, and all the rest "nicknames" since Derrida is clear that they cannot be proper names: There is nothing "proper" about them.

9. Also see in this connection Derrida's reflections on the idiom "apprendre à vivre enfin" in *Specters of Marx: The State of the Debt, the Work of Mourning, and the New International*, trans. Peggy Kamuf, introduction by Bernd Magnus and Stephen Cullenberg (Routledge: New York, 1994), xvii–xx; and generally, *Apprendre à vivre enfin.*

10. Derrida, "The Deaths of Roland Barthes," in *The Work of Mourning*, ed. Pascale-Anne Brault and Michael Naas (Chicago: University of Chicago Press, 2001), 41.

11. For Levinas's use of the expression, see *Totality and Infinity: An Essay on Exteriority*, trans. Alphonso Lingis (The Hague: Martinus Nijhoff, 1979), 80.

12. For the dating of Derrida's renewed interest in Blanchot, see *The Ear of the Other: Otobiography, Transference, Translation*, ed. Christie V. McDonald, trans. Peggy Kamuf (New York: Schocken Books, 1985), 78.

13. Maurice Blanchot, *The Infinite Conversation*, trans. Susan Hanson (Minneapolis: University of Minnesota Press, 1993), 73.

14. Derrida, *Speech and Phenomena*, 54.

15. See Maurice Blanchot, "Literature and the Right to Death," trans. Lydia Davis, in *The Work of Fire*, gen. trans. Charlotte Mandell (Stanford, Calif.: Stanford University Press, 1995), 323.

16. Jacques Derrida, *Politics of Friendship*, trans. George Collins (London: Verso, 1997), 122.

17. T. S. Eliot, "The Hollow Men," in *Collected Poems 1909–1962* (London: Faber and Faber, 1963), 91–92.

18. See Nicolas Abraham and Maria Torok, "Mourning and Melancholia: Introjection *versus* Incorporation," in *The Shell and the Kernel*, ed. and trans. Nicholas T. Rand (Chicago: University of Chicago Press, 1994), 125–38.

19. Jacques Derrida, "*Fors*: The Anglish Words of Nicolas Abraham and Maria Torok," in Nicolas Abraham and Maria Torok, *The Wolf Man's Magic Word*, trans. Nicholas Rand (Minneapolis: University of Minnesota Press, 1986), xxxv. For Derrida's remarks on the priority of melancholy over mourning, see his *Memoirs: For Paul de Man*, trans. Cecile Lindsay et al. (New York: Columbia University Press, 1986), 31–35.

20. Derrida distinguishes between specters and ghosts on the basis of Abraham and Torok's theory of transgenerational haunting, which is distinct from spectral return. See *The Shell and the Kernel*, chaps. 9–11.

21. See Michel Henry, *The Essence of Manifestation*, trans. Girard Etzkorn (The Hague: Martinus Nijhoff, 1973), §32; and Gilles Deleuze, *Pure Immanence: Essays on a Life*, intro. John Rajchman, trans. Anne Boyman (New York: Zone Books, 2001), 27, 31.

22. See Derrida, *Specters of Marx*, xviii.

23. See Jacques Derrida, *On Touching—Jean-Luc Nancy*, trans. Christine Irizarry (Stanford, Calif.: Stanford University Press, 2005), 328n3. Also see *Speech and Phenomena*, 103.

24. See Jacques Derrida, "Living On: Border Lines," in *Deconstruction and Criticism*, ed. Geoffrey Hartman (London: Routledge and Kegan Paul, 1979), 75–176. Derrida cites Blanchot on *survivre* on page 107. Also see Jacques Derrida, "Des tours de Babel," in his *Psyche: Inventions of the Other*, 2 vols., ed. Peggy Kamuf and Elizabeth Rottenberg (Stanford, Calif.: Stanford University Press, 2007), 1:203.

25. Max Brod, ed., *The Diaries of Franz Kafka, 1914–1923* (New York: Schocken Books, 1965), 196.

26. Maurice Blanchot, "After the Fact," in *Vicious Circles: Two Fictions and "After the Fact,"* trans. Paul Auster (Barrytown, N.Y.: Station Hill Press, 1985), 60.

27. See Derrida's comments in "'This Strange Institution Called Literature': An Interview with Jacques Derrida," in *Acts of Literature*, ed. Derek Attridge (New York: Routledge, 1992), 45.

28. For the view on the singular as not being able to be lodged in the present moment, see Jacques Derrida, "Politics and Friendship," in *Negotiations: Interventions and Interviews, 1971–2001*, ed. and trans. Elizabeth Rottenberg (Stanford, Calif.: Stanford University Press, 2002), 180.

29. Jacques Derrida, *Of Grammatology*, corrected ed., trans. Gayatri Chakravorty Spivak (Baltimore: Johns Hopkins University Press, 1997), 60.

30. Iris Murdoch, for example, assumes that Derrida is "thoroughly uneasy" with experience as a concept. See her *Metaphysics as a Guide to Morals* (London: Chatto and Windus, 1992), 157.

31. Derrida, *Of Grammatology*, 60.

32. Jacques Derrida, "Signature Event Context," in *Margins of Philosophy*, trans. Alan Bass (Chicago: University of Chicago Press, 1982), 318.

33. Ibid.

34. Jacques Derrida, "A 'Madness' Must Watch Over Thinking," *Points . . . : Interviews, 1974–1994*, ed. Elisabeth Weber, trans. Peggy Kamuf et al. (Stanford, Calif.: Stanford University Press, 1995), 362.

35. Ibid.

36. Jacques Derrida, *Aporias*, trans. Thomas Dutoit (Stanford, Calif.: Stanford University Press, 1993), 15.

37. Also see Derrida, *On Touching—Jean-Luc Nancy*, 111.

38. Jacques Derrida, *The Other Heading: Reflections on Today's Europe*, trans. Pascale-Anne Brault and Michael B. Naas (Bloomington: Indiana University Press, 1992), 41.

39. Plato, *Republic* 509b.

40. Emmanuel Levinas, *Totality and Infinity: An Essay on Exteriority*, trans. Alphonso Lingis (The Hague: Martinus Nijhoff, 1979), 293.

41. Derrida, *Aporias*, 22. Also see Jacques Derrida, *The Gift of Death and Literature in Secret*, 2nd ed., trans. David Wills (Chicago: University of Chicago Press, 2008), 82–116.

42. Jacques Derrida and Bernard Stiegler, *Echographies of Television: Filmed Interviews*, trans. Jennifer Bajorek (Cambridge: Polity Press, 2002), 11.

43. Derrida, "A 'Madness' Must Watch Over Thinking," 355.

44. The distinction is Kant's. See his *Critique of Pure Reason*, A213.

45. Derrida, "'Madness' Must Watch Over Thinking, 355.

46. Jacques Derrida and Elisabeth Roudinesco, *For What Tomorrow . . . A Dialogue*, trans. Jeff Fort (Stanford, Calif.: Stanford University Press, 2004), 3–4.

47. Ibid., 4.

48. See Maurice Blanchot, *The Unavowable Community*, trans. Pierre Joris (Barrytown, N.Y.: Station Hill Press, 1988), and Jean-Luc Nancy, *The Inoperative Community*, ed. Peter Connor, trans. Peter Connor et al. (Minneapolis: University of Minnesota Press, 1991). For Derrida's comments on Blanchot and Nancy, see *Politics of Friendship*, 47–48.

49. For caveats about "culture," with which Derrida would tend to agree, see Raymond Williams, *Culture* (London: Fontana, 1981), 10–14.

50. Derrida, *Politics of Friendship*, 35.

51. Jacques Derrida, "Hostipitality," trans. Gil Anidjar, in *Acts of Religion*, ed. Gil Anidjar (New York: Routledge, 2002), 364.

52. Derrida quotes Shakespeare's *Hamlet* 1.5 in *Specters of Marx*, 3.

53. Jacques Derrida, "Psyche: Invention of the Other," in his *Psyche*: *Inventions of the Other*, 2 vols., ed. Peggy Kamuf and Elizabeth Rottenberg (Stanford, Calif.: Stanford University Press, 2007), 1:15.

54. See Derrida, *H.C. for Life,* 27.

55. See Jacques Derrida, *Rogues: Two Essays on Reason*, trans. Pascale-Anne Brault and Michael Naas (Stanford, Calif.: Stanford University Press, 2005), 110.

56. For a level-headed analysis of mystical phenomena considered as full intuitions, see Herbert Thurston, *The Physical Phenomena of Mysticism*, ed. J. H. Crehan (Fort Collins, Colo.: Roman Catholic Books, 1951).

57. See Saint Thomas Aquinas, *Summa theologiae*, 2a2ae, q. 27, art. 6.

58. Derrida, "Faith and Knowledge," 16.

59. Ibid., 18.

60. See Thomas Aquinas, *Faith, Reason and Theology: Questions I–IV of His Commentary on the "De Trinitate" of Boethius*, trans. and intro. Armand Maurer, Mediaeval Sources in Translation (Toronto: Pontifical Institute of Mediaeval Studies, 1987), q. III art. 1, reply. Aquinas cites Cicero's *De officiis* 1.7.23.

61. "Kantian intuitionism" is, of course, Robert Audi's notion, as developed in *The Good in the Right: A Theory of Intuition and Intrinsic Value* (Princeton: Princeton University Press, 2004), chap. 3.

62. Derrida, "Faith and Knowledge," 18.

63. Simone Weil, *Notebooks*, 2 vols. (New York: Putnam's Sons, 1956), 1:205.

64. Iris Murdoch, *The Sovereignty of Good* (1970; London: Routledge, 2001), 36.

65. Ibid.

66. Derrida, *Gift of Death*, 69. My emphasis.

67. Murdoch, *Sovereignty of Good*, 46.

68. I take my list from W. D. Ross. On this list, see Audi, *Good in the Right,* 188–95.

69. See Robert Audi, *Moral Knowledge and Ethical Character* (Oxford: Oxford University Press, 1997), 34, and *Good in the Right*, 24.

70. Derrida, *Rogues*, 60. For lack of space, I leave aside the important question whether the best criticism of this position is the one proposed by the young Derrida. See his "Violence and Metaphysics," in *Writing and Difference*, trans. Alan Bass (London: Routledge and Kegan Paul, 1978), 126.

71. See John F. Benton, "Consciousness of Self and Perceptions of Individuality," in *Renaissance and Renewal in the Twelfth Century*, ed. Robert L. Benson, Giles Constable, and Carol D. Lanham (Toronto: University of Toronto Press, 1991), 285.

72. It is worth observing that, for the Levinas of *Otherwise Than Being*, the human psyche has the structure of "the other in the same." There is sheer otherness inside the self, then, but it is the otherness of the other person, not that of God.

73. On the question of full intuition, see Audi, *Moral Knowledge and Ethical Character*, 39, 46, 55.

74. See, for example, Derrida, *Ear of the Other,* 106–7.

75. The distinction is Jean Wahl's; see his *Existence humaine et transcendance* (Neuchâtel: Éditions de la Baconnière, 1944), 37.

76. See, among other places, John Milbank, "Can a Gift Be Given? Prolegomena to a Future Trinitarian Metaphysic," *Modern Theology* 11, no. 1 (1995): 119–61.

77. See Jacques Derrida, "Scribble (writing/power)," trans. Cary Plotkin, *Yale French Studies*, no. 58 (1979): 117–47.

## Marc Nichanian, *Mourning and Reconciliation*

I dedicate this text to Catherine Coquio in order to rectify an omission. In fact, the second chapter of my book *La perversion historiographique* (Paris: Léo Scheer, 2006), translated by Gil Anidjar as *The Historiographic Perversion* (New York: Columbia University Press, 2009), was first written as a long letter addressed to her (that was in March 1999). It was there that I understood what a "crime without truth" was, in which every request for forgiveness would be only a redoubling of the crime, that is to say, a further attack on the victim. I explain all this here. In the course of this explanation, I am dumbfounded again by the violence of the crime without truth and even more dumbfounded, all of a sudden, by this redoubling of the crime that is a request for forgiveness *motivated by the will to reconciliation*. But is there another way to request forgiveness, a radical way, without the will to reconciliation? That is without doubt the question.

1. See http://www.ozurdiliyoruz.com.

2. Here is the reaction in its entirety, with no commentary on my part. Any commentary would only increase the confusion further.

*Thank you.*

*Thank you to the citizens of Turkey who have just issued a petition in order to request forgiveness, individually, to the Armenians of today.*

*They decided publicly, in their soul and conscience, to no longer tolerate the denial to which they have been submitted for nearly 94 years. By their unprecedented gesture, they recognize that the negation of the victims of the genocide of 1915 has as its consequence the negation of the moral injuries done to survivors and their descendants.*

*Conscious of the risks that they run, I decide, in turn, to respond otherwise than with indifference, critique, or delay.*

*As a citizen of the world and child of surviving Armenians, I express my gratitude to the signatories for their courage.*

*Denial and deceit made and continue to make the bed of extremism, generating hatred and suffering. All forms of violence should now belong to a foregone past.*

*Today the time can come for the truth which pacifies, for a new encounter and for sharing. This is the way opened by Hrant Dink. I believe in the strong determination of men and women, on both sides, to accelerate this process at the human level.*

*Turkish civil society has a right to know, freely and individually, everything that happened. Everywhere, even in Turkey, the information and the books exist, testimonies and traces are still there, words are loosened in spite of and against the denegations of the State.*

*In this context, I welcome this initiative as an authentic sign of hope and historic progress and, personally, I support it.*

France, January 19, 2009

3. Vladimir Jankélévitch, "Should We Pardon Them?" trans. Ann Hobart, *Critical Inquiry* 22, no. 3 (1996): 567. These lines were taken from an article published initially in 1965, in the *Revue administrative*, an article that reacted against attempts to place statutes of limitation on Hitlerian crimes.

4. Ibid., 569.

5. Ibid., 562.

6. Cf. *Hegel's Phenomenology of Spirit*, trans. A. V. Miller (Oxford: Oxford University Press, 1977), 288; *Phänomenologie des Geistes* (Frankfurt: Suhrkamp 1970), 353. Derrida remarked on this irony of the *Gemeinwesen* in *Glas*, and then more briefly in *The Gift of Death*. Mark Sanders, in a quite remarkable essay, takes up the question starting from other premises ("Ambiguities of Mourning: Law, Custom, and Testimony of Women before South Africa's Truth and Reconciliation Commission," in *Loss*, ed. David Eng and David Kazanjian [Berkeley: University of California Press 2003], 91). I am going to return to this at greater length at the end.

7. Translator's note: The word translated here as "right" is *droit*, which means both "law" and "right," and is notoriously problematic in translation. *Droit* appears most frequently in the latter half of the essay, especially in the fourth section, where it has been translated according to context.

8. See Homer, *The Iliad*, ed. Bernard Knox, trans. Robert Fagles, (New York: Penguin Classics 1990), 486; Homer, *The Iliad*, vol. 2, trans. A. T. Murray (1924), revised by William F. Wyatt (1999) (Loeb Classical Library) 471. Wyatt revised Murray's "You, cursed" to "Curse you." See also Homère, *L'Iliade*, trans. Eugène Lasserre (Paris: Garnier, 1952), 402; Homère, *L'Iliade*, trans. Paul Mazon, ed. Jean-Pierre Vernant, (Paris: Les Belles Lettres), 2002.

9. Nicole Loraux, *The Divided City*, trans. Corinne Pache and Jeff Port (New York: Zone Books, 2002), 159. The citation comes from the famous article "De l'amnistie et de son contraire," published initially in the proceedings of a colloquium at Royaumont, *Usages de l'oubli* (Paris: Le Seuil, 1988). There are two English translations of this article. One has been placed as an appendix in Loraux's *Mothers in Mourning* (Ithaca, N.Y.: Cornell University Press, 1998); the other appears in *The Divided City*.

10. Re-reading these lines, I tell myself that the "unforgetful," here, would be rather Hector, logically. This being so, Hector is the nonforgetting *potentially* and not actually, not yet. He therefore represents, in advance, the survivor, the one who will never forget. This is the *double-bind* of the genocidal will. Achilles prohibits mourning in advance by getting rid of the nonforgetting. In this way, he provokes unquenchable nonforgetting. It is for this reason, moreover, that *álastos* is so difficult to translate.

11. Barbara Cassin, "Amnistie et pardon: Pour une ligne de partage entre éthique et politique [Amnesty and Forgiving: For a Dividing Line between Ethics and Politics]," *Vérité, réconciliation, réparation* (special issue of the journal *Le Genre Humain*), ed. Barbara Cassin, Olivier Cayla and Philippe-Joseph Salazar (Paris: Seuil, 2004). Hereafter cited parenthetically in the text. In addition to the essay mentioned, Barbara Cassin has also signed her name to the introduction of the edition under the title: "*Dire la vérité, faire la réconciliation, manquer la réparation* [Speak the Truth, Accomplish (literally: Do) Reconciliation, Miss Reparation]." Jacques Derrida lent his support to this edition with a text (in fact, a session of his seminar) titled "*Versöhnung, ubuntu, pardon: quel genre* [Reconciliaion, *Ubuntu*, Pardon: Which Genre?]," regarding which we are going to say a few words further on.

12. Translator's note: "Human rights" and "human wrongs" are in English in the original.

13. Let us open another parenthesis, apropos of the failures of this transitional justice. On February 4, 2003, the organization called the International Center for Transitional Justice (ICTJ, of American inspiration and based in New York) produced an analysis of the "applicability" of the Geneva Conventions of 1948 concerning genocide to the events that took place at the beginning of the twentieth century in the Ottoman Empire, in sum, the extermination of the Armenians of the Empire. This analysis was requested by the members of the Turkish Armenian Reconciliation Commission (TARC). The text of this analysis can be found online, for example on the Armenian News network site, dated February 10, 2003. Once again, let us not fear being vulgar in the extreme:

All of this turned to shit. The anger of the American emissary is expressed in a book of great violence. Cf. David Phillips, *Unsilencing the Past: Track-Two Diplomacy and Turkish-Armenian Reconciliation* (Oxford: Berghahn Books, 2005).

14. Translator's note: The word "forensic" is in English in the original.

15. Here is what one reads in the introductory essay to the special issue of *Le Genre Humain*, written by Barbara Cassin, Olivier Cayla, and Philippe-Joseph Salazar:

> One of the possible responses (with regard to the problem of reversing wrongs into rights) . . . then perceives itself as the subject of a common decisive and deciding speech in the form of a sovereign 'we' and not as subjected to the racist norm formally attributable to the external source of a European, colonial sovereignty. (14)

Such confirmation of the discourse of sovereignty and the ensuing confidence in the eradication of colonialism by means of a "decisive" speech will never cease to amaze me. Which is not to say that the authors are unaware of the problem. Thus they ask:

> Could one say . . . that the victims were robbed of all participation in reconstruction? That they have been summoned to join in it following a Christian-inspired ritual, through which the colonialism of Western culture operates, once again, in a surreptitious but nonetheless violent manner? (18)

16. "The word of reconciliation is the *objectively* existent Spirit" (*Hegel's Phenomenology*, 408; *Phänomenologie des Geistes*, 493).

17. Derrida, "*Versöhnung, ubuntu, pardon: quel genre?*" 112. Let us add this: Derrida does not insist unduly on the very word of *Versöhnung* in German, which means "reconciliation" in the form of a theater of sons or of a universal understanding within the Son, which is, after all, impressive. Is that *also* what Hegel meant, when he spoke of the "word (of) reconciliation"? Another fortuitous word in German. In her day, Safaa Fathy filmed a session of Derrida's Parisian seminar, the same which we now have before our eyes under the title "Réconciliation, *Versöhnung*. . . ." The debut of this session is one sequence of her film, *D'ailleurs Derrida*, produced in 1999 by Montparnasse. There Derrida is heard insisting on the fact that in Hegel (or in Derrida's explanation of Hegel), it is not a matter of the word *Versöhnung* but instead of the dialogical event that speaks of reconciliation and that, in speaking of it, enacts it. Who would have been able to foresee that the Hegelian dialogic in its modern realization would make the discourse of the executioner and of the victim intersect, the discourse of avowal and the discourse of testimony, until they become indiscernible at the heart of the monolingualism of the reconciled spirit?

18. *Le Genre Humain*, 19.

19. Antje Krog, *Country of My Skull* (Johannesburg: South Africa Random House, 1998), available in the French translation by Georges-Marie Leroy under the title *La Douleur des mots* (Arles: Actes Sud, 2004).

20. Gillian Slovo, *Red Dust* (New York: Norton, 2000); French translation by Jean Guiloineau, *Poussière rouge* (Paris: Editions Christian Bourgois, 2001). The following summary of the novel is adapted from the French publisher's online description, no longer available: Sarah Barcant is a prosecutor in New York. Ben Hoffman, who had been her professor in the past, her friend and her mentor, asks her to return to Smitrivier, their small town in South Africa. The Truth and Reconciliation Commission must convene there in order to respond to the request for amnesty submitted by the former police officer Dirk Hendricks. Sarah will be the lawyer of Alex Mpondo, former "terrorist," savagely tortured by Hendricks. But behind this process another truth is hidden. Did the information extracted from Mpondo under torture cause the death of his friend, Steve Sizela, who "disappeared"

after also having been savagely tortured? The whole world expects a truth—Alex Mpondo, Steve's parents, Pieter Muller, Dirk Hendricks's former superior—and beyond these, an entire city and a nation, torn by a half-century of apartheid, which looks painfully into its past. About the author, the inside jacket of the book says this: "Born in South Africa, Gillian Slovo is a novelist, living in London. She is the daughter of the anti-apartheid activists Joe Slovo, who was part of Nelson Mandela's government, and Ruth First, who was killed by a mail bomb while in exile." In February 2002 the book received the RFI-Témoin du Monde prize, which gave rise to a colloquium co-organized by Radio France International, AIRCRIGE, the "Centre Littérature et savoirs à l'épreuve de la violence politique, Génocide et transmission" (CRLC Paris IV) and the Research Center "Ecritures du roman contemporain de langue anglaise" (Paris IV). I take up again here what I was able to say of the novel on that occasion, at the invitation of Catherine Coquio.

21. Translator's note: The English word "remains" captures part of what is indicated by the French "*ce qui reste.*" The verb *rester*, the impersonal form *il reste*, and the noun form appear throughout the rest of the essay and have been translated with variations of the English words "remain," "remainder," and "the rest" as appropriate.

22. For a more consequential development of the modern novel in its confrontation with testimony, as the genre which is devoted to the remainder, to that which remains, thus to the rest, I refer to my book *Le Roman de la Catastrophe* (Geneva: Métis Presses, 2008). It happens that the novel in question, which is analyzed and interpreted throughout, is an Armenian novel from the post-catastrophic period (published in Cairo in three volumes in 1932–43), titled *Mnatsortats*, a title which could be translated as "The Survivors," or, more simply, as "Remnants." It is a novel that wanted "to approach the Catastrophe," according to the formulation of the author, Hagop Oshagan, in an interview from 1931. The novel has been left unfinished. The author was never able to penetrate the scene of the Catastrophe, to make the "force of the word" equal to that of the event. He was obsessed by testimony. But at the time, the spirit was not yet reconciled with itself. The theater of testimony had not yet reached the limits of the known world in making the word of reconciliation resound. I said therefore in the introduction of the book (pardon me for citing it): "It could be that the novel tests and receives 'that which remains.' In this way, it could be that it is an obligatory passage, the only memory that remains for us, the modern experience par excellence. One could say in this case, correcting or aping Hölderlin: 'That which remains, the novelists ground it.' But precisely, they ground nothing. They do nothing other than to register the passage of the specter. Thus they create a type of event which is not that of historiography" (27).

23. The references to *Red Dust* will be given within the text. Here, as in all the citations that follow, the italics are mine.

24. Of course, one could apply what I say here to all instances of "crime without truth," which are also crimes that aim at the "death of the witness." A Brazilian author, Idelber Avelar, said some luminous things about this in his book, *The Letter of Violence: Essays on Narrative, Ethics, and Politics* (New York: Palgrave, 2004), particularly in the gripping chapter on the nature and the effects of torture, titled "From Plato to Pinochet: Torture, Confession, and the History of Truth." I content myself here with one citation: "For survivors, this promise [of narrativity] takes the form of a *retrospective construction of a witness*, right there where all witnessing had been eliminated" (48, author's emphasis). Cf. also the note that I devoted to Avelar's propositions on the "virtual place of the witness" in *Le Roman de la Catastrophe*, 287.

25. Nichanian, *Historiographic Perversion*, 122.

26. Of course, the entire beginning of the session of the seminar of 1999 on reconciliation insists precisely on the Hegelian moment in the history of reconciliation.

27. I will not develop this link, though it is essential. I explained at length the emergence of philology as an "institution of mourning" in chapter 3 of my book *Le Deuil de la philologie* (Geneva: Métis Presses 2007).

28. I refer the reader to my book, *The National Revolution* (London: Gomidas Books, 2002); but also to my essay "Catastrophic Mourning," in *Loss: The Politics of Mourning*, ed. David L. Eng and David Kazanjian (Berkeley: University of California Press, 2003), and to the interview (with David Kazanjian) which appeared in the same volume under the title "Between Genocide and Catastrophe."

29. I gave the reference to this article in note 6 above, concerning Antigone as the eternal irony of being-together.

30. Sanders, "Ambiguities of Mourning," 82.

31. Ibid., 83.

32. Here, I refer the reader to the categories established by Mahmood Mamdani in *Citizen and Subject: Contemporary Africa and the Legacy of Late Colonialism* (Princeton: Princeton University Press, 1996), categories and analyses that he then applies in order to study the sociology of the genocidal will in *When Victims Become Killers: Colonialism, Nativism, and the Genocide in Rwanda* (Princeton: Princeton University Press, 2001).

33. I have taken this development from my essay, "Retour d'humanisme: Humanisme, orientalisme et philologie chez Edward Said," in *Retours du Colonial*, ed. Catherine Coquio (Nantes: L'Atalante, 2007).

34. "Irony . . . consists of not saying anything, declaring that one doesn't have any knowledge of something, but doing that in order to interrogate, to have someone or something (the lawyer, the law) speak or think. *Eironeia* dissimulates, it is the act of questioning by feigning ignorance, by pretending" (Jacques Derrida, *The Gift of Death* [Chicago: University of Chicago Press, 1995], 76). It is equally in this way that Nicole Loraux, in her first great work, *The Invention of Athens* (Brooklyn: Zone Books, 2006), interrogated the conciliatory foundation of being-together by the *demos* by means of a usurpation of mourning. She did this without referring much to Antigone. Her object was the funerary oration, the official ceremony par excellence, in which the Athenian State regularly put to the test its own foundation as ideality, in regularly repeating therefore the exclusion of women and of the ancient custom of mourning. Since then, interpretations of Sophocles' *Antigone* have been produced that are entirely inspired by this inaugural work. Cf., for example, Blake Tyrell and Larry Benett, *Recapturing Sophocles' Antigone* (Lanham, Md.: Rowman Littlefield, 1998).

35. Walter Benjamin, "On the Concept of History," in *Selected Writings*, vol. 4 1938–1970, ed. Howard Eiland and Michael Jennings, trans. Edmund Jephcott et al. (Cambridge, Mass.: Belknap Press of Harvard University Press 2003), 391.


## Michal Ben-Naftali, *The Painter of Postmodern Life*

1. Jacques Derrida, *Rogues: Two Essays on Reason*, trans. Pascale-Anne Brault and Michael Naas (Stanford, Calif.: Stanford University Press, 2005), 39.

2. Ibid., 13.

3. Jacques Derrida, *H.C. Pour la vie, c'est à dire* (Paris: Galilée, 2002), 27. Quoted in Derrida, *H.C. for Life, That Is to Say . . .*, trans. Laurent Milesi and Stefan Herbrechter (Stanford, Calif.: Stanford University Press, 2006), 24.

4. Jacques Derrida, *Adieu to Emmanuel Levinas*, trans. Pascale-Anne Brault and Michael Naas (Stanford, Calif.: Stanford University Press, 1999), 1.

5. Jacques Derrida, *Politics of Friendship*, trans. George Collins (New York: Verso, 1997), 160.

6. Maurice Blanchot, *The Book to Come*, trans. Charlotte Mandell (Stanford, Calif.: Stanford University Press, 2003), 207.

7. In his conference "The Book to Come," Derrida relates to Blanchot's work, and in particular to his discussion of Mallarmé's *Un coup de dés*. See Jacques Derrida, "The Book to Come," in *Paper Machine*, trans. Rachel Bowlby (Stanford, Calif.: Stanford University Press, 2005).

8. Blanchot, *The Book to Come*, 235.

9. "*Whereas* the presumed fictive structure of every work exonerates its signatory from responsibility, before political or civic law, for its sense and references . . . while at the same time increasing in inverse proportion, to infinity, responsibility for the singular event constituted by every work . . ." (Jacques Derrida, "Literature in Secret: An Impossible Filiation", in *The Gift of Death*, 2nd ed., and *Literature in Secret*, trans. David Wills [Chicago: University of Chicago Press, 2008], 156).

10. Derrida, *Literature in Secret*, 137.

11. Jacques Derrida, *Mémoires for Paul de Man*, trans. Cecile Lindsay (New York: Columbia University Press, 1986), 1.

12. See Jacques Derrida, *The Gift of Death*, trans. David Wills (Chicago: University of Chicago Press, 1995), chap. 3.

13. Derrida, "Literature in Secret," 132.

14. Jacques Derrida, *Paper Machine*, trans. Rachel Bowlby (Stanford, Calif.: Stanford University Press, 2005), 36.

15. "Je ne saurai jamais *ni* dessiner *ni* regarder un dessin" (Jacques Derrida, *Mémoires d'aveugle* [Paris: Editions de la Réunion des musées nationaux, 1990], 43). "I will never know *either* how to draw *or* how to look at a drawing" (Jacques Derrida, *Memoirs of the Blind*, trans. Pascale-Anne Brault and Michael Naas [Chicago: University of Chicago Press 1993], 36).

16. See Michel Henri, *Voir l'invisible: Sur Kandinsky* (Paris: PUF, 1988).

17. See Jacques Derrida, "Unsealing ('the old new language?')," in *Points . . . : Interviews, 1974–1994*, ed. Elisabeth Weber, trans. Peggy Kamuf et al. (Stanford, Calif.: Stanford University Press, 1995); Jacques Derrida, "Abraham, L'Autre," in *Judéités—Questions pour Jacques Derrida*, ed. Joseph Cohen and Raphaël Zagury-Orly (Paris: Galilée, 2003).

18. Jacques Derrida, *Sovereignties in Question: The Poetics of Paul Celan*, ed. Thomas Dutoit and Outi Pasanen (New York: Fordham University Press, 2005), 87–91.

19. Jacques Derrida, *Monolingualism of the Other, or The Prosthesis of Origin*, trans. Patrick Mensah (Stanford, Calif.: Stanford University Press 1998), 20.

20. See ibid., 54.

21. Derrida, "Unsealing"; Derrida, "Abraham, L'Autre."

22. The framework of this essay does not enable me to elaborate this point concerning Derrida's complex and problematic generalization of the notion of "sacrifice."

23. See Derrida, *Memoirs of the Blind*, 23.

24. See Jacques Derrida, "Qu-est-ce qu'une traduction 'relevante'?" in *L'Herne Derrida*, ed. Marie-Louise Mallet and Ginette Michaud (Paris: Édition de l'Herne, 2004), 561–76.

25. Jacques Derrida, *Béliers* (Paris: Galilée, 2003); English translation: "Rams," in Derrida, *Sovereignties in Question: The Poetics of Paul Celan* (New York: Fordham University Press, 2005).

26. From the prayer "Kol Nidrei."

27. Derrida, *Adieu to Emmanuel Levinas*, 92.

28. Derrida, *Politics of Friendship*, 35.

29. Derrida, *Politics of Friendship*, 122.

30. Ibid., 172: "This enemy was a companion, a brother, he was like myself, the figure of my *own* projection. . . . My truth in painting."

31. Derrida, *Adieu to Emmanuel Levinas*, 95.

32. Derrida, "Rams," 160.

33. Jacques Derrida, *Edmund Husserl's* Origin of Geometry: *An Introduction*, trans. John Leavey Jr. (Lincoln: University of Nebraska Press, 1989).

34. In "Rams," Derrida speaks of a "cogito of adieu," 140.

35. Hannah Arendt, *The Jew as Pariah: Jewish Identity and Politics in the Modern Age*, ed. Ron H. Feldman (New York: Grove Press, 1978).

36. Derrida, *Paper Machine*, 129.

37. Derrida, *Adieu to Emmanuel Levinas*, 81.

38. Derrida, *H.C. Pour la vie; H.C. for Life*.

39. Derrida, "Literature in Secret," 137.

40. Ibid., 142.

41. Ibid., 144.

42. Ibid., 148.

43. Ibid.

## Sherene Seikaly, *Return to the Present*

I am indebted to Sharif Waked, Yigal Nizri, and Agnes Czajka for their critical engagement, incisive comments, and generous suggestions. Shiva Balaghi's organization of and invitation to participate in the event "Reading Lebanon" (Hagop Kevorkian Center for Near Eastern Studies and the Vera List Center for Art and Politics, New School, March 2007) was crucial to developing central portions of this essay.

1. Scholars and activists, in particular the Boycott Divestment Sanctions Movement, have realized political and theoretical achievements through comparing South African *apartheid* to the Zionist enterprise in Israel/Palestine. But broad historical comparisons can blur and collapse significant historical and political differences. The neologism of *aparthood* opens a window to understanding the last one hundred years of enforced separation between Palestinians and other Palestinians as similar to *and* different from the system of racial segregation and discrimination in South Africa. (The origin of the world *apartheid* is from Afrikaans, meaning literally "separateness," from the Dutch *apart* (separate) and *heid* (equivalent of -hood).

2. Gayatri Chakravorty Spivak cites Derrida from *Margins of Philosophy*, trans. Alan Bass (Chicago: University of Chicago Press, 1982), 21, and *Speech and Phenomena and Other Essays on Husserl's*

*Theory of Signs,* trans. David B. Allison (Evanston, Ill.: Northwestern University Press, 1973): "The unconscious is not . . . a hidden, virtual, and potential self-presence. . . . There is no chance that the mandating subject 'exists' somewhere, that it is present or is 'itself,' and still less chance that it will become conscious." Gayatri Chakravorty Spivak, "Translator's Preface," in *Of Grammatology,* trans. Gayatri Chakravorty Spivak (Baltimore: Johns Hopkins University Press, 1974), xliv.

3. In a speech to the International Committee for the Support of Algerian Intellectuals (CISIA) and the League of the Rights of Man, at the Grand Amphitheater of the Sorbonne on February 7, 1994, Derrida explained: "All I say is inspired above all and after all by a painful love for Algeria, an Algeria where I was born, which I left literally for the first time only at nineteen, before the war of independence, an Algeria to which I have often come back and which in the end I know to have never really ceased inhabiting or bearing in my innermost, a love for Algeria to which if not the love of citizenry, and the the patriotic tie to a Nation-state, is nonetheless what makes it impossible to dissociate here the heart, the thinking, and the political position-taking—and thus dictates all that I will say." Jacques Derrida, "Taking a Stand for Algeria," *College Literature* 30, no. 1, *Algeriad* (2003): 117.

4. For an intellectual profile of Maimonides and his significance to both Jewish and Islamic philosophy during the shift away from Judeo-Arabic Mediterranean culture to European intellectual power, see Sarah Stroumsa, *Maimonides in His World: Portrait of a Mediterranean Thinker* (Princeton: Princeton University Press, 2009), 1.

5. Gil Anidjar, in "Muslim Jews," provides an insightful reflection on conversion as a narrative turn. He builds on the groundbreaking work of Ella Shohat and Ammiel Alcalay, whose interventions destabilized the political and rhetorical opposition between "Arab" and "Jew." Anidjar uses the "implausible" phrase "Muslim Jew" in order to "highlight a peculiar feature of the shift from race (or ethnicity) to religion, namely whereas racial discourse sought to *forbid* miscegenation, the current discourse of religion appears efficiently to make it *impossible,* to function so as to make certain modes of co-presence unthinkable or nonsensical, and minimally paradoxical." (Gil Anidjar, "Muslim Jews," *Qui Parle* 18, no. 1 [2009]: 2, 11). I am grateful to Yigal Nizri for leading me to this piece. See also Ella Shohat, "Sephardim in Israel: Zionism from the Standpoint of Its Jewish Victims," *Social Text* 19/20 (Autumn 1988): 1–35; Ella Shohat, *Taboo Memories, Diasporic Voices* (Durham, N.C.: Duke University Press, 2006); Ammiel Alcalay, *After Jews and Arabs: Remaking Levantine Culture* (Minneapolis: Univeristy of Minnesota Press, 1993); and Gil Anidjar, *Semites: Race, Religion, Literature* (Stanford, Calif.: Stanford University Press, 2008).

6. Judith Butler, "Jacques Derrida," *London Review of Books* 26, no. 21 (2004): 32.

7. Jacques Derrida, "Jean-François Lyotard," *The Work of Mourning,* ed. Pascale-Anne Brault and Michael Naas (Chicago: University of Chicago Press, 2001), 223, as cited in Butler, "Jacques Derrida."

8. Butler, "Jacques Derrida," 32.

9. Derrida, *Speech and Phenomena,* 68: "Every now is always already comprised by a trace or a residue of a previous experience, that precludes us ever being contained in a 'now' moment."

10. The Israeli Jewish colony now called Ein Hod (Spring of Glory) located in the Southern Carmel hills nine miles south of Haifa, was originally Ayn Hawd (Spring of the Trough), a seven-hundred-year-old Palestinian village, whose inhabitants were expelled by Israeli force in 1948 and dispersed in the West Bank and Jordan. Muhammed Abu al-Hayja and his immediate family were the only ones remaining in the village vicinity. They built a small village on what had been their pastures, less than a mile away from the original village. For an exploration of how the people of Ein Hod and Ayn Hawd remember, and forget, see Susan Slyomovics, *The Object of Memory: Arab*

*and Jew Narrate the Palestinian Village* (Philadelphia: University of Pennsylvania Press, 1998). See also the film *500 Dunam on the Moon* (Rachel Leah Jones, 2002).

11. Derrida, *Of Grammatology*, 61.

12. As cited in Anton Shammas, "Autocartogrophy," *Threepenny Review,* no. 63 (1995): 8.

13. Jan Verwoert (in "The Boss: On the Unresolved Question of Authority in Joseph Beuys' Oeuvre and Public Image," *Eflux Journal* 12, no. 1 [2008]: n. 1) reflects on the tension between constructing and dismantling auratic authority in Joseph Beuys's work and persona. In discussing the installation piece "I Like America and America Likes Me" (1974), Verwoert touches on the comedy of living with the failure of communication and the connections between authority and conviviality. The installation engages a situation wherein "two unequal characters for whom communication constantly fails, somehow find a way to deal with each other and the failure of their communication simply because they live together in close proximity." This failure of communication describes the experience of living with the spectral presence of the other in Haifa, amid Israeli state and popular active denial of the possibility of that presence.

14. On February 7, 2003, speaking on the war in Iraq, Defense Secretary Donald Rumsfeld said to U.S. troops in Aviano, Italy: "It is unknowable how long that conflict will last. It could last six days, six weeks. I doubt six months." Susan Page, "Confronting Iraq," *USA Today*, April 1, 2003.

15. "Prime Minister Ehud Olmert Addresses Meeting of Heads of Local Authorities," *Israel Ministry of Foreign Affairs,* July 31, 2006.

16. Notable in this regard was Yossef Gorni's description of the 2006 war on Lebanon as Israel's "second war of independence." "Second War of Independence," *Haaretz*, July 30, 2006. See Yitzhak Laor, "You are Terrorists, We are Virtuous," *London Review of Books* 28, no. 16 (2006): 11–12.

17. See "Hezbollah Warns Israel Over Raids," *BBC News*, July 12, 2006.

18. Jon Elmer ("Good Night Battle of Britain, Good Morning Gaza," *Briarpatch Magazine* 39, no, 12 [2005]: 11) analyzes Israel's "pioneering" role in the use of asymmetrical air power. He cites Avi Dichter, Israel's internal security chief during the second intifada on Israel's well-honed assassination policy: "Its effectiveness is amazing. The State of Israel has brought preventative assassination to the level of real art." Elmer continues: "Dichter added with pride: 'When a Palestinian child draws a sky nowadays, he will not draw it without a helicopter." See also excerpted edition in the *Journal of Palestine Studies* 35, no. 139 (2006): 191–93.

19. "I wouldn't have gone to war, Peres tells Winograd Commission," *IsraelNews Ynet News*, March 22, 2007. The Winograd Commission, officially named the "Commission of Inquiry into the Events of Military Engagement in Lebanon 2006," was appointed by the Israeli government, chaired by retired judge Eliyahu Winograd.

20. Here Shammas is referring to Dante's description of Hebrew as the "language of grace," in the face of Babel's "language of confusion." Anton Shammas, "At Half-Mast—Myths, Symbols, and Rituals of the Emerging State: A Personal Testimony of an 'Israeli-Arab,'" in *New Perspectives on Israeli History: The Early Years of the State*, ed. Laurence J. Silberstein (New York: New York University Press, 1991), 217.

21. Ibid., 217–18.

22. Ibid., 218.

23. Antonio Vásquez-Arroyo, "Agamben, Derrida, and the Genres of Political Theory," *Theory and Event* 8, no. 1 (2005). Vásquez-Arroyo critiques Derrida's discussion of the first act of violence against the foreigner in *On Hospitality* (trans. Anne Dufourmantelle [Stanford, Calif.: Stanford

University Press, 2000]). Derrida addresses Socrates' plea as a foreigner to the language of the courts as a correlation to the situation of the foreigner forced "to ask for hospitality in a language not his own, the one imposed on him by the master of the house, the host, the king, the authorities, the nation, the State, the father, etc." (Derrida, *On Hospitality,* 15). Vásquez-Arroyo concedes that Derrida criticizes how "modes of speech colonize the foreigner and thus [make] coarse . . . an otherwise subversive edge in the foreigner's claims" (11), but he goes on to say that the political dimension of the question of home and homelessness, and the way that the language of collectivity and power might be necessary conditions for "being at home politically," are absent in Derrida's discussion. I am interested here in how a condition of enforced hospitality is key to the impossibilities of "living together" in Israel and Palestine.

24. ISA: RG 5/1456/32: Administration Report-Public Works Department, April 1937–March 1938.

25. Edward Said, "Invention, Memory, and Place," *Critical Inquiry* 26, no. 2 (2000):184.

26. Timothy Mitchell, *Rule of Experts: Egypt, Techno-Politics, Modernity* (Berkeley: University of California Press, 2002), 13.

27. The Knesset passed the Nationality and Entry into Israel Law (Temporary Order) on July 31, 2003. It prohibits granting residency or citizenship status to Palestinians from the 1967 occupied territories who are married to Israeli citizens. The Knesset has renewed and extended this emergency regulation, originally enacted for one year, for the last nine years. On March 21, 2007, the Knesset expanded the ban on family unification when a spouse resides in or is a citizen of Lebanon, Syria, Iran, or Iraq. This law deliberately targets Palestinians in Israel and separates them from their families in the occupied territories and the Arab world. See the work of Adalah: The Legal Center for Arab Minority Rights in Israel for more information: http://www.adalah.org/eng/famunif.php.

This ban on family unification is one among many painful ironies, given Derrida's point about questions "to which Jews are particularly sensitive: the question of hospitality to foreigners, immigrants with or without permits, the questions of civil union and of marriage, the question of national memory" ("Avowing," 24).

28. Edward Said, *The Question of Palestine* (London: Routledge and Kegan Paul, 1980), 23: "The full irony of this remarkable epistemological achievement—and I use the philosophical term because there is no other one adequate to expressing the sheer blotting out from knowledge of almost a million natives—is enhanced when we remember that in 1948, at the moment that Israel declared itself a state, it legally owned a little more than 6 percent of the land of Palestine and its population of Jews consisted of a fraction of the total population."

29. Gabriel Piterberg, "Erasures," *New Left Review* 10 (July–August 2001): 31.

30. Ibid., 32.

31. Massad is citing Gilles Deleuze here. Joseph Massad, "The Legacy of Jean-Paul Sartre," *Al Ahram Weekly*, January 30, 2005.

32. Joseph A. Massad, "Forget Semitism!" this volume, 112–13.

33. Manu Goswami, *Producing India: From Colonial Economy to National Space* (Chicago: University of Chicago Press, 2004), 6.

34. Derrida's words, quoted above, are important reminders: "The adverb 'together' in the expression 'living together' does not refer to the totality of a natural, biological, or genetic ensemble, to the cohesiveness of an organism or of some social body (family, ethnic group, nation) that would be measured with this organic metaphor." ("Avowing," 26). Additionally,

God is the name and the element of that which makes possible an absolutely pure and absolutely self-present self-knowledge. From Descartes to Hegel and in spite of all the differences that separate the different places and moments in the structure of that epoch, God's infinite understanding is the other name for the logos as self-presence. The logos can be infinite and self-present, it can be *produced as auto-affection,* only through the *voice:* an order of the signifier by which the subject takes from itself into itself, does not borrow outside of itself the signifier that it emits and that affects it at the same time. Such is at least the experience—or consciousness—of the voice: of hearing (understanding)-oneself-speak [*s'entendre-parler*]. That experience lives and proclaims itself as the exclusion of writing, that is to say of the invoking of an "exterior," "sensible," "spatial" signifier interrupting self-presence. (Derrida, *Of Grammatology,* 98)

Jack Reynolds (*Merleau-Ponty and Derrida: Intertwining Embodiment and Alterity* [Athens: Ohio University Press, 2004], 36) provides a cogent discussion of Derrida's critique of Ferdinand de Saussure's argument that language and writing are two distinct systems, the second existing for the purpose of representing the first.

Derrida vehemently disagrees with this type of hierarchy and instead argues that all that can be claimed of writing—for instance, that it is derivative and merely refers to other signs—is equally true of speech. But as well as criticizing such a position for certain unjustifiable presuppositions, including the idea that we are self-identical with ourselves in "hearing" ourselves think, Derrida makes explicit the manner in which such a hierarchy is rendered untenable from within Saussure's own text.

## Elisabeth Weber, *Living—with—Torture—Together*

1. Darius Rejali, *Torture and Democracy* (Princeton: Princeton University Press, 2009), 30.

2. Irgun (also known as "Etzel") was formed in 1931 and existed until the foundation of the State of Israel in 1948, when it was absorbed into the Israeli military. The group's goal was to defend the right of every Jew to enter Palestine and to carry out armed retaliation against Arabs who attacked Jews. Several authors described the militant group as a "terrorist" organization: for example, in 1946, *New York Times* reporter Julian Louis Meltzer ("Zionists condemn Palestine Terror," *New York Times,* December 24, 1946, 1). The Israeli historian Tom Segev describes Irgun as an "anti-British terrorist group" in *The Seventh Million: The Israelis and the Holocaust,* trans. Haim Watzman (New York: Hill and Wang, 1993), 33. Segev quotes the German writer Arnold Zweig, who had fled the Nazis and emigrated to Palestine, and wrote to Sigmund Freud a day after Irgun had detonated a bomb in a busy Arab marketplace in Jerusalem: "A terrible vengeance will descend upon us all. . . . The Jews, who came to this country against the will of the Arab majority and who since 1919 have been incapable of winning the goodwill of the Arabs, had only one thing in their favor: their moral position, their passive endurance. Their aggression as immigrants and the aggression of the Arab terrorists cancelled each other out. But if they now throw bombs, I see a dark future ahead for us all" (39).

3. Jacques Derrida, "Avowing—The Impossible: 'Returns,' Repentance, and Reconciliation," this volume, 30. Further references will be made parenthetically in the text.

4. This idea is at the heart of Julie Carlson's work. See, for example, her *England's First Family of Writers: Mary Wollstonecraft, William Godwin, Mary Shelley* (Baltimore: Johns Hopkins University Press, 2007).

5. See also "Avowing," 37–38: "Those whom I call, in this undeniable but unjustifiable hierarchy, *my own,* are not those who belong to me; it is the ensemble of those with whom, precisely, it is

*given to me*, prior to any choice, to 'live together,' in all the dimensions of what one calls so easily a community: my family, my congeners, countrymen, coreligionists, my neighbors [*mes voisins*], my close ones, those who speak my language."

6. As Darius Rejali shows, besides applying the old, and still-prevailing techniques of inflicting severe physical pain (beating, kicking, slamming detainees against walls, etc.), modern democracies have developed so-called clean or stealth techniques, that make use of electricity, water, temperature control, noise, music, drugs, stress positions, and, as was evident in Abu Ghraib, sexual humiliation—all techniques that leave no visible scars. See Rejali's magnum opus *Torture and Democracy*.

7. Alfred McCoy, *A Question of Torture* (New York: Henry Holt, 2006), 32–51.

8. This report was written in 2004. Its release was delayed three times before being finally obtained on August 24, 2009; Greg Miller, "CIA's Black Sites, Illuminated," *Los Angeles Times*, August 31, 2009, 1, available at http://www.latimes.com/news/nationworld/nation/la-na-cia-detainee31 -2009aug31,0,1893773.story. See also the reaction from the Center for Constitutional Rights, CCR: http://www.ccrjustice.org/newsroom/press-releases/cia-inspector-general%2526%2523039%3Bs -torture-report%3A-first-reactions-ccr-senior-mana.

9. See McCoy, *Question of Torture*, 121–23.

10. See, for example, Jacques Derrida, "Faith and Knowledge," in *Acts of Religion*, ed. Gil Anidjar (New York: Routledge, 2002), 88–89.

11. Ariel Dorfman, "The Tyranny of Terror," in *Torture*, ed. Sanford Levinson (Oxford: Oxford University Press, 2004), 5. In his criticism of "torture warrants," Dorfman alludes to Alan Dershowitz, whose essay "Tortured Reasoning" is also included in Levinson's collection; see in particular *Torture*, 257. For another critique of "torture warrants," see McCoy, *Question of Torture*, 111.

12. See McCoy, *Question of Torture*, 121–23.

13. Ibid., 100–101.

14. The use of the singular ("the enemy") is an absurdity that seeks to establish an identifiable "whole" ("ensemble") where there is none. The use of the singular was one of the hallmarks of the Bush administration's statements about detainees in Guantánamo and other American-run prisons overseas. According to a document dated November 2008 by the New York City–based Center for Constitutional Rights (CCR), "of the more than 770 detainees who have endured Guantánamo since it opened in 2002, over 500 have been released without formal criminal charges or trial. So far, of the 250 or more who remain in detention, only 23 have been charged with a crime. Two have been convicted and one has pled guilty." On January 22, 2009, President Obama issued an executive order to close the facility within one year. Nonetheless, on the tenth anniversary of the prison camp in January 2012, 171 men remained imprisoned in Guantánamo without charge or trial, of whom 89 have been "unanimously cleared by the C.I.A., F.B.I., N.S.C. and Department of Defense for transfer or resettlement." However, as Vincent Warren observes, "Provisions in the 2012 National Defense Authorization Act effectively prevent the release . . . and codify a system of indefinite detention that should make us all shudder" (Vincent Warren, "Congress Should Close Guantánamo," *New York Times*, January 9, 2012. http://www.nytimes.com/roomfordebate/2012/01/09/guantanamo-10-years -later/congress-should-close-guantanamo?scp=6&sq=guantanamo&st=cse).

15. Eric Fair, "An Iraq Interrogator's Nightmare," *Washington Post*, February 9, 2007, http:// www.washingtonpost.com/wp-dyn/content/article/2007/02/08/AR2007020801680.html.

16. Eric Fair, in "No More: No Torture, No Exceptions," *Washington Monthly*, January–March 2008, http://www.washingtonmonthly.com/features/2008/0801.torture.html.

17. The by-now famous "ticking time-bomb" scenario has been discredited as entirely fictitious. See, for example, McCoy, *Question of Torture*, 190–95.

18. UN Convention on Torture and Other Cruel, Inhuman or Degrading Treatment or Punishment, Article 2. http://www2.ohchr.org/english/law/cat.htm.

19. See Jacques Derrida, "Autoimmunity: Real and Symbolic Suicides," in Giovanna Borradori, *Philosophy in a Time of Terror: Dialogues with Jürgen Habermas and Jacques Derrida* (Chicago: University of Chicago Press 2003), 106; see also 114.

20. I need to leave aside the huge question of the torturer's compassion, or rather the necessity to make himself or herself impervious to it. Françoise Sironi's work is here of great importance, for example her *Bourreaux et victimes: Psychologie de la torture* (Paris: Odile Jacob, 1999). "*L'étude de la torture en tant que système m'a permis de mettre en évidence le fait suivant: on ne naît pas tortionnaire, on le devient; soit par une violente expérience de déculturation, soit par une initiation spécifique qui utilise des techniques traumatiques* [The study of torture as a system has allowed me to clearly reveal the following fact: one isn't born a torturer, one becomes one, either through a violent experience of de-culturation, or through a specific initiation that uses traumatizing techniques]" (129).

21. Veena Das, "Language and Body," quoted in Rejali, *Torture and Democracy*, 31.

22. Rejali, *Torture and Democracy*, 31.

23. Ibid.

24. Geoffrey Bennington and Jacques Derrida, *Jacques Derrida*, trans. Geoffrey Bennington (Chicago: University of Chicago Press, 1993), 58.

25. Derrida gave the address in 1998 at the occasion of an annual conference held in Paris, the Colloque des intellectuels juifs de langue française. See "Avowing," 20.

26. Jacques Derrida, *Politiques de l'amitié* (Paris: Galilée 1994), 63; *Politics of Friendship*, trans. G. Collins (London: Verso 1997), 43. The "Perhaps" was first introduced into philosophy as an unheard-of dimension by Nietzsche, to whom *Politics of Friendship* dedicates a long section, especially chapters 2 and 3.

27. Derrida, *Politics of Friendship*, 7; *Politiques de l'amitié*, 23.

28. Derrida, *Politics of Friendship*, 39, translation modified; *Politiques de l'amitié*, 59. "*Le pouvoir et l'être*": Derrida adds the definite article to both verbs, because they can serve, in French, as substantives as well, in which case they are translated as "power" and "being."

29. "The Hebrew Bible documents the early evolution of the emotion of the mercy connected with mother-love in the ascription of it to God. The ancient Hebrews had several words for pity and the more emotionally charged mercy. . . . The most distinctive Hebraic word is derived from *rechem* 'womb' that yields the plural *rachamim* 'mercies' (once translated 'bowels of mercy') and the verb *racham* 'to love' or 'to have mercy' (as a noun, also 'womb'). Although male-oriented interpreters of the Bible were formerly inclined to relate this word for mercy to the *brotherly* feeling of those born from the same womb, today scholars favor the equally venerable and now more convincing interpretation that roots this kind of mercy in the courageous and steadfast love of the *mother* for the offspring of her womb. In the Hebrew Bible the literal sense of womb-mercy is represented in the hard emotional decision of the true mother in the strategy of King Solomon to divide in half a living child in dispute between two harlots (1 Kings 3:16–28). With the sudden threat of death to her child the real mother's 'womb grew hot (*kamar*), and she said "Oh my Lord, give her the living child, and by no means slay it" (v. 26). Then the king answered, "Give the living child to the first woman . . . she is its mother."' The waxing hot of the womb in compassion is also ascribed to Joseph

in Egypt, when he, as deputy of Pharaoh, entertained his brothers (Genesis 43), especially verse 30: 'Then Joseph made haste, for his *rachamim* yearned for his brother,' Benjamin, the youngest and the one among them who was also son of Rachel, dead in her last childbirth. Mother-love, womb-love, womb-mercy in the Hebrew eventually evolved into a generic word for steadfast love and was ascribed to God himself (cf. Psalm 25:6; Isaiah 49:15, 54:7; Hosea 2:19, 14:5; Zechariah 1:16) and then to men, such as the compassionate Joseph. . . . In Islam a man, like a woman, is enjoined to be merciful in one adjectival form of the noun for 'womb' (*rahm, rahim*). More important, Allah is called the Merciful and the Compassionate, the two adjectives being both variants derived from womb-mercy, in the subtitle of every chapter of the Koran, except surah 9. And the Job of the Old Testament, taken over by the Koran in surah 40:07, speaks of Allah as 'the most merciful of merciful ones,' while Allah himself says in surah 7:156: 'My mercy encompasses all things.'" George H. Williams, "Mercy as the Basis of a Non-Elitist Ecological Ethic," in *Festschrift in Honor of Charles Speel*, edited by Thomas J. Sienkewicz and James E. Betts (Monmouth, Ill.: Monmouth College, 1997), 31–32. I thank Aaron Gross for sharing his erudition on the concept "Rachamim" so generously with me.

30. Emmanuel Levinas, *Otherwise than Being, or Beyond Essence*, trans. Alphonso Lingis (Pittsburgh: Dusquesne University Press, 1998), 75.

31. Cf. Elisabeth de Fontenay, *Le Silence des Bêtes: La philosophie à l'épreuve de l'animalité* (Paris: Fayard, 1998), 703. These "cardinal criteria" mutually imply each other: "world, hand, death, vertical posture, *logos*, glance, questioning" (703). See also Jacques Derrida, *The Animal That Therefore I Am*, ed. Marie-Louise Mallet, trans. David Wills (New York: Fordham University Press 2008), 30–31.

32. Derrida, *Animal That Therefore I Am*, 24.

33. As Derrida formulates it in the context of the suffering of animals, ibid., 28, translation slightly altered.

34. Ibid., 28–29.

35. Ibid., 26. On this subject, see also Frans de Waal's book *The Age of Empathy* (New York: Three Rivers Press, 2009). I am indebted to Aaron Gross for sharing his work on animals and animal rights with me. His illuminating dissertation "The Question of the Animal and Religion: Dietary Practices, Subjectivity and Ethics in Jewish Traditions" will hopefully be published in the near future.

36. Derrida, *Animal That Therefore I Am*, 29.

37. As Ernst Bloch notes, Thomasius, a scholar of natural law and "anti-wig in epitome," had "caused a sensation [*machte Furore*]," when he dared, in 1687, to announce at the University of Leipzig a lecture in German, rather than Latin. His fearless and methodical book against the prosecution of witches had caused the King of Prussia, Friedrich Wilhelm I, to make the prosecution of witches illegal in 1714. Cf. Ernst Bloch, *Christian Thomasius, ein deutscher Gelehrter ohne Misere* (1953; Frankfurt: Suhrkamp, 1967), 8, 13. Influenced by Thomasius, the Elector Friedrich I insisted in 1721 that "torture could only be applied after the monarch had consented to each particular case. . . . In 1754, all torture was abolished in Prussia, the earliest date of complete abolition in European history." Edward Peters, *Torture* (New York: Basic Blackwell, 1985), 90. See also 76 for Peters's brief mention of Thomasius.

38. *De tortura ex foris Christianorum proscribenda, Über die Folter, die aus den Gerichten der Christen verbannt werden muss.* Even though Thomasius contributed significantly to the abolition of torture in Prussia, a German translation of his treatise was published only in 1960: Christian Thom-

asius, *Über die Folter: Untersuchungen zur Geschichte der Folter*, ed. and trans. Rolf Lieberwirth (Weimar: Hermann Böhlaus Nachfolger, 1960). See also Uwe Wesel, "Das Fiasko des Strafrechts," *Die Zeit* 49 (2005).

39. Michel Foucault, *Discipline and Punish: The Birth of the Prison*, trans. Alan Sheridan (New York: Vintage 1979), 7.

40. One might see here evidence of a return to the old "spectacle" regime.

41. In Greek and Roman antiquity and in European countries inspired by Roman law, the standard procedure in criminal cases stipulated that the state had the right to punish only once the accused had confessed. In absence of a confession, the "queen of proof [*Confessio regina probationis*]," and in absence of two eyewitnesses of guilt or innocence, torture was applied. Thomasius denounces torture that targets the victim *before* any conviction of guilt, which Foucault comments on briefly under the name of judicial torture (Foucault, *Discipline and Punish*, 40–42). But the implications of Thomasius's critique also reach the practice of punitive torture as described in detail by Foucault, by which the convicted person was made to suffer a "thousand deaths" before his or her execution (12).

42. See Peters, *Torture*, 54–55.

43. Thomasius, *Über die Folter*, 122–23. In this edition, the Latin text (even-numbered pages) faces the German translation (uneven-numbered pages). In the following, pages from this text will be given in parentheses. As Thomasius specifies, Ludovicus Vives had made the same point. With Cicero and Ulpian (who nonetheless did not categorically oppose the use of torture) Thomasius notes that people who are tortured will end up confessing to anything the torturer wants to hear, and that this is precisely why one should not believe a testimony given under torture (122–23). On Cicero and Ulpian, see Werner Riess, "Die historische Entwicklung der römischen Folter- und Hinrichtungspraxis in kulturvergleichender Perspektive," *Historia: Zeitschrift für Alte Geschichte* 51, no. 2 (2002): 208.

44. Thomasius, *Über die Folter*, 118–19. "Oh what an all too godless twistedness/evilness [*perversitas*] in punishing! Is there anything more unjust?" Ibid.

45. Commenting on examples from the twentieth century, Elaine Scarry points out that calling the confession obtained under torture "betrayal" is nothing short of becoming complicit with the torturer: The implication that confessing torture victims are "traitors" perpetuates the destruction of their world that torture has caused. The "contempt" with which the collapse of the world of the victim is met becomes obvious in this word choice. Scarry also uses the concept of self-betrayal: "There is a second equally crucial and equally cruel bond between physical pain and interrogation that further explains their inevitable appearance together. Just as the interrogation, like the pain, is a way of wounding, so the pain, like the interrogation, is a vehicle of self-betrayal. Torture systematically prevents the prisoner from being an agent of anything and simultaneously pretends that he is the agent of some things." The "unseen sense of self-betrayal in pain" is "objectified in forced confession" and in "forced exercises that make the prisoner's body an active agent, an actual cause of his pain." Elaine Scarry, *The Body in Pain* (Oxford: Oxford University Press, 1985), 29–30, 47.

46. Peter Schröder, *Christian Thomasius zur Einführung* (Hamburg: Junius, 1999), 68.

47. For example, Thomasius, *Über die Folter*, 160: "*mortales.*"

48. See also ibid., 174–75: "Is it compatible with natural reason to force people to their own death?"

49. The German translation reads here simply "death [*zu ihrem eigenen Tod zu zwingen*]," but this translation is not precise enough. On the resonance of this "*Zerfleischen*" with Jean Améry's

"*Verfleischlichung*" ("fleshization" or "meatization"), see my "'Torture was the Essence of National Socialism': Reading Jean Améry Today," in *Speaking about Torture,* ed. Julie Carlson and Elisabeth Weber (New York: Fordham University Press, 2012).

50. Riess, "Die historische Entwicklung der römischen Folter- und Hinrichtungspraxis," 215n50. Riess sees here a parallel to the Roman "infamy" that followed certain punishments.

51. This is, of course, a counterargument to "living together we must," or, in any case, a modality of it which cannot be simply placed on a continuum and which calls for an investigation of its own.

52. In her seminal study *Torture and Truth*, Page duBois shows how already in Greek antiquity, the separation between slaves who could be "tortured" and "free men and women" who in principle could not, was constantly threatened and could not be sustained. Page duBois, *Torture and Truth* (New York: Routledge, 1991), 40–45, 62. See also Peters, *Torture*: "From the second half of the thirteenth century to the end of the eighteenth, torture was part of the ordinary criminal procedure of the Latin Church and of most of the states of Europe" (54). "By the end of the fifteenth century every man might be tortured, as the groundwork of early modern criminal law was firmly and professionally laid out" (62). Alfred McCoy convincingly traces the "slippery slope" from the hypothesis of "selective, surgical" use of torture of the few to "torture in general"; see, for example, *Question of Torture*, 190–95.

53. See also Foucault quoting Damhoudère's description of the executioner's cruelty towards the condemned man, exercising "'every cruelty with regard to the evil-doing patients, treating them, buffeting and killing them as if they had a beast in their hands'" (*Discipline and Punish*, 51).

54. See McCoy, *Question of Torture*, 157–60, and Darius Rejali, "Viewpoint: The Real Shame of Abu Ghraib." *Time*, May 20, 2004, http://www.time.com/time/nation/article/0,8599,640375,00.html.

55. Rejali, "Real Shame of Abu Ghraib."

56. Ibid.

57. Marc Nichanian, *The Historiographic Perversion*, trans. Gil Anidjar (New York: Columbia University Press, 2009), 118, 120–21.

58. Whereas in the U.S. "war on terror" the victims of torture have been almost exclusively Muslim men, it should be noted that the treatment of inmates of the U.S. prison system frequently also amounts to torture. The title of a recent "position paper" by the Center for Constitutional Rights on the "Death Row Experience from a Human Rights Perspective" bluntly summarizes the analyses presented in the document by asserting "The United States Tortures before It Kills" (http://ccrjustice.org/files/deathrow_torture_position_paper.pdf). However, conditions of torture are not limited to death row. Colin Dayan has shown that "the now-famous 'torture memos'" which "redefined the meaning of torture and extended the limits of permissible pain" actually "rely upon the last 30 years of court decisions, which have gradually eviscerated the Eighth Amendment's prohibition of 'cruel and unusual punishments'" (Colin Dayan, *The Story of Cruel and Unusual* [Cambridge: MIT Press, 2007], 5). The "realm of constitutional minimums—situated between mere need and bare survival," Dayan explains, "set the stage for Guantánamo Bay and Abu Ghraib. I recall the words of Marine Brigadier General Michael R. Lehnert at Guantánamo Bay in 2002: 'There is no torture, no whips, no bright lights, no drugging. We are a nation of laws.' But what kind of laws? Laws that permit indefinite solitary confinement in state-of-the-art units, with cell doors, unit doors, and shower doors operated remotely from a control center and physical contact limited to touching through a security door by a correctional officer while being placed in restraints. Inmates have described life in the massive, windowless super-maximum prison as akin to 'living in a tomb'" (53–54). Commenting on

solitary confinement, Dayan notes that "over the past two and a half decades, an intimate dialogue between courts and prison administrators has normalized what was once the most severe deprivation. The subject is couched in euphemisms: first 'disciplinary segregation,' and later 'administrative segregation' (nominally based on security classification rather than wrongdoing). Since prison officials claim that these units are non-punitive, they are difficult to fight under either the Eighth or the Fourteenth Amendments. Since the 1980s, the United Nations Commission on Human Rights, the United Nations Committee Against Torture, the Red Cross, human-rights organizations such as Amnesty International and Human Rights Watch, and civil-rights organizations such as the ACLU and the Center for Constitutional Rights, have criticized the darkly authoritarian and abusive conditions of prisons in the United States, focusing on super-maximum imprisonment, where inmates deemed incorrigible are locked down for 23 to 24 hours a day, their food delivered through a slot in the steel door of their 80-square-foot cell" (54–55). Most recently, in May 2011, the U.S. Supreme Court upheld a ruling by a panel of three federal judges holding that conditions in California's prisons amount to a violation of the Eighth Amendment ban on cruel and unusual punishment. The fifty-two-page court opinion, authored by Justice Kennedy, described among others the dismal conditions for mentally or physically ill inmates: "Prisoners in California with serious mental illness do not receive minimal, adequate care. Because of a shortage of treatment beds, suicidal inmates may be held for prolonged periods in telephone-booth-sized cages without toilets. A psychiatric expert reported observing an inmate who had been held in such a cage for nearly 24 hours, standing in a pool of his own urine, unresponsive and nearly catatonic. Prison officials explained they had 'no place to put him.' Other inmates awaiting care may be held for months in administrative segregation, where they endure harsh and isolated conditions and receive only limited mental health services. Wait times for mental health care range as high as 12 months. In 2006, the suicide rate in California's prisons was nearly 80% higher than the national average for prison populations; and a court-appointed Special Master found that 72.1% of suicides involved 'some measure of inadequate assessment, treatment, or intervention, and were therefore most probably foreseeable and/or preventable.' Prisoners suffering from physical illness also receive severely deficient care. California's prisons were designed to meet the medical needs of a population at 100% of design capacity and so have only half the clinical space needed to treat the current population. A correctional officer testified that, in one prison, up to 50 sick inmates may be held together in a 12- by 20-foot cage for up to five hours awaiting treatment. The number of staff is inadequate, and prisoners face significant delays in access to care. A prisoner with severe abdominal pain died after a 5-week delay in referral to a specialist; a prisoner with 'constant and extreme' chest pain died after an 8-hour delay in evaluation by a doctor; and a prisoner died of testicular cancer after a 'failure of MDs to work up for cancer in a young man with 17 months of testicular pain.' . . . Many prisoners, suffering from severe but not life-threatening conditions, experience prolonged illness and unnecessary pain" (Supreme Court of the United States, No. 09-1233, Edmund G. Brown Jr., Governor of California, et al., Appellants, *v.* Marciano Plata et al., on appeal from the United States District Courts for the Eastern Districts and the Northern Districts of California, http://www.supremecourt.gov/opinions/10pdf/09-1233.pdf, pp. 5–7). The opinion also quotes Doyle W. Scott, the former head of Texas prisons, who described "conditions in California's prisons as 'appalling,' 'inhumane,' and 'unacceptable' and stated that 'in more than 35 years of prison work experience, I have never seen anything like it'" (5).

59. Rejali, "Real Shame of Abu Ghraib."

60. Ibid.

61. Martin Hengel, "Crucifixion," in *The Cross of the Son of God*, trans. Jon Bowden (London: SCM Press, 1986), 116.

62. See, for example, ibid., 138. Hengel writes that only the Carthaginians "tended to crucify especially generals and admirals who had either been defeated or who proved too willful."

63. Darius Rejali, "Speak Frankly about Torture," http://academic.reed.edu/poli_sci/faculty /rejali/rejali/articles/Speak_Frankly.htm

64. Alfred McCoy, "The U.S. Has a History of Using Torture," George Mason University's History News Network, http://hnn.us/articles/32497.html; see also McCoy, *Question of Torture*, 129–30.

65. Hengel, "Crucifixion," 114. Hengel quotes sources that show that crucifixion was practiced among the Persians, Indians, Assyrians, Scythians, and later by the Greeks and Romans, whose historians were, however, "fond of stressing *barbarian* crucifixions, and playing down their own use of this form of execution" (115).

66. See for example McCoy, *A Question of Torture*, 130. For the CIA "torture paradigm" see above, 246.

67. Avital Ronell, *Finitude's Score: Essays for the End of the Millennium* (Lincoln: University of Nebraska Press, 1994), 269, 272.

68. Scott Higham and Joe Stephens, "New Details of Prison Abuse Emerge: Abu Ghraib Detainees' Statements Describe Sexual Humiliation and Savage Beatings," *Washington Post*, May 21, 2004, A01, http://www.washingtonpost.com/ac2/wp-dyn/A43783-2004May20.

69. See, for example, Rosa Brooks, "America Tortures (Yawn)," *Los Angeles Times*, February 23, 2007, http://www.latimes.com/news/printedition/asection/la-oe-brooks23feb23,0,6991987.column. See also Maura Moynihan, "Torture Chic: Why Is the Media Glorifying Inhumane, Sadistic Behavior?" *AlterNet*, February 3, 2009, http://www.alternet.org/rights/124739/.

70. This idea is developed in Derrida's *Rogues* and *Politics of Friendship*. See Jacques Derrida, *Rogues: Two Essays on Reason*, trans. Pascale-Anne Brault and Michael Naas (Stanford, Calif.: Stanford University Press 2005), 92, and *Politics of Friendship*, 1–24, 99–106.

71. According to the website of Human Rights First, the number of scenes of torture on TV shows has significantly increased between 1995 and 2005 (with a peak in 2003). Perhaps most important, "The characters who torture have changed. It used to be that only villains on television tortured. Today, 'good guys' and heroic American characters torture—and this torture is depicted as necessary, effective and even patriotic." The website also features interviews with former interrogators and retired military leaders, who deplore "that the portrayal of torture in popular culture is having an undeniable impact on how interrogations are conducted in the field." U.S. soldiers are "imitating the techniques they have seen on television—because they think such tactics work," in stark contrast to trained interrogators' experience. See http: //www.humanrightsfirst.org/us_law /etn/primetime/index.asp.

72. Derrida, "Autoimmunity," 117.

73. See Ronell, *Finitude's Score*, 269, 272.

74. Talal Asad, "Horror at Suicide Terrorism," in *On Suicide Bombing* (New York: Columbia University Press, 2007), 84, 86.

75. Ibid., 86. Regarding our "secular age," see Gil Anidjar's analysis, summarized in this succinct formulation: "Secularism is a name Christianity gave itself when it invented 'religion,' named its other or others as 'religions'" (Gil Anidjar, *Semites: Race, Religion, Literature* [Stanford, Calif.: Stanford University Press, 2008], 48).

## Michal Govrin, *From Jerusalem to Jerusalem—A Dedication*

1. The essay is based on a lecture with this title given at the Levinas-Derrida Conference, organized by Raphael Orly-Zagori and Joseph Cohen, June 1, 2008, in Tel Aviv.

2. Jacques Derrida, "Che Cos'è La Poesia?" in *Poesia* (1988). Hebrew translation by Michal Govrin: "Mahi Shira?" *Hadarim* 9 (1990): 47–50. It was the first translation into Hebrew of any of Derrida's texts, the selection was his own.

3. Paul Celan, "The Poles [*Die Pole*]," in *Poems of Paul Celan*, trans. Michael Hamburger (New York: Persea Books, 1989), 345.

4. Derrida, *Adieu à Emmanuel Levinas* (Paris: Galilée, 1997); *Adieu to Emmanuel Levinas*, trans. Pascale-Anne Brault and Michael Naas (Stanford, Calif.: Stanford University Press, 1999).

5. Regarding Emmanuel Levinas's influence and my intensive meetings with him in the mid-1970s about my creative work, see Michal Govrin, "Literary Reverberations of the Zohar," in *New Developments in Zohar Studies*, ed. Ronit Meroz (Tel Aviv: Tel Aviv University, 2007), 23–52.

6. Author's note: Is this a reminder of the passage from Psalms: "Our feet stand at your gates Jerusalem"?

7. Derrida, *Adieu to Emmanuel Levinas,* 101; *Adieu à Emmanuel Levinas*, 177.

8. It was David Brezis who took me to Jacques Derrida's seminar at ENS (École Normale Supérieure) in the summer of 1979. Brezis's thought and our conversations over the years opened before me in greater depth both deconstruction and its philosophical and exegetical contexts.

9. Exodus 20:4 and Deuteronomy 5:8, King James Version.

10. Through reading the interpretations of the Talmud and Rashi of these verses and of the scene of God's self-revelation to Moses in Exodus 33:7–23, I followed the shift from image to a revelation through language and letters. The debate continued in my essay "Jewish Ritual as a Genre of Sacred Theater," *Conservative Judaism* 36, no. 3 (1983), and in Jacques Derrida's *Ulysse gramophone* (Paris: Galilée, 1987).

11. In several places Derrida mistakenly dates this visit to 1982, and conflates it as one continuous signifier with his arrest in Prague.

12. Jacques Derrida, *D'un ton apocalyptique adopté naguère en philosophie* (Paris: Galilée, 1983).

13. Michal Govrin, "Chant d'Outre-Tombe," in *Le Passage des frontières, Autour du travail de Jacques Derrida, Colloque de Cerisy* (Paris: Galilée, 1994). In the exchange of letters between Ilana Shmueli and Celan during the last months of his life, obscurities are revealed that add considerably to what was veiled in the poems.

Paul Celan and Ilana Shmueli, *Correspondance 1965–1970*, trans. Bertrand Badiou (Paris: Editions du Seuil, 2006).

14. Michal Govrin, *The Name* [HaShem], trans. Barbara Harshav (New York: Riverhead, 1998).

15. Pinchas Govrin, *We Were Like Dreamers* [Hayinu Kekholmim] (Jerusalem: Carmel, 2005).

16. The parable, as it first fell into my hands, in the adaptation of Martin Buber, in *The Hidden Light* [Or HaGanuz] (Jerusalem: Schocken, 1971), 95–96.

Before blowing the shofar the Baal Shem Tov said:

There was a King who was very wise and built around his palace many barriers one before another, something to behold, dug moats between each wall, lodged bears and lions and a host of other frightening beasts there so that people would be frightened of coming near him. The King commanded that great fortunes be scattered before the gates of the walls. And messengers went out to say that anyone who comes to the King will be granted wealth and honor by the King. Many of the citizens of the state came and wanted to go in. Some came to the first gate and saw all the frightening things and fell back. And there was one who got in and found money and when he saw before him the terrible walls went home to enjoy his money. But the one who loved the King paid no mind to any of these, for his heart overflowed to see the King's countenance. And when he stood up to leap over the walls and moats he noticed that they were all illusions, and there the King was sitting before him on his throne and reaching out his hand toward him.

17. Govrin, "Chant d'outre tombe," 236.

18. Emphasis mine on "say."

19. From a recording of oral remarks by Jacques Derrida.

20. As I'll evoke later, it is in the book *Adieu à Emmanuel Levinas* that Derrida further addresses the erotic feminine aspect of Jerusalem that was opened during this session.

21. Jacques Derrida, *Psyché: inventions de l'autre* (Paris: Galilée, 1987), 546; Jacques Derrida, "How to Avoid Speaking: Denials," trans. Ken Frieden, in *Derrida and Negative Theology*, ed. Harold G. Coward and Toby Foshay (Albany: State University of New York Press, 1992), 83.

22. Stéphane Moses, trans., "Une lettre de Gershom Scholem à Franz Rosenzweig, Jérusalem, le 7 Teweth 5687 [12 December 1926]," *Archives de Sciences Sociales et Religieuses* 60/61 (1985); G. Scholem, "Thoughts about Our Language," in *On the Possibility of Jewish Mysticism* (Philadelphia: Jewish Publication Society, 1997).

23. Emphasis mine. Derrida, ". . . la voie apocalyptique sur laquelle nous sommes de toute façon engagés . . ." *Les yeux de la langue, L'abîme et le volcan, Magazine Littéraire* 430 (2004): 45.

24. Michal Govrin and Lillian Kalpisch (illustrator), *The Making of the Sea, A Chronicle of Exegesis* (Jerusalem: Carmel, 2000). Also published in Yoram Merose, *"Forbidden Game,"* trans. Peter Cole, Ramat Gan Museum Catalogue, 1993.

The address in Hebrew leads to the described journey back to Jerusalem:

The Turning toward you in speech, you, now. (Written at a height of thirty five thousand feet, less place than a place of motion, a place of hovering, erased as it comes into being). The turning toward you from within the hovering, the unfolding of distance, the tension which is splayed, the longing that decides, which is spread, which is now being made explicit between us, me and you.

The turning toward you from behind the curtain. Explicitly, masculine of feminine, in a Hebrew that instantly determines its addressee—*att* or *atta*, female or male.

The turning toward you in Hebrew, *Ivrit*, a language wholly encased in a crossing, *ma'avar*, in what lies across, *me'ever*, in a division inscribed between the two banks of the Jordan—that fine line, almost dry, of the mythical river that distinguishes at once between the nations and Israel.

The turning toward you in Hebrew, a language whose being is wholly a crossing, or passage, a distance—the very passage, in the forcing of the voice through the straits of silence, already implying the cancellation of distance, *korban haKirva*, an offering on inwardness, of nearness, a burning.

(Again and again returning, like waves, the memory of border, the separation, the cut and the hovering, the wound at the place of departure.)

. . . The turning toward you while hovering, for there, in the question of turning through language, the passage, or direction of motion is almost blurred—the wash of the waves or their ebbing—what's commonly seen as the manner of man or the manner of woman, penetration or reception. A bisexual sense of address in reception. In the turning aside of the head, in receiving the offering, the inwardness, the burning, *korban*, the near, *kirvah*.

. . . And in other words, the place. The longing for it or from it, the turning toward, and from, the place. The longing for impossible entrance or the surrendering to the already present, in each place, from creation.

The turning which is unfolding (meaning, surrendering) at the place of the fold (the pain) at the moment of consecration, The place of pain and consecration, The covenant's pieces. The blood's birth.

25. Michal Govrin, *Snapshots* [Hevzekim], trans. Barbara Harshav (New York: Riverhead, 2008).

26. In my lecture at Tel Aviv I quoted the Hebrew translation by Michal Ben Naftali of the essay "Avowing—The Impossible"; the translation was made at my request for a book in preparation titled *From Jerusalem to Jerusalem*. I am grateful to Michal Ben Naftali not only for the translation but for a unique journey *à deux*—if not *à trois*.

27. Catherine Malabou and Jacques Derrida, *Jacques Derrida, La contre-allée*, (Paris: Quinzaine littéraire-Louis Vuitton, 1999), 259–61; *Counterpath: Traveling with Jacques Derrida* (Stanford, Calif.: Stanford University Press, 2004), 263–67.

28. An expression used by Nechama Gesser in the Lacanian seminar "Why Jerusalem?" held in Mishkenot Sha'ananim, Jerusalem, in 2007. An attitude dividing Israeli culture, symbolized as an "opposition between Tel Aviv and Jerusalem." (Its echoes are expressed in the poem "Who's Afraid of Jerusalem," which is the opening of my *And So Said Jerusalem, Poems and Hymns* [Amra Yerushalaim, Mizmorim VeShirim], trans. Betsy Rosenberg (Jerusalem: Devarim/Carmel, 2008).

29. Malabou and Derrida, *Counterpath*, 15.

30. Ibid., 21–23. Without entering into the required discussion here regarding the identity of the Derrida's "marrano," I will merely note the tension between the gaze from without and the personal identification. Further on, in a confessional tone, Derrida describes being torn between anticipation of the "event" and terror lest it arrive.

31. Derrida, *Adieu to Emmanuel Levinas*, 185–86. Also relevant is 149n114:

This verse is re-translated, interpreted, reinscribed and meditated upon in *Chant d'Outre Tombe* by Michal Govrin, in order to introduce [in particular] a reading of Celan's "Jerusalem" ("*sag, dass Jerusalem ist*").... A passion that has not let go of the West for some twenty-five centuries. The passion to conquer this city-woman-wound. A passionate madness ... the desire to be in Jerusalem, to possess her.... The desire to be the conqueror of Jerusalem, her sole possessor and lover, this exclusive passion might have as its origin and model the God of the Bible: "Get up, Lord, so as to go into your *place of repose*.... For the Eternal *has made his choice* in Zion. He *desired* it as his dwelling. This will be my *place of repose for ever*. There I will dwell for I *lusted* [*ivitiha*] after her."

For the mytho-theological key to understanding the roots of the conflict over the possession of Jerusalem see also Govrin, *The Name, Snapshots*, and "Martyrs and Survivors? Thoughts on the Mythical Dimension of the Story War," *Partisan Review* (2003): www.michalgovrin.com/English /essays; "Martyres et survivants? Réflexion sur la dimension mythique de la 'guerre pour l'histoire,'" *Temps Modernes* 634 (2003): www.michalgovrin.com/French. (The translation of the concept "The Story War" in the title of the essay [*la guerre pour histoire*] was made in consultation with Jacques Derrida during his last visit to Jerusalem.)

32. David Shapiro et al., *Body of Prayer: Written Words, Voices* (New York: Irwin S. Chanin School of Architecture of the Cooper Union, 2001).

33. Ibid., 65.

34. Ibid., 87, 89.

35. Frederic Brenner, *Diaspora: Homelands in Exile* (New York: Harper Collins, 2003), 19. It is also interesting to note how much the Hassidic courts of Mea She'arim are usually perceived in Israeli secular consciousness as places of violence and exclusion.

36. See *Judéités: Questions pour Jacques Derrida*, ed. J. Cohen and R. Zagury-Orly (Paris: Galilée, 2003), partially translated as *Judeites: Questions for Jacques Derrida*, ed. B. Bergo, J. Cohen and R. Zagury-Orly, trans. B. Bergo and M. Smith (New York: Fordham University Press, 2007).

37. I hope this debate will be transcribed and published in the future.

38. A description of the event first published in Michal Govrin, "An Open Contradiction, with No Ending, or Conclusion," *Haaretz*, October 22, 2004.

39. Jean Halperin, *Comment vivre ensemble? Actes du xxxvii Colloque des intellectuels juifs de langue française* (Paris: Michel, 2001).

### Richard Falk, *How to Live Together Well: Interrogating the Israel/Palestine Conflict*

I thank Giovanna Borradori for her encouragement, and for valuable conceptual and editorial advice, particularly her willingness to share an extensive awareness and clear comprehension of the Derrida corpus.

1. What is meant here is that both Israelis and Palestinians must demonstrate as much or more of a commitment to an outcome of the conflict that would be experienced as fair and respectful by the other side than to obtaining advantages for their own side. Without this encompassing mutuality there is no possibility of real peace between the two peoples. It is more essential for Israel, as the occupier and oppressor, to manifest such a dramatic change of heart, which will be initially difficult for the Palestinians to comprehend as credible. Admittedly, satisfying this requirement may make peace appear unattainable, and that may be the only truthful assessment, given the hold of Machiavellian realism on the political imagination. Does that mean that an outcome less than "peace" should be automatically dismissed?

2. An important ambiguity, not commented on by Derrida, should be taken into account throughout this chapter. References to "Israelis" and to "Israel" tend to suggest a monolithic reality that obscures a spectrum of Jewish attitudes (including toward a variety of Zionisms), and more important, the reality that 20 percent of the population of pre-1967 Israel is Palestinian, and has been living as a second-class, discriminated, and mainly alienated minority in a self-proclaimed Jewish state. Such conditions are themselves incompatible with Articles 26 and 27 of the International Covenant of Civil and Political Rights. It should also be emphasized that the conditions that exist at present should not be treated as symmetrical in assessing the burdens of the conflict on Israelis and Palestinians living under occupation. In every material, political, and psychological sense conditions are grossly unequal to the disadvantage of the Palestinians, which is particularly true given the unlawful character of an occupation that has gone on since 1967, entailing severe encroachment on fundamental human rights.

3. Giovanna Borradori, *Philosophy in a Time of Terror: Dialogues with Jürgen Habermas and Jacques Derrida* (Chicago: University of Chicago Press, 2003), 117.

4. Ibid., 117–18n1; I would personally question whether Israel, given its increasingly harsh approach to internal dissent and to its Palestinian minority, deserves the characterization of "another democracy," although the inverted quotes in the Derrida text suggests an intention to question whether the Israeli claim to be the only democracy in the Middle East is to be accepted at face value.

5. Ibid., 118.

6. Such a formulation deliberately indicts the search for inauthentic peace of the kind now being proposed under the banner of a "two-state solution" that somehow embeds fundamental inequality and denial of rights in a structure called "peace." This inequality is exhibited by the subordinated and conditional sovereignty of a future Palestinian state as compared to the dominant and unconditionally sovereign Israeli state, and by the permanent consignment of the 1.3 million Palestinian minority in Israel to second-class citizenship, and by the denial of rights to Palestinians living as refugees or in exile. As Edward Said has pointed out, the Abrahamic formulation often excludes Islam, and implicitly claims moral hegemony for the Judeo-Christian tradition, making it easier to overlook the elemental claims of Palestinians for respect of their fundamental rights. This discriminatory outlook is reinforced by overlooking Christian Palestinians, a significant minority, and regarding the Palestinians as Muslim and Arab, thereby pandering to Western, and particularly American, prejudices that have intensified in the post-9/11 political environment.

7. A variation on "the security dilemma" is depicted by Robert Jervis in *Perception and Misperception in International Politics* (Princeton, N.J.: Princeton University Press, 1976), 58–116.

8. Best articulated by Henry Siegman, "Imposing Middle East Peace," *Nation*. January 25, 2010, 18–20; but see Meron Benvenisti, "The Case for Shared Sovereignty," *Nation*, June 18, 2007, 11–16.

9. It is not a word game to insist that the impossible is necessary. It is a way of criticizing conventional endorsements of a two-state solution as an outcome that would not bring peace, and at this stage, given Israeli policies associated with the settler movement enacted for more than forty years and a cumulative effort at ethnic cleansing in East Jerusalem, the preconditions for a viable Palestinian sovereign state are missing, even if the Israeli political will existed, which is not the case. Impossible is meant here not in the Derridean positive sense, but in a negative sense of pretending that there exists a correspondence between the words "two-state solution" and "an end of the conflict."

10. It was the Holocaust, as perceived at the end of World War II, which generated the sovereignty-transcending idea of "Crimes against Humanity," which represents a large move to curb the absolutist pretensions of Westphalian modernity. For Derrida's comment on this development see *Philosophy in a Time of Terror*, 132–33; for Habermas's comment see ibid., 38.

11. The provenance of the reference to perpetual peace is, of course, to Kant's famous essay bearing that name, but also conveyed with a subtle irony of Kant's given his association of the name with an innkeeper's sign, which promises a different form of "perpetual peace."

12. Borradori, *Philosophy in a Time of Terror*, 119.

13. For a subtle and sophisticated inquiry into the ethics and politics of assassination in the context of Gandhi see Ashis Nandy, "Final Encounter: The Politics of the Assassination of Gandhi," in *At the Edge of Psychology: Essays in Politics and Culture* (Bombay, India: Oxford University Press, 1990), 70–98.

14. I have argued frequently to this effect. See Richard Falk, "International Law and the Peace Process," *Hastings International and Comparative Law Review* 28, no. 3 (2005): 331–48.

15. As has been often noted, the Palestinians, along with the Arab countries bordering Israel, rejected the UN partition plan, contending that the imposition of a Jewish homeland was unacceptable and colonialist.

16. For an excellent study of the evolution of the conflict, which confirms the impression that the Palestinian side was victimized in terms of rights and reasonable expectations at every stage, see Victor Kattan, *From Coexistence to Conquest: International Law and the Origins of the Arab-Israeli Conflict, 1891–1949* (London: Pluto, 2009).

17. For Edward Said's still influential views, which have a certain prophetic character, having been largely vindicated by subsequent events, see *The End of the Peace Process* (New York: Pantheon, 2000).

18. Frantz Fanon, *The Wretched of the Earth* (Harmondsworth, UK: Penguin, 1967); Haunani-Kay Trask, *From a Native Daughter: Colonialism and Sovereignty in Hawaii* (Monroe, Maine: Common Courage Press, 1993).

19. Widely read authors such as Sam Harris, *The End of Faith: Religion, Terror, and the Future* (New York: Norton, 2004), and Christopher Hitchens, *God Is Not Great: How Religion Poisons Everything* (New York: Twelve, 2007) have reinforced the tendency to demonize religion and to treat religion as reducible to its extremist embodiments.

20. For my attempt to portray this dual face of religion see Richard Falk, *Religion and Humane Global Governance* (New York: Palgrave, 2001); for an impressive grappling with these issues see Nader Hashemi, *Islam, Secularism, and Liberal Democracy* (Oxford: Oxford University Press, 2009).

21. For representative critical reflections from Jewish and Muslim perspectives see Marc H. Ellis, *Israel and Palestine out of the Ashes: The Search for Jewish Identity in the Twenty-First Century* (London: Pluto, 2002); Chandra Muzaffar, ed., *Religion and Global Governance* (Kuala Lumpur: Arah Publications, 2008).

22. Politics is being conceived here as the art of the possible, a rationalistic calculation resting on some sort of agreed bargain that is not receptive to nor particularly concerned about considerations based on empathy or equity.

23. I did witness in 2005 a revealing acknowledgment by an important actor, the former British Prime Minister John Major, who at a private breakfast in London contended that significant progress in conflict resolution occurred only after he and others treated the IRA as a political actor rather than a terrorist organization; he contrasted such an approach with the demonization of al-Qaeda by George W. Bush in the aftermath of the 9/11 attacks.

24. Such a posture has been made easier to adopt by Hamas's 2006 electoral victory in Gaza combined with its continual proposals for a long-term cease-fire with an implied acceptance of a sovereign Israel with 1967 borders.

25. Borradori, *Philosophy in a Time of Terror,* 116–17.

26. See Saree Makdisi, *Palestine Inside Out: An Everyday Occupation* (New York: Norton, 2008), 263–98 especially; Virginia Tilley, *The One-State Solution: A Breakthrough for Peace in the Israeli-Palestinian Deadlock* (Ann Arbor: University of Michigan Press, 2005); Ali Abinimah, *One Country: A Bold Proposal to End the Israeli-Palestinian Impasse* (New York: Metropolitan, 2006).

27. Here, Derrida follows and extends the thinking of Walter Benjamin in his "Critique of Violence," in *Selected Writings,* vol. 1: *1913–1926,* trans. Edmund Jephcott (Cambridge, Mass.: Belknap Press of Harvard University Press, 1996).

28. For general insight into this political perspective see Mary Kaldor, *Global Civil Society: An Answer to War* (Cambridge, UK: Polity, 2001); see also Richard Falk on globalization from below in *Predatory Globalization: A Critique* (Cambridge: Polity, 1999).

29. Howard Zinn, *A People's History of the United States: 1492–Present* (New York: Harper-Collins, 2003); Eric Wolf, *Europe and the People without History* (Berkeley: University of California Press, 1982).

30. Although initiated in 2005, BDS (that is, the boycott, divestment, and sanctions movement) has become a serious challenge to Israel after the Gaza attacks at the end of 2009. See http://www.bdsmovement.net for information.

31. The Geneva Accord or Geneva Initiative was a comprehensive unofficial text of a peace agreement prepared by prominent Israelis and Palestinians, released in 2003. The Israeli participants were viewed as much further removed from government policy than were the Palestinians who took part; see Dennis Ross, *The Missing Peace: The Inside Story of the Fight for Middle East Peace* (New York: Farrar, Straus and Giroux, 2004).

32. See Nassim Nicholas Talib, *The Black Swan: The Impact of the Highly Improbable*, 2nd ed. (New York: Random House, 2010).

# Contributors

**Jacques Derrida** (1930–2004) was Directeur d'Études at the École des Hautes Études en Sciences Sociales, Paris, and Professor of Humanities at the University of California, Irvine. Among the more than sixty books he authored are *Of Grammatology* (1976), *Writing and Difference* (1978), *Margins of Philosophy* (1984), *Of Spirit: Heidegger and the Question* (1989), *Specters of Marx* (1993), *Politics of Friendship* (1997), *Adieu: To Emmanuel Levinas* (1999), *Acts of Religion* (ed. Gil Anidjar, 2002), *Rogues: Two Essays on Reason* (2004), *Sovereignties in Question: The Poetics of Paul Celan* (2005), *The Animal That Therefore I Am* (2008), *The Beast and the Sovereign, Volumes I and II* (2009 and 2012).

**Gil Anidjar** teaches in the Religion Department and in Middle Eastern, South Asian, and African Studies at Columbia University. He edited Jacques Derrida's *Acts of Religion* (2002).

**Ellen T. Armour** holds the E. Rhodes and Leona B. Carpenter Chair in Feminist Theology at Vanderbilt Divinity School. She is the author of *Deconstruction, Feminist Theology, and the Problem of Difference: Subverting the Race/Gender Divide* (1999) and coeditor of *Bodily Citations: Judith Butler and Religion* (2006), as well as a number of articles and book chapters. Her current book project, tentatively titled "Signs and Wonders: Theology after Modernity," will diagnose and craft a theological response to the shifts in our understanding of "man" and "his" others (sexed/raced, animal, and divine) as modernity declines.

**Michal Ben-Naftali** is a writer, a translator, and an editor of the series "The French" for the publishing house Hakibbutz Hameuchad. She lectures at Tel Aviv University, at the Bezalel and the Hamidrasha Schools for the Arts. Her books include *Chronicle of Separation* (2000), *The Visitation of Hannah Arendt* (2006), *Childhood, a Book—A Novella* (2007), *On Retreat: Four Essays* (2009), and *Spirit* (2012). Among her translations are *Derrida Reads Shakespeare* (2007); *The Gift of Death* by Jacques Derrida (2008); *Love Stories* by Julia Kristeva (2006); *Nadja* by André Breton (2007); *Blanchot Anthology—The Book to Come, The Literary Space* (2011). She received the Prime Minister's Prize for Israeli Authors in 2007 and the Haaretz Prize for the best essay in 2008.

**A. R. Bjerke** works on Christian theology and modern continental philosophy. She received her PhD in Religious Studies from University of California, Santa Barbara, in 2012.

Her dissertation compares theories of intuition in William of Ockham and Immanuel Kant. Her other interests include feminist theory, Hegel, and contemporary animal studies.

**Richard Falk** is the UN Human Rights Council's Special Rapporteur for the Occupied Palestinian Territories. He is Albert G. Milbank Professor of International Law Emeritus at Princeton University, and since 2002, Research Professor of Global and International Studies at the University of California, Santa Barbara. He also directs a project titled "Global Climate Change, Human Security, and Democracy" under the auspices of the Orfaela Center at UCSB. He was Chair of the Board of the Nuclear Age Peace Foundation until the end of 2011. Among his recent books are *The Great Terror War* (2003), *The Decline of World Order* (2004), *Achieving Human Rights* (2009), and *The Path to Zero* (2012).

**Michal Govrin** is a novelist, poet, and theater director. She is the academic chair of the Theater Department of the Emunah College in Jerusalem and a visiting professor at Tel Aviv University. Among the pioneers of Jewish experimental theater, Govrin has directed award-winning performances in all the major theaters in Israel. Govrin has published ten books of poetry and fiction. In 2010 she was selected by the Salon du Livre of Paris as one of the most influential writers of the past thirty years. *Body of Prayer* (2000) was printed in New York under the coauthorship of Jacques Derrida and David Shapiro. Among her novels, *The Name* (*HaShem*) (1995) received the Kugel Literary Prize in Israel and was nominated for the Koret Jewish Book Award in its English translation (1998; 1999). *Snapshots* (*Hevzekim*) (2002) was awarded the 2003 Acum Prize for the Best Literary Achievement of the Year, and was published in English and French translations. Govrin's other books include *Hold on to the Sun: Stories and Legends* (1984), three books of poetry, and *And So Said Jerusalem: Hymns and Poems*, with original drawings by Orna Millo (2008). An anthology of her short stories, poetry and personal essays, *Hold On to the Sun, True Stories and Tales*, edited by Judith G. Miller with a long interview, was published in 2010.

**Atar Hadari** was born in Israel, raised in England, and trained as an actor and writer at the University of East Anglia before studying poetry and playwrighting with Derek Walcott at Boston University. His *Songs from Bialik: Selected Poems of Hayim Nahman Bialik* (2000) was a finalist for the American Literary Translators' Association Award; his poems have won the Daniel Varoujan award from New England Poetry Club, a Petra Kenney award, and the Paumanok poetry award, and have appeared in *Poetry, American Poetry Review,* the *TLS,* and other journals.

**Kevin Hart** is Chairman and Edwin B. Kyle Professor of Christian Studies in the Department of Religious Studies at the University of Virginia. He also holds courtesy professorships in the Departments of English and French. In addition, he is Eric D'Arcy Professor of Philosophy at the Australian Catholic University. Among his recent scholarly books are

*Jean-Luc Marion: The Essential Writings* (2012), *Clandestine Encounters: Philosophy in the Narratives of Maurice Blanchot* (2010), and *The Exorbitant: Emmanuel Levinas between Jews and Christians* (2010). His collections of poetry are *Flame Tree: Selected Poems* (2002), *Young Rain* (2008), and *Morning Knowledge* (2011).

**Dana Hollander** is Associate Professor in the Department of Religious Studies at McMaster University, where she is also an associate member of the Department of Philosophy and a member of the MA Program in Cultural Studies and Critical Theory. Her research areas are recent European philosophy, modern Jewish thought, and German-Jewish studies. Her book *Exemplarity and Chosenness: Rosenzweig and Derrida on the Nation of Philosophy* (2008) presents an account of Derrida's philosophy that is centered on his explorations of the relationship of cultural particularity and philosophical universality, including those that concern the question of Jewishness. Her current project is on ethics, law, and "the neighbor" in the works of Hermann Cohen.

**Priya Kumar** is Associate Professor in the English department at the University of Iowa, where she teaches postcolonial studies and South Asian literature. She is the author of *Limiting Secularism: The Ethics of Coexistence in Indian Literature and Film* (2008), which considers the fraught question of religious coexistence in post-Partition India and its entanglement with the concept of secularism. Informed by Jacques Derrida's work on hospitality and living together, *Limiting Secularism* examines literary and cinematic narratives that direct us to the possibility of an ethical relationship with those who have been rendered outside the conditional circles of religious community and nation. Kumar has also published essays on the Partition of the Indian subcontinent, on South Asian literature, and on Hindi cinema. Currently, she is working on a second book project on cross-border migrations within the Indian subcontinent. She has also coedited a special issue of the *South Asian Review* on diaspora.

**Joseph Massad** is Associate Professor of modern Arab politics and intellectual history at Columbia University. He is the author of *Colonial Effects: The Making of National Identity in Jordan* (2001), *The Persistence of the Palestinian Question: Essays on Zionism and the Palestinians* (2006), and *Desiring Arabs* (2007). An earlier version of his essay in this volume has appeared in French under the title "*Oublier le sémitisme*" in his book *La persistance de la question palestinienne* (2009).

**Marc Nichanian** was Professor of Armenian Studies at Columbia University from 1996 to 2007 and is currently Visiting Professor at Sabanci University, Istanbul, in the Department of Cultural Studies. As editor of the Armenian language series *GAM*, a philosophical review, he published six volumes from 1980 to 2005. His recent publications in French include *La Perversion historiographique* (2006; translated into English by Gil Anidjar under the title *The Historiographic Perversion*, 2008), and a three-volume study, *Entre l'art et le témoignage* (2006–8), on Armenian literature in the twentieth century, of which the first volume is also available in English: *Writers of Disaster* (2002). He has translated Walter Benjamin, Friedrich Nietzsche, Ernst Jünger, Maurice Blanchot, Jean-Luc Nancy, among others, into Armenian. The series of five lectures he gave in 2009 in Istanbul has been published in Turkish translation: *Edebiyat ve Felaket* (Literature and Catastrophe, 2011).

**William Robert** is Assistant Professor in the Department of Religion at Syracuse University. He is the author of *Trials: Of Antigone and Jesus* (2010).

**Sherene Seikaly** is Assistant Professor of History at the American University in Cairo, coeditor of the *Arab Studies Journal* and cofounder and coeditor of *Jadaliyya*. She was the Qatar Postdoctoral Fellow at Georgetown University (2007–8) and Postdoctoral Fellow at the Middle East in Europe Program at the Wissenschaftskolleg zu Berlin (2008–9). Situated at the intersections of studies on consumption, political economy, and colonialism, Seikaly's manuscript in progress, "Meatless Days: Consumption and Capitalism in Wartime Palestine," explores economic thought, economic management, and consumption as key sites of subject formation. It traces how Palestinian businessmen, Palestinian reformers, and British colonial officials shaped new understandings and experiences of the "healthy" economy, home, and body.

**Elisabeth Weber** teaches German and Comparative Literature at the University of California, Santa Barbara. She is the author of *Verfolgung und Trauma: Zu Emmanuel Levinas' Autrement qu'être ou au-delà de l'essence* (1990), and the editor of *Questioning Judaism* (2004). She has edited several works by Jacques Derrida and has translated into German texts by Jacques Derrida, Emmanuel Levinas, and Félix Guattari. Together with Julie Carlson, she is coeditor of *Speaking about Torture* (2012).

**Raef Zreik** graduated from Hebrew University, where he earned his LLB and LLM. For many years, he was a practicing lawyer and political activist within the Palestinian community in Israel. In 2001 he earned a second LLM from Columbia Law School, and in 2007 an SJD degree from Harvard Law School. His dissertation deals with Kant's concept of right and the distinction between right and virtue. Currently he teaches jurisprudence and property law at Carmel Academic Center, Haifa, and serves as codirector of the Minerva Center for the Humanities at Tel Aviv University. His fields of research and writing include legal and political theory, citizenship and identity, and Israel-Palestine issues.

# Index

Abdülhamīd, 192
Abraham: circumcision of, 53; ethic of, 126; forgiveness for, 39–40, 126; hospitality by, 157; memory of, 61, 69–70; messianism of, 75; as Orientalist, 71–72, 79; in Qur'an, 71; religions of, 69–72, 135–36; sacrifice by, 5–8, 14, 21, 34–36, 131, 136, 155, 182, 215, 221–22
Abraham, Nicolas, 172, 328n20
"Absence and Negation" (conference), 266
Abu Ghraib prison, 13, 246, 251–52, 255–56, 258, 346n58
activism, 14–15, 104–5, 116, 118, 244, 254
"Acts of Genre" (Bennington, Derrida), 134
*Acts of Religion* (Anidjar), 306n8
*Adieu to Emmanuel Levinas* (Derrida), 49, 55, 117, 123, 213, 222, 261, 269, 274, 315n42, 316n47, 350n20, 351n31
Akbar, 89, 96, 98, 310n44
Algeria, 1, 9, 27, 29, 128, 138
"Ambiguities of Mourning" (Sanders), 207–9
Amir, Yigal, 282
amnesty, conditions for, 195–96
"Amnistie et pardon: Pour une ligne de partage entre éthique et politique (Cassin), 195
*Among the Ruins* (Essayan), 206–7
"And So Said Jerusalem" (Govrin, M.), 259–60, 349n1
Anidjar, Gil, 70–72, 74, 90, 93, 136, 303n49, 306n5, 306n8, 338n5
animals, mistreatment of, 13, 33, 251, 344n31, 344n33, 344n35
*Antigone* (Sophocles), 192, 207, 209–10, 335n34

anti-Semitism, 54–55, 267; compatibility of, 57–58; as exclusion, 14; historiography of, 62, 64–68; persecution as, 128, 301n4; Zionism and, 50, 58, 61, 66
apartheid, 1, 24, 33, 77, 118, 194–95, 227, 289, 316n53, 337n1
*aparthood*, of community, 12, 227, 337n1
aporias: avowals of, 26, 126; of forgiveness, 6, 8–9, 126; impossibility of, 15, 181; of justice, 250; of living together, 224–25, 227, 250; of prayer, 12; of responsibility, 141–42; by singular and universal, 174–75
Aquinas, 181
Arab Revolt (1936–1939), 233
Arabs: depiction of, 68; Jews and, 90, 109, 307n25; Muslims and, 60; Orientalism for, 67–68; as Saracens, 62, 302n10, 304n52; as Semites, 63, 65, 68
Arafat, Yasser, 291
archive, as site of memory, 52–56, 204, 297n6
*Archive Fever* (Derrida), 14, 46–49, 52–53, 55, 57–58, 297n5, 297n8, 300n41
Arendt, Hannah, 62–66, 218, 224
Aristotle, 31, 178, 251
Armenia, 10, 17, 191–92, 331n2
*L'Arrêt de mort* (Blanchot), 171
Arya dharma, 96
Aryanism, 61–63, 65–66, 68–69, 79
Asad, Talal, 257, 301n47
assimilationism, 66–67, 108–9
atheism, 45, 270
Audi, Robert, 183, 330n61
Augustine, 134
Auschwitz, 31–32, 142, 265
autochthony, 13, 82, 85–93, 95, 102. *See also étranger*
Avelar, Idelber, 334n24

avowals: of aporias, 26, 126; as confession, 211; as current, 31; for forgiveness, 125, 222; of impossible, 125, 156; initiative for, 23; language of, 219–20; for reconciliation, 194–95; before stranger, 35; of unavowable, 30, 37, 39, 81, 100, 155–58, 166–67, 305n2. *See also* globalization
"Avowing—The Impossible: Returns, Repentance, and Reconciliation, A Lesson" (Derrida), 7–14, 30, 75–76, 79–82, 84, 100–101, 104, 106, 111–12, 114–15, 119, 124–30, 133–35, 148, 150–51, 153–55, 158, 161–67, 169, 205, 211–12, 218–22, 225–34, 236–39, 243–47, 249–52, 256, 258, 265, 267–68, 270, 272–75, 280–82, 288, 300n35, 304n64, 308n28, 321n32, 323n1, 323n10, 340n27, 340n34, 341n5, 343n25, 351n26

Baal Shem Tov, Israel, 264, 349n16
Babar, 96
Baeck, Leo, 31, 36
Bagram prison, 13, 246, 251
Baishya, Amit, 309n37
Balfour Declaration, 66
Balibar, Etienne, 88, 93
Barth, Karl, 179, 185
Barthes, Roland, 213
Bauman, Zygmunt, 84, 91, 306n12
BDS movement. *See* Boycott Divestment Sanctions Movement
Beardsworth, Richard, 3, 293n14
Beccaria, Cesare, 252
*Before Absence* (Darwish), 227
"Before the Law" (Kafka), 264
Begin, Menachem, 73
Beit-Hallahmi, Benjamin, 49, 66, 299n22